Western Europe

phrasebooks

Western Europe phrasebook
4th edition – February 2007

Published by
Lonely Planet Publications Pty Ltd ABN 36 005 607 983
90 Maribyrnong St, Footscray, Victoria 3011, Australia

Lonely Planet Offices
Australia Locked Bag 1, Footscray, Victoria 3011
USA 150 Linden St, Oakland CA 94607
UK 72–82 Rosebery Ave, London, EC1R 4RW

Cover illustration
Europa by Yukiyoshi Kamimura

ISBN 978 1 74104 059 3

10 9 8 7 6 5 4 3 2

Printed by C&C Offset Printing Co Ltd, China

acknowledgments

This book is based on existing editions of Lonely Planet's phrasebooks as well as new content. It was developed with the help of the following people:

- Karin Vidstrup Monk for the Danish chapter
- Annelies Mertens for the Dutch chapter
- Michael Janes for the French chapter
- Gunter Muehl for the German chapter
- Thanasis Spilias for the Greek chapter
- Karina Coates, Pietro Iagnocco and Susie Walker for the Italian chapter
- Anne Stensletten for the Norwegian chapter
- Robert Landon and Anabela de Azevedo Teixeira Sobrinho for the Portuguese chapter
- Marta López for the Spanish chapter
- Emma Koch for the Swedish chapter
- Arzu Kürklü for the Turkish chapter

Editor Branislava Vladisavljevic would also like to thank Elmar Duenschede (German), Floriana Badalotti (Italian), Gina Tsarouhas (Greek), Gus Balbontin (Spanish), Jean-Pierre Masclef (French), William Goulay (Turkish) and Yukiyoshi Kamimura (Portuguese) for additional language expertise.

Lonely Planet Language Products

Publishing Manager: Chris Rennie
Commissioning Editor: Karin Vidstrup Monk
Editor: Branislava Vladisavljevic
Assisting Editors: Vanessa Battersby & Francesca Coles
Managing Editor: Annelies Mertens
Project Manager: Adam McCrow
Layout Designer: Laura Jane
Managing Layout Designer: Sally Darmody
Cartographer: Wayne Murphy
Series Designer & Illustrations: Yukiyoshi Kamimura
Production Manager: Jennifer Bilos

contents

Western Europe

Danish	Greek
Dutch	Italian
French	Norwegian
German	Portuguese

Scandinavia: same scale as main map

NORWEGIAN SEA
NORWAY
Oslo
SWEDEN
Stockholm
Gulf of Bothnia
Finland
Estonia
Skagerrak
BALTIC SEA
DENMARK
Latvia

Estonia
Latvia
See inset
Russia
BALTIC SEA
Lithuania
Kaliningrad (Russia)
Belarus
Poland
Ukraine
Slovakia
Moldova
Hungary
Romania
Bosnia & Hercegovina
Serbia
Montenegro
Bulgaria
FYROM
Albania
BLACK SEA
Armenia
Istanbul
Ankara
TURKEY
Thessaloniki
Aegean Sea
Ionian Sea
GREECE
Izmir
Athens
Syria
Nicosia (Lefkosia)
Sea of Crete
SEA
Crete
CYPRUS
Lebanon
Iraq

Spanish
Swedish
Turkish

Note: Language areas are approximate only. For more details see the relevant introduction.

western europe – at a glance

One of the most rewarding things about travelling through Western Europe is the rich variety of cuisine, customs, architecture and history. The flipside of course is that you'll encounter a number of very different languages. Most languages spoken in Western Europe, including English, belong to what's known as the Indo-European language family, believed to have originally developed from one language spoken thousands of years ago. Luckily for English speakers, all but one use Roman script.

The Romance languages (French, Italian, Spanish and Portuguese) all developed from Vulgar Latin, which spread through Western Europe during the rule of the Roman Empire. The freedom with which English has borrowed Latin-based vocabulary means you'll quickly recognise many words from these languages. The Germanic languages – Dutch and German – are more closely related to English. The Scandinavian languages (Danish, Norwegian and Swedish) form the northern branch of the Germanic languages tree, having developed from Old Norse, the language of the Vikings. Their big advantage is that, being so closely related, once you've got the hang of one language, the others should seem quite familiar. Greek, the language of the *Iliad* and the *Odyssey,* forms a single branch of the Indo-European language family and uses Greek script. Finally, Turkish is part of the Ural-Altaic language family, which includes languages spoken from the Balkan Peninsula to northeast Asia. Arabic script was replaced by Roman script for Turkish in the early 20th century.

did you know?

- The European Union (EU) was established by the Maastricht Treaty in 1992. It developed from the European Economic Community, founded by the Treaty of Rome in 1957. Since the 2004 enlargement, it has 25 member states and 20 official languages.
- The EU flag is a circle of 12 gold stars on a blue background – the number 12 representing wholeness.
- The EU anthem is the 'Ode to Joy' from Beethoven's Ninth Symphony.
- Europe Day, 9 May, commemorates the 1950 declaration by French Foreign Minister Robert Schuman, which marks the creation of the European Union.
- The euro has been in circulation since E-Day, 1 January 2002. The euro's symbol (€) was inspired by the Greek letter epsilon (ε) – Greece being the cradle of European civilisation and ε being the first letter of the word 'Europe'.
- The Eurovision Song Contest, held each May, has been running since 1956. For the larger part of the competition's history, the performers were only allowed to sing in their country's national language, but that's no longer the case.

Danish

danish alphabet				
Aa aa	*Bb* bey	*Cc* sey	*Dd* dey	*Ee* ey
Ff ef	*Gg* gey	*Hh* haw	*Ii* ee	*Jj* yawdh
Kk kaw	*Ll* el	*Mm* em	*Nn* en	*Oo* oh
Pp pey	*Qq* koo	*Rr* er	*Ss* es	*Tt* tey
Uu oo	*Vv* vey	*Ww* *do*·belt vey	*Xx* eks	*Yy* ew
Zz zet	*Ææ* e	*Øø* eu	*Åå* aw	

danish

introduction

What do the fairy tales of Hans Christian Andersen and the existentialist philosophy of Søren Kierkegaard have in common (apart from pondering the complexities of life and human character)? Danish (*dansk* dansk), of course – the language of the oldest European monarchy. Danish contributed to the English of today as a result of the Viking conquests of the British Isles in the form of numerous personal and place names, as well as many basic words.

As a member of the Scandinavian or North Germanic language family, Danish is closely related to Swedish and Norwegian. It's particularly close to one of the two official written forms of Norwegian, *Bokmål* – Danish was the ruling language in Norway between the 15th and 19th centuries, and was the base of this modern Norwegian literary language. In pronunciation, however, Danish differs considerably from both of its neighbours thanks to its softened consonants and often 'swallowed' sounds. Among the foreign influences on Danish, German is the most notable: a consequence of both warfare and trade through centuries.

Writing in Danish starts with the runic alphabet – used mainly on stone for the common ancestor of all Scandinavian languages as far back as AD 200 – which flourished during the Viking age from the 9th century. The earliest examples of what can be considered Danish text date from that period, when Danish began to take shape as a distinct language. The Roman alphabet in which Danish is written today was first introduced by Christian missionaries. It started replacing the runic alphabet in the 12th century and was modified through a series of spelling reforms.

The current international status of Danish (with about 5.5 million speakers) is the legacy of its historical expansion. It's the official language of Denmark and has co-official status – with Greenlandic and Faroese respectively – in Greenland and the Faroese Islands, which are autonomous Danish territories. Until 1944 it was the official language of Iceland and today is taught in schools there as the first foreign language. Danish is also a minority language in the area of Schleswig-Holstein in northern Germany, where it has some 30,000 speakers. And if all that isn't enough, just think of the whole corpus of words for which English is indebted to its old Viking conquerors – one of those essential words thought to have Danish origin is 'smile', so whenever you're taking photos on your travels, remember to thank the Danes!

pronunciation

vowel sounds

The Danish vowel system has long and short versions of each vowel, and additional 'combined vowels' or diphthongs. Most of the vowels have equivalents in English – but as ever, it's best to listen carefully to native speakers and follow their lead. By using our coloured pronunciation guides, you're sure to be understood.

symbol	english equivalent	danish example	transliteration
a	act	*plads*	plas
aa	father	*trafik*	traa·*feek*
ai	aisle	*jeg*	yai
aw	saw	*håndklæde*	*hawn*·kle·dhe
e	bet	*hotel*	hoh·*tel*
ee	see	*turist*	too·*reest*
eu	nurse	*købe*	*keu*·be
ew	ee pronounced with rounded lips	*cykel*	*sew*·kel
ey	as in 'bet', but longer	*bestille*	bey·*sti*·le
i	hit	*forsinket*	for·*sing*·ket
o	pot	*postkontor*	post·kon·*tohr*
oh	oh	*postkontor*	post·kon·*tohr*
oo	soon	*forbudt*	for·*boot*
ow	how	*afgangshal*	*ow*·gaangs·hal
oy	toy	*toilet*	toy·*let*

word stress

In Danish, stress often falls on the first syllable in a word. Compound words can have more than one syllable stressed. In this chapter, the stressed syllables are in italics.

consonant sounds

Most Danish consonants are also found in English, including the 'soft' sounds (such as dh). However, the consonants in Danish can be 'swallowed' and even omitted completely, creating, in conjunction with vowels, a glottal stop or *stød* steudh. Its sounds rather like the Cockney pronunciation of the 'tt' in 'bottle'.

symbol	english equivalent	danish example	transliteration
b	bed	*bord*	bohr
ch	cheat	*chips*	cheeps
d	dog	*dansk*	dansk
dh	that	*hvid*	veedh
f	fat	*finde*	*fi*·ne
g	go	*glas*	glas
h	hat	*hente*	*hen*·te
j	joke	*juice*	joos
k	kit	*koncert*	kon·*sert*
l	lot	*lang*	laang
m	man	*maskine*	mas·*kee*·ne
n	not	*nogle*	*noh*·le
ng	ring	*synge*	*sewng*·e
p	pet	*penge*	*peng*·e
r	red (trilled)	*rejse*	*rai*·se
s	sun	*seng*	seng
sh	shot	*chokolade*	shoh·koh·*la*·dhe
t	top	*ting*	ting
v	very	*vin*	veen
w	win	*whiskey, peber*	*wees*·kee, *pey*·wa
y	yellow	*jeg*	yai

language difficulties

Do you speak English?		
Taler De/du engelsk? **pol/inf**		*ta*·la dee/doo *eng*·elsk
Do you understand?		
Forstår De/du? **pol/inf**		for·*stawr* dee/doo
I (don't) understand.		
Jeg forstår (ikke).		yai for·*stawr* (*i*·ke)
What does (*hyggelig*) mean?		
Hvad betyder (hyggelig)?		va bi·*tew*·dha (*hew*·ge·lee)

How do you ...?	*Hvordan ...?*	vor·*dan* ...
pronounce this	*udtaler man det*	*oodh*·ta·la man dey
write (*hyggelig*)	*skriver man (hyggelig)*	*skree*·va man (*hew*·ge·lee)
Could you please ...?	*Kunne De/du ...?* **pol/inf**	*koo*·ne dee/doo ...
repeat that	*gentage det*	*gen*·ta dey
speak more slowly	*tale langsommere*	*ta*·la *laang*·so·ma
write it down	*skrive det ned*	*skree*·ve dey nidh

essentials

Yes.	*Ja.*	ya
No.	*Nej.*	nai
Please.	*Vær så venlig.*	ver saw *ven*·lee
Thank you (very much).	*(Mange) Tak.*	(*mang*·e) taak
You're welcome.	*Selv tak.*	sel taak
Excuse me.	*Undskyld mig.*	*awn*·skewl mai
Sorry.	*Undskyld.*	*awn*·skewl

numbers

0	*nul*	nawl	16	*seksten*	*sais*·ten
1	*en*	in	17	*sytten*	*sew*·ten
2	*to*	toh	18	*atten*	*a*·ten
3	*tre*	trey	19	*nitten*	*ni*·ten
4	*fire*	feer	20	*tyve*	*tew*·ve
5	*fem*	fem	21	*enogtyve*	*eyn*·o·tew·ve
6	*seks*	seks	22	*toogtyve*	*toh*·o·tew·ve
7	*syv*	sew	30	*tredive*	*traadh*·ve
8	*otte*	*aw*·te	40	*fyrre*	*fewr*·re
9	*ni*	nee	50	*halvtreds*	hal·*tres*
10	*ti*	tee	60	*tres*	tres
11	*elleve*	*el*·ve	70	*halvfjerds*	hal·*fyers*
12	*tolv*	tol	80	*firs*	feers
13	*tretten*	*traa*·ten	90	*halvfems*	hal·*fems*
14	*fjorten*	*fyor*·ten	100	*hundrede*	*hoon*·re·dhe
15	*femten*	*fem*·ten	1000	*tusind*	*too*·sen

time & dates

What time is it?	*Hvad er klokken?*	va ir *klo*·ken
It's one o'clock.	*Klokken er et.*	*klo*·ken ir it
It's (two) o'clock.	*Klokken er (to).*	*klo*·ken ir (toh)
Quarter past (one).	*Kvarter over (et).*	kvaar·*teyr o*·va (it)
Half past (one).	*Halv (to).* (lit: half two)	hal (toh)
Quarter to (eight).	*Kvarter i (otte).*	kvaar·*teyr* ee (*aw*·te)
At what time ...?	*Hvad tid ...?*	va teedh ...
At ...	*Klokken ...*	*klo*·ken ...
am (morning)	*om morgenen*	om *mor*·nen
pm (afternoon)	*om eftermiddagen*	om *ef*·taa·mi·da·en
pm (evening)	*om aftenen*	om *aaft*·nen
Monday	*mandag*	*man*·da
Tuesday	*tirsdag*	*teers*·da
Wednesday	*onsdag*	*awns*·da
Thursday	*torsdag*	*tors*·da
Friday	*fredag*	*fre*·da
Saturday	*lørdag*	*leur*·da
Sunday	*søndag*	*seun*·da

January	*januar*	*ya*·noo·ar
February	*februar*	*feb*·roo·ar
March	*marts*	maarts
April	*april*	a·*preel*
May	*maj*	mai
June	*juni*	*yoo*·nee
July	*juli*	*yoo*·lee
August	*august*	ow·*gawst*
September	*september*	sip·*tem*·ba
October	*oktober*	ohk·*toh*·ba
November	*november*	noh·*vem*·ba
December	*december*	dey·*sem*·ba

What date is it today?
Hvilken dato er det i dag? — *vil*·ken *da*·toh ir dey ee da

It's (15 December).
Det er den (femtende december). — dey ir den (*fem*·te·ne dey·*sem*·ba)

since (May)	*siden (maj)*	*see*·dhen (mai)
until (June)	*indtil (juni)*	*in*·til (*yoo*·nee)
yesterday	*i går*	ee gawr
last night	*i går aftes*	ee gawr *aaf*·tes
today	*i dag*	ee da
tonight	*i aften*	ee *aaf*·ten
tomorrow	*i morgen*	ee morn
last/next ...	*sidste/næste ...*	*sees*·te/*nes*·te ...
week	*uge*	*oo*·e
month	*måned*	*maw*·nedh
year	*år*	awr
yesterday ...	*i går ...*	ee gawr ...
morning	*morges*	*mo*·res
afternoon	*eftermiddags*	*ef*·taa·mi·das
evening	*aftes*	*aaf*·tes
tomorrow ...	*i morgen ...*	ee morn ...
morning	*tidlig*	*teedh*·lee
afternoon	*eftermiddag*	*ef*·taa·mi·da
evening	*aften*	*aaf*·ten

weather

What's the weather like?	*Hvordan er vejret?*	vor·*dan* ir *vey*·ret
It's …		
cloudy	*Det er overskyet.*	dey ir *o*·*va*·skew·et
cold	*Det er koldt.*	dey ir kolt
hot	*Det er varmt.*	dey ir vaarmt
raining	*Det regner.*	dey *rain*·a
snowing	*Det sner.*	dey sneyr
sunny	*Solen skinner.*	*soh*·len *ski*·na
warm	*Det er varmt.*	dey ir vaarmt
windy	*Det blæser.*	dey *ble*·sa
spring	*forår* n	*for*·awr
summer	*sommer*	*so*·ma
autumn	*efterår* n	*ef*·taa·awr
winter	*vinter*	*vin*·ta

border crossing

I'm here …	*Jeg er …*	yai ir …
in transit	*i transit*	ee traan·*seet*
on business	*på forretningsrejse*	paw for·*rat*·nings·rai·se
on holiday	*på ferie*	paw *feyr*·ye
I'm here for …	*Jeg er her i …*	yai ir heyr ee …
(10) days	*(ti) dage*	(tee) *da*·e
(three) weeks	*(tre) uger*	(trey) *oo*·a
(two) months	*(to) måneder*	(toh) *maw*·ne·dha

I'm going to (Valby).
Jeg skal til (Valby). — yai skal til (*val*·bew)

I'm staying at the (Hotel Europa).
Jeg bor på (Hotel Europa). — yai bohr paw (hoh·*tel* e·oo·*roh*·pa)

I have nothing to declare.
Jeg har ingenting at fortolde. — yai haar *ing*·en·ting at for·*to*·le

I have something to declare.
Jeg har noget at fortolde. — yai haar *naw*·et at for·*to*·le

That's (not) mine.
Det er (ikke) mit. — dey ir (*i*·ke) meet

transport

tickets & luggage

Where can I buy a ticket?
Hvor kan jeg købe en billet? — vor ka yai *keu*·be in bi·*let*

Do I need to book a seat?
Er det nødvendigt at bestille plads? — ir dey neudh·*ven*·deet at bey·*sti*·le plas

One … ticket (to Odense), please.	*En … billet (til Odense), tak.*	in … bee·*let* (til *oh*·dhen·se) taak
one-way	*enkelt*	*eng*·kelt
return	*retur*	rey·*toor*

I'd like to … my ticket, please.	*Jeg vil gerne … min billet, tak.*	yai vil *gir*·ne … meen bee·*let* taak
cancel	*afbestille*	*ow*·bey·sti·le
change	*ændre*	*en*·dre
collect	*hente*	*hen*·te
confirm	*bekræfte*	bey·*kref*·te

I'd like a … seat, please.	*Jeg vil gerne have en … plads, tak.*	yai vil *gir*·ne ha in … plas taak
nonsmoking	*ikke-ryger*	*i*·ke·*rew*·a
smoking	*ryger*	*rew*·a

How much is it?
Hvor meget koster det? — vor *maa*·yet *kos*·ta dey

Is there air conditioning?
Er der aircondition? — ir deyr eyr·kon·*dee*·shen

Is there a toilet?
Er der et toilet? — ir deyr it toy·*let*

How long does the trip take?
Hvor længe varer turen? — vor *leng*·e *vaa*·ra *too*·ren

Is it a direct route?
Er det en direkte forbindelse? — ir deyr in *dee*·rek·te for·*bi*·nel·se

I'd like a luggage locker.
Jeg vil gerne have et bagageskab med lås. — yai vil *gir*·ne ha it ba·*gaa*·she·skaab me laws

My luggage has been …	*Min bagage er blevet …*	meen ba·*gaa*·she ir *bley*·vet …
damaged	*beskadiget*	bey·*ska*·dhee·et
lost	*væk*	vek
stolen	*stjålet*	*styaw*·let

getting around

Where does flight (71) arrive/depart?
Hvor ankommer/afgår fly nummer (71)?
vor *an*·ko·ma/*ow*·gawr flew *naw*·ma (eyn·o·hal·*fyers*)

Where's (the) …?	*Hvor er …?*	vor ir …
arrivals hall	*ankomsthallen*	*an*·komst·*ha*·len
departures hall	*afgangshallen*	*ow*·gaangs·*ha*·len
duty-free shop	*den toldfri butik*	den *tol*·free boo·*teek*
gate (12)	*gate (tolv)*	gayt (tol)

Is this the … to (Aarhus)?	*Er dette … til (Århus)?*	ir *dey*·te … til (*awr*·hoos)
boat	*båden*	*baw*·dhen
bus	*bussen*	*boo*·sen
plane	*flyet*	*flew*·et
train	*toget*	*taw*·et

What time's the … bus?	*Hvad tid er den … bus?*	va teedh ir den … boos
first	*første*	*feurs*·te
last	*sidste*	*sees*·te
next	*næste*	*nes*·te

At what time does (the train) arrive/leave?
Hvornår ankommer/afgår (toget)?
vor·*nawr an*·ko·ma/*ow*·gawr (*taw*·et)

How long will (the train) be delayed?
Hvor meget er (toget) forsinket?
vor *maa*·yet ir (*taw*·et) for·*sing*·ket

What station/stop is this?
Hvad station/stoppested er dette?
va sta·*shohn*/*sto*·pe·stedh ir *dey*·te

What's the next station/stop?
Hvad er næste station/stoppested?
va ir *nes*·te sta·*shohn*/*sto*·pe·stedh

Does it stop at (Østerport)?
Stopper den/det på (Østerport)?
sto·pa den/dey paw (*eus*·ta·port)

Please tell me when we get to (Roskilde).
Sig venligst til når vi kommer til (Roskilde). — see *ven*·leest til nawr vee *ko*·ma til (*ros*·kee·le)

How long do we stop here?
Hvor længe stopper vi her? — vor *leng*·e *sto*·pa vee heyr

Is this seat available?
Er denne plads fri? — ir *de*·ne plas free

That's my seat.
Det er min plads. — dey ir meen plas

I'd like a taxi ...	*Jeg vil gerne have en taxa ...*	yai vil *gir*·ne ha in *tak*·sa ...
at (9am)	*klokken (ni om morgenen)*	*klo*·ken (nee om *mor*·nen)
now	*nu*	noo
tomorrow	*i morgen*	ee morn

Is this taxi available?
Er denne taxa fri? — ir *de*·ne *tak*·sa free

How much is it to ...?
Hvad koster det til ...? — va *kos*·ta dey til ...

Please put the meter on.
Vær venlig at sætte taxametret. — ver *ven*·lee at *se*·te tak·sa·*mey*·tret

Please take me to (this address).
Vær venlig at køre mig til (denne adresse). — ver *ven*·lee at *keu*·re mai til (*de*·ne a·*draa*·se)

Please ...	*Venligst ...*	*ven*·leest ...
slow down	*kør langsommere*	keur *laang*·so·ma
stop here	*stop her*	stop heyr
wait here	*vent her*	vent heyr

car, motorbike & bicycle hire

I'd like to hire a ...	*Jeg vil gerne leje en ...*	yai vil *gir*·ne *lai*·ye in ...
bicycle	*cykel*	*sew*·kel
car	*bil*	beel
motorbike	*motorcykel*	*moh*·tor·sew·kel

with …	*med …*	me …
a driver	*chauffør*	*shoh*·feur
air conditioning	*air-conditioning*	*eyr*·kon·dee·shoh·ning
antifreeze	*defroster*	dey·*fros*·ta

How much for … hire?	*Hvor meget koster det per …?*	vor *maa*·yet *kos*·ta dey peyr …
hourly	*time*	*tee*·me
daily	*dag*	da
weekly	*uge*	*oo*·e

air	*luft* n	lawft
oil	*olie*	*ohl*·ye
petrol	*benzin* n	ben·*seen*
tyres	*dæk* n pl	dek

I need a mechanic.
Jeg har brug for en mekaniker. — yai haar broo for in mi·*ka*·ni·ka

I've run out of petrol.
Jeg er løbet tør for benzin. — yai ir *leu*·bet teur for ben·*seen*

I have a flat tyre.
Jeg er punkteret. — yai ir pawng·*tey*·ret

directions

Where's the …?	*Hvor er …?*	vor ir …
bank	*der en bank*	deyr in baank
city centre	*bycentrum*	*bew*·sen·trawm
hotel	*der et hotel*	deyr it hoh·*tel*
market	*der et marked*	deyr it *maar*·kedh
police station	*politistationen*	poh·lee·*tee*·sta·shoh·nen
post office	*der et postkontor*	deyr it *post*·kon·tohr
public toilet	*der et offentligt toilet*	deyr it *o*·fent·leet toy·*let*
tourist office	*turistkontoret*	too·*reest*·kon·toh·ret

Is this the road to (Kronborg Slot)?
Fører denne vej til (Kronborg Slot)? — *feu*·ra *de*·ne vai til (*krohn*·borg slot)

Can you show me (on the map)?
Kan De/du vise mig det (på kortet)? pol/inf — kan dee/doo *vee*·se mai dey (paw *kor*·tet)

What's the address?
Hvad er adressen? — va ir a·*draa*·sen

How far (away) is it?
Hvor langt (væk) er det? — vor laangt (vek) ir dey

How do I get there?
Hvordan kommer jeg derhen? — vor·*dan ko*·ma yai deyr·*hen*

Can I get there by bicycle?
Kan jeg cykle derhen? — kan yai *sewk*·le deyr·*hen*

Turn …	*Drej …*	drai …
at the corner	*ved hjørnet*	vi *yeur*·nedh
at the traffic lights	*ved trafiklyset*	vi traa·*feek*·lew·set
left/right	*til venstre/højre*	til *vens*·tre/*hoy*·re
It's …	*Det er …*	dey ir …
behind …	*bag …*	ba …
far (away)	*langt (væk)*	laangt (vek)
here	*her*	heyr
in front of …	*foran …*	*fo*·ran …
left	*til venstre*	til *vens*·tre
near (to …)	*nær (ved …)*	ner (vi …)
next to …	*ved siden af …*	vi *see*·dhen a …
on the corner	*på hjørnet*	paw *yeur*·net
opposite …	*på modsate side af …*	paw *mohdh*·sa·te *see*·dhe a …
right	*til højre*	til *hoy*·re
straight ahead	*lige ud*	*li*·e oodh
there	*der*	deyr
by bicycle	*på cykel*	paw *sew*·kel
by bus	*med bus*	me boos
by taxi	*med taxa*	me *tak*·sa
by train	*med tog*	me taw
on foot	*til fods*	til fohdhs
north	*nord*	nohr
south	*syd*	sewdh
east	*øst*	eust
west	*vest*	vest

signs

Indgang/Udgang	*in*·gaang/*udh*·gaang	**Entrance/Exit**
Åben/Lukket	*aw*·ben/*law*·ket	**Open/Closed**
Ledige værelser	*ley*·dhee·e *verl*·sa	**Rooms Available**
Alt optaget	alt *op*·ta·yet	**No Vacancies**
Information	in·for·ma·*shohn*	**Information**
Politistation	poh·lee·*tee*·sta·shohn	**Police Station**
Forbudt	for·*boot*	**Prohibited**
Toilet	toy·*let*	**Toilets**
Herrer	*hey*·ra	**Men**
Damer	*daa*·ma	**Women**
Varm/Kold	vaarm/kol	**Hot/Cold**

accommodation

finding accommodation

Where's a ...?	*Hvor er der ...?*	vor ir deyr ...
camping ground	*en campingplads*	in *kaam*·ping·plas
guesthouse	*et gæstehus*	it *ges*·te·hoos
hotel	*et hotel*	it hoh·*tel*
youth hostel	*et ungdomsherberg*	it *awng*·doms·heyr·beyrg
Can you recommend somewhere ...?	*Kan De/du anbefale et ... sted?* **pol/inf**	kan dee/doo *an*·bey·fa·le it ... stedh
cheap	*billigt*	*bee*·leet
good	*godt*	got

Can you recommend somewhere nearby?
Kan De/du anbefale et sted i nærheden? **pol/inf** — kan dee/doo *an*·bey·fa·le it stedh ee *ner*·hey·dhen

I'd like to book a room, please.
Jeg vil gerne bestille et værelse. — yai vil *gir*·ne bey·*sti*·le it *verl*·se

I have a reservation.
Jeg har en reservation. — yai haar in rey·ser·vaa·*shohn*

My name's ...
Mit navn er ... — meet nown ir ...

Do you have a twin room?
Har I et værelse med to senge? — haar ee it *verl*·se me toh *seng*·e

Do you have a ... room?	*Har I et ... værelse?*	haar ee it ... *verl*·se
single	*enkelt*	*eng*·kelt
double	*dobbelt*	*do*·belt

How much is it per ...?	*Hvor meget koster det per ...?*	vor *maa*·yet *kos*·ta dey peyr ...
night	*nat*	nat
person	*person*	per·*sohn*

Can I pay ...?	*Kan jeg betale med ...?*	kan yai bey·*taa*·le me ...
by credit card	*kreditkort*	kre·*deet*·kort
with a travellers cheque	*rejsecheck*	*rai*·se·shek

I'd like to stay for (two) nights.
Jeg vil gerne blive (to) nætter. — yai vil *gir*·ne *blee*·ve (toh) *ne*·ta

From (2 July) to (6 July).
Fra (anden juli) til (sjette juli). — fraa (*a*·nen *yoo*·lee) til (*sye*·te *yoo*·lee)

Can I see it?
Må jeg se det? — maw yai sey dey

Am I allowed to camp here?
Må jeg campere her? — maw yai kaam·*pey*·a heyr

Is there a campsite nearby?
Er der en campingplads i nærheden? — ir deyr in *kaam*·ping·plas ee *ner*·hey·dhen

requests & queries

When's breakfast served?
Hvornår er der morgenmad? — vor·*nawr* ir deyr *morn*·madh

Where's breakfast served?
Hvor serveres der morgenmad? — vor ser·*vey*·res deyr *morn*·madh

Please wake me at (eight).
Vær så venlig at vække mig klokken (otte). — ver saw *ven*·lee at *ve*·ke mai *klo*·ken (*aw*·te)

Could I have my key, please?
Må jeg få min nøgle, tak? — maw yai faw meen *noy*·le taak

Can I get another (quilt)?
Må jeg få en ekstra dyne? — maw yai faw en *eks*·tra (*dew*·ne)

Is there a/an ...?	*Er der ...?*	ir deyr ...
elevator	*en elevator*	in ey·ley·*va*·tor
safe	*et pengeskab*	it *peng*·e·skaab

The room is too ...	*Det her værelse er for ...*	dey heyr *verl*·se ir for ...
expensive	*dyrt*	dewrt
noisy	*larmende*	*laar*·me·ne
small	*lille*	*lee*·le

The ... doesn't work.	*... virker ikke.*	... *veer*·ka *i*·ke
air conditioning	*Air-conditioningen*	*eyr*·kon·dee·shoh·ning·en
fan	*Viften*	*vif*·ten
toilet	*Toilettet*	toy·*le*·tet

This ... isn't clean.	*... er snavset.*	... ir *snow*·set
pillow	*Denne pude*	*de*·ne *poo*·dhe
sheet	*Dette lagen*	*dey*·te *la*·yen
towel	*Dette håndklæde*	*dey*·te *hawn*·kle·dhe

checking out

What time is checkout?
Hvad tid er checkout? — va teedh ir chek·*owt*

Can I leave my luggage here?
Kan jeg efterlade min bagage her? — kan yai *ef*·ta·la·dhe meen ba·*gaa*·she heyr

Could I have my ..., please?	*Må jeg få ..., tak?*	maw yai faw ... taak
deposit	*mit depositum*	meet dey·*poh*·see·tawm
passport	*mit pas*	meet pas
valuables	*mine værdigenstande*	*mee*·ne ver·*dee*·gen·sta·ne

communications & banking

the internet

Where's the local Internet café?
Hvor er den lokale internet café? — vor ir den loh·*ka*·le *in*·ta·net ka·*fey*

How much is it per hour?
Hvad koster det per time? — va *kos*·ta dey peyr *tee*·me

I'd like to ...	*Jeg vil gerne ...*	yai vil *gir*·ne ...
check my email	*checke mine emails*	*che*·ke *mee*·ne *ee*·mayls
get Internet access	*have internet adgang*	ha *in*·ta·net *adh*·gaang
use a printer	*benytte en printer*	bey·*new*·te in *preen*·ta
use a scanner	*benytte en skanner*	bey·*new*·te in *ska*·na

mobile/cell phone

I'd like a ...	*Jeg vil gerne ...*	yai vil *gir*·ne ...
mobile/cell phone for hire	*leje en mobil-telefon*	*lai*·ye in moh·*beel*·tey·ley·*fohn*
SIM card for your network	*have et SIM-kort til jeres netværk*	ha it *seem*·kort til *ye*·res *net*·verk

What are the rates?
Hvad er taksterne? — va ir *taaks*·ta·ne

telephone

What's your phone number?
Hvad er Deres/dit telefonnummer? pol/inf — va ir *de*·res/deet tey·ley·*fohn*·naw·ma

The number is ...
Nummeret er ... — *naw*·ma·et ir ...

Where's the nearest public phone?
Hvor er den nærmeste telefonboks? — vor ir den *ner*·mes·te tey·ley·*fohn*·boks

I'd like to buy a phonecard.
Jeg vil gerne købe et telefonkort. — yai vil *gir*·ne *keu*·be it tey·ley·*fohn*·kort

I want to …	*Jeg vil gerne …*	yai vil *gir*·ne …
call (Singapore)	*ringe til (Singapore)*	*ring*·e til (*seeng*·ga·pohr)
make a local call	*ringe lokalt*	*ring*·e loh·*kalt*
reverse the charges	*have at modtageren betaler*	ha at *mohdh*·ta·yaan bey·*ta*·la
How much does … cost?	*Hvor meget koster …?*	vo *maa*·yet *kos*·ta …
a (three)-minute call	*det for (tre) minutter*	dey for (trey) mee·*noo*·ta
each extra minute	*hvert ekstra minut*	vert *eks*·traa mee·*noot*
It's … per minute.	*… per minut.*	… peyr mee·*noot*
(one) euro	*(En) euro*	(eyn) *euw*·roh
(three) kroner	*(Tre) kroner*	(trey) *kroh*·na

post office

I want to send a …	*Jeg vil gerne sende …*	yai vil *gir*·ne *sen*·ne …
fax	*en fax*	in faaks
letter	*et brev*	it brev
parcel	*en pakke*	in *paa*·ke
postcard	*et postkort*	it *post*·kort
I want to buy …	*Jeg vil gerne købe …*	yai vil *gir*·ne *keu*·be …
an envelope	*en konvolut*	in kon·voh·*loot*
stamps	*frimærker*	*free*·mer·ka
Please send it (to Australia) by …	*Kan I sende det (til Australien) per …*	kan ee *sen*·ne dey (til ow·*straa*·lee·en) peyr …
airmail	*luftpost*	*lawft*·post
express mail	*eksprespost*	eks·*pres*·post
registered mail	*anbefalet post*	*an*·bey·fa·let post
surface mail	*pakkepost*	*paa*·ke·post
Is there any mail for me?	*Er der post til mig?*	ir deyr post til mai

bank

Where's a/an ...?	*Hvor er der ...?*	vor ir deyr ...
ATM	*en hæveautomat*	in *he*·ve·ow·toh·mat
foreign exchange office	*et vekselkontor*	it *veks*·le·kon·tohr
I'd like to ...	*Jeg vil gerne ...*	yai vil *gir*·ne ...
arrange a transfer	*foretage en overførsel*	*fo*·re·ta in *o*·va·feur·sel
cash a cheque	*veksle en check*	*veks*·le in shek
change money	*veksle nogle penge*	*veks*·le *noh*·le *peng*·e
change travellers cheques	*veksle rejsechecks*	*veks*·le *rai*·se·sheks
get a cash advance	*få et forskud*	faw it *for*·skoodh
withdraw money	*hæve penge*	*he*·ve *peng*·e
What's the ...?	*Hvad ...?*	va ...
charge for that	*koster det*	*kos*·ta dey
exchange rate	*er vekselkursen*	ir *veks*·le·koor·sen
It's ...	*Det ...*	dey ...
(12) euros	*koster (tolv) euroer*	*kos*·ta (tol) *euw*·roh
(50) kroner	*koster (halvtreds) kroner*	*kos*·ta (hal·*tres*) *kroh*·na
free	*er gratis*	ir *graa*·tees

What time does the bank open?
Hvornår åbner banken? — vor·*nawr awb*·na *baang*·ken

Has my money arrived yet?
Er mine penge kommet? — ir *mee*·ne *peng*·e *ko*·met

sightseeing

getting in

What time does it open/close?
Hvornår åbner/lukker de? — vor·*nawr awb*·na/*law*·ka de

What's the admission charge?
Hvad koster adgang? — va *kos*·ta *adh*·gaang

Is there a discount for students/children?
Er der studenterabat/børnerabat? — ir deyr stoo·*den*·ta·raa·*bat*/*beur*·ne·raa·*bat*

I'd like a …	*Jeg vil gerne have …*	yai vil *gir*·ne ha …
catalogue	*et katalog*	it ka·ta·*loh*
guide	*en rejsehåndbog*	in *rai*·se·*hawn*·borw
local map	*et lokalkort*	it loh·*kal*·kort

I'd like to see …	*Jeg vil gerne se …*	yai vil *gir*·ne sey …
What's that?	*Hvad er det?*	va ir dey
Can I take a photo?	*Må jeg tage et foto?*	maw yai ta it *foh*·toh

tours

When's the next …?	*Hvornår er den næste …?*	vor·*nawr* ir den *nes*·te …
boat trip	*bådtur*	*bawdh*·toor
day trip	*dagstur*	*dows*·toor
tour	*ekskursion*	eks·koor·*shohn*

Is … included?	*Er … inkluderet?*	ir … in·kloo·*dey*·ret
accommodation	*ophold*	*op*·hol
the admission charge	*entreen*	ang·*trey*·en
food	*mad*	madh
transport	*transport*	traans·*port*

How long is the tour?
Hvor lang er turen? vor laang ir *too*·ren

What time should we be back?
Hvornår kommer vi tilbage? vor·*nawr* *ko*·ma vee til·*bu*·ye

sightseeing

castle	*slot* n	slot
cathedral	*katedral*	ka·te·*draal*
church	*kirke*	*keer*·ke
main square	*storetorv* n	*stoh*·re·torw
monastery	*kloster* n	*klos*·ta
monument	*monument* n	moh·noo·*ment*
museum	*museum* n	moo·*se*·awm
old city	*den gamle bydel*	den *gaam*·le *bew*·deyl
palace	*palads* n	pa·*las*
ruins	*ruiner*	roo·*ee*·na
stadium	*stadion* n	*sta*·dee·on
statue	*statue*	*sta*·too·e

shopping

enquiries

Where's a ...?	*Hvor er der ...?*	vor ir deyr ...
bank	*en bank*	in baank
bookshop	*en boghandel*	in *borw*·ha·nel
camera shop	*en fotohandel*	in *foh*·toh·ha·nel
department store	*et stormagasin*	it *stohr*·maa·ga·seen
grocery store	*en købmand*	in *keub*·man
market	*et marked*	it *maar*·kedh
newsagency	*en kiosk*	in kee·*osk*
supermarket	*et supermarked*	it *soo*·pa·maar·kedh

Where can I buy (a padlock)?
Hvor kan jeg købe (en hængelås)? — vor kan yai *keu*·be (in *heng*·e·laws)

I'm looking for ...
Jeg leder efter ... — yai *li*·dha *ef*·ta ...

Can I have a look?
Må jeg se? — maw yai sey

Do you have any others?
Har I andre? — haar ee *aan*·dre

Does it have a guarantee?
Er der garanti? — ir deyr gaa·raan·*tee*

Can I have it sent abroad?
Kan jeg få det sendt udenlands? — kan yai faw dey sent *oo*·dhen·lans

Can I have my (watch) repaired?
Kan jeg få mit (ur) repareret? — kan yai faw meet (oor) rey·paa·*rey*·ret

It's faulty.
Det er i stykker. — dey ir ee *stew*·ka

I'd like ..., please.	*Jeg vil gerne ..., tak.*	yai vil *gir*·ne ... taak
a bag	*have en pose*	ha in *poh*·se
a refund	*have en refundering*	ha in re·fawn·*dey*·ring
to return this	*returnere dette*	rey·toor·*ney*·re *dey*·te

paying

How much is it?
Hvor meget koster det? — vor *maa*·yet *kos*·ta dey

Can you write down the price?
Kan De/du skrive prisen ned? pol/inf — ka dee/doo *skree*·ve *pree*·sen nidh

That's too expensive.
Det er for dyrt. — dey ir for dewrt

What's your lowest price?
Hvad er jeres laveste pris? — va ir *ye*·res *la*·ve·ste prees

I'll give you (five) euros.
Jeg vil betale (fem) euro. — yai vil bey·*ta*·le (fem) *eu*·roh

I'll give you (20) kroner.
Jeg vil betale (tyve) kroner. — yai vil bey·*ta*·le (*tew*·ve) *kroh*·na

There's a mistake in the bill. (restaurant/shop)
Der er en fejl i regningen/ kvitteringen. — deyr ir in fail ee *rai*·ning·en/ kvee·*tey*·ring·en

Do you accept ...?	*Tager I ...?*	ta ee ...
credit cards	*kreditkort*	kre·*deet*·kort
debit cards	*hævekort*	*he*·ve·kort
travellers cheques	*rejsechecks*	*rai*·se·sheks

I'd like ..., please.	*Jeg vil gerne have ..., tak.*	yai vil *gir*·ne ha ... taak
a receipt	*en kvittering*	in kvee·*tey*·ring
my change	*mine byttepenge*	*mee*·ne *bew*·te·peng·e

clothes & shoes

Can I try it on?
Må jeg prøve? — maw yai *preu*·ve

My size is (40).
Jeg er størrelse (fyrre). — yai ir *steu*·rel·se (*fewr*·re)

It doesn't fit.
Det passer ikke. — dey *pa*·sa *i*·ke

small	*lille*	*lee*·le
medium	*medium*	*mey*·dee·awm
large	*stor*	stohr

books & music

I'd like a …	*Jeg vil gerne have en …*	yai vil *gir*·*ne* ha in …
newspaper	*avis*	a·*vees*
(in English)	*(på engelsk)*	(paw *eng*·elsk)
pen	*kuglepen*	*koo*·le·pen

Is there an English-language bookshop?
Er der en engelsksproget boghandel? — ir deyr in *eng*·elsk·*spraw*·wet *borw*·ha·nel

I'm looking for something by (Kim Larsen).
Jeg leder efter noget af (Kim Larsen). — yai *li*·dha *ef*·ta *naw*·et a (keem *laar*·sen)

Can I listen to this?
Må jeg lytte til den? — maw yai *lew*·te til den

photography

Could you …?	*Kan I …?*	kan ee …
burn a CD from my memory card	*brænde en CD fra mit hukommelseskort*	*bre*·ne in *sey*·dey fraa meet hoo·*ko*·mel·ses·kort
develop this film	*fremkalde denne film*	*frem*·ka·le *de*·ne feelm
load my film	*sætte min film i*	*se*·te meen feelm ee

I need a/an … film for this camera.	*Jeg har brug for … film til dette kamera.*	yai haar broo for … feelm til *dey*·te *ka*·me·raa
APS	*APS-*	aa pey es
B&W	*sort-hvid*	*sort*·veedh
colour	*farve*	*faar*·ve
slide	*dias-*	*dee*·as
(200) speed	*(to hundrede) ISO*	(toh *hoon*·re·dhe) *ee*·soh

When will it be ready?
Hvornår er den færdig? — vor·*nawr* ir den *fer*·dee

meeting people

greetings, goodbyes & introductions

Hello.	*Goddag.*	go·*da*
Hi.	*Hej/Dav.*	hai/dow
Good night.	*Godnat.*	go·*nat*
Goodbye.	*Farvel.*	faar·*vel*
Bye.	*Hej hej.*	hai hai
See you later.	*Vi ses.*	vee seys
Mr	*Hr*	heyr
Mrs	*Fru*	froo
Miss	*Frøken*	*freu*·ken

How are you?
Hvordan går det? — vor·*dan* gawr dey

Good, thanks.
Godt, tak. — got taak

What's your name?
Hvad hedder De/du? pol/inf — va *hey*·dha dee/doo

My name is ...
Mit navn er ... — mit nown ir ...

I'm pleased to meet you.
Hyggeligt at møde Dem/dig. pol/inf — *hew*·ge·leet at *meu*·dhe dem/dai

This is my ...	*Det er min ...*	dey ir meen ...
boyfriend	*kæreste*	*ker*·ste
brother	*bror*	brohr
daughter	*datter*	*da*·ta
father	*far*	faar
friend	*ven/veninde* m/f	ven/ven·*i*·ne
girlfriend	*kæreste*	*ker*·ste
husband	*mand*	man
mother	*mor*	mohr
partner (intimate)	*kæreste*	*ker*·ste
sister	*søster*	*seus*·ta
son	*søn*	seun
wife	*kone*	*koh*·ne

Here's my ...	*Her er min ...*	heyr ir meen ...
What's your ...?	*Hvad er Deres/ din ...?* pol/inf	va ir *de*·res/ deen ...
address	*adresse*	a·*draa*·se
email address	*email adresse*	*ee*·mayl a·*draa*·se

Here's my ...	*Her er mit ...*	heyr ir meet ...
What's your ...?	*Hvad er Deres/ dit ...?* pol/inf	va ir *de*·res/ deet ...
fax number	*fax nummer*	faks *naw*·ma
phone number	*telefonnummer*	tey·ley·*fohn*·naw·ma

occupations

What's your occupation?
Hvad laver De/du? pol/inf — va *la*·va dee/doo

I'm a/an ...	*Jeg er ...*	yai ir ...
artist	*kunstner*	*kawnst*·na
business person	*forretningsdrivende*	for·*rat*·nings·dree·ve·ne
farmer	*landmand*	*lan*·man
manual worker	*arbejder*	*aar*·bai·da
office worker	*kontorarbejder*	kon·*tohr*·aar·bai·da
scientist	*forsker*	*fors*·ka
student	*studerende*	stoo·*dey*·re·ne
tradesperson	*næringsdrivende*	*ne*·rings·dree·ven·e

background

Where are you from?
Hvor kommer De/du fra? pol/inf — vor *ko*·ma dee/doo fraa

I'm from ...	*Jeg er fra ...*	yai ir fraa ...
Australia	*Australien*	ow·*straa*·lee·en
Canada	*Kanada*	*ka*·na·da
England	*England*	*eng*·lan
New Zealand	*New Zealand*	new *see*·lan
the USA	*USA*	oo es a

Are you married?	*Er De/du gift?*	ir dee/doo geeft
I'm married.	*Jeg er gift.*	yai ir geeft
I'm single.	*Jeg er ugift.*	yai ir *oo*·geeft

age

How old ...?	*Hvor gammel er ...?*	vor *gaa*·mel ir ...
are you	*du*	doo
is your daughter	*din datter*	deen *da*·ta
is your son	*din søn*	deen seun
I'm ... years old.	*Jeg er ... år gammel.*	yai ir ... awr *gaa*·mel
He/She is ... years old.	*Han/Hun er ... år gammel.*	han/hoon ir ... awr *gaa*·mel

feelings

I'm (not) ...	*Jeg er (ikke) ...*	yai ir (*i*·ke) ...
Are you ...?	*Er du ...?*	ir doo ...
happy	*glad*	gladh
hungry	*sulten*	*sool*·ten
sad	*trist*	treest
thirsty	*tørstig*	*teus*·tee
Are you cold?	*Fryser du?*	*frew*·sa doo
I'm (not) cold.	*Jeg fryser (ikke).*	yai *frew*·sa (*i*·ke)
Are you hot?	*Har du det varmt?*	haar doo dey vaarmt
I'm (not) hot.	*Jeg har det (ikke) varmt.*	yai haar dey (*i*·ke) vaarmt

entertainment

going out

Where can I find ...?	*Hvor kan jeg finde ...?*	vor kan yai *fi*·ne ...
clubs	*natklubber*	*nat*·kloo·ba
gay venues	*bøsseklubber*	*beu*·se·kloo·ba
pubs	*pubber*	*paw*·ba
I feel like going to a/the ...	*Jeg har lyst til at tage ...*	yai haar lewst til at ta ...
concert	*til koncert*	til kon·*sert*
movies	*i biografen*	ee bee·oh·*graa*·fen
party	*til fest*	til fest
restaurant	*på restaurant*	paw res·toh·*rang*
theatre	*i teatret*	ee tey·*a*·la

interests

Do you like ...?	*Kan De/du lide ...?* pol/inf	kan dee/doo lee ...
I (don't) like ...	*Jeg synes (ikke) om ...*	yai sewns (*i*·ke) om ...
art	*kunst*	kawnst
cooking	*madlavning*	*madh*·low·ning
movies	*film*	feelm
reading	*at læse*	at *le*·se
shopping	*at handle*	at *han*·le
sport	*sport*	sport
travelling	*at rejse*	at *rai*·se
Do you like to ...?	*Kan De/du lide at ...?* pol/inf	kan dee/doo lee at ...
dance	*danse*	*dan*·se
go to concerts	*gå til koncert*	gaw til kon·*sert*
listen to music	*høre musik*	*heu*·re moo·*seek*

food & drink

finding a place to eat

Can you recommend a ...?	*Kan De/du anbefale en ...?* pol/inf	kan dee/doo *an*·bey·fa·le in ...
bar	*bar*	baar
café	*café*	ka·*fey*
restaurant	*restaurant*	res·toh·*rang*
I'd like ..., please.	*Jeg vil gerne ..., tak.*	yai vil *gir*·ne ... taak
a table for (four)	*have et bord til (fire)*	ha it bohr til (feer)
the (non)smoking section	*sidde i (ikke-) rygerafdelingen*	*si*·dha ee (*i*·ke·) *rew*·a·ow·*dey*·ling·en

ordering food

breakfast	*morgenmad*	*morn*·madh
lunch	*frokost*	*froh*·kost
dinner	*middag*	*mi*·da
snack n	*mellemmåltid*	*me*·lem·mawl·teedh

What would you recommend?		
Hvad kan De/du anbefale? **pol/inf**		va kan dee/doo *an*·bey·fa·le
I'd like (the) ..., please.	*Jeg vil gerne have ..., tak.*	yai vil *gir*·ne ha ... taak
bill	*regningen*	*rai*·ning·en
drink list	*vinkortet*	*veen*·kor·tet
menu	*menuen*	me·*new*·en
that dish	*den ret*	den ret

drinks

(cup of) coffee ...	*(en kop) kaffe ...*	(in kop) *ka*·fe ...
(cup of) tea ...	*(en kop) te ...*	(in kop) tey ...
with milk	*med mælk*	me melk
without sugar	*uden sukker*	*oo*·dhen *saw*·ka
boiled water	*kogt vand*	kogt van
(orange) juice	*(appelsin)juice*	(aa·pel·*seen*·)joos
mineral water	*mineralvand/danskvand*	mee·ne·*ral*·van/*dansk*·van
soft drink	*sodavand*	*soh*·da·van

in the bar

I'll have (a gin).	*(En gin), tak.*	(in jeen) taak
I'll buy you a drink.	*Jeg giver en drink.*	yai geer in drink
What would you like?	*Hvad vil du have?* **inf**	va vil doo ha
Cheers!	*Skål!*	skawl
cocktail	*cocktail*	*kok*·tayl
cognac	*konjak*	*kon*·yak
a shot of (whisky)	*et shot (whiskey)*	it shot (*wees*·kee)
snaps	*snaps*	snaaps
a ... of beer	*øl*	... eul
bottle	*en flaske*	in *flas*·ke
glass	*et glas*	it glas
a bottle of ...	*en flaske ...*	in *flas*·ke ...
a glass of ...	*et glas ...*	it glas ...
red wine	*rødvin*	*reudh*·veen
sparkling wine	*mousserende vin*	moo·*sey*·ra·ne veen
white wine	*hvidvin*	*veedh*·veen

self-catering

What's the local speciality?
Hvad er den lokale specialitet? va ir den loh·*ka*·le spey·sha·lee·*teyt*

What's that?
Hvad er det? va ir dey

How much is it?
Hvor meget koster det? vor *maa*·yet *kos*·ta dey

I'd like ...	*Jeg vil gerne have ...*	yai vil *gir*·ne ha ...
(100) grams	*(hundrede) gram*	(*hoon*·re·dhe) graam
(two) kilos	*(to) kilo*	(toh) *kee*·lo
(three) pieces	*(tre) stykker*	(trey) *stew*·ka
(six) slices	*(seks) skiver*	(seks) *skee*·va

Less.	*Mindre.*	*min*·dra
Enough.	*Nok.*	nok
More.	*Mere.*	*mey*·a

special diets & allergies

Is there a vegetarian restaurant near here?
Er der en vegetarisk restaurant i nærheden? ir deyr in vey·gey·*taa*·reesk res·toh·*rang* ee *ner*·hey·dhen

Do you have vegetarian food?
Har I vegetarmad? haar ee vey·ge·*taar*·madh

Could you prepare a meal without ...?	*Kan I lave et måltid uden ...?*	kan ee *la*·ve it *mawl*·teedh *oo*·dhen ...
butter	*smør*	smeur
eggs	*æg*	eg
meat stock	*kødboullion*	*keudh*·boo·lee·yong

I'm allergic to ...	*Jeg er allergisk over for ...*	yai ir a·*ler*·geesk *o*·va for ...
dairy produce	*mælkeprodukter*	*mel*·ke·proh·*dawk*·ta
gluten	*gluten*	*gloo*·ten
MSG	*monosodium glutamat*	moh·noh·*soh*·dee·awm gloo·ta·*mat*
nuts	*nødder*	*neu*·dha
seafood	*skaldyr*	*skaal*·dewr

menu reader

boller i karry	*bo*·la ee *kaa*·ree	*meatballs in a curry sauce, served with rice or potatoes*
budding	*boo*·dhing	*a kind of pudding flavoured with rum or almonds, served warm*
bøf med løg	beuf me loy	*hamburger served with fried onions, potatoes & brown gravy*
bøftartar	*beuf*·ta·taar	*beef tartar raw ground beef topped with a raw egg yolk, raw onions & capers*
champignoner	shaam·peen·*yong*·a	*mushrooms*
dyrlægens natmad	*dewr*·le·yens *nat*·madh	*liver pâté on sourdough ryebread, with a slice of salt beef, raw onions & beef jelly*
engelsk bøf	*eng*·elsk beuf	*sirloin steak*
fiskesuppe	*fis*·ke saw·pe	*fish soup, usually creamy*
flæskesteg	*fles*·ke·stai	*pork roast served with potatoes, brown gravy & pickled cucumbers*
forel	foh·*rel*	*trout*
frikadeller	fri·ka·*dhe*·la	*pork & veal meatballs*
fromage	froh·*ma*·she	*a kind of mousse flavoured with lemon, served cold*
fyldt hvidkålshoved n	fewlt *veedh*·kawls·hoh·vedh	*ground beef wrapped in cabbage leaves*
gravad laks	*gra*·vadh laks	*gravlax – traditional salt-cured raw salmon with a sweet mustard sauce*
grønsagssuppe	*greun*·sas·saw·pe	*vegetable soup*
gule ærter	*goo*·le *eyr*·ta	*split pea soup, served with pork*
hakkebøf	*haa*·ke·beuf	*hamburger*
havregrød	*how*·re·greudh	*porridge*
hønsekødssuppe	*heun*·se·keudh·saw·pe	*chicken soup*
jordbær med fløde	*yohr*·beyr me *fleu*·dhe	*strawberries with cream*
kartoffel	kaar·*to*·fel	*potato*
kogt torsk	kogt torsk	*poached cod in mustard sauce, served with boiled potatoes*

konditorkager	kon·*dee*·tor·ka·ya	*French pastries*
koteletter	ko·te·*le*·ta	*meat chops*
lammesteg	*laa*·me·stai	*roast lamb*
leverpostej	ley·va·poo·*stai*	*liver pâté*
marineret sild	maa·ree·*ney*·ret seel	*pickled herring, served with raw onions*
medisterpølse	mey·*dees*·ta·*peul*·se	*large fried sausage*
mørbrad	*meur*·braadh	*sirloin*
oksesteg	*ok*·se·stai	*roast beef*
ostemad	aws·te·*madh*	*open cheese sandwich*
pandekager	*pa*·ne·ka·ya	*crepes with jam, sugar or ice cream*
rejemad	*rai*·ye·maadh	*small shrimp served on bread with mayonnaise & lemon slices*
rejer	*rai*·ya	*shrimps*
rødgrød med fløde	*reudh*·greudh me *fleu*·dhe	*fruit pudding (red currant, raspberry, strawberry) served with cream*
røget ål	*reu*·yet awl	*smoked eel*
røget laks	*reu*·yet laks	*smoked salmon with scrambled eggs*
røget sild	*reu*·yet seel	*smoked herring on rye bread with raw onions, chives & a raw egg yolk*
røræg	*reur*·eg	*scrambled eggs*
spaghetti med kødsovs	spa·*ge*·tee me *keudh*·saws	*spaghetti with ground beef in a tomato sauce*
stegt ål med stuvede kartofler	stegt awl me *stoo*·ve·dhe kaar·*tof*·la	*fried eel with boiled potatoes in a white sauce*
stegt flæsk med persillesovs	stegt flesk me per·*si*·le·saws	*fried pork strips served with potatoes*
stegt sild	stegt seel	*fried herring, rolled in rye flour & served with potatoes & a white parsley sauce*
syltede agurker	*sewl*·te·dhe a·*goor*·ka	*pickled cucumbers*
wienerbrød n	*vee*·na·breudh	*Danish pastry*
æggekage	e·ge·*ka*·ye	*egg dish (made with flour) with bacon*
øllebrød	*eu*·le·breudh	*a smooth beer & bread dish served hot with milk or whipped cream*

emergencies

basics

Help!	*Hjælp!*	yelp
Stop!	*Stop!*	stop
Go away!	*Gå væk!*	gaw vek
Thief!	*Tyv!*	tew
Fire!	*Ildebrand!*	*ee*·le·braan
Watch out!	*Pas på!*	pas paw

Call ...!	*Ring efter ...!*	ring *ef*·ta ...
a doctor	*en læge*	in *le*·ye
an ambulance	*en ambulance*	in aam·boo·*laang*·se
the police	*politiet*	poh·lee·*tee*·et

It's an emergency!
Det er et nødstilfælde! dey ir it *neudhs*·til·fe·le

Could you help me, please?
Kan De/du hjælpe mig? pol/inf kan dee/doo *yel*·pe mai

I have to use the telephone.
Jeg skal bruge en telefon. yai skal *broo*·e en tey·ley·*fohn*

I'm lost.
Jeg er faret vild. yai ir *faa*·ret veel

Where's the toilet?
Hvor er toilettet? vor ir toy·*le*·tet

police

Where's the police station?
Hvor er politistationen? vor ir poh·lee·*tee*·sta·shoh·nen

I want to report an offence. (minor/serious)
Jeg vil gerne anmelde en lovovertrædelse/forbrydelse. yai vil *gir*·ne *an*·me·le in *law*·o·va·tre·dhel·se/for·*breu*·dhel·se

I have insurance.
Jeg har forsikring. yai haar for·*sik*·ring

I've been ...	*Jeg er blevet ...*	yai ir *bley*·vet ...
assaulted	*overfaldet*	*o*·va·fa·let
raped	*voldtaget*	*vol*·ta·yet
robbed	*bestjålet*	bey·*styaw*·let

I've lost my …	*Jeg har mistet …*	yai haar *mis*·tet …
backpack	*min rygsæk*	meen *reug*·sek
bags	*min bagage*	meen ba·*gaa*·she
credit card	*mit kreditkort*	meet kre·*deet*·kort
handbag	*min håndtaske*	meen *hawn*·tas·ke
jewellery	*mine smykker*	*mee*·ne *smew*·ka
money	*mine penge*	*mee*·ne *peng*·e
passport	*mit pas*	meet pas
travellers cheques	*mine rejsechecks*	*mee*·ne *rai*·se·sheks
wallet	*min pung*	meen pawng

I want to contact my …	*Jeg vil gerne kontakte …*	yai vil *gir*·ne kon·*taak*·te …
consulate	*mit konsulat*	meet kon·soo·*lat*
embassy	*min ambassade*	meen aam·ba·*sa*·dhe

health

medical needs

Where's the nearest …?	*Hvor er der …?*	vor ir deyr …
dentist	*en tandlæge*	in *tan*·le·ye
doctor	*en læge*	in *le*·ye
hospital	*et hospital*	it hos·pi·*tal*
(night) pharmacist	*et (nat)apotek*	it (*nat*·)aa·poh·*tek*

I need a doctor (who speaks English).
Jeg har brug for en læge (som taler engelsk). — yai haar broo for in *le*·ye (som *ta*·la *eng*·elsk)

Could I see a female doctor?
Må jeg få en kvindelig læge? — maw yai faw in *kvi*·ne·lee *le*·ye

I've run out of my medication.
Jeg er løbet tør for medicin. — yai ir *leu*·bet teur for mey·dee·*seen*

DANSK – health

symptoms, conditions & allergies

I'm sick.	*Jeg er syg.*	yai ir sew
It hurts here.	*Det gør ondt her.*	dey geur awnt heyr
I have (a) …	*Jeg har …*	yai haar …
asthma	*astma*	*ast*·ma
bronchitis	*bronkitis*	brawng·*kee*·tees
constipation	*forstoppelse*	for·*sto*·pel·se
cough	*hoste*	*hoh*·ste
diabetes	*sukkersyge*	*saw*·ka·sew·ye
diarrhoea	*diarré*	dee·a·*rey*
fever	*feber*	*fey*·ba
headache	*hovedpine*	*hoh*·vedh·pee·ne
heart condition	*hjerteproblemer*	*yer*·te·proh·bley·ma
nausea	*kvalme*	*kval*·me
pain	*smerter*	*smeyr*·ta
sore throat	*ondt i halsen*	awnt ee *hal*·sen
toothache	*tandpine*	tan·*pee*·ne
I'm allergic to …	*Jeg er allergisk over for …*	yai ir a·*ler*·geesk *o*·va for …
antibiotics	*antibiotika*	an·tee·bee·*oh*·tee·ka
anti-inflammatories	*betændelseshæmmende medicin*	bey·*te*·nel·ses·ha·me·ne mey·dee·*seen*
aspirin	*aspirin*	as·pee·*reen*
bees	*bier*	*bee*·a
codeine	*kodein*	koh·dey·*een*
penicillin	*penicillin*	pen·sey·*leen*
antiseptic	*antiseptisk*	an·tee·*sep*·teesk
bandage	*forbindning*	for·*bi*·ning
condoms	*kondomer*	kon·*doh*·ma
contraceptives	*preservativer*	pre·*seyr*·va·tee·va
diarrhoea medicine	*diarré medicin*	dee·a·*rey* mey·dee·*seen*
insect repellent	*insektspray*	in·*sekt*·spray
laxatives	*afføringsmiddel*	*ow*·feu·rings·mee·dhel
painkillers	*smertestillende middel*	*smer*·te·sti·le·ne mee·*dhel*
rehydration salts	*vanddrivende piller*	*van*·dree·ve·ne *pi*·la
sleeping tablets	*sovepiller*	*so*·ve·pi·la

english–danish dictionary

In this dictionary, words are marked as n (noun), a (adjective), v (verb), sg (singular), pl (plural), inf (informal) and pol (polite) where necessary. Note that Danish nouns are either 'common gender' (masculine or feminine forms but never referred to as such) or neuter. Common gender takes the indefinite article *en* (a) while the neuter forms take the article *et* (a). Every Danish noun needs to be learned with its indefinite article (*en* or *et*). We've only indicated the neuter nouns with ⓝ after the translation. Note also that the ending 't' is added to adjectives for the neuter form (ie when they accompany indefinite singular nouns).

A

accident *ulykke oo*·lew·ke
accommodation *indkvartering in*·kvaar·tey·ring
adaptor *adapter* a·*dap*·ter
address n *adresse* a·*draa*·se
after *efter ef*·ter
air conditioning *aircondition eyr*·kon·dee·shen
airplane *fly* ⓝ flew
airport *lufthavn lawft*·hawn
alcohol *alkohol al*·koh·hol
all a *alt/alle* sg/pl alt/*a*·le
allergy *allergi* a·ler·*gee*
ambulance *ambulance* am·boo·*lang*·se
and *og* o
ankle *ankel aang*·kel
arm *arm* aarm
ashtray *askebæger* ⓝ *as*·ke·be·ya
ATM *hæveautomat he*·ve·ow·toh·mat

B

baby *baby bey*·bee
back (body) *ryg* reug
backpack *rygsæk reug*·sek
bad *dårlig(t) dawr*·lee(t)
bag *taske tas*·ke
baggage claim *bagageudlevering* ba·*gaa*·she·oodh·ley·vey·ring
bank *bank* baank
bar *bar* baar
bathroom *badeværelse* ⓝ *ba*·dhe·*verl*·se
battery *batteri* ⓝ ba·ta·*ree*
beautiful *smuk(t)* smawk(t)
bed *seng* seng
beer *øl* eul
before *før* feur
behind *bag* ba
bicycle *cykel sew*·kel
big *stor(t)* stohr(t)
bill *regning rai*·ning
black *sort* sohrt
blanket *tæppe* ⓝ *te*·pe
blood group *blodgruppe blohdh*·groo·pe
blue *blå* blaw
boat *båd* bawdh
book (make a reservation) v *bestille* bey·*sti*·le
bottle *flaske flas*·ke
bottle opener *proptrækker prop*·trai·ka
boy *dreng* draing
brakes (car) *bremser brem*·sa
breakfast *morgenmad morn*·madh
broken (faulty) *i stykker* ee *stew*·ka
bus *bus* boos
business *forretninger* for·*rat*·ning·a
buy *købe keu*·be

C

café *café* ka·*fey*
camera *kamera* ⓝ *ka*·me·raa
camp site *campingplads kaam*·ping·plas
cancel *aflyse ow*·lew·se
can opener *dåseåbner daw*·se·awb·na
car *bil* beel
cash n *kontanter* kon·*tan*·ta
cash (a cheque) v *veksle (en check) veks*·le (in shek)
cell phone *mobiltelefon* moh·*beel*·tey·ley·*fohn*
centre *center* ⓝ *sen*·ta
change (money) v *veksle (penge) veks*·le (*peng*·e)
cheap *billig(t) bee*·lee(t)
check (bill) *regning rai*·ning
check-in n *check-in* chek·*in*
chest *bryst* ⓝ breust
child *barn* ⓝ baarn
cigarette *cigaret* see·ga·*ret*

A

DICTIONARY

city *storby* stohr·bew
clean a *ren(t)* ren(t)
closed *lukket* law·ket
coffee *kaffe* ka·fe
coins *mønter* meun·ta
cold a *kold(t)* kol(t)
collect call *modtageren betaler* mohdh·ta·yaan bey·ta·la
come *komme* ko·me
computer *computer* kom·pyoo·ta
condom *kondom* ⓝ kon·dohm
contact lenses *kontaktlinser* kon·takt·lin·sa
cook v *lave mad* la·ve madh
cost n *udgift* oodh·geeft
credit card *kreditkort* ⓝ kre·deet·kort
cup *kop* kop
currency exchange *vekslekontor* ⓝ veks·le·kon·tohr
customs (immigration) *told* tol

D

dangerous *farlig(t)* faar·lee(t)
Danish (language) *dansk* dansk
Danish a *dansk* dansk
date (time) *dato* da·toh
day *dag* day
delay n *forsinkelse* for·sing·kel·se
Denmark *Danmark* dan·mark
dentist *tandlæge* tan·le·ye
depart *afrejse* ow·rai·se
diaper *ble* bley
dictionary *ordbog* ohr·borw
dinner *middag* mi·da
direct *direkte* dee·rek·te
dirty *snavset* snow·set
disabled *handikappet* han·dee·ka·pet
discount n *rabat* raa·bat
doctor *læge* le·ye
double bed *dobbeltseng* ⓝ do·belt·seng
double room *dobbeltværelse* ⓝ do·belt·verl·se
drink n *drink* drink
drive v *køre* keu·re
drivers licence *kørekort* ⓝ keu·re·kort
drugs (illicit) *stoffer* sto·fa
dummy (pacifier) *sut* soot

E

ear *øre* ⓝ eu·re
east *øst* eust
eat *spise* spee·se
economy class *økonomiklasse* eu·koh·noh·mee·kla·se
electricity *elektricitet* ey·lek·tree·see·teyt
elevator *elevator* ey·ley·va·tor
email *email* ee·meyl
embassy *ambassade* aam·ba·sa·dhe
emergency *nødstilfælde* ⓝ neudhs·til·fe·le
English (language) *engelsk* eng·elsk
entrance *indgang* in·gaang
evening *aften* aaf·ten
exchange rate *vekslekurs* veks·le·koors
exit n *udgang* oodh·gaang
expensive *dyr(t)* dewr(t)
express mail *eksprespost* eks·pres·post
eye *øje* ⓝ oy·e

F

far (away) *langt (væk)* laangt (vek)
fast *hurtig(t)* hoor·tee(t)
father *far* faar
film (camera) *film* feelm
finger *finger* fing·aa
first-aid kit *førstehjælp* feur·ste·yelp
first class *første klasse* feur·ste kla·se
fish n *fisk* fisk
food *mad* madh
foot *fod* fohdh
fork *gaffel* gaa·fel
free (of charge) *gratis* graa·tees
friend *ven/veninde* ⓜ/ⓕ ven/ven·i·ne
fruit *frugt* frawgt
full *fuld(t)* fool(t)
funny *skæg(t)* skeg(t)

G

gift *gave* gaa·ve
girl *pige* pee·ye
glass (drinking) *glas* ⓝ glas
glasses *briller* bre·la
go *gå* gaw
good *god(t)* gohdh/got
green *grøn* greun
guide (person) n *guide* gaid

H

half n *halv* hal
hand *hånd* hawn
handbag *håndtaske* hawn·tas·ke

D

english–danish

happy *glad* gladh
have *have* ha/*ha*·ve
he *han* han
head *hoved* ⓝ *hoh*·vedh
heart *hjerte* ⓝ *yer*·te
heat n *varme* *vaar*·me
heavy *tung(t)* tawng(t)
help v *hjælpe* *yel*·pe
here *her* heyr
high *høj(t)* hoy(t)
highway *motorvej* *moh*·tor·vai
hike v *vandre* *vaan*·dre
holidays *ferie* *feyr*·ye
homosexual a *homoseksuel* *hoh*·moh·*sek*·soo·el
hospital *hospital* ⓝ hos·pi·*tal*
hot *varm(t)* vaarm(t)
hotel *hotel* ⓝ hoh·*tel*
hungry *sulten(t)* *sool*·ten(t)
husband *mand* man

I

I *jeg* yai
identification (card) *ID-kort* ⓝ *ee*·dey·kort
ill *syg(t)* sew(t)
important *vigtig(t)* *vig*·tee(t)
included *inklusive* *in*·kloo·seev
injury *skade* *ska*·dhe
insurance *forsikring* for·*sik*·ring
Internet *internet* *in*·ta·net
interpreter *tolk* tolk

J

jewellery *smykker* *smew*·ka
job *job* ⓝ job

K

key *nøgle* *noy*·le
kilogram *kilogram* ⓝ *kee*·lo·graam
kitchen *køkken* ⓝ *keu*·ken
knife *kniv* kneev

L

laundry (place) *møntvaskeri* ⓝ *meunt*·vas·ka·ree
lawyer *advokat* adh·voh·*kaat*
left (direction) *venstre* *ven*·stre
left-luggage office *rejsegodskontor* ⓝ *rai*·se·gaws·kon·*tohr*
leg *ben* beyn
lesbian a *lesbisk* *les*·beesk
less *mindre* *min*·dra
letter (mail) *brev* ⓝ brev
lift (elevator) *elevator* ey·ley·*va*·tor
light n *lys* lews
like v *kunne lide* *koo*·ne *lee*·dhe
lock n *lås* laws
long *lang(t)* laang(t)
lost *mistet* *mis*·tet
lost-property office *hittegodskontor* ⓝ *hee*·te·gaws·kon·*tohr*
love v *elske* *els*·ke
luggage *bagage* ba·*gaa*·she
lunch *frokost* *froh*·kost

M

mail n *post* post
man *mand* maan
map *kort* ⓝ kort
market *marked* ⓝ *maar*·kedh
matches *tændstikker* *ten*·sti·ka
meat *kød* keudh
medicine *medicin* me·dee·*seen*
menu *menu* me·*new*
message *besked* bey·*skeydh*
milk *mælk* melk
minute *minut* ⓝ mee·*noot*
mobile phone *mobiltelefon* moh·*beel*·tey·ley·*fohn*
money *penge* *peng*·e
month *måned* *maw*·nedh
morning *morgen* *mawr*·en
mother *mor* mohr
motorcycle *motorcykel* *moh*·tor·sew·kel
motorway *motorvej* *moh*·tor·vai
mouth *mund* mawn
music *musik* moo·*seek*

N

name *navn* ⓝ nown
napkin *serviet* seyr·vee·*yet*
nappy *ble* bley
near *nær(t)* ner(t)
neck *hals* hals
new *ny(t)* new(t)
news *nyheder* *new*·hey·dha

newspaper *avis* a·vees
night *nat* nat
no *nej* nai
noisy *støjende* sto·ye·ne
nonsmoking *ikke-ryger* i·ke·rew·a
north *nord* nohr
nose *næse* ne·se
now *nu* noo
number *nummer* ⓝ naw·ma

O

oil (engine) *olie* ohl·ye
old *gammel* gaa·mel
one-way ticket *enkeltbillet* eng·kelt·bee·let
open a *åben(t)* aw·ben(t)
outside *udenfor* oo·dhen·for

P

package *pakke* paa·ke
paper *papir* ⓝ pa·peer
park (car) v *parkere* paar·key·ra
passport *pas* ⓝ pas
pay *betale* bey·taa·le
pen *pen* pen
petrol *benzin* ben·seen
pharmacy *apotek* ⓝ aa·poh·tek
phonecard *telefonkort* ⓝ tey·ley·fohn·kort
photo *fotografi* ⓝ foh·toh·graa·fee
plate *tallerken* ta·ler·ken
police *politi* ⓝ poh·lee·tee
postcard *postkort* ⓝ post·kort
post office *postkontor* ⓝ post·kon·tohr
pregnant *gravid* graa·veedh
price *pris* prees

Q

quiet *stille* sti·le

R

rain n *regn* rain
razor *barbermaskine* baar·beyr·ma·skee·ne
receipt n *kvittering* kvee·tey·ring
red *rød* reudh
refund n *refundering* rey·foon·dey·ring
registered mail *anbefalet post* an·bey·fa·let post
rent v *leje* lai·ye
repair v *reparere* rey·paa·rey·ra
reservation *reservation* rey·sa·vaa·shohn
restaurant *restaurant* res·toh·rang
return v *returnere* rey·toor·ney·ra
return ticket *returbillet* rey·toor·bee·let
right (direction) *højre* hoy·re
road *vej* vai
room *værelse* ⓝ verl·se

S

safe a *sikker(t)* si·ka(t)
sanitary napkin *bind* ⓝ bin
seat *siddeplads* si·dhe·plas
send *sende* se·ne
service station *benzinstation* ben·seen·sta·shohn
sex *sex* seks
shampoo *shampoo* shaam·poh
share (a dorm) *dele* dey·le
shaving cream *barberskum* baar·beyr·skawm
she *hun* hoon
sheet (bed) *lagen* ⓝ la·yen
shirt *skjorte* skyor·te
shoes *sko* skoh
shop n *butik* boo·teek
short *kort* kort
shower n *brusebad* ⓝ broo·se·badh
single room *enkeltværelse* ⓝ eng·kelt·verl·se
skin *hud* hoodh
skirt *nederdel* ney·dha·deyl
sleep v *sove* so·ve
slowly *langsomt* laang·somt
small *lille* lee·le
smoke (cigarettes) v *ryge* rew·ye
soap *sæbe* se·be
some *nogle* noh·le
soon *snart* snart
south *syd* sewdh
souvenir shop *souvenirbutik* soo·ve·neer·boo·teek
speak *tale* ta·le
spoon *ske* skey
stamp *frimærke* ⓝ free·mer·ke
stand-by ticket *stand-by billet* stand·bai bee·let
station (train) *station* sta·shohn
stomach *mave* ma·ve
stop v *stoppe* sto·pe
stop (bus) n *busstoppested* ⓝ boos·sto·pe·stedh
street *gade* ga·dhe
student *studerende* stoo·dey·re·ne
sun *sol* sohl

O

english–danish

sunscreen *solcreme sohl*·kreym
swim v *svømme sveu*·me

T

tampons *tamponer* taam·*pong*·a
taxi *taxi tak*·see
teaspoon *teske tey*·skey
teeth *tænder ten*·a
telephone n *telefon* tey·ley·*fohn*
television *fjernsyn* ⓝ *fyern*·sewn
temperature (weather) *temperatur* tem·praa·*toor*
tent *telt* ⓝ telt
that (one) *den/det* ⓝ *(der)* den/dey (deyr)
they *de* dey
thirsty *tørstig(t) teurs*·tee(t)
this (one) *denne/dette* ⓝ *(her) de*·ne/*dey*·te (heyr)
throat *hals* hals
ticket *billet* bee·*let*
time *tid* tidh
tired *træt* tret
tissues *ansigtsservietter an*·sigts·ser·vee·*e*·ta
today *i dag* ee da
toilet *toilet* toy·*let*
tomorrow *i morgen* ee morn
tonight *i aften* ee *aaf*·ten
toothbrush *tandbørste taan*·beurs·te
toothpaste *tandpasta taan*·paas·taa
torch (flashlight) *lygte lewg*·te
tour n *tur* toor
tourist office *turistkontor* ⓝ too·*reest*·kon·tohr
towel *håndklæde* ⓝ *hawn*·kle·dhe
train *tog* ⓝ taw
translate *oversætte o*·va·se·te
travel agency *rejseagent rai*·se·a·*gent*
travellers cheque *rejsecheck rai*·se·shek
trousers *bukser bawk*·sa
twin beds *to senge* toh *seng*·e
tyre *dæk* ⓝ dek

U

underwear *undertøj aw*·na·toy
urgent *vigtig(t) vig*·tee(t)

V

vacant *ledig(t) ley*·dhee(t)
vacation *ferie feyr*·ye
vegetable n *grønsag greun*·saa
vegetarian a *vegetarisk* vey·gey·*taa*·reesk
visa *visum* ⓝ *vee*·sawm

W

waiter *tjener tye*·na
walk v *gå* gaw
wallet *pung* pawng
warm a *varm(t)* vaarm(t)
wash (something) *vaske vas*·ke
watch n *ur* ⓝ oor
water *vand* van
we *vi* vee
weekend *weekend wee*·kend
west *vest* vest
wheelchair *kørestol keu*·re·stohl
when *hvornår* vor·*nawr*
where *hvor* vor
white *hvid* veedh
who *hvem* vem
why *hvorfor vor*·for
wife *kone koh*·ne
window *vindue* ⓝ *vin*·doo
wine *vin* veen
with *med* medh
without *uden oo*·dhen
woman *kvinde kvi*·ne
write *skrive skree*·ve

Y

yellow *gul* gool
yes *ja* ya
yesterday *i går* ee gawr
you sg inf *du* doo
you sg pol *De* dee
you pl *I* ee

Dutch

dutch alphabet

Aa aa	*Bb* bey	*Cc* sey	*Dd* dey	*Ee* ey
Ff ef	*Gg* khey	*Hh* haa	*Ii* ee	*Jj* yey
Kk kaa	*Ll* el	*Mm* em	*Nn* en	*Oo* oh
Pp pey	*Qq* kew	*Rr* er	*Ss* es	*Tt* tey
Uu ew	*Vv* vey	*Ww* wey	*Xx* iks	*Yy* *eep*·see·lon/ey
Zz zet				

dutch

introduction

If you like to indulge in *booze* or *cookies*, have ever tried to *sketch* a *landscape*, are known to *bluff* or act *aloof*, dream of becoming a *mannequin* or going on a *cruise*, hate your *boss*, believe in *Santa Claus*, or you're simply a *Yankee* from *Brooklyn* or *Harlem*, you should know that all these words and many more came from Dutch (*Nederlands* *ney*·duhr·lants). Dutch is the third largest member of the Germanic language family, after English and German, and shares common roots with these languages. In grammar, in particular, it's close to German, but Dutch pronunciation presents a challenge for German and English speakers alike, due to some unusual sounds it employs.

Don't be confused when you hear the term Flemish (*Vlaams* vlaams) – from a linguistic point of view, it's really the same language as Dutch, but for historical and cultural reasons this is the name often used to refer to the language spoken in the north of Belgium. There are slight differences between this variety and the Dutch spoken in the Netherlands (they are indicated with Ⓝ/Ⓑ in this chapter). However, both the Netherlands and Belgium are members of the *Nederlandse Taalunie* (Dutch Language Union), the supreme authority on modern language standards. In both countries Dutch has official status (shared in Belgium with French and German).

The boundaries of various local dialects throughout both the Netherlands and Belgium are historical rather than political. The standard language is based on the northern dialects, mainly as spoken around Amsterdam. One of the major influences on the modern language came from the Bible translation of 1637, known as the *Staten-Bijbel*. Dutch is written with the 26-letter Roman alphabet, just like English.

With over 20 million speakers, Dutch has a strong presence on the world linguistic stage. Its global influence came with the expansion of the Dutch empire during the 16th and 17th centuries. Thanks to the explorers and traders who brought Dutch to many corners of the globe, today it has official status in Aruba, the Dutch Antilles and Suriname. There are still Dutch speakers in Indonesia, although the local varieties that developed in this former colony of the Netherlands are now virtually extinct. In New York (formerly known as New Amsterdam), a simplified form of Dutch was still in use during the 18th century. But the greatest achievement of the Dutch linguistic expansion is its famous offspring – Afrikaans, now considered a separate language and spoken by around six million people in South Africa.

pronunciation

vowel sounds

Dutch is rich in vowels – it's important to distinguish between the long and short versions of each vowel sound. There are also a few combined vowels or 'diphthongs' that can be a bit tricky for English speakers to pronounce (eg the öy sound, which has no equivalent in English). If you listen carefully to native speakers and follow our coloured pronunciation guides, you shouldn't have any problems being understood.

symbol	english equivalent	dutch example	transliteration
a	run	*vak*	vak
aa	father	*vaak*	vaak
aw	saw	*lauw, koud*	law, kawt
e	bet	*bed*	bet
ee	see	*niet*	neet
eu	nurse	*leuk*	leuk
ew	ee pronounced with rounded lips	*u, uur*	ew, ewr
ey	as in 'bet', but longer	*beet, reis, mijn*	beyt, reys, meyn
i	hit	*ik*	ik
o	pot	*bot*	bot
oh	oh	*boot*	boht
oo	zoo	*boer*	boor
öy	her year (without the 'r')	*buik*	böyk
u	put	*hut*	hut
uh	ago	*het, een*	huht, uhn

word stress

There are no universal rules on stress in Dutch. Just follow our pronunciation guides, in which the stressed syllables are indicated with italics.

consonant sounds

Dutch consonants are pretty straightforward to pronounce, as most are identical to those in English. You might need a little practice with the kh sound, which is guttural and harsher than the English 'h' (it sounds like a hiss produced between the tongue and the back roof of the mouth).

symbol	english equivalent	dutch example	transliteration
b	bed	*bed*	bet
ch	cheat	*kindje*	*kin*·chuh
d	dog	*dag*	dakh
f	fat	*fiets*	feets
g	go	*gate*	geyt
h	hat	*hoed*	hoot
k	kit	*klok*	klok
kh	as the 'ch' in the Scottish *loch*	*goed, schat*	khoot, skhat
l	lot	*lied*	leet
m	man	*man*	man
n	not	*niet*	neet
ng	ring	*haring*	*haa*·ring
p	pet	*pot*	pot
r	red (trilled)	*rechts*	rekhs
s	sun	*slapen*	*slaa*·puhn
sh	shot	*alsjeblieft*	a·shuh·*bleeft*
t	top	*tafel*	*taa*·fuhl
v	very	*vlucht*	vlukht
w	win	*water*	*waa*·tuhr
y	yes	*je*	yuh
z	zero	*zomer*	*zoh*·muhr
zh	pleasure	*garage*	kha·*raa*·zhuh

tools

language difficulties

Do you speak English?		
Spreekt u Engels? pol		spreykt ew *eng*·uhls
Do you understand?		
Begrijpt u? pol		buh·*khreypt* ew
I (don't) understand.		
Ik begrijp het (niet).		ik buh·*khreyp* huht (neet)
What does (*verboden*) mean?		
Wat betekent (verboden)?		wat buh·*tey*·kuhnt (vuhr·*boh*·duhn)
Could you please speak more slowly?		
Kunt u alstublieft wat trager spreken? pol		kunt ew al·stew·*bleeft* wat *traa*·khuhr *sprey*·kuhn
How do you ...?	*Hoe ...?*	hoo ...
pronounce this	*spreek je dit uit*	spreyk yuh dit öyt
write (*dank u wel*)	*schrijf je (dank u wel)*	skhreyf yuh (dangk ew wel)
Could you please ...?	*Kunt u dat alstublieft ...?* pol	kunt ew dat al·stew·*bleeft* ...
repeat that	*herhalen*	her·*haa*·luhn
write it down	*opschrijven*	*op*·skhrey·vuhn

essentials

Yes.	*Ja.*	yaa
No.	*Nee.*	ney
Please.	*Alstublieft.* pol	al·stew·*bleeft*
	Alsjeblieft. inf	a·shuh·*bleeft*
Thank you (very much).	*Dank u (wel).* pol	dangk ew (wel)
	Dank je (wel). inf	dangk yuh (wel)
Thanks.	*Bedankt.*	buh·*dangt*
You're welcome.	*Graag gedaan.*	khraakh khuh·*daan*
Excuse me.	*Pardon.*	par·*don*
Sorry.	*Sorry.*	*so*·ree

numbers					
0	*nul*	nul	16	*zestien*	*zes*·teen
1	*één*	eyn	17	*zeventien*	*zey*·vuhn·teen
2	*twee*	twey	18	*achttien*	*akh*·teen
3	*drie*	dree	19	*negentien*	*ney*·khuhn·teen
4	*vier*	veer	20	*twintig*	*twin*·tikh
5	*vijf*	veyf	21	*eenentwintig*	*eyn*·en·twin·tikh
6	*zes*	zes	22	*tweeëntwintig*	*twey*·en·twin·tikh
7	*zeven*	*zey*·vuhn	30	*dertig*	*der*·tikh
8	*acht*	akht	40	*veertig*	*feyr*·tikh
9	*negen*	*ney*·khuhn	50	*vijftig*	*feyf*·tikh
10	*tien*	teen	60	*zestig*	*ses*·tikh
11	*elf*	elf	70	*zeventig*	*sey*·vuhn·tikh
12	*twaalf*	twaalf	80	*tachtig*	*takh*·tikh
13	*dertien*	*der*·teen	90	*negentig*	*ney*·khuhn·tikh
14	*veertien*	*veyr*·teen	100	*honderd*	*hon*·duhrt
15	*vijftien*	*veyf*·teen	1000	*duizend*	*döy*·zuhnt

time & dates

What time is it?	*Hoe laat is het?*	hoo laat is huht
It's one o'clock.	*Het is één uur.*	huht is eyn ewr
It's (two) o'clock.	*Het is (twee) uur.*	huht is (twey) ewr
Quarter past (one).	*Kwart over (één).*	kwart *oh*·vuhr (eyn)
Half past (one).	*Half (twee).* (lit: half two)	half (twey)
Quarter to (eight).	*Kwart voor (acht).*	kwart vohr (akht)
At what time ...?	*Hoe laat ...?*	hoo laat ...
At ...	*Om ...*	om ...
in the morning	*'s morgens/'s ochtends*	*smor*·khuhns/*sokh*·tuhns
in the afternoon	*'s middags*	*smi*·dakhs
in the evening	*'s avonds*	*saa*·vonts
Monday	*maandag*	*maan*·dakh
Tuesday	*dinsdag*	*dins*·dakh
Wednesday	*woensdag*	*woons*·dakh
Thursday	*donderdag*	*don*·duhr·dakh
Friday	*vrijdag*	*vrey*·dakh
Saturday	*zaterdag*	*zaa*·tuhr·dakh
Sunday	*zondag*	*zon*·dakh

January	*januari*	ya·new·*waa*·ree
February	*februari*	fey·brew·*waa*·ree
March	*maart*	maart
April	*april*	a·*pril*
May	*mei*	mey
June	*juni*	*yew*·nee
July	*juli*	*yew*·lee
August	*augustus*	aw·*khus*·tus
September	*september*	sep·*tem*·buhr
October	*oktober*	ok·*toh*·buhr
November	*november*	noh·*vem*·buhr
December	*december*	dey·*sem*·buhr

What date is it today?
De hoeveelste is het vandaag? — duh hoo·*veyl*·stuh is huht van·*daakh*

It's (9 January).
Het is (negen januari). — huht is (*ney*·khuhn ya·new·*waa*·ree)

since (May)	*sinds (mei)*	sins (mey)
until (June)	*tot (juni)*	tot (*yew*·nee)
yesterday	*gisteren*	*khis*·tuh·ruhn
today	*vandaag*	van·*daakh*
tonight (before midnight)	*vanavond*	va·*naa*·vont
tonight (after midnight)	*vannacht*	va·*nakht*
tomorrow	*morgen*	*mor*·khuhn
last/next night (before midnight)	*gisteravond/ morgenavond*	*khis*·tuhr·*aa*·vont/ *mor*·khuhn·*aa*·vont
last/next year	*vorig/komend jaar*	*voh*·rikh/*koh*·muhnt yaar
last/next …	*vorige/komende …*	*voh*·ri·khuh/*koh*·muhn·duh …
night (after midnight)	*nacht*	nakht
week	*week*	weyk
month	*maand*	maant
yesterday/tomorrow …	*gister-/morgen- …*	*khis*·tuhr·/*mor*·khuhn· …
morning	*ochtend*	*okh*·tuhnt
afternoon	*middag*	*mi*·dakh
evening	*avond*	*aa*·vont

weather

What's the weather like?
Hoe is het weer? — hoo is huht weyr

It's …	*Het is …*	huht is …
cloudy	*bewolkt*	buh·*wolkt*
cold	*koud*	kawt
foggy	*mistig*	*mis*·tikh
hot	*zeer warm*	zeyr warm
rainy	*regenachtig*	*rey*·khuhn·akh·tikh
sunny	*zonnig*	*zo*·nikh
warm	*warm*	warm
It's …	*Het …*	huht …
freezing	*vriest*	vreest
raining	*regent*	*rey*·khuhnt
snowing	*sneeuwt*	sneywt
windy	*waait*	waayt
spring	*lente*	*len*·tuh
summer	*zomer*	*zoh*·muhr
autumn	*herfst*	herfst
winter	*winter*	*win*·tuhr

border crossing

I'm here …	*Ik ben hier …*	ik ben heer …
in transit	*op doorreis*	op *doh*·reys
on business	*voor zaken*	vohr *zaa*·kuhn
on holiday	*met vakantie*	met va·*kan*·see
I'm here for …	*Ik ben hier voor …*	ik ben heer vohr …
(10) days	*(tien) dagen*	(teen) *daa*·khuhn
(three) weeks	*(drie) weken*	(dree) *wey*·kuhn
(two) months	*(twee) maanden*	(twey) *maan*·duhn

I'm going to (Den Helder).
Ik ben op weg naar (Den Helder). — ik ben op wekh naar (duhn *hel*·duhr)

I'm staying at the (Hotel Industrie).
Ik verblijf in (Hotel Industrie). — ik vuhr·*bleyf* in (hoh·*tel* in·dus·*tree*)

I have nothing to declare.
Ik heb niets aan te geven. — ik hep neets aan tuh *khey*·vuhn

I have something to declare.
Ik heb iets aan te geven. — ik hep eets aan tuh *khey*·vuhn

That's (not) mine.
Dat is (niet) van mij. — dat is (neet) van mey

I didn't know I had to declare it.
Ik wist niet dat ik het moest aangeven. — ik wist neet dat ik huht moost *aan*·khey·vuhn

transport

tickets & luggage

Where can I buy a ticket?
Waar kan ik een kaartje/ticket kopen? Ⓝ/Ⓑ — waar kan ik uhn *kaar*·chuh/ti·*ket* *koh*·puhn

Do I need to book a seat?
Moet ik een zitplaats reserveren? — moot ik uhn *zit*·plaats rey·zer·*vey*·ruhn

One ... (to Antwerp), please.	*Een ... (naar Antwerpen) graag.*	uhn ... (naar *ant*·wer·puhn) khraakh
one-way ticket	*enkele reis*	*eng*·kuh·luh reys
return ticket	*retourtje*	ruh·*toor*·chuh

I'd like to ... my ticket, please.	*Ik wil graag mijn kaartje/ticket ...* Ⓝ/Ⓑ	ik wil khraakh meyn *kaar*·chuh/ti·*ket* ...
cancel	*annuleren*	a·new·*ley*·ruhn
change	*wijzigen*	*wey*·zi·khuhn
collect	*afhalen*	*af*·haa·luhn
confirm	*bevestigen*	buh·*ves*·ti·khuhn

I'd like a ... seat, please.	*Ik wil graag ...*	ik wil khraakh ...
nonsmoking	*niet-roken*	*neet*·roh·kuhn
smoking	*roken*	*roh*·kuhn

How much is it?
Hoeveel kost het? — hoo·*veyl* kost huht

Is there air conditioning?
Is er airconditioning? — is uhr *eyr*·kon·di·shuh·ning

Is there a toilet?
Is er een toilet? — is uhr uhn twa·*let*

How long does the trip take?
Hoe lang duurt de reis? — hoo lang dewrt duh reys

Is it a direct route?
Is het een rechtstreekse verbinding? — is huht uhn *rekh*·streyk·suh vuhr·*bin*·ding

I'd like a luggage locker.
Ik wil graag een bagagekluis. — ik wil khraakh uhn ba·*khaa*·zhuh·klöys

My luggage has been ...	*Mijn bagage is ...*	meyn ba·*khaa*·zhuh is ...
damaged	*beschadigd*	buh·*skhaa*·dikht
lost	*verloren*	vuhr·*loh*·ruhn
stolen	*gestolen*	khuh·*stoh*·luhn

getting around

Where does flight (KL1082) arrive?
Waar komt vlucht (KL1082) aan? — waar komt vlukht (kaa el teen *twey*·en·takh·tikh) aan

Where does flight (KL1083) depart?
Waar vertrekt vlucht (KL1083)? — waar vuhr·*trekt* vlukht (kaa el teen *dree*·en·takh·tikh)

Where's (the) ...?	*Waar is ...?*	waar is ...
arrivals hall	*de aankomsthal*	duh *aan*·komst·hal
departures hall	*de vertrekhal*	duh vuhr·*trek*·hal
duty-free shop	*de duty-free*	duh dew·tee·*free*
gate (12)	*gate (twaalf)*	geyt (twaalf)

Is this the ... to (Amsterdam)?	*Is dit ... naar (Amsterdam)?*	is dit ... naar (am·stuhr·*dam*)
boat	*de boot*	duh boht
bus	*de bus*	duh bus
plane	*het vliegtuig*	huht *vleekh*·töykh
train	*de trein*	duh treyn

What time's the ... bus?	*Hoe laat gaat de ... bus?*	hoo laat khaat duh ... bus
first	*eerste*	*eyr*·stuh
last	*laatste*	*laat*·stuh
next	*volgende*	*vol*·khuhn·duh

At what time does (the train) leave?
Hoe laat vertrekt (de trein)? hoo laat vuhr·*trekt* (duh treyn)

At what time does (the train) arrive?
Hoe laat komt (de trein) aan? hoo laat komt (duh treyn) aan

How long will it be delayed?
Hoeveel vertraging is er? hoo·*veyl* vuhr·*traa*·khing is uhr

What station is this?
Welk station is dit? welk sta·*syon* is dit

What stop is this?
Welke stop is dit? *wel*·kuh stop is dit

What's the next station?
Welk is het volgende station? welk is huht *vol*·khuhn·duh sta·*syon*

What's the next stop?
Welk is de volgende stop? welk is duh *vol*·khuhn·duh stop

Does it stop at (Berchem)?
Stopt het in (Berchem)? stopt huht in (*ber*·khuhm)

Please tell me when we get to (Dordrecht).
Kunt u me laten weten wanneer we in (Dordrecht) aankomen? pol kunt ew muh *laa*·tuhn *wey*·tuhn wa·*neyr* wuh in (*dòr*·drekht) *aan*·koh·muhn

How long do we stop here?
Hoe lang houden we hier halt? hoo lang *haw*·duhn wuh heer halt

Is this seat available?
Is deze zitplaats vrij? is *dey*·zuh *zit*·plaats vrey

That's my seat.
Dat is mijn zitplaats. dat is meyn *zit*·plaats

I'd like a taxi . . .	*Ik wil graag een taxi . . .*	ik wil khraakh uhn *tak*·see . . .
at (9am)	*om (negen uur 's morgens)*	om (*ney*·khuhn ewr *smor*·khuhns)
now	*nu*	new
tomorrow	*voor morgen*	vohr *mor*·khuhn

Is this taxi available?
Is deze taxi vrij? — is *dey*·zuh *tak*·see vrey

How much is it to ...?
Hoeveel kost het naar ...? — hoo·*veyl* kost huht naar ...

Please take me to (this address).
Breng me alstublieft naar (dit adres). pol — breng muh al·stew·*bleeft* naar (dit a·*dres*)

Please slow down.
Rijd alstublieft wat langzamer. pol — reyt al·stew·*bleeft* wat *lang*·zaa·muhr

Please stop here.
Stop hier alstublieft. pol — stop heer al·stew·*bleeft*

Please wait here.
Wacht hier alstublieft. pol — wakht heer al·stew·*bleeft*

car, motorbike & bicycle hire

I'd like to hire a ...	*Ik wil graag een ... huren.*	ik wil khraakh uhn ... *hew*·ruhn
bicycle	*fiets*	feets
car	*auto*	*aw*·toh
motorbike	*motorfiets*	*moh*·tor·feets
with ...	*met ...*	met ...
air conditioning	*airconditioning*	*eyr*·kon·di·shuh·ning
antifreeze	*antivries*	an·tee·*vrees*
snow chains	*sneeuwkettingen*	*sneyw*·ke·ting·uhn
How much for ... hire?	*Hoeveel is het per ...?*	hoo·*veyl* is huht puhr ...
hourly	*uur*	ewr
daily	*dag*	dakh
weekly	*week*	weyk
How much is it per ...?	*Hoeveel is het per ...?*	hoo·*veyl* is huht puhr ...
morning	*ochtend*	*okh*·tuhnt
afternoon	*middag*	*mi*·dakh
air	*lucht*	lukht
oil	*olie*	*oh*·lee
petrol	*benzine*	ben·*zee*·nuh
tyres	*banden*	*ban*·duhn

I need a mechanic.
Ik heb een monteur/mecanicien nodig. Ⓝ/Ⓑ — ik hep uhn mon·*teur*/mey·ka·nee·*sye* *noh*·dikh

I've run out of petrol.
Ik zit zonder benzine. — ik zit *zon*·duhr ben·*zee*·nuh

I have a flat tyre.
Ik heb een lekke band. — ik hep uhn *le*·kuh bant

directions

Where's the ...?	*Waar is ...?*	waar is ...
bank	*de bank*	duh bangk
city centre	*het stadscentrum*	huht *stat*·sen·truhm
hotel	*het hotel*	huht hoh·*tel*
market	*de markt*	duh mart
police station	*het politiebureau*	huht po·*leet*·see·bew·roh
post office	*het postkantoor*	huht *post*·kan·tohr
public toilet	*het openbaar toilet*	huht *oh*·puhn·baar twa·*let*
tourist office	*de VVV* Ⓝ	duh vey·vey·*vey*
	het toerismebureau Ⓑ	huht too·*ris*·muh·bew·roh

Is this the road to (Katwijk)?
Gaat deze weg naar (Katwijk)? — khaat *dey*·zuh wekh naar (*kat*·weyk)

Can you show me (on the map)?
Kunt u het aanwijzen (op de kaart)? pol — kunt ew huht *aan*·wey·zuhn (op duh kaart)

What's the address?
Wat is het adres? — wat is huht a·*dres*

How far is it?
Hoe ver is het? — hoo ver is huht

How do I get there?
Hoe kom ik er? — hoo kom ik uhr

Can I get there by (bicycle)?
Kun je er met de (fiets) heen? — kun yuh uhr met duh (feets) heyn

Turn left/right ...	*Sla linksaf/rechtsaf ...*	slaa *lings*·af/*rekhs*·af ...
at the corner	*op de hoek*	op duh hook
at the traffic lights	*bij de verkeerslichten*	bey duh vuhr·*keyrs*·likh·tuhn

It's ...	*Het is ...*	huht is ...
behind ...	*achter ...*	*akh*·tuhr ...
far away	*ver*	ver
here	*hier*	heer
in front of ...	*voor ...*	vohr ...
left	*links*	lingks
near	*dichtbij*	dikht·*bey*
near to ...	*dicht bij ...*	dikht bey ...
next to ...	*naast ...*	naast ...
opposite ...	*tegenover ...*	tey·khuh·*noh*·vuhr ...
right	*rechts*	rekhs
straight ahead	*rechtdoor*	rekh·*dohr*
there	*daar*	daar

north	*noord*	nohrt
south	*zuid*	zöyt
east	*oost*	ohst
west	*west*	west

by bicycle	*met de fiets*	met duh feets
by bus	*met de bus*	met duh bus
by taxi	*met de taxi*	met duh *tak*·see
by train	*met de trein*	met duh treyn
on foot	*te voet*	tuh voot

signs

Ingang/Uitgang	*in*·khang/*öyt*·khang	**Entrance/Exit**
Open/Gesloten	*oh*·puhn/khuh·*sloh*·tuhn	**Open/Closed**
Kamers Vrij	*kaa*·muhrs vrey	**Rooms Available**
Volzet	vol *zet*	**No Vacancies**
Inlichtingen	*in*·likh·ting·uhn	**Information**
Politiebureau	po·*leet*·see·bew·roh	**Police Station**
Verboden	vuhr·*boh*·duhn	**Prohibited**
Toiletten/WC's	twa·*le*·tuhn/wey·*seys*	**Toilets**
Heren	*hey*·ruhn	**Men**
Dames	*daa*·muhs	**Women**
Warm/Koud	warm/kawt	**Hot/Cold**

accommodation

finding accommodation

Where's a …?	*Waar vind ik een …?*	waar vint ik uhn …
camping ground	*camping*	*kem*·ping
guesthouse	*pension*	pen·*syon*
hotel	*hotel*	hoh·*tel*
youth hostel	*jeugdherberg*	*yeukht*·her·berkh
Can you recommend somewhere …?	*Kunt u iets … aanbevelen?* **pol**	kunt ew eets … *aan*·buh·vey·luhn
cheap	*goedkoops*	khoot·*kohps*
good	*goeds*	khoots
nearby	*dichtbij*	dikht·*bey*

I'd like to book a room, please.
Ik wil graag een kamer reserveren. — ik wil khraakh uhn *kaa*·muhr rey·zer·*vey*·ruhn

I have a reservation.
Ik heb een reservatie. — ik hep uhn rey·zer·*vaa*·see

My name's …
Mijn naam is … — meyn naam is …

Do you have a … room?	*Heeft u een …?* **pol**	heyft ew uhn …
single	*eenpersoonskamer*	*eyn*·puhr·sohns·kaa·muhr
double	*tweepersoonskamer met een dubbel bed*	*twey*·puhr·sohns·kaa·muhr met uhn *du*·buhl bet
twin	*tweepersoonskamer met twee enkele bedden*	*twey*·puhr·sohns·kaa·muhr met twey *eng*·kuh·luh *be*·duhn
How much is it per …?	*Hoeveel is het per …?*	hoo·*veyl* is huht puhr …
night	*nacht*	nakht
person	*persoon*	puhr·*sohn*
Can I pay …?	*Kan ik met … betalen?*	kan ik met … buh·*taa*·luhn
by credit card	*mijn kredietkaart*	meyn krey·*deet*·kaart
with a travellers cheque	*een reischeque*	uhn *reys*·shek

I'd like to stay for (two) nights.
(Twee) overnachtingen graag. — (twey) oh·vuhr·*nakh*·ting·uhn khraakh

From (2 July) to (6 July).
Van (twee juli) tot (zes juli). — van (twey *yew*·lee) tot (zes *yew*·lee)

Can I see it?
Kan ik een kijkje nemen? kan ik uhn *keyk*·yuh *ney*·muhn

Am I allowed to camp here?
Mag ik hier kamperen? makh ik heer kam·*pey*·ruhn

Is there a camping ground nearby?
Is er een camping in de buurt? is uhr uhn *kem*·ping in duh bewrt

requests & queries

When's breakfast served?
Hoe laat wordt het ontbijt geserveerd? hoo laat wort huht ont·*beyt* khuh·ser·*veyrt*

Where's breakfast served?
Waar wordt het ontbijt geserveerd? waar wort huht ont·*beyt* khuh·ser·*veyrt*

Please wake me at (seven).
Maak mij wakker om (zeven) uur alstublieft. pol maak mey *wa*·kuhr om (*zey*·vuhn) ewr al·stew·*bleeft*

Could I have my key, please?
Kan ik mijn sleutel hebben alstublieft? pol kan ik meyn *sleu*·tuhl *he*·buhn al·stew·*bleeft*

Can I get another (blanket)?
Kan ik een nog een (deken) hebben alstublieft? pol kan ik nokh uhn (*dey* kuhn) *he*·buhn al·stew·*bleeft*

Is there an elevator/a safe?
Heeft u een lift/kluis? pol heyft ew uhn lift/klöys

The room is too ...	*De kamer is te ...*	duh *kaa*·muhr is tuh ...
expensive	*duur*	dewr
noisy	*lawaaierig*	la·*waa*·yuh·rikh
small	*klein*	kleyn

The ... doesn't work.	*... is stuk.*	... is stuk
air conditioning	*De airconditioning*	duh *eyr*·kon·di·shuh·ning
fan	*De ventilator*	duh ven·tee·*laa*·tor
toilet	*Het toilet*	huht twa·*let*

This ... isn't clean.	*... is niet schoon.*	... is neet skhohn
pillow	*Dit kussen*	dit *ku*·suhn
sheet	*Dit laken*	dit *laa*·kuhn
towel	*Deze handdoek*	*dey*·zuh *han*·dook

checking out

What time is checkout?
Hoe laat is het uitchecken? — hoo laat is huht *öyt*·che·kuhn

Can I leave my luggage here?
Kan ik mijn bagage hier laten? — kan ik meyn ba·*khaa*·zhuh heer *laa*·tuhn

Could I have my . . ., please? pol	*Kan ik mijn . . . hebben alstublieft?*	kan ik meyn . . . *he*·buhn al·stew·*bleeft*
deposit	*borg*	borkh
passport	*paspoort*	*pas*·pohrt
valuables	*waardevolle bezittingen*	*waar*·duh·vo·luh buh·*zi*·ting·uhn

communications & banking

the internet

Where's the local Internet café?
Waar is het plaatselijke internetcafé? — waar is huht *plaat*·suh·luh·kuh *in*·tuhr·net·ka·fey

How much is it per hour?
Hoeveel is het per uur? — hoo·*veyl* is huht puhr ewr

I'd like to . . .	*Ik wil graag . . .*	ik wil khraakh . . .
check my email	*mijn e-mails checken*	meyn *ee*·meyls *che*·kuhn
get Internet access	*op het internet gaan*	op huht *in*·tuhr·net khaan
use a printer	*een printer gebruiken*	uhn *prin*·tuhr khuh·*bröy*·kuhn
use a scanner	*een scanner gebruiken*	uhn *ska*·nuhr khuh·*bröy*·kuhn

mobile/cell phone

I'd like a . . .	*Ik wil graag een . . .*	ik wil khraakh uhn . . .
mobile/cell phone for hire	*mobiele telefoon huren* Ⓝ	moh·*bee*·luh tey·ley·*fohn* *hew*·ruhn
	GSM huren Ⓑ	khey·es·*em* *hew*·ruhn
SIM card for your network	*sim-kaart voor uw netwerk*	*sim*·kaart vohr ew *net*·werk

What are the rates? *Wat zijn de tarieven?* — wat zeyn duh ta·*ree*·vuhn

telephone

What's your phone number?
Wat is uw/jouw telefoonnummer? pol/inf — wat is ew/yaw tey·ley·*foh*·nu·muhr

The number is ...
Het nummer is ... — huht *nu*·muhr is ...

Where's the nearest public phone?
Waar is de dichstbijzijnde openbare telefoon? — waar is duh dikhs·bey·*zeyn*·duh oh·puhn·*baa*·ruh tey·ley·*fohn*

I'd like to buy a phonecard.
Ik wil graag een telefoonkaart kopen. — ik wil khraakh uhn tey·ley·*fohn*·kaart *koh*·puhn

I want to ...	*Ik wil ...*	ik wil ...
call (Ireland)	*(Ierland) bellen*	(*eer*·lant) *be*·luhn
make a local call	*een lokaal telefoon gesprek maken*	uhn loh·*kaal* tey·ley·*fohn*·khuh·*sprek maa*·kuhn
reverse the charges	*dat de ontvanger betaalt*	dat duh ont·*vang*·uhr buh *taalt*
How much does ... cost?	*Hoeveel kost ...?*	hoo·*veyl* kost
a (three)-minute call	*een gesprek van (drie) minuten*	uhn khuh·*sprek* van (dree) mee·*new*·tuhn
each extra minute	*het per extra minuut*	huht puhr *eks*·traa mee·*newt*
(One euro) per minute.	*(Één euro) per minuut.*	(eyn *ew*·roh) puhr mee·*newt*

post office

I want to send a	*Ik wil een ... sturen.*	ik wil uhn ... *stew*·ruhn
fax	*fax*	faks
letter	*brief*	breef
parcel	*pakje*	*pak*·yuh
postcard	*ansichtkaart*	*an*·sikht·kaart
I want to buy a/an ...	*Ik wil een ... kopen.*	ik wil uhn ... *koh*·puhn
envelope	*envelop*	en·vuh·*lop*
stamp	*postzegel*	*post*·zey·khuhl

Please send it (to Australia) by …	*Stuur het alstublieft (naar Australië) per …* pol	stewr huht al·stew·*bleeft* (naar aw·*straa*·lee·yuh) puhr …
airmail	*luchtpost*	*lukht*·post
express mail	*exprespost*	eks·*pres*·post
registered mail	*aangetekende post*	*aan*·khuh·tey·kuhn·duh post
surface mail	*gewone post*	khuh·*woh*·nuh post
Is there any mail for me?	*Is er post voor mij?*	is uhr post vohr mey

bank

Where's a/an …?	*Waar vind ik een …?*	waar vint ik uhn …
ATM	*pin-automaat* Ⓝ	*pin*·aw·toh·maat
	geldautomaat Ⓑ	*khelt*·aw·toh·maat
foreign exchange office	*wisselkantoor*	*wi*·suhl·kan·tohr
I'd like to …	*Ik wil graag …*	ik wil khraakh …
Where can I …?	*Waar kan ik …?*	waar kan ik …
arrange a transfer	*geld overmaken*	khelt *oh*·vuhr·maa·kuhn
cash a cheque	*een cheque innen*	uhn shek *i*·nuhn
change a travellers cheque	*een reischeque innen*	uhn *reys*·shek *i*·nuhn
change money	*geld wisselen*	khelt *wi*·suh·luhn
get a cash advance	*een voorschot bekomen*	uhn *vohr*·skhot buh·*koh*·muhn
withdraw money	*geld afhalen*	khelt *af*·haa·luhn
What's the …?	*Wat is de …?*	wat is duh …
charge for that	*kost hiervoor*	kost *heer*·vohr
commission	*commissie*	ko·*mi*·see
exchange rate	*wisselkoers*	*wi*·suhl·koors
It's …	*Het is …*	huht is …
(12) euros	*(twaalf) euro*	(twaalf) *ew*·roh
free	*gratis*	*khraa*·tis

What time does the bank open?
Hoe laat gaat de bank open? — hoo laat khaat duh bangk *oh*·puhn

Has my money arrived yet?
Is mijn geld al aangekomen? — is meyn khelt al *aan*·khuh·koh·muhn

sightseeing

getting in

What time does it open/close?
Hoe laat gaat het open/dicht? — hoo laat khaat huht *oh*·puhn/dikht

What's the admission charge?
Wat is de toegangsprijs? — wat is duh *too*·khangs·preys

Is there a discount for students/children?
Is er korting voor studenten/kinderen? — is uhr *kor*·ting vohr stew·*den*·tuhn/*kin*·duh·ruhn

I'd like a ...	*Ik wil graag een ...*	ik wil khraakh uhn ...
catalogue	*cataloog*	ka·ta·*lohkh*
guide	*gids*	khits
map (building)	*plattegrond*	pla·tuh·*khront*
map (town)	*kaart*	kaart

I'd like to see ...	*Ik wil graag ... zien.*	ik wil khraakh ... zeen
What's that?	*Wat is dat?*	wat is dat
Can I take a photo?	*Mag ik een foto nemen?*	makh ik uhn *foh*·toh *ney*·muhn

tours

When's the next ...?	*Wanneer is de volgende ...?*	wa·*neyr* is duh *vol*·khuhn·duh ...
day trip	*daguitstap*	*dakh*·öyt·stap
tour	*rondleiding*	*ront*·ley·ding

Is ... included?	*Is ... inbegrepen?*	is ... in·buh·*khrey*·puhn
accommodation	*accommodatie*	a·koh·moh·*daa*·see
the admission charge	*de toegangsprijs*	duh *too*·khangs·preys
food	*het eten*	huht *ey*·tuhn
transport	*het transport*	huht trans·*port*

How long is the tour?
Hoe lang duurt de rondleiding? — hoo lang dewrt duh *ront*·ley·ding

What time should we be back?
Hoe laat moeten we terug zijn? — hoo laat *moo*·tuhn wuh tuh·*rukh* zeyn

sightseeing

bridge	*brug*	brukh
castle	*kasteel* n	kas·*teyl*
cathedral	*kathedraal*	ka·tey·*draal*
church	*kerk*	kerk
main square	*stadsplein* n	*stats*·pleyn
(wind)mill	*(wind)molen*	(wint·)*moh*·luhn
monastery	*klooster* n	*kloh*·stuhr
monument	*monument* n	mo·new·*ment*
museum	*museum* n	mew·*see*·yum
old city	*oude stad*	*aw*·duh stat
palace	*paleis* n	pa·*leys*
ruins	*ruines*	*rwee*·nuhs
stadium	*stadion* n	*staa*·dyon
statue	*standbeeld* n	*stant*·beylt

shopping

enquiries

Where's a ... ?	*Waar vind ik een ...?*	waar vint ik uhn ...
bank	*bank*	bangk
bookshop	*boekhandel*	*book*·han·duhl
camera shop	*fotozaak*	*foh*·toh·zaak
department store	*warenhuis* Ⓝ	*waa*·ruhn·höys
	grootwarenhuis Ⓑ	khroht·*waa*·ruhn·höys
grocery store	*kruidenier*	kröy·duh·*neer*
market	*markt*	mart
newsagency	*krantenzaak*	*kran*·tuhn·zaak
supermarket	*supermarkt*	*sew*·puhr·mart

Where can I buy (a padlock)?
Waar kan ik (een hangslot) kopen? — waar kan ik (uhn *hang*·slot) *koh*·puhn

I'm looking for ...
Ik ben op zoek naar ... — ik ben op zook naar ...

Can I look at it?
Kan ik het even zien? — kan ik huht *ey*·vuhn zeen

Do you have any others?
Heeft u nog andere? pol — heyft ew nokh *an*·duh·ruh

Does it have a guarantee?
Komt het met garantie? — komt huht met kha·*ran*·see

Can I have it sent abroad?
Kan ik het naar het buitenland sturen? — kan Ik huht naar huht *böy*·tuhn·lant *stew*·ruhn

Can I have my ... repaired here?
Kan ik mijn ... hier laten herstellen? — kan ik meyn ... heer *laa*·tuhn her·*ste*·luhn

It's faulty.
Het werkt niet. — huht werkt neet

I'd like ..., please.	*Ik wil graag ...*	ik wil khraakh ...
a bag	*een draagtasje*	uhn *draakh*·ta·shuh
a refund	*mijn geld terug*	meyn gelt tuh·*rukh*
to return this	*dit retourneren*	dit ruh·toor·*ney*·ruhn

paying

How much is it?
Hoeveel kost het? — hoo·*veyl* kost huht

Can you write down the price?
Kunt u de prijs opschrijven? pol — kunt ew duh preys *op*·skhrey·vuhn

That's too expensive.
Dat is te duur. — dat is tuh dewr

What's your lowest price?
Wat is uw beste prijs? pol — wat is ew *bes*·tuh preys

I'll give you (five) euros.
Ik wil er (vijf) euro voor betalen. — ik wil uhr (veyf) *ew*·roh vohr buh·*taa*·luhn

There's a mistake in the bill.
Er zit een fout in de rekening. — uhr zit eyn fawt in duh *rey*·kuh·ning

Do you accept ...?	*Accepteert u ...?* pol	ak·sep·*teyrt* ew ...
credit cards	*kredietkaarten*	krey·*deet*·kaar·tuhn
debit cards	*debetkaarten*	*dey*·bet·kaar·tuhn
travellers cheques	*reischeques*	*reys*·sheks

I'd like ..., please.	*Ik wil graag ...*	ik wil khraakh ...
a receipt	*een kwitantie*	uhn kwee·*tan*·see
my change	*mijn wisselgeld*	meyn *wi*·suhl·gelt

clothes & shoes

Can I try it on?	*Kan ik het passen?*	kan ik huht *pa*·suhn
My size is (40).	*Ik heb maat (veertig).*	ik hep maat (*feyr*·tikh)
It doesn't fit.	*Het past niet.*	huht past neet
small	*small*	smal
medium	*medium*	*mey*·dyum
large	*large*	larsh

books & music

I'd like a ...	*Ik wil graag een ...*	ik wil khraakh uhn ...
newspaper (in English)	*krant (in het Engels)*	krant (in huht *eng*·uhls)
pen	*balpen*	*bal*·pen

Is there an English-language bookshop?
Is er een Engelstalige boekhandel? is uhr uhn *eng*·uhls·taa·li·khuh *book*·han·duhl

I'm looking for something by (Hugo Claus).
Ik ben op zoek naar iets van (Hugo Claus). ik ben op zook naar eets van (*hew*·khoh klaws)

Can I listen to this?
Kan ik hier naar dit luisteren? kan ik heer naar dit *löy*·stuh·ruhn

photography

Could you ...?	*Kunt u ...?* pol	kunt ew ...
burn a CD from my memory card	*deze geheugenkaart op cd zetten*	*dey*·zuh khuh·*heu*·khuhn·kaart op sey·*dey* *ze*·tuhn
develop this film	*deze film ontwikkelen*	*dey*·zuh film ont·*wi*·kuh·luhn
load my film	*mijn film laden*	meyn film *laa*·duhn
I need a/an ... film for this camera.	*Ik heb een ... nodig voor dit fototoestel.*	ik hep uhn ... *noh*·dikh vohr dit *foh*·toh·too·stel
APS	*APS film*	aa·pey·*es* film
B&W	*zwart-wit film*	zwart·*wit* film
colour	*kleurenfilm*	*kleu*·ruhn·film
slide	*diafilm*	*dee*·ya·film
(200) speed	*film van (tweehonderd) ASA*	film van (*twey*·hon·duhrt) *aa*·sa
When will it be ready?	*Wanneer is het klaar?*	wa·*neyr* is huht klaar

meeting people

greetings, goodbyes & introductions

Hello/Hi.	*Goedendag/Dag/Hallo.*	khoo·duh·*dakh*/dakh/ha·*loh*
Good evening.	*Goedenavond.*	khoo·duh·*naa*·vont
Good night.	*Goedenacht.*	khoo·duh·*nakht*
Goodbye/Bye.	*Dag.*	dakh
See you later.	*Tot ziens.*	tot seens

Mr	*Meneer*	muh·*neyr*
Mrs	*Mevrouw*	muh·*vraw*
Miss	*Juffrouw*	*yu*·fraw

How are you?
Hoe gaat het met u/jou? pol/inf — hoo khaat huht met ew/yaw

Fine. And you?
Goed. En met u/jou? pol/inf — khoot en met ew/yaw

What's your name?
Hoe heet u/je? pol/inf — hoo heyt ew/yuh

My name is ...
Ik heet ... — ik heyt ...

I'm pleased to meet you.
Aangenaam. — *aan*·khuh·naam

This is my ...	*Dit is mijn ...*	dit is meyn ...
boyfriend	*vriend*	vreent
brother	*broer*	broor
daughter	*dochter*	*dokh*·tuhr
father	*vader*	*vaa*·duhr
fiancé(e)	*verloofde*	vuhr·*lohf*·duh
friend	*vriend/vriendin* m/f	vreent/vreen·*din*
girlfriend	*vriendin*	vreen·*din*
husband	*man*	man
mother	*moeder*	*moo*·duhr
partner (intimate)	*partner*	*part*·nuhr
sister	*zus*	zus
son	*zoon*	zohn
wife	*vrouw*	vraw

Here's my ...	*Dit is mijn ...*	dit is meyn ...
What's your ...?	*Wat is uw/ jouw ...?* **pol/inf**	wat is ew/ yaw ...
address	*adres*	a·*dres*
email address	*e-mailadres*	*ee*·meyl·a·dres
fax number	*faxnummer*	*faks*·nu·muhr
phone number	*telefoonnummer*	tey·ley·*foh*·nu·muhr

occupations

What's your occupation?
Wat is uw/jouw beroep? **pol/inf** — wat is ew/yaw buh·*roop*

I'm a/an ...	*Ik ben ...*	ik ben ...
artist	*kunstenaar* **m**	*kun*·stuh·naar
	kunstenares **f**	kun·stuh·naa·*res*
businessperson	*zakenman* **m**	*zaa*·kuh·man
	zakenvrouw **f**	*zaa*·kuh·vraw
farmer	*boer/boerin* **m/f**	boor/boo·*rin*
manual worker	*arbeider* **m**	*ar*·bey·duhr
	arbeidster **f**	*ar*·beyt·stuhr
scientist	*wetenschapper* **m&f**	*wey*·tuhn·skha·puhr
student	*student* **m&f**	stew·*dent*

background

Where are you from?
Waar komt u vandaan? **pol** — waar komt ew van·*daan*
Waar kom je vandaan? **inf** — waar kom yuh van·*daan*

I'm from ...	*Ik kom uit ...*	ik kom öyt ...
Australia	*Australië*	aw·*straa*·lee·yuh
Canada	*Canada*	*ka*·na·da
England	*Engeland*	*eng*·uh·lant
New Zealand	*Nieuw-Zeeland*	neew·*zey*·lant
the USA	*de Verenigde Staten*	duh vuh·*rey*·nikh·duh *staa*·tuhn
Are you married?	*Bent u getrouwd?* **pol**	bent ew khuh·*trawt*
	Ben je getrouwd? **inf**	ben yuh khuh·*trawt*
I'm married.	*Ik ben getrouwd.*	ik ben khuh·*trawt*
I'm single.	*Ik ben vrijgezel.*	ik ben *vrey*·khuh·zel

age

How old ...?	*Hou oud ...?*	hoo awt ...
are you	*ben je* **inf**	ben yuh
is your daughter	*is jouw dochter* **inf**	is yaw *dokh*·tuhr
is your son	*is jouw zoon* **inf**	is yaw zohn
I'm ... years old.	*Ik ben ... jaar.*	ik ben ... yaar
He/She is ... years old.	*Hij/Zij is ... jaar.*	hey/zey is ... yaar

feelings

I'm (not) ...	*Ik ben (niet) ...*	ik ben (neet) ...
Are you ...?	*Ben jij ...?* **inf**	ben yey ...
happy	*blij*	bley
sad	*droef*	droof
I'm (not) ...	*Ik heb (geen) ...*	ik hep (kheyn) ...
Are you ...?	*Heb je ...?* **inf**	hep yey ...
hungry	*honger*	*hong*·uhr
thirsty	*dorst*	dorst
I'm (not) ...	*Ik heb het (niet) ...*	ik hep huht (neet) ...
Are you ...?	*Heb jij het ...?* **inf**	hep yey huht ...
cold	*koud*	kawt
hot	*warm*	warm

entertainment

going out

Where can I find ...?	*Waar vind ik de ...?*	waar vint ik duh ...
(night)clubs	*(nacht)clubs*	(*nakht*·)klups
gay venues	*homotenten*	*hoh*·moh·ten·tuhn
pubs	*kroegen/cafés* Ⓝ/Ⓑ	*khroo*·khuhn/ka·*feys*
I feel like going to ...	*Ik heb zin om naar ... te gaan.*	ik hep zin om naar ... tuh khaan
a/the concert	*een/het concert*	uhn/huht kon·*sert*
the movies	*de bioscoop*	duh bee·yos·*kohp*
a/the party	*een/het feestje*	uhn/huht *fey*·shuh
a restaurant	*op restaurant*	op res·toh·*rant*
the theatre	*het toneel*	huht toh·*neyl*

interests

Do you like ...?	*Hou je van ...?* inf	haw yuh van ...
I (don't) like ...	*Ik hou (niet) van ...*	ik haw (neet) van ...
art	*kunst*	kunst
cooking	*koken*	*koh*·kuhn
movies	*films*	films
reading	*lezen*	*ley*·zuhn
shopping	*winkelen*	*wing*·kuh·luhn
sport	*sport*	sport
travelling	*reizen*	*rey*·zuhn

Do you like to dance?
Hou je van dansen? inf — haw yuh van *dan*·suhn

Do you like to listen to music?
Luister je graag naar muziek? inf — *löys*·tuhr yuh khraakh naar mew·*zeek*

food & drink

finding a place to eat

Can you recommend a ...?	*Kunt u een ... aanbevelen?* pol	kunt ew uhn ... *aan*·buh·vey·luhn
bar	*bar*	bar
café	*eethuisje/taverne* Ⓝ/Ⓑ	*eyt*·höy·shuh/ta·*ver*·nuh
restaurant	*restaurant*	res·toh·*rant*
I'd like ..., please.	*Ik wil graag ...*	ik wil khraakh ...
a table for (four)	*een tafel voor (vier)*	uhn *taa*·fuhl vohr (veer)
the (non)smoking section	*(niet-)roken*	(*neet*·)roh·kuhn

ordering food

breakfast	*ontbijt* n	ont·*beyt*
lunch	*middageten* n	*mi*·dakh·ey·tuhn
dinner	*avondeten* n	*aa*·vont·ey·tuhn
snack	*snack*	snek/snak Ⓝ/Ⓑ
today's special	*dagschotel*	*dakh*·shoh·tuhl

What would you recommend?
Wat kunt u aanbevelen? pol — wat kunt ew *aan*·buh·vey·luhn

I'd like (the) ..., please.	*..., graag.*	... khraakh
bill	*De rekening*	duh *rey*·kuh·ning
drink list	*De drankkaart*	duh *drang*·kaart
menu	*De menu*	duh muh·*new*
that dish	*Dat gerecht*	dat guh·*rekht*
wine list	*De wijnkaart*	duh *weyn*·kaart

drinks

(cup of) coffee ...	*(een tas) koffie ...*	(uhn tas) *ko*·fee ...
(cup of) tea ...	*(een tas) thee ...*	(uhn tas) tey ...
with milk	*met melk*	met melk
without sugar	*zonder suiker*	*zon*·duhr *söy*·kuhr
(orange) juice	*(sinaasappel)sap*	(see·*naas*·a·puhl·)sap
soft drink	*frisdrank*	*fris*·drangk
flat mineral water	*spa blauw/plat* Ⓝ/Ⓑ	spa blaw/plat
mineral/bottled water	*mineraalwater* n	mee·ney·*raal*·waa·tuhr
sparkling mineral water	*spa rood/bruis* Ⓝ/Ⓑ	spa roht/bröys

in the bar

I'll have ...	*Voor mij ...*	vohr mey ...
My shout/round.	*Mijn rondje.*	meyn *ron*·chuh
What would you like? inf	*Wat wil je drinken?*	wat wil yuh *dring*·kuhn
Cheers!	*Proost!*	prohst
brandy	*brandewijn*	*bran*·duh·weyn
gin	*jenever*	zhuh·*ney*·vuhr
a shot of (whisky)	*een glas (whisky)*	uhn khlas (*wis*·kee)
strong alcoholic drink	*borrel*	*bo*·ruhl
beer on tap	*bier van 't vat*	beer vant vat
bottled beer	*bier op fles*	beer op fles
a bottle/glass of beer	*een flesje/glas bier*	uhn *fle*·shuh/khlas beer
a bottle/glass of ...	*een fles/glas ...*	uhn fles/khlas ...
red wine	*rode wijn*	*roh*·duh weyn
sparkling wine	*mousserende wijn* Ⓝ	moo·*sey*·ruhn·duh weyn
	schuimwijn Ⓑ	*skhöym*·weyn
white wine	*witte wijn*	*wi*·tuh weyn

self-catering

What's the local speciality?
Wat is het streekgerecht? — wat is huht *streyk*·khuh·rekht

What's that?
Wat is dat? — wat is dat

How much is (a kilo of cheese)?
Hoeveel kost (een kilo kaas)? — hoo·*veyl* kost (uhn *kee*·loh kaas)

I'd like ...	*Ik wil graag ...*	ik wil khraakh ...
(100) grams	*(honderd) gram*	(*hon*·duhrt) khram
(two) kilos	*(twee) kilo*	(twey) *kee*·loh
(three) pieces	*(drie) stuks*	(dree) stuks
(six) slices	*(zes) plakken/sneetjes* Ⓝ/Ⓑ	(zes) *pla*·kuhn/*sney*·chuhs

Less.	*Minder.*	*min*·duhr
Enough.	*Dat is genoeg.*	dat is khuh·*nookh*
More.	*Meer.*	meyr

special diets & allergies

Is there a vegetarian restaurant near here?
Is er hier een vegetarisch restaurant in de buurt? — is uhr heer uhn vey·khey·*taa*·ris res·toh·*rant* in duh bewrt

Do you have vegetarian food?
Heeft u vegetarische maaltijden? — heyft ew vey·khey·*taa*·ri·suh *maal*·tey·duhn

Could you prepare a meal without ...?	*Zou u een maaltijd zonder ... kunnen klaarmaken?*	zaw ew uhn *maal*·teyt *zon*·duhr ... *ku*·nuhn *klaar*·maa·kuhn
butter	*boter*	*boh*·ter
eggs	*eieren*	*ey*·yuh·ruhn
meat stock	*vleesbouillon*	*vleys*·boo·yon

I'm allergic to ...	*Ik ben allergisch voor ...*	ik ben a·*ler*·khis vohr ...
dairy produce	*zuivelproducten*	*zöy*·vuhl·pro·duk·tuhn
gluten	*gluten*	*khlew*·tuhn
MSG	*MSG/vetsin*	em·es·*khey*/vet·*seen*
nuts	*noten*	*noh*·tuhn
seafood	*vis, schaal- en schelpdieren*	vis skhaal en *skhelp*·dee·ruhn

menu reader

aardappels	*aart*·a·puhls	*potatoes*
appelmoes	*a*·puhl·moos	*apple sauce*
beignet	bey·*nye*	*fritter*
beschuit	buh·*shöyt*	*typical Dutch light crisp bread (often round)*
biefstuk tartaar	*beef*·stuk tar·*taar*	*raw minced beef with eggs & spices*
bloedworst	*bloot*·worst	*black pudding • blood sausage – called* **pens** pens *or* **beuling** *beu*·ling *in Belgium*
boterham	*boh*·tuhr·ham	*sandwich (of sliced bread)*
brood n	broht	*bread*
croque monsieur	krok muh·*sye*	*toasted sandwich with cheese & ham*
drop	drop	*sweet or salty liquorice*
ei/eieren n	ey/*ey*·yuh·ruhn	*egg/eggs*
flensjes	*flen*·shuhs	*small thin pancakes*
friet/frieten/frit(es)	freet/*free*·tuhn/frit	*chips (also called* **patat** pa·*tat)*
gebak n	khuh·*bak*	*cakes & pastries*
gehakt n	khuh·*hakt*	*minced meat*
gevogelte n	khuh·*voh*·khuhl·tuh	*fowl*
groenten	*khroon*·tuhn	*vegetables*
hagelslag	*haa*·khuhl·slakh	*chocolate vermicelli*
haring	*haa*·ring	*herring*
hutsepot	*hut*·suh·pot	*stew of potatoes, onions & carrots*
jachtschotel	*yakht*·skhoh·tuhl	*oven dish with meat & potatoes*
kaas	kaas	*cheese*
karbonade	kar·boh·*naa*·duh	*chop – also called* **kotelet** ko·tuh·*let*
lekkerbekje n	*le*·kuhr·bek·yuh	*deep-fried fish fillet*
muisjes	*möy*·shuhs	*sugar-coated aniseed*

oliebol	*oh*·lee·bol	*dough fritter*
ontbijtkoek	ont·*beyt*·kook	*gingerbread-style honey cake – called* **peperkoek** *pey*·puhr·kook *in Belgium*
paddestoelen	*pa*·duh·stoo·luhn	*mushrooms*
poffertjes	*po*·fuhr·chuhs	*small puffed-up pancakes served with butter & icing sugar*
puree	pew·*rey*	*mash*
rolmops	*rol*·mops	*pickled herring with gherkin/onion*
(slag)room	(*slakh*·)rohm	*(whipped) cream*
saucijzebroodje n	saw·*sey*·zuh·broh·chuh	*sausage roll – in Belgium called* **worstebrood** *wor*·stuh·broht
schaal- en schelpdieren	skhaal en *skhelp*·dee·ruhn	*crustaceans & shellfish*
slakken	*sla*·kuhn	*snails – in Belgium called* **escargots** es·kar·*khohs*
spek	spek	*bacon*
stamppot/stoemp	*stam*·pot/stoomp	*mashed potatoes & vegetables*
stoofschotel	*stohf*·skhoh·tuhl	*casserole*
stoofvlees n	*stohf*·vleys	*beef stew traditionally served with fries*
tompoes	tom·*poos*	*custard slice with icing*
uitsmijter	*öyt*·smey·tuhr	*sliced bread with cold meat covered with eggs & served with a garnish*
vlaai	vlaay	*sweet tart/cake/pie*
vlees n	vleys	*meat*
vogelnestje n	*voh*·khuhl·ne·shuh	*'bird's nest' – meat loaf with egg inside*
waterzooi	*waa*·tuhr·zohy	*creamy soup with potatoes, vegetables & chicken or fish*
wild n	wilt	*game*
worst	worst	*sausage*

emergencies

basics

Help!	*Help!*	help
Stop!	*Stop!*	stop
Go away!	*Ga weg!*	khaa wekh
Thief!	*Dief!*	deef
Fire!	*Brand!*	brant
Watch out!	*Pas op!*	pas op
Call . . .!	*Bel . . .!*	bel . . .
a doctor	*een doktor*	uhn *dok*·tuhr
an ambulance	*een ambulance*	uhn am·bew·*lans*
the police	*de politie*	duh poh·*leet*·see

It's an emergency!
Het is een noodgeval. — huht is uhn *noht*·khuh·val

Could you help me, please?
Kunt u mij alstublieft helpen? pol — kunt ew mey al·stew·*bleeft hel*·puhn

I have to use the telephone.
Ik heb een telefoon nodig. — ik hep uhn tey·ley·*fohn noh*·dikh

I'm lost.
Ik ben de weg kwijt. — ik ben duh wekh kweyt

Where are the toilets?
Waar zijn de toiletten? — waar zeyn duh twa·*le*·tuhn

police

Where's the police station?
Waar is het politiebureau? — waar is huht poh·*leet*·see·bew·roh

I want to report an offence. (minor/serious)
Ik wil aangifte doen van een overtreding/misdrijf. — ik wil *aan*·khif·tuh doon van uhn oh·vuhr·*trey*·ding/*mis*·dreyf

I have insurance.
Ik heb verzekering. — ik hep vuhr·*zey*·kuh·ring

I've been . . .	*Ik ben . . .*	ik ben . . .
assaulted	*aangevallen*	*aan*·khuh·va·luhn
raped	*verkracht*	vuhr·*khrakht*
robbed	*bestolen*	buh·*stoh*·luhn

I've lost my …	*Ik heb mijn … verloren.*	ik hep meyn … vuhr·*loh*·ruhn
My … was/were stolen.	*Mijn … is/zijn gestolen.*	meyn … is/zeyn khuh·*stoh*·luhn
backpack	*rugzak*	*rukh*·zak
bags	*tassen*	*ta*·suhn
credit card	*kredietkaart*	krey·*deet*·kaart
handbag	*handtas*	*han*·tas
jewellery	*juwelen*	yew·*wey*·luhn
money	*geld*	khelt
passport	*paspoort*	*pas*·pohrt
travellers cheques	*reischeques*	*reys*·sheks
wallet	*portefeuille*	por·tuh·*föy*
I want to contact my …	*Ik wil contact opnemen met mijn …*	ik wil kon·*takt* op·*ney*·muhn met meyn …
consulate	*consulaat*	kon·sew·*laat*
embassy	*ambassade*	am·ba·*saa*·duh

health

medical needs

Where's the nearest …?	*Waar is de dichtsbijzijnde …?*	waar is duh dikhs·bey·*zeyn*·duh …
dentist	*tandarts*	*tan*·darts
doctor	*dokter*	*dok*·tuhr
(night) pharmacist	*(nacht)apotheek*	(*nakht*·)a·poh·*teyk*

Where's the nearest hospital?
Waar is het dichtsbijzijnde ziekenhuis? — waar is huht dikhs·bey·*zeyn*·duh *zee*·kuhn·höys

I need a doctor (who speaks English).
Ik heb een dokter nodig (die Engels spreekt). — ik hep uhn *dok*·tuhr *noh*·dikh (dee *eng*·uhls spreykt)

Could I see a female doctor?
Zou ik een vrouwelijke dokter kunnen zien? — zaw ik uhn *vraw*·wuh·ley·kuh *dok*·tuhr *ku*·nuhn zeen

I've run out of my medication.
Mijn medicijnen zijn op. — meyn mey·dee·*sey*·nuhn zeyn op

symptoms, conditions & allergies

I'm sick.	*Ik ben ziek.*	ik ben zeek
It hurts here.	*Hier doet het pijn.*	heer doot huht peyn
I have nausea.	*Ik ben misselijk.*	ik ben *mi*·suh·luhk
I have (a) …	*Ik heb …*	ik hep …
asthma	*astma*	*ast*·ma
bronchitis	*bronchitis*	bron·*khee*·tees
constipation	*last van constipatie*	last van kon·stee·*paa*·see
cough	*een hoest*	uhn hoost
diabetes	*diabetes/ suikerziekte*	dee·ya·*bey*·tes/ *söy*·kuhr·zeek·tuh
diarrhoea	*diarree*	dee·ya·*rey*
fever	*koorts*	kohrts
headache	*hoofdpijn*	*hohft*·peyn
heart condition	*een hartkwaal*	uhn *hart*·kwaal
pain	*pijn*	peyn
sore throat	*keelpijn*	*keyl*·peyn
toothache	*kiespijn*	*kees* peyn
I'm allergic to …	*Ik ben allergisch voor …*	ik ben a·*ler*·khis vohr …
antibiotics	*antibiotica*	an·tee·bee·*yoh*·tee·ka
anti inflammatories	*ontstekingsremmende medicijnen*	ont·*stey*·kings·re·muhn·duh mey·dee·*sey*·nuhn
aspirin	*aspirine*	as·pee·*ree*·nuh
bees	*bijen*	*bey*·yuhn
codeine	*codeïne*	koh·dey·*ee*·nuh
penicillin	*penicilline*	pey·nee·see·*lee*·nuh
antiseptic n	*ontsmettend middel* **n**	ont·*sme*·tuhnt *mi*·duhl
bandage	*verband* **n**	vuhr·*bant*
condoms	*condooms* **n pl**	kon·*dohms*
contraceptives	*anticonceptiemiddelen* **n pl**	an·tee·kon·*sep*·see·mi·duh·luhn
diarrhoea medicine	*middel tegen diarree* **n**	*mi*·duhl *tey*·khuhn dee·ya·*rey*
insect repellent	*insectverdrijvend middel* **n**	*in*·sekt·vuhr·drey·vuhnt *mi*·duhl
laxatives	*laxeermiddelen* **n pl**	lak·*seyr*·mi·duh·luhn
painkillers	*pijnstillers*	*peyn*·sti·luhrs
rehydration salts	*rehydratatie-oplossing*	rey·hee·dra·*ta*·see·op·lo·sing
sleeping tablets	*slaappillen*	*slaa*·pi·luhn

english–dutch dictionary

In this dictionary, words are marked as n (noun), a (adjective), v (verb), sg (singular), pl (plural), inf (informal) and pol (polite) where necessary. Note that Dutch nouns are either masculine, feminine or neuter. Masculine and feminine forms (known as 'common gender') take the definite article *de* (the) while neuter forms take the article *het* (the). Every Dutch noun needs to be learned with its definite article (*de* or *het*). Only in archaic forms is the distinction between masculine and feminine still relevant, so we've only indicated the neuter nouns with ⓝ after the translation. We've also used the symbols Ⓝ/Ⓑ for some words which are different in the Netherlands and Belgium respectively.

A

accident *ongeval* ⓝ *on*·khuh·val
accommodation *accommodatie* a·koh·moh·*daa*·see
adaptor *adapter* a·*dap*·tuhr
address n *adres* ⓝ a·*dres*
after *na* naa
air-conditioned *met airconditioning* met *eyr*·kon·dee·shuh·ning
airplane *vliegtuig* ⓝ *vleekh*·töykh
airport *luchthaven* *lukht*·haa·vuhn
alcohol *alcohol* *al*·koh·hol
all a *alle* *a*·luh
allergy *allergie* a·ler·*khee*
ambulance *ambulance* am·bew·*lans*
and *en* en
ankle *enkel* *eng*·kuhl
arm *arm* arm
ashtray *asbak* *as*·bak
ATM *pin-automaat/geldautomaat* Ⓝ/Ⓑ *pin*·aw·toh·maat/*khelt*·aw·toh·maat

B

baby *baby* *bey*·bee
back (body) *rug* rukh
backpack *rugzak* *rukh*·zak
bad *slecht* slekht
bag *tas* tas
baggage claim *bagage afhalen* ba·*khaa*·zhuh *af*·haa·luhn
bank *bank* bangk
bar *bar* bar
bathroom *badkamer* *bat*·kaa·muhr
battery *batterij* ba·tuh·*rey*
beautiful *mooi* mohy
bed *bed* ⓝ bet
beer *bier* ⓝ beer
before *voor* vohr
behind *achter* *akh*·tuhr
Belgian a *Belgisch* *bel*·khis
Belgium *België* *bel*·khee·yuh
bicycle *fiets* feets
big *groot* khroht
bill *rekening* *rey*·kuh·ning
black *zwart* zwart
blanket *deken* *dey*·kuhn
blood group *bloedgroep* *bloot*·khroop
blue *blauw* blaw
boat *boot* boht
book (make a reservation) v *reserveren* rey·zer·*vey*·ruhn
bottle *fles* fles
bottle opener *flesopener* *fles*·oh·puh·nuhr
boy *jongen* *yong*·uhn
brakes (car) *remmen* *re*·muhn
breakfast *ontbijt* ⓝ ont·*beyt*
broken (faulty) *stuk* stuk
bus *bus* bus
business *zaken* *zaa*·kuhn
buy *kopen* *koh*·puhn

C

café *eethuisje* ⓝ/*taverne* Ⓝ/Ⓑ *eyt*·höy·shuh/ta·*ver*·nuh
camera *fototoestel* ⓝ *foh*·toh·too·stel
camping ground *camping* *kem*·ping
camp site *kampeerplaats* kam·*peyr*·plaats
cancel *annuleren* a·new·*ley*·ruhn
can opener *blikopener* *blik*·oh·puh·nuhr
car *auto* *aw*·toh
cash n *baar geld* ⓝ baar khelt
cash (a cheque) v *(een cheque) innen* (uhn shek) *i*·nuhn
cell phone *mobiele telefoon/GSM* Ⓝ/Ⓑ moh·*bee*·luh tey·ley·*fohn*/khey·es·*em*
centre n *centrum* ⓝ *sen*·truhm
change (money) v *(geld) wisselen* (khelt) *wi*·suh·luhn

A

DICTIONARY

cheap *goedkoop* khoot·*kohp*
check (bill) *rekening* rey·kuh·ning
check-in n *check-in* chek·in
chest *borst* borst
child *kind* ⓝ kint
cigarette *sigaret* see·kha·*ret*
city *stad* stat
clean a *schoon* skhoon
closed *gesloten* khuh·*sloh*·tuhn
coffee *koffie* *ko*·fee
coins *muntstukken* ⓝ pl *munt*·stu·kuhn
cold a *koud* kawt
collect call *collect call* ko·*lekt* kawl
come *komen* *koh*·muhn
computer *computer* kom·*pyoo*·tuhr
condom *condoom* ⓝ kon·*dohm*
contact lenses *contaktlenzen* kon·*takt*·len·zuhn
cook v *bereiden* be·*rey*·duhn
cost n *kost* kost
credit card *kredietkaart* krey·*deet*·kaart
cup *tas* tas
currency exchange *wisselkantoor* ⓝ *wi*·suhl·kan·tohr
customs (immigration) *douane* doo·*waa*·nuh

D

dangerous *gevaarlijk* khuh·*vaar*·luhk
date (time) *datum* *daa*·tum
day *dag* dakh
delay n *vertraging* vuhr·*traa*·khing
dentist *tandarts* *tan*·darts
depart *vertrekken* vuhr·*tre*·kuhn
diaper *luier* *löy*·yuhr
dictionary *woordenboek* ⓝ *wohr*·duhn·book
dinner *avondeten* ⓝ *aa*·vont·ey·tuhn
direct *rechtstreeks* rekh·*streyks*
dirty *vuil* vöyl
disabled *gehandicapt* khuh·*han*·dee·kapt
discount n *korting* *kor*·ting
doctor *dokter* *dok*·tuhr
double bed *dubbel bed* ⓝ *du*·buhl bet
double room *tweepersoonskamer* *twey*·puhr·sohns·kaa·muhr
drink n *drinken* *dring*·kuhn
drive v *rijden* *rey*·duhn
drivers licence *rijbewijs* ⓝ *rey*·buh·weys
drugs (illicit) *drugs* drukhs
dummy (pacifier) *fopspeen* *fop*·speyn
Dutch (language) *Nederlands* ⓝ *ney*·duhr·lants
Dutch a *Nederlands* *ney*·duhr·lants

E

ear *oor* n ohr
east *oost* ohst
eat *eten* *ey*·tuhn
economy class *economy klas* ey·*ko*·no·mee klas
electricity *elektriciteit* ey·lek·tree·see·*teyt*
elevator *lift* lift
email *e-mail* *ee*·meyl
embassy *ambassade* am·ba·*saa*·duh
emergency *noodgeval* ⓝ *noht*·khuh·val
English (language) *Engels* ⓝ *eng*·uhls
entrance *ingang* *in*·khang
evening *avond* *aa*·vont
exchange rate *wisselkoers* *wi*·suhl·koors
exit n *uitgang* *öyt*·khang
expensive *duur* dewr
express mail *exprespost* eks·*pres*·post
eye *oog* ⓝ ohkh

F

far *ver* ver
fast *snel* snel
father *vader* *vaa*·duhr
film (camera) *film* film
finger *vinger* *ving*·uhr
first-aid kit *verbandkist* vuhr·*bant*·kist
first class *eerste klas* *eyr*·stuh klas
fish n *vis* vis
Flanders *Vlaanderen* *vlaan*·duh·ruhn
Flemish (language) *Vlaams* ⓝ vlaams
Flemish a *Vlaams* vlaams
food *eten* ⓝ *ey*·tuhn
foot *voet* voot
fork *vork* vork
free (of charge) *gratis* *khraa*·tis
French (language) *Frans* ⓝ frans
friend *vriend/vriendin* ⓜ/ⓕ vreend/vreen·*din*
fruit *fruit* ⓝ freyt
full *vol* vol
funny *grappig* *khra*·pikh

G

German (language) *Duits* ⓝ döyts
gift *cadeau* ⓝ ka·*doh*
girl *meisje* ⓝ *mey*·shuh
glass (drinking) *glas* ⓝ khlas
glasses *bril* bril

go *gaan* khaan
good *goed* khoot
green *groen* khroon
guide n *gids* khits

H

half n *helft* helft
hand *hand* hant
handbag *handtas* *han*·tas
happy *blij* bley
have *hebben* *he*·buhn
he *hij* hey
head *hoofd* ⓝ hohft
heart *hart* ⓝ hart
heat n *warmte* *warm*·tuh
heavy *zwaar* zwaar
help v *helpen* *hel*·puhn
here *hier* heer
high *hoog* hohkh
highway *snelweg* *snel*·wekh
hike v *trekken* *tre*·kuhn
holidays *vakantie* va·*kant*·see
homosexual n&a *homosexueel* hoh·moh·sek·sew·*weyl*
hospital *ziekenhuis* ⓝ *zee*·kuhn·höys
hot *warm* warm
hotel *hotel* ⓝ hoh·*tel*
(to be) hungry *honger (hebben)* *hong*·uhr (*he*·buhn)
husband *man* man

I

I *ik* ik
identification (card) *identiteitsbewijs* ⓝ ee·den·tee·*teyts*·buh·weys
ill *ziek* zeek
important *belangrijk* buh·*lang*·reyk
included *inbegrepen* *in*·buh·khrey·puhn
injury *verwonding* vuhr·*won*·ding
insurance *verzekering* vuhr·*zey*·kuh·ring
Internet *internet* ⓝ *in*·tuhr·net
interpreter *vertaler* vuhr·*taa*·luhr

J

jewellery *juwelen* ⓝ pl yew·*wey*·luhn
job *baan/werk* ⓝ Ⓝ/Ⓑ baan/werk

K

key *sleutel* *sleu*·tuhl
kilogram *kilogram* *kee*·lo(·khram)
kitchen *keuken* *keu*·kuhn
knife *mes* ⓝ mes

L

laundry (place) *wasserette* wa·suh·*ret*
lawyer *advokaat* at·voh·*kaat*
left (direction) *links* lingks
left-luggage office *garderobe/vestiaire* Ⓝ/Ⓑ khar·duh·*roh*·buh/ves·*tyeyr*
leg *been* ⓝ beyn
lesbian a *lesbisch* *les*·bis
less *minder* *min*·duhr
letter (mail) *brief* breef
lift (elevator) *lift* lift
light n *licht* ⓝ likht
like v *houden van* *haw*·duhn van
lock n *slot* ⓝ slot
long *lang* lang
lost *verloren* vuhr·*loh*·ruhn
lost-property office *verloren voorwerpen* vuhr·*loh*·ruhn *vohr*·wer·puhn
love v *houden van* *haw*·duhn van
luggage *bagage* ba·*khaa*·zhuh
lunch *middageten* ⓝ *mi*·dakh·ey·tuhn

M

mail n *post* post
man *man* man
map (building) *plattegrond* pla·tuh·*khront*
map (town) *kaart* kaart
market *markt* mart
matches *lucifers* *lew*·see·fers
meat *vlees* ⓝ vleys
medicine *medicijn* ⓝ mey·dee·*seyn*
menu *menu* ⓜ&ⓝ muh·*new*
message *bericht* ⓝ buh·*rikht*
milk *melk* melk
minute *minuut* mee·*newt*
mobile phone *mobiele telefoon/GSM* Ⓝ/Ⓑ moh·*bee*·luh tey·ley·*fohn*/khey·es·*em*
money *geld* ⓝ khelt
month *maand* maant
morning *ochtend* *okh*·tuhnt
mother *moeder* *moo*·duhr
motorcycle *motorfiets* *moh*·tor·feets
motorway *snelweg* *snel*·wekh
mouth *mond* mont
music *muziek* mew·*zeek*

DICTIONARY

N

name *naam* naam
napkin *servet* ⓝ ser·*vet*
nappy *luier* *löy*·yuhr
near *dicht bij* dikht bey
neck *nek* nek
(the) Netherlands *Nederland* *ney*·duhr·lant
new *nieuw* neew
news *nieuws* ⓝ neews
newspaper *krant* krant
night *nacht* nakht
no *nee* ney
noisy *lawaaierig* la·*waa*·yuh·rikh
nonsmoking *niet-roken* *neet*·roh·kuhn
north *noord* nohrt
nose *neus* neus
now *nu* new
number *nummer* ⓝ *nu*·muhr

O

oil (engine) *olie* *oh*·lee
old *oud* awt
one-way ticket *enkele reis* *eng*·kuh·luh reys
open a *open* *oh*·puhn
outside *buiten* *böy*·tuhn

P

package *pakje* ⓝ *pak*·yuh
paper *papier* ⓝ pa·*peer*
park (car) v *parkeren* par·*key*·ruhn
passport *paspoort* ⓝ *pas*·pohrt
pay *betalen* buh·*taa*·luhn
pen *balpen* *bal*·pen
petrol *benzine* ben·*zee*·nuh
pharmacy *apotheek* a·poh·*teyk*
phonecard *telefoonkaart* tey·ley·*fohn*·kaart
photo *foto* *foh*·toh
plate *bord* ⓝ bort
police *politie* po·*leet*·see
postcard *ansichtkaart* *an*·sikht·kaart
post office *postkantoor* ⓝ *post*·kan·tohr
pregnant *zwanger* *zwang*·uhr
price *prijs* preys

Q

quiet *stil* stil

R

rain n *regen* *rey*·khuhn
razor (electrical) *scheerapparaat* ⓝ *skheyr*·a·pa·raat
razor (manual) *scheermesje* ⓝ *skheyr*·me·shuh
receipt n *kwitantie* kwee·*tan*·see
red *rood* roht
refund n *terugbetaling* tuh·*rukh*·buh·taa·ling
registered mail *aangetekende post*
aan·khuh·tey·kuhn·duh post
rent v *huren* *hew*·ruhn
repair v *herstellen* her·*ste*·luhn
reservation *reservatie* rey·ser·*vaa*·see
restaurant *restaurant* ⓝ res·toh·*rant*
return v *terugkomen* tuh·*rukh*·koh·muhn
return ticket *retourtje* ⓝ ruh·*toor*·chuh
right (direction) *rechts* rekhs
road *weg* wekh
room *kamer* *kaa*·muhr

S

safe a *veilig* *vey*·likh
sanitary napkin *maandverband* ⓝ *maant*·vuhr·bant
seat *zitplaats* *zit*·plaats
send *sturen* *stew*·ruhn
service station *tankstation* ⓝ *tank*·sta·syon
sex *seks* seks
shampoo *shampoo* *sham*·poh
share *delen* *dey*·luhn
shaving cream *scheerschuim* ⓝ *skheyr*·skhöym
she *zij* zey
sheet (bed) *laken* ⓝ *laa*·kuhn
shirt *hemd* ⓝ hemt
shoes *schoenen* *skhoo*·nuhn
shop n *winkel* *wing*·kuhl
short *kort* kort
shower n *douche* *doo*·shuh
single room *eenpersoonskamer*
eyn·puhr·sohns·kaa·muhr
skin *huid* höyt
skirt *rok* rok
sleep v *slapen* *slaa*·puhn
slowly *traag* traakh
small *klein* kleyn
smoke (cigarettes) v *roken* *roh*·kuhn
soap *zeep* zeyp
some *enkele* *eng*·kuh·luh
soon *gauw* khaw
south *zuid* zöyt
souvenir shop *souvenirwinkel* soo·vuh·*neer*·wing·kuhl

english–dutch

speak *spreken* sprey·kuhn
spoon *lepel* ley·puhl
stamp *postzegel* post·zey·khuhl
stand-by ticket *stand-by ticket* ⓝ *stent*·baay *ti*·ket
station (train) *station* ⓝ sta·*syon*
stomach *maag* maakh
stop v *stoppen* *sto*·puhn
stop (bus) n *(bus)stop* *(bus·)*stop
street *straat* straat
student *student* stew·*dent*
sun *zon* zon
sunscreen *zonnebrandolie* *zo*·nuh·brant·oh·lee
swim v *zwemmen* *zwe*·muhn

T

tampons *tampons* *tam*·pons
taxi *taxi* *tak*·see
teaspoon *lepeltje* ⓝ *ley*·puhl·chuh
teeth *tanden* *tan*·duhn
telephone n *telefoon* tey·ley·*fohn*
television *televisie* tey·ley·*vee*·zee
temperature (weather) *temperatuur* tem·pey·ra·*tewr*
tent *tent* tent
that (one) *die* ⓜ&ⓕ/*dat* ⓝ dee/dat
they *zij* zey
(to be) thirsty *dorst (hebben)* dorst (*he*·buhn)
this (one) *deze* ⓜ&ⓕ/*dit* ⓝ *dey*·zuh/dit
throat *keel* keyl
ticket *kaartje* ⓝ/*ticket* ⓝ Ⓝ/Ⓑ *kaar*·chuh/*ti*·*ket*
time *tijd* teyt
tired *moe* moo
tissues *tissues* ti·*sews*
today *vandaag* van·*daakh*
toilet *toilet* ⓝ/*WC* twa·*let*/wey·*sey*
tomorrow *morgen* *mor*·khuhn
tonight (after midnight) *vannacht* va·*nakht*
tonight (before midnight) *vanavond* va·*naa*·vont
toothbrush *tandenborstel* *tan*·duhn·bors·tuhl
toothpaste *tandpasta* *tant*·pas·ta
torch (flashlight) *zaklantaarn* *zak*·lan·taarn
tour n *rondleiding* *ront*·ley·ding
tourist office *VVV/toerismebureau* ⓝ Ⓝ/Ⓑ
vey·vey·*vey*/too·*ris*·muh·bew·roh
towel *handdoek* *han*·dook
train *trein* treyn
translate *vertalen* vuhr·*taa*·luhn
travel agency *reisbureau* ⓝ *reys*·bew·roh
travellers cheque *reischeque* *reys*·shek
trousers *broek* brook
twin beds *enkele bedden* *eng*·kuh·luh *be*·duhn
tyre *band* bant

U

underwear *ondergoed* ⓝ *on*·duhr·khoot
urgent *dringend* *dring*·uhnt

V

vacant *vrij* vrey
vacation *vakantie* va·*kan*·see
vegetable n *groente* *khroon*·tuh
vegetarian a *vegetarisch* vey·khey·*taa*·ris
visa *visum* ⓝ *vee*·sum

W

waiter *ober* *oh*·buhr
walk v *gaan* khaan
wallet *portefeuille* por·tuh·*föy*
warm a *warm* warm
wash (something) *wassen* *wa*·suhn
watch n *horloge* ⓝ hor·*loh*·khuh
water *water* ⓝ *waa*·tuhr
we *wij* wey
weekend *weekeinde* ⓝ *weyk*·eyn·duh
west *west* west
wheelchair *rolstoel* *rol*·stool
when *wanneer* wa·*neyr*
where *waar* waar
white *wit* wit
who *wie* wee
why *waarom* waa·*rom*
wife *vrouw* vraw
window *raam* ⓝ raam
wine *wijn* weyn
with *met* met
without *zonder* *zon*·duhr
woman *vrouw* vraw
write *schrijven* *skhrey*·vuhn

Y

yellow *geel* kheyl
yes *ja* yaa
yesterday *gisteren* *khis*·tuh·ruhn
you sg inf *je* yuh
you sg pol *u* ew
you pl *jullie* *yu*·lee

French

french alphabet				
Aa a	*Bb* be	*Cc* se	*Dd* de	*Ee* eu
Ff ef	*Gg* zhe	*Hh* ash	*Ii* i	*Jj* zhi
Kk ka	*Ll* el	*Mm* em	*Nn* en	*Oo* o
Pp pe	*Qq* kew	*Rr* er	*Ss* es	*Tt* te
Uu ew	*Vv* ve	*Ww* dubl ve	*Xx* iks	*Yy* i grek
Zz zed				

french

FRANÇAIS

introduction

What do you think of when the word 'French' comes up? A *bon vivant*, drinking an *apéritif tête-à-tête* with a friend at a *café*, while studying the *a la carte* menu and making some witty *double entendres*? Are you getting *déjà vu* yet? Chances are you already know a few fragments of French (*français* fron·sey) – *bonjour*, *oui*, *au revoir*, *bon voyage* and so on. Even if you missed out on French lessons, though, that first sentence (forgive the stereotyping) is evidence that you probably know quite a few French words without realising it. And thanks to the Norman invasion of England in the 11th century, many common English words have a French origin – some estimate, in fact, that three-fifths of everyday English vocabulary arrived via French.

So, after centuries of contact with English, French offers English speakers a relatively smooth path to communicating in another language. The structure of a French sentence won't come as a surprise and the sounds of the language are generally common to English as well. The few sounds that do differ will be familiar to most through television and film examples of French speakers – the silent 'h' and the throaty 'r', for example. French is a distant cousin of English, but is most closely related to its Romance siblings, Italian and Spanish. These languages developed from the Latin spoken by the Romans during their conquests of the 1st century BC.

Almost 30 countries cite French as an official language (not always the only language, of course), in many cases due to France's colonisation of various countries in Africa, the Pacific and the Caribbean. It's the mother tongue of around 80 million people in places like Belgium, Switzerland, Luxembourg, Monaco, Canada and Senegal as well as France, and another 50 million speak it as a second language. French was the language of international diplomacy until the early 20th century, and is still an official language of a number of international organisations, including the Red Cross, the United Nations and the International Olympic Committee.

As well as the advantage of learning a language that's spoken all around the world, there are more subtle benefits to French. Being told of a wonderful vineyard off the tourist track, for example, or discovering that there's little truth in the cliché that the French are rude. And *regardez* the significant body of literature (the Nobel Prize for Literature has gone to French authors a dozen times), film and music … You'll find the reasons to speak French just keep growing.

pronunciation

vowel sounds

Generally, French vowel sounds are short and don't glide into other vowels. Note that the ey in *café* is close to the English sound, but it's shorter and sharper.

symbol	english equivalent	french example	transliteration
a	run	*tasse*	tas
ai	aisle	*travail*	tra·vai
air	fair	*faire*	fair
e	bet	*fesses*	fes
ee	see	*lit*	lee
eu	nurse	*deux*	deu
ew	ee pronounced with rounded lips	*tu*	tew
ey	as in 'bet', but longer	*musée*	moo·zey
o	pot	*pomme*	pom
oo	moon	*chou*	shoo

There are also four nasal vowels in French. They're pronounced as if you're trying to force the sound out of your nose rather than your mouth. In French, nasal vowels cause the following nasal consonant sound to be omitted, but a 'hint' of what the implied consonant is can sometimes be heard. We've used nasal consonant sounds (m, n, ng) with the nasal vowel to help you produce the sound with more confidence. Since the four nasal sounds can be quite close, we've simplified it this way:

symbol	english equivalent	french example	transliteration
om/on/ong	like the 'o' in 'pot', plus nasal consonant sound	*mouton*	moo·ton
um/un/ung	similar to the 'a' in 'bat', plus nasal consonant sound	*magasin*	ma·ga·zun

consonant sounds

symbol	english equivalent	french example	transliteration
b	bed	*billet*	bee·yey
d	dog	*date*	dat
f	fat	*femme*	fam
g	go	*grand*	gron
k	kit	*carte*	kart
l	lot	*livre*	leev·re
m	man	*merci*	mair·see
n	not	*non*	non
ny	canyon	*signe*	see·nye
ng	ring	*cinquante*	sung·kont
p	pet	*parc*	park
r	run (throaty)	*rue*	rew
s	sun	*si*	see
sh	shot	*changer*	shon·zhey
t	top	*tout*	too
v	very	*verre*	vair
w	win	*oui*	wee
y	yes	*payer*	pe·yey
z	zero	*vous avez*	voo·za·vey
zh	pleasure	*je*	zhe

word stress

Syllables in French words are, for the most part, equally stressed. English speakers tend to stress the first syllable, so try adding a light stress on the final syllable to compensate. The rhythm of a French sentence is based on breaking the phrase into meaningful sections, then stressing the final syllable pronounced in each section. The stress at these points is characterised by a slight rise in intonation.

language difficulties

Do you speak English?
Parlez-vous anglais? par·ley·voo ong·gley

Do you understand?
Comprenez-vous? kom·pre·ney·voo

I understand.
Je comprends. zhe kom·pron

I don't understand.
Je ne comprends pas. zhe ne kom·pron pa

What does (*beaucoup*) mean?
Que veut dire (beaucoup)? ke veu deer (bo·koo)

How do you ...?	*Comment ...?*	ko·mon ...
pronounce this	*le prononcez-vous*	le pro·non·sey voo
write (*bonjour*)	*est-ce qu'on écrit (bonjour)*	es kon ey·kree (bon·zhoor)
Could you please ...?	*Pourriez-vous ..., s'il vous plaît?*	poo·ree·yey voo ... seel voo pley
repeat that	*répéter*	rey·pey·tey
speak more slowly	*parler plus lentement*	par·ley plew lon·te·mon
write it down	*l'écrire*	ley·kreer

essentials

Yes.	*Oui.*	wee
No.	*Non.*	non
Please.	*S'il vous plaît.*	seel voo pley
Thank you (very much).	*Merci (beaucoup).*	mair·see (bo·koo)
You're welcome.	*Je vous en prie.*	zhe voo zon·pree
Excuse me.	*Excusez-moi.*	ek·skew·zey·mwa
Sorry.	*Pardon.*	par·don

numbers

0	*zéro*	zey·ro	16	*seize*	sez
1	*un*	un	17	*dix-sept*	dee·set
2	*deux*	deu	18	*dix-huit*	dee·zweet
3	*trois*	trwa	19	*dix-neuf*	deez·neuf
4	*quatre*	ka·tre	20	*vingt*	vung
5	*cinq*	sungk	21	*vingt et un*	vung tey un
6	*six*	sees	22	*vingt-deux*	vung·deu
7	*sept*	set	30	*trente*	tront
8	*huit*	weet	40	*quarante*	ka·ront
9	*neuf*	neuf	50	*cinquante*	sung·kont
10	*dix*	dees	60	*soixante*	swa·sont
11	*onze*	onz	70	*soixante-dix*	swa·son·dees
12	*douze*	dooz	80	*quatre-vingts*	ka·tre·vung
13	*treize*	trez	90	*quatre-vingt-dix*	ka·tre·vung·dees
14	*quatorze*	ka·torz	100	*cent*	son
15	*quinze*	kunz	1000	*mille*	meel

time & dates

What time is it?	*Quelle heure est-il?*	kel eur ey·teel
It's one o'clock.	*Il est une heure.*	ee·ley ewn eu
It's (10) o'clock.	*Il est (dix) heures.*	ee·ley (deez) eu
Quarter past (one).	*Il est (une) heure et quart.*	ee·ley (ewn) eu ey kar
Half past (one).	*Il est (une) heure et demie.*	ee·ley (ewn) eu ey de·mee
Quarter to (one).	*Il est (une) heure moins le quart.*	ee·ley (ewn) eu mwun le kar
At what time ...?	*À quelle heure ...?*	a kel eu ...
At ...	*À ...*	a ...
in the morning	*du matin*	dew ma·tun
in the afternoon	*de l'après-midi*	de la·prey·mee·dee
in the evening	*du soir*	dew swar
Monday	*lundi*	lun·dee
Tuesday	*mardi*	mar·dee
Wednesday	*mercredi*	mair·kre·dee
Thursday	*jeudi*	zheu·dee
Friday	*vendredi*	von·dre·dee
Saturday	*samedi*	sam·dee
Sunday	*dimanche*	dee·monsh

January	*janvier*	zhon·vyey
February	*février*	feyv·ryey
March	*mars*	mars
April	*avril*	a·vreel
May	*mai*	mey
June	*juin*	zhwun
July	*juillet*	zhwee·yey
August	*août*	oot
September	*septembre*	sep·tom·bre
October	*octobre*	ok·to·bre
November	*novembre*	no·vom·bre
December	*décembre*	dey·som·bre

What date is it today?
C'est quel jour aujourd'hui? sey kel zhoor o·zhoor·dwee

It's (18 October).
C'est le (dix-huit octobre). sey le (dee·zwee tok·to·bre)

since (May)	*depuis (mai)*	de·pwee (mey)
until (June)	*jusqu'à (juin)*	zhoos·ka (zhwun)
today	*aujourd'hui*	o·zhoor·dwee
tonight	*ce soir*	se swar
last ...		
night	*hier soir*	ee·yair swar
week	*la semaine dernière*	la se·men dair·nyair
month	*le mois dernier*	le mwa dair·nyey
year	*l'année dernière*	la·ney dair·nyair
next ...		
week	*la semaine prochaine*	la se·men pro·shen
month	*le mois prochain*	le mwa pro·shen
year	*l'année prochaine*	la·ney pro·shen
yesterday/tomorrow ...	*hier/demain ...*	ee·yair/de·mun ...
morning	*matin*	ma·tun
afternoon	*après-midi*	a·pre·mee·dee
evening	*soir*	swar

weather

What's the weather like?	*Quel temps fait-il?*	kel tom fey·teel
It's ...		
cloudy	*Le temps est couvert.*	le tom ey koo·vair
cold	*Il fait froid.*	eel fey frwa
hot	*Il fait chaud.*	eel fey sho
raining	*Il pleut.*	eel pleu
snowing	*Il neige.*	eel nezh
sunny	*Il fait beau.*	eel fey bo
warm	*Il fait chaud.*	eel fey sho
windy	*Il fait du vent.*	eel fey dew von
spring	*printemps* m	prun·tom
summer	*été* m	ey·tey
autumn	*automne* m	o·ton
winter	*hiver* m	ee·vair

border crossing

I'm here ...	*Je suis ici ...*	zhe swee zee·see ...
in transit	*de passage*	de pa·sazh
on business	*pour le travail*	poor le tra·vai
on holiday	*pour les vacances*	poor ley va·kons
I'm here for ...	*Je suis ici pour ...*	zhe swee zee·see poor ...
(10) days	*(dix) jours*	(dees) zhoor
(three) weeks	*(trois) semaines*	(trwa) se·men
(two) months	*(deux) mois*	(deu) mwa

I'm going to (Paris).
Je vais à (Paris). zhe vey a (pa·ree)

I'm staying at the (Hotel Grand).
Je loge à (l'hotel Grand). zhe lozh a (lo·tel gron)

I have nothing to declare.
Je n'ai rien à déclarer. zhe ney ryun a dey·kla·rey

I have something to declare.
J'ai quelque chose à déclarer. zhey kel·ke·shoz a dey·kla·rey

That's not mine.
Ce n'est pas à moi se ney pa a mwa

transport

tickets & luggage

Where can I buy a ticket?
Où peut-on acheter un billet? — oo pe·ton ash·tey um bee·yey

Do I need to book a seat?
Est-ce qu'il faut réserver une place? — es·keel fo rey·zer·vey ewn plas

One ... ticket (to Bordeaux), please.	*Un billet ... (pour Bordeaux), s'il vous plaît.*	um bee·yey ... (poor bor·do) seel voo pley
one-way	*simple*	sum·ple
return	*aller et retour*	a·ley ey re·toor
I'd like to ... my ticket, please.	*Je voudrais ... mon billet, s'il vous plaît.*	zhe voo·drey ... mom bee·yey seel voo pley
cancel	*annuler*	a·new·ley
change	*changer*	shon·zhey
collect	*retirer*	re·tee·rey
confirm	*confirmer*	kon·feer·mey
I'd like a ... seat, please.	*Je voudrais une place ..., s'il vous plaît.*	zhe voo·drey ewn plas ... seel voo pley
(non)smoking	*non-fumeur*	non few·me
smoking	*fumeur*	few·me

How much is it?
C'est combien? — sey kom·byun

Is there air conditioning?
Est-qu'il y a la climatisation? — es·keel ya la klee·ma·tee·za·syon

Is there a toilet?
Est-qu'il y a des toilettes? — es·keel ya dey twa·let

How long does the trip take?
Le trajet dure combien de temps? — le tra·zhey dewr kom·byun de tom

Is it a direct route?
Est-ce que c'est direct? — es·ke sey dee·rekt

I'd like a luggage locker.
Je voudrais une consigne automatique. — zhe voo·drey ewn kon·see·nye o·to·ma·teek

My luggage has been ...	*Mes bagages ont été ...*	mey ba·gazh on tey·tey ...
damaged	*endommagés*	on·do·ma·zhey
lost	*perdus*	per·dew
stolen	*volés*	vo·ley

getting around

Where does flight (008) arrive?
Où atterí le vol (008)? oo a·te·ree le vol (zey·ro zey·ro weet)

Where does flight (008) depart?
D'où décolle le vol (008)? doo dey·kol le vol (zey·ro zey·ro weet)

Where's (the) ...?	*Où se trouve ...?*	oo se troo·ve ...
arrivals hall	*le hall d'arrivée*	le hol da·ree·vey
departures hall	*le hall des departs*	le hol dey dey·par
duty-free shop	*le magasin duty-free*	le ma·ga·zun dyoo·tee free
gate (12)	*porte (douze)*	port (dooz)

Is this the ... to (Nice)?	*Est ce ... pour (Nice)?*	es se ... poor (nees)
boat	*le bateau*	le ba·to
bus	*le bus*	le bews
plane	*l'avion*	la vyon
train	*le train*	le trun

What time's the ... bus?	*Le ... bus passe à quelle heure?*	le ... bews pas a kel e
first	*premier*	pre·myey
last	*dernier*	dalr·nyey
next	*prochain*	pro·shun

At what time does it arrive/leave?
A quelle heure est ce qu'il arrive/part? a kel eur es se keel a·ree·ve/par

How long will it be delayed?
De combien de temps est-il retardé? de kom·byun de tom es·teel re·tar·dey

What station is this?
C'est quelle gare? sey kel gar

What's the next station?
Quelle est la prochaine gare? kel ey la pro·shen gar

Does it stop at (Amboise)?
Est-ce qu'il s'arrête à (Amboise)? es·kil sa·ret a (om·bwaz)

Please tell me when we get to (Nantes).
Pouvez-vous me dire quand nous arrivons à (Nantes)? — poo·vey·voo me deer kon noo za·ree·von a (nont)

How long do we stop here?
Combien de temps on s'arrête ici? — kom·byun de tom on sa·ret ee·see

Is this seat available?
Est-ce que cette place est libre? — es·ke set plas ey lee·bre

That's my seat.
C'est ma place. — sey ma plas

I'd like a taxi ...	*Je voudrais un taxi ...*	zhe voo·drey un tak·see ...
at (9am)	*à (neuf heures du matin)*	a (neu veur dew ma·tun)
now	*maintenant*	mun·te·non
tomorrow	*demain*	de·mun

Is this taxi available?
Vous êtes libre? — voo·zet lee·bre

How much is it to ...?
C'est combien pour aller à ...? — sey kom·byun poor a·ley a ...

Please put the meter on.
Mettez le compteur, s'il vous plaît. — me·tey le kon·teseel voo pley

Please take me to (this address).
Conduisez-moi à (cette adresse), s'il vous plaît. — kon·dwee·zey mwa a (set a·dres) seel voo pley

Please ...	*..., s'il vous plaît.*	... seel voo pley
slow down	*Roulez plus lentement*	roo·ley plew lont·mon
stop here	*Arrêtez-vous ici*	a·rey·tey voo ee·see
wait here	*Attendez ici*	a·ton·dey ee·see

car, motorbike & bicycle hire

I'd like to hire a ...	*Je voudrais louer ...*	zhe voo·drey loo·wey ...
bicycle	*un vélo*	un vey·lo
car	*une voiture*	ewn vwa·tewr
motorbike	*une moto*	ewn mo·to

with ...	*avec ...*	a·vek ...
a driver	*un chauffeur*	un sho·feur
air conditioning	*climatisation*	klee·ma·tee·za·syon

How much for ... hire?	*Quel est le tarif par ...?*	kel ey le ta·reef par ...
hourly	*heure*	eur
daily	*jour*	zhoor
weekly	*semaine*	se·men

air	*air* m	air
oil	*huile* f	weel
petrol	*essence* f	es·sons
tyres	*pneus* f pl	pneu

I need a mechanic.
J'ai besoin d'un mécanicien. zhey be·zwun dun mey·ka·nee·syun

I've run out of petrol.
Je suis en panne d'essence. zhe swee zon pan de·sons

I have a flat tyre.
Mon pneu est à plat. mom pneu ey ta pla

directions

Where's the ...?	*Où est-ce qu'il y a ...?*	oo es·keel ya ...
bank	*la banque*	la bongk
city centre	*le centre-ville*	ler son·tre·veel
hotel	*l'hôtel*	lo·tel
market	*le marché*	le mar·shey
police station	*le commissariat de police*	le kom·mee·sar ya de po·lees
post office	*le bureau de poste*	le bew·ro de post
public toilet	*des toilettes*	dey twa·let
tourist office	*l'office de tourisme*	lo·fees de too·rees·me

Is this the road to (Toulouse)?
C'est la route pour (Toulouse)? sey la root poor (too·looz)

Can you show me (on the map)?
Pouvez vous m'indiquer (sur la carte)? poo·vey·voo mun·dee·key (sewr la kart)

What's the address?
Quelle est l'adresse? kel ey la·dres

How far is it?
C'est loin? sey lwun

How do I get there?
Comment faire pour y aller? ko·mon fair poor ee a·ley

Turn …	*Tournez …*	toor·ney …
at the corner	*au coin*	o kwun
at the traffic lights	*aux feux*	o feu
left/right	*à gauche/droite*	a gosh/drwat
It's …	*C'est …*	sey …
behind …	*derrière …*	dair·yair …
far away	*loin d'ici*	lwun dee·see
here	*ici*	ee·see
in front of …	*devant …*	de·von …
left	*à gauche*	a gosh
near (to …)	*près (de …)*	prey (de …)
next to …	*à côté de …*	a ko·tey de …
opposite …	*en face de …*	on fas de …
right	*à droite*	a drwat
straight ahead	*tout droit*	too drwa
there	*là*	la
north	*nord* m	nor
south	*sud* m	sewd
east	*est* m	est
west	*ouest* m	west
by bus	*en bus*	om bews
by taxi	*en taxi*	on tak·see
by train	*en train*	on trun
on foot	*à pied*	a pyey

signs

Entrée/Sortie	on·trey/sor·tee	**Entrance/Exit**
Ouvert/Fermé	oo·vair/fair·mey	**Open/Closed**
Chambre Libre	shom·bre lee·bre	**Rooms Available**
Complet	kom·pley	**No Vacancies**
Renseignements	ron·sen·ye·mon	**Information**
Commissariat De Police	ko·mee·sar·ya de po·lees	**Police Station**
Interdit	in·teyr·dee	**Prohibited**
Toilettes	twa·let	**Toilets**
Hommes	om	**Men**
Femmes	fam	**Women**
Chaude/Froide	shod/frwad	**Hot/Cold**

accommodation

finding accommodation

Where's a ...?	*Où est-ce qu'on peut trouver ...?*	oo es·kon peu troo·vey ...
camping ground	*un terrain de camping*	un tey·run de kom·peeng
guesthouse	*une pension*	ewn pon·see·on
hotel	*un hôtel*	un o·tel
youth hostel	*une auberge de jeunesse*	ewn o·bairzh de zhe·nes

Can you recommend somewhere ...?	*Est-ce que vous pouvez recommander un logement ...?*	es·ke voo poo·vey re·ko·mon·dey un lozh·mon ...
cheap	*pas cher*	pa shair
good	*de bonne qualité*	de bon ka·lee·tey
nearby	*près d'ici*	prey dee·see

I'd like to book a room, please.
Je voudrais réserver une chambre, s'il vous plaît. — zhe voo·drey rey·zair·vey ewn shom·bre seel voo pley

I have a reservation.
J'ai une réservation. — zhey ewn rey·zair·va·syon

My name is ...
Mon nom est ... — mon nom ey ...

Do you have a ... room?	*Avez-vous une chambre ...?*	a·vey·voo ewn shom·bre ...
single	*à un lit*	a un lee
double	*avec un grand lit*	a·vek ung gron lee
twin	*avec des lits jumeaux*	a·vek dey lee zhew·mo

Can I pay by ...?	*Est-ce qu'on peut payer avec ...?*	es·kom peu pey·yey a·vek ...
credit card	*une carte de crédit*	ewn kart de krey·dee
travellers cheque	*des chèques de voyage*	dey shek de vwa·yazh

How much is it per ...?	*Quel est le prix par ...?*	kel ey le pree par ...
night	*nuit*	nwee
person	*personne*	pair·son

I'd like to stay for (two) nights.
Je voudrais rester pour (deux) nuits. zhe voo·drey res·tey poor (der) nwee

From (July 2) to (July 6).
Du (deux juillet) au (six juillet). dew (de zhwee·yey) o (see zhwee·yey)

Can I see it?
Est-ce que je peux la voir? es·ke zhe peu la vwar

Am I allowed to camp here?
Est-ce que je peux camper ici? es·ke zhe peu kom·pey ee·see

Where's the nearest camp site?
Où est le terrain de camping le plus proche? oo ey ler tey·run de kom·peeng le plew prosh

requests & queries

When/Where is breakfast served?
Quand/Où le petit déjeuner est-il servi? kon/oo le pe·tee dey·zhe·ney ey·teel sair·vee

Please wake me at (seven).
Réveillez-moi à (sept) heures, s'il vous plaît. rey·vey·yey·mwa a (set) eur seel voo pley

Could I have my key, please?
Est-ce que je pourrais avoir la clé, s'il vous plaît? es·ke zhe poo·rey a·vwar la kley seel voo pley

Can I get another (blanket)?
Est-ce que je peux avoir une autre (couverture)? es·ke zhe pe a·vwar ewn o·tre (koo·vair·tewr)

Is there a/an ...?	*Avez-vous un ...?*	a·vey·voo un ...
elevator	*ascenseur*	a·son·seur
safe	*coffre-fort*	ko·fre·for

The room is too ...	*C'est trop ...*	sey tro ...
expensive	*cher*	shair
noisy	*bruyant*	brew·yon
small	*petit*	pe·tee

The … doesn't work.	*… ne fonctionne pas.*	… ne fong·syon pa
air conditioning	*La climatisation*	klee·ma·tee·za·syon
fan	*Le ventilateur*	le von·tee·la·teur
toilet	*Les toilettes*	le twa·let

This … isn't clean.	*… n'est pas propre.*	… ney pa pro·pre
pillow	*Cet oreiller*	set o·rey·yey
sheet	*Ce drap*	se drap
towel	*Cette serviette*	set sair·vee·et

checking out

What time is checkout?
Quand faut-il régler? kon fo·teel rey·gley

Can I leave my luggage here?
Puis-je laisser mes bagages? pweezh ley·sey mey ba·gazh

Could I have my …, please?	*Est-ce que je pourrais avoir …, s'il vous plaît?*	es·ke zhe poo·rey a·vwar … seel voo pley
deposit	*ma caution*	ma ko·syon
passport	*mon passeport*	mon pas·por
valuables	*mes biens précieux*	mey byun prey·syeu

communications & banking

the internet

Where's the local Internet café?
Où est le cybercafé du coin? oo ey le see·bair·ka·fey dew kwun

How much is it per hour?
C'est combien l'heure? sey kom·byun leur

I'd like to …	*Je voudrais …*	zhe voo·drey …
check my email	*consulter mon courrier électronique*	kon·sewl·tey mong koor·yey ey·lek·tro·neek
get Internet access	*me connecter à l'internet*	me ko·nek·tey a lun·tair·net
use a printer	*utiliser une imprimante*	ew·tee·lee·zey ewn um·pree·mont
use a scanner	*utiliser un scanner*	ew·tee·lee·zey un ska·nair

mobile/cell phone

I'd like a ...	*Je voudrais ...*	zhe voo·drey ...
mobile/cell phone for hire	*louer un portable*	loo·ey um por·ta·ble
SIM card for your network	*une carte SIM pour le réseau*	ewn kart seem poor le rey·zo

What are the rates?	*Quels sont les tarifs?*	kel son ley ta·reef

telephone

What's your phone number?
Quel est votre numéro de téléphone? — kel ey vo·tre new·mey·ro de tey·ley·fon

The number is ...
Le numéro est ... — le new·mey·ro ey ...

Where's the nearest public phone?
Où est le téléphone public le plus proche? — oo ey le tey·ley·fon pewb·leek le plew prosh

I'd like to buy a phone card.
Je voudrais acheter une carte téléphonique. — zhe voo·drey ash·tey ewn kart tey·ley·fo·neek

I want to ...	*Je veux ...*	zhe ve ...
call (Singapore)	*téléphoner avec préavis (à Singapour)*	tey·ley·fo·ney a·vek prey·a·vee (a sung·ga·poor)
make a local call	*faire un appel local*	fair un a·pel lo·kal
reverse the charges	*téléphoner en PCV*	tey·ley·fo·ney om pey·sey·vey

How much does ... cost?	*Quel est le prix ...?*	kel ey le pree ...
a (three)-minute call	*d'une communication de (trois) minutes*	dewn ko·mew·nee·ka·syon de (trwa) mee·newt
each extra minute	*de chaque minute supplémentaire*	de shak mee·newt sew·pley·mon·tair

It's (one euro) per (minute).
(Un euro) pour (une minute). — (un eu·ro) poor (ewn mee·newt)

post office

I want to send a …	*Je voudrais envoyer …*	zhe voo·drey on·vwa·yey …
fax	*un fax*	un faks
letter	*une lettre*	ewn le·tre
parcel	*un colis*	ung ko·lee
postcard	*une carte postale*	ewn kart pos·tal
I want to buy a/an …	*Je voudrais acheter …*	zhe voo·drey ash·tey …
envelope	*une enveloppe*	ewn on·vlop
stamp	*un timbre*	un tum·bre
Please send it (to Australia) by …	*Envoyez-le (en Australie) …, s'il vous plaît.*	on·vwa·yey·le (on os·tra·lee) … seel voo pley
airmail	*par avion*	par a·vyon
express mail	*en exprès*	on neks·pres
registered mail	*en recommandé*	on re·ko·mon·dey
surface mail	*par voie de terre*	par vwa de tair

Is there any mail for me?
Y a-t-il du courrier pour moi? ya·teel dew koor·yey poor mwa

bank

Where's a/an …?	*Où est …?*	oo ey …
ATM	*le guichet automatique*	le gee·shey o·to·ma·teek
foreign exchange office	*le bureau de change*	le bew·ro de shonzh
I'd like to …	*Je voudrais …*	zhe voo·drey …
arrange a transfer	*faire un virement*	fair un veer·mon
cash a cheque	*encaisser un chèque*	ong·key·sey un shek
change a travellers cheque	*changer des chèques de voyage*	shon·zhey dey shek de vwa·yazh
change money	*changer de l'argent*	shon·zhey de lar·zhon
get a cash advance	*une avance de crédit*	ewn a·vons de krey·dee
withdraw money	*retirer de l'argent*	re·tee·rey de lar·zhon
What's the …?	*Quel est …?*	kel ey …
charge for that	*le tarif*	le ta·reef
exchange rate	*le taux de change*	le to de shonzh

It's …	C'est …	sey …
(12) euros	*(douze) euros*	(dooz) eu·ro
free	*gratuit*	gra·twee

What time does the bank open?
À quelle heure ouvre la banque? — a kel eur oo·vre la bongk

Has my money arrived yet?
Mon argent est-il arrivé? — mon ar·zhon ey·teel a·ree·vey

sightseeing

getting in

What time does it …?	*Quelle est l'heure …?*	kel ey leur …
close	*de fermeture*	de fer·me·tewr
open	*d'ouverture*	doo·vair·tewr

What's the admission charge?
Quel est le prix d'admission? — kel ey le pree dad·mee·syon

Is there a discount for children/students?
Il y a une réduction pour les enfants/étudiants? — eel ya ewn rey·dewk·syon poor ley zon·fon/zey·tew·dyon

I'd like a …	*Je voudrais …*	zhe voo·drey …
catalogue	*un catalogue*	ung ka·ta·log
guide	*un guide*	ung geed
local map	*une carte de la région*	ewn kart de la rey·zhyon

I'd like to see …	*J'aimerais voir …*	zhem·rey vwar …
What's that?	*Qu'est-ce que c'est?*	kes·ke sey
Can I take photos?	*Je peux prendre des photos?*	zhe peu pron·dre dey fo·to

tours

When's the next …?	*C'est quand la prochaine …?*	sey kon la pro·shen …
day trip	*excursion d'une journée*	eks·kewr·syon dewn zhoor·ney
tour	*excursion*	eks·kewr·syon

Is … included?	*Est-ce que … est inclus/incluse?* m/f	es·ke … ey tung·klew/tung·klewz
accommodation	*le logement* m	le lozh·mon
the admission charge	*l'admission* f	lad·mee·syon
food	*la nourriture* f	la noo·ree·tewr
transport	*le transport* m	le trons·por

How long is the tour?
L'excursion dure combien de temps? — leks·kewr·syon dewr kom·byun de tom

What time should we be back?
On doit rentrer pour quelle heure? — on dwa ron·trey poor kel eur

sightseeing

castle	*château* m	sha·to
cathedral	*cathédrale* f	ka·tey·dral
church	*église* f	ey·gleez
main square	*place centrale* f	plas son·tral
monastery	*monastère* m	mo·na·stair
monument	*monument* m	mo·new·mon
museum	*musée* m	mew·zey
old city	*vieille ville* f	vyey veel
palace	*palais* m	pa·ley
ruins	*ruines* f pl	rween
stadium	*stade* m	stad
statues	*statues* f pl	sta·tew

shopping

enquiries

Where's a …?	*Où est …?*	oo es …
bank	*la banque*	la bongk
bookshop	*la librairie*	la lee·brey·ree
camera shop	*le magasin photo*	le ma·ga·zun fo·to
department store	*le grand magasin*	le gron ma·ga·zun
grocery store	*l'épicerie*	ley·pee·sree
market	*le marché*	le mar·shey
newsagency	*le marchand de journaux*	le mar·shon de zhoor·no
supermarket	*le supermarché*	le sew·pair·mar·shey

Where can I buy (a padlock)?
Où puis-je acheter (un cadenas)? oo pweezh ash·tey (un kad·na)

I'm looking for ...
Je cherche ... zhe shairsh ...

Can I look at it?
Est-ce que je peux le voir? es·ke zhe peu le vwar

Do you have any others?
Vous en avez d'autres? voo zon a·vey do·tre

Does it have a guarantee?
Est-ce qu'il y a une garantie? es keel ya ewn ga·ron·tee

Can I have it sent overseas?
Pouvez-vous me l'envoyer à l'étranger? poo·vey·voo me lon·vwa·yey a ley·tron·zhey

Can I have my ... repaired?
Puis-je faire réparer ...? pwee·zhe fair rey·pa·rey ...

It's faulty.
C'est défectueux. sey dey·fek·tweu

I'd like ..., please.	*Je voudrais ..., s'il vous plaît.*	zhe voo·drey ... seel voo pley
a bag	*un sac*	un sak
a refund	*un remboursement*	un rom·boors·mon
to return this	*rapporter ceci*	ra·por·tey se·see

paying

How much is it?
C'est combien? sey kom·byun

Can you write down the price?
Pouvez-vous écrire le prix? poo·vey·voo ey·kreer le pree

That's too expensive.
C'est trop cher. sey tro shair

Can you lower the price?
Vous pouvez baisser le prix? voo poo·vey bey·sey le pree

I'll give you (five) euros.
Je vous donnerai (cinq) euros. zhe voo don·rey (sungk) eu·ro

There's a mistake in the bill.
Il y a une erreur dans la note. eel ya ewn ey·reur don la not

Do you accept . . .?	*Est-ce que je peux payer avec . . .?*	es·ke zhe pe pey·yey a·vek . . .
credit cards	*une carte de crédit*	ewn kart de krey·dee
debit cards	*une carte de débit*	ewn kart de dey·bee
travellers cheques	*des chèques de voyages*	dey shek de vwa·yazh

I'd like . . ., please.	*Je voudrais . . ., s'il vous plaît.*	zhe voo·drey . . . seel voo pley
a receipt	*un reçu*	un re·sew
my change	*ma monnaie*	ma mo·ney

clothes & shoes

Can I try it on?	*Puis-je l'essayer?*	pwee·zhe ley·sey·yey
My size is (42).	*Je fais du (quarante-deux).*	zhe fey dew (ka·ront·deu)
It doesn't fit.	*Ce n'est pas la bonne taille.*	se ney pa la bon tai

small	*petit*	pe·tee
medium	*moyen*	mwa·yen
large	*grand*	gron

books & music

I'd like a . . .	*Je voudrais . . .*	zhe voo·drey . . .
newspaper (in English)	*un journal (en anglais)*	un zhoor·nal (on ong·gley)
pen	*un stylo*	un stee·lo

Is there an English-language bookshop?
Y a-t-il une librairie anglaise? ya·teel ewn lee·brey·ree ong·gleyz

I'm looking for something by (Camus).
Je cherche quelque chose de (Camus). zhe shairsh kel·ke shoz de (ka·mew)

Can I listen to this?
Je peux l'écouter ici? zhe peu ley·koo·tey ee·see

photography

Can you ...?	*Pouvez-vous ...?*	poo·vey·voo ...
burn a CD from my memory card	*copier un CD de ma carte memoire*	ko·pyey un se·de de ma kart mey·mwar
develop this film	*développer cette pellicule*	dey·vlo·pey set pey·lee·kewl
load my film	*charger ma pellicule*	shar·zhey ma pey·lee·kewl

I need a/an ... film for this camera.	*J'ai besoin d'une pellicule ... pour cet appareil.*	zhey be·zwun dewn pey·lee·kewl ... poor sey·ta·pa·rey
APS	*APS*	a·pey·es
B&W	*en noir et blanc*	on nwar ey·blong
colour	*couleur*	koo·leur
slide	*diapositive*	dya·po·zee·teev
(200) speed	*rapidité (deux cent)*	ra·pee·dee·tey (deu son)

When will it be ready?
Quand est-ce que cela sera prêt? kon tes·ke se·la se·ra prey

meeting people

greetings, goodbyes & introductions

Hello.	*Bonjour.*	bon·zhoor
Hi.	*Salut.*	sa·lew
Good night.	*Bonsoir.*	bon·swar
Goodbye.	*Au revoir.*	o re·vwar
See you later.	*À bientôt.*	a byun·to

Mr	*Monsieur*	me·syeu
Mrs	*Madame*	ma·dam
Miss	*Mademoiselle*	mad·mwa·zel

How are you?	*Comment allez-vous?*	ko·mon ta·ley·voo
Fine, thanks. And you?	*Bien, merci. Et vous?*	byun mair·see ey voo
What's your name?	*Comment vous appelez-vous?*	ko·mon voo za·pley·voo
My name is ...	*Je m'appelle ...*	zhe ma·pel ...
I'm pleased to meet you.	*Enchanté/Enchantée.* m/f	on·shon·tey

This is my …	*Voici mon/ma …* m/f	vwa·see mon/ma …
boyfriend	*petit ami*	pe·tee ta·mee
brother	*frère*	frair
daughter	*fille*	fee·ye
father	*père*	pair
friend	*ami/amie* m/f	a·mee
girlfriend	*petite amie*	pe·teet a·mee
husband	*mari*	ma·ree
mother	*mère*	mair
partner (intimate)	*partenaire*	par·te·nair
sister	*sœur*	seur
son	*fils*	fees
wife	*femme*	fam

Here's my …	*Voici mon …*	vwa·see mon …
What's your …?	*Quel est votre …?* pol	kel ey vo·tre …
	Quel est ton …? inf	kel ey ton …
address	*adresse*	a·dress
email address	*e-mail*	ey·mel
fax number	*numéro de fax*	new·mey·ro de faks
phone number	*numéro de téléphone*	new·mey·ro de tey·ley·fon

occupations

What's your occupation?

Vous faites quoi comme métier? pol — voo fet kwa kom mey·tyey

Tu fais quoi comme métier? inf — tew fey kwa kom mey·tyey

I'm a/an …	*Je suis un/une …* m/f	zhe swee zun/zewn …
artist	*artiste* m&f	ar·teest
businessperson	*homme/femme d'affaires* m/f	om/fem da·fair
farmer	*agriculteur* m	a·gree·kewl·teur
	agricultrice f	a·gree·kewl·trees
manual worker	*ouvrier/ouvrière* m/f	oo·vree·yey/oo·vree·yair
office worker	*employé/employée de bureau* m/f	om·plwa·yey de bew·ro
scientist	*scientifique* m&f	syon·tee·feek
student	*étudiant/étudiante* m/f	ey·tew·dyon/ey·tew·dyont
tradesperson	*ouvrier qualifié* m&f	oo·vree·yey ka·lee·fyey

background

Where are you from?	*Vous venez d'où?* pol	voo ve·ney doo
	Tu viens d'où? inf	tew vyun doo
I'm from …	*Je viens …*	zhe vyun …
Australia	*d'Australie*	dos·tra·lee
Canada	*du Canada*	dew ka·na·da
England	*d'Angleterre*	dong·gle·tair
New Zealand	*de la Nouvelle-Zélande*	de la noo·vel·zey·lond
the USA	*des USA*	dey zew·es·a

Are you married?
Est-ce que vous êtes marié(e)? m/f pol — es·ke voo zet mar·yey
Est-ce que tu es marié(e)? m/f inf — es·ke tew ey mar·yey

I'm married.
Je suis marié/mariée. m/f — zhe swee mar·yey

I'm single.
Je suis célibataire. m&f — zhe swee sey·lee·ba·tair

age

How old …?	*Quel âge …?*	kel azh …
are you	*avez-vous* pol	a·vey·voo
	as-tu inf	a·tew
is your daughter	*a votre fille* pol	a vo·tre fee·ye
is your son	*a votre fils* pol	a vo·tre fees
I'm … years old.	*J'ai … ans.*	zhey … on
He/She is … years old.	*Il/Elle a … ans.*	eel/el a … on

feelings

I'm (not) …	*Je (ne) suis (pas)…*	zhe (ne) swee (pa) …
Are you …?	*Êtes-vous …?* pol	et voo …
	Es-tu …? inf	ey·tew …
happy	*heureux/heureuse* m/f	er·reu/er·reuz
sad	*triste* m&f	treest

FRANÇAIS – meeting people

I'm ...	*J'ai ...*	zhey ...
I'm not ...	*Je n'ai pas ...*	zhe ney pa ...
Are you ...?	*Avez-vous ...?* pol	a·vey voo ...
	As-tu ...? inf	a·tew ...
cold	*froid/froide* m/f	frwa/frwad
hot	*chaud/chaude* m/f	sho/shod
hungry	*faim* m&f	fum
thirsty	*soif* m&f	swaf

entertainment

going out

Where can I find ...?	*Où sont les ...?*	oo son ley ...
clubs	*clubs*	kleub
gay venues	*boîtes gaies*	bwat gey
pubs	*pubs*	peub
I feel like going to a/the ...	*Je voudrais aller ...*	zhe voo·drey a·ley ...
concert	*à un concert*	a ung kon·sair
movies	*au cinéma*	o see·ney·ma
party	*à la fête*	a la feyt
restaurant	*au restaurant*	o res·to·ron
theatre	*au théâtre*	o tey·a·tre

interests

Do you like ...?	*Aimes-tu ...?* inf	em·tew ...
I like ...	*J'aime ...*	zhem ...
I don't like ...	*Je n'aime pas ...*	zhe nem pa ...
art	*l'art*	lar
cooking	*cuisiner*	kwee·zee·ney
movies	*le cinéma*	le see·ney·ma
nightclubs	*les boites*	ley bwat
reading	*lire*	leer
shopping	*faire des courses*	fair dey koors
sport	*le sport*	le spor
travelling	*voyager*	vwa·ya·zhey

Do you like to . . .?	*Aimes-tu . . .?* **inf**	em·tew . . .
dance	*danser*	don·sey
go to concerts	*aller aux concerts*	a·ley o kon·sair
listen to music	*écouter de la musique*	ey·koo·tey de la mew·zeek

food & drink

finding a place to eat

Can you recommend a . . .?	*Est-ce que vous pouvez me conseiller . . .?*	es·ke voo poo·vey me kon·sey·yey . . .
bar	*un bar*	um bar
café	*un café*	ung ka·fey
restaurant	*un restaurant*	un res·to·ron
I'd like . . ., please.	*Je voudrais . . ., s'il vous plaît.*	zhe voo·drey . . . seel voo pley
a table for (five)	*une table pour (cinq) personnes*	ewn ta·ble poor (sungk) pair·son
the (non)smoking section	*un endroit pour (non-)fumeurs*	un on·drwa poor non·few·me

ordering food

breakfast	*petit déjeuner* **m**	pe·tee dey·zhe·ney
lunch	*déjeuner* **m**	dey·zhe·ney
dinner	*dîner* **m**	dee·ney
snack	*casse-croûte* **m**	kas·kroot

What would you recommend?
Qu'est-ce que vous conseillez? kes·ke voo kon·sey·yey

I'd like (the) . . ., please.	*Je voudrais . . ., s'il vous plaît.*	zhe voo·drey . . . seel voo pley
bill	*l'addition*	la·dee·syon
drink list	*la carte des boissons*	la kart dey bwa·son
menu	*la carte*	la kart
that dish	*ce plat*	ser pla
wine list	*la carte des vins*	la kart dey vun

drinks

(cup of) coffee …	*(un) café …*	(ung) ka·fey …
(cup of) tea …	*(un) thé …*	(un) tey …
with milk	*au lait*	o ley
without sugar	*sans sucre*	son sew·kre
(orange) juice	*jus (d'orange)* m	zhew (do·ronzh)
soft drink	*boisson non-alcoolisée* f	bwa·son non·al·ko·lee·zey
… water	*eau …*	o …
hot	*chaude*	shod
sparkling mineral	*minérale gazeuse*	mee·ney·ral ga·zeuz
still mineral	*minérale non-gazeuse*	mee·ney·ral nong·ga·zeuz

in the bar

I'll have …	*Je prends …*	zhe pron …
I'll buy you a drink.	*Je vous offre un verre.*	zhe voo zo·fre un vair
What would you like?	*Qu'est-ce que vous voulez?*	kes·ke voo voo·ley
Cheers!	*Santé!*	son·tey
brandy	*cognac* m	ko·nyak
champagne	*champagne* m	shom·pan·ye
cocktail	*cocktail* m	kok·tel
a shot of (whisky)	*un petit verre de (whisky)*	um pe·tee vair de (wees·kee)
a bottle of … wine	*une bouteille de vin …*	ewn boo·tey de vun …
a glass of … wine	*un verre de vin …*	un vair de vun …
red	*rouge*	roozh
sparkling	*mousseux*	moo·seu
white	*blanc*	blong
a … of beer	*… de bière*	… de byair
glass	*un verre*	un vair
bottle	*une bouteille*	ewn boo·tey

self-catering

What's the local speciality?
Quelle est la spécialité locale? kel ey la spey·sya·lee·tey lo·kal

What's that?
Qu'est-ce que c'est, ça? kes·ke sey sa

How much is (a kilo of cheese)?
C'est combien (le kilo de fromage)? sey kom·byun (le kee·lo de fro·mazh)

I'd like …	*Je voudrais …*	zhe voo·drey …
(200) grams	*(deux cents) grammes*	(deu son) gram
(two) kilos	*(deux) kilos*	(deu) kee·lo
(three) pieces	*(trois) morceaux*	(trwa) mor·so
(six) slices	*(six) tranches*	(sees) tronsh

Less.	*Moins.*	mwun
Enough.	*Assez.*	a·sey
More.	*Plus.*	plew

special diets & allergies

Is there a vegetarian restaurant near here?
Y a-t-il un restaurant végétarien par ici? ya·teel un res·to·ron vey·zhey·ta·ryun par ee·see

Do you have vegetarian food?
Vous faites les repas végétarien? voo fet ley re·pa vey·zhey·ta·ryun

Could you prepare a meal without …?	*Pouvez-vous préparer un repas sans …?*	poo·vey·voo prey·pa·rey un re·pa son …
butter	*beurre*	beur
eggs	*œufs*	zeu
meat stock	*bouillon gras*	boo·yon gra

I'm allergic to …	*Je suis allergique …*	zhe swee za·lair·zheek …
dairy produce	*aux produits laitiers*	o pro·dwee ley·tyey
gluten	*au gluten*	o glew·ten
MSG	*au glutamate de sodium*	o glew·ta·mat de so·dyom
nuts	*au noix*	no nwa
seafood	*aux fruits de mer*	o frwee de mair

menu reader

baba au rhum m	ba·ba o rom	*small sponge cake, often with raisins, soaked in a rum-flavoured syrup*
béarnaise f	bey·ar·neyz	*white sauce of wine or vinegar beaten with egg yolks & flavoured with herbs*
blanquette de veau f	blong·ket de vo	*veal stew in white sauce with cream*
bombe glacée f	bom·be gla·sey	*ice cream with candied fruits, glazed chestnuts & cream*
bouillabaisse f	bwee·ya·bes	*fish soup stewed in a broth with garlic, orange peel, fennel, tomatoes & saffron*
brioche f	bree·yosh	*small roll or cake sometimes flavoured with nuts, currants or candied fruits*
brochette f	bro·shet	*grilled skewer of meat or vegetables*
consommé m	kon·so·mey	*clarified meat or fish-based broth*
contre-filet m	kon·tre·fee·ley	*beef sirloin roast*
coulis m	koo·lee	*fruit or vegetable purée, used as a sauce*
croque-madame m	krok·ma·dam	*grilled or fried ham & cheese sandwich, topped with a fried egg*
croquembouche m	kro·kom·boosh	*cream puffs dipped in caramel*
croque-monsieur m	krok·mes·yeu	*grilled or fried ham & cheese sandwich*
croustade f	kroo·stad	*puff pastry filled with fish, seafood, meat, mushrooms or vegetables*
dijonnaise	dee·zho·nez	*dishes with a mustard-based sauce*
estouffade f	es·too·fad	*meat stewed in wine with carrots & herbs*
friand m	free·yon	*pastry stuffed with minced sausage meat, ham & cheese, or almond cream*
fricandeau m	free·kon·do	*veal fillet simmered in white wine, vegetables herbs & spices • a pork pâté*

fricassée f	free·ka·sey	*lamb, veal or poultry in a thick creamy sauce with mushrooms & onions*
grenadin m	gre·na·dun	*veal (or sometimes poultry) fillet, wrapped in a thin slice of bacon*
michette f	mee·shet	*savoury bread stuffed with cheese, olives, onions & anchovies*
pan-bagnat m	pun ban·ya	*small round bread loaves, filled with onions, vegetables, anchovies & olives*
plateau de fromage m	pla·to de fro·mazh	*cheese board or platter*
pomme duchesse f	pom dew·shes	*fritter of mashed potato, butter & egg yolk*
pot-au-feu m	po·to·fe	*beef, root vegetable & herb stockpot*
potée f	po·tey	*meat & vegetables cooked in a pot*
profiterole m	pro·fee·trol	*small pastry with savoury or sweet fillings*
puits d'amour m	pwee da·moor	*puff pastry filled with custard or jam*
quenelle f	ke·nel	*fish or meat dumpling, often poached*
quiche f	keesh	*tart with meat, fish or vegetable filling*
raclette f	ra·klet	*hot melted cheese, served with potatoes & gherkins*
ragoût m	ra·goo	*stew of meat, fish and/or vegetables*
ratatouille f	ra·ta·too·ye	*vegetable stew*
roulade f	roo·lad	*slice of meat or fish rolled around stuffing*
savarin m	sa·va·run	*sponge cake soaked with a rum syrup & filled with custard, cream & fruits*
savoie f	sav·wa	*light cake made with beaten egg whites*
tartiflette f	tar·tee·flet	*dish of potatoes, cheese & bacon*
velouté m	ver·loo·tey	*rich, creamy soup, usually prepared with vegetables, shellfish or fish purée*
vol-au-vent m	vo·lo·von	*puff pastry filled with a mixture of sauce & meat, seafood or vegetables*

emergencies

basics

Help!	*Au secours!*	o skoor
Stop!	*Arrêtez!*	a·rey·tey
Go away!	*Allez-vous-en!*	a·ley·voo·zon
Thief!	*Au voleur!*	o vo·leur
Fire!	*Au feu!*	o feu
Watch out!	*Faites attention!*	fet a·ton·syon

Call . . .!	*Appelez . . .!*	a·pley . . .
a doctor	*un médecin*	un meyd·sun
an ambulance	*une ambulance*	ewn om·bew·lons
the police	*la police*	la po·lees

It's an emergency!
C'est urgent! — sey tewr·zhon

Could you help me, please?
Est-ce que vous pourriez m'aider, s'il vous plaît? — es·ke voo poo·ryey mey·dey seel voo pley

Could I use the telephone?
Est-ce que je pourrais utiliser le téléphone? — es·ke zhe poo·rey ew·tee·lee·zey le tey·ley·fon

I'm lost.
Je suis perdu/perdue. m/f — zhe swee pair·dew

Where are the toilets?
Où sont les toilettes? — oo son ley twa·let

police

Where's the police station?
Où est le commissariat de police? — oo ey le ko·mee·sar·ya de po·lees

I want to report an offence.
Je veux signaler un délit. — zhe veu see·nya·ley un dey·lee

I have insurance.
J'ai une assurance. — zhey ewn a·sew·rons

I've been assaulted.
J'ai été attaqué/attaquée. m/f — zhey ey·tey a·ta·key

I've been raped.
J'ai été violé/violée. m/f — zhey ey·tey vyo·ley

I've been robbed.
On m'a volé. — on ma vo·ley

I've lost my ...	*J'ài perdu ...*	zhey pair·dew ...
My ... was/were stolen.	*On m'a volé ...*	on ma vo·ley ...
backpack	*mon sac à dos*	mon sak a do
bags	*mes valises*	mey va·leez
credit card	*ma carte de crédit*	ma kart de krey·dee
handbag	*mon sac à main*	mon sak a mun
jewellery	*mes bijoux*	mey bee·zhoo
money	*mon argent*	mon ar·zhon
passport	*mon passeport*	mom pas·por
travellers cheques	*mes chèques de voyage*	mey shek de vwa·yazh
wallet	*mon portefeuille*	mom por·te·feu·ye

I want to contact my ...	*Je veux contacter mon ...*	zher veu kon·tak·tey mon ...
consulate	*consulat*	kon·sew·la
embassy	*ambassade*	om·ba·sad

health

medical needs

Where's the nearest ...?	*Où y a t-il ... par ici?*	oo ee a teel ... par ee·see
dentist	*un dentiste*	un don·teest
doctor	*un médecin*	un meyd·sun
hospital	*un hôpital*	u·no·pee·tal
(night) pharmacist	*une pharmacie (de nuit)*	ewn far·ma·see (de nwee)

I need a doctor (who speaks English).
J'ai besoin d'un médecin (qui parle anglais). — zhey be·zwun dun meyd·sun (kee parl ong·gley)

Could I see a female doctor?
Est-ce que je peux voir une femme médecin? — es·ke zhe peu vwar ewn fam meyd·sun

I've run out of my medication.
Je n'ai plus de médicaments. — zhe ney plew de mey·dee·ka·mon

symptoms, conditions & allergies

I'm sick.	*Je suis malade.*	zhe swee ma·lad
It hurts here.	*J'ai une douleur ici.*	zhey ewn doo·leur ee·see
I have (a) ...	*J'ai ...*	zhey ...
asthma	*de l'asthme*	de las·me
bronchitis	*la bronchite*	la bron·sheet
constipation	*la constiptation*	la kon·stee·pa·syon
cough	*la toux*	la too
diarrhoea	*la diarrhée*	la dya·rey
fever	*la fièvre*	la fyev·re
headache	*mal à la tête*	mal a la tet
heart condition	*maladie de cœur*	ma·la·dee de keur
nausea	*la nausée*	la no·zey
pain	*une douleur*	ewn doo·leur
sore throat	*mal à la gorge*	mal a la gorzh
toothache	*mal aux dents*	mal o don
I'm allergic to ...	*Je suis allergique ...*	zhe swee za·lair·zheek ...
antibiotics	*aux antibiotiques*	o zon·tee·byo·teek
anti-inflammatories	*aux antiinflammatoires*	o zun·tee·un·fla·ma·twar
aspirin	*à l'aspirine*	a las·pee·reen
bees	*aux abeilles*	o za·bey·ye
codeine	*à la codéine*	a la ko·dey·een
penicillin	*à la pénicilline*	a la pey·nee·see·leen
antiseptic	*antiseptique* m	on·tee·sep·teek
bandage	*pansement* m	pons·mon
condoms	*préservatifs* m pl	prey·zair·va·teef
contraceptives	*contraceptifs* m pl	kon·tre·sep·teef
diarrhoea medicine	*médecine pour la diarrhée* f	med·seen poor la dya·ey
insect repellent	*repulsif anti-insectes* m	rey·pewl·seef on·tee·un·sekt
laxatives	*laxatifs* m pl	lak·sa·teef
painkillers	*analgésiques* m pl	a·nal·zhey·zeek
rehydration salts	*sels de réhydratation* m pl	seyl de rey·ee·dra·ta·syon
sleeping tablets	*somnifères* m pl	som·nee·fair

english–french dictionary

French nouns and adjectives in this dictionary have their gender indicated by ⓜ (masculine) or ⓕ (feminine). If it's a plural noun, you'll also see pl. Words are also marked as n (noun), a (adjective), v (verb), sg (singular), pl (plural), inf (informal) and pol (polite) where necessary.

A

accident *accident* ⓜ ak·see·don
accommodation *logement* ⓜ lozh·mon
adaptor *adaptateur* ⓜ a·dap·ta·teur
address *adresse* ⓕ a·dres
after *après* a·prey
air-conditioned *climatisé* kee·ma·tee·zey
airplane *avion* ⓜ a·vyon
airport *aéroport* ⓜ a·ey·ro·por
alcohol *alcool* ⓜ al·kol
all a *tout/toute* ⓜ/ⓕ too/toot
allergy *allergie* ⓕ a·lair·zhee
ambulance *ambulance* ⓕ om·bew·lons
and *et* ey
ankle *cheville* ⓕ she·vee·ye
arm *bras* ⓜ bra
ashtray *cendrier* ⓜ son·dree·yey
ATM *guichet automatique de banque* ⓜ gee·shey o·to·ma·teek de bonk

B

baby *bébé* ⓜ bey·bey
back (body) *dos* ⓜ do
backpack *sac à dos* ⓜ sak a do
bad *mauvais/mauvaise* ⓜ/ⓕ mo·vey/mo·veyz
bag *sac* ⓜ sak
baggage claim *retrait des bagages* ⓜ re·trey dey ba·gazh
bank *banque* ⓕ bonk
bar *bar* ⓜ bar
bathroom *salle de bain* ⓕ sal de bun
battery (car) *batterie* ⓕ bat·ree
battery (general) *pile* ⓕ peel
beautiful *beau/belle* ⓜ/ⓕ bo/bel
bed *lit* ⓜ lee
beer *bière* ⓕ byair
before *avant* a·von
behind *derrière* dair·yair
Belgium *Belgique* ⓕ bel·zheek
bicycle *vélo* ⓜ vey·lo
big *grand/grande* ⓜ/ⓕ gron/grond
bill *addition* ⓕ a·dee·syon
black *noir/noire* ⓜ/ⓕ nwar
blanket *couverture* ⓕ koo·vair·tewr
blood group *groupe sanguin* ⓜ groop song·gun
blue *bleu/bleue* ⓜ/ⓕ bler
book (make a reservation) v *réserver* rey·zair·vey
bottle *bouteille* ⓕ boo·tey
bottle opener *ouvre-bouteille* ⓜ oo·vre·boo·tey
boy *garçon* ⓜ gar·son
brakes (car) *freins* ⓜ frun
breakfast *petit déjeuner* ⓜ pe·tee dey·zheu·ney
broken (faulty) *défectueux/défectueuse* ⓜ/ⓕ dey·fek·tweu/dey·fek·tweuz
bus *(auto)bus* ⓜ (o·to)bews
business *affaires* ⓕ a·fair
buy *acheter* ash·tey

C

café *café* ⓜ ka·fey
camera *appareil photo* ⓜ a·pa·rey fo·to
camp site *terrain de camping* ⓜ tey·run de kom·peeng
cancel *annuler* a·new·ley
can opener *ouvre-boîte* ⓜ oo·vre·bwat
car *voiture* ⓕ vwa·tewr
cash *argent* ⓜ ar·zhon
cash (a cheque) v *encaisser* ong·key·sey
cell phone *téléphone portable* ⓜ tey·ley·fon por·ta·ble
centre *centre* ⓜ son·tre
change (money) v *échanger* ey·shon·zhey
cheap *bon marché* ⓜ&ⓕ bon mar·shey
check (bill) *addition* ⓕ la·dee·syon
check-in n *enregistrement* ⓜ on·re·zhee·stre·mon
chest *poitrine* ⓕ pwa·treen
child *enfant* ⓜ&ⓕ on·fon
cigarette *cigarette* ⓕ see·ga·ret
city *ville* ⓕ veel
clean a *propre* ⓜ&ⓕ pro·pre
closed *fermé/fermée* ⓜ/ⓕ fair·mey
coffee *café* ⓜ ka·fey
coins *pièces* ⓕ pyes
cold a *froid/froide* ⓜ/ⓕ frwa/frwad

collect call *appel en PCV* ⓜ a·pel on pey·sey·vey
come *venir* ve·neer
computer *ordinateur* ⓜ or·dee·na·teur
condom *préservatif* ⓜ prey·zair·va·teef
contact lenses *verres de contact* ⓜ vair de kon·takt
cook v *cuire* kweer
cost *coût* ⓜ koo
credit card *carte de crédit* ⓕ kart de krey·dee
cup *tasse* ⓕ tas
currency exchange *taux de change* ⓜ to de shonzh
customs (immigration) *douane* ⓕ dwan

D

dangerous *dangereux/dangereuse* ⓜ/ⓕ don·zhreu/don·zhreuz
date (time) *date* ⓕ dat
day *date de naissance* ⓕ dat de ney·sons
delay *retard* ⓜ re·tard
dentist *dentiste* ⓜ don·teest
depart *partir* par·teer
diaper *couche* ⓕ koosh
dictionary *dictionnaire* ⓜ deek·syo·nair
dinner *dîner* ⓜ dee·ney
direct *direct/directe* ⓜ/ⓕ dee·rekt
dirty *sale* ⓜ&ⓕ sal
disabled *handicapé/handicapée* ⓜ/ⓕ on·dee·ka·pey
discount *remise* ⓕ re·meez
doctor *médecin* ⓜ meyd·sun
double bed *grand lit* ⓜ gron lee
double room *chambre pour deux personnes* ⓕ shom·bre poor de pair·son
drink *boisson* ⓕ bwa·son
drive v *conduire* kon·dweer
drivers licence *permis de conduire* ⓜ pair·mee de kon·dweer
drugs (illicit) *drogue* ⓕ drog
dummy (pacifier) *tétine* ⓕ tey·teen

E

ear *oreille* ⓕ o·rey
east *est* ⓜ est
eat *manger* mon·zhey
economy class *classe touriste* ⓕ klas too·reest
electricity *électricité* ⓕ ey·lek·tree·see·tey
elevator *ascenseur* ⓜ a·son·seur
email *e-mail* ⓜ ey·mel
embassy *ambassade* ⓕ om·ba·sad
emergency *cas urgent* ⓜ ka ewr·zhon
English (language) *anglais/anglaise* ⓜ/ⓕ ong·gley/ong·gleyz
entrance *entrée* ⓕ on·trey
evening *soir* ⓜ swar
exchange rate *taux de change* ⓜ to de shonzh
exit *sortie* ⓕ sor·tee
expensive *cher/chère* ⓜ/ⓕ shair
express mail *exprès* eks·pres
eye *œil* ⓜ eu·yee

F

far *lointain/lointaine* ⓜ/ⓕ lwun·tun/lwun·ten
fast *rapide* ⓜ&ⓕ ra·peed
father *père* ⓜ pair
film (camera) *pellicule* ⓕ pey·lee·kewl
finger *doigt* ⓜ dwa
first-aid kit *trousse à pharmacie* ⓕ troos a far·ma·see
first class *première classe* ⓕ pre·myair klas
fish *poisson* ⓜ pwa·son
food *nourriture* ⓕ noo·ree·tewr
foot *pied* ⓜ pyey
fork *fourchette* ⓕ foor·shet
France *France* frons
free (of charge) *gratuit/gratuite* ⓜ/ⓕ gra·twee/gra·tweet
French (language) *Français* fron·sey
friend *ami/amie* ⓜ/ⓕ a·mee
fruit *fruit* ⓜ frwee
full *plein/pleine* ⓜ/ⓕ plun/plen
funny *drôle* ⓜ&ⓕ drol

G

gift *cadeau* ⓜ ka·do
girl *fille* ⓕ fee·ye
glass (drinking) *verre* ⓜ vair
glasses *lunettes* ⓕ pl lew·net
go *aller* a·ley
good *bon/bonne* ⓜ/ⓕ bon
green *vert/verte* ⓜ/ⓕ vair
guide n *guide* ⓜ geed

H

half *moitié* ⓕ mwa·tyey
hand *main* ⓕ mun
handbag *sac à main* ⓜ sak a mun
happy *heureux/heureuse* ⓜ/ⓕ eu·reu/eu·reuz
have *avoir* a·vwar

he *il* eel
head *tête* ⓕ tet
heart *cœur* ⓜ keur
heat *chaleur* ⓕ sha·leur
heavy *lourd/lourde* ⓜ/ⓕ loor/loord
help v *aider* ey·dey
here *ici* ee·see
high *haut/haute* ⓜ/ⓕ o/ot
highway *autoroute* ⓕ o·to·root
hike v *faire la randonnée* fair la ron·do·ney
holiday *vacances* ⓕ pl va·kons
homosexual n *homosexuel/homosexuelle* ⓜ/ⓕ o·mo·sek·swel
hospital *hôpital* ⓜ o·pee·tal
hot *chaud/chaude* ⓜ/ⓕ sho/shod
hotel *hôtel* ⓜ o·tel
(be) hungry *avoir faim* a·vwar fum
husband *mari* ⓜ ma·ree

I

I *je* zhe
identification (card) *carte d'identité* ⓕ kart dee·don·tee·tey
ill *malade* ⓜ&ⓕ ma·lad
important *important/importante* ⓜ/ⓕ um·por·ton/um·por·tont
included *compris/comprise* ⓜ/ⓕ kom·pree/kom·preez
injury *blessure* ⓕ bley·sewr
insurance *assurance* ⓕ a·sew·rons
Internet *Internet* ⓜ un·tair·net
interpreter *interprète* ⓜ&ⓕ un·tair·pret

J

jewellery *bijoux* ⓜ pl bee·zhoo
job *travail* ⓜ tra·vai

K

key *clé* ⓕ kley
kilogram *kilogramme* ⓜ kee·lo·gram
kitchen *cuisine* ⓕ kwee·zeen
knife *couteau* ⓜ koo·to

L

laundry (place) *blanchisserie* ⓕ blon·shees·ree
lawyer *avocat/avocate* ⓜ/ⓕ a·vo·ka/a·vo·kat
left (direction) *à gauche* a gosh
left-luggage office *consigne* ⓕ kon·see·nye
leg *jambe* ⓕ zhomb
lesbian n *lesbienne* ⓕ les·byen
less *moins* mwun
letter (mail) *lettre* ⓕ ley·trer
lift (elevator) *ascenseur* ⓜ a·son·seur
light *lumière* ⓕ lew·myair
like v *aimer* ey·mey
lock *serrure* ⓕ sey·rewr
long *long/longue* ⓜ/ⓕ long(k)
lost *perdu/perdue* ⓜ/ⓕ pair·dew
lost-property office *bureau des objets trouvés* ⓜ bew·ro dey zob·zhey troo·vey
love v *aimer* ey·mey
luggage *bagages* ⓜ pl ba·gazh
lunch *déjeuner* ⓜ dey·zheu·ney

M

mail *courrier* ⓜ koo·ryey
man *homme* ⓜ om
map *carte* ⓕ kart
market *marché* ⓜ mar·shey
matches *allumettes* ⓕ pl a·lew·met
meat *viande* ⓕ vyond
medicine *médecine* ⓕ med·seen
menu *carte* kart
message *message* ⓜ mey·sazh
milk *lait* ⓜ ley
minute *minute* ⓕ mee·newt
mobile phone *téléphone portable* ⓜ tey·ley·fon por·ta·ble
money *argent* ⓜ ar·zhon
month *mois* ⓜ mwa
morning *matin* ⓜ ma·tun
mother *mère* ⓕ mair
motorcycle *moto* ⓕ mo·to
motorway *autoroute* ⓕ o·to·root
mouth *bouche* ⓕ boosh
music *musique* ⓕ mew·zeek

N

name *nom* ⓜ nom
napkin *serviette* ⓕ sair·vyet
nappy *couche* ⓕ koosh
near *près de* prey de
neck *cou* ⓜ koo
new *nouveau/nouvelle* ⓜ/ⓕ noo·vo/noo·vel

news *les nouvelles* ley noo·vel
newspaper *journal* ⓜ zhoor·nal
night *nuit* ⓕ nwee
no *non* non
noisy *bruyant/bruyante* ⓜ/ⓕ brew·yon/brew·yont
nonsmoking *non-fumeur* non·few·meur
north *nord* ⓜ nor
nose *nez* ⓜ ney
now *maintenant* mun·te·non
number *numéro* ⓜ new·mey·ro

O

oil (engine) *huile* ⓕ weel
old *vieux/vieille* ⓜ/ⓕ vyeu/vyey
one-way ticket *billet simple* ⓜ bee·yey sum·ple
open a *ouvert/ouverte* ⓜ/ⓕ oo·vair/oo·vairt
outside *dehors* de·or

P

package *paquet* ⓜ pa·key
paper *papier* ⓜ pa·pyey
park (car) v *garer (une voiture)* ga·rey (ewn vwa·tewr)
passport *passeport* ⓜ pas·por
pay *payer* pey·yey
pen *stylo* ⓜ stee·lo
petrol *essence* ⓕ ey·sons
pharmacy *pharmacie* ⓕ far·ma·see
phonecard *télécarte* ⓕ tey·ley·kart
photo *photo* ⓕ fo·to
plate *assiette* ⓕ a·syet
police *police* ⓕ po·lees
postcard *carte postale* ⓕ kart pos·tal
post office *bureau de poste* ⓜ bew·ro de post
pregnant *enceinte* on·sunt
price *prix* ⓜ pree

Q

quiet *tranquille* ⓜ&ⓕ trong·keel

R

rain n *pluie* ⓕ plwee
razor *rasoir* ⓜ ra·zwar
receipt *reçu* ⓜ re·sew
red *rouge* roozh
refund *remboursement* ⓜ rom·boor·se·mon
registered mail *en recommandé* on re·ko·mon·dey
rent v *louer* loo·ey
repair v *réparer* rey·pa·rey
reservation *réservation* ⓕ rey·zair·va·syon
restaurant *restaurant* ⓜ res·to·ron
return v *revenir* rev·neer
return ticket *aller retour* ⓜ a·ley re·toor
right (direction) *à droite* a drwat
road *route* ⓕ root
room *chambre* ⓕ shom·bre

S

safe a *sans danger* ⓜ&ⓕ son don·zhey
sanitary napkin *serviette hygiénique* ⓕ sair·vyet ee·zhyey·neek
seat *place* ⓕ plas
send *envoyer* on·vwa·yey
service station *station-service* ⓕ sta·syon·sair·vees
sex *sexe* ⓜ seks
shampoo *shampooing* ⓜ shom·pwung
share (a dorm) *partager* par·ta·zhey
shaving cream *mousse à raser* ⓕ moos a ra·zey
she *elle* el
sheet (bed) *drap* ⓜ dra
shirt *chemise* ⓕ she·meez
shoes *chaussures* ⓕ pl sho·sewr
shop *magasin* ⓜ ma·ga·zun
short *court/courte* ⓜ/ⓕ koor/koort
shower *douche* ⓕ doosh
single room *chambre pour une personne* ⓕ shom·bre poor ewn pair·son
skin *peau* ⓕ po
skirt *jupe* ⓕ zhewp
sleep v *dormir* dor·meer
slowly *lentement* lon·te·mon
small *petit/petite* ⓜ/ⓕ pe·tee/pe·teet
smoke (cigarettes) v *fumer* few·mey
soap *savon* ⓜ sa·von
some *quelques* kel·ke
soon *bientôt* byun·to
south *sud* ⓜ sewd
souvenir shop *magasin de souvenirs* ⓜ ma·ga·zun de soov·neer
speak *parler* par·ley
spoon *cuillère* ⓕ kwee·yair
stamp *timbre* ⓜ tum·bre
stand-by ticket *billet stand-by* ⓜ bee·yey stond·bai
station (train) *gare* ⓕ gar
stomach *estomac* ⓜ es·to·ma
stop v *arrêter* a·rey·tey

stop (bus) *arrêt* ⓜ a·rey
street *rue* ⓕ rew
student *étudiant/étudiante* ⓜ/ⓕ ey·tew·dyon/ey·tew·dyont
sun *soleil* ⓜ so·ley
sunscreen *écran solaire* ⓜ ey·kron so·lair
swim v *nager* na·zhey
Switzerland *Suisse* swees

T

tampons *tampons* ⓜ pl tom·pon
taxi *taxi* ⓜ tak·see
teaspoon *petite cuillère* ⓕ pe·teet kwee·yair
teeth *dents* ⓕ don
telephone n *téléphone* ⓜ tey·ley·fon
television *télé(vision)* ⓕ tey·ley(vee·zyon)
temperature (weather) *température* ⓕ tom·pey·ra·tewr
tent *tente* ⓕ tont
that (one) *cela* se·la
they *ils/elles* ⓜ/ⓕ eel/el
(be) thirsty *avoir soif* a·vwar swaf
this (one) *ceci* se·see
throat *gorge* ⓕ gorzh
ticket *billet* ⓜ bee·yey
time *temps* ⓜ tom
tired *fatigué/fatiguée* ⓜ/ⓕ fa·tee·gey
tissues *mouchoirs en papier* ⓜ pl moo·shwar om pa·pyey
today *aujourd'hui* o·zhoor·dwee
toilet *toilettes* ⓕ pl twa·let
tomorrow *demain* de·mun
tonight *ce soir* se swar
toothbrush *brosse à dents* ⓕ bros a don
toothpaste *dentifrice* ⓜ don·tee·frees
torch (flashlight) *lampe de poche* ⓕ lomp de posh
tour *voyage* ⓜ vwa·yazh
tourist office *office de tourisme* ⓜ o·fees·de too·rees·me
towel *serviette* ⓕ sair·vyet
train *train* ⓜ trun
translate *traduire* tra·dweer
travel agency *agence de voyage* ⓕ a·zhons de vwa·yazh
travellers cheque *chèque de voyage* ⓜ shek de vwa·yazh
trousers *pantalon* ⓜ pon·ta·lon
twin beds *lits jumeaux* ⓜ pl dey lee zhew·mo
tyre *pneu* ⓜ pneu

U

underwear *sous-vêtements* ⓜ soo·vet·mon
urgent *urgent/urgente* ⓜ/ⓕ ewr·zhon/ewr·zhont

V

vacant *libre* ⓜ&ⓕ lee·bre
vacation *vacances* ⓕ pl va·kons
vegetable n *légume* ⓜ ley·gewm
vegetarian a *végétarien/végétarienne* ⓜ/ⓕ vey·zhey·ta·ryun/vey·zhey·ta·ryen
visa *visa* ⓜ vee·za

W

waiter *serveur/serveuse* ⓜ/ⓕ sair·veur/sair·veurz
walk v *marcher* mar·shey
wallet *portefeuille* ⓜ por·te·feu·ye
warm a *chaud/chaude* ⓜ/ⓕ sho/shod
wash (something) *laver* la·vey
watch *montre* ⓕ mon·tre
water *eau* ⓕ o
we *nous* noo
weekend *week-end* ⓜ week·end
west *ouest* ⓜ west
wheelchair *fauteuil roulant* ⓜ fo·teu·ye roo·lon
when *quand* kon
where *où* oo
white *blanc/blanche* ⓜ/ⓕ blong/blonsh
who *qui* kee
why *pourquoi* poor·kwa
wife *femme* ⓕ fam
window *fenêtre* ⓕ fe·ney·tre
wine *vin* ⓜ vun
with *avec* a·vek
without *sans* son
woman *femme* ⓕ fam
write *écrire* ey·kreer

Y

yellow *jaune* zhon
yes *oui* wee
yesterday *hier* ee·yair
you sg inf *tu* tew
you sg pol *vous* voo
you pl *vous* voo

German

german alphabet

Aa a	*Bb* be	*Cc* tse	*Dd* de	*Ee* e
Ff ef	*Gg* ge	*Hh* ha	*Ii* i	*Jj* yot
Kk ka	*Ll* el	*Mm* em	*Nn* en	*Oo* o
Pp pe	*Qq* ku	*Rr* er	*Ss* es	*Tt* te
Uu u	*Vv* fau	*Ww* ve	*Xx* iks	*Yy* *ewp*·si·lon
Zz tset				

german

DEUTSCH

introduction

Romantic, flowing, literary . . . not usually how German (*Deutsch* doytsh) is described, but maybe it's time to reconsider. After all, this is the language that's played a major role in the history of Europe and remains one of the most widely spoken languages on the continent. It's taught throughout the world and chances are you're already familiar with a number of German words that have entered English – *kindergarten*, *kitsch* and *hamburger*, for example, are all of German origin.

German is spoken by around 100 million people, and is the official language of Germany, Austria and Liechtenstein, as well as one of the official languages of Belgium, Switzerland and Luxembourg. German didn't spread across the rest of the world with the same force as English, Spanish or French. Germany only became a unified nation in 1871 and never established itself as a colonial power. After the reunification of East and West Germany, however, German has become more important in global politics and economics. Its role in science has long been recognised and German literature lays claim to some of the most famous written works ever printed. Just think of the enormous influence of Goethe, Nietzsche, Freud and Einstein.

German is usually divided into two forms – Low German (*Plattdeutsch* *plat*·doytsh) and High German (*Hochdeutsch* *hokh*·doytsh). Low German is an umbrella term used for the dialects spoken in Northern Germany. High German is considered the standard form and is understood throughout German-speaking communities, from the Swiss Alps to the cosy cafés of Vienna; it's also the form used in this phrasebook.

Both German and English belong to the West Germanic language family, along with a number of other languages including Dutch and Yiddish. The primary reason why German and English have grown apart is that the Normans, on invading England in 1066, brought with them a large number of non-Germanic words. As well as the recognisable words, the grammar of German will also make sense to an English speaker. Even with a slight grasp of German grammar, you'll still manage to get your point across. On the other hand, German tends to join words together (while English uses a number of separate words) to express a single notion. You shouldn't be intimidated by this though – after a while you'll be able to tell parts of words and recognising 'the Football World Cup qualifying match' hidden within *Fussballweltmeisterschaftsqualifikationsspiel* won't be a problem at all!

pronunciation

vowel sounds

German vowels can be short or long, which influences the meaning of words. They're pronounced crisply and distinctly, so *Tee* (tea) is tey, not *tey*·ee.

symbol	english equivalent	german example	transliteration
a	run	*hat*	hat
aa	father	*habe*	*haa*·be
ai	aisle	*mein*	main
air	fair	*Bär*	bair
aw	saw	*Boot*	bawt
e	bet	*Männer*	*me*·ner
ee	see	*fliegen*	*flee*·gen
eu	nurse	*schön*	sheun
ew	ee pronounced with rounded lips	*zurück*	tsu·*rewk*
ey	as in 'bet', but longer	*leben*	*ley*·ben
i	hit	*mit*	mit
o	pot	*Koffer*	*ko*·fer
oo	zoo	*Schuhe*	*shoo*·e
ow	now	*Haus*	hows
oy	toy	*Leute, Häuser*	*loy*·te, *hoy*·zer
u	put	*unter*	*un*·ter

word stress

Almost all German words are pronounced with stress on the first syllable. While this is a handy rule of thumb, you can always rely on the coloured pronunciation guides, which show the stressed syllables in italics.

consonant sounds

All German consonant sounds exist in English except for the kh and r sounds. The kh sound is generally pronounced at the back of the throat, like the 'ch' in 'Bach' or the Scottish 'loch'. The r sound is pronounced at the back of the throat, almost like saying g, but with some friction, a bit like gargling.

symbol	english equivalent	german example	transliteration
b	bed	*Bett*	bet
ch	cheat	*Tschüss*	chews
d	dog	*dein*	dain
f	fat	*vier*	feer
g	go	*gehen*	*gey*·en
h	hat	*helfen*	*hel*·fen
k	kit	*kein*	kain
kh	loch	*Ich*	ikh
l	lot	*laut*	lowt
m	man	*Mann*	man
n	not	*nein*	nain
ng	ring	*singen*	*zing*·en
p	pet	*Preis*	prais
r	run (throaty)	*Reise*	*rai*·ze
s	sun	*heiß*	hais
sh	shot	*schön*	sheun
t	top	*Tag*	taak
ts	hits	*Zeit*	tsait
v	very	*wohnen*	*vaw*·nen
y	yes	*ja*	yaa
z	zero	*sitzen*	*zi*·tsen
zh	pleasure	*Garage*	ga·*raa*·zhe

tools

language difficulties

Do you speak English?
Sprechen Sie Englisch? — *shpre*·khen zee *eng*·lish

Do you understand?
Verstehen Sie? — fer·*shtey*·en zee

I (don't) understand.
Ich verstehe (nicht). — ikh fer·*shtey*·e (nikht)

What does (*Kugel*) mean?
Was bedeutet (Kugel)? — vas be·*doy*·tet (*koo*·gel)

How do you ...?	*Wie ...?*	vee ...
pronounce this	*spricht man dieses Wort aus*	shprikht man *dee*·zes vort ows
write (*Schweiz*)	*schreibt man (Schweiz)*	shraipt man (shvaits)

Could you please ...?	*Könnten Sie ...?*	*keun*·ten zee ...
repeat that	*das bitte wiederholen*	das *bi*·te vee·der·*haw*·len
speak more slowly	*bitte langsamer sprechen*	*bi*·te *lang*·za·mer *shpre*·khen
write it down	*das bitte aufschreiben*	das *bi*·te *owf*·shrai·ben

essentials

Yes.	*Ja.*	yaa
No.	*Nein.*	nain
Please.	*Bitte.*	*bi*·te
Thank you.	*Danke.*	*dang*·ke
Thank you very much.	*Vielen Dank.*	*fee*·len dangk
You're welcome.	*Bitte.*	*bi*·te
Excuse me.	*Entschuldigung.*	ent·*shul*·di·gung
Sorry.	*Entschuldigung.*	ent·*shul*·di·gung

numbers

0	*null*	nul	16	*sechzehn*	*zeks*·tseyn
1	*eins*	ains	17	*siebzehn*	*zeep*·tseyn
2	*zwei*	tsvai	18	*achtzehn*	*akht*·tseyn
3	*drei*	drai	19	*neunzehn*	*noyn*·tseyn
4	*vier*	feer	20	*zwanzig*	*tsvan*·tsikh
5	*fünf*	fewnf	21	*einundzwanzig*	*ain*·unt·tsvan·tsikh
6	*sechs*	zeks	22	*zweiundzwanzig*	*tsvai*·unt·tsvan·tsikh
7	*sieben*	*zee*·ben	30	*dreißig*	*drai*·tsikh
8	*acht*	akht	40	*vierzig*	*feer*·tsikh
9	*neun*	noyn	50	*fünfzig*	*fewnf*·tsikh
10	*zehn*	tseyn	60	*sechzig*	*zekh*·tsikh
11	*elf*	elf	70	*siebzig*	*zeep*·tsikh
12	*zwölf*	zveulf	80	*achtzig*	*akht*·tsikh
13	*dreizehn*	*drai*·tseyn	90	*neunzig*	*noyn*·tsikh
14	*vierzehn*	*feer*·tseyn	100	*hundert*	*hun*·dert
15	*fünfzehn*	*fewnf*·tseyn	1000	*tausend*	*tow*·sent

time & dates

What time is it?	*Wie spät ist es?*	vee shpeyt ist es
It's one o'clock.	*Es ist ein Uhr.*	es ist ain oor
It's (10) o'clock.	*Es ist (zehn) Uhr.*	es ist (tseyn) oor
Quarter past (one).	*Viertel nach (eins).*	*fir*·tel naakh (ains)
Half past (one).	*Halb (zwei).* (lit: half two)	halp (tsvai)
Quarter to (one).	*Viertel vor (eins).*	*fir*·tel fawr (ains)
At what time ...?	*Um wie viel Uhr ...?*	um vee feel oor ...
At ...	*Um ...*	um ...
am	*vormittags*	*fawr*·mi·taaks
pm (midday–6pm)	*nachmittags*	*naakh*·mi·taaks
pm (6pm–midnight)	*abends*	*aa*·bents
Monday	*Montag*	*mawn*·taak
Tuesday	*Dienstag*	*deens*·taak
Wednesday	*Mittwoch*	*mit*·vokh
Thursday	*Donnerstag*	*do*·ners·taak
Friday	*Freitag*	*frai*·taak
Saturday	*Samstag*	*zams*·taak
Sunday	*Sonntag*	*zon*·taak

January	*Januar*	*yan*·u·aar
February	*Februar*	*fey*·bru·aar
March	*März*	merts
April	*April*	a·*pril*
May	*Mai*	mai
June	*Juni*	*yoo*·ni
July	*Juli*	*yoo*·li
August	*August*	ow·*gust*
September	*September*	zep·*tem*·ber
October	*Oktober*	ok·*taw*·ber
November	*November*	no·*vem*·ber
December	*Dezember*	de·*tsem*·ber

What date is it today?
Der Wievielte ist heute? — dair *vee*·feel·te ist *hoy*·te

It's (18 October).
Heute ist (der achtzehnte Oktober). — *hoy*·te ist dair (*akh*·tseyn·te ok·*taw*·ber)

since (May)	*seit (Mai)*	zait (mai)
until (June)	*bis (Juni)*	bis (*yoo*·ni)
yesterday	*gestern*	*ges*·tern
today	*heute*	*hoy*·te
tonight	*heute Abend*	*hoy*·te *aa*·bent
tomorrow	*morgen*	*mor*·gen
last …		
night	*vergangene Nacht*	fer·*gang*·e·ne nakht
week	*letzte Woche*	*lets*·te *vo*·khe
month	*letzten Monat*	*lets*·ten *maw*·nat
year	*letztes Jahr*	*lets*·tes yaar
next …		
week	*nächste Woche*	*neykhs*·te *vo*·khe
month	*nächsten Monat*	*neykhs*·ten *maw*·nat
year	*nächstes Jahr*	*neykhs*·tes yaar
yesterday/ tomorrow …	*gestern/ morgen …*	*ges*·tern/ *mor*·gen …
morning	*Morgen*	*mor*·gen
afternoon	*Nachmittag*	*naakh*·mi·taak
evening	*Abend*	*aa*·bent

weather

What's the weather like?	*Wie ist das Wetter?*	vee ist das *ve*·ter
It's ...		
cloudy	*Es ist wolkig.*	es ist *vol*·kikh
cold	*Es ist kalt.*	es ist kalt
hot	*Es ist heiß.*	es ist hais
raining	*Es regnet.*	es *reyg*·net
snowing	*Es schneit.*	es shnait
sunny	*Es ist sonnig.*	es ist *zo*·nikh
warm	*Es ist warm.*	es ist varm
windy	*Es ist windig.*	es ist *vin*·dikh
spring	*Frühling* m	*frew*·ling
summer	*Sommer* m	*zo*·mer
autumn	*Herbst* m	herpst
winter	*Winter* m	*vin*·ter

border crossing

I'm here ...	*Ich bin hier ...*	ikh bin heer ...
in transit	*auf der Durchreise*	owf dair *durkh*·rai·ze
on business	*auf Geschäftsreise*	owf ge·*shefts*·rai·ze
on holiday	*im Urlaub*	im *oor*·lowp
I'm here for ...	*Ich bin hier für ...*	ikh bin heer fewr ...
(10) days	*(zehn) Tage*	(tseyn) *taa*·ge
(three) weeks	*(drei) Wochen*	(drai) *vo*·khen
(two) months	*(zwei) Monate*	(tsvai) *maw*·na·te

I'm going to (Salzburg).
Ich gehe nach (Salzburg). — ikh *gey*·e nakh *zalts*·boorg

I'm staying at the (Hotel Park).
Ich wohne im (Hotel Park). — ikh *vaw*·ne im (ho·*tel* park)

I have nothing to declare.
Ich habe nichts zu verzollen. — ikh *haa*·be nikhts tsoo fer·*tso*·len

I have something to declare.
Ich habe etwas zu verzollen. — ikh *haa*·be *et*·vas tsoo fer·*tso*·len

That's (not) mine.
Das ist (nicht) meins. — das ist (nikht) mains

transport

tickets & luggage

Where can I buy a ticket?
Wo kann ich eine Fahrkarte kaufen? — vaw kan ikh *ai*·ne *faar*·kar·te *kow*·fen

Do I need to book a seat?
Muss ich einen Platz reservieren lassen? — mus ikh *ai*·nen plats re·zer·*vee*·ren *la*·sen

One … ticket to (Berlin), please.	*Einen … nach (Berlin), bitte.*	*ai*·nen … naakh (ber·*leen*) *bi*·te
one-way	*einfache Fahrkarte*	*ain*·fa·khe *faar*·kar·te
return	*Rückfahrkarte*	*rewk*·faar·kar·te
I'd like to … my ticket, please.	*Ich möchte meine Fahrkarte bitte …*	ikh *meukh*·te *mai*·ne *faar*·kar·te *bi*·te …
cancel	*zurückgeben*	tsu·*rewk*·gey·ben
change	*ändern lassen*	*en*·dern *la*·sen
collect	*abholen*	ab·*ho*·len
confirm	*bestätigen lassen*	be·*shtey*·ti·gen *la*·sen
I'd like a … seat, please.	*Ich hätte gern einen …*	ikh *he*·te gern *ai*·nen …
nonsmoking	*Nichtraucherplatz*	*nikht*·row·kher·plats
smoking	*Raucherplatz*	*row*·kher·plats

How much is it?
Was kostet das? — vas *kos*·tet das

Is there air conditioning?
Gibt es eine Klimaanlage? — gipt es *ai*·ne *klee*·ma·an·*laa*·ge

Is there a toilet?
Gibt es eine Toilette? — gipt es *ai*·ne to·a·*le*·te

How long does the trip take?
Wie lange dauert die Fahrt? — vee *lang*·e *dow*·ert dee faart

Is it a direct route?
Ist es eine direkte Verbindung? — ist es *ai*·ne di·*rek*·te fer·*bin*·dung

I'd like a luggage locker.
Ich hätte gern ein Gepäckschließfach. — ikh *he*·te gern ain ge·*pek*·shlees·fakh

My luggage has been ...	*Mein Gepäck ist ...*	main ge·*pek* ist ...
damaged	*beschädigt*	be·*shey*·dikht
lost	*verloren gegangen*	fer·*law*·ren ge·*gang*·en
stolen	*gestohlen worden*	ge·*shtaw*·len *vor*·den

getting around

Where does flight (D4) arrive?
Wo ist die Ankunft des Fluges (D4)? vaw ist dee *an*·kunft des *floo*·ges (de feer)

Where does flight (D4) depart?
Wo ist die der Abflug des Fluges (D4)? vaw ist dair *ab*·flug des *floo*·ges (de feer)

Where's the ...?	*Wo ist ...?*	vaw ist ...
arrivalls hall	*Ankunftshalle*	an·kunfts·*ha*·le
departures hall	*Abflughalle*	ab·flug·*ha*·le

Is this the ... to (Hamburg)?	*Fährt ... nach (Hamburg)?*	fairt ... nakh (*ham*·burg)
boat	*das Boot*	das bawt
bus	*der Bus*	dair bus
plane	*das Flugzeug*	das *flook*·tsoyk
train	*der Zug*	dair tsook

What time's the ... bus?	*Wann fährt der ... Bus?*	van fairt dair ... bus
first	*erste*	*ers*·te
last	*letzte*	*lets*·te
next	*nächste*	*neykhs*·te

At what time does it leave?
Wann fährt es ab? van fairt es ap

At what time does it arrive?
Wann kommt es an? van komt es an

How long will it be delayed?
Wie viel Verspätung wird es haben? vee feel fer·*shpey*·tung virt es *haa*·ben

What station/stop is this?
Welcher Bahnhof/Halt ist das? *vel*·kher *baan*·hawf/halt ist das

What's the next station/stop?
Welches ist der nächste Bahnhof/Halt? *vel*·khes ist dair *neykhs*·te *baan*·hawf/halt

Does it stop at (Freiburg)?
Hält es in (Freiburg)? — helt *es* in (*frai*·boorg)

Please tell me when we get to (Kiel).
Könnten Sie mir bitte sagen, wann wir in (Kiel) ankommen? — *keun*·ten zee meer *bi*·te *zaa*·gen van veer in (keel) *an*·ko·men

How long do we stop here?
Wie lange halten wir hier? — vee *lan*·ge *hal*·ten veer heer

Is this seat available?
Ist dieser Platz frei? — ist *dee*·zer plats frai

That's my seat.
Dieses ist mein Platz. — *dee*·zes ist main plats

I'd like a taxi ...	*Ich hätte gern ein Taxi für ...*	ikh *he*·te gern ain *tak*·si fewr ...
at (9am)	*(neun Uhr vormittags)*	(noyn oor *fawr*·mi·taaks)
now	*sofort*	zo·*fort*
tomorrow	*morgen*	*mor*·gen

Is this taxi available?
Ist dieses Taxi frei? — ist *dee*·zes *tak*·si frai

How much is it to ...?
Was kostet es bis ...? — vas *kos*·tet es bis ...

Please put the meter on.
Schalten Sie bitte den Taxameter ein. — *shal*·ten zee *bi*·te deyn tak·sa·*mey*·ter ain

Please take me to (this address).
Bitte bringen Sie mich zu (dieser Adresse). — *bi*·te *bring*·en zee mikh tsoo (*dee*·zer a·*dre*·se)

Please ...	*Bitte ...*	*bi*·te ...
slow down	*fahren Sie langsamer*	*faa*·ren zee *lang*·za·mer
stop here	*halten Sie hier*	*hal*·ten zee heer
wait here	*warten Sie hier*	*var*·ten zee heer

car, motorbike & bicycle hire

I'd like to hire a …	*Ich möchte … mieten.*	ikh *meukh*·te … *mee*·ten
bicycle	*ein Fahrrad*	ain *faar*·raat
car	*ein Auto*	ain *ow*·to
motorbike	*ein Motorrad*	ain *maw*·tor·raat
with …	*mit …*	mit …
a driver	*Fahrer*	*faa*·rer
air conditioning	*Klimaanlage*	*klee*·ma·an·*laa*·ge
How much for … hire?	*Wie viel kostet es pro …?*	vee feel *kos*·tet es praw …
hourly	*Stunde*	*shtun*·de
daily	*Tag*	taak
weekly	*Woche*	*vo*·khe
air	*Luft* f	luft
oil	*Öl* n	eul
petrol	*Benzin* n	ben·*tseen*
tyres	*Reifen* m pl	*rai*·fen

I need a mechanic.
Ich brauche einen Mechaniker. — ikh *brow*·khe *ai*·nen me·*khaa*·ni·ker

I've run out of petrol.
Ich habe kein Benzin mehr. — ikh *haa*·be kain ben·*tseen* mair

I have a flat tyre.
Ich habe eine Reifenpanne. — ikh *haa*·be *ai*·ne *rai*·fen·pa·ne

directions

Where's the …?	*Wo ist …?*	vaw ist …
bank	*die Bank*	dee bangk
city centre	*die Innenstadt*	*i*·nen·shtat
hotel	*das Hotel*	das ho·*tel*
market	*der Markt*	dair markt
police station	*das Polizeirevier*	das po·li·*tsai*·re·veer
post office	*das Postamt*	das *post*·amt
public toilet	*die öffentliche Toilette*	dee *eu*·fent·li·khe to·a·*le*·te
tourist office	*das Fremdenverkehrsbüro*	das *frem*·den·fer·kairs·bew·raw

Is this the road to (Frankfurt)?
Führt diese Straße nach (Frankfurt)? — fewrt *dee*·ze *shtraa*·se naakh (*frank*·foort)

Can you show me (on the map)?
Können Sie es mir (auf der Karte) zeigen? — *keu*·nen zee es meer (owf dair *kar*·te) *tsai*·gen

What's the address?
Wie ist die Adresse? — vee ist dee a·*dre*·se

How far is it?
Wie weit ist es? — vee *vait* ist es

How do I get there?
Wie kann ich da hinkommen? — vee kan ikh daa *hin*·ko·men

Turn …	*Biegen Sie … ab.*	*bee*·gen zee … ap
at the corner	*an der Ecke*	an dair *e*·ke
at the traffic lights	*bei der Ampel*	bai dair *am*·pel
left/right	*links/rechts*	lingks/rekhts

It's …	*Es ist …*	es ist …
behind …	*hinter …*	*hin*·ter …
far away	*weit weg*	vait vek
here	*hier*	heer
in front of …	*vor …*	fawr …
left	*links*	lingks
near (to …)	*nahe (zu …)*	*naa*·e (zoo …)
next to …	*neben …*	*ney*·ben …
on the corner	*an der Ecke*	an dair *e*·ke
opposite …	*gegenüber …*	gey·gen·*ew*·ber …
right	*rechts*	rekhts
straight ahead	*geradeaus*	ge·raa·de·*ows*
there	*dort*	dort

north	*Norden* m	*nor*·den
south	*Süden* m	*zew*·den
east	*Osten* m	*os*·ten
west	*Westen* m	*ves*·ten

by bus	*mit dem Bus*	mit deym *bus*
by taxi	*mit dem Taxi*	mit deym *tak*·si
by train	*mit dem Zug*	mit deym *tsook*
on foot	*zu Fuß*	tsoo *foos*

signs

Eingang/Ausgang	*ain*·gang/*ows*·gang	**Entrance/Exit**
Offen/Geschlossen	*o*·fen/ge·*shlo*·sen	**Open/Closed**
Zimmer Frei	*tsi*·mer frai	**Rooms Available**
Ausgebucht	*ows*·ge·bukht	**No Vacancies**
Auskunft	*ows*·kunft	**Information**
Polizeirevier	po·li·*tsai*·re·veer	**Police Station**
Verboten	fer·*baw*·ten	**Prohibited**
Toiletten/WC	to·a·*le*·ten/vee·*tsee*	**Toilets**
Herren	*her*·en	**Men**
Damen	*daa*·men	**Women**
Heiß/Kalt	hais/kalt	**Hot/Cold**

accommodation

finding accommodation

Where's a/an ...?	*Wo ist ...?*	vaw ist ...
camping ground	*ein Campingplatz*	ain *kem*·ping·plats
guesthouse	*eine Pension*	*ai*·ne paang·*zyawn*
hotel	*ein Hotel*	ain ho·*tel*
inn	*ein Gasthof*	ain *gast*·hawf
youth hostel	*eine Jugendherberge*	*ai*·ne *yoo*·gent·her·ber·ge

Can you recommend somewhere ...?	*Können Sie etwas ... empfehlen?*	*keu*·nen zee *et*·vas ... emp·*fey*·len
cheap	*Billiges*	*bi*·li·ges
good	*Gutes*	*goo*·tes
luxurious	*Luxuriöses*	luk·su·ri·*eu*·ses
nearby	*in der Nähe*	in dair *ney*·e

I'd like to book a room, please.
Ich möchte bitte ein Zimmer reservieren. — ikh *meukh*·te *bi*·te ain *tsi*·mer re·zer·*vee*·ren

I have a reservation.
Ich habe eine Reservierung. — ikh *haa*·be *ai*·ne re·zer·*vee*·rung

My name's ...
Mein Name ist ... — main *naa*·me ist ...

Do you have a … room?	*Haben Sie ein …?*	*haa*·ben zee ain …
single	*Einzelzimmer*	*ain*·tsel·tsi·mer
double	*Doppelzimmer mit einem Doppelbett*	*do*·pel·tsi·mer mit *ai*·nem *do*·pel·bet
twin	*Doppelzimmer mit zwei Einzelbetten*	*do*·pel·tsi·mer mit tsvai *ain*·tsel·be·ten
Can I pay by …?	*Nehmen Sie …?*	*ney*·men zee …
credit card	*Kreditkarten*	kre·*deet*·kar·ten
travellers cheque	*Reiseschecks*	*rai*·ze·sheks
How much is it per …?	*Wie viel kostet es pro …?*	vee feel *kos*·tet es praw …
night	*Nacht*	nakht
person	*Person*	per·*zawn*

I'd like to stay for (two) nights.
Ich möchte für (zwei) Nächte bleiben. — ikh *meukh*·te fewr (tsvai) *nekh*·te *blai*·ben

From (July 2) to (July 6).
Vom (zweiten Juli) bis zum (sechsten Juli). — vom (*tsvai*·ten *yoo*·li) bis tsum (*zeks*·ten *yoo*·li)

Can I see it?
Kann ich es sehen? — kan ikh es *zey*·en

Am I allowed to camp here?
Kann ich hier zelten? — kan ikh heer *tsel*·ten

Is there a camp site nearby?
Gibt es in der Nähe einen Zeltplatz? — gipt es in dair *ney*·e *ai*·nen *tselt*·plats

requests & queries

When/Where is breakfast served?
Wann/Wo gibt es Frühstück? — van/vaw gipt es *frew*·shtewk

Please wake me at (seven).
Bitte wecken Sie mich um (sieben) Uhr. — *bi*·te *ve*·ken zee mikh um (*zee*·ben) oor

Could I have my key, please?
Könnte ich bitte meinen Schlüssel haben? — *keun*·te ikh *bi*·te *mai*·nen *shlew*·sel *haa*·ben

Can I get another (blanket)?
Kann ich noch (eine Decke) bekommen? — kan ikh nokh (*ai*·ne *de*·ke) be·*ko*·men

Is there a/an ...?	*Haben Sie ...?*	*haa*·ben zee ...
elevator	*einen Aufzug*	*ai*·nen *owf*·tsook
safe	*einen Safe*	*ai*·nen sayf

The room is too ...	*Es ist zu ...*	es ist tsoo ...
expensive	*teuer*	*toy*·er
noisy	*laut*	lowt
small	*klein*	klain

The ... doesn't work.	*... funktioniert nicht.*	... fungk·tsyo·*neert* nikht
air conditioning	*Die Klimaanlage*	dee *klee*·ma·an·laa·ge
fan	*Der Ventilator*	dair ven·ti·*laa*·tor
toilet	*Die Toilette*	dee to·a·*le*·te

This ... isn't clean.	*Dieses ... ist nicht sauber.*	*dee*·zes ... ist nikht *zow*·ber
pillow	*Kopfkissen*	*kopf*·ki·sen
sheet	*Bettlaken*	*bet*·laa·ken
towel	*Handtuch*	*hant*·tookh

checking out

What time is checkout?
Wann muss ich auschecken? — van mus ikh *ows*·che·ken

Can I leave my luggage here?
Kann ich meine Taschen hier lassen? — kan ikh *mai*·ne *ta*·shen heer *la*·sen

Could I have my ..., please?	*Könnte ich bitte ... haben?*	*keun*·te ikh *bi*·te ... *haa*·ben
deposit	*meine Anzahlung*	*mai*·ne *an*·tsaa·lung
passport	*meinen Pass*	*mai*·nen *pas*
valuables	*meine Wertsachen*	*mai*·ne *vert*·za·khen

communications & banking

the internet

Where's the local Internet café?
Wo ist hier ein Internet-Café? — vaw ist heer ain *in*·ter·net·ka·fey

How much is it per hour?
Was kostet es pro Stunde? — vas *kos*·tet es praw *shtun*·de

I'd like to ...	*Ich möchte ...*	ikh *meukh*·te ...
check my email	*meine E-Mails checken*	*mai*·ne *ee*·mayls *che*·ken
get Internet access	*Internetzugang haben*	*in*·ter·net·tsoo·gang *haa*·ben
use a printer	*einen Drucker benutzen*	*ai*·nen *dru*·ker be·*nu*·tsen
use a scanner	*einen Scanner benutzen*	*ai*·nen *ske*·ner be·*nu*·tsen

mobile/cell phone

I'd like a ...	*Ich hätte gern ...*	ikh *he*·te gern ...
mobile/cell phone for hire	*ein Miethandy*	ain *meet*·hen·di
SIM card for your network	*eine SIM-Karte für Ihr Netz*	*ai*·ne *zim*·kar·te fewr eer nets

What are the rates?
Wie hoch sind die Gebühren? vee hawkh zint dee ge·*bew*·ren

telephone

What's your phone number?
Wie ist Ihre Telefonnummer? vee ist *ee*·re te·le·*fawn*·nu·mer

The number is ...
Die Nummer ist ... dee *nu*·mer ist ...

Where's the nearest public phone?
Wo ist das nächste öffentliche Telefon? vaw ist das *neykhs*·te *eu*·fent·li·khe te·le·*fawn*

I'd like to buy a phonecard.
Ich möchte eine Telefonkarte kaufen. ikh *meukh*·te *ai*·ne te·le·*fawn*·kar·te *kow*·fen

I want to ...	*Ich möchte ...*	ikh *meukh*·te ...
call (Singapore)	*(nach Singapur) telefonieren*	(naakh *zing*·a·poor) te·le·fo·*nee*·ren
make a local call	*ein Ortsgespräch machen*	ain awrts·ge·*shpreykh* *ma*·khen
reverse the charges	*ein R-Gespräch führen*	ain *air*·ge·shpreykh *few*·ren

How much does … cost?	*Wie viel kostet …?*	vee feel *kos*·tet …
a (three)-minute call	*ein (drei)-minutiges Gespräch*	ain *(drai)*·mi·noo·ti·ges ge·*shpreykh*
each extra minute	*jede zusätzliche Minute*	*yey*·de tsoo·*zeyts*·li·khe mi·*noo*·te

It's (one euro) per (minute).
(Ein Euro) für (eine Minute). (ain *oy*·ro) fewr (*ai*·ne mi·*noo*·te)

post office

I want to send a …	*Ich möchte … senden.*	ikh *meukh*·te … *zen*·den
fax	*ein Fax*	ain faks
letter	*einen Brief*	*ai*·nen breef
parcel	*ein Paket*	ain pa·*keyt*
postcard	*eine Postkarte*	*ai*·ne *post*·kar·te

I want to buy a/an …	*Ich möchte … kaufen.*	ikh *meukh*·te … *kow*·fen
envelope	*einen Umschlag*	*ai*·nen *um*·shlaak
stamp	*eine Briefmarke*	*ai*·ne *breef*·mar·ke

Please send it (to Australia) by …	*Bitte schicken Sie das (nach Australien) per …*	*bi*·te *shi*·ken zee das (nakh ows·*traa*·li·en) per …
airmail	*Luftpost*	*luft*·post
express mail	*Expresspost*	eks·*pres*·post
registered mail	*Einschreiben*	*ain*·shrai·ben
surface mail	*Landbeförderung*	*lant*·be·feur·de·rung

Is there any mail for me?	*Ist Post für mich da?*	ist post fewr mikh da

bank

Where's a/an …?	*Wo ist …?*	vaw ist …
ATM	*der Geldautomat*	dair *gelt*·ow·to·maat
foreign exchange office	*die Geldwechselstube*	dee *gelt*·vek·sel·shtoo·be

I'd like to …	*Ich möchte …*	ikh *meukh*·te …
Where can I …?	*Wo kann ich …?*	vaw kan ikh …
arrange a transfer	*einen Transfer tätigen*	*ai*·nen trans·*fer tey*·ti·gen
cash a cheque	*einen Scheck einlösen*	*ai*·nen shek *ain*·leu·zen
change a travellers cheque	*einen Reisescheck einlösen*	*ai*·nen *rai*·ze·shek *ain*·leu·zen
change money	*Geld umtauschen*	gelt *um*·tow·shen
get a cash advance	*eine Barauszahlung*	*ai*·ne *baar*·ows·tsaa·lung
withdraw money	*Geld abheben*	gelt *ap*·hey·ben

What's the …?	*Wie …?*	vee …
charge for that	*hoch sind die Gebühren dafür*	hawkh zint dee ge·*bew*·ren da·*fewr*
exchange rate	*ist der Wechselkurs*	ist dair *vek*·sel·kurs

It's …	*Das …*	das …
(12) euros	*kostet (zwölf) euro*	*kos*·tet (zveulf) *oy*·ro
free	*ist umsonst*	ist um·*zonst*

What time does the bank open?
Wann macht die Bank auf? van makht dee bangk owf

Has my money arrived yet?
Ist mein Geld schon angekommen? ist main gelt shawn *an*·ge·ko·men

sightseeing

getting in

What time does it open/close?
Wann macht es auf/zu? van makht es owf/tsoo

What's the admission charge?
Was kostet der Eintritt? vas *kos*·tet dair *ain*·trit

Is there a discount for children/students?
Gibt es eine Ermäßigung für Kinder/Studenten? gipt es *ai*·ne er·*mey*·si·gung fewr *kin*·der/shtu·*den*·ten

I'd like a ...	*Ich hätte gern ...*	ikh *he*·te gern ...
catalogue	*einen Katalog*	*ai*·nen ka·ta·*lawg*
guide	*einen Reiseführer*	*ai*·nen *rai*·ze·few·rer
local map	*eine Karte von hier*	*ai*·ne *kar*·te fon heer

I'd like to see ...	*Ich möchte ... sehen.*	ikh *meukh*·te ... *zey*·en
What's that?	*Was ist das?*	vas ist das
Can I take a photo?	*Kann ich fotografieren?*	kan ikh fo·to·gra·*fee*·ren

tours

When's the next ...?	*Wann ist der/die nächste ...?* **m/f**	van ist dair/dee *neykhs*·te ...
day trip	*Tagesausflug* **m**	*taa*·ges·ows·flook
tour	*Tour* **f**	toor

Is ... included?	*Ist ... inbegriffen?*	ist ... *in*·be·gri·fen
accommodation	*die Unterkunft*	dee *un*·ter·kunft
the admission charge	*der Eintritt*	dair *ain*·trit
food	*das Essen*	das *e*·sen
transport	*die Beförderung*	dee be·*feur*·de·rung

How long is the tour?
Wie lange dauert die Führung? — vee *lang*·e *dow*·ert dee *few*·rung

What time should we be back?
Wann sollen wir zurück sein? — van *zo*·len veer tsu·*rewk* zain

sightseeing

castle	*Burg* **f**	burk
cathedral	*Dom* **m**	dawm
church	*Kirche* **f**	*kir*·khe
main square	*Hauptplatz* **m**	*howpt*·plats
monastery	*Kloster* **n**	*klaws*·ter
monument	*Denkmal* **n**	*dengk*·maal
museum	*Museum* **n**	mu·*zey*·um
old city	*Altstadt* **f**	*alt*·stat
palace	*Schloss* **n**	shlos
ruins	*Ruinen* **f pl**	ru·*ee*·nen
stadium	*Stadion* **n**	*shtaa*·di·on
statues	*Statuen* **f pl**	*shtaa*·tu·e

shopping

enquiries

Where's a . . .?	*Wo ist . . .?*	vaw ist . . .
bank	*die Bank*	dee bangk
bookshop	*die Buchhandlung*	dee *bookh*·hand·lung
camera shop	*das Fotogeschäft*	das fo·to·ge·*sheft*
department store	*das Warenhaus*	das *vaa*·ren·hows
grocery store	*der Lebensmittelladen*	dair *ley*·bens·mi·tel·laa·den
market	*der Markt*	dair markt
newsagency	*der Zeitungshändler*	dair *tsai*·tungks·hen·dler
supermarket	*der Supermarkt*	dair *zoo*·per·markt

Where can I buy (a padlock)?
Wo kann ich (ein Vorhängeschloss) kaufen? — vaw kan ikh (ain *fawr*·heng·e·shlos) *kow*·fen

I'm looking for . . .
Ich suche nach . . . — ikh *zoo*·khe nakh . . .

Can I look at it?
Können Sie es mir zeigen? — *keu*·nen zee es meer *tsai*·gen

Do you have any others?
Haben Sie noch andere? — *haa*·ben zee nokh *an*·de·re

Does it have a guarantee?
Gibt es darauf Garantie? — gipt es da·*rowf* ga·ran·*tee*

Can I have it sent overseas?
Kann ich es ins Ausland verschicken lassen? — kan ikh es ins *ows*·lant fer·*shi*·ken *la*·sen

Can I have my . . . repaired?
Kann ich mein . . . reparieren lassen? — kan ikh main . . . re·pa·*ree*·ren *la*·sen

It's faulty.
Es ist fehlerhaft. — es ist *fey*·ler·haft

I'd like ..., please.	*Ich möchte bitte ...*	ikh *meukh*·te *bi*·te ...
a bag	*eine Tüte*	*ai*·ne *tew*·te
a refund	*mein Geld zurückhaben*	main gelt tsu·*rewk*·haa·ben
to return this	*dieses zurückgeben*	*dee*·zes tsu·*rewk*·gey·ben

paying

How much is it?
Wie viel kostet das? — vee feel *kos*·tet das

Can you write down the price?
Können Sie den Preis aufschreiben? — *keu*·nen zee deyn prais *owf*·shrai·ben

That's too expensive.
Das ist zu teuer. — das ist tsoo *toy*·er

Can you lower the price?
Können Sie mit dem Preis heruntergehen? — *keu*·nen zee mit dem prais he·*run*·ter·gey·en

I'll give you (five) euros.
Ich gebe Ihnen (fünf) euro. — ikh *gey*·be *ee*·nen (fewnf) *oy*·ro

There's a mistake in the bill.
Da ist ein Fehler in der Rechnung. — daa ist ain *fey*·ler in dair *rekh*·nung

Do you accept ...?	*Nehmen Sie ...?*	*ney*·men zee ...
credit cards	*Kreditkarten*	kre·*deet*·kar·ten
debit cards	*Debitkarten*	*dey*·bit·kar·ten
travellers cheques	*Reiseschecks*	*rai*·ze·sheks

I'd like ..., please.	*Ich möchte bitte ...*	ikh *meukh*·te *bi*·te ...
a receipt	*eine Quittung*	*ai*·ne *kvi*·tung
my change	*mein Wechselgeld*	main *vek*·sel·gelt

clothes & shoes

Can I try it on?	*Kann ich es anprobieren?*	kan ikh es *an*·pro·bee·ren
My size is (40).	*Ich habe Größe (vierzig).*	ikh *haa*·be *greu*·se (*feer*·tsikh)
It doesn't fit.	*Es passt nicht.*	es past nikht

small	*klein*	klain
medium	*mittelgroß*	*mi*·tel·graws
large	*groß*	graws

books & music

I'd like a ...	*Ich hätte gern ...*	ikh *he*·te gern ...
newspaper (in English)	*eine Zeitung (auf Englisch)*	*ai*·ne *tsai*·tung (owf *eng*·lish)
pen	*einen Kugelschreiber*	*ai*·nen *koo*·gel·shrai·ber

Is there an English-language bookshop?
Gibt es einen Buchladen für englische Bücher? — gipt es *ai*·nen *bookh*·laa·den fewr *eng*·li·she *bew*·kher

I'm looking for something by (Herman Hesse).
Ich suche nach etwas von (Herman Hesse). — ikh *zoo*·khe nakh *et*·vas fon (*her*·man *he*·se)

Can I listen to this?
Kann ich mir das anhören? — kan ikh meer das *an*·heu·ren

photography

Can you ...?	*Können Sie ...?*	*keu*·nen zee ...
burn a CD from my memory card	*eine CD von meiner Speicherkarte brennen*	*ai*·ne tse de von *mai*·ner *shpai*·kher·*kar*·te *bre*·nen
develop this film	*diesen Film entwickeln*	*dee*·zen film ent·*vi*·keln
load my film	*mir den Film einlegen*	meer deyn film *ain*·ley·gen

I need a ... film for this camera.	*Ich brauche einen ... für diese Kamera.*	ikh *brow*·khe *ai*·nen ... fewr *dee*·ze *ka*·me·ra
APS	*APS-Film*	aa·pey·*es*·film
B&W	*Schwarzweißfilm*	shvarts·*vais*·film
colour	*Farbfilm*	*farp*·film
slide	*Diafilm*	*dee*·a·film
(200) speed	*(zweihundert)-ASA-Film*	(*tsvai*·hun·dert)·*aa*·za·film

When will it be ready?	*Wann ist er fertig?*	van ist air *fer*·tikh

meeting people

greetings, goodbyes & introductions

Hello. (Austria)	*Servus.*	zer·vus
Hello. (Germany)	*Guten Tag.*	goo·ten taak
Hello. (Switzerland)	*Grüezi.*	grew·e·tsi
Hi.	*Hallo.*	ha·lo
Good night.	*Gute Nacht.*	goo·te nakht
Goodbye.	*Auf Wiedersehen.*	owf vee·der·zey·en
Bye.	*Tschüss/Tschau.*	chews/chow
See you later.	*Bis später.*	bis shpey·ter
Mr	*Herr*	her
Mrs	*Frau*	frow
Miss	*Fräulein*	froy·lain
How are you?	*Wie geht es Ihnen?*	vee geyt es ee·nen
Fine. And you?	*Danke, gut. Und Ihnen?*	dang·ke goot unt ee·nen
What's your name?	*Wie ist Ihr Name?*	vee ist eer naa·me
My name is …	*Mein Name ist …*	main naa·me ist …
I'm pleased to meet you.	*Angenehm.*	an·ge·neym
This is my …	*Das ist mein/meine …* m/f	das ist main/mai·ne …
brother	*Bruder*	broo·der
daughter	*Tochter*	tokh·ter
father	*Vater*	faa·ter
friend	*Freund/Freundin* m/f	froynt/froyn·din
husband	*Mann*	man
mother	*Mutter*	mu·ter
partner (intimate)	*Partner/Partnerin* m/f	part·ner/part·ne·rin
sister	*Schwester*	shves·ter
son	*Sohn*	zawn
wife	*Frau*	frow
Here's my …	*Hier ist meine …*	heer ist mai·ne …
What's your …?	*Wie ist Ihre …?*	vee ist ee·re …
address	*Adresse*	a·dre·se
email address	*E-mail-Adresse*	ee·mayl·a·dre·se
fax number	*Faxnummer*	faks·nu·mer
phone number	*Telefonnummer*	te·le·fawn·nu·mer

meeting people – GERMAN

occupations

What's your occupation?	*Als was arbeiten Sie?* **pol**	als vas *ar*·bai·ten zee
	Als was arbeitest du? **inf**	als vas *ar*·bai·test doo
I'm a/an ...	*Ich bin ein/eine ...* **m/f**	ikh bin ain/*ai*·ne ...
artist	*Künstler/Künstlerin* **m/f**	*kewnst*·ler/*kewnst*·le·rin
business person	*Geschäftsmann* **m**	ge·*shefts*·man
	Geschäftsfrau **f**	ge·*shefts*·frow
farmer	*Bauer/Bäuerin* **m/f**	*bow*·er/*boy*·e·rin
manual worker	*Arbeiter/Arbeiterin* **m/f**	*ar*·bai·ter/*ar*·bai·te·rin
office worker	*Büroangestellte* **m&f**	bew·*raw*·an·ge·shtel·te
scientist	*Wissenschaftler* **m**	*vi*·sen·shaft·ler
	Wissenschaftlerin **f**	*vi*·sen·shaft·le·rin
student	*Student/Studentin* **m/f**	shtu·*dent*/shtu·*den*·tin

background

Where are you from?	*Woher kommen Sie?* **pol**	*vaw*·hair *ko*·men zee
	Woher kommst du? **inf**	*vaw*·hair komst doo
I'm from ...	*Ich komme aus ...*	ikh *ko*·me ows ...
Australia	*Australien*	ows·*traa*·li·en
Canada	*Kanada*	*ka*·na·daa
England	*England*	*eng*·lant
New Zealand	*Neuseeland*	noy·*zey*·lant
the USA	*den USA*	deyn oo·es·*aa*
Are you married?	*Sind Sie verheiratet?* **pol**	zint zee fer·*hai*·ra·tet
	Bist du verheiratet? **inf**	bist doo fer·*hai*·ra·tet
I'm married.	*Ich bin verheiratet.*	ikh bin fer·*hai*·ra·tet
I'm single.	*Ich bin ledig.*	ikh bin *ley*·dikh

age

How old ...?	*Wie alt ...?*	vee alt ...
are you	*sind Sie* **pol**	zint zee
	bist du **inf**	bist doo
is your daughter	*ist Ihre Tochter* **pol**	ist *ee*·re *tokh*·ter
is your son	*ist Ihr Sohn* **pol**	ist eer zawn
I'm ... years old.	*Ich bin ... Jahre alt.*	ikh bin ... *yaa*·re alt
He/She is ... years old.	*Er/Sie ist ... Jahre alt.*	air/zee ist ... *yaa*·re alt

feelings

I'm (not) ...	*Ich bin (nicht) ...*	ikh bin (nikht) ...
Are you ...?	*Sind Sie ...?* **pol**	zint zee ...
	Bist du ...? **inf**	bist doo ...
happy	*glücklich*	*glewk*·likh
sad	*traurig*	*trow*·rikh
I'm (not) ...	*Ich habe (kein) ...*	ikh *haa*·be (kain) ...
Are you ...?	*Haben Sie ...?* **pol**	*haa*·ben zee ...
	Hast du ...? **inf**	hast doo ...
hungry	*Hunger*	*hung*·er
thirsty	*Durst*	durst
I'm (not) ...	*Mir ist (nicht) ...*	meer ist (nikht) ...
Are you ...?	*Ist Ihnen/dir ...?* **pol/inf**	ist *ee*·nen/deer ...
cold	*kalt*	kalt
hot	*heiß*	hais

entertainment

going out

Where can I find ...?	*Wo sind die ...?*	vaw zint dee ...
clubs	*Klubs*	klups
gay venues	*Schwulen- und Lesbenkneipen*	*shvoo*·len unt *les*·ben·knai·pen
pubs	*Kneipen*	*knai*·pen
I feel like going to a/the ...	*Ich hätte Lust, ... zu gehen.*	ikh *he*·te lust ... tsoo *gey*·en
concert	*zum Konzert*	tsoom kon·*tsert*
movies	*ins Kino*	ins *kee*·no
party	*zu eine Party*	tsoo *ai*·ne *par*·ti
restaurant	*in ein Restaurant*	in ain res·to·*rang*
theatre	*ins Theater*	ins te·*aa*·ter

interests

Do you like …?	*Magst du …?* **inf**	maakst doo …
I (don't) like …	*Ich mag (keine/ keinen) …* **m/f**	ikh maak (*kai*·ne/ *kai*·nen) …
art	*Kunst* **f**	kunst
sport	*Sport* **m**	shport
I (don't) like …	*Ich … (nicht) gern.*	ikh … (nikht) gern
cooking	*koche*	*ko*·khe
reading	*lese*	*ley*·ze
travelling	*reise*	*rai*·ze

Do you like to dance?
Tanzt du gern? **inf** — tantst doo gern

Do you like music?
Hörst du gern Musik? **inf** — heurst doo gern mu·*zeek*

food & drink

finding a place to eat

Can you recommend a …?	*Können Sie … empfehlen?*	*keu*·nen zee … emp·*fey*·len
bar	*eine Kneipe*	*ai*·ne *knai*·pe
café	*ein Café*	ain ka·*fey*
restaurant	*ein Restaurant*	ain res·to·*rang*
I'd like …, please.	*Ich hätte gern …, bitte.*	ikh *he*·te gern … *bi*·te
a table for (five)	*einen Tisch für (fünf) Personen*	*ai*·nen tish fewr (fewnf) per·*zaw*·nen
the (non)smoking section	*einen (Nicht-) rauchertisch*	*ai*·nen (*nikht*·) *row*·kher·tish

ordering food

breakfast	*Frühstück* **n**	*frew*·shtewk
lunch	*Mittagessen* **n**	*mi*·taak·e·sen
dinner	*Abendessen* **n**	*aa*·bent·e·sen
snack	*Snack* **m**	snek

What would you recommend?		
Was empfehlen Sie?		vas emp·*fey*·len zee
I'd like (the) ..., please.	*Bitte bringen Sie ...*	*bi*·te *bring*·en zee ...
bill	*die Rechnung*	dee *rekh*·nung
drink list	*die Getränkekarte*	dee ge·*treng*·ke·kar·te
menu	*die Speisekarte*	dee *shpai*·ze·kar·te
that dish	*dieses Gericht*	*dee*·zes ge·*rikht*

drinks

(cup of) coffee ...	*(eine Tasse) Kaffee ...*	(*ai*·ne *ta*·se) *ka*·fey ...
(cup of) tea ...	*(eine Tasse) Tee ...*	(*ai*·ne *ta*·se) tey ...
with milk	*mit Milch*	mit milkh
without sugar	*ohne Zucker*	*aw*·ne *tsu*·ker
(orange) juice	*(Orangen)Saft* **m**	(o·*rang*·zhen·)zaft
mineral water	*Mineralwasser* **n**	mi·ne·*raal*·va·ser
soft drink	*Softdrink* **m**	*soft*·dringk
(boiled) water	*(heißes) Wasser* **n**	(*hai*·ses) *va*·ser

in the bar

I'll have ...	*Ich hätte gern ...*	ikh *he*·te gern ...
I'll buy you a drink.	*Ich gebe dir einen aus.* **inf**	ikh *gey*·be deer *ai*·nen ows
What would you like?	*Was möchtest du?* **inf**	vas *meukh*·test doo
Cheers!	*Prost!*	prawst
brandy	*Weinbrand* **m**	*vain*·brant
cognac	*Kognak* **m**	*ko*·nyak
cocktail	*Cocktail* **m**	*kok*·tayl
a shot of (whisky)	*einen (Whisky)*	*ai*·nen (*vis*·ki)
a bottle of ...	*eine Flasche ...*	*ai*·ne *fla*·she ...
a glass of ...	*ein Glas ...*	ain glaas ...
red wine	*Rotwein*	*rawt*·vain
sparkling wine	*Sekt*	zekt
white wine	*Weißwein*	*vais*·vain
a ... of beer	*... Bier*	... beer
bottle	*eine Flasche*	*ai*·ne *fla*·she
glass	*ein Glas*	ain glaas

self-catering

What's the local speciality?
Was ist eine örtliche Spezialität? — vas ist *ai*·ne *eurt*·li·khe shpe·tsya·li·*teyt*

What's that?
Was ist das? — vas ist das

How much is (a kilo of cheese)?
Was kostet (ein Kilo Käse)? — vas *kos*·tet (ain *kee*·lo *key*·ze)

I'd like ...	*Ich möchte ...*	ikh *meukh*·te ...
(100) grams	*(hundert) Gramm*	(hun·dert) gram
(two) kilos	*(zwei) Kilo*	(tsvai) *kee*·lo
(three) pieces	*(drei) Stück*	(drai) shtewk
(six) slices	*(sechs) Scheiben*	(zeks) *shai*·ben

Less.	*Weniger.*	*vey*·ni·ger
Enough.	*Genug.*	ge·*nook*
More.	*Mehr.*	mair

special diets & allergies

Is there a vegetarian restaurant near here?
Gibt es ein vegetarisches Restaurant hier in der Nähe? — gipt es ain vege·*tar*·ish·shes res·to·*rang* heer in dair *ney*·e

Do you have vegetarian food?
Haben Sie vegetarisches Essen? — *haa*·ben zee ve·ge·*taa*·ri·shes *e*·sen

Could you prepare a meal without ...?	*Können Sie ein Gericht ohne ... zubereiten?*	*keu*·nen zee ain ge·*rikht aw*·ne ... *tsoo*·be·rai·ten
butter	*Butter*	*bu*·ter
eggs	*Eiern*	*ai*·ern
meat stock	*Fleischbrühe*	*flaish*·brew·e

I'm allergic to ...	*Ich bin allergisch gegen ...*	ikh bin a·*lair*·gish *gey*·gen ...
dairy produce	*Milchprodukte*	*milkh*·pro·duk·te
gluten	*Gluten*	*gloo*·ten
MSG	*Natrium-glutamat*	*naa*·tri·um·glu·ta·maat
nuts	*Nüsse*	*new*·se
seafood	*Meeresfrüchte*	*mair*·res·frewkh·te

Bayrisch Kraut n	*bai*·rish krowt	*shredded cabbage cooked with sliced apples, wine & sugar*
Berliner m	ber·*lee*·ner	*jam doughnut*
Cervelatwurst f	ser·ve·*laat*·vurst	*spicy pork & beef sausage*
Erdäpfelgulasch n	*ert*·ep·fel·goo·lash	*spicy sausage & potato stew*
gekochter Schinken m	ge·*kokh*·ter *shing*·ken	*cooked ham*
Graupensuppe f	*grow*·pen·zu·pe	*barley soup*
Greyerzer m	*grai*·er·tser	*a smooth, rich cheese*
Grießklößchensuppe f	*grees*·kleus·khen·zu·pe	*soup with semolina dumplings*
Gröstl n	greustl	*grated fried potatoes with meat*
Grünkohl mit Pinkel m	*grewn*·kawl mit *ping*·kel	*cabbage with sausages*
Holsteiner Schnitzel n	*hol*·shtai·ner *shni*·tsel	*veal schnitzel with fried egg & seafood*
Husarenfleisch n	hu·*zaa*·ren·flaish	*braised beef, veal & pork fillets with sweet peppers, onions & sour cream*
Hutzelbrot n	*hu*·tsel·brawt	*bread made of prunes & other dried fruit*
Kaiserschmarren m	*kai*·zer·shmar·ren	*pancakes with raisins, fruit compote or chocolate sauce*
Kaisersemmeln f pl	*kai*·zer·ze·meln	*Austrian bread rolls*
Katenwurst f	*kaa*·ten·vurst	*country-style smoked sausage*
Königinsuppe f	*keu*·ni·gin·zu·pe	*creamy chicken soup*
Königstorte f	*keu*·niks·tor·te	*rum-flavoured fruit cake*
Krautsalat m	*krowt*·za·laat	*coleslaw*
Leipziger Allerlei n	*laip*·tsi·ger *a*·ler·lai	*mixed vegetable stew*
Linzer Torte f	*lin*·tser *tor*·te	*latticed tart with jam topping*

Nudelauflauf m	*noo*·del·owf·lowf	*pasta casserole*
Obatzter m	*aw*·bats·ter	*Bavarian soft cheese mousse*
Ochsenschwanzsuppe f	*ok*·sen·shvants·zu·pe	*oxtail soup*
Palatschinken m	*pa*·lat·shing·ken	*pancakes filled with jam or cheese*
Rollmops m	*rol*·mops	*pickled herring fillet rolled around chopped onions or gherkins*
Sauerbraten m	*zow*·er·braa·ten	*marinated roasted beef served with a sour cream sauce*
Sauerkraut n	*zow*·er·krowt	*pickled cabbage*
Schafskäse m	*shaafs*·key·ze	*sheep's milk feta*
Schmorbraten m	*shmawr*·braa·ten	*beef pot roast*
Schnitzel n	*shni*·tsel	*pork, veal or chicken breast rolled in breadcrumbs & fried*
Strammer Max m	*shtra*·mer maks	*ham, sausage or pork sandwich, served with fried eggs & onions*
Streichkäse m	*shtraikh*·key·ze	*any kind of soft cheese spread*
Streuselkuchen m	*shtroy*·zel·koo·khen	*coffee cake topped with cinnamon*
Strudel m	*shtroo*·del	*loaf-shaped pastry with a sweet or savoury filling*
Tascherl n	*ta*·sherl	*pastry with meat, cheese or jam*
Voressen n	*fawr*·e·sen	*meat stew*
Weinkraut n	*vain*·krowt	*white cabbage, braised with apples & simmered in wine*
Wiener Schnitzel n	*vee*·ner *shni*·tsel	*crumbed veal schnitzel*
Wiener Würstchen n	*vee*·ner *vewrst*·khen	*frankfurter (sausage)*
Zwetschgendatschi m	*tsvetsh*·gen·dat·shi	*damson plum tart*
Zwiebelsuppe f	*tsvee*·bel·zu·pe	*onion soup*
Zwiebelwurst f	*tsvee*·bel·vurst	*liver & onion sausage*

emergencies

basics

Help!	*Hilfe!*	*hil*·fe
Stop!	*Halt!*	halt
Go away!	*Gehen Sie weg!*	*gey*·en zee vek
Thief!	*Dieb!*	deeb
Fire!	*Feuer!*	*foy*·er
Watch out!	*Vorsicht!*	for·*zikht*

Call ...!	*Rufen Sie ...!*	*roo*·fen zee ...
a doctor	*einen Arzt*	*ai*·nen artst
an ambulance	*einen Krankenwagen*	*ai*·nen *krang*·ken·vaa·gen
the police	*die Polizei*	dee po·li·*tsai*

It's an emergency!
Es ist ein Notfall! — es ist ain *nawt*·fal

Could you help me, please?
Könnten Sie mir bitte helfen? — *keun*·ten zee meer *bi*·te *hel*·fen

I have to use the telephone.
Ich muss das Telefon benutzen. — ikh mus das te·le·*fawn* be·*nu*·tsen

I'm lost.
Ich habe mich verirrt. — ikh *haa*·be mikh fer·*irt*

Where are the toilets?
Wo ist die Toilette? — vo ist dee to·a·*le*·te

police

Where's the police station?
Wo ist das Polizeirevier? — vaw ist das po·li·*tsai*·re·veer

I want to report an offence.
Ich möchte eine Straftat melden. — ikh *meukh*·te *ai*·ne *shtraat*·taat *mel*·den

I have insurance.
Ich bin versichert. — ikh bin fer·*zi*·khert

I've been ...	*Ich bin ... worden.*	ikh bin ... *vor*·den
assaulted	*angegriffen*	*an*·ge·gri·fen
raped	*vergewaltigt*	fer·ge·*val*·tikht
robbed	*bestohlen*	be·*shtaw*·len

I've lost my . . .	*Ich habe . . . verloren.*	ikh *haa*·be . . . fer·*law*·ren
My . . . was/ were stolen.	*Man hat mir . . . gestohlen.*	man hat meer . . . ge·*shtaw*·len
backpack	*meinen Rucksack*	*mai*·nen *ruk*·zak
bags	*meine Reisetaschen*	*mai*·ne *rai*·ze·ta·shen
credit card	*meine Kreditkarte*	*mai*·ne kre·*deet*·karte
handbag	*meine Handtasche*	*mai*·ne *hant*·ta·she
jewellery	*meinen Schmuck*	*mai*·nen shmuk
money	*mein Geld*	main gelt
passport	*meinen Pass*	*mai*·nen pas
travellers cheques	*meine Reiseschecks*	*mai*·ne *rai*·ze·sheks
wallet	*meine Brieftasche*	*mai*·ne *breef*·ta·she

I want to contact my . . .	*Ich mochte mich mit . . . in Verbindung setzen.*	ikh *meukh*·te mikh mit . . . in fer·*bin*·dung *ze*·tsen
consulate	*meinem Konsulat*	*mai*·nem kon·zu·*laat*
embassy	*meiner Botschaft*	*mai*·ner *bawt*·shaft

health

medical needs

Where's the nearest . . .?	*Wo ist der/die/das nächste . . . ?* **m/f/n**	vaw ist dair/dee/das *neykhs*·te . . .
dentist	*Zahnarzt* **m**	*tsaan*·artst
doctor	*Arzt* **m**	artst
hospital	*Krankenhaus* **n**	*krang*·ken·hows
(night) pharmacist	*(Nacht)Apotheke* **f**	(*nakht*·)a·po·*tey*·ke

I need a doctor (who speaks English).
Ich brauche einen Arzt (der Englisch spricht). — ikh *brow*·khe *ai*·nen artst (dair *eng*·lish shprikht)

Could I see a female doctor?
Könnte ich von einer Ärztin behandelt werden? — *keun*·te ikh fon *ai*·ner *erts*·tin be·*han*·delt *ver*·den

I've run out of my medication.
Ich habe keine Medikamente mehr. — ikh *haa*·be *kai*·ne me·di·ka·*men*·te mair

symptoms, conditions & allergies

I'm sick.	*Ich bin krank.*	ikh bin krangk
It hurts here.	*Es tut hier weh.*	es toot heer *vey*
I have (a) …	*Ich habe …*	ikh *haa*·be …
asthma	*Asthma*	*ast*·ma
bronchitis	*Bronchitis*	bron·*khee*·tis
constipation	*Verstopfung*	fer·*shtop*·fung
cough	*Husten*	*hoos*·ten
diarrhoea	*Durchfall*	*durkh*·fal
fever	*Fieber*	*fee*·ber
headache	*Kopfschmerzen*	*kopf*·shmer·tsen
heart condition	*Herzbeschwerden*	*herts*·be·shver·den
nausea	*Übelkeit*	*ew*·bel·kait
pain	*Schmerzen*	*shmer*·tsen
sore throat	*Halsschmerzen*	*hals*·shmer·tsen
toothache	*Zahnschmerzen*	*tsaan*·shmer·tsen
I'm allergic to …	*Ich bin allergisch gegen …*	ikh bin a·*lair*·gish *gey*·gen …
antibiotics	*Antibiotika*	an·ti·bi·*aw*·ti·ka
anti-inflammatories	*entzündungshemmende Mittel*	en·*tsewn*·dungks·he·men·de *mi*·tel
aspirin	*Aspirin*	as·pi·*reen*
bees	*Bienen*	*bee*·nen
codeine	*Kodein*	ko·de·*een*
penicillin	*Penizillin*	pe·ni·tsi·*leen*
antiseptic	*Antiseptikum* n	an·ti·*zep*·ti·kum
bandage	*Verband* m	fer·*bant*
condoms	*Kondom* n	kon·*dawm*
contraceptives	*Verhütungsmittel* n	fer·*hew*·tungks·mi·tel
diarrhoea medicine	*Mittel gegen Durchfall* n	*mi*·tel *gey*·gen *durkh*·fal
insect repellent	*Insektenschutzmittel* n	in·*zek*·ten·shuts·mi·tel
laxatives	*Abführmittel* n	*ap*·fewr·mi·tel
painkillers	*Schmerzmittel* n	*shmerts*·mi·tel
rehydration salts	*Kochsalzlösung* n	kokh·zalts·*leu*·zung
sleeping tablets	*Schlaftabletten* f pl	*shlaaf*·ta·ble·ten

english–german dictionary

German nouns in this dictionary have their gender indicated by ⓜ (masculine), ⓕ (feminine) or ⓝ (neuter). If it's a plural noun, you'll also see pl. Words are also marked as n (noun), a (adjective), v (verb), sg (singular), pl (plural), inf (informal) and pol (polite) where necessary.

A

accident *Unfall* ⓜ *un*·fal
accommodation *Unterkunft* ⓕ *un*·ter·kunft
adaptor *Adapter* ⓜ a·*dap*·ter
address *Adresse* ⓕ a·*dre*·se
after *nach* naakh
air-conditioned *mit Klimaanlage* ⓕ mit *klee*·ma·an·laa·ge
airplane *Flugzeug* ⓝ *flook*·tsoyk
airport *Flughafen* ⓜ *flook*·haa·fen
alcohol *Alkohol* ⓜ *al*·ko·hawl
all a *alle* *a*·le
allergy *Allergie* ⓕ a·lair·*gee*
ambulance *Krankenwagen* ⓜ *krang*·ken·vaa·gen
and *und* unt
ankle *Knöchel* ⓜ *kneu*·khel
arm *Arm* ⓜ arm
ashtray *Aschenbecher* ⓜ *a*·shen·be·kher
ATM *Geldautomat* ⓜ *gelt*·ow·to·maat
Austria *Österreich* ⓝ *eus*·ter·raikh

B

baby *Baby* ⓝ *bay*·bi
back (body) *Rücken* ⓜ *rew*·ken
backpack *Rucksack* ⓜ *ruk*·zak
bad *schlecht* shlekht
bag *Tasche* ⓕ *ta*·she
baggage claim *Gepäckausgabe* ⓕ ge·*pek*·ows·gaa·be
bank *Bank* ⓕ bangk
bar *Lokal* ⓝ lo·*kaal*
bathroom *Badezimmer* ⓝ *baa*·de·tsi·mer
battery *Batterie* ⓕ ba·te·*ree*
beautiful *schön* sheun
bed *Bett* ⓝ bet
beer *Bier* ⓝ beer
before *vor* fawr
behind *hinter* *hin*·ter
Belgium ⓝ *Belgien* *bel*·gi·en
bicycle *Fahrrad* ⓝ *faar*·raat
big *groß* graws
bill *Rechnung* ⓕ *rekh*·nung
black *schwarz* shvarts
blanket *Decke* ⓕ *de*·ke
blood group *Blutgruppe* ⓕ *bloot*·gru·pe
blue *blau* blow
book (make a reservation) v *buchen* *boo*·khen
bottle *Flasche* ⓕ *fla*·she
bottle opener *Flaschenöffner* ⓜ *fla*·shen·euf·ner
boy *Junge* ⓜ *yung*·e
brakes (car) *Bremsen* ⓕ pl *brem*·zen
breakfast *Frühstück* ⓝ *frew*·shtewk
broken (faulty) *kaputt* ka·*put*
bus *Bus* ⓜ bus
business *Geschäft* ⓝ ge·*sheft*
buy *kaufen* *kow*·fen

C

café *Café* ⓝ ka·*fey*
camera *Kamera* ⓕ *ka*·me·ra
camp site *Zeltplatz* ⓜ *tselt*·plats
cancel *stornieren* shtor·*nee*·ren
can opener *Dosenöffner* ⓜ *daw*·zen·euf·ner
car *Auto* ⓝ *ow*·to
cash *Bargeld* ⓝ *baar*·gelt
cash (a cheque) v *(einen Scheck) einlösen* (*ai*·nen shek) *ain*·leu·zen
cell phone *Handy* ⓝ *hen*·di
centre *Zentrum* ⓝ *tsen*·trum
change (money) v *wechseln* *vek*·seln
cheap *billig* *bi*·likh
check (bill) *Rechnung* ⓕ *rekh*·nung
check-in *Abfertigungsschalter* ⓜ *ap*·fer·ti·gungks·shal·ter
chest *Brustkorb* ⓜ *brust*·korp
child *Kind* ⓝ kint
cigarette *Zigarette* ⓕ tsi·ga·*re*·te
city *Stadt* ⓕ shtat
clean a *sauber* *zow*·ber

closed *geschlossen* ge·*shlo*·sen
coffee *Kaffee* ⓜ *ka*·fey
coins *Münzen* ⓕ pl *mewn*·tsen
cold a *kalt* kalt
collect call *R-Gespräch* ⓝ *air*·ge·shpreykh
come *kommen* *ko*·men
computer *Computer* ⓜ kom·*pyoo*·ter
condom *Kondom* ⓝ kon·*dawm*
contact lenses *Kontaktlinsen* ⓕ pl kon·*takt*·lin·zen
cook v *kochen* *ko*·khen
cost *Preis* ⓜ prais
credit card *Kreditkarte* ⓕ kre·*deet*·kar·te
cup *Tasse* ⓕ *ta*·se
currency exchange *Geldwechsel* ⓜ *gelt*·vek·sel
customs (immigration) *Zoll* ⓜ tsol

D

dangerous *gefährlich* ge·*fair*·likh
date (time) *Datum* ⓝ *daa*·tum
day *Tag* ⓜ taak
delay n *Verspätung* ⓕ fer·*shpey*·tung
dentist *Zahnarzt/Zahnärztin* ⓜ/ⓕ *tsaan*·artst/*tsaan*·erts·tin
depart *abfahren* *ap*·faa·ren
diaper *Windel* ⓕ *vin*·del
dictionary *Wörterbuch* ⓝ *veur*·ter·bookh
dinner *Abendessen* ⓝ *aa*·bent·e·sen
direct *direkt* di·*rekt*
dirty *schmutzig* *shmu*·tsikh
disabled *behindert* be·*hin*·dert
discount n *Rabatt* ⓜ ra·*bat*
doctor *Arzt/Ärztin* ⓜ/ⓕ artst/*erts*·tin
double bed *Doppelbett* ⓝ *do*·pel·bet
double room *Doppelzimmer mit einem Doppelbett* ⓝ *do*·pel·tsi·mer mit *ai*·nem *do*·pel·bet
drink *Getränk* ⓝ ge·*trengk*
drive v *fahren* *faa*·ren
drivers licence *Führerschein* ⓜ *few*·rer·shain
drugs (illicit) *Droge* ⓕ *draw*·ge
dummy (pacifier) *Schnuller* ⓜ *shnu*·ler

E

ear *Ohr* ⓝ awr
east *Osten* ⓜ *os*·ten
eat *essen* *e*·sen
economy class *Touristenklasse* ⓕ tu·*ris*·ten·kla·se
electricity *Elektrizität* ⓕ e·lek·tri·tsi·*teyt*
elevator *Lift* ⓜ lift
email *E-Mail* *e*·mayl
embassy *Botschaft* ⓕ *bawt*·shaft
emergency *Notfall* ⓜ *nawt*·fal
English (language) *Englisch* ⓝ *eng*·lish
entrance *Eingang* ⓜ *ain*·gang
evening *Abend* ⓜ *aa*·bent
exchange rate *Wechselkurs* ⓜ *vek*·sel·kurs
exit *Ausgang* ⓜ *ows*·gang
expensive *teuer* *toy*·er
express mail *Expresspost* ⓕ eks·*pres*·post
eye *Auge* ⓝ *ow*·ge

F

far *weit* vait
fast *schnell* shnel
father *Vater* ⓜ *faa*·ter
film (camera) *Film* ⓜ film
finger *Finger* ⓜ *fing*·er
first-aid kit *Verbandskasten* ⓜ fer·*bants*·kas·ten
first class *erste Klasse* ⓕ *ers*·te *kla*·se
fish *Fisch* ⓜ fish
food *Essen* ⓝ *e*·sen
foot *Fuß* ⓜ foos
fork *Gabel* ⓕ *gaa*·bel
free (of charge) *gratis* *graa*·tis
friend *Freund/Freundin* ⓜ/ⓕ froynt/*froyn*·din
fruit *Frucht* ⓕ frukht
full *voll* fol
funny *lustig* *lus*·tikh

G

German (language) *Deutsch* ⓝ doytsh
Germany *Deutschland* ⓝ *doytsh*·lant
gift *Geschenk* ⓝ ge·*shengk*
girl *Mädchen* ⓝ *meyt*·khen
glass (drinking) *Glas* ⓝ glaas
glasses *Brille* ⓕ *bri*·le
go *gehen* *gey*·en
good *gut* goot
green *grün* grewn
guide *Führer* ⓜ *few*·rer

H

half *Hälfte* ⓕ *helf*·te
hand *Hand* ⓕ hant
handbag *Handtasche* ⓕ *hant*·ta·she
happy *glücklich* *glewk*·likh

have *haben* haa·ben
he *er* air
head *Kopf* ⓜ kopf
heart *Herz* ⓝ herts
heat n *Hitze* ⓕ *hi*·tse
heavy *schwer* shvair
help v *helfen* *hel*·fen
here *hier* heer
high *hoch* hawkh
highway *Autobahn* ⓕ *ow*·to·baan
hike v *wandern* *van*·dern
holiday *Urlaub* ⓜ *oor*·lowp
homosexual *homosexuell* haw·mo·zek·su·*el*
hospital *Krankenhaus* ⓝ *krang*·ken·hows
hot *heiß* hais
hotel *Hotel* ⓝ ho·*tel*
hungry *hungrig* *hung*·rikh
husband *Ehemann* ⓜ *ey*·e·man

I

I *ich* ikh
identification (card) *Personalausweis* ⓜ
per·zo·*naal*·ows·vais
ill *krank* krangk
important *wichtig* *vikh*·tikh
included *inbegriffen* *in*·be·gri·fen
injury *Verletzung* ⓕ fer·*le*·tsung
insurance *Versicherung* ⓕ fer·*zi*·khe·rung
Internet *Internet* ⓝ *in*·ter·net
interpreter *Dolmetscher/Dolmetscherin* ⓜ/ⓕ
dol·met·sher/*dol*·met·she·rin

J

jewellery *Schmuck* ⓜ shmuk
job *Arbeitsstelle* ⓕ *ar*·baits·shte·le

K

key *Schlüssel* ⓜ *shlew*·sel
kilogram *Kilogramm* ⓝ *kee*·lo·gram
kitchen *Küche* ⓕ *kew*·khe
knife *Messer* ⓝ *me*·ser

L

laundry (place) *Waschküche* ⓕ *vash*·kew·khe
lawyer *Rechtsanwalt/Rechtsanwältin* ⓜ/ⓕ
rekhts·an·valt/*rekhts*·an·vel·tin
left (direction) *links* lingks
left-luggage office *Gepäckaufbewahrung* ⓕ
ge·*pek*·owf·be·vaa·rung
leg *Bein* ⓝ bain
lesbian *Lesbierin* ⓕ *les*·bi·e·rin
less *weniger* *vey*·ni·ger
letter (mail) *Brief* ⓜ breef
lift (elevator) *Lift* ⓜ lift
light *Licht* ⓝ likht
like v *mögen* *meu*·gen
lock *Schloss* ⓝ shlos
long *lang* lang
lost *verloren* fer·*law*·ren
lost-property office *Fundbüro* ⓝ *funt*·bew·raw
love v *lieben* *lee*·ben
luggage *Gepäck* ⓝ ge·*pek*
lunch *Mittagessen* ⓝ *mi*·taak·e·sen

M

mail *Post* ⓕ post
man *Mann* ⓜ man
map *Karte* ⓕ *kar*·te
market *Markt* ⓜ markt
matches *Streichhölzer* ⓝ pl *shtraikh*·heul·tser
meat *Fleisch* ⓝ flaish
medicine *Medizin* ⓕ me·di·*tseen*
menu *Speisekarte* ⓕ *shpai*·ze·kar·te
message *Mitteilung* ⓕ *mi*·tai·lung
milk *Milch* ⓕ milkh
minute *Minute* ⓕ mi·*noo*·te
mobile phone *Handy* ⓝ *hen*·di
money *Geld* ⓝ gelt
month *Monat* ⓜ *maw*·nat
morning *Morgen* ⓜ *mor*·gen
mother *Mutter* ⓕ *mu*·ter
motorcycle *Motorrad* ⓝ *maw*·tor·raat
motorway *Autobahn* ⓕ *ow*·to·baan
mouth *Mund* ⓜ munt
music *Musik* ⓕ mu·*zeek*

N

name *Name* ⓜ *naa*·me
napkin *Serviette* ⓕ zer·*vye*·te
nappy *Windel* ⓕ *vin*·del
near *nahe* *naa*·e
neck *Hals* ⓜ hals
new *neu* noy
news *Nachrichten* ⓕ pl *naakh*·rikh·ten

newspaper *Zeitung* ⓕ tsai·tung
night *Nacht* ⓕ nakht
no *nein* nain
noisy *laut* lowt
nonsmoking *Nichtraucher* nikht·row·kher
north *Norden* ⓜ nor·den
nose *Nase* ⓕ naa·ze
now *Jetzt* yetst
number *Zahl* ⓕ tsaal

O

oil (engine) *Öl* ⓝ eul
old *alt* alt
one-way ticket *einfache Fahrkarte* ⓕ ain·fa·khe faar·kar·te
open a *offen* o·fen
outside *draußen* drow·sen

P

package *Paket* ⓝ pa·keyt
paper *Papier* ⓝ pa·peer
park (car) v *parken* par·ken
passport *(Reise)Pass* ⓜ (rai·ze·)pas
pay *bezahlen* be·tsaa·len
pen *Kugelschreiber* ⓜ koo·gel·shrai·ber
petrol *Benzin* ⓝ ben·tseen
pharmacy *Apotheke* ⓕ a·po·tey·ke
phonecard *Telefonkarte* ⓕ te·le·fawn·kar·te
photo *Foto* ⓝ faw·to
plate *Teller* ⓜ te·ler
police *Polizei* ⓕ po·li·tsai
postcard *Postkarte* ⓕ post·kar·te
post office *Postamt* ⓝ post·amt
pregnant *schwanger* shvang·er
price *Preis* ⓜ prais

Q

quiet *ruhig* roo·ikh

R

rain n *Regen* ⓜ rey·gen
razor *Rasierer* ⓜ ra·zee·rer
receipt *Quittung* ⓕ kvi·tung
red *rot* rawt
refund *Rückzahlung* ⓕ rewk·tsaa·lung
registered mail *Einschreiben* ⓝ ain·shrai·ben
rent v *mieten* mee·ten
repair v *reparieren* re·pa·ree·ren
reservation *Reservierung* ⓕ re·zer·vee·rung
restaurant *Restaurant* ⓝ res·to·raang
return v *zurückkommen* tsu·rewk·ko·men
return ticket *Rückfahrkarte* ⓕ rewk·faar·kar·te
right (direction) *rechts* rekhts
road *Straße* ⓕ shtraa·se
room *Zimmer* ⓝ tsi·mer

S

safe a *sicher* zi·kher
sanitary napkin *Damenbinden* ⓕ pl daa·men·bin·den
seat *Platz* ⓜ plats
send *senden* zen·den
service station *Tankstelle* ⓕ tangk·shte·le
sex *Sex* ⓜ seks
shampoo *Shampoo* ⓝ sham·poo
share (a dorm) *teilen (mit)* tai·len (mit)
shaving cream *Rasiercreme* ⓕ ra·zeer·kreym
she *sie* zee
sheet (bed) *Bettlaken* ⓝ bet·laa·ken
shirt *Hemd* ⓝ hemt
shoes *Schuhe* ⓜ pl shoo·e
shop n *Geschäft* ⓝ ge·sheft
short *kurz* kurts
shower *Dusche* ⓕ doo·she
single room *Einzelzimmer* ⓝ ain·tsel·tsi·mer
skin *Haut* ⓕ howt
skirt *Rock* ⓜ rok
sleep v *schlafen* shlaa·fen
slowly *langsam* lang·zaam
small *klein* klain
smoke (cigarettes) v *rauchen* row·khen
soap *Seife* ⓕ zai·fe
some *einige* ai·ni·ge
soon *bald* balt
south *Süden* ⓜ zew·den
souvenir shop *Souvenirladen* ⓜ zu·ve·neer·laa·den
speak *sprechen* shpre·khen
spoon *Löffel* ⓜ leu·fel
stamp *Briefmarke* ⓕ breef·mar·ke
stand-by ticket *Standby-Ticket* ⓝ stend·bai·ti·ket
station (train) *Bahnhof* ⓜ baan·hawf
stomach *Magen* ⓜ maa·gen
stop v *anhalten* an·hal·ten
stop (bus) *Bushaltestelle* ⓕ bus·hal·te·shte·le
street *Straße* ⓕ shtraa·se

O

english–german

student *Student/Studentin* ⓜ/ⓕ shtu·*dent*/shtu·*den*·tin
sun *Sonne* ⓕ *zo*·ne
sunscreen *Sonnencreme* ⓕ *zo*·nen·kreym
swim v *schwimmen* *shvi*·men
Switzerland *Schweiz* ⓕ shvaits

T

tampons *Tampons* ⓜ pl *tam*·pons
taxi *Taxi* ⓝ *tak*·si
teaspoon *Teelöffel* ⓜ *tey*·leu·fel
teeth *Zähne* ⓜ pl *tsey*·ne
telephone *Telefon* ⓝ te·le·*fawn*
television *Fernseher* ⓜ *fern*·zey·er
temperature (weather) *Temperatur* ⓕ tem·pe·ra·*toor*
tent *Zelt* ⓝ tselt
that (one) *jene* *yey*·ne
they *sie* zee
thirsty *durstig* *durs*·tikh
this (one) *diese* *dee*·ze
throat *Kehle* ⓕ *key*·le
ticket (transport) *Fahrkarte* ⓕ *faar*·kar·te
ticket (sightseeing) *Eintrittskarte* ⓕ *ain*·trits·kar·te
time *Zeit* ⓕ tsait
tired *müde* *mew*·de
tissues *Papiertaschentücher* ⓝ pl pa·*peer*·ta·shen·tew·kher
today *heute* *hoy*·te
toilet *Toilette* ⓕ to·a·*le*·te
tomorrow *morgen* *mor*·gen
tonight *heute Abend* *hoy*·te *aa*·bent
toothbrush *Zahnbürste* ⓕ *tsaan*·bewrs·te
toothpaste *Zahnpasta* ⓕ *tsaan*·pas·ta
torch (flashlight) *Taschenlampe* ⓕ *ta*·shen·lam·pe
tour *Tour* ⓕ toor
tourist office *Fremdenverkehrsbüro* ⓝ *frem*·den·fer·kairs·bew·raw
towel *Handtuch* ⓝ *hant*·tookh
train *Zug* ⓜ tsook
translate *übersetzen* ew·ber·*ze*·tsen
travel agency *Reisebüro* ⓝ *rai*·ze·bew·raw
travellers cheque *Reisescheck* ⓜ *rai*·ze·shek
trousers *Hose* ⓕ *haw*·ze
twin beds *zwei Einzelbetten* ⓝ pl tsvai *ain*·tsel·be·ten
tyre *Reifen* ⓜ *rai*·fen

U

underwear *Unterwäsche* ⓕ *un*·ter·ve·she
urgent *dringend* *dring*·ent

V

vacant *frei* frai
vacation *Ferien* pl *fair*·i·en
vegetable *Gemüse* ⓝ ge·*mew*·ze
vegetarian a *vegetarisch* ve·ge·*taa*·rish
visa *Visum* ⓝ *vee*·zum

W

waiter *Kellner/Kellnerin* ⓜ/ⓕ *kel*·ner/*kel*·ne·rin
walk v *gehen* *gey*·en
wallet *Brieftasche* ⓕ *breef*·ta·she
warm a *warm* varm
wash (something) *waschen* *va*·shen
watch *Uhr* ⓕ oor
water *Wasser* ⓝ *va*·ser
we *wir* veer
weekend *Wochenende* ⓝ *vo*·khen·en·de
west *Westen* ⓜ *ves*·ten
wheelchair *Rollstuhl* ⓜ *rol*·shtool
when *wann* van
where *wo* vaw
white *weiß* vais
who *wer* vair
why *warum* va·*rum*
wife *Ehefrau* ⓕ *ey*·e·frow
window *Fenster* ⓝ *fens*·ter
wine *Wein* ⓜ vain
with *mit* mit
without *ohne* *aw*·ne
woman *Frau* ⓕ frow
write *schreiben* *shrai*·ben

Y

yellow *gelb* gelp
yes *ja* yaa
yesterday *gestern* *ges*·tern
you sg inf *du* doo
you sg pol *Sie* zee
you pl *Sie* zee

Greek

greek alphabet				
Α α *al*·pha	Β β *vi*·ta	Γ γ *gha*·ma	Δ δ *dhel*·ta	Ε ε *ep*·si·lon
Ζ ζ *zi*·ta	Η η *i*·ta	Θ θ *thi*·ta	Ι ι *yio*·ta	Κ κ *ka*·pa
Λ λ *lam*·dha	Μ μ mi	Ν ν ni	Ξ ξ ksi	Ο ο *o*·mi·kron
Π π pi	Ρ ρ ro	Σ σ/ς* *sigh*·ma	Τ τ taf	Υ υ *ip*·si·lon
Φ φ fi	Χ χ hi	Ψ ψ psi	Ω ω o·*me*·gha	

* The letter Σ has two forms for the lower case – σ and ς. The second one is used at the end of words.

ΕΛΛΗΝΙΚΑ

introduction

Aristotle, Plato, Homer, Sappho and Herodotus can't all be wrong in their choice of language – if you've ever come across arcane concepts such as 'democracy', exotic disciplines like 'trigonometry' or a little-known neurosis termed 'the Oedipus complex', then you'll have some inkling of the widespread influence of Greek (Ελληνικά e·li·ni·*ka*). With just a little Modern Greek under your belt, you'll have a richer understanding of this language's impact on contemporary Western culture.

Modern Greek is a separate branch of the Indo-European language family, with Ancient Greek its only (extinct) relative. The first records of written Ancient Greek date from the 14th to the 12th centuries BC. By the 9th century BC, the Greeks had adapted the Phoenician alphabet to include vowels – the first alphabet to do so – and the script in use today came to its final form some time in the 5th century BC. The Greek script was the foundation for both the Cyrillic and the Latin alphabet.

Although written Greek has been remarkably stable over the millennia, the spoken language has evolved considerably. In the 5th century, the dialect spoken around Athens (known as 'Attic') became the dominant speech as a result of the city-state's cultural and political prestige. Attic gained even greater influence as the medium of administration for the vast empire of Alexander the Great, and remained the official language of the Eastern Roman Empire and the Orthodox Church after the demise of the Hellenistic world. Once the Ottoman Turks took Constantinople in 1453, the Attic dialect lost its official function. In the meantime, the common language, known as Koine (Κοινή ki·*ni*), continued to evolve, absorbing vocabulary from Turkish, Italian, Albanian and other Balkan languages.

When an independent Greece returned to the world stage in 1832, it needed to choose a national language. Purists advocated a slightly modernised version of Attic known as Καθαρεύουσα ka·tha·*re*·vu·sa (from the Greek word for 'clean'), which no longer resembled the spoken language. However, Koine had strong support as it was spoken and understood by the majority of Greeks, and in the end it gained official recognition, although it was banned during the military dictatorship (1967–74).

Today, Greek is the official language of Greece and a co-official language of Cyprus, and has over 13 million speakers worldwide. Start your Greek adventure with this chapter – and if you're having one of those days when you're dying to say 'It's all Greek to me!', remember that in your shoes, a Greek speaker would say: Αυτά για μένα είναι Κινέζικα af·*ta* yia *me*·na *i*·ne ki·*ne*·zi·ka (This is Chinese to me)!

pronunciation

vowel sounds

Greek vowels are pronounced separately even when they're written in sequence, eg ζώο *zo*·o (animal). You'll see though, in the table below, that some letter combinations correspond to a single sound – ουρά (queue) is pronounced u·*ra*. When a word ending in a vowel is followed by another word that starts with the same or a similar vowel sound, one vowel is usually omitted and the two words are pronounced as if they were one – Σε ευχαριστώ se ef·kha·ris·*to* becomes Σ' ευχαριστώ sef·kha·ris·*to* (Thank you). Note that the apostrophe (') is used in written Greek to show that two words are joined together.

symbol	english equivalent	greek example	transliteration
a	father	αλλά	a·*la*
e	bet	πλένομαι	*ple*·no·me
i	hit	πίσω, πόλη, υποφέρω, είδος, οικογένεια, υιός	*pi*·so, *po*·li, i·po·*fe*·ro, *i*·dhos, i·ko·*ye*·ni·a, i·*os*
ia	nostalgia	ζητιάνος	zi·*tia*·nos
io	ratio	πιο	pio
o	pot	πόνος, πίσω	*po*·nos, *pi*·so
u	put	ουρά	u·*ra*

word stress

Stress can fall on any of the last three syllables. In our pronunciation guides, the stressed syllable is always in italics, but in written Greek, the stressed syllable is always indicated by an accent over the vowel, eg καλά ka·*la* (good). If a vowel is represented by two letters, it's written on the second letter, eg ζητιάνος zi·*tia*·nos (beggar). If the accent is marked on the first of these two letters, they should be read separately, eg Μάιος *ma*·i·os (May). Where two vowels occur together but are not stressed, a diaeresis (¨) is used to indicate that they should be pronounced separately, eg λαϊκός la·i·*kos* (popular).

consonant sounds

Most Greek consonant sounds are also found in English – only the guttural gh and kh might need a bit of practice. Double consonants are only pronounced once – άλλος *a*·los (other). However, you'll notice that sometimes two Greek letters in combination form one single consonant sound – the combination of the letters μ and π makes the sound b, and the combination of the letters ν and τ makes the sound d.

symbol	english equivalent	greek example	transliteration
b	bed	μπαρ	bar
d	dog	ντομάτα	do·*ma*·ta
dh	that	δεν	dhen
dz	adds	τζάμι	dza·*mi*
f	fat	φως, αυτή	fos, af·*ti*
g	go	γκαρσόν	gar·*son*
gh	guttural sound, between 'goat' and 'loch'	γάτα	*gha*·ta
h	hat	χέρι	*he*·ri
k	kit	καλά	ka·*la*
kh	loch (guttural sound)	χαλί	kha·*li*
l	let	λάδι	*la*·dhi
m	man	μαζί	ma·*zi*
n	not	ναός	na·*os*
ng	ring	ελέγχω	e·*leng*·kho
p	pet	πάνω	*pa*·no
r	red (trilled)	ράβω	*ra*·vo
s	sun	στυλό	sti·*lo*
t	top	τι	ti
th	thin	θέα	*the*·a
ts	hats	τσέπη	*tse*·pi
v	very	βίζα, αύριο	*vi*·za, *av*·ri·o
y	yes	γέρος	*ye*·ros
z	zero	ζέστη	*ze*·sti

tools

language difficulties

Do you speak English?		
Μιλάς Αγγλικά;		mi·*las* ang·gli·*ka*
Do you understand?		
Καταλαβαίνεις;		ka·ta·la·*ve*·nis
I understand.		
Καταλαβαίνω.		ka·ta·la·*ve*·no
I don't understand.		
Δεν καταλαβαίνω.		dhen ka·ta·la·*ve*·no
What does (μώλος) mean?		
Τι σημαίνει (μώλος);		ti si·*me*·ni (*mo*·los)

How do you ...?	Πως ...;	pos ...
pronounce this	προφέρεις αυτό	pro·*fe*·ris af·*to*
write (Madhuri)	γράφουν (Μαδουρή)	*ghra*·foun (ma·dhu·*ri*)

Could you please ...?	Θα μπορούσες παρακαλώ να ...;	tha bo·*ru*·ses pa·ra·ka·*lo* na ...
repeat that	το επαναλάβεις	to e·pa·na·*la*·vis
speak more slowly	μιλάς πιο σιγά	mi·*las* pio si·*gha*
write it down	το γράψεις	to *ghrap*·sis

essentials

Yes.	Ναι.	ne
No.	Οχι.	*o*·hi
Please.	Παρακαλώ.	pa·ra·ka·*lo*
Thank you (very much).	Ευχαριστώ (πολύ).	ef·kha·ri·*sto* (po·*li*)
You're welcome.	Παρακαλώ.	pa·ra·ka·*lo*
Excuse me.	Με συγχωρείτε.	me sing·kho·*ri*·te
Sorry.	Συγνώμη.	si·*ghno*·mi

numbers					
0	μυδέν	mi·*dhen*	15	δεκαπέντε	dhe·ka·*pe*·de
1	ένας/μία/ένα m/f/n	e·nas/*mi*·a/*e*·na	16	δεκαέξι	dhe·ka·*ek*·si
2	δύο	*dhi*·o	17	δεκαεφτά	dhe·ka·ef·*ta*
3	τρεις m&f	tris	18	δεκαοχτώ	dhe·ka·okh·*to*
	τρία n	*tri*·a	19	δεκαεννέα	dhe·ka·e·*ne*·a
4	τέσσερις m&f	*te*·se·ris	20	είκοσι	*i*·ko·si
	τέσσερα n	*te*·se·ra	21	είκοσι ένας/μία/ ένα m/f/n	*i*·ko·si e·nas/*mi*·a/ e·na
5	πέντε	*pe*·de			
6	έξι	*ek*·si			
7	εφτά	ef·*ta*	22	είκοσι δύο	*i*·ko·si *dhi*·o
8	οχτώ	okh·*to*	30	τριάντα	tri·*a*·da
9	εννέα	e·*ne*·a	40	σαράντα	sa·*ra*·da
10	δέκα	*dhe*·ka	50	πενήντα	pe·*ni*·da
11	έντεκα	*e*·de·ka	60	εξήντα	ek·*si*·da
12	δώδεκα	*dho*·dhe·ka	70	εβδομήντα	ev·dho·*mi*·da
13	δεκατρείς m&f	dhe·ka·*tris*	80	ογδόντα	ogh·*dho*·da
	δεκατρία n	dhe·ka·*tri*·a	90	ενενήντα	e·ne·*ni*·da
14	δεκατέσσερις m&f	dhe·ka·*te*·se·ris	100	εκατό	e·ka·*to*
	δεκατέσσερα n	dhe·ka·*te*·se·ra	1000	χίλια	*hi*·lia

time & dates

What time is it?	Τι ώρα είναι;	ti *o*·ra *i*·ne
It's one o'clock.	Είναι (μία) η ώρα.	*i*·ne (*mi*·a) i *o*·ra
It's (10) o'clock.	Είναι (δέκα) η ώρα.	*i*·ne (*dhe*·ka) i *o*·ra
Quarter past (10).	(Δέκα) και τέταρτο.	(*dhe*·ka) ke *te*·tar·to
Half past (10).	(Δέκα) και μισή.	(*dhe*·ka) ke mi·*si*
Quarter to (10).	(Δέκα) παρά τέταρτο.	(*dhe*·ka) pa·*ra* *te*·tar·to
At what time ...?	Τι ώρα ...;	ti *o*·ra ...
At ...	Στις ...	stis ...
Monday	Δευτέρα	dhef·*te*·ra
Tuesday	Τρίτη	*tri*·ti
Wednesday	Τετάρτη	te·*tar*·ti
Thursday	Πέμπτη	*pem*·ti
Friday	Παρασκευή	pa·ra·ske·*vi*
Saturday	Σάββατο	*sa*·va·to
Sunday	Κυριακή	ki·ria·*ki*

January	Ιανουάριος	i·a·nu·*a*·ri·os
February	Φεβρουάριος	fev·ru·*a*·ri·os
March	Μάρτιος	*mar*·ti·os
April	Απρίλιος	a·*pri*·li·os
May	Μάιος	*ma*·i·os
June	Ιούνιος	i·*u*·ni·os
July	Ιούλιος	i·*u*·li·os
August	Αύγουστος	*av*·ghu·stos
September	Σεπτέμβριος	sep·*tem*·vri·os
October	Οκτώβριος	ok·*tov*·ri·os
November	Νοέμβριος	no·*em*·vri·os
December	Δεκέμβριος	dhe·*kem*·vri·os

What date is it today?
Τι ημερομηνία είναι σήμερα; — ti i·me·ro·mi·*ni*·a *i*·ne *si*·me·ra

It's (18 October).
Είναι (δεκαοχτώ Οκτωβρίου). — *i*·ne (dhe·ka·okh·*to* ok·tov·*ri*·u)

since (May)	από (το Μάιο)	a·*po* (to *ma*·i·o)
until (June)	μέχρι (τον Ιούνιο)	*meh*·ri (ton i·*u*·ni·o)
yesterday	χτες	khtes
today	σήμερα	*si*·me·ra
tonight	απόψε	a·*pop*·se
tomorrow	αύριο	*av*·ri·o
last ...		
night	την περασμένη νύχτα	tin pe·raz·*me*·ni *nikh*·ta
week	την περασμένη εβδομάδα	tin pe·raz·*me*·ni ev·dho·*ma*·dha
month	τον περασμένο μήνα	ton pe·raz·*me*·no *mi*·na
year	τον περασμένο χρόνο	ton pe·raz·*me*·no *khro*·no
next ...		
week	την επόμενη εβδομάδα	tin e·*po*·me·ni ev·dho·*ma*·dha
month	τον επόμενο μήνα	ton e·*po*·me·no *mi*·na
year	τον επόμενο χρόνο	ton e·*po*·me·no *khro*·no
yesterday/ tomorrow ...	χτες/ αύριο το ...	khtes/ *av*·ri·o to ...
morning	πρωί	pro·*i*
afternoon	απόγευμα	a·*po*·yev·ma
evening	βράδι	*vra*·dhi

ΕΛΛΗΝΙΚΑ – tools

weather

What's the weather like?	Πως είναι ο καιρός;	pos *i*·ne o ke·*ros*
It's …		
cloudy	Είναι συννεφιά.	*i*·ne si·ne·*fia*
cold	Κάνει κρύο.	*ka*·ni *kri*·o
hot	Κάνει πολλή ζέστη.	*ka*·ni po·*li ze*·sti
raining	Βρέχει.	*vre*·hi
snowing	Χιονίζει.	hio·*ni*·zi
sunny	Είναι λιακάδα.	*i*·ne lia·*ka*·dha
warm	Κάνει ζέστη.	*ka*·ni *ze*·sti
windy	Φυσάει.	fi·*sa*·i
spring	άνοιξη f	*a*·nik·si
summer	καλοκαίρι n	ka·lo·*ke*·ri
autumn	φθινόπωρο n	fthi·*no*·po·ro
winter	χειμώνας m	hi·*mo*·nas

border crossing

I'm here …	Είμαι εδώ…	*i*·me e·*dho*…
in transit	τράνζιτ	*tran*·zit
on business	για δουλειά	yia dhu·*lia*
on holiday	σε διακοπές	se dhia·ko·*pes*
I'm here for (three) …	Είμαι εδώ για (τρεις) …	*i*·me e·*dho* yia (tris) …
days	μέρες	*me*·res
weeks	εβδομάδες	ev·dho·*ma*·dhes
months	μήνες	*mi*·nes

I'm going to (Limassol).
Πηγαίνω στη (Λεμεσό). — pi·*ye*·no sti (le·me·*so*)

I'm staying at the (Xenia).
Μένω στο (Ξενία). — *me*·no sto (kse·*ni*·a)

I have nothing to declare.
Δεν έχω τίποτε να δηλώσω. — dhen *e*·kho *ti*·po·te na dhi·*lo*·so

I have something to declare.
Εχω κάτι να δηλώσω. — *e*·kho *ka*·ti na dhi·*lo*·so

That's (not) mine.
Αυτό (δεν) είναι δικό μου. — af·*to* (dhen) *i*·ne dhi·*ko* mu

transport

tickets & luggage

Where can I buy a ticket?	Που αγοράζω εισιτήριο;	pu a·gho·*ra*·zo i·si·*ti*·ri·o
Do I need to book a seat?	Χρειάζεται να κλείσω θέση;	khri·*a*·ze·te na *kli*·so *the*·si
One ... ticket to (Patras), please.	Ενα εισιτήριο ... για την (Πάτρα), παρακαλώ.	*e*·na i·si·*ti*·ri·o ... yia tin (*pa*·tra) pa·ra·ka·*lo*
one-way	απλό	a·*plo*
return	με επιστροφή	me e·pi·stro·*fi*
I'd like to ... my ticket, please.	Θα ήθελα να ... το εισιτήριό μου, παρακαλώ.	tha *i*·the·la na ... to i·si·*ti*·ri·*o* mu pa·ra·ka·*lo*
cancel	ακυρώσω	a·ki·*ro*·so
change	αλλάξω	a·*lak*·so
confirm	επικυρώσω	e·pi·ki·*ro*·so
I'd like a ... seat.	Θα ήθελα μια θέση ...	tha *i*·the·la mia *the*·si ...
nonsmoking	στους μη καπνίζοντες	stus mi kap·*ni*·zo·des
smoking	στους καπνίζοντες	stus kap·*ni*·zo·des

How much is it?
Πόσο κάνει; — *po*·so *ka*·ni

Is there air conditioning?
Υπάρχει έρκοντίσιον; — i·*par*·hi e·kon·*di*·si·on

Is there a toilet?
Υπάρχει τουαλέτα; — i·*par*·hi tu·a·*le*·ta

How long does the trip take?
Πόσο διαρκεί το ταξίδι; — *po*·so dhi·ar·*ki* to tak·*si*·dhi

Is it a direct route?
Πηγαίνει κατ'ευθείαν; — pi·*ye*·ni ka·tef·*thi*·an

Where can I find a luggage locker?
Που μπορώ να βρω τη φύλαξη αντικειμένων; — pu bo·*ro* na vro ti *fi*·lak·si a·di·ki·*me*·non

My luggage has been ...	Οι αποσκευές μου έχουν ...	i a·pos·ke·*ves* mu *e*·khun ...
damaged	πάθει ζημιά	*pa*·thi zi·*mia*
lost	χαθεί	kha·*thi*
stolen	κλαπεί	kla·*pi*

getting around

Where does flight (10) arrive/depart?
Που προσγειώνεται/ απογειώνεται η πτήση (δέκα); — pu pros·yi·*o*·ne·te/ a·po·yi·*o*·ne·te i *pti*·si (*dhe*·ka)

Where's (the) ...?	Που είναι ...;	pu *i*·ne ...
arrivals hall	η αίθουσα των αφίξεων	i *e*·thu·sa tona·*fik*·se·on
departures hall	η αίθουσα των αναχωρήσεων	i *e*·thu·sa ton *a*·na kho·*ri*·se·on
duty-free shop	τα αφορολόγητα	ta a·fo·ro·*lo*·yi·ta
gate (nine)	η θύρα (εννέα)	i *thi*·ra (e·*ne*·a)

Is this the ... to (Athens)?	Είναι αυτό το ... για την (Αθήνα);	*i*·ne af·*to* to ... yia tin (a·*thi*·na)
boat	πλοίο	*pli*·o
bus	λεωφορείο	le·o·fo·*ri*·o
ferry	φέρυ	*fe*·ri
plane	αεροπλάνο	a·e·ro·*pla*·no
train	τρένο	*tre*·no

What time's the ... (bus)?	Πότε είναι το (λεωφορείο);	*po*·te *i*·ne to (le·o·fo·*ri*·o)
first	πρώτο	*pro*·to
last	τελευταίο	te·lef·*te*·o
next	επόμενο	e·*po*·me·no

At what time does it arrive/depart?
Τι ώρα φτάνει/φεύγει; — ti *o*·ra *fta*·ni/*fev*·yi

What time does it get to (Thessaloniki)?
Τι ώρα φτάνει στη (Θεσσαλονίκη); — ti *o*·ra *fta*·ni sti (the·sa·lo·*ni*·ki)

How long will it be delayed?
Πόση ώρα θα καθυστερήσει; — *po*·si *o*·ra tha ka·thi·ste·*ri*·si

What station is this?
Ποιος σταθμός είναι αυτός; — pios stath·*mos* *i*·ne af·*tos*

What stop is this?
Ποια στάση είναι αυτή; — pia *sta*·si *i*·ne af·*ti*

What's the next station?
Ποιος είναι ο επόμενος σταθμός; — pios *i*·ne o e·*po*·me·nos stath·*mos*

What's the next stop?
Ποια είναι η επόμενη στάση; — pia *i*·ne i e·*po*·me·ni *sta*·si

Does it stop at (Iraklio)?
Σταματάει στο (Ηράκλειο); — sta·ma·*ta*·i sto (i·*ra*·kli·o)

Please tell me when we get to (Thessaloniki).
Παρακαλώ πέστε μου όταν φτάσουμε στη (Θεσσαλονίκη). — pa·ra·ka·*lo* *pe*·ste mu *o*·tan *fta*·su·me sti (the·sa·lo·*ni*·ki)

How long do we stop here?
Πόση ώρα θα σταματήσουμε εδώ; — *po*·si *o*·ra tha sta·ma·*ti*·su·me e·*dho*

Is this seat available?
Είναι αυτή η θέση ελεύθερη; — *i*·ne af·*ti* i *the*·si e·*lef*·the·ri

That's my seat.
Αυτή η θέση είναι δική μου. — af·*ti* i *the*·si *i*·ne dhi·*ki* mu

I'd like a taxi …	Θα ήθελα ένα ταξί …	tha *i*·the·la *e*·na tak·*si* …
at (9am)	στις (εννέα πριν το μεσημέρι)	stis (e·*ne*·a prin to me·si·*me*·ri)
now	τώρα	*to*·ra
tomorrow	αύριο	*av*·ri·o

Is this taxi available?
Είναι αυτό το ταξί ελεύθερο; — *i*·ne af·*to* to tak·*si* e·*lef*·the·ro

How much is it to …?
Πόσο κάνει για …; — *po*·so *ka*·ni yia …

Please put the meter on.
Παρακαλώ βάλε το ταξίμετρο. — pa·ra·ka·*lo* *va*·le to tak·*si*·me·tro

Please take me to (this address).
Παρακαλώ πάρε με σε (αυτή τη διεύθυνση). — pa·ra·ka·*lo* *pa*·re me se (af·*ti* ti dhi·*ef*·thin·si)

Please …	Παρακαλώ …	pa·ra·ka·*lo* …
slow down	πήγαινε πιο σιγά	*pi*·ye·ne pio si·*gha*
stop here	σταμάτα εδώ	sta·*ma*·ta e·*dho*
wait here	περίμενε εδώ	pe·*ri*·me·ne e·*dho*

car, motorbike & bicycle hire

I'd like to hire a …	Θα ήθελα να ενοικιάσω ένα …	tha *i*·the·la na e·ni·ki·*a*·so *e*·na …
bicycle	ποδήλατο	po·*dhi*·la·to
car	αυτοκίνητο	af·to·*ki*·ni·to
motorbike	μοτοσικλέτα	mo·to·si·*kle*·ta

with …	με …	me …
a driver	οδηγό	o·dhi·*gho*
air conditioning	έρκοντίσιον	e·kon·*di*·si·on
How much for … hire?	Πόσο νοικάζεται την …;	*po*·so ni·*kia*·ze·te tin …
hourly	ώρα	*o*·ra
daily	ημέρα	i·*me*·ra
weekly	εβδομάδα	ev·dho·*ma*·dha
air	αέρας m	a·*e*·ras
oil	λάδι αυτοκινήτου n	*la*·dhi af·to·ki·*ni*·tu
petrol	βενζίνα f	ven·*zi*·na
tyres	λάστιχα n	*la*·sti·kha
I need a mechanic.	Χρειάζομαι μηχανικό.	khri·*a*·zo·me mi·kha·ni·*ko*
I've run out of petrol.	Μου τελείωσε η βενζίνα.	mu te·*li*·o·se i ven·*zi*·na
I have a flat tyre.	Μ'έπιασε λάστιχο.	*me*·pia·se *la*·sti·kho

directions

Where's the …?	Που είναι …?	pu *i*·ne …
bank	η τράπεζα	i *tra*·pe·za
city centre	το κέντρο της πόλης	to *ke*·dro tis *po*·lis
hotel	το ξενοδοχείο	to kse·no·dho·*hi*·o
market	η αγορά	i a·gho·*ra*
police station	ο αστυνομικός σταθμός	o a·sti·no·mi·*kos* stath·*mos*
post office	το ταχυδρομείο	to ta·hi·dhro·*mi*·o
public toilet	τα δημόσια αποχωρητήρια	ta dhi·*mo*·si·a a·po·kho·ri·*ti*·ria
tourist office	το τουριστικό γραφείο	to tu·ri·sti·*ko* ghra·*fi*·o

Is this the road to (Lamia)?
Είναι αυτός ο δρόμος για (τη Λαμία); — *i*·ne af·*tos* o *dhro*·mos yia (ti la·*mi*·a)

Can you show me (on the map)?
Μπορείς να μου δείξεις (στο χάρτη); — bo·*ris* na mu *dhik*·sis (sto *khar*·ti)

What's the address?
Ποια είναι η διεύθυνση; — pia *i*·ne i dhi·*ef*·thin·si

How far is it?
Πόσο μακριά είναι; — *po*·so ma·kri·*a i*·ne

How do I get there?
Πως πηγαίνω εκεί; — pos pi·*ye*·no e·*ki*

Turn …	Στρίψε …	*strip*·se …
at the corner	στη γωνία	sti gho·*ni*·a
at the traffic lights	στα φανάρια	sta fa·*na*·ria
left/right	αριστερά/δεξιά	a·ris·te·*ra*/dhek·si·*a*
It's …	Είναι …	*i*·ne …
behind …	πίσω …	*pi*·so …
far away	μακριά	ma·kri·*a*
here	εδώ	e·*dho*
in front of …	μπροστά από …	bros·*ta* a·*po* …
near …	κοντά …	ko·*da* …
next to …	δίπλα από …	*dhip*·la a·*po* …
on the corner	στη γωνία	sti gho·*ni*·a
opposite …	απέναντι …	a·*pe*·na·di …
straight ahead	κατ'ευθείαν	ka·tef·*thi*·an
there	εκεί	e·*ki*
by bus	με λεωφορείο	me le·o·fo·*ri*·o
by boat	με πλοίο	me *pli*·o
by taxi	με ταξί	me tak·*si*
by train	με τρένο	me *tre*·no
on foot	με πόδια	me *po*·dhia
north	βόρια	*vo*·ri·a
south	νότια	*no*·ti·a
east	ανατολικά	a·na·to·li·*ka*
west	δυτικά	dhi·ti·*ka*

signs

Είσοδος/Έξοδος	*i*·so·dhos/*ek*·so·dhos	**Entrance/Exit**
Ανοικτός/Κλειστός	a·nik·*tos*/kli·*stos*	**Open/Closed**
Ελεύθερα Δωμάτια	e·*lef*·the·ra dho·*ma*·ti·a	**Rooms Available**
Πλήρες	*pli*·res	**No Vacancies**
Πληροφορίες	pli·ro·fo·*ri*·es	**Information**
Αστυνομικός Σταθμός	a·sti·no·mi·*kos* stath·*mos*	**Police Station**
Απαγορεύεται	a·pa·gho·*re*·ve·te	**Prohibited**
Τουαλέτες	tu·a·*le*·tes	**Toilets**
Ανδρών	an·*dhron*	**Men**
Γυναικών	yi·ne·*kon*	**Women**
Ζεστό/Κρύο	zes·*to*/*khri*·o	**Hot/Cold**

accommodation

finding accommodation

Where's a ...?	Που είναι ...;	pu *i*·ne ...
camping ground	χώρος για κάμπινγκ	*kho*·ros yia *kam*·ping
guesthouse	ξενώνας	kse·*no*·nas
hotel	ξενοδοχείο	kse·no·dho·*hi*·o
youth hostel	γιουθ χόστελ	yiuth *kho*·stel
Can you recommend somewhere ...?	Μπορείτε να συστήσετε κάπου ...;	bo·*ri*·te na si·*sti*·se·te *ka*·pu ...
cheap	φτηνό	fti·*no*
good	καλό	ka·*lo*
nearby	κοντινό	ko·di·*no*

I'd like to book a room, please.
Θα ήθελα να κλείσω ένα δωμάτιο, παρακαλώ. — tha *i*·the·la na *kli*·so *e*·na dho·*ma*·ti·o pa·ra·ka·*lo*

I have a reservation.
Εχω κάνει κάποια κράτηση. — *e*·kho *ka*·ni *ka*·pia *kra*·ti·si

My name's ...
Με λένε ... — me *le*·ne ...

Do you have a ... room?	Εχετε ένα ... δωμάτιο;	*e*·he·te *e*·na ... dho·*ma*·ti·o
single	μονό	mo·*no*
double	διπλό	dhi·*plo*
twin	δίκλινο	*dhi*·kli·no
How much is it per ...?	Πόσο είναι για κάθε ...;	*po*·so *i*·ne yia *ka*·the ...
night	νύχτα	*nikh*·ta
person	άτομο	*a*·to·mo
Can I pay ...?	Μπορώ να πληρώσω με ...;	bo·*ro* na pli·*ro*·so me ...
by credit card	πιστωτική κάρτα	pi·sto·ti·*ki* *kar*·ta
with a travellers cheque	ταξιδιωτική επιταγή	tak·si·dhio·ti·*ki* e·pi·ta·*yi*

For (three) nights/weeks.
Για (τρεις) νύχτες/εβδομάδες. — yia (tris) *nikh*·tes/ev·dho·*ma*·dhes

From (2 July) to (6 July).
Από (τις δύο Ιουλίου) μέχρι (τις έξι Ιουλίου). — a·*po* (tis *dhi*·o i·u·*li*·u) *me*·khri (tis *ek*·si i·u·*li*·u)

Can I see it?
Μπορώ να το δω; — bo·*ro* na to dho

Am I allowed to camp here?
Μπορώ να κατασκηνώσω εδώ; — bo·*ro* na ka·ta·ski·*no*·so e·*dho*

Where can I find a camp site?
Που μπορώ να βρω το χώρο του κάμπινγκ; — pu bo·*ro* na vro to *kho*·ro tu *kam*·ping

requests & queries

When/Where is breakfast served?
Πότε/Που σερβίρεται το πρόγευμα; — *po*·te/pu ser·*vi*·re·te to *pro*·yev·ma

Please wake me at (seven).
Παρακαλώ ξύπνησέ με στις (εφτά). — pa·ra·ka·*lo* *ksip*·ni·*se* me stis (ef·*ta*)

Could I have my key, please?
Μπορώ να έχω το κλειδί μου παρακαλώ; — bo·*ro* na *e*·kho to kli·*dhi* mu pa·ra·ka·*lo*

Can I get another (blanket)?
Μπορώ να έχω και άλλη (κουβέρτα); — bo·*ro* na *e*·kho ke *a*·li (ku·*ver*·ta)

This (towel) isn't clean.
Αυτή (η πετσέτα) δεν είναι καθαρό. — af·*ti* (i pet·*se*·ta) dhen *i*·ne ka·tha·*ri*

Is there a/an ...?	Εχετε ...;	*e*·he·te ...
elevator	ασανσέρ	a·san·*ser*
safe	χρηματοκιβώτιο	khri·ma·to·ki·*vo*·ti·o

The room is too ...	Είναι πάρα πολύ ...	*i*·ne *pa*·ra po·*li* ...
expensive	ακριβό	a·kri·*vo*
noisy	θορυβώδες	tho·ri·*vo*·dhes
small	μικρό	mi·*kro*

The ... doesn't work.	... δεν λειτουργεί.	... dhen li·tur·*ghi*
air conditioning	Το έρκοντίσιον	to er·kon·*di*·si·on
fan	Ο ανεμιστήρας	o a·ne·mi·*sti*·ras
toilet	Η τουαλέτα	i tu·a·*le*·ta

checking out

What time is checkout?
Τι ώρα είναι η αναχώρηση; — ti *o*·ra *i*·ne i a·na·*kho*·ri·si

Can I leave my luggage here?
Μπορώ να αφήσω τις βαλίτσες μου εδώ; — bo·*ro* na a·*fi*·so tis va·*lit*·ses mu e·*dho*

Could I have my ..., please?	Μπορώ να έχω ... μου παρακλώ;	bo·*ro* na *e*·kho ... mu pa·ra·ka·*lo*
deposit	την προκαταβολή	tin pro·ka·ta·vo·*li*
passport	το διαβατήριό	to dhia·va·*ti*·rio
valuables	τα κοσμήματά	ta koz·*mi*·ma·*ta*

communications & banking

the internet

Where's the local Internet cafe?
Που είναι το τοπικό καφενείο με διαδίκτυο; — pu *i*·ne to to·pi·*ko* ka·fe·*ni*·o me dhi·a·*dhik*·ti·o

How much is it per hour?
Πόσο κοστίζει κάθε ώρα; — *po*·so ko·*sti*·zi *ka*·the *o*·ra

I'd like to ...	Θα ήθελα να ...	tha *i*·the·la na ...
check my email	ελέγξω την ηλεκτρονική αλληλογραφία μου	e·*lenk*·so tin i·lek·tro·ni·*ki* a·li·lo·ghra·*fi*·a mu
get Internet access	έχω πρόσβαση στο διαδίκτυο	*e*·kho *pros*·va·si sto dhi·a·*dhik*·ti·o
use a printer	χρησιμοποιήσω έναν εκτυπωτή	khri·si·mo·pi·*i*·so *e*·nan ek·ti·po·*ti*
use a scanner	χρησιμοποιήσω ένα σκάνερ	khri·si·mo·pi·*i*·so *e*·na *ska*·ner

communications & banking – GREEK

mobile/cell phone

I'd like a …	Θα ήθελα …	tha *i*·the·la …
mobile/cell phone for hire	να νοικιάσω ένα κινητό τηλέφωνο	na ni·*kia*·so *e*·na ki·ni·*to* ti·*le*·fo·no
SIM card for your network	μια κάρτα SIM για το δίκτυό σας	mia *kar*·ta sim yia to *dhik*·*tio* sas
What are the rates?	Ποιες είναι οι τιμές;	pies *i*·ne i ti·*mes*

telephone

What's your phone number?
Τι αριθμό τηλεφώνου έχεις; — ti a·rith·*mo* ti·le·*fo*·nu *e*·his

The number is …
Ο αριθμός είναι … — o a·rith·*mos* *i*·ne …

Where's the nearest public phone?
Που είναι το πιο κοντινό δημόσιο τηλέφωνο; — pu *i*·ne to pio ko·di·*no* dhi·*mo*·si·o ti·*le*·fo·no

I'd like to buy a phonecard.
Θέλω να αγοράσω μια τηλεφωνική κάρτα. — *the*·lo na a·gho·*ra*·so mia ti·le·fo·ni·*ki* *kar*·ta

I want to …	Θέλω να …	*the*·lo na …
call (Singapore)	τηλεφωνήσω (στη Σιγγαπούρη)	ti·le·fo·*ni*·so (sti sing·ga·*pu*·ri)
make a local call	κάνω ένα τοπικό τηλέφωνο	*ka*·no *e*·na to·pi·*ko* ti·*le*·fo·no
reverse the charges	αντιστρέψω τα έξοδα	a·di·*strep*·so ta *ek*·so·dha

How much does … cost?	Πόσο κοστίζει …;	*po*·so ko·*sti*·zi …
a (three)- minute call	ένα τηλεφώνημα (τριών) λεπτών	*e*·na ti·le·*fo*·ni·ma (tri·*on*) lep·*ton*
each extra minute	κάθε έξτρα λεπτό	*ka*·the *eks*·tra lep·*to*

It's (40c) per (30) seconds.
(Σαράντα λεπτά) για (τριάντα) δευτερόλεπτα. — (sa·*ra*·da lep·*ta*) yia (tri·*a*·da) dhef·te·*ro*·lep·ta

ΕΛΛΗΝΙΚΑ – communications & banking

post office

I want to send a …	Θέλω να στείλω …	*the*·lo na *sti*·lo …
fax	ένα φαξ	*e*·na faks
letter	ένα γράμμα	*e*·na *ghra*·ma
parcel	ένα δέμα	*e*·na *dhe*·ma
postcard	μια κάρτα	mia *kar*·ta
I want to buy a/an …	Θέλω να αγοράσω ένα …	*the*·lo na a·gho·*ra*·so *e*·na …
envelope	φάκελο	*fa*·ke·lo
stamp	γραμματόσημο	ghra·ma·*to*·si·mo
Please send it (to Australia) by …	Παρακαλώ στείλτε το … (στην Αυστραλία).	pa·ra·ka·*lo* *stil*·te to … (stin af·stra·*li*·a)
airmail	αεροπορικώς	a·e·ro·po·ri·*kos*
express mail	εξπρές	eks·*pres*
registered mail	συστημένο	si·sti·*me*·no
surface mail	δια ξηράς	dhia ksi·*ras*

Is there any mail for me?
Υπάρχουν γράμματα για μένα; — i·*par*·khun *ghra*·ma·ta yia *me*·na

bank

Where's a/an …?	Που είναι …;	pu *i*·ne …
ATM	μια αυτόματη μηχανή χρημάτων	mia af·*to*·ma·ti mi·kha·*ni* khri·*ma*·ton
foreign exchange office	ένα γραφείο αλλαγής χρημάτων	*e*·na ghra·*fi*·o a·la·*yis* khri·*ma*·ton
I'd like to …	Θα ήθελα να …	tha *i*·the·la na …
Where can I …?	Που μπορώ να …;	pu bo·*ro* na …
arrange a transfer	τακτοποιήσω μια μεταβίβαση	tak·to·pi·*i*·so mia me·ta·*vi*·va·si
cash a cheque	εξαργυρώσω μια επιταγή	ek·sar·yi·*ro*·so mia e·pi·ta·*yi*
change a travellers cheque	αλλάξω μια ταξιδιωτική επιταγή	a·*lak*·so mia tak·si·dhio·ti·*ki* e·pi·ta·*yi*
change money	αλλάξω χρήματα	a·*lak*·so *khri*·ma·ta
get a cash advance	κάνω μια ανάληψη σε μετρητά	*ka*·no mia a·*na*·lip·si se me·tri·*ta*
withdraw money	αποσύρω χρήματα	a·po·*si*·ro *khri*·ma·ta

What's the ...?	Ποια είναι ... ;	pia *i*·ne ...
charge for that	η χρέωση για αυτό	i *khre*·o·si yia af·*to*
exchange rate	η τιμή συναλλάγματος	i ti·*mi* si·na·*lagh*·ma·tos
It's (12) ...	Κάνει (δώδεκα) ...	*ka*·ni (*dho*·dhe·ka) ...
Cyprus pounds	λίρες Κύπρου	*li*·res *ki*·pru
euros	ευρώ	ev·*ro*

It's free.
Είναι δωρεάν. *i*·ne dho·re·*an*

What time does the bank open?
Τι ώρα ανοίγει η τράπεζα; ti *o*·ra a·*ni*·yi i *tra*·pe·za

Has my money arrived yet?
Εχουν φτάσει τα χρήματά μου; *e*·khun *fta*·si ta *khri*·ma·*ta* mu

sightseeing

getting in

What time does it open/close?
Τι ώρα ανοίγει/κλείνει; ti *o*·ra a·*ni*·yi/*kli*·ni

What's the admission charge?
Πόσο κοστίζει η είσοδος; *po*·so ko·*sti*·zi i *i*·so·dhos

Is there a discount for students/children?
Υπάρχει έκπτωση για σπουδαστές/παιδιά; i·*par*·hi *ek*·pto·si yia spu·dha·*stes*/pe·*dhia*

I'd like a ...	Θα ήθελα ...	tha *i*·the·la ...
catalogue	ένα κατάλογο	*e*·na ka·*ta*·lo·gho
guide	έναν οδηγό	*e*·nan o·dhi·*gho*
local map	ένα τοπικό χάρτη	*e*·na to·pi·*ko* *khar*·ti
I'd like to see ...	Θα ήθελα να δω ...	tha *i*·the·la na dho ...
What's that?	Τι είναι εκείνο;	ti *i*·ne e·*ki*·no
Can I take a photo?	Μπορώ να πάρω μια φωτογραφία;	bo·*ro* na *pa*·ro mia fo·to·ghra·*fi*·a

tours

When's the next tour?
Πότε είναι η επόμενη περιήγηση; *po*·te *i*·ne i e·*po*·me·ni pe·ri·*i*·yi·si

When's the next ...?	Πότε είναι το επόμενο ...;	*po*·te *i*·ne to e·*po*·me·no ...
boat trip	ταξίδι με τη βάρκα	tak·*si*·dhi me ti *var*·ka
day trip	ημερήσιο ταξίδι	i·me·*ri*·si·o tak·*si*·dhi

Is ... included?	Συμπεριλαμβάνεται ...;	si·be·ri·lam·*va*·ne·te ...
accommodation	κατάλυμα	ka·*ta*·li·ma
the admission charge	τιμή εισόδου	ti·*mi* i·*so*·dhu
food	φαγητό	fa·yi·*to*
transport	μεταφορά	me·ta·fo·*ra*

How long is the tour?
Πόση ώρα διαρκεί η περιήγηση; *po*·si *o*·ra dhi·ar·*ki* i pe·ri·*i*·yi·si

What time should we be back?
Τι ώρα πρέπει να επιστρέψουμε; ti *o*·ra *pre*·pi na e·pi·*strep*·su·me

sightseeing

amphitheatre	αμφιθέατρο n	am·fi·*the*·a·tro
castle	κάστρο n	*ka*·stro
cathedral	μητρόπολη f	mi·*tro*·po·li
church	εκκλησία f	e·kli·*si*·a
fresco	φρέσκο n	*fres*·ko
labyrinth	λαβύρινθος m	la·*vi*·rin·thos
main square	κεντρική πλατεία f	ken·dhri·*ki* pla·*ti*·a
monastery	μοναστήρι n	mo·na·*sti*·ri
monument	μνημείο n	mni·*mi*·o
mosaic	μωσαϊκό n	mo·sa·i·*ko*
museum	μουσείο n	mu·*si*·o
old city	αρχαία πόλι	ar·*khe*·a *po*·li
palace	παλάτι n	pa·*la*·ti
ruins	ερρίπια n pl	e·*ri*·pi·a
sculpture	γλυπτική f	ghlip·ti·*ki*
stadium	στάδιο n	*sta*·dhi·o
statue	άγαλμα n	*a*·ghal·ma
temple	ναός m	na·*os*

shopping

enquiries

Where's a ...?	Που είναι ...;	pu *i*·ne ...
bank	μια τράπεζα	mia *tra*·pe·za
bookshop	ένα βιβλιοπωλείο	e·na viv·li·o·po·*li*·o
camera shop	ένα κατάστημα φωτογραφικών ειδών	e·na ka·*ta*·sti·ma fo·to·ghra·fi·*kon* i·*dhon*
department store	ένα κατάστημα	e·na ka·*ta*·sti·ma
grocery store	ένα οπωροπωλείο	e·na o·po·ro·po·*li*·o
kiosk	ένα περίπτερο	e·na pe·*rip*·te·ro
market	μια αγορά	mia a·gho·*ra*
newsagency	το εφημεριδοπωλείο	to e·fi·me·ri·dho·po·*li*·o
supermarket	ένα σούπερμάρκετ	e·na *su*·per·*mar*·ket

Where can I buy (a padlock)?
Που μπορώ να αγοράσω (μια κλειδαριά);
pu bo·*ro* na a·gho·*ra*·so (mia kli·dha·*ria*)

I'd like to buy ...
Θα ήθελα να αγοράσω ...
tha *i*·the·la na a·gho·*ra*·so ...

Can I look at it?
Μπορώ να το κοιτάξω;
bo·*ro* na to ki·*tak*·so

Do you have any others?
Εχετε άλλα;
e·he·te *a*·la

Does it have a guarantee?
Εχει εγγύηση;
e·hi e·*gi*·i·si

Can I have it sent overseas?
Μπορείς να το στείλεις στο εξωτερικό;
bo·*ris* na to *sti*·lis sto ek·so·te·ri·*ko*

Can I have ... repaired?
Μπορώ να επισκευάσω εδώ ...;
bo·*ro* na e·pi·ske·*va*·so e·*dho* ...

Can I have a bag, please?
Μπορώ να έχω μια τσάντα, παρακαλώ;
bo·*ro* na *e*·kho mia *tsa*·da pa·ra·ka·*lo*

It's faulty.
Είναι ελαττωματικό.
i·ne e·la·to·ma·ti·*ko*

I'd like ..., please.	Θα ήθελα ..., παρακαλώ.	tha *i*·the·la ... pa·ra·ka·*lo*
a refund	επιστροφή χρημάτων	e·pi·stro·*fi* khri·*ma*·ton
to return this	να επιστρέψω αυτό	na e·pi·*strep*·so af·*to*

paying

How much is it?
Πόσο κάνει; — *po*·so *ka*·ni

Can you write down the price?
Μπορείς να γράψεις την τιμή; — bo·*ris* na *ghrap*·sis tin ti·*mi*

That's too expensive.
Είναι πάρα πολύ ακριβό. — *i*·ne *pa*·ra po·*li* a·kri·*vo*

Can you lower the price?
Μπορείς να κατεβάσεις την τιμή; — bo·*ris* na ka·te·*va*·sis tin ti·*mi*

I'll give you (five) euros.
Θα σου δώσω (πέντε) ευρώ. — tha su *dho*·so (*pe*·de) ev·*ro*

I'll give you (five) Cyprus pounds.
Θα σου δώσω (πέντε) λίρες Κύπρου. — tha su *dho*·so (*pe*·de) *li*·res *ki*·pru

There's a mistake in the bill.
Υπάρχει κάποιο λάθος στο λογαριασμό. — i·*par*·hi *ka*·pio *la*·thos sto lo·gha·riaz·*mo*

Do you accept ...?	Δέχεστε ...;	*dhe*·he·ste ...
credit cards	πιστωτικές κάρτες	pi·sto·ti·*kes* *kar*·tes
debit cards	χρεωτικές κάρτες	khre·o·ti·*kes* *kar*·tes
travellers cheques	ταξιδιωτικές επιταγές	tak·si·dhio·ti·*kes* e·pi·ta·*yes*

I'd like my change, please.
Θα ήθελα τα ρέστα μου, παρακαλώ. — tha *i*·the·la ta *re*·sta mu pa·ra·ka·*lo*

Can I have a receipt, please?
Μπορώ να έχω μια απόδειξη, παρακαλώ; — bo·*ro* na *e*·kho mia a·*po*·dhik·si pa·ra·ka·*lo*

clothes & shoes

Can I try it on?	Μπορώ να το προβάρω;	bo·*ro* na to pro·*va*·ro
My size is (40).	Το νούμερό μου είναι (σαράντα).	to *nu*·me·*ro* mu *i*·ne (sa·*ra*·da)
It doesn't fit.	Δε μου κάνει.	dhe mu *ka*·ni
small	μικρό	mi·*kro*
medium	μεσαίο	me·*se*·o
large	μεγάλο	me·*gha*·lo

shopping – GREEK

books & music

I'd like a ...	Θα ήθελα ...	tha *i*·the·la ...
newspaper (in English)	μια εφημερίδα (στα Αγγλικά)	mia e·fi·me·*ri*·dha (sta ang·gli·*ka*)
pen	ένα στυλό	*e*·na sti·*lo*

Is there an English-language bookshop?
Υπάρχει ένα βιβλιοπωλείο Αγγλικής γλώσσας; — i·*par*·hi *e*·na viv·li·o·po·*li*·o ang·gli·*kis ghlo*·sas

I'm looking for something by (Anna Vissi).
Ψάχνω για κάτι (της Αννας Βίσση). — *psakh*·no yia *ka*·ti (tis *a*·nas *vi*·si)

Can I listen to this?
Μπορώ να το ακούσω; — bo·*ro* na to a·*ku*·so

photography

Can you ...?	Μπορείς να ...;	bo·*ris* na ...
develop this film	εμφανίσεις αυτό το φιλμ	em·fa·*ni*·sis af·*to* to film
load my film	βάλεις το φιλμ στη μηχανή μου	*va*·lis to film sti mi·kha·*ni* mu
transfer photos from my camera to CD	μεταφέρεις φωτογραφίες από την φωτογραφική μου μηχανή στο CD	me·ta·*fe*·ris fo·to·ghra·*fi*·es a·*po* ti fo·to·ghra·fi·*ki* mu mi·kha·*ni* sto si·*di*
I need a/an ... film for this camera.	Χρειάζομαι φιλμ ... για αυτή τη μηχανή.	khri·*a*·zo·me film ... yia af·*ti* ti mi·kha·*ni*
APS	APS	*e*·i·pi·es
B&W	μαυρόασπρο	mav·*ro*·a·spro
colour	έγχρωμο	*eng*·khro·mo
slide	σλάιντ	*sla*·id
(200) speed	ταχύτητα (διακοσίων)	ta·*hi*·ti·ta (dhia·ko·*si*·on)
When will it be ready?	Πότε θα είναι έτοιμο;	*po*·te tha *i*·ne *e*·ti·mo

meeting people

greetings, goodbyes & introductions

Hello/Hi.	Γεια σου.	yia su
Good night.	Καληνύχτα.	ka·li·*nikh*·ta
Goodbye/Bye.	Αντίο.	a·*di*·o
Mr	Κύριε	*ki*·ri·e
Mrs	Κυρία	ki·*ri*·a
Miss	Δις	dhes·pi·*nis*
How are you?	Τι κάνεις;	ti *ka*·nis
Fine. And you?	Καλά. Εσύ;	ka·*la* e·*si*
What's your name?	Πως σε λένε;	pos se *le*·ne
My name is ...	Με λένε ...	me *le*·ne ...
I'm pleased to meet you.	Χαίρω πολύ.	*he*·ro po·*li*
This is my ...	Από εδώ ... μου.	a·*po* e·*dho* ... mu
boyfriend	ο φίλος	o *fi*·los
brother	ο αδερφός	o a·dher·*fos*
daughter	η κόρη	i *ko*·ri
father	ο πατέρας	o pa·*te*·ras
friend	ο φίλος/η φίλη m/f	o *fi*·los/i *fi*·li
girlfriend	η φιλενάδα	i fi·le·*na*·dha
husband	ο σύζυγός	o *si*·zi·*ghos*
mother	η μητέρα	i mi·*te*·ra
partner (intimate)	ο/η σύντροφός m/f	o/i *si*·dro·*fos*
sister	η αδερφή	i a·dher·*fi*
son	ο γιος	o yios
wife	η σύζυγός	i *si*·zi·*ghos*
Here's my ...	Εδώ είναι ... μου.	e·*dho* *i*·ne ... mu
What's your ...?	Ποιο είναι ... σου;	pio *i*·ne ... su
email address	το ημέιλ	to i·*me*·il
fax number	το φαξ	to faks
phone number	το τηλέφωνό	to ti·*le*·fo·*no*

Here's my address.
Εδώ είναι η διεύθυνσή μου. — e·*dho* *i*·ne i dhi·*ef*·thin·*si* mu

What's your address?
Ποια είναι η δική σου διεύθυνση; — pia *i*·ne i dhi·*ki* su dhi·*ef*·thin·si

meeting people – GREEK

occupations

What's your occupation?	Τι δουλειά κάνεις;	ti dhu·*lia* *ka*·nis
I'm a/an ...	Είμαι/Δουλεύω ...	*i*·me/dhou·*lev*·o ...
businessperson	επιχειρηματίας m&f	e·pi·hi·ri·ma·*ti*·as
farmer	γεωργός m&f	ye·or·*ghos*
manual worker	εργάτης/εργάτρια m/f	er·*gha*·tis/er·*gha*·tri·a
office worker	σε γραφείο	se ghra·*phi*·o
scientist	επιστήμονας m&f	e·pi·*sti*·mo·nas
tradesperson	έμπορος m&f	*e*·bo·ros

background

Where are you from?	Από που είσαι;	a·*po* pu *i*·se
I'm from ...	Είμαι από ...	*i*·me a·*po* ...
Australia	την Αυστραλία	tin af·stra·*li*·a
Canada	τον Καναδά	ton ka·na·*dha*
England	την Αγγλία	tin ang·*gli*·a
New Zealand	την Νέα Ζηλανδία	tin *ne*·a zi·lan·*dhi*·a
the USA	την Αμερική	tin A·me·ri·*ki*
Are you married?	Είσαι παντρεμένος/ παντρεμένη; m/f	*i*·se pa·dre·*me*·nos/ pa·dre·*me*·ni
I'm married.	Είμαι παντρεμένος/ παντρεμένη. m/f	i·*me* pa·dre·*me*·nos/ pa·dre·*me*·ni
I'm single.	Είμαι ανύπαντρος/ ανύπαντρη. m/f	i·*me* a·*ni*·pa·dros/ a·*ni*·pa·dri

age

How old ...?	Πόσο χρονών ...;	*po*·so khro·*non* ...
are you	είσαι	*i*·se
is your daughter	είναι η κόρη σου	*i*·ne i *ko*·ri su
is your son	είναι ο γιος σου	*i*·ne o yios su
I'm ... years old.	Είμαι ... χρονών.	*i*·me ... khro·*non*
He/She is ... years old.	Αυτός/αυτή είναι ... χρονών.	af·*tos*/af·*ti* *i*·ne ... khro·*non*

feelings

I'm (not) ...	(Δεν) Είμαι ...	(dhen) *i*·me ...
Are you ...?	Είσαι ...;	*i*·se ...
happy	ευτυχισμένος m	ef·ti·hiz·*me*·nos
	ευτυχισμένη f	ef·ti·hiz·*me*·ni
hot	ζεστός/ζεστή m/f	ze·*stos*/ze·*sti*
hungry	πεινασμένος m	pi·naz·*me*·nos
	πεινασμένη f	pi·naz·*me*·ni
sad	στενοχωρημένος m	ste·no·kho·ri·*me*·nos
	στενοχωρημένη f	ste·no·kho·ri·*me*·ni
thirsty	διψασμένος m	dhip·saz·*me*·nos
	διψασμένη f	dhip·saz·*me*·ni

entertainment

going out

Where can I find ...?	Που μπορώ να βρω ...;	pu bo·*ro* na vro ...
clubs	κλαμπ	klab
gay venues	Χώρους συνάντησης για γκέη	*kho*·rus si·*na*·di·sis yia *ge*·i
pubs	μπυραρίες	bi·ra·*ri*·es
I feel like going to a/the ...	Εχω όρεξι να πάω σε ...	*e*·kho *o*·rek·si na *pa*·o se ...
concert	κονσέρτο	kon·*ser*·to
the movies	φιλμ	film
party	πάρτυ	*par*·ti
restaurant	εστιατόριο	e·sti·a·*to*·ri·o
theatre	θέατρο	*the*·a·tro

interests

Do you like ...?	Σου αρέσει ...;	su a·*re*·si ...
I (don't) like ...	(Δεν) μου αρέσει ...	(dhen) mu a·*re*·si ...
cooking	η μαγειρική	i ma·yi·ri·*ki*
reading	το διάβασμα	to *dhia*·vaz·ma

Do you like ...?	Σου αρέσουν ...;	su a·*re*·sun ...
I (don't) like ...	(Δεν) μου αρέσουν τα ...	(dhen) mu a·*re*·sun ta ...
art	καλλιτεχνικά	ka·li·tekh·ni·*ka*
movies	φιλμ	film
nightclubs	νάιτ κλαμπ	*na*·it klab
sport	σπορ	spor

Do you like to ...?	Σου αρέσει να ...;	sou a·*re*·si na ...
dance	χορεύεις	kho·*re*·vis
go to concerts	πηγαίνεις σε κονσέρτα	pi·*ye*·nis se kon·*ser*·ta
listen to music	ακούς μουσική	a·*kus* mu·si·*ki*

food & drink

finding a place to eat

Can you recommend a ...?	Μπορείς να συστήσεις ...;	bo·*ris* na si·*sti*·sis ...
bar	ένα μπαρ	*e*·na bar
café	μία καφετέρια	*mi*·a ka·fe·*te*·ria
restaurant	ένα εστιατόριο	e·sti·a·*to*·ri·o

I'd like ..., please.	Θα ήθελα ..., παρακαλώ.	tha *i*·thela ... pa·ra·ka·*lo*
a table for (five)	ένα τραπέζι για (πέντε)	*e*·na tra·*pe*·zi yia (*pe*·de)
the (non)smoking section	στους (μη) καπνίζοντες	stus (mi) kap·*ni*·zo·des

ordering food

breakfast	πρόγευμα n	*pro*·yev·ma
lunch	γεύμα n	*yev*·ma
dinner	δείπνο n	*dhip*·no
snack	μεζεδάκι n	me·ze·*dha*·ki

What would you recommend?
Τι θα συνιστούσες; — ti tha si·ni·*stu*·ses

I'd like (a/the) ..., please.	Θα ήθελα ..., παρακαλώ.	tha *i*·the·la ... pa·ra·ka·*lo*
bill	το λογαριασμό	to lo·gha·riaz·*mo*
drink list	τον κατάλογο με τα ποτά	ton ka·*ta*·lo·gho me ta po·*ta*
menu	το μενού	to me·*nu*
that dish	εκείνο το φαγητό	e·*ki*·no to fa·yi·*to*

drinks

(cup of) coffee ...	(ένα φλυτζάνι) καφέ ...	(*e*·na fli·*dza*·ni) ka·*fe* ...
(cup of) tea ...	(ένα φλυτζάνι) τσάι ...	(*e*·na fli·*dza*·ni) *tsa*·i ...
with milk	με γάλα	me *gha*·la
without sugar	χωρίς ζάχαρη	kho·*ris* *za*·kha·ri
(orange) juice	χυμός (πορτοκάλι) m	hi·*mos* (por·to·*ka*·li)
soft drink	αναψυκτικό n	a·nap·sik·ti·*ko*
... water	... νερό	... ne·*ro*
hot	ζεστό	ze·*sto*
(sparkling) mineral	(γαζόζα) μεταλλικό	(gha·*zo*·za) me·ta·li·*ko*

in the bar

I'll have ...	Θα πάρω ...	tha *pa*·ro ...
I'll buy you a drink.	Θα σε κεράσω εγώ.	tha se ke·*ra*·so e·*gho*
What would you like?	Τι θα ήθελες;	ti tha *i*·the·les
Cheers!	Εις υγείαν!	is i·*yi*·an
brandy	μπράντι n	*bran*·di
champagne	σαμπάνια f	sam·*pa*·nia
a glass/bottle of beer	ένα ποτήρι/μπουκάλι μπύρα	*e*·na po·*ti*·ri/bu·*ka*·li *bi*·ra
ouzo	ούζο n	*u*·zo
a shot of (whisky)	ένα (ουίσκι)	*e*·na (u·*i*·ski)
a glass/bottle of ... wine	ένα ποτηρι/μπουκαλι ... κρασί	*e*·na po·*ti*·ri/bu·*ka*·li ... kra·*si*
red	κόκκινο	*ko*·ki·no
sparkling	σαμπάνια	sam·*pa*·nia
white	άσπρο	*a*·spro

self-catering

What's the local speciality?
Ποιες είναι οι τοπικές λιχουδιές; — pies *i*·ne i to·pi·*kes* li·khu·*dhies*

What's that?
Τι είναι εκείνο; — ti *i*·ne e·*ki*·no

How much is (a kilo of cheese)?
Πόσο κάνει (ένα κιλό τυρί); — *po*·so *ka*·ni (*e*·na ki·*lo* ti·*ri*)

I'd like ...	Θα ήθελα ...	tha *i*·the·la ...
(100) grams	(εκατό) γραμμάρια	(e·ka·*to*) ghra·*ma*·ria
(two) kilos	(δύο) κιλά	(*dhi*·o) ki·*la*
(three) pieces	(τρία) κομμάτια	(*tri*·a) ko·*ma*·tia
(six) slices	(έξι) φέτες	(*ek*·si) *fe*·tes

Less.	Πιο λίγο.	pio *li*·gho
Enough.	Αρκετά.	ar·ke·*ta*
More.	Πιο πολύ.	pio po·*li*

special diets & allergies

Is there a vegetarian restaurant near here?
Υπάρχει ένα εστιατόριο χορτοφάγων εδώ κοντά; — i·*par*·hi *e*·na e·sti·a·*to*·ri·o hor·to·*fa*·ghon e·*dho* ko·*da*

Do you have vegetarian food?
Εχετε φαγητό για χορτοφάγους; — *e*·he·te fa·yi·*to* yia khor·to·*fa*·ghus

I don't eat ...	Δεν τρώγω ...	dhen *tro*·gho ...
butter	βούτυρο	*vu*·ti·ro
eggs	αβγά	av·*gha*
meat stock	ζουμί από κρέας	zu·*mi* a·*po* *kre*·as

I'm allergic to ...	Είμαι αλλεργικός/ αλλεργική ... m/f	*i*·me a·ler·yi·*kos* a·ler·yi·*ki* ...
dairy produce	στα γαλακτικά	sta gha·lak·ti·*ka*
gluten	στη γλουτένη	sti ghlu·*te*·ni
MSG	στο MSG	sto em es dzi
nuts	στους ξηρούς καρπούς	stus ksi·*rus* kar·*pus*
seafood	στα θαλασσινά	sta tha·la·si·*na*

ΕΛΛΗΝΙΚΑ – food & drink

αρνί κοκκινιστό n	ar·*ni* ko·ki·ni·*sto*	lamb braised in white wine
αστακός m	a·sta·*kos*	lobster, boiled or chargrilled
γιαουρτογλού f	yia·ur·to·*ghlu*	grilled meat & yogurt pie
γιουβέτσι n	yiu·*vet*·si	casserole of meat & seafood with tomatoes & pasta
δάχτυλα n pl	*dhakh*·ti·la	deep-fried, nut-filled pastries
ελιές τσακιστές f pl	e·*lies* tsa·ki·*stes*	marinated green olives
ελιές τουρσί f pl	e·*lies* tur·*si*	pickled olives
ιμάμ-μπαϊλντί n	i·*mam*·ba·il·*di*	stuffed eggplant
καβούρι βραστό n	ka·*vu*·ri vra·*sto*	boiled crab with dressing
κακαβιά f	ka·ka·*via*	saltwater fish soup
καλαμάρι Λεβριανά n	ka·la·*ma*·ri lev·ria·*na*	squid stewed in wine
καλαμάρι τηγανητό n	ka·la·*ma*·ri ti·gha·ni·*to*	battered & fried squid rings
καρυδόπιτα f	ka·ri·*dho*·pi·ta	rich moist walnut cake
καταΐφι n	ka·ta·*i*·fi	syrupy nut-filled rolls
κεφτέδες m pl	kef·*te*·dhes	lamb, pork or veal rissoles
κοντοσούβλι n	kon·do·*suv*·li	spit-roast pieces of lamb or pork
κοφίσι n	ko·*fi*·si	fish pie
κρεατόπιτα f	kre·a·*to*·pi·ta	lamb or veal pie
λάχανα με λαρδί n pl	*la*·kha·na me lar·*dhi*	greens & bacon casserole
μηλοπιτάκια n pl	mi·lo·pi·*ta*·kia	apple & walnut pies
μπακλαβάς m pl	ba·kla·*vas*	nut-filled pastry in honey syrup
μπάμιες γιαχνί f pl	*ba*·mies yia·*khni*	braised okra
μπιζελόσουπα f	bi·ze·*lo*·su·pa	fragrant pea soup with dill
μπουρδέτο n	bur·*dhe*·to	salt cod stew

μπριάμι n	bri·*a*·mi	mixed vegetables casserole
μπριζόλες f pl	bri·*zo*·les	chops • steak
μύδια κρασάτα n pl	*mi*·dhia kra·*sa*·ta	poached mussels in wine sauce
ντολμάδες m pl	dol·*ma*·dhes	stuffed vine or cabbage leaves
ντοματόσουπα f	do·ma·*to*·su·pa	tomato soup with pasta
παλικάρια n pl	pa·li·*ka*·ri·a	boiled legumes & grains
ρέγγα f	*reng*·ga	smoked herrings, plain or grilled
ριζάδα f	ri·*za*·dha	thick soup with rice & shellfish
σαλιγκάρια n pl	sa·ling·*ga*·ri·a	snails cooked in the shell
σουβλάκι n	suv·*la*·ki	seasoned or marinated meat or fish, skewered & chargrilled
σπανακόπιτα f	spa·na·*ko*·pi·ta	spinach pie
συκόψωμο n	si·*kop*·so·mo	heavy aromatic fig cake
ταβάς m	ta·*vas*	seasoned beef or lamb casserole
τζατζίκι n	dza·*dzi*·ki	cucumber, yogurt & garlic salad
τυρόπιτα f	ti·*ro*·pi·ta	cheese pie
φακές σούπα f pl	fa·*kes su*·pa	lentil soup
φασολάδα f	fa·so·*la*·dha	thick fragrant bean soup
χαλβάς m	khal·*vas*	sweet of sesame seeds & honey, with pistachio or almonds
χαμψοπίλαφο n	kham·pso·*pi*·la·fo	onion & anchovy pilau
χόρτα τσιγάρι n pl	*khor*·ta tsi·*gha*·ri	lightly fried wild greens
χορτόπιτα f	khor·*to*·pi·ta	pie with seasonal greens
χορτοσαλάτα f	khor·to·sa·*la*·ta	warm salad of greens & dressing
χταπόδι βραστό n	khta·*po*·dhi vra·*sto*	boiled octopus
χωριάτικη σαλάτα f	kho·ri·*a*·ti·ki sa·*la*·ta	salad of tomatoes, cucumber, olives & feta

emergencies

basics

Help!	Βοήθεια!	vo·*i*·thia
Stop!	Σταμάτα!	sta·*ma*·ta
Go away!	Φύγε!	*fi*·ye
Thief!	Κλέφτης!	*klef*·tis
Fire!	Φωτιά!	fo·*tia*
Watch out!	Προσεχε!	*pro*·se·he

Call . . .!	Κάλεσε . . .!	*ka*·le·se . . .
an ambulance	το ασθενοφόρο	to as·the·no·*fo*·ro
the doctor	ένα γιατρό	e·na yia·*tro*
the police	την αστυνομία	tin a·sti·no·*mi*·a

It's an emergency.
Είναι μια έκτακτη ανάγκη. — *i*·ne mia *ek*·tak·ti a·*na*·gi

Could you help me, please?
Μπορείς να βοηθήσεις, παρακαλώ; — bo·*ris* na vo·i·*thi*·sis pa·ra·ka·*lo*

Can I make a phone call?
Μπορώ να κάνω ένα τηλεφώνημα; — bo·*ro* na *ka*·no *e*·na ti·le·*fo*·ni·ma

I'm lost.
Εχω χαθεί. — *e*·kho kha·*thi*

Where are the toilets?
Που είναι η τουαλέτα; — pu *i*·ne I tu·a·*le*·ta

police

Where's the police station?
Που είναι ο αστυνομικός σταθμός; — pu *i*·ne o a·sti·no·mi·*kos* stath·*mos*

I want to report an offence.
Θέλω να αναφερω μια παρανομια. — *the*·lo na a·na·*fe*·ro mia pa·ra·no·*mi*·a

I have insurance.
Εχω ασφάλεια. — *e*·kho as·*fa*·li·a

I've been . . .	Με έχουν . . .	me *e*·khun . . .
assaulted	κακοποιήσει	ka·ko·pi·*i*·si
raped	βιάσει	vi·*a*·si
robbed	ληστέψει	li·*step*·si

emergencies – GREEK

I've lost my ...	Εχασα ... μου.	*e*·kha·sa ... mu
My ... was/were stolen.	Εκλεψαν ... μου.	*e*·klep·san ... mu
backpack	το σακίδιό	to sa·*ki*·dhio
bags	τις βαλίτσες	tis va·lits·*es*
credit card	την πιστωτική κάρτα	tin pi·sto·ti·*ki* *kar*·ta
handbag	την τσάντα	tin *tsa*·da
jewellery	τα κοσμήματά	ta koz·*mi*·ma·*ta*
money	τα χρήματά	ta *khri*·ma·*ta*
passport	το διαβατήριό	to dhia·va·*ti*·rio
travellers cheques	τις ταξιδιωτικές επιταγές	tis tak·si·dhio·ti·*kes* e·pi·ta·*yes*
wallet	το πορτοφόλι	to por·to·*fo*·li

I want to contact my ...	Θέλω να έρθω σε επαφή με ... μου.	*the*·lo na *er*·tho se e·pa·*fi* me ... mu
consulate	τηνπρεσβεία	tin prez·*vi*·a
embassy	το προξενείο	to pro·ksee·*ni*·o

health

medical needs

Where's the nearest ...?	Που είναι ο πιο κοντινός ...;	pu *i*·ne o pio ko·di·*nos* ...
dentist	οδοντίατρος	o·dho·*di*·a·tros
doctor	γιατρός	yia·*tros*

Where's the nearest ...?	Που είναι το πιο κοντινό...;	pu *i*·ne to pio ko·di·*no* ...
hospital	νοσοκομείο	no·so·ko·*mi*·o
(night) pharmacy	(νυχτερινό) φαρμακείο	(nikh·te·ri·*no*) far·ma·*ki*·o

I need a doctor (who speaks English).
Χρειάζομαι ένα γιατρό (που να μιλάει αγγλικά). — khri·*a*·zo·me *e*·na yia·*tro* (pu na mi·*la*·i ang·gli·*ka*)

Could I see a female doctor?
Μπορώ να δω μια γυναίκα γιατρό; — bo·*ro* na dho mia yi·*ne*·ka yia·*tro*

I've run out of my medication.
Μου έχουν τελειώσει τα φάρμακά μου. — mu *e*·khun te·li·*o*·si ta *far*·ma·*ka* mu

symptoms, conditions & allergies

I'm sick.	Είμαι άρρωστος/άρρωστη m/f	i·*me a*·ro·stos/*a*·ro·sti
It hurts here.	Πονάει εδώ.	po·*na*·i e·*dho*
I have (a/an) …	Εχω …	e·kho …
asthma	άσθμα n	*as*·thma
bronchitis	βροχίτιδα f	vro·*hl*·ti·dha
constipation	δυσκοιλιότητα f	dhis·ki·li·*o*·ti·ta
cough	βήχα m	*vi*·kha
diarrhoea	διάρροια f	dhi·*a*·ri·a
fever	πυρετό m	pi·re·*to*
headache	πονοκέφαλο m	po·no·*ke*·fa·lo
heart condition	καρδιακή κατάσταση f	kar·dhi·a·*ki* ka·*ta*·sta·si
nausea	ναυτία f	naf·*ti*·a
pain	πόνο m	*po*·no
sore throat	πονόλαιμο m	po·*no*·le·mo
toothache	πονόδοντο	po·*no*·dho·do
I'm allergic to …	Είμαι αλλεργικός/ αλλεργική … m/f	*i*·me a·ler·yi·*kos* a·ler·yi·*ki* …
antibiotics	στα αντιβιωτικά	sta a·di·vi·o·ti·*ka*
anti-inflammatories	στα αντιφλεγμονώδη	sta a·di·flegh·mo·*no*·dhi
aspirin	στην ασπιρίνη	stin as·pi·*ri*·ni
bees	στις μέλισσες	stis *me*·li·ses
codeine	στην κωδεΐνη	stin ko·dhe·*i*·ni
penicillin	στην πενικιλλίνη	stin pe·ni·ki·*li*·ni
antiseptic	αντισηπτικό n	a·di·sip·ti·*ko*
bandage	επίδεσμος m	e·*pi*·dhez·mos
condoms	προφυλακτικά n	pro·fi·lak·ti·*ka*
contraceptives	αντισυλληπτικά n pl	a·di·si·lip·ti·*ka*
diarrhoea medicine	φάρμακο διάροιας	*far*·ma·ko *dhiar*·ghias
insect repellent	εντομοαπωθητικό n	e·do·mo·a·po·thi·ti·*ko*
laxatives	καθαρτικό n	ka·thar·ti·*ko*
painkillers	παυσίπονα	paf·*si*·po·na
rehydration salts	ενυδρωτικά άλατα n pl	en·i·dhro·ti·*ka a*·la·ta
sleeping tablets	υπνωτικά χάπια n pl	ip·no·ti·*ka kha*·pia

english–greek dictionary

Greek nouns in this dictionary have their gender indicated by ⓜ (masculine), ⓕ (feminine) or ⓝ (neuter). If it's a plural noun you'll also see pl. Adjectives are given in the masculine form only. Words are also marked as n (noun), a (adjective), v (verb), sg (singular), pl (plural), inf (informal) and pol (polite) where necessary.

A

accident ατύχημα ⓝ a·*ti*·hi·ma
accommodation κατάλυμα ⓝ ka·*ta*·li·ma
adaptor μετασχηματιστής ⓜ me·ta·shi·ma·ti·*stis*
address διεύθυνση ⓕ dhi·*ef*·thin·si
aeroplane αεροπλάνο ⓝ a·e·ro·*pla*·no
after μετά me·*ta*
air-conditioned με έρκοντίσιον me er·kon·*di*·si·on
airport αεροδρόμιο ⓝ a·e·ro·*dhro*·mi·o
alcohol αλκοόλ ⓝ al·ko·*ol*
all όλοι ⓜ *o*·li
allergy αλλεργία ⓕ a·ler·*yi*·a
ambulance νοσοκομειακό ⓝ no·so·ko·mi·a·*ko*
and και ke
ankle αστράγαλος ⓜ a·*stra*·gha·los
arm χέρι ⓝ *he*·ri
ashtray σταχτοθήκη ⓕ stakh·to·*thi*·ki
ATM αυτόματη μηχανή χρημάτων ⓕ af·*to*·ma·ti mi·kha·*ni* khri·*ma*·ton

B

baby μωρό ⓝ mo·*ro*
back (body) πλάτη ⓕ *pla*·ti
backpack σακίδιο ⓝ sa·*ki*·dhi·o
bad κακός ka·*kos*
bag σάκος ⓜ *sa*·kos
baggage claim παραλαβή αποσκευών ⓕ pa·ra·la·*vi* a·po·ske·*von*
bank τράπεζα ⓕ *tra*·pe·za
bar μπαρ ⓝ bar
bathroom μπάνιο ⓝ *ba*·nio
battery μπαταρία ⓕ ba·ta·*ri*·a
beautiful όμορφος *o*·mor·fos
bed κρεβάτι ⓝ kre·*va*·ti
beer μπύρα ⓕ *bi*·ra
before πριν prin
behind πίσω *pi*·so
bicycle ποδήλατο ⓝ po·*dhi*·la·to
big μεγάλος me·*gha*·los
bill λογαριασμός ⓜ lo·gha·riaz·*mos*
black a μαύρος *mav*·ros
blanket κουβέρτα ⓕ ku·*ver*·ta
blood group ομάδα αίματος ⓕ o·*ma*·dha *e*·ma·tos
blue a μπλε ble
boat βάρκα ⓕ *var*·ka
book (make a reservation) v κλείσω θέση *kli*·so *the*·si
bottle μπουκάλι ⓝ bu·*ka*·li
bottle opener ανοιχτήρι ⓝ a·nikh·*ti*·ri
boy αγόρι ⓝ a·*gho*·ri
brakes (car) φρένα ⓝ pl *fre*·na
breakfast πρωινό ⓝ *pro*·i·no
broken (faulty) ελαττωματικός e·la·to·ma·ti·*kos*
bus λεωφορείο ⓝ le·o·fo·*ri*·o
business επιχείρηση ⓕ e·pi·*hi*·ri·si
buy αγοράζω a·gho·*ra*·zo

C

café καφετέρια ⓝ ka·fe·*te*·ria
camera φωτογραφική μηχανή ⓕ fo·to·ghra·fi·*ki* mi·kha·*ni*
camp site χώρος για κάμπινγκ ⓜ *kho*·ros yia *kam*·ping
cancel ακυρώνω a·ki·*ro*·no
can opener ανοιχτήρι ⓝ a·nikh·*ti*·ri
car αυτοκίνητο ⓝ af·to·*ki*·ni·to
cash μετρητά ⓝ pl me·tri·*ta*
cash (a cheque) v εξαργυρώνω ek·sar·yi·*ro*·no
cell phone κινητό ⓝ ki·ni·*to*
centre κέντρο ⓝ *ke*·dro
change (money) v αλλάζω a·*la*·zo
cheap φτηνός fti·*nos*
check (bill) λογαριασμός ⓜ lo·gha·riaz·*mos*
check-in ρεσεψιόν ⓕ re·sep·*sion*
chest στήθος ⓝ *sti*·thos
child παιδί ⓝ pe·*dhi*
cigarette τσιγάρο ⓝ tsi·*gha*·ro
city πόλι ⓕ *po*·li
clean a καθαρός ka·tha·*ros*
closed κλεισμένος kliz·*me*·nos
coffee καφές ⓜ ka·*fes*
coins κέρματα ⓝ pl *ker*·ma·ta
cold a κρυωμένος kri·o·*me*·nos

collect call κλήση με αντιστροφή της επιβάρυνσης ⓕ
kli·si me a·dis·tro·*fi* tis e·pi·*va*·rin·sis
come έρχομαι *er*·kho·me
computer κομπιούτερ ⓝ kom·*piu*·ter
condom προφυλακτικό ⓝ pro·fi·lak·ti·*ko*
contact lenses φακοί επαφής ⓜ pl fa·*ki* e·pa·*fis*
cook v μαγειρεύω ma·yi·*re*·vo
cost τιμή ⓕ ti·*mi*
credit card πιστωτική κάρτα ⓕ pi·sto·ti·*ki* *kar*·ta
cup φλυτζάνι ⓝ fli·*dza*·ni
currency exchange τιμή συναλλάγματος ⓕ
ti·*mi* si·na·*lagh*·ma·tos
customs (immigration) τελωνείο ⓝ te·lo·*ni*·o
Cypriot (nationality) Κύπριος/Κύπρια ⓜ/ⓕ
ki·pri·os/*ki*·pri·a
Cypriot a κυπριακός/κυπριακή ⓜ/ⓕ
ki·pri·a·*kos*/ki·pri·a·*ki*
Cyprus Κύπρος ⓕ *ki*·pros

D

dangerous επικίνδυνος e·pi·*kin*·dhi·nos
date (time) ημερομηνία ⓕ i·me·ro·mi·*ni*·a
day ημέρα ⓕ i·*me*·ra
delay καθυστέρηση ⓕ ka·thi·*ste*·ri·si
dentist οδοντίατρος ⓜ&ⓕ o·dho·*di*·a·tros
depart αναχωρώ a·na·kho·*ro*
diaper πάνα ⓕ *pa*·na
dictionary λεξικό ⓝ lek·si·*ko*
dinner δείπνο ⓝ *dhip*·no
direct άμεσος *a*·me·sos
dirty βρώμικος *vro*·mi·kos
disabled ανάπηρος a·*na*·pi·ros
discount έκπτωση ⓕ *ek*·pto·si
doctor γιατρός ⓜ&ⓕ yia·*tros*
double bed διπλό κρεβάτι ⓝ dhi·*plo* kre·*va*·ti
double room διπλό δωμάτιο ⓝ dhi·*plo* dho·*ma*·ti·o
drink ποτό ⓝ po·*to*
drive v οδηγώ o·dhi·*gho*
drivers licence άδεια οδήγησης ⓕ *a*·dhi·a o·*dhi*·yi·sis
drugs (illicit) ναρκωτικό ⓝ nar·ko·ti·*ko*
dummy (pacifier) πιπίλα ⓕ pi·*pi*·la

E

ear αφτί ⓝ af·*ti*
east ανατολή ⓕ a·na·to·*li*
eat τρώγω *tro*·gho
economy class τουριστική θέση ⓕ tu·ri·sti·*ki* *the*·si
electricity ηλεκτρισμός ⓜ i·lek·triz·*mos*
elevator ασανσέρ ⓝ a·san·*ser*
email ημέιλ ⓝ i·*me*·il
embassy πρεσβεία ⓕ pre·*zvi*·a
emergency έκτακτη ανάγκη ⓕ *ek*·tak·ti a·*na*·gi
English (language) Αγγλικά ⓝ ang·gli·*ka*
entrance είσοδος ⓕ *i*·so·dhos
evening βράδι ⓝ *vra*·dhi
exchange rate τιμή συναλλάγματος ⓕ
ti·*mi* si·na·*lagh*·ma·tos
exit έξοδος ⓕ *ek*·so·dhos
expensive ακριβός a·kri·*vos*
express mail επείγον ταχυδρομείο ⓝ
e·*pi*·ghon ta·hi·dhro·*mi*·o
eye μάτι ⓝ *ma*·ti

F

far μακριά ma·kri·*a*
fast γρήγορος *ghri*·gho·ros
father πατέρας ⓜ pa·*te*·ras
film (camera) φιλμ ⓝ film
finger δάκτυλο ⓝ *dhak*·ti·lo
first-aid kit κυτίο πρώτων βοηθειών ⓝ
ki·*ti*·o *pro*·ton vo·i·thi·*on*
first class πρώτη τάξη ⓕ *pro*·ti *tak*·si
fish ψάρι ⓝ *psa*·ri
food φαγητό ⓝ fa·yi·*to*
foot πόδι ⓝ *po*·dhi
fork πιρούνι ⓝ pi·*ru*·ni
free (of charge) δωρεάν dho·re·*an*
friend φίλος/φίλη ⓜ/ⓕ *fi*·los/*fi*·li
fruit φρούτα ⓝ pl *fru*·ta
full γεμάτο ye·*ma*·to
funny αστείος a·*sti*·os

G

gift δώρο ⓝ *dho*·ro
girl κορίτσι ⓝ ko·*rit*·si
glass (drinking) ποτήρι ⓝ po·*ti*·ri
glasses γιαλιά ⓝ yia·*lia*
go πηγαίνω pi·*ye*·no
good καλός ka·*los*
Greece Ελλάδα ⓕ e·*la*·dha
Greek (language) Ελληνικά ⓝ e·li·ni·*ka*
Greek (nationality) Έλληνες ⓜ pl *e*·li·nes
green πράσινος *pra*·si·nos
guide οδηγός ⓜ&ⓕ o·dhi·*ghos*

H

half μισό ⓝ mi·*so*
hand χέρι ⓝ *he*·ri
handbag τσάντα ⓕ *tsa*·da
happy ευτυχισμένος ef·ti·hiz·*me*·nos
have έχω *e*·kho
he αυτός ⓜ af·*tos*
head κεφάλι ⓝ ke·*fa*·li
heart καρδιά ⓕ kar·*dhia*
heat ζέστη ⓕ *ze*·sti
heavy βαρύς va·*ris*
help v βοηθώ vo·i·*tho*
here εδώ e·*dho*
high ψηλός psi·*los*
highway δημόσιος δρόμος ⓜ dhi·*mo*·si·os *dhro*·mos
hike v πεζοπορώ pe·zo·po·*ro*
holiday διακοπές ⓕ dhia·ko·*pes*
homosexual ομοφυλόφιλος ⓜ o·mo·fi·*lo*·fi·los
hospital νοσοκομείο ⓝ no·so·ko·*mi*·o
hot ζεστός ze·*stos*
hotel ξενοδοχείο ⓝ kse·no·dho·*hi*·o
hungry πεινασμένος pi·naz·*me*·nos
husband σύζυγος ⓜ *si*·zi·ghos

I

I εγώ e·*gho*
identification (card) ταυτότητα ⓕ taf·*to*·ti·ta
ill άρρωστος *a*·ro·stos
important σπουδαίος spu·*dhe*·os
included συμπεριλαμβανομένου
si·be·ri·lam·va·no·*me*·nu
injury πληγή ⓕ pli·*yi*
insurance ασφάλεια ⓕ as·*fa*·li·a
Internet διαδίκτυο ⓝ dhi·a·*dhik*·ti·o
interpreter διερμηνέας ⓜ&ⓕ dhi·er·mi·*ne*·as

J

jewellery κοσμήματα ⓝ pl koz·*mi*·ma·ta
job δουλειά ⓕ dhu·*lia*

K

key κλειδί ⓝ kli·*dhi*
kilogram χιλιόγραμμο ⓝ hi·*lio*·gra·mo
kitchen κουζίνα ⓕ ku·*zi*·na
knife μαχαίρι ⓝ ma·*he*·ri

L

laundry (place) πλυντήριο ⓝ pli·*di*·ri·o
lawyer δικηγόρος ⓜ&ⓕ dhi·ki·*gho*·ros
left (direction) αριστερός ⓜ a·ri·ste·*ros*
left-luggage office γραφείο φύλαξη αποσκευών ⓝ
gra·*fi*·o *fi*·lak·si a·po·ske·*von*
leg πόδι ⓝ *po*·dhi
lesbian λεσβία ⓕ les·*vi*·a
less λιγότερο li·*gho*·te·ro
letter (mail) γράμμα ⓝ *ghra*·ma
lift (elevator) ασανσέρ ⓝ a·san·*ser*
light φως ⓝ fos
like v μου αρέσει mu a·*re*·si
lock κλειδαριά ⓕ kli·dha·*ria*
long μακρύς ma·*kris*
lost χαμένος kha·*me*·nos
lost-property office γραφείο απωλεσθέντων
αντικειμένων ⓝ gra·*fi*·o a·po·les·*the*·don a·di·ki·*me*·non
love v αγαπώ a·gha·*po*
luggage αποσκευές ⓕ pl a·po·ske·*ves*
lunch μεσημεριανό φαγητό ⓝ me·si·me·ria·*no* fa·yi·*to*

M

mail (letters) αλληλογραφία ⓕ a·li·lo·ghra·*fi*·a
mail (postal system) ταχυδρομείο ⓝ ta·hi·dhro·*mi*·o
man άντρας ⓜ *a*·dras
map χάρτης ⓜ *khar*·tis
market αγορά ⓕ a·gho·*ra*
matches σπίρτα ⓝ pl *spir*·ta
meat κρέας ⓝ *kre*·as
medicine φάρμακο ⓝ *far*·ma·ko
menu μενού ⓝ me·*nu*
message μήνυμα ⓝ *mi*·ni·ma
milk γάλα ⓝ *gha*·la
minute λεπτό ⓝ lep·*to*
mobile phone κινητό ⓝ ki·ni·*to*
money χρήματα ⓝ *khri*·ma·ta
month μήνας ⓜ *mi*·nas
morning πρωί ⓝ pro·*i*
mother μητέρα ⓕ mi·*te*·ra
motorcycle μοτοσυκλέτα ⓕ mo·to·si·*kle*·ta
motorway αυτοκινητόδρομος ⓜ af·to·ki·ni·*to*·dhro·mos
mouth στόμα ⓝ *sto*·ma
music μουσική ⓕ mu·si·*ki*

N

name όνομα ⓝ *o*·no·ma
napkin πετσετάκι ⓝ pet·se·*ta*·ki
nappy πάνα ⓕ *pa*·na

near κοντά ko·*da*
neck λαιμός ⓜ le·*mos*
new νέος *ne*·os
news νέα ⓝ *ne*·a
newspaper εφημερίδα ⓕ e·fi·me·*ri*·dha
night νύχτα ⓕ *nikh*·ta
no όχι *o*·hi
noisy a θορυβώδης tho·ri·*vo*·dhis
nonsmoking μη καπνίζοντες mi kap·*ni*·zo·des
north βοράς ⓜ vo·*ras*
nose μύτη ⓕ *mi*·ti
now τώρα *to*·ra
number αριθμός ⓜ a·rith·*mos*

O

oil (engine) λάδι αυτοκινήτου ⓝ *la*·dhi af·to·ki·*ni*·tu
old παλιός pa·*lios*
one-way ticket απλό εισιτήριο ⓝ a·*plo* i·si·*ti*·ri·o
open a ανοιχτός a·nikh·*tos*
outside έξω *ek*·so

P

package πακέτο ⓝ pa·*ke*·to
paper χαρτί ⓝ khar·*ti*
park (car) v παρκάρω par·*ka*·ro
passport διαβατήριο ⓝ dhia·va·*ti*·ri·o
pay v πληρώνω pli·*ro*·no
pen στυλό ⓝ sti·*lo*
petrol πετρέλαιο ⓝ pe·*tre*·le·o
pharmacy φαρμακείο ⓝ far·ma·*ki*·o
phonecard τηλεκάρτα ⓕ ti·le·*kar*·ta
photo φωτογραφία ⓕ fo·to·gra·*fi*·a
plate πιάτο ⓝ *pia*·to
police αστυνομία ⓕ a·sti·no·*mi*·a
postcard κάρτα ⓕ *kar*·ta
post office ταχυδρομείο ⓝ ta·hi·dhro·*mi*·o
pregnant έγκυος *e*·gi·os
price τιμή ⓕ ti·*mi*

Q

quiet ήσυχος *i*·si·khos

R

rain βροχή vro·*hi*
razor ξυριστική μηχανή ⓕ ksi·ri·sti·*ki* mi·kha·*ni*
receipt απόδειξη ⓕ a·*po*·dhik·si
red κόκκινο *ko*·ki·no
refund n επιστροφή χρημάτων ⓕ e·pi·stro·*fi* khri·*ma*·ton
registered mail συστημένο sis·ti·*me*·no
rent v ενοικιάζω e·ni·ki·*a*·zo
repair v επισκευάζω e·pi·ske·*va*·zo
reservation κράτηση ⓕ *kra*·ti·si
restaurant εστιατόριο ⓝ e·sti·a·*to*·ri·o
return v επιστρέφω e·pi·*stre*·fo
return ticket εισιτήριο μετ' επιστροφής ⓝ i·si·*ti*·ri·o me·te·pis·tro·*fis*
right (direction) δεξιός dhek·si·*os*
road δρόμος ⓜ *dhro*·mos
room δωμάτιο ⓝ dho·*ma*·ti·o

S

safe a ασφαλής as·fa·*lis*
sanitary napkin πετσετάκι υγείας ⓝ pet·se·*ta*·ki i·*yi*·as
seat θέση ⓕ *the*·si
send στέλνω *stel*·no
service station βενζινάδικο ⓝ ven·zi·*na*·dhi·ko
sex σεξ ⓝ seks
shampoo σαμπουάν ⓝ sam·pu·*an*
share (a dorm) μοιράζομαι mi·*ra*·zo·me
shaving cream κρέμα ξυρίσματος ⓕ *kre*·ma ksi·*riz*·ma·tos
she αυτή af·*ti*
sheet (bed) σεντόνι ⓝ se·*do*·ni
shirt πουκάμισο ⓝ pu·*ka*·mi·so
shoes παπούτσια ⓝ pl pa·*put*·si·a
shop μαγαζί ⓝ ma·gha·*zi*
short κοντός ko·*dos*
shower ντους ⓝ duz
single room μονό δωμάτιο ⓝ mo·*no* dho·*ma*·tio
skin δέρμα ⓝ *dher*·ma
skirt φούστα ⓕ *fu*·sta
sleep v κοιμάμαι ki·*ma*·me
slowly αργά ar·*gha*
small μικρός mi·*kros*
smoke (cigarettes) v καπνίζω kap·*ni*·zo
soap σαπούνι ⓝ sa·*pu*·ni
some μερικοί me·ri·*ki*
soon σύντομα *si*·do·ma
south νότος ⓜ *no*·tos
souvenir shop κατάστημα για σουβενίρ ⓝ ka·*ta*·sti·ma yia su·ve·*nir*
speak μιλάω mi·*la*·o
spoon κουτάλι ⓝ ku·*ta*·li
stamp γραμματόσημο ⓝ ghra·ma·*to*·si·mo

O

english–greek

stand-by ticket εισιτήριο σταντ μπάι ⓝ i·si·*ti*·ri·o stand *ba*·i
station (train) σταθμός ⓜ stath·*mos*
stomach στομάχι ⓝ sto·*ma*·hi
stop v σταματάω sta·ma·*ta*·o
stop (bus) στάση ⓕ *sta*·si
street οδός ⓕ o·*dhos*
student σπουδαστής/σπουδάστρια ⓜ/ⓕ spu·dha·*stis*/spu·*dha*·stri·a
sun ήλιος ⓜ *i*·li·os
sunscreen αντιηλιακό ⓝ a·di·i·li·a·*ko*
swim v κολυμπώ ko·li·*bo*

T

tampon ταμπόν ⓝ ta·*bon*
taxi ταξί ⓝ tak·*si*
teaspoon κουτάλι τσαγιού ⓝ ku·*ta*·li tsa·*yiu*
teeth δόντια ⓝ *dho*·dia
telephone τηλέφωνο ⓝ ti·*le*·fo·no
television τηλεόραση ⓕ ti·le·*o*·ra·si
temperature (weather) θερμοκρασία ⓕ ther·mo·kra·*si*·a
tent τέντα ⓕ *te*·da
that (one) εκείνο e·*ki*·no
they αυτοί af·*ti*
thirsty διψασμένος dhip·saz·*me*·nos
this (one) αυτός ⓜ af·*tos*
throat λαιμός ⓜ le·*mos*
ticket εισιτήριο ⓝ i·si·*ti*·ri·o
time ώρα ⓕ *o*·ra
tired κουρασμένος ku·raz·*me*·nos
tissues χαρτομάντηλα ⓝ pl khar·to·*ma*·di·la
today σήμερα *si*·me·ra
toilet τουαλέτα ⓕ tu·a·*le*·ta
tomorrow αύριο *av*·ri·o
tonight απόψε a·*pop*·se
toothbrush οδοντόβουρτσα ⓕ o·dho·*do*·vur·tsa
toothpaste οδοντόπαστα ⓕ o·dho·*do*·pa·sta
torch (flashlight) φακός ⓜ fa·*kos*
tour περιήγηση ⓕ pe·ri·*i*·yi·si
tourist office τουριστικό γραφείο ⓝ tu·ri·sti·*ko* ghra·*fi*·o
towel πετσέτα ⓕ pet·*se*·ta
train τρένο ⓝ *tre*·no
translate v μεταφράζω me·ta·*fra*·zo
travel agency ταξιδιωτικό γραφείο ⓝ tak·si·dhi·o·ti·*ko* ghra·*fi*·o
travellers cheque ταξιδιωτική επιταγή ⓕ tak·si·dhi·o·ti·*ki* e·pi·ta·*yi*
trousers παντελόνι ⓝ pa·de·*lo*·ni
twin beds δίκλινο δωμάτιο ⓝ *dhi*·kli·no dho·*ma*·ti·o
tyre λάστιχο ⓝ *la*·sti·kho

U

underwear εσώρουχα ⓝ pl e·*so*·ru·kha
urgent επείγον e·*pi*·ghon

V

vacant ελεύθερος e·*lef*·the·ros
vacation διακοπές ⓕ dhia·ko·*pes*
vegetable λαχανικά ⓝ pl la·kha·ni·*ka*
vegetarian n χορτοφάγος ⓜ&ⓕ khor·to·*fa*·ghos
visa βίζα ⓕ *vi*·za

W

waiter γκαρσόν ⓝ gar·*son*
walk v περπατάω per·pa·*ta*·o
wallet πορτοφόλι ⓝ por·to·*fo*·li
warm a ζεστός ze·*stos*
wash (something) v πλένω *ple*·no
watch ρολόι ⓝ ro·*lo*·i
water νερό ⓝ ne·*ro*
we εμείς e·*mis*
weekend Σαββατοκύριακο ⓝ sa·va·to·*ki*·ria·ko
west δύση ⓕ *dhi*·si
wheelchair αναπηρική καρέκλα ⓕ a·na·pi·ri·*ki* ka·*re*·kla
when όταν *o*·tan
where πού pu
white άσπρος *as*·pros
who ποιος pios
why γιατί yia·*ti*
wife σύζυγος ⓕ *si*·zi·ghos
window παράθυρο ⓝ pa·*ra*·thi·ro
wine κρασί ⓝ kra·*si*
with με me
without χωρίς kho·*ris*
woman γυναίκα ⓕ yi·*ne*·ka
write v γράφω *ghra*·fo

Y

yellow a κίτρινος *ki*·tri·nos
yes ναι ne
yesterday χτες khtes
you sg inf εσύ e·*si*
you sg pol & pl εσείς e·*sis*

Italian

italian alphabet				
Aa a	*Bb* bee	*Cc* chee	*Dd* dee	*Ee* e
Ff *e*·fe	*Gg* jee	*Hh* *a*·ka	*Ii* ee	*Ll* *e*·le
Mm *e*·me	*Nn* *e*·ne	*Oo* o	*Pp* pee	*Qq* koo
Rr *e*·re	*Ss* *e*·se	*Tt* tee	*Uu* oo	*Vv* voo
Zz *tse*·ta				

italian

introduction

All you need for *la dolce vita* is to be able to tell your *Moschino* from your *macchiato* and your *Fellini* from your *fettuccine*. Happily, you'll find Italian (*italiano* ee·ta·*lya*·no) an easy language to start speaking as well as a beautiful one to listen to. When even a simple sentence sounds like an aria it can be difficult to resist striking up a conversation – and thanks to widespread migration and the huge popularity of Italian culture and cuisine, you're probably familiar with words like *ciao*, *pasta* and *bella* already.

There are also many similarities between Italian and English which smooth the way for language learners. Italian is a Romance language – a descendent of Latin, the language of the Romans (as are French, Spanish, Portuguese and Romanian), and English has been heavily influenced by Latin, particularly via contact with French.

Up until the 19th century, Italy was a collection of autonomous states, rather than a nation-state. As a result, Italian has many regional dialects, including Sardinian and Sicilian. Some dialects are so different from standard Italian as to be considered distinct languages in their own right. It wasn't until the 19th century that the Tuscan dialect – the language of Dante, Boccaccio and Petrarch – became the standard language of the nation, and the official language of schools, media and administration. 'Standard Italian' is the variety that will take you from the top of the boot to the very toe – all the language in this phrasebook is in standard Italian.

The majority of the approximately 65 million people who speak Italian live, of course, in Italy. However, the language also has official status in San Marino, Vatican City, parts of Switzerland, Slovenia and the Istrian peninsula of Croatia. Italian was the official language of Malta during the period of the Knights of St John (1530–1798) and afterwards shared that status with English during the British rule. Only in 1934 was Italian withdrawn and substituted with the native Maltese language. Today, Maltese people are generally fluent in Italian. It might surprise you to learn that Italian is also spoken in the African nation of Eritrea, which was a colony of Italy from 1880 until 1941. Most Eritreans nowadays speak Italian only as a second language. Italian is widely used in Albania, Monaco and France, and spoken by large communities of immigrants worldwide. This chapter is designed to help you on your adventures in the Italian-speaking world – so, as the Italians would say, *In bocca al lupo!* een *bo*·ka·*loo*·po (lit: in the mouth of the wolf) – good luck!

pronunciation

vowel sounds

Italian vowel sounds are generally shorter than those in English. They also tend not to run together to form vowel sound combinations (diphthongs), though it can often sound as if they do to English speakers.

symbol	english equivalent	italian example	transliteration
a	father	*pane*	*pa*·ne
ai	aisle	*mai*	mai
ay	say	*vorrei*	vo·*ray*
e	bet	*letto*	*le*·to
ee	see	*vino*	*vee*·no
o	pot	*molo*	*mo*·lo
oo	zoo	*frutta*	*froo*·ta
oy	toy	*poi*	poy
ow	how	*ciao, autobus*	chow, *ow*·to·boos

word stress

In Italian, you generally emphasise the second-last syllable of a word. When a written word has an accent marked on a vowel, though, the stress is on that syllable. The stressed syllable is always italicised in our pronunciation guides. The characteristic sing-song quality of an Italian sentence is created by pronouncing the syllables evenly and rhythmically, then swinging down on the last word.

consonant sounds

In addition to the sounds described on the next page, Italian consonants can also have a stronger, more emphatic pronunciation. The actual sounds are basically the same, though meaning can be altered between a normal consonant sound and this double consonant sound. The phonetic guides in this book don't distinguish between the two forms. Refer to the written Italian beside each phonetic guide as the cue –

if the word is written with a double consonant, use the stronger form. Even if you never distinguish them, you'll always be understood in context. Here are some examples where this 'double consonant' effect can make a difference:

sonno	*son*·no	**sleep**	*sono*	*so*·no	**I am**
pappa	*pap*·pa	**baby food**	*papa*	*pa*·pa	**pope**

symbol	english equivalent	italian example	transliteration
b	bed	*bello*	*be*·lo
ch	cheat	*centro*	*chen*·tro
d	dog	*denaro*	de·*na*·ro
dz	adds	*mezzo, zaino*	*me*·dzo, *dzai*·no
f	fat	*fare*	*fa*·re
g	go	*gomma*	*go*·ma
j	joke	*cugino*	ku·*jee*·no
k	kit	*cambio, quanto*	*kam*·byo, *kwan*·to
l	lot	*linea*	*lee*·ne·a
ly	million	*figlia*	*fee*·lya
m	man	*madre*	*ma*·dre
n	not	*numero*	*noo*·me·ro
ny	canyon	*bagno*	*ba*·nyo
p	pet	*pronto*	*pron*·to
r	red (stronger and rolled)	*ristorante*	ree·sto·*ran*·te
s	sun	*sera*	*se*·ra
sh	shot	*sciare*	*shya*·re
t	top	*teatro*	te·*a*·tro
ts	hits	*grazie, sicurezza*	*gra*·tsye, see·koo·*re*·tsa
v	very	*viaggio*	*vya*·jo
w	win	*uomo*	*wo*·mo
y	yes	*italiano*	ee·ta·*lya*·no
z	zero	*casa*	*ka*·za

language difficulties

Do you speak English?
Parla inglese? — *par*·la een·*gle*·ze

Do you understand?
Capisce? — ka·*pee*·she

I (don't) understand.
(Non) capisco. — (non) ka·*pee*·sko

What does (*giorno*) mean?
Che cosa vuol dire (giorno)? — ke *ko*·za vwol *dee*·re (*jor*·no)

How do you . . .?	*Come si . . .?*	*ko*·me see . . .
pronounce this	*pronuncia questo*	pro·*noon*·cha *kwe*·sto
write (*arrivederci*)	*scrive (arrivederci)*	*skree*·ve (a·ree·ve·*der*·chee)

Could you please . . .?	*Può . . . per favore?*	pwo . . . per fa·*vo*·re
repeat that	*ripeterlo*	ree·*pe*·ter·lo
speak more slowly	*parlare più lentamente*	par·*la*·re pyoo len·ta·*men*·te
write it down	*scriverlo*	*skree*·ver·lo

essentials

Yes.	*Sì.*	see
No.	*No.*	no
Please.	*Per favore.*	per fa·*vo*·re
Thank you (very much).	*Grazie (mille).*	*gra*·tsye (*mee*·le)
You're welcome.	*Prego.*	*pre*·go
Excuse me.	*Mi scusi.* pol	mee *skoo*·zee
	Scusami. inf	*skoo*·za·mee
Sorry.	*Mi dispiace.*	mee dees·*pya*·che

numbers

0	*zero*	*dze*·ro	16	*sedici*	*se*·dee·chee
1	*uno*	*oo*·no	17	*diciassette*	dee·cha·*se*·te
2	*due*	*doo*·e	18	*diciotto*	dee·*cho*·to
3	*tre*	tre	19	*diciannove*	dee·cha·*no*·ve
4	*quattro*	*kwa*·tro	20	*venti*	*ven*·tee
5	*cinque*	*cheen*·kwe	21	*ventuno*	ven·*too*·no
6	*sei*	say	22	*ventidue*	ven·tee·*doo*·e
7	*sette*	*se*·te	30	*trenta*	*tren*·ta
8	*otto*	*o*·to	40	*quaranta*	kwa·*ran*·ta
9	*nove*	*no*·ve	50	*cinquanta*	cheen·*kwan*·ta
10	*dieci*	*dye*·chee	60	*sessanta*	se·*san*·ta
11	*undici*	*oon*·dee·chee	70	*settanta*	se·*tan*·ta
12	*dodici*	*do*·dee·chee	80	*ottanta*	o·*tan*·ta
13	*tredici*	*tre*·dee·chee	90	*novanta*	no·*van*·ta
14	*quattordici*	kwa·*tor*·dee·chee	100	*cento*	*chen*·to
15	*quindici*	*kween*·dee·chee	1000	*mille*	*mee*·le

time & dates

What time is it?	*Che ora è?*	ke *o*·ra e
It's one o'clock.	*È l'una.*	e *loo*·na
It's (two) o'clock.	*Sono le (due).*	*so*·no le (*doo*·e)
Quarter past (one).	*(L'una) e un quarto.*	(*loo*·na) e oon *kwar*·to
Half past (one).	*(L'una) e mezza.*	(*loo*·na) e *me*·dza
Quarter to (eight).	*(Le otto) meno un quarto.*	(le *o*·to) *me*·no oon *kwar*·to
At what time ...?	*A che ora ...?*	a ke *o*·ra ...
At ...	*Alle ...*	*a*·le ...
am	*di mattina*	dee ma·*tee*·na
pm	*di pomeriggio*	dee po·me·*ree*·jo
Monday	*lunedì*	loo·ne·*dee*
Tuesday	*martedì*	mar·te·*dee*
Wednesday	*mercoledì*	mer·ko·le·*dee*
Thursday	*giovedì*	jo·ve·*dee*
Friday	*venerdì*	ve·ner·*dee*
Saturday	*sabato*	*sa*·ba·to
Sunday	*domenica*	do·*me*·nee·ka

January	*gennaio*	je·*na*·yo
February	*febbraio*	fe·*bra*·yo
March	*marzo*	*mar*·tso
April	*aprile*	a·*pree*·le
May	*maggio*	*ma*·jo
June	*giugno*	*joo*·nyo
July	*luglio*	*loo*·lyo
August	*agosto*	a·*gos*·to
September	*settembre*	se·*tem*·bre
October	*ottobre*	o·*to*·bre
November	*novembre*	no·*vem*·bre
December	*dicembre*	dee·*chem*·bre

What date is it today?
Che giorno è oggi? — ke *jor*·no e *o*·jee

It's (15 December).
È (il quindici) dicembre. — e (eel *kween*·dee·chee) dee·*chem*·bre

since (May)	*da (maggio)*	da (*ma*·jo)
until (June)	*fino a (giugno)*	*fee*·no a (*joo*·nyo)
yesterday	*ieri*	*ye*·ree
today	*oggi*	*o*·jee
tonight	*stasera*	sta·*se*·ra
tomorrow	*domani*	do·*ma*·nee
last …		
night	*ieri notte*	*ye*·ree *no*·te
week	*la settimana scorsa*	la se·tee·*ma*·na *skor*·sa
month	*il mese scorso*	eel *me*·ze *skor*·so
year	*l'anno scorso*	*la*·no *skor*·so
next …		
week	*la settimana prossima*	la se·tee·*ma*·na *pro*·see·ma
month	*il mese prossimo*	eel *me*·ze *pro*·see·mo
year	*l'anno prossimo*	*la*·no *pro*·see·mo
yesterday/tomorrow …	*ieri/domani …*	*ye*·ree/do·*ma*·nee …
morning	*mattina*	ma·*tee*·na
afternoon	*pomeriggio*	po·me·*ree*·jo
evening	*sera*	*se*·ra

weather

What's the weather like?	*Che tempo fa?*	ke *tem*·po fa
It's ...		
cloudy	*È nuvoloso.*	e noo·vo·*lo*·zo
cold	*Fa freddo.*	fa *fre*·do
hot	*Fa caldo.*	fa *kal*·do
raining	*Piove.*	*pyo*·ve
snowing	*Nevica.*	ne·*vee*·ka
sunny	*È soleggiato.*	e so·le·*ja*·to
warm	*Fa bel tempo.*	fa bel *tem*·po
windy	*Tira vento.*	*tee*·ra *ven*·to
spring	*primavera* f	pree·ma·*ve*·ra
summer	*estate* f	es·*ta*·te
autumn	*autunno* m	ow·*too*·no
winter	*inverno* m	een·*ver*·no

border crossing

I'm here ...	*Sono qui ...*	*so*·no kwee ...
in transit	*in transito*	een *tran*·see·to
on business	*per affari*	per a·*fa*·ree
on holiday	*in vacanza*	een va·*kan*·tsa
I'm here for ...	*Sono qui per ...*	*so*·no kwee per ...
(10) days	*(dieci) giorni*	(*dye*·chee) *jor*·nee
(three) weeks	*(tre) settimane*	(tre) se·tee·*ma*·ne
(two) months	*(due) mesi*	(*doo*·e) *me*·zee

I'm going to (Perugia).
Vado a (Perugia). — *va*·do a (pe·*roo*·ja)

I'm staying at the (Minerva Hotel).
Alloggio al (Minerva). — a·*lo*·jo al (mee·*ner*·va)

I have nothing to declare.
Non ho niente da dichiarare. — non o *nyen*·te da dee·kya·*ra*·re

I have something to declare.
Ho delle cose da dichiarare. — o *de*·le *ko*·ze da dee·kya·*ra*·re

That's (not) mine.
(Non) è mio/mia. m/f — (non) e *mee*·o/*mee*·a

transport

tickets & luggage

Where can I buy a ticket?
Dove posso comprare un biglietto? — do·ve *po*·so kom·*pra*·re oon bee·*lye*·to

Do I need to book a seat?
Bisogna prenotare un posto? — bee·*zo*·nya pre·no·*ta*·re oon *pos*·to

One … ticket (to Rome), please.	*Un biglietto … (per Roma), per favore.*	oon bee·*lye*·to … (per *ro*·ma) per fa·*vo*·re
one-way	*di sola andata*	dee *so*·la an·*da*·ta
return	*di andata e ritorno*	dee an·*da*·ta e ree·*tor*·no
I'd like to … my ticket, please.	*Vorrei … il mio biglietto, per favore.*	vo·*ray* … eel *mee*·o bee·*lye*·to per fa·*vo*·re
cancel	*cancellare*	kan·che·*la*·re
change	*cambiare*	kam·*bya*·re
collect	*ritirare*	ree·tee·*ra*·re
confirm	*confermare*	kon·fer·*ma*·re
I'd like a … seat, please.	*Vorrei un posto …, per favore.*	vo·*ray* oon *pos*·to … per fa·*vo*·re
nonsmoking	*per non fumatori*	per non foo·ma·*to*·ree
smoking	*per fumatori*	per foo·ma·*to*·ree

How much is it?
Quant'è? — kwan·*te*

Is there air conditioning?
C'è l'aria condizionata? — che *la*·rya kon·dee·tsyo·*na*·ta

Is there a toilet?
C'è un gabinetto? — che oon ga·bee·*ne*·to

How long does the trip take?
Quanto ci vuole? — *kwan*·to chee *vwo*·le

Is it a direct route?
È un itinerario diretto? — e oo·nee·tee·ne·*ra*·ryo dee·*re*·to

I'd like a luggage locker.
Vorrei un armadietto per il bagaglio. — vo·*ray* oon ar·ma·*dye*·to per eel ba·*ga*·lyo

My luggage has been …	*Il mio bagaglio è stato …*	eel *mee*·o ba·*ga*·lyo e *sta*·to …
damaged	*danneggiato*	da·ne·*ja*·to
lost	*perso*	*per*·so
stolen	*rubato*	roo·*ba*·to

getting around

Where does flight (004) arrive?
Dove arriva il volo (004)? — do·ve a·*ree*·va eel *vo*·lo (*dze*·ro *dze*·ro *kwa*·tro)

Where does flight (004) depart?
Da dove parte il volo (004)? — da *do*·ve *par*·te eel *vo*·lo (*dze*·ro *dze*·ro *kwa*·tro)

Where's the …?	*Dove sono …?*	*do*·ve *so*·no …
arrivalls hall	*gli arrivi*	lyee a·*ree*·vee
departures hall	*le partenze*	le par·*ten*·dze

Is this the … to (Venice)?	*È questo/questa … per (Venezia)?* m/f	e *kwes*·to/*kwes*·ta … per (ve·*ne*·tsya)
boat	*la nave* f	la *na*·ve
bus	*l'autobus* m	*low*·to·boos
plane	*l'aereo* m	la·*e*·re·o
train	*il treno* m	eel *tre*·no

What time's the … bus?	*A che ora passa … autobus?*	a ke *o*·ra *pa*·sa … *ow*·to·boos
first	*il primo*	eel *pree*·mo
last	*l'ultimo*	*lool*·tee·mo
next	*il prossimo*	eel *pro*·see·mo

At what time does it arrive/leave?
A che ora arriva/parte? — a ke *o*·ra a·*ree*·va/*par*·te

How long will it be delayed?
Di quanto ritarderà? — dee *kwan*·to ree·tar·de·*ra*

What station/stop is this?
Che stazione/fermata è questa? — ke sta·*tsyo*·ne/fer·*ma*·ta e *kwe*·sta

What's the next station/stop?
Qual'è la prossima stazione/fermata? — kwa·*le* la *pro*·see·ma sta·*tsyo*·ne/fer·*ma*·ta

Does it stop at (Milan)?
Si ferma a (Milano)? — see *fer*·ma a (mee·*la*·no)

Please tell me when we get to (Taranto).
Mi dica per favore quando arriviamo a (Taranto). — mee *dee*·ka per fa·*vo*·re *kwan*·do a·ree·*vya*·mo a (ta·*ran*·to)

How long do we stop here?
Per quanto tempo ci fermiamo qui? — per *kwan*·to *tem*·po chee fer·*mya*·mo kwee

Is this seat available?
È libero questo posto? — e *lee*·be·ro *kwe*·sto *pos*·to

That's my seat.
Quel posto è mio. — kwel *pos*·to e *mee*·o

I'd like a taxi ...	*Vorrei un tassì ...*	vo·*ray* oon ta·*see* ...
at (9am)	*alle (nove di mattina)*	*a*·le (*no*·ve dee ma·*tee*·na)
now	*adesso*	a·*de*·so
tomorrow	*domani*	do·*ma*·nee

Is this taxi available?
È libero questo tassì? — e *lee*·be·ro *kwe*·sto ta·*see*

How much is it to ...?
Quant'è per ...? — kwan·*te* per ...

Please put the meter on.
Usi il tassametro, per favore. — *oo*·zee eel ta·sa·*me*·tro per fa·*vo*·re

Please take me to (this address).
Mi porti a (questo indirizzo), per piacere. — mee *por*·tee a (*kwe*·sto een·dee·*ree*·tso) per pya·*che*·re

Please ...	*..., per favore.*	... per fa·*vo*·re
slow down	*Rallenti*	ra·*len*·tee
stop here	*Si fermi qui*	see *fer*·mee kwee
wait here	*Mi aspetti qui*	mee as·*pe*·tee kwee

car, motorbike & bicycle hire

I'd like to hire a/an ...	*Vorrei noleggiare ...*	vo·*ray* no·le·*ja*·re ...
bicycle	*una bicicletta*	*oo*·na bee·chee·*kle*·ta
car	*una macchina*	*oo*·na *ma*·kee·na
motorbike	*una moto*	*oo*·na *mo*·to

with ...	*con ...*	kon ...
a driver	*un'autista*	oo·now·*tee*·sta
air conditioning	*aria condizionata*	*a*·rya kon·dee·tsyo·*na*·ta

How much for ... hire?	*Quanto costa ...?*	*kwan*·to *kos*·ta ...
hourly	*all'ora*	a·*lo*·ra
daily	*al giorno*	al *jor*·no
weekly	*alla settimana*	*a*·la se·tee·*ma*·na

air	*aria* f	*a*·rya
oil	*olio* m	*o*·lyo
petrol	*benzina* f	ben·*dzee*·na
tyres	*gomme* f pl	*go*·me

I need a mechanic.
Ho bisogno di un meccanico. — o bee·*zo*·nyo dee oon me·*ka*·nee·ko

I've run out of petrol.
Ho esaurito la benzina. — o e·zow·*ree*·to la ben·*dzee*·na

I have a flat tyre.
Ho una gomma bucata. — o *oo*·na *go*·ma boo·*ka*·ta

directions

Where's the ...?	*Dov'è ...?*	do·*ve* ...
bank	*la banca*	la *ban*·ka
city centre	*il centro città*	eel *chen*·tro chee·*ta*
hotel	*l'albergo*	lal·*ber*·go
market	*il mercato*	eel mer·*ka*·to
police station	*il posto di polizia*	eel *pos*·to dee po·lee·*tsee*·a
post office	*l'ufficio postale*	loo·*fee*·cho pos·*ta*·le
public toilet	*il gabinetto pubblico*	eel ga·bee·*ne*·to *poo*·blee·ko
tourist office	*l'ufficio del turismo*	loo·*fee*·cho del too·*reez*·mo

Is this the road to (Milan)?
Questa strada porta a (Milano)? — *kwe*·sta *stra*·da *por*·ta a (mee·*la*·no)

Can you show me (on the map)?
Può mostrarmi (sulla pianta)? — pwo mos·*trar*·mee (*soo*·la *pyan*·ta)

What's the address?
Qual'è l'indirizzo? — kwa·*le* leen·dee·*ree*·tso

How far is it?
Quant'è distante? — kwan·*te* dees·*tan*·te

How do I get there?
Come ci si arriva? — *ko*·me chee see a·*ree*·va

Turn …	*Giri …*	*jee*·ree …
at the corner	*all'angolo*	a·*lan*·go·lo
at the traffic lights	*al semaforo*	al se·*ma*·fo·ro
left/right	*a sinistra/destra*	a see·*nee*·stra/*de*·stra
It's …	*È …*	e …
behind …	*dietro …*	*dye*·tro …
far away	*lontano*	lon·*ta*·no
here	*qui*	kwee
in front of …	*davanti a …*	da·*van*·tee a …
left	*a sinistra*	a see·*nee*·stra
near (to …)	*vicino (a …)*	vee·*chee*·no (a …)
next to …	*accanto a …*	a·*kan*·to a …
on the corner	*all'angolo*	a *lan*·go·lo
opposite …	*di fronte a …*	dee *fron*·te a …
right	*a destra*	a *de*·stra
straight ahead	*sempre diritto*	*sem*·pre dee·*ree*·to
there	*là*	la
by bus	*con l'autobus*	kon *low*·to·boos
by taxi	*con il tassì*	*ko*·neel ta·*see*
by train	*con il treno*	*ko*·neel *tre*·no
on foot	*a piedi*	a *pye*·dee
north	*nord* m	nord
south	*sud* m	sood
east	*est* m	est
west	*ovest* m	*o*·vest

signs

Entrata/Uscita	en·*tra*·ta/oo·*shee*·ta	**Entrance/Exit**
Aperto/Chiuso	a·*per*·to/*kyoo*·zo	**Open/Closed**
Camere Libere	*ka*·me·re *lee*·be·re	**Rooms Available**
Completo	kom·*ple*·to	**No Vacancies**
Informazioni	een·for·ma·*tsyo*·nee	**Information**
Posto di Polizia	*pos*·to dee po·lee·*tsee*·a	**Police Station**
Proibito	pro·ee·*bee*·to	**Prohibited**
Gabinetti	ga·bee·*ne*·tee	**Toilets**
Uomini	*wo*·mee·nee	**Men**
Donne	*do*·ne	**Women**
Caldo/Freddo	*kal*·do/*fre*·do	**Hot/Cold**

accommodation

finding accommodation

Where's a/an ...?	*Dov'è ...?*	do·*ve* ...
camping ground	*un campeggio*	oon kam·*pe*·jo
guesthouse	*una pensione*	*oo*·na pen·*syo*·ne
inn	*una locanda*	oo·na lo·*kan*·da
hotel	*un albergo*	oo·nal·*ber*·go
youth hostel	*un ostello della gioventù*	oo·nos·*te*·lo *de*·la jo·ven·*too*

Can you recommend somewhere ...?	*Può consigliare qualche posto ...?*	pwo kon·see·*lya*·re *kwal*·ke *pos*·to ...
cheap	*economico*	e·ko·*no*·mee·ko
good	*buono*	*bwo*·no
nearby	*vicino*	vee·*chee*·no

I'd like to book a room, please.
Vorrei prenotare una camera, per favore. — vo·*ray* pre·no·*ta*·re *oo*·na *ka*·me·ra per fa·*vo*·re

I have a reservation.
Ho una prenotazione. — o *oo*·na pre·no·ta·*tsyo*·ne

My name's ...
Mi chiamo ... — mee *kya*·mo ...

Do you have a ... room?	*Avete una camera ...?*	a·*ve*·te *oo*·na *ka*·me·ra ...
single	*singola*	*seen*·go·la
double	*doppia con letto matrimoniale*	do·*pya* kon le·*to* ma·tree·mo·*nya*·le
twin	*doppia a due letti*	*do*·pya a *doo*·e *le*·tee

How much is it per ...?	*Quanto costa per ...?*	*kwan*·to *kos*·ta per ...
night	*una notte*	*oo*·na *no*·te
person	*persona*	per·*so*·na

Can I pay by ...?	*Posso pagare con ...?*	*po*·so pa·*ga*·re kon ...
credit card	*la carta di credito*	la *kar*·ta dee *kre*·dee·to
travellers cheque	*un assegno di viaggio*	oo·na·*se*·nyo dee vee·*a*·jo

I'd like to stay for (two) nights.		
Vorrei rimanere (due) notti.		vo·*ray* ree·ma·*ne*·re (*doo*·e) *no*·tee
From (July 2) to (July 6).		
Dal (due luglio) al (sei luglio).		dal (*doo*·e *loo*·lyo) al (say *loo*·lyo)
Can I see it?		
Posso vederla?		*po*·so ve·*der*·la
Am I allowed to camp here?		
Si può campeggiare qui?		see pwo kam·pe·*ja*·re kwee
Is there a camp site nearby?		
C'è un campeggio qui vicino?		che oon kam·*pe*·jo kwee vee·*chee*·no

requests & queries

When's breakfast served?	
A che ora è la prima colazione?	a ke *o*·ra e la *pree*·ma ko·la·*tsyo*·ne
Where's breakfast served?	
Dove si prende la prima colazione?	*do*·ve see *pren*·de la *pree*·ma ko·la·*tsyo*·ne
Please wake me at (seven).	
Mi svegli alle (sette), per favore.	mee *sve*·lyee *a*·le (*se*·te) per fa·*vo*·re
Could I have my key, please?	
Posso avere la chiave, per favore?	*po*·so a·*ve*·re la *kya*·ve per fa·*vo*·re
Can I get another (blanket)?	
Può darmi un altra (coperta)?	pwo *dar*·mee oo·*nal*·tra (ko·*per*·ta)
This (sheet) isn't clean.	
Questo (lenzuolo) non è pulito.	*kwe*·sto (len·*tzwo*·lo) non e poo·*lee*·to

Is there a/an ...?	*C'è ...?*	che ...
elevator	*un ascensore*	oo·na·shen·*so*·re
safe	*una cassaforte*	*oo*·na ka·sa·*for*·te

The room is too ...	*La camera è troppo ...*	la *ka*·me·ra e *tro*·po ...
expensive	*cara*	*ka*·ra
noisy	*rumorosa*	roo·mo·*ro*·za
small	*piccola*	*pee*·ko·la

The ... doesn't work.	*... non funziona.*	... non foon·*tsyo*·na
air conditioning	*L'aria condizionata*	*la*·rya kon·dee·tsyo·*na*·ta
fan	*Il ventilatore*	eel ven·tee·la·*to*·re
toilet	*Il gabinetto*	eel ga·bee·*ne*·to

checking out

What time is checkout?		
A che ora si deve lasciar libera la camera?		a ke o·*ra* see *de*·ve la·*shar* *lee*·be·ra la *ka*·me·ra
Can I leave my luggage here?		
Posso lasciare ili mio bagaglio qui?		*po*·so la·*sha*·re eel *mee*·o ba·*ga*·lyo kwee

Could I have my ..., please?	*Posso avere ..., per favore?*	*po*·so a·*ve*·re ... per fa·*vo*·re
deposit	*la caparra*	la ka·*pa*·ra
passport	*il mio passaporto*	eel *mee*·o pa·sa·*por*·to
valuables	*i miei oggetti di valore*	ee myay o·*je*·tee dee va·*lo*·re

communications & banking

the internet

Where's the local Internet café?		
Dove si trova l'Internet point?		*do*·ve see *tro*·va *leen*·ter·net poynt
How much is it per hour?		
Quanto costa all'ora?		*kwan*·to *kos*·ta a·*lo*·ra

I'd like to ...	*Vorrei ...*	vo·*ray* ...
check my email	*controllare le mie email*	kon·tro·*la*·re le *mee*·e e·mayl
get Internet access	*usare Internet*	oo·*za*·re *een*·ter·net
use a printer	*usare una stampante*	oo·*za*·re *oo*·na stam·*pan*·te
use a scanner	*scandire*	skan·*dee*·re

mobile/cell phone

I'd like a ...	*Vorrei ...*	vo·*ray* ...
mobile/cell phone for hire	*un cellulare da noleggiare*	oon che·loo·*la*·re da no·le·*ja*·re
SIM card for your network	*un SIM card per la rete telefonica*	oon seem kard per la *re*·te te·le·*fo*·nee·ka
What are the rates?	*Quali sono le tariffe?*	*kwa*·lee *so*·no le ta·*ree*·fe

telephone

What's your phone number?
Qual'è il Suo/tuo numero di telefono? pol/inf — kwa·*le* eel *soo*·o/*too*·o *noo*·me·ro dee te·*le*·fo·no

The number is ...
Il numero è ... — eel *noo*·me·ro e ...

Where's the nearest public phone?
Dov'è il telefono pubblico più vicino? — do·*ve* eel te·*le*·fo·no *poo*·blee·ko pyoo vee·*chee*·no

I'd like to buy a phonecard.
Vorrei comprare una scheda telefonica. — vo·*ray* kom·*pra*·re *oo*·na *ske*·da te·le·*fo*·nee·ka

I want to ...	*Vorrei ...*	vo·*ray* ...
call (Singapore)	*fare una chiamata a (Singapore)*	*fa*·re *oo*·na kya·*ma*·ta a (seen·ga·*po*·re)
make a local call	*fare una chiamata locale*	*fa*·re *oo*·na kya·*ma*·ta lo·*ka*·le
reverse the charges	*fare una chiamata a carico del destinatario*	*fa*·re *oo*·na kya·*ma*·ta a *ka*·ree·ko del des·tee·na·*ta*·ryo

How much does ... cost?	*Quanto costa ...?*	*kwan*·to *kos*·ta ...
a (three)-minute call	*una telefonata di (tre) minuti*	*oo*·na te·le·fo·*na*·ta dee (tre) mee·*noo*·tee
each extra minute	*ogni minuto in più*	*o*·nyee mee·*noo*·to een pyoo

It's (one euro) per (minute).
(Un euro) per (un minuto). — (oon e·*oo*·ro) per (oon mee·*noo*·to)

post office

I want to send a ...	*Vorrei mandare ...*	vo·*ray* man·*da*·re ...
fax	*un fax*	oon faks
letter	*una lettera*	*oo*·na *le*·te·ra
parcel	*un pacchetto*	oon pa·*ke*·to
postcard	*una cartolina*	*oo*·na kar·to·*lee*·na

I want to buy ...	*Vorrei comprare ...*	vo·*ray* kom·*pra*·re ...
an envelope	*una busta*	*oo*·na *boo*·sta
stamps	*dei francobolli*	day fran·ko·*bo*·lee

Please send it (to Australia) by ...	*Lo mandi ... (in Australia), per favore.*	lo *man*·dee ... (een ow·*stra*·lya) per fa·*vo*·re
airmail	*via aerea*	*vee*·a a·*e*·re·a
express mail	*posta prioritaria*	*pos*·ta pryo·ree·*ta*·rya
registered mail	*posta raccomandata*	*pos*·ta ra·ko·man·*da*·ta
surface mail	*posta ordinaria*	*pos*·ta or·dee·*na*·rya
Is there any mail for me?	*C'è posta per me?*	che *pos*·ta per me

bank

Where's a/an ...?	*Dov'è ... più vicino?*	do·*ve* ... pyoo vee·*chee*·no
ATM	*il Bancomat*	eel *ban*·ko·mat
foreign exchange office	*il cambio*	eel *kam*·byo

I'd like to ...	*Vorrei ...*	vo·*ray* ...
Where can I ...?	*Dove posso ...?*	*do*·ve *po*·so ...
arrange a transfer	*trasferire soldi*	tras·fe·*ree*·re *sol*·dee
cash a cheque	*riscuotere un assegno*	ree·*skwo*·te·re oo·na·*se*·nyo
change a travellers cheque	*cambiare un assegno di viaggio*	kam·*bya*·re oo·na·*se*·nyo dee vee·*a*·jo
change money	*cambiare denaro*	kam·*bya*·re de·*na*·ro
get a cash advance	*prelevare con carta di credito*	pre·le·*va*·re kon *kar*·ta dee *kre*·dee·to
withdraw money	*fare un prelievo*	*fa*·re oon pre·*lye*·vo

What's the ...?	*Quant'è ...?*	kwan·*te* ...
commission	*la commissione*	la ko·mee·*syo*·ne
exchange rate	*il cambio*	eel *kam*·byo

It's ...	*È ...*	e ...
(12) euros	*(dodici) euro*	(*do*·dee·chee) e·*oo*·ro
free	*gratuito*	gra·too·*ee*·to

What's the charge for that?
Quanto costa? — *kwan*·to *kos*·ta

What time does the bank open?
A che ora apre la banca? — a ke *o*·ra *a*·pre la *ban*·ka

Has my money arrived yet?
È arrivato il mio denaro? — e a·ree·*va*·to eel *mee*·o de·*na*·ro

sightseeing

getting in

What time does it open/close?
A che ora apre/chiude? — a ke *o*·ra *a*·pre/*kyoo*·de

What's the admission charge?
Quant'è il prezzo d'ingresso? — kwan·*te* eel *pre*·tso deen·*gre*·so

Is there a discount for children/students?
C'è uno sconto per bambini/studenti? — che *oo*·no *skon*·to per bam·*bee*·nee/stoo·*den*·tee

I'd like a ...	*Vorrei ...*	vo·*ray* ...
catalogue	*un catalogo*	oon ka·*ta*·lo·go
guide	*una guida*	*oo*·na *gwee*·da
local map	*una cartina della zona*	*oo*·na kar·*tee*·na *de*·la *dzo*·na

I'd like to see ...	*Vorrei vedere ...*	vo·*ray* ve·*de*·re ...
What's that?	*Cos'è?*	ko·*ze*
Can I take a photo?	*Posso fare una foto?*	*po*·so *fa*·re *oo*·na *fo*·to

tours

When's the next ...?	*A che ora parte la prossima ...?*	a ke *o*·ra *par*·te la *pro*·see·ma ...
day trip	*escursione in giornata*	es·koor·*syo*·ne een jor·*na*·ta
tour	*gita turistica*	*jee*·ta too·*ree*·stee·ka

Is ... included?	*È incluso ...?*	e een·*kloo*·zo ...
accommodation	*l'alloggio*	la·*lo*·jo
the admission charge	*il prezzo d'ingresso*	eel *pre*·tso deen·*gre*·so
food	*il vitto*	eel *vee*·to
transport	*il trasporto*	eel tras·*por*·to

How long is the tour?
Quanto dura la gita? — *kwan*·to *doo*·ra la *jee*·ta

What time should we be back?
A che ora dovremmo ritornare? — a ke *o*·ra dov·*re*·mo ree·tor·*na*·re

sightseeing

castle	*castello* m	kas·*te*·lo
cathedral	*duomo* m	*dwo*·mo
church	*chiesa* f	*kye*·za
main square	*piazza principale* f	*pya*·tsa preen·chee·*pa*·le
monastery	*monastero* m	mo·nas·*te*·ro
monument	*monumento* m	mo·noo·*men*·to
museum	*museo* m	moo·*ze*·o
old city	*centro storico* m	*chen*·tro *sto*·ree·ko
palace	*palazzo* m	pa·*la*·tso
ruins	*rovine* f pl	ro·*vee*·ne
stadium	*stadio* m	*sta*·dyo
statues	*statue* f pl	*sta*·too·e

shopping

enquiries

Where's a ... ?	*Dov'è ... ?*	do·*ve* ...
bank	*la banca*	la *ban*·ka
bookshop	*la libreria*	la lee·bre·*ree*·a
camera shop	*il fotografo*	eel fo·*to*·gra·fo
department store	*il grande magazzino*	eel *gran*·de ma·ga·*dzee*·no
grocery store	*la drogheria*	la dro·ge·*ree*·a
market	*il mercato*	eel mer·*ka*·to
newsagency	*l'edicola*	le·*dee*·ko·la
supermarket	*il supermercato*	eel soo·per·mer·*ka*·to

Where can I buy (a padlock)?
Dove posso comprare (un lucchetto)? — do·ve *po*·so kom·*pra*·re (oon loo·*ke*·to)

I'm looking for ...
Sto cercando ... — sto cher·*kan*·do ...

Can I look at it?
Posso dare un'occhiata? — *po*·so *da*·re oo·no·*kya*·ta

Do you have any others?
Ne avete altri? — ne a·*ve*·te *al*·tree

Does it have a guarantee?
Ha la garanzia? — a la ga·ran·*tsee*·a

Can I have it sent overseas?
Può spedirlo all'estero? — pwo spe·*deer*·lo a·*les*·te·ro

Can I have my ... repaired?
Posso far aggiustare ... qui? — *po*·so far a·joo·*sta*·re ... kwee

It's faulty.
È difettoso. — e dee·fe·*to*·zo

I'd like (a) ..., please.	*Vorrei ..., per favore.*	vo·*ray* ... per fa·*vo*·re
bag	*un sacchetto*	oon sa·*ke*·to
refund	*un rimborso*	oon reem·*bor*·so
to return this	*restituire questo*	res·tee·*twee*·re *kwe*·sto

paying

How much is it?
Quant'è? — kwan·*te*

Can you write down the price?
Può scrivere il prezzo? — pwo *skree*·ve·re eel *pre*·tso

That's too expensive.
È troppo caro. — e *tro*·po *ka*·ro

Can you lower the price?
Può farmi lo sconto? — pwo *far*·mee lo *skon*·to

I'll give you (five) euros.
Le offro (cinque) euro. — le *o*·fro (*cheen*·kwe) e·*oo*·ro

There's a mistake in the bill.
C'è un errore nel conto. — che oon e·*ro*·re nel *kon*·to

Do you accept ...?	*Accettate ...?*	a·che·*ta*·te ...
credit cards	*la carta di credito*	la *kar*·ta dee *kre*·dee·to
debit cards	*la carta di debito*	la *kar*·ta dee *de*·bee·to
travellers cheques	*gli assegni di viaggio*	lyee a·*se*·nyee dee vee·*a*·jo

I'd like . . ., please.	*Vorrei . . ., per favore.*	vo·*ray* . . . per fa·*vo*·re
a receipt	*una ricevuta*	*oo*·na ree·che·*voo*·ta
my change	*il mio resto*	eel *mee*·o *res*·to

clothes & shoes

Can I try it on?	*Potrei provarmelo?*	po·*tray* pro·*var*·me·lo
My size is (40).	*Sono una taglia (quaranta).*	*so*·no *oo*·na *ta*·lya (kwa·*ran*·ta)
It doesn't fit.	*Non va bene.*	non va *be*·ne
small	*piccola*	*pee*·ko·la
medium	*media*	*me*·dya
large	*forte*	*for*·te

books & music

I'd like a . . .	*Vorrei . . .*	vo·*ray* . . .
newspaper (in English)	*un giornale (in inglese)*	oon jor·*na*·le (een een·*gle*·ze)
pen	*una penna*	*oo*·na *pe*·na

Is there an English-language bookshop?
C'è una libreria specializzata in lingua inglese? — che *oo*·na lee·bre·*ree*·a spe·cha·lee·*dza*·ta een *leen*·gwa een·*gle*·ze

I'm looking for something by (Alberto Moravia).
Sto cercando qualcosa di (Alberto Moravia). — sto cher·*kan*·do kwal·*ko*·za dee (al·*ber*·to mo·*ra*·vee·a)

Can I listen to this?
Potrei ascoltarlo? — po·*tray* as·kol·*tar*·lo

photography

Can you . . .?	*Potrebbe . . .?*	po·*tre*·be . . .
burn a CD from my memory card	*masterizzare un CD dalla mia memory card*	mas·te·ree·*tsa*·re oon chee dee *da*·la *mee*·a *me*·mo·ree kard
develop this film	*sviluppare questo rullino*	svee·loo·*pa*·re *kwe*·sto roo·*lee*·no
load my film	*inserire il mio rullino*	een·se·*ree*·re eel *mee*·o roo·*lee*·no

I need a/an … film for this camera.	*Vorrei un rullino … per questa macchina fotografica.*	vo·*ray* oon roo·*lee*·no … per *kwe*·sta *ma*·kee·na fo·to·*gra*·fee·ka
APS	*da APS*	da a·pee·*e*·se
B&W	*in bianco e nero*	een *byan*·ko e *ne*·ro
colour	*a colori*	a *ko*·lo·ree
slide	*per diapositive*	per dee·a·po·zee·*tee*·ve
(200) speed	*da (duecento) ASA*	da (*doo*·e *chen*·to) *a*·za
When will it be ready?	*Quando sarà pronto?*	*kwan*·do sa·*ra* *pron*·to

meeting people

greetings, goodbyes & introductions

Hello.	*Buongiorno.*	bwon·*jor*·no
Hi.	*Ciao.*	chow
Good night.	*Buonanotte.*	bwo·na·*no*·te
Goodbye.	*Arrivederci.*	a·ree·ve·*der*·chee
Bye.	*Ciao.*	chow
See you later.	*A più tardi.*	a pyoo *tar*·dee
Mr	*Signore*	see·*nyo*·re
Mrs	*Signora*	see·*nyo*·ra
Miss	*Signorina*	see·nyo·*ree*·na
How are you?	*Come sta?* **pol**	*ko*·me sta
	Come stai? **inf**	*ko*·me stai
Fine. And you?	*Bene. E Lei?* **pol**	*be*·ne e lay
	Bene. E tu? **inf**	*be*·ne e too
What's your name?	*Come si chiama?* **pol**	*ko*·me see *kya*·ma
	Come ti chiami? **inf**	*ko*·me tee *kya*·mee
My name is …	*Mi chiamo …*	mee *kya*·mo …
I'm pleased to meet you.	*Piacere.*	pya·*che*·re

This is my …	*Le/Ti presento …* pol/inf	le/tee pre·*zen*·to …
boyfriend	*mio ragazzo*	*mee*·o ra·*ga*·tso
brother	*mio fratello*	*mee*·o fra·*te*·lo
daughter	*mia figlia*	*mee*·a *fee*·lya
father	*mio padre*	*mee*·o *pa*·dre
friend	*il mio amico* m	eel *mee*·o a·*mee*·ko
	la mia amica f	la *mee*·a a·*mee*·ka
girlfriend	*mia ragazza*	*mee*·a ra·*ga*·tsa
husband	*mio marito*	*mee*·o ma·*ree*·to
mother	*mia madre*	*mee*·a *ma*·dre
partner (intimate)	*il mio compagno* m	eel *mee*·o kom·*pa*·nyo
	la mia compagna f	la *mee*·a kom·*pa*·nya
sister	*mia sorella*	*mee*·a so·*re*·la
son	*mio figlio*	*mee*·o *fee*·lyo
wife	*mia moglie*	*mee*·a *mo*·lye

Here's my …	*Ecco il mio …*	e·ko eel *mee*·o …
What's your …?	*Qual'è il*	kwa·*le* eel
	Suo/tuo …? pol/inf	*soo*·o/*too*·o …
address	*indirizzo*	een·dee·*ree*·tso
email address	*indirizzo di email*	een·dee·*ree*·tso dee *e*·mayl
fax number	*numero di fax*	*noo*·me·ro dee faks
phone number	*numero di telefono*	*noo*·me·ro dee te·*le*·fo·no

occupations

What's your occupation?	*Che lavoro fa/fai?* pol/inf	ke la·*vo*·ro fa/fai

I'm a/an …	*Sono …*	*so*·no …
artist	*artista* m&f	ar·*tees*·ta
business person	*uomo/donna d'affari* m/f	*wo*·mo/*do*·na da·*fa*·ree
farmer	*agricoltore* m	a·gree·kol·*to*·re
	agricoltrice f	a·gree·kol·*tree*·che
manual worker	*manovale* m&f	ma·no·*va*·le
office worker	*impiegato/a* m/f	eem·pye·*ga*·to/a
scientist	*scienziato/a* m/f	shen·tsee·*a*·to/a
student	*studente* m	stoo·*den*·te
	studentessa f	stoo·den·*te*·sa
tradesperson	*operaio/a* m/f	o·pe·*ra*·yo/a

background

Where are you from?	*Da dove viene/vieni?* **pol/inf**	da *do*·ve *vye*·ne/*vye*·nee
I'm from ...	*Vengo ...*	*ven*·go ...
Australia	*dall'Australia*	dal·ow·*stra*·lya
Canada	*dal Canada*	dal *ka*·na·da
England	*dall'Inghilterra*	da·leen·geel·*te*·ra
New Zealand	*dalla Nuova Zelanda*	*da*·la *nwo*·va ze·*lan*·da
the USA	*dagli Stati Uniti*	*da*·lyee *sta*·tee oo·*nee*·tee
Are you married?	*È sposato/a?* **m/f pol**	e spo·*za*·to/a
	Sei sposato/a? **m/f inf**	say spo·*za*·to/a
I'm married.	*Sono sposato/a.* **m/f**	*so*·no spo·*za*·to/a
I'm single.	*Sono celibe/nubile.* **m/f**	*che*·lee·be/*noo*·bee·le

age

How old ...?	*Quanti anni ...?*	*kwan*·tee *a*·nee ...
are you	*ha/hai* **pol/inf**	a/ai
is your daughter	*ha Sua/tua figlia* **pol/inf**	a *soo*·a/*too*·a *fee*·lya
is your son	*ha Suo/tuo figlio* **pol/inf**	a *soo*·o/*too*·o *fee*·lyo
I'm ... years old.	*Ho ... anni.*	o ... *a*·nee
He/She is ... years old.	*Ha ... anni.*	a ... *a*·nee

feelings

I'm (not) ...	*(Non) Ho ...*	(non) o ...
Are you ...?	*Ha/Hai ...?* **pol/inf**	a/ai ...
cold	*freddo*	*fre*·do
hot	*caldo*	*kal*·do
hungry	*fame*	*fa*·me
thirsty	*sete*	*se*·te
I'm (not) ...	*(Non) Sono ...*	(non) *so*·no ...
Are you ...?	*È/Sei ...?* **pol/inf**	e/say ...
happy	*felice*	fe·*lee*·che
sad	*triste*	*tree*·ste

entertainment

going out

Where can I find ...?	*Dove sono ...?*	*do*·ve *so*·no ...
clubs	*dei clubs*	day kloob
gay venues	*dei locali gay*	day lo·*ka*·lee ge
pubs	*dei pub*	day pab
I feel like going to a/the ...	*Ho voglia d'andare ...*	o *vo*·lya dan·*da*·re ...
concert	*a un concerto*	a oon kon·*cher*·to
movies	*al cinema*	al *chee*·nee·ma
party	*a una festa*	a *oo*·na *fes*·ta
restaurant	*in un ristorante*	een oon rees·to·*ran*·te
theatre	*a teatro*	a te·*a*·tro

interests

Do you like ...?	*Ti piace/piacciono ...?* sg/pl	tee *pya*·che/pya·*cho*·no ...
I (don't) like ...	*(Non) Mi piace/piacciono ...* sg/pl	(non) mee *pya*·che/pya·*cho*·no ...
art	*l'arte* sg	*lar*·te
cooking	*cucinare* sg	koo·chee·*na*·re
movies	*i film* pl	ee feelm
nightclubs	*le discoteche* pl	le dees·ko·*te*·ke
reading	*leggere* sg	*le*·je·re
shopping	*lo shopping* sg	lo *sho*·ping
sport	*lo sport* sg	lo sport
travelling	*viaggiare* sg	vee·a·*ja*·re
Do you like to ...?	*Ti piace ...?*	tee *pya*·che ...
dance	*ballare*	ba·*la*·re
go to concerts	*andare ai concerti*	an·*da*·re ai kon·*cher*·tee
listen to music	*ascoltare la musica*	as·kol·*ta*·re la *moo*·zee·ka

food & drink

finding a place to eat

Can you recommend a ...?	*Potrebbe consigliare un ...?*	po·*tre*·be kon·see·*lya*·re oon ...
bar	*locale*	lo·*ka*·le
café	*bar*	bar
restaurant	*ristorante*	rees·to·*ran*·te
I'd like ..., please.	*Vorrei ..., per favore.*	vo·*ray* ... per fa·*vo*·re
a table for (four)	*un tavolo per (quattro)*	oon *ta*·vo·lo per (*kwa*·tro)
the (non)smoking section	*(non) fumatori*	(non) foo·ma·*to*·ree

ordering food

breakfast	*prima colazione* **f**	*pree*·ma ko·la·*tsyo*·ne
lunch	*pranzo* **m**	*pran*·dzo
dinner	*cena* **f**	*che*·na
snack	*spuntino* **m**	spoon·*tee*·no

What would you recommend?
Cosa mi consiglia? — *ko*·za mee kon·*see*·lya

I'd like (the) ..., please.	*Vorrei ..., per favore.*	vo·*ray* ... per fa·*vo*·re
bill	*il conto*	eel *kon*·to
drink list	*la lista delle bevande*	la *lee*·sta *de*·le be·*van*·de
menu	*il menù*	eel me·*noo*
that dish	*questo piatto*	*kwe*·sto *pya*·to

drinks

(cup of) coffee …	*(un) caffè …*	(oon) ka·*fe* …
(cup of) tea …	*(un) tè …*	(oon) te …
with milk	*con latte*	kon *la*·te
without sugar	*senza zucchero*	*sen*·tsa *tsoo*·ke·ro
orange juice (bottled)	*succo d'arancia* m	*soo*·ko da·*ran*·cha
orange juice (fresh)	*spremuta d'arancia* f	spre·*moo*·ta da·*ran*·cha
soft drink	*bibita* f	*bee*·bee·ta
… water	*acqua …*	*a*·kwa …
boiled	*bollita*	bo·*lee*·ta
mineral	*minerale*	mee·ne·*ra*·le
sparkling mineral	*frizzante*	free·*tsan*·te
still mineral	*naturale*	na·too·*ra*·le

in the bar

I'll have …	*Prendo …*	*pren*·do …
I'll buy you a drink.	*Ti offro da bere.* inf	tee *of*·ro da *be*·re
What would you like?	*Cosa prendi?*	*ko*·za *pren*·dee
Cheers!	*Salute!*	sa·*loo*·te
brandy	*cognac* m	*ko*·nyak
champagne	*champagne* m	sham·*pa*·nye
cocktail	*cocktail* m	*kok*·tayl
a shot of (whisky)	*un sorso di (whisky)*	oon *sor*·so dee (*wee*·skee)
a … of beer	*… di birra*	… dee *bee*·ra
bottle	*una bottiglia*	*oo*·na bo·*tee*·lya
glass	*un bicchiere*	oon bee·*kye*·re
a bottle of …	*una bottiglia di*	*oo*·na bo·*tee*·lya dee
wine	*vino …*	*vee*·no …
a glass of …	*un bicchiere di*	oon bee·*kye*·re dee
wine	*vino …*	*vee*·no …
red	*rosso*	*ro*·so
sparkling	*spumante*	spoo·*man*·te
white	*bianco*	*byan*·ko

self-catering

What's the local speciality?
Qual'è la specialità di questa regione? — kwa·*le* la spe·cha·lee·*ta* dee *kwe*·sta re·*jo*·ne

What's that?
Cos'è? — ko·*ze*

How much is (a kilo of cheese)?
Quanto costa (un chilo di formaggio)? — *kwan*·to *kos*·ta (oon *kee*·lo dee for·*ma*·jo)

I'd like ...	*Vorrei ...*	vo·*ray* ...
100 grams	*un etto*	oo·*ne*·to
(two) kilos	*(due) chili*	(*doo*·e) *kee*·lee
(three) pieces	*(tre) pezzi*	(tre) *pe*·tsee
(six) slices	*(sei) fette*	(say) *fe*·te

Less.	*Meno.*	*me*·no
Enough.	*Basta.*	*bas*·ta
More.	*Più.*	pyoo

special diets & allergies

Is there a vegetarian restaurant near here?
C'è un ristorante vegetariano qui vicino? — che oon rees·to·*ran*·te ve·je·ta·*rya*·no kwee vee·*chee*·no

Do you have vegetarian food?
Avete piatti vegetariani? — a·*ve*·te *pya*·tee ve·je·ta·*rya*·nee

Could you prepare a meal without ...?	*Potreste preparare un pasto senza ...?*	po·*tres*·te pre·pa·*ra*·re oon *pas*·to *sen*·tsa ...
butter	*burro*	*boo*·ro
eggs	*uova*	*wo*·va
meat stock	*brodo di carne*	*bro*·do dee *kar*·ne

I'm allergic to ...	*Sono allergico/a ...* m/f	*so*·no a·*ler*·jee·ko/a ...
dairy produce	*ai latticini*	ai la·tee·*chee*·nee
gluten	*al glutine*	al *gloo*·tee·ne
MSG	*al glutammato monosodico*	al glu·ta·*ma*·to mo·no·*so*·dee·ko
nuts	*alle noci*	*a*·le *no*·chee
seafood	*ai frutti di mare*	ai *froo*·tee dee *ma*·re

menu reader

acciughe f pl	a·*choo*·ge	*anchovies*
arancini m pl	a·ran·*chee*·nee	*rice balls stuffed with a meat mixture*
babà m	ba·*ba*	*dessert containing sultanas*
baccalà m	ba·ka·*la*	*dried salted cod*
bagna cauda f	*ban*·ya *cow*·da	*anchovy, olive oil & garlic dip*
brioche m	bree·*osh*	*breakfast pastry*
bruschetta f	broos·*ke*·ta	*toasted bread with olive oil & toppings*
budino m	boo·*dee*·no	*milk-based pudding*
cacciucco m	ka·*choo*·ko	*seafood stew with wine, garlic & herbs*
cannelloni m pl	ka·ne·*lo*·nee	*pasta stuffed with spinach, minced roast veal, ham, eggs, parmesan & spices*
caponata f	ka·po·*na*·ta	*eggplant with a tomato sauce*
ciabatta f	cha·*ba*·ta	*crisp, flat & long bread*
conchiglie f pl	kon·*kee*·lye	*pasta shells*
costine f pl	kos·*tee*·ne	*ribs*
cozze f pl	*ko*·tse	*mussels*
crostata f	kro·*sta*·ta	*fruit tart*
crostini m pl	kro·*stee*·nee	*bread toasted with savoury toppings*
farinata f	fa·ree·*na*·ta	*thin, flat bread made from chickpea flour*
fettuccine f pl	fe·too·*chee*·ne	*long ribbon-shaped pasta*
focaccia f	fo·*ka*·cha	*flat bread filled or topped with cheese, ham, vegetables & other ingredients*
frittata f	free·*ta*·ta	*thick omelette slice, served hot or cold*
funghi m pl	*foon*·gee	*mushrooms*
gamberoni m pl	gam·be·*ro*·nee	*prawns*
gelato m	je·*la*·to	*ice cream*

gnocchi m pl	*nyo*·kee	*small (usually potato) dumplings*
grappa f	*gra*·pa	*distilled grape must*
involtini m pl	een·vol·*tee*·nee	*stuffed rolls of meat or fish*
linguine f pl	leen·*gwee*·ne	*long thin ribbons of pasta*
lumache f pl	loo·*ma*·ke	*snails*
maccheroni m pl	ma·ke·*ro*·nee	*refers to any tube pasta*
mascarpone m	mas·kar·*po*·ne	*very soft & creamy cheese*
minestrone m	mee·ne·*stro*·ne	*traditional vegetable soup*
ostriche f pl	*os*·tree·ke	*oysters*
pancetta f	pan·*che*·ta	*salt-cured bacon*
panzanella f	pan·tsa·*ne*·la	*tomato, onion, garlic, olive oil, bread & basil salad*
penne f pl	*pe*·ne	*short & tubular pasta*
pesto m	*pes*·to	*paste of garlic, basil, pine nuts & parmesan*
polpette m	pol·*pe*·te	*meatballs*
prosciutto m	pro·*shoo*·to	*any type of thinly sliced ham*
quattro formaggi	*kwa*·tro for·*ma*·jee	*pasta sauce with four different cheeses*
quattro stagioni	*kwa*·tro sta·*jo*·nee	*pizza with different toppings on each quarter*
ragù m	ra·*goo*	*meat sauce (sometimes vegetarian)*
ravioli m pl	ra·vee·*o*·lee	*pasta squares usually stuffed with meat, parmesan cheese & breadcrumbs*
rigatoni m pl	ree·ga·*to*·nee	*short, fat tubes of pasta*
risotto m	ree·*zo*·to	*rice dish cooked in broth*
spaghetti m pl	spa·*ge*·tee	*ubiquitous long thin strands of pasta*
tagliatelle f	ta·lya·*te*·le	*long, ribbon-shaped pasta*
tiramisù m	tee·ra·mee·*soo*	*layered sponge cake soaked in coffee*
tortellini m pl	tor·te·*lee*·nee	*pasta filled with meat, parmesan & egg*
vongole f pl	*von*·go·le	*clams*

emergencies

basics

Help!	*Aiuto!*	ai·*yoo*·to
Stop!	*Fermi!*	*fer*·mee
Go away!	*Vai via!*	vai *vee*·a
Thief!	*Ladro!*	*la*·dro
Fire!	*Al fuoco!*	al *fwo*·ko
Watch out!	*Attenzione!*	a·ten·*tsyo*·ne
Call ...!	*Chiami ...!*	*kya*·mee ...
a doctor	*un medico*	oon *me*·dee·ko
an ambulance	*un'ambulanza*	o·nam·boo·*lan*·tsa
the police	*la polizia*	la po·lee·*tsee*·a

It's an emergency!
È un'emergenza! — e oo·ne·mer·*jen*·tsa

Could you help me, please?
Mi può aiutare, per favore? — mee pwo ai·yoo·*ta*·re per fa·*vo*·re

I have to use the telephone.
Devo fare una telefonata. — *de*·vo *fa*·re *oo*·na te·le·fo·*na*·ta

I'm lost.
Mi sono perso/a. m/f — mee *so*·no *per*·so/a

Where are the toilets?
Dove sono i gabinetti? — *do*·ve *so*·no ee ga·bee·*ne*·tee

police

Where's the police station?
Dov'è il posto di polizia? — do·*ve* eel *pos*·to dee po·lee·*tsee*·a

I want to report an offence.
Voglio fare una denuncia. — *vo*·lyo *fa*·re *oo*·na de·*noon*·cha

I have insurance.
Ho l'assicurazione. — o la·see·koo·ra·*tsyo*·ne

I've been ...	*Sono stato/a ...* m/f	*so*·no *sta*·to/a ...
assaulted	*aggredito/a* m/f	a·gre·*dee*·to/a
raped	*violentato/a* m/f	vyo·len·*ta*·to/a
robbed	*derubato/a* m/f	roo·*ba*·to/a

I've lost my ...	*Ho perso ...*	o *per*·so ...
My ... was/were stolen.	*Mi hanno rubato ...*	mee *a*·no roo·*ba*·to ...
backpack	*il mio zaino*	eel *mee*·o *dzai*·no
bags	*i miei bagagli*	ee mee·*ay* ba·*ga*·lyee
credit card	*la mia carta di credito*	la *mee*·a *kar*·ta dee *kre*·dee·to
handbag	*la mia borsa*	la *mee*·a *bor*·sa
jewellery	*i miei gioielli*	ee mee·*ay* jo·*ye*·lee
money	*i miei soldi*	ee mee·*ay sol*·dee
passport	*il mio passaporte*	eel *mee*·o pa·sa·*por*·te
travellers cheques	*i miei assegni di viaggio*	ee mee·*ay* a·*se*·nyee dee vee·*a*·jo
wallet	*portafoglio*	por·ta·*fo*·lyo

I want to contact my ...	*Vorrei contattare ...*	vo·*ray* kon·ta·*ta*·re ...
consulate	*il mio consolato*	eel *mee*·o kon·so·*la*·to
embassy	*la mia ambasciata*	la *mee*·a am·ba·*sha*·ta

health

medical needs

Where's the nearest ...?	*Dov'è ... più vicino/a?* m/f	do·*ve* ... pyoo vee·*chee*·no/a
dentist	*il dentista* m	eel den·*tee*·sta
doctor	*il medico* m	eel *me*·dee·ko
hospital	*l'ospedale* m	los·pe·*da*·le
(night) pharmacist	*la farmacia (di turno)* f	la far·ma·*chee*·a (dee *toor*·no)

I need a doctor (who speaks English).
Ho bisogno di un medico (che parli inglese). — o bee·*zo*·nyo dee oon *me*·dee·ko (ke *par*·lee een·*gle*·ze)

Could I see a female doctor?
Posso vedere una dottoressa? — *po*·so ve·*de*·re *oo*·na do·to·*re*·sa

I've run out of my medication.
Ho finito la mia medicina. — o fee·*nee*·to la *mee*·a me·dee·*chee*·na

ITALIANO – health

symptoms, conditions & allergies

I'm sick.	*Mi sento male.*	mee *sen*·to *ma*·le
It hurts here.	*Mi fa male qui.*	mee fa *ma*·le kwee
I have (a) ...	*Ho ...*	o ...
asthma	*asma*	*as*·ma
bronchitis	*la bronchite*	la bron·*kee*·te
constipation	*la stitichezza*	la stee·tee·*ke*·tsa
cough	*la tosse*	la *to*·se
diarrhoea	*la diarrea*	la dee·a·*re*·a
fever	*la febbre*	la *fe*·bre
headache	*mal di testa*	mal dee *tes*·ta
heart condition	*un problema cardiaco*	oon pro·*ble*·ma kar·*dee*·a·ko
nausea	*la nausea*	la *now*·ze·a
pain	*un dolore*	oon do·*lo*·re
sore throat	*mal di gola*	mal dee *go*·la
toothache	*mal di denti*	mal dee *den*·tee
I'm allergic to ...	*Sono allergico/a ...* m/f	*so*·no a·*ler*·jee·ko/a ...
antibiotics	*agli antibiotici*	*a*·lyee an·tee·bee·*o*·tee chee
anti-inflammatories	*agli antinfiammatori*	*a*·lyee an·teen·fya·ma·*to*·ree
aspirin	*all'aspirina*	a·las·pee·*ree*·na
bees	*alle api*	*a*·le *a*·pee
codeine	*alla codeina*	*a*·la ko·de·*ee*·na
penicillin	*alla penicillina*	*a*·la pe·nee·chee·*lee*·na
antiseptic	*antisettico* m	an·tee·*se*·tee·ko
bandage	*fascia* f	*fa*·sha
condoms	*preservativi* m pl	pre·zer·va·*tee*·vee
contraceptives	*contraccettivi* m pl	kon·tra·che·*tee*·vee
diarrhoea medicine	*antidissenterico* m	an·tee·dee·sen·*te*·ree·ko
insect repellent	*repellente per gli insetti* m	re·pe·*len*·te per lyee een·*se*·tee
laxatives	*lassativi* m pl	la·sa·*tee*·vee
painkillers	*analgesico* m	a·nal·*je*·zee·ko
rehydration salts	*sali minerali* m pl	*sa*·lee mee·ne·*ra*·lee
sleeping tablets	*sonniferi* m pl	so·*nee*·fe·ree

english–italian dictionary

Italian nouns in this dictionary, and adjectives affected by gender, have their gender indicated by ⓜ (masculine) or ⓕ (feminine). If it's a plural noun, you'll also see pl. Words are also marked as n (noun), a (adjective), v (verb), sg (singular), pl (plural), inf (informal) and pol (polite) where necessary.

A

accident *incidente* ⓜ een·chee·*den*·te
accommodation *alloggio* ⓜ a·*lo*·jo
adaptor *presa multipla* ⓕ *pre*·sa *mool*·tee·pla
address *indirizzo* ⓜ een·dee·*ree*·tso
after *dopo* *do*·po
air-conditioned *ad aria condizionata* ad *a*·rya kon·dee·*tsyo*·na·ta
airplane *aereo* ⓜ a·*e*·re·o
airport *aeroporto* ⓜ a·e·ro·*por*·to
alcohol *alcol* ⓜ *al*·kol
all a *tutto/a* *too*·to/a
allergy *allergia* ⓕ a·ler·*jee*·a
ambulance *ambulanza* ⓕ am·boo·*lan*·tsa
and *e* e
ankle *caviglia* ⓕ ka·*vee*·lya
arm *braccio* ⓜ *bra*·cho
ashtray *portacenere* ⓜ por·ta·*che*·ne·re
ATM *Bancomat* ⓜ *ban*·ko·mat

B

baby *bimbo/a* ⓜ/ⓕ *beem*·bo/a
back (body) *schiena* ⓕ *skye*·na
backpack *zaino* ⓜ *dzai*·no
bad *cattivo/a* ⓜ/ⓕ ka·*tee*·vo/a
bag *borsa* ⓕ *bor*·sa
baggage claim *ritiro bagagli* ⓜ ree·*tee*·ro ba·*ga*·lyee
bank *banca* ⓕ *ban*·ka
bar *locale* ⓜ lo·*ka*·le
bathroom *bagno* ⓜ *ba*·nyo
battery *pila* ⓕ *pee*·la
beautiful *bello/a* ⓜ/ⓕ *be*·lo/a
bed *letto* ⓜ *le*·to
beer *birra* ⓕ *bee*·ra
before *prima* *pree*·ma
behind *dietro* *dye*·tro
bicycle *bicicletta* ⓕ bee·chee·*kle*·ta
big *grande* *gran*·de
bill *conto* ⓜ *kon*·to
black *nero/a* ⓜ/ⓕ *ne*·ro/a
blanket *coperta* ⓕ ko·*per*·ta
blood group *gruppo sanguigno* ⓜ *groo*·po san·*gwee*·nyo
blue *azzurro/a* ⓜ/ⓕ a·*dzoo*·ro/a
boat *barca* ⓕ *bar*·ka
book (make a reservation) v *prenotare* pre·no·*ta*·re
bottle *bottiglia* ⓕ bo·*tee*·lya
bottle opener *apribottiglie* ⓜ a·pree·bo·*tee*·lye
boy *ragazzo* ⓜ ra·*ga*·tso
brakes (car) *freno* ⓜ *fre*·no
breakfast *(prima) colazione* ⓕ (*pree*·ma) ko·la·*tsyo*·ne
broken (faulty) *rotto/a* ⓜ/ⓕ *ro*·to/a
bus *autobus* ⓜ *ow*·to·boos
business *affari* ⓜ pl a·*fa*·ree
buy *comprare* kom·*pra*·re

C

café *bar* ⓜ bar
camera *macchina fotografica* ⓕ *ma*·kee·na fo·to·*gra*·fee·ka
camp site *campeggio* ⓜ kam·*pe*·jo
cancel *cancellare* kan·che·*la*·re
can opener *apriscatole* ⓜ a·pree·*ska*·to·le
car *macchina* ⓕ *ma*·kee·na
cash *soldi* ⓜ pl *sol*·dee
cash (a cheque) v *riscuotere un assegno* ree·*skwo*·te·re oon a·*se*·nyo
cell phone *telefono cellulare* ⓜ te·*le*·fo·no che·loo·*la*·re
centre *centro* ⓜ *chen*·tro
change (money) v *cambiare* kam·*bya*·re
cheap *economico/a* ⓜ/ⓕ e·ko·*no*·mee·ko/a
check (bill) *conto* ⓜ *kon*·to
check-in *registrazione* ⓕ re·jee·stra·*tsyo*·ne
chest *petto* ⓜ *pe*·to
child *bambino/a* ⓜ/ⓕ bam·*bee*·no/a
cigarette *sigaretta* ⓕ see·ga·*re*·ta
city *città* ⓕ chee·*ta*
clean a *pulito/a* ⓜ/ⓕ poo·*lee*·to/a
closed *chiuso/a* ⓜ/ⓕ *kyoo*·zo/a
coffee *caffè* ⓜ ka·*fe*
coins *monete* ⓕ pl mo·*ne*·te

cold a *freddo/a* ⓜ/ⓕ *fre*·do/a
collect call *chiamata a carico del destinatario* ⓕ kya·*ma*·ta a *ka*·ree·ko del des·tee·na·*ta*·ryo
come *venire* ve·*nee*·re
computer *computer* ⓜ kom·*pyoo*·ter
condom *preservativo* ⓜ pre·zer·va·*tee*·vo
contact lenses *lenti a contatto* ⓕ pl *len*·tee a kon·*ta*·to
cook v *cucinare* koo·chee·*na*·re
cost *prezzo* ⓜ *pre*·tso
credit card *carta di credito* ⓕ *kar*·ta dee *kre*·dee·to
cup *tazza* ⓕ *ta*·tsa
currency exchange *cambio valuta* ⓜ *kam*·byo va·*loo*·ta
customs (immigration) *dogana* ⓕ do·*ga*·na

D

dangerous *pericoloso/a* ⓜ/ⓕ pe·ree·ko·*lo*·zo/a
date (time) *data* ⓕ *da*·ta
day *giorno* ⓜ *jor*·no
delay *ritardo* ⓜ ree·*tar*·do
dentist *dentista* ⓜ/ⓕ den·*tee*·sta
depart *partire* par·*tee*·re
diaper *pannolino* ⓜ pa·no·*lee*·no
dictionary *vocabolario* ⓜ vo·ka·bo·*la*·ryo
dinner *cena* ⓕ *che*·na
direct *diretto/a* ⓜ/ⓕ dee·*re*·to/a
dirty *sporco/a* ⓜ/ⓕ *spor*·ko/a
disabled *disabile* dee·*za*·bee·le
discount *sconto* ⓜ *skon*·to
doctor *medico* ⓜ *me*·dee·ko
double bed *letto matrimoniale* ⓜ *le*·to ma·tree·mo·*nya*·le
double room *camera doppia* ⓕ *ka*·me·ra *do*·pya
drink *bevanda* ⓕ be·*van*·da
drive v *guidare* gwee·*da*·re
drivers licence *patente di guida* ⓕ pa·*ten*·te dee *gwee*·da
drugs (illicit) *droga* ⓕ *dro*·ga
dummy (pacifier) *ciucciotto* ⓜ choo·*cho*·to

E

ear *orecchio* ⓜ o·*re*·kyo
east *est* ⓜ est
eat *mangiare* man·*ja*·re
economy class *classe turistica* ⓕ *kla*·se too·*ree*·stee·ka
electricity *elettricità* ⓕ e·le·tree·chee·*ta*
elevator *ascensore* ⓜ a·shen·*so*·re
email *email* ⓜ *e*·mayl
embassy *ambasciata* ⓕ am·ba·*sha*·ta
emergency *emergenza* ⓕ e·mer·*jen*·tsa
English (language) *inglese* een·*gle*·ze
entrance *entrata* ⓕ en·*tra*·ta
evening *sera* ⓕ *se*·ra
exchange rate *tasso di cambio* ⓜ *ta*·so dee *kam*·byo
exit *uscita* ⓕ *ta*·so dee *kam*·byo
expensive *caro/a* ⓜ/ⓕ *ka*·ro/a
express mail *posta prioritaria* ⓕ *pos*·ta pree·o·ree·*ta*·rya
eye *occhio* ⓜ *o*·kyo

F

far *lontano/a* ⓜ/ⓕ lon·*ta*·no/a
fast *veloce* ve·*lo*·che
father *padre* ⓜ *pa*·dre
film (camera) *rullino* ⓜ roo·*lee*·no
finger *dito* ⓜ *dee*·to
first-aid kit *valigetta del pronto soccorso* ⓕ va·lee·*je*·ta del *pron*·to so·*kor*·so
first class *prima classe* ⓕ *pree*·ma *kla*·se
fish n *pesce* ⓜ *pe*·she
food *cibo* ⓜ *chee*·bo
foot *piede* ⓜ *pye*·de
fork *forchetta* ⓕ for·*ke*·ta
free (of charge) *gratuito/a* ⓜ/ⓕ gra·*too*·ee·to/a
friend *amico/a* ⓜ/ⓕ a·*mee*·ko/a
fruit *frutta* ⓕ *froo*·ta
full *pieno/a* ⓜ/ⓕ *pye*·no/a
funny *divertente* dee·ver·*ten*·te

G

gift *regalo* ⓜ re·*ga*·lo
girl *ragazza* ⓕ ra·*ga*·tsa
glass (drinking) *bicchiere* ⓜ bee·*kye*·re
glasses *occhiali* ⓜ pl o·*kya*·lee
go *andare* an·*da*·re
good *buono/a* ⓜ/ⓕ *bwo*·no/a
green *verde* *ver*·de
guide n *guida* ⓕ *gwee*·da

H

half *mezzo* ⓜ *me*·dzo
hand *mano* ⓕ *ma*·no
handbag *borsetta* ⓕ bor·*se*·ta
happy *felice* ⓜ/ⓕ fe·*lee*·che
have *avere* a·*ve*·re
he *lui* *loo*·ee
head *testa* ⓕ *tes*·ta
heart *cuore* ⓜ *kwo*·re
heat n *caldo* ⓜ *kal*·do

heavy *pesante* pe·*zan*·te
help v *aiutare* a·yoo·*ta*·re
here *qui* kwee
high *alto/a* ⓜ/ⓕ *al*·to/a
highway *autostrada* ⓕ *ow*·to·stra·da
hike v *fare un'escursione a piedi*
fa·re oon es·koor·*syo*·ne a *pye*·de
holiday *vacanze* ⓕ pl va·*kan*·tse
homosexual n *omosessuale* ⓜ&ⓕ o·mo·se·*swa*·le
hospital *ospedale* ⓜ os·pe·*da*·le
hot *caldo/a* ⓜ/ⓕ *kal*·do/a
hotel *albergo* ⓜ al·*ber*·go
hungry *affamato/a* ⓜ/ⓕ a·fa·*ma*·to
husband *marito* ⓜ ma·*ree*·to

I

I *io* *ee*·o
identification (card) *carta d'identità* ⓕ
kar·ta dee·den·tee·*ta*
ill *malato/a* ⓜ/ⓕ ma·*la*·to/a
important *importante* eem·por·*tan*·te
included *compreso/a* ⓜ/ⓕ kom·*pre*·zo/a
injury *ferita* ⓕ fe·*ree*·ta
insurance *assicurazione* ⓕ a·see·koo·ra·*tsyo*·ne
Internet *Internet* ⓜ *een*·ter·net
interpreter *interprete* ⓜ/ⓕ een·*ter*·pre·te
Italy *Italia* ⓕ ee·*ta*·lya
Italian (language) *italiano* ⓜ ee·ta·*lya*·no

J

jewellery *gioielli* ⓜ pl jo·*ye*·lee
job *lavoro* ⓜ la·*vo*·ro

K

key *chiave* ⓕ *kya*·ve
kilogram *chilo* ⓜ *kee*·lo
kitchen *cucina* ⓕ koo·*chee*·na
knife *coltello* ⓜ kol·*te*·lo

L

laundry (place) *lavanderia* ⓕ la·van·de·*ree*·a
lawyer *avvocato/a* ⓜ/ⓕ a·vo·*ka*·to/a
left (direction) *sinistra* see·*nee*·stra
left-luggage office *deposito bagagli* ⓜ
de·*po*·zee·to ba·*ga*·lyee
leg *gamba* ⓕ *gam*·ba
lesbian n *lesbica* ⓕ *lez*·bee·ka
less *(di) meno* (dee) *me*·no
letter (mail) *lettera* ⓕ *le*·te·ra
lift (elevator) *ascensore* ⓜ a·shen·*so*·re
light *luce* ⓕ *loo*·che
like v *piacere* pya·*che*·re
lock *serratura* ⓕ se·ra·*too*·ra
long *lungo/a* ⓜ/ⓕ *loon*·go/a
lost *perso/a* ⓜ/ⓕ *per*·so/a
lost-property office *ufficio oggetti smarriti* ⓜ
oo·*fee*·cho o·*je*·tee sma·*ree*·tee
love v *amare* a·*ma*·re
luggage *bagaglio* ⓜ ba·*ga*·lyo
lunch *pranzo* ⓜ *pran*·dzo

M

mail *posta* ⓕ *pos*·ta
man *uomo* ⓜ *wo*·mo
map *pianta* ⓕ *pyan*·ta
market *mercato* ⓜ mer·*ka*·to
matches *fiammiferi* ⓜ pl fya·*mee*·fe·ree
meat *carne* ⓕ *kar*·ne
medicine *medicina* ⓕ me·dee·*chee*·na
menu *menu* ⓜ me·*noo*
message *messaggio* ⓜ me·*sa*·jo
milk *latte* ⓜ *la*·te
minute *minuto* ⓜ mee·*noo*·to
mobile phone *telefono cellulare* ⓜ te·*le*·fo·no che·loo·*la*·re
money *denaro* ⓜ de·*na*·ro
month *mese* ⓜ *me*·ze
morning *mattina* ⓕ ma·*tee*·na
mother *madre* ⓕ *ma*·dre
motorcycle *moto* ⓕ *mo*·to
motorway *autostrada* ⓕ *ow*·to·stra·da
mouth *bocca* ⓕ *bo*·ka
music *musica* ⓕ *moo*·zee·ka

N

name *nome* ⓜ *no*·me
napkin *tovagliolo* ⓜ to·va·*lyo*·lo
nappy *pannolino* ⓜ pa·no·*lee*·no
near *vicino (a)* vee·*chee*·no (a)
neck *collo* ⓜ *ko*·lo
new *nuovo/a* ⓜ/ⓕ *nwo*·vo/a
news *notizie* ⓕ pl no·*tee*·tsye
newspaper *giornale* ⓜ jor·*na*·le
night *notte* ⓕ *no*·te
no *no* no

noisy *rumoroso/a* ⓜ/ⓕ roo·mo·ro·zo/a
nonsmoking *non fumatore* non foo·ma·to·re
north *nord* ⓜ nord
nose *naso* ⓜ na·zo
now *adesso* a·de·so
number *numero* ⓜ noo·me·ro

O

oil (engine) *olio* ⓜ o·lyo
old *vecchio/a* ⓜ/ⓕ ve·kyo/a
one-way ticket *biglietto di solo andata* bee·lye·to dee so·lo an·da·ta
open a *aperto/a* ⓜ/ⓕ a·per·to/a
outside *fuori* fwo·ree

P

package *pacchetto* ⓜ pa·ke·to
paper *carta* ⓕ kar·ta
park (car) v *parcheggiare* par·ke·ja·re
passport *passaporto* ⓜ pa·sa·por·to
pay *pagare* pa·ga·re
pen *penna (a sfera)* ⓕ pe·na (a sfe·ra)
petrol *benzina* ⓕ ben·dzee·na
pharmacy *farmacia* ⓕ far·ma·chee·a
phonecard *scheda telefonica* ⓕ ske·da te·le·fo·nee·ka
photo *foto* ⓕ fo·to
plate *piatto* ⓜ pya·to
police *polizia* ⓕ po·lee·tsee·a
postcard *cartolina* ⓕ kar·to·lee·na
post office *ufficio postale* ⓜ oo·fee·cho pos·ta·le
pregnant *incinta* een·cheen·ta
price *prezzo* ⓜ pre·tso

Q

quiet *tranquillo/a* ⓜ/ⓕ tran·kwee·lo/a

R

rain n *pioggia* ⓕ pyo·ja
razor *rasoio* ⓜ ra·zo·yo
receipt *ricevuta* ⓕ ree·che·voo·ta
red *rosso/a* ⓜ/ⓕ ro·so/a
refund *rimborso* ⓜ reem·bor·so
registered mail *posta raccomandata* ⓕ pos·ta ra·ko·man·da·ta
rent v *prendere in affitto* pren·de·re een a·fee·to
repair v *riparare* ree·pa·ra·re
reservation *prenotazione* ⓕ pre·no·ta·tsyo·ne
restaurant *ristorante* ⓜ rees·to·ran·te
return v *ritornare* ree·tor·na·re
return ticket *biglietto di andata e ritorno* bee·lye·to dee an·da·ta e ree·tor·no
right (direction) *destra* de·stra
road *strada* ⓕ stra·da
room *camera* ⓕ ka·me·ra

S

safe a *sicuro/a* ⓜ/ⓕ see·koo·ro/a
sanitary napkins *assorbenti igienici* ⓜ pl as·or·ben·tee ee·je·nee·chee
seat *posto* ⓜ pos·to
send *mandare* man·da·re
service station *stazione di servizio* ⓕ sta·tsyo·ne dee ser·vee·tsyo
sex *sesso* ⓜ se·so
shampoo *shampoo* ⓜ sham·poo
share (a dorm) *condividere* kon·dee·vee·de·re
shaving cream *crema da barba* ⓕ kre·ma da bar·ba
she *lei* lay
sheet (bed) *lenzuolo* ⓜ len·tswo·lo
shirt *camicia* ⓕ ka·mee·cha
shoes *scarpe* ⓕ pl skar·pe
shop *negozio* ⓜ ne·go·tsyo
short *corto/a* ⓜ/ⓕ kor·to/a
shower *doccia* ⓕ do·cha
single room *camera singola* ⓕ ka·me·ra seen·go·la
skin *pelle* ⓕ pe·le
skirt *gonna* ⓕ go·na
sleep v *dormire* dor·mee·re
slowly *lentamente* len·ta·men·te
small *piccolo/a* ⓜ/ⓕ pee·ko·lo/a
smoke (cigarettes) v *fumare* foo·ma·re
soap *sapone* ⓜ sa·po·ne
some *alcuni/e* ⓜ/ⓕ pl al·koo·nee/al·koo·ne
soon *fra poco* fra po·ko
south *sud* ⓜ sood
souvenir shop *negozio di souvenir* ⓜ ne·go·tsyo dee soo·ve·neer
speak *parlare* par·la·re
spoon *cucchiaio* ⓜ koo·kya·yo
stamp *francobollo* ⓜ fran·ko·bo·lo
stand-by ticket *in lista d'attesa* een lee·sta da·te·za
station (train) *stazione* ⓕ sta·tsyo·ne
stomach *stomaco* ⓜ sto·ma·ko
stop v *fermare* fer·ma·re
stop (bus) *fermata* ⓕ fer·ma·ta

street *strada* ⓕ *stra*·da
student *studente/studentessa* ⓜ/ⓕ stoo·*den*·te/stoo·den·*te*·sa
sun *sole* ⓜ *so*·le
sunscreen *crema solare* ⓕ *kre*·ma so·*la*·re
swim v *nuotare* nwo·*ta*·re
Switzerland *Svizzera* ⓕ svee·*tse*·ra

T

tampons *assorbenti interni* ⓜ pl a·sor·*ben*·tee een·*ter*·nee
taxi *tassì* ⓜ ta·*see*
teaspoon *cucchiaino* ⓜ koo·kya·*ee*·no
teeth *denti* ⓜ pl *den*·tee
telephone *telefono* ⓜ te·*le*·fo·no
television *televisione* ⓕ te·le·vee·*zyo*·ne
temperature (weather) *temperatura* ⓕ tem·pe·ra·*too*·ra
tent *tenda* ⓕ *ten*·da
that (one) *quello/a* ⓜ/ⓕ *kwe*·lo/a
they *loro* *lo*·ro
thirsty *assetato/a* ⓜ/ⓕ a·se·*ta*·to
this (one) *questo/a* ⓜ/ⓕ *kwe*·sto/a
throat *gola* ⓕ *go*·la
ticket *biglietto* ⓜ bee·*lye*·to
time *tempo* ⓜ *tem*·po
tired *stanco/a* ⓜ/ⓕ *stan*·ko/a
tissues *fazzolettini di carta* ⓜ pl fa·tso·le·*tee*·nee dee *kar*·ta
today *oggi* *o*·jee
toilet *gabinetto* ⓜ ga·bee·*ne*·to
tomorrow *domani* do·*ma*·nee
tonight *stasera* sta·*se*·ra
toothbrush *spazzolino da denti* ⓜ spa·tso·*lee*·no da *den*·tee
toothpaste *dentifricio* ⓜ den·tee·*free*·cho
torch (flashlight) *torcia elettrica* ⓕ *tor*·cha e·*le*·tree·ka
tour *gita* ⓕ *jee*·ta
tourist office *ufficio del turismo* ⓜ oo·*fee*·cho del too·*reez*·mo
towel *asciugamano* ⓜ a·shoo·ga·*ma*·no
train *treno* ⓜ *tre*·no
translate *tradurre* tra·*doo*·re
travel agency *agenzia di viaggio* ⓕ a·jen·*tsee*·a dee vee·*a*·jo
travellers cheque *assegno di viaggio* ⓜ a·*se*·nyo dee vee·*a*·jo
trousers *pantaloni* ⓜ pl pan·ta·*lo*·nee
twin beds *due letti* *doo*·e *le*·tee
tyre *gomma* ⓕ *go*·ma

U

underwear *biancheria intima* ⓜ byan·ke·*ree*·a *een*·tee·ma
urgent *urgente* ⓜ/ⓕ oor·*jen*·te

V

vacant *libero/a* ⓜ/ⓕ *lee*·be·ro/a
vacation *vacanza* ⓕ va·*kan*·tsa
vegetable *verdura* ⓕ ver·*doo*·ra
vegetarian a *vegetariano/a* ⓜ/ⓕ ve·je·ta·*rya*·no/a
visa *visto* ⓜ *vee*·sto

W

waiter *cameriere/a* ⓜ/ⓕ ka·mer·*ye*·re/a
walk v *camminare* ka·mee·*na*·re
wallet *portafoglio* ⓜ por·ta·*fo*·lyo
warm a *tiepido/a* ⓜ/ⓕ *tye*·pee·do/a
wash (something) *lavare* la·*va*·re
watch *orologio* ⓜ o·ro·*lo*·jo
water *acqua* ⓕ *a*·kwa
we *noi* noy
weekend *fine settimana* ⓜ *fee*·ne se·tee·*ma*·na
west *ovest* ⓜ *o*·vest
wheelchair *sedia a rotelle* ⓕ *se*·dya a ro·*te*·le
when *quando* *kwan*·do
where *dove* *do*·ve
white *bianco/a* ⓜ/ⓕ *byan*·ko/a
who *chi* kee
why *perché* per·*ke*
wife *moglie* ⓕ *mo*·lye
window *finestra* ⓕ fee·*nes*·tra
wine *vino* ⓜ *vee*·no
with *con* kon
without *senza* *sen*·tsa
woman *donna* ⓕ *do*·na
write *scrivere* *skree*·ve·re

Y

yellow *giallo/a* ⓜ/ⓕ *ja*·lo/a
yes *sì* see
yesterday *ieri* *ye*·ree
you sg inf *tu* too
you sg pol *Lei* lay
you pl *voi* voy

Norwegian

norwegian alphabet				
Aa a	*Bb* be	*Cc* se	*Dd* de	*Ee* e
Ff ef	*Gg* ge	*Hh* haw	*Ii* ee	*Jj* ye
Kk kaw	*Ll* el	*Mm* em	*Nn* en	*Oo* o
Pp pe	*Qq* koo	*Rr* er	*Ss* es	*Tt* te
Uu oo	*Vv* ve	*Ww* *daw*-bel ve	*Xx* eks	*Yy* ew
Zz set	*Ææ* ey	*Øø* eu	*Åå* aw	

norwegian

NORSK

introduction

Norwegian (*norsk* nawrsk), the language from which words such as *fjord*, *reindeer*, *slalom* and *quisling* came into English, has gone a long way since the Vikings roamed the northern seas and the ancient heroic sagas were composed. The ancestor of modern Norwegian ventured as far as Russia, Greenland and even Canada. After centuries of subdued existence in the shadow of Danish, Norwegian ended up in the 21st century as two official languages and many local dialects.

Together with Swedish, Danish, Icelandic and Faroese, Norwegian belongs to the North Germanic (or Scandinavian) group of languages, all of which developed from Old Norse, the language spoken during the Viking era, in the 9th century. The earliest written records of Old Norse, in the form of old runes, can be traced back to around AD 200 and represent the oldest inscriptions in any Germanic language. After the spread of Christianity among the Nordic people in the 12th century, the Roman alphabet gradually came into use. Between the 15th and the 19th century, while Norway was under Denmark's rule, Danish had official status and was used as the written language among the educated urban population.

The 19th century national revival movement resulted in the unique linguistic situation of modern Norway. The two official written forms of Norwegian, actually quite similar and understood by all speakers, are known as *Bokmål* *bok*·mawl (literally 'book language') and *Nynorsk* *new*·nawrsk (or 'new Norwegian'). The former developed as the urban-Norwegian variety of Danish, with spelling adapted to reflect Norwegian sounds. The latter is based on the rural dialects spoken by the common people during Danish rule, and draws on the heritage of Old Norwegian. Both varieties are written standards, and are used in written communication only. The spoken language has numerous local dialects. Both written forms are represented in schools, administration and the media. *Bokmål* is predominant in the cities, while *Nynorsk* is more common in the western fjords and the central mountains. It's estimated that out of the 5 million speakers of Norwegian around 85% use *Bokmål* and about 15% use *Nynorsk*.

If the differences in some Norwegian spellings are making you go *berserk* (which, by the way, is a word originating from Old Norse), you should know that as part of Norwegian linguistic policy, many words have two or more officially authorised spellings, and people can choose elements of either written form.

pronunciation

vowel sounds

Length is a distinctive feature of the vowel sounds in Norwegian, as each vowel can be either long or short. Generally, they're long when followed by one consonant and short when followed by two or more consonants. The length of vowels often affects meaning, as in *mat* maat (food) and *matt* mat (faint), or *sur* soor (bad mood) and *surr* sur (confusion).

symbol	english equivalent	norwegian example	transliteration
a	run	*katt*	kat
aa	father	*dag*	daag
ai	aisle	*jeg*	yai
aw	saw	*dato*	*daa*·taw
e	bet	*mett*	met
ee	see	*fin*	feen
eu	nurse	*øre*	*eu*·re
ew	ee pronounced with a flared upper lip	*dyr*	dewr
ey	as in 'bet', but longer	*penger*	*peyng*·er
i	hit	*litt*	lit
o	pot	*noe*	*no*·e
oo	zoo	*mulig*	*moo*·li
ow	cow	*Europa*	ow·*roo*·pa
oy	toy	*boikott*	*boy*·kot
u	put	*ku*	ku

consonant sounds

As shown in the table below, Norwegian consonants all have equivalents in English.

symbol	english equivalent	norwegian example	transliteration
b	bed	*bord*	boor
ch	cheat	*kjempe*	*chem*·pe
d	dog	*dere*	*de*·re
f	fat	*flere*	*fle*·re
g	go	*gul*	gool
h	hat	*hus*	hoos
k	kit	*kabel*	*ka*·bel
l	lot	*lys*	lews
m	man	*mange*	*mang*·e
n	not	*Norge*	*nawr*·ge
ng	ring	*ting*	ting
p	pet	*pølse*	*peul*·se
r	red	*rabatt*	ra·*bat*
s	sun	*sol*	sol
sh	shot	*sjø*	sheu
t	top	*topp*	top
v	very	*være*	*ve*·re
y	yes	*jente*	*yen*·te

word stress

Most Norwegian words have stress on the first syllable, and sometimes there's more than one stressed syllable in a word. Words of Latin origin tend to have stress on the last syllable, though. In the pronunciation guides throughout this chapter, the stressed syllables are always in italics.

tools

language difficulties

Do you speak English?
Snakker du engelsk? — *sna*·ker doo *eyng*·elsk

Do you understand?
Forstår du? — fawr·*stawr* doo

I understand.
Jeg forstår. — yai fawr·*stawr*

I don't understand.
Jeg forstår ikke. — yai fawr·*stawr i*·key

What does (*fint*) mean?
Hva betyr (fint)? — vaa be·*tewr* (feent)

How do you ...?	*Hvordan ...?*	*vor*·dan ...
pronounce this	*uttales dette*	ut·*taa*·les de·*tey*
write (*morsom*)	*skrives (morsom)*	*skree*·ves (*mawr*·som)

Could you please ...?	*Kan du ...?*	kan doo ...
repeat that	*gjenta det*	*yen*·taa de
speak more slowly	*snakke langsommere*	*sna*·key *lang*·so·me·re
write it down	*skrive det*	*skree*·ve de

essentials

Yes.	*Ja.*	yaa
No.	*Nei.*	ney
Please.	*Vær så snill.*	veyr saw snil
Thank you (very much).	*(Tusen) Takk.*	(*too*·sen) tak
You're welcome.	*Ingen årsak.*	*ing*·en *awr*·saak
Excuse me.	*Unnskyld.*	*ewn*·shewl
Sorry.	*Beklager, tilgi meg.*	bey·*klaa*·geyr *til*·yee mai

numbers					
0	*null*	nool	16	*seksten*	*sai*·sten
1	*en*	en	17	*sytten*	*sew*·ten
2	*to*	taw	18	*atten*	*a*·ten
3	*tre*	trey	19	*nitten*	*nee*·ten
4	*fire*	*fee*·re	20	*tjue*	*shoo*·e
5	*fem*	fem	21	*tjueen*	*shoo*·e·en
6	*seks*	seks	22	*tjueto*	*shoo*·e·taw
7	*sju*	shoo	30	*tretti*	*trey*·tee
8	*åtte*	*aw*·te	40	*førti*	*feur*·tee
9	*ni*	nee	50	*femti*	*fem*·tee
10	*ti*	tee	60	*seksti*	*seks*·tee
11	*elleve*	*el*·ve	70	*sytti*	*sew*·tee
12	*tolv*	tawl	80	*åtti*	*aw*·tee
13	*tretten*	*trey*·ten	90	*nitti*	*nee*·tee
14	*fjorten*	*fyaw*·ten	100	*hundre*	*hun*·dre
15	*femten*	*fem*·ten	1000	*tusen*	*tu*·sen

time & dates

What time is it?	*Hva er klokka?*	vaa eyr *klaw*·ka
It's one o'clock.	*Klokka er ett.*	*klaw*·ka eyr et
It's (two) o'clock.	*Klokka er (to).*	*klaw*·ka eyr (taw)
Quarter past (one).	*Kvart over (ett).*	kvaat *aw*·ver (et)
Half past (one).	*Halv (to).* (lit: half two)	haal (taw)
Quarter to (eight).	*Kvart på (åtte).*	kvaat paw (*aw*·te)
At what time ...?	*Når ...?*	nawr ...
At ...	*Klokka ...*	*klaw*·ka ...
in the morning	*om formiddagen*	awm *fawr*·mi·dan
in the afternoon	*om ettermiddagen*	awm *e*·ter·mi·dan
in the evening	*om kvelden*	awm *kve*·len
Monday	*mandag*	*maan*·daa
Tuesday	*tirsdag*	*teers*·daa
Wednesday	*onsdag*	*awns*·daa
Thursday	*torsdag*	*tawrs*·daa
Friday	*fredag*	*frey*·daa
Saturday	*lørdag*	*leu*·daa
Sunday	*søndag*	*seun*·daa

January	*januar*	yaa·nu·*aar*
February	*februar*	fe·broo·*aar*
March	*mars*	maars
April	*april*	aa·*preel*
May	*mai*	mai
June	*juni*	*yoo*·nee
July	*juli*	*yoo*·lee
August	*august*	ow·*goost*
September	*september*	sep·*tem*·ber
October	*oktober*	awk·*taw*·ber
November	*november*	naw·*veym*·ber
December	*desember*	de·*seym*·ber

What date is it today?
Hvilken dato er det i dag? — *veel*·keyn *daa*·taw eyr de ee daag

It's (15 December).
Det er den (femtende desember). — de eyr den (*fem*·te·ne de·*seym*·ber)

since (May)	*siden (mai)*	*see*·den (mai)
until (June)	*til (juni)*	til (*yoo*·nee)
last ...		
night	*i natt*	ee nat
week	*sist uke*	sist *oo*·ke
month	*sist måned*	sist *maw*·ne
year	*i fjor*	ee fyor
next ...	*neste ...*	*nes*·te ...
week	*uke*	*oo*·ke
month	*måned*	*maw*·ne
year	*år*	awr
yesterday ...	*i går ...*	ee gawr ...
morning	*morges*	*maw*·res
afternoon	*ettermiddag*	e·*ter*·mee·daa
evening	*kveld*	kvel
tomorrow ...	*i morgen ...*	ee *maw*·ren ...
morning	*tidlig*	*teed*·lee
afternoon	*ettermiddag*	e·*ter*·mee·daa
evening	*kveld*	kvel

weather

What's the weather like?
Hvordan er været? — *vor*·dan eyr *veyr*·re

It's ...

cloudy	*Det er overskyet.*	de eyr *aw*·ver·shew·et
cold	*Det er kaldt.*	de eyr kalt
hot	*Det er veldig varmt.*	de eyr *vel*·dee varmt
warm	*Det er varmt.*	de eyr varmt
raining	*Det regner.*	de *rai*·ner
snowing	*Det snør.*	de sneur
sunny	*Solen skinner.*	*saw*·len *shi*·ner
windy	*Det blåser.*	de *blaw*·ser

spring	*vår*	vawr
summer	*sommer*	*saw*·mer
autumn	*høst*	heust
winter	*vinter*	*veen*·ter

border crossing

I'm here ...	*Jeg ...*	yai ...
in transit	*skal videre med fly*	skal *vee*·de·re mey flew
on business	*er på forretningsreise*	eyr paw faw·*ret*·neengs·*rai*·se
on holiday	*er på ferie*	eyr paw *fe*·ree·e

I'm here for ...	*Jeg skal være her i ...*	yai skal *vey*·re heyr ee ...
(10) days	*(ti) dager*	(tee) *daa*·ger
(three) weeks	*(tre) uker*	(trey) *oo*·ker
(two) months	*(to) måneder*	(taw) *maw*·ner

I'm going to (Hamar).
Jeg skal til (Hamar). — yai skal til (*haa*·mar)

I'm staying at the (Grand Hotel).
Jeg bor på (Grand hotell). — yai boor paw (graan hoo·*tel*)

I have nothing to declare.
Jeg har ingenting å fortolle. — yai haar *ing*·en·teeng aw fawr·*taw*·le

I have something to declare.
Jeg har noe å fortolle. — yai haar *naw*·e aw fawr·*taw*·le

That's (not) mine.
Det er (ikke) mitt. — de eyr (*i*·key) mit

transport

tickets & luggage

Where can I buy a ticket?
Hvor kan jeg kjøpe billett? — vor kan yai *sheu*·pe bee·*let*

Do I need to book a seat?
Er det nødvendig å bestille sitteplass? — eyr de neu·*ven*·dee aw be·*sti*·le *see*·te·plas

One … ticket (to Bergen), please.	*Jeg vil gjerne ha … (til Bergen), takk.*	yai vil *yer*·ne haa … (til *ber*·gen) tak
one-way	*enveisbillett*	*en*·veys·bee·*let*
return	*returbillett*	re·*toor*·bi·*let*
I'd like to … my ticket, please.	*Jeg vil gjerne … min billett, takk.*	yai vil *yer*·ne … meen bee·*let* tak
cancel	*avbestille*	*av*·be·sti·le
change	*endre*	*en*·dre
collect	*hente*	*hen*·te
confirm	*bekrefte*	be·*kref*·te
I'd like a … seat, please.	*Jeg vil gjerne ha … plass, takk.*	yai vil *yer*·ne haa … plas tak
nonsmoking	*ikkerøyke*	*i*·key·*roy*·ke
smoking	*røyke*	*roy*·ke

How much is it?
Hvor mye koster det? — vor *mew*·e *kaws*·ter de

Is there air conditioning?
Er det luftkjøling? — eyr de *luft*·sheu·ling

Is there a toilet?
Er det toalett? — eyr de to·aa·*let*

How long does the trip take?
Hvor lenge tar reisen? — vor *leng*·e taar *rai*·sen

Is it a direct route?
Er det en direkterute? — eyr de en dee·*rek*·te·*roo*·te

I'd like a luggage locker.
Jeg vil gjerne ha en oppbevaringsboks. — yai vil *yer*·ne haa en awp·be·*vaa*·reengs·bawks

My luggage has been ...	*Bagasjen min er ...*	ba·*gaa*·shen meen eyr ...
damaged	*skadet*	*ska*·det
lost	*blitt borte*	blit *bawr*·te
stolen	*stjålet*	*styaw*·let

getting around

Where does flight (SK50) arrive?
Hvor ankommer flyrute (SK50)? vor *an*·kaw·mer *flew*·roo·te (*es*·kaw *fem*·tee)

Where does flight (SK50) depart?
Hvor går flyrute (SK50) fra? vor gawr *flew*·*roo*·te (*es*·kaw *fem*·tee) fra

Where's the ...?	*Hvor er ...?*	vor eyr ...
arrivals hall	*ankomsthallen*	*an*·kawmst·*ha*·len
departures hall	*avgangshallen*	*av*·gangs·*ha*·len
duty-free shop	*tollfri butikk*	*tawl*·free boo·*tik*
gate (12)	*utqanq (tolv)*	*oot*·gang (tawl)

Is this the ... to (Oslo)?	*Er dette ... til (Oslo)?*	er de·*tey* ... til (*os*·law)
boat	*båten*	*baw*·ten
bus	*bussen*	*bu*·sen
plane	*flyet*	*flew*·e
train	*toget*	*taw*·ge

What time's the ... bus?	*Når går ... buss?*	nawr gawr ... bus
first	*første*	*feur*·ste
last	*siste*	*si*·ste
next	*neste*	*ne*·ste

At what time does it arrive/leave?
Når ankommer/går den? nawr *an*·kaw·mer/gawr den

How long will it be delayed?
Hvor mye er det forsinket? vor *mew*·e eyr de fawr·*sin*·ket

What station/stop is this?
Hvilke stasjon/stopp er dette? *veel*·key staa·*shawn*/stawp eyr de·*tey*

What's the next station/stop?
Hva er neste stasjon/stopp? vaa eyr *nes*·te staa·*shawn*/stawp

Does it stop at (Majorstua)?
Stopper denne på (Majorstua)? *staw*·per *dey*·ne paw (maa·*yoor*·stu·a)

Please tell me when we get to (Oslo).
Kan du si fra når vi kommer til (Oslo)? kan doo see fraa nawr vee *kaw*·mer til (*os*·law)

How long do we stop here?
Hvor lenge stopper vi her? — vor *leng*·e *staw*·per vee heyr

Is this seat available?
Er denne plassen ledig? — eyr *dey*·ne *pla*·sen *le*·dee

That's my seat.
Dette er min plass. — de·*tey* eyr meen plas

I'd like a taxi …	*Jeg vil gjerne ha en drosje …*	yai vil *yer*·ne haa en *draw*·shey …
at (9am)	*klokka (ni om morgenen)*	*klaw*·ka (nee awm *mawr*·ge·nen)
now	*nå*	naw
tomorrow	*i morgen*	ee *maw*·ren

Is this taxi available?
Er denne drosjen ledig? — er *dey*·ne *draw*·sheyn *le*·dee

How much is it to …?
Hvor mye koster det å kjøre til …? — vor *mew*·e *kaws*·ter de aw *sheu*·re til …

Please put the meter on.
Kan du være så snill å skru på taksameteret? — kan doo *vey*·re saw snil aw skroo paw tak·saa·*me*·te·re

Please take me to (this address).
Kan du kjøre meg til (denne adressen)? — kan doo *sheu*·re mai til (*dey*·ne a·*dre*·sen)

Please …	*Vær så snill å …*	veyr saw snil aw …
slow down	*kjør litt saktere*	*sheur* lit *sak*·te·re
stop here	*stoppe her*	*sto*·pe heyr
wait here	*vente her*	*ven*·te heyr

car, motorbike & bicycle hire

I'd like to hire a …	*Jeg vil gjerne leie en …*	yai vil *yer*·ne *lai*·e en …
bicycle	*sykkel*	*sew*·kel
car	*bil*	beel
motorbike	*motorsykkel*	maw·tor·*sew*·kel

with …	*med …*	mey …
a driver	*sjåfør*	shaw·*feur*
air conditioning	*klimaanlegg*	*klee*·ma·an·leg
antifreeze	*frostvæske*	*frawst*·ves·ke
snow chains	*kjettinger*	*shey*·teeng·er

How much for … hire?	*Hvor mye koster det …?*	vor *mew*·e *kaws*·ter de …
hourly	*pr. time*	per *tee*·me
daily	*pr. dag*	per daag
weekly	*pr. uke*	per *oo*·ke

air	*luft*	luft
oil	*olje*	*ol*·ye
petrol	*bensin*	ben·*seen*
tyres	*dekk*	dek

I need a mechanic.
Jeg trenger et verksted. — yai *treng*·er et *verk*·stey

I've run out of petrol.
Jeg har gått tom for bensin. — yai haar gawt tawm fawr ben·*seen*

I have a flat tyre.
Jeg har punktert. — yey haar poonk·*tert*

directions

Where's the …?	*Hvor er …?*	vor eyr …
bank	*banken*	*ban*·ken
city centre	*sentrum*	*sent*·rum
hotel	*hotellet*	hoo·*te*·ley
market	*torget*	*tawr*·gey
police station	*politistasjonen*	po·lee·*tee*·sta·*shaw*·nen
post office	*postkontoret*	*pawst*·kawn·taw·rey
public toilet	*offentlig toalett*	*aw*·fent·lee to·aa·*let*
tourist office	*turistinformasjon*	tu·*reest*·in·fawr·ma·*shawn*

Is this the road to (Gol)?
Er dette veien til (Gol)? — eyr de·*tey vai*·en til (gol)

Can you show me (on the map)?
Kan du vise meg (på kartet)? — kan doo *vee*·sey mai (paw *kar*·te)

What's the address?
Hva er adressen? — va eyr aa·*dre*·seyn

How far is it?
Hvor langt er det? — vor langt eyr de

How do I get there?
Hvordan kommer jeg meg dit? — vor·*dan kaw*·mer yai mai deet

Turn …	*Ta av …*	taa av …
at the corner	*på hjørne*	paw *yeur*·ney
at the traffic lights	*i lyskrysset*	ee *lews*·krew·sey
left/right	*til venstre/høyre*	til *vens*·trey/*hoy*·rey
It's …	*Det er …*	de eyr …
behind …	*bak …*	baak …
far away	*langt*	laangt
here	*her*	heyr
in front of …	*foran …*	*faw*·ran …
left	*venstre*	*vens*·trey
near to …	*nær …*	neyr …
next to …	*ved siden av …*	vey *see*·den aav …
on the corner	*på hjørne*	paw *yeur*·ney
opposite …	*ovenfor …*	*aw*·ven·fawr …
right	*høyre*	*hoy*·rey
straight ahead	*rett fram*	ret fram
there	*der*	deyr
by bus	*med buss*	mey bus
by taxi	*med drosje*	mey *draw*·shey
by train	*med tog*	mey tawg
on foot	*til fots*	til fots
north	*nord*	noor
south	*sør*	seur
east	*øst*	eust
west	*vest*	vest

signs

Inngang/Utgang	*in*·gang/*oot*·gang	**Entrance/Exit**
Åpen/Stengt	*aw*·pen/stengt	**Open/Closed**
Rom ledig	rom *le*·dee	**Rooms Available**
Fult	fult	**No Vacancies**
Informasjon	in·fawr·ma·*shawn*	**Information**
Politistasjon	po·lee·*tee*·sta·*shawn*	**Police Station**
Forbudt	fawr·*boot*	**Prohibited**
Toaletter/WC	to·aa·*le*·ter/*ve*·se	**Toilets**
Herrer	*hey*·rer	**Men**
Damer	*da*·mer	**Women**
Varmt/Kaldt	varmt/kalt	**Hot/Cold**

accommodation

finding accommodation

Where's a …?	*Hvor finnes det …?*	vor *fi*·nes de …
camping ground	*en campingplass*	en *keym*·ping·plas
guesthouse	*et gjestgiveri*	et *yest*·gi·ve·ree
hotel	*et hotell*	et hoo·*tel*
youth hostel	*et ungdomsherberge*	et *ong*·dawms·heyr·beyrg
Can you recommend somewhere …?	*Kan du anbefale et … sted?*	kan doo *an*·be·fa·le et … stey
cheap	*billig*	*bi*·lee
good	*godt*	gawt
nearby	*nærliggende*	*neyr*·li·gen·de

I'd like to book a room, please.
Jeg vil gjerne bestille et rom. — yai vil *yer*·ne be·*sti*·le et rom

I have a reservation.
Jeg har bestilt. — yai har be·*stilt*

My name's …
Jeg heter … — yai *he*·ter …

Do you have a … room?	*Finnes det et …?*	*fi*·nes de et …
single	*enkeltrom*	*eyn*·kelt·rom
double	*dobbeltrom*	*daw*·belt·rom
twin	*tomansrom*	*taw*·mans·rom
How much is it per …?	*Hvor mye koster det pr. …?*	vor *mew*·e *kaws*·ter de peyr …
night	*dag*	daag
person	*person*	*peyr*·son
Can I pay by …?	*Tar du imot …?*	tar doo ee·*mot* …
credit card	*kredittkort*	kre·*dit*·kawrt
travellers cheque	*reisesjekker*	*rai*·se·*shey*·ker

I'd like to stay for (two) nights.
Jeg har tenkt å bli her i (to) dager. — yai har tenkt aw bli heyr ee (taw) *da*·ger

From (July 2) to (July 6).
Fra (andre juli) til (sjette juli). — fra (*an*·dre *yoo*·lee) til (*shey*·te *yoo*·lee)

Can I see it?
Kan jeg få se det? — kan yai faw se de

Am I allowed to camp here?
Kan jeg slå opp telt her? — kan yai slaw awp telt heyr

Is there a camp site nearby?
Er det en campingplass i nærheten? — eyr de en *kam*·ping·plas ee *neyr*·he·ten

requests & queries

When's breakfast served?
Når serveres frokost? — nawr seyr·*vey*·res *fro*·kost

Where's breakfast served?
Hvor serveres frokost? — vor seyr·*vey*·res *fro*·kost

Please wake me at (seven).
Vær så snill å vekke meg klokka (sju). — veyr saw snil aw *vey*·ke mai *klaw*·ka (shoo)

Could I have my key, please?
Kan jeg få nøkkelen, takk? — kan yai faw *neu*·ke·len tak

Can I get another (blanket)?
Kan jeg få et ekstra (teppe)? — kan yai faw et *eks*·tra (*te*·pe)

This ... isn't clean.	*Dette ... er ikke rent.*	*de*·tey ... eyr *i*·key rent
sheet	*lakenet*	*la*·ke·net
towel	*håndkledet*	*hawn*·kle

Is there a/an ...?	*Er det ...?*	eyr de ...
elevator	*heis*	hais
safe	*safe*	saif

The room is too ...	*Rommet er for ...*	*ro*·me eyr fawr ...
expensive	*dyrt*	dewrt
noisy	*bråkete*	*braw*·ke·te
small	*lite*	*lee*·te

The ... doesn't work.	*... virker ikke.*	... *vir*·ker *i*·key
air conditioning	*Luftkjøling*	*luft*·sheu·ling
fan	*Viften*	*vif*·ten
toilet	*Toalettet*	*to*·aa·*le*·te

checking out

What time is checkout?
Når må jeg sjekke ut? — nawr maw yai *shey*·ke oot

Can I leave my luggage here?
Kan jeg la bagasjen stå her? — kan yai laa ba·*gaa*·shen staw heyr

Could I have my ..., please?	*Kan jeg få tilbake ..., takk?*	kan yai faw til·*baa*·ke ... tak
deposit	*depositumet mitt*	de·*po*·see·tu·me mit
passport	*passet mitt*	*pa*·se mit
valuables	*verdisakene mine*	ver·*dee*·sa·ke·ne *mee*·ne

communications & banking

the internet

Where's the local Internet café?
Finnes det en Internettkafé her? — *fi*·nes de en *in*·ter·net·ka·*fe* heyr

How much is it per hour?
Hvor mye koster det pr. time? — vor *mew*·e *kaws*·ter de peyr *tee*·me

I'd like to ...	*Jeg vil gjerne ...*	yai vil *yer*·ne ...
check my email	*sjekke e-post*	*shey*·ke *e*·pawst
get Internet access	*bruke Internett*	*broo*·ke *in*·ter·net
use a printer	*ta utskrift*	taa *ut*·skrift
use a scanner	*bruke skanner*	*broo*·ke *ska*·ner

mobile/cell phone

I'd like a ...	*Jeg vil gjerne ...*	yai vil *yer*·ne ...
mobile/cell phone for hire	*leie en mobiltelefon*	*ley*·e en mo·*beel*·te·le·*fon*
SIM card for your network	*ha et norsk SIM-kort*	haa et nawrsk *seem*·kawrt

What are the rates?
Hva koster det? — va *kaws*·ter de

telephone

What's your phone number?
Hva er ditt telefonnummer? — va eyr dit te·le·*fon*·no·mer

The number is …
Nummeret er … — *no*·me·re eyr …

Where's the nearest public phone?
Hvor er nærmeste telefonkiosk? — vor eyr *neyr*·me·ste te·le·*fon*·shosk

I'd like to buy a phonecard.
Jeg ønsker å kjøpe et telefonkort. — yai *eun*·sker aw *shaw*·pe et te·le·*fon*·kawrt

I want to …	*Jeg vil …*	yai vil …
call (Singapore)	*ringe til (Singapore)*	*ring*·e til (*seeng*·aa·pawr)
make a local call	*ringe et lokalt nummer*	*ring*·e et lo·*kalt* *no*·mer
reverse the charges	*ringe på noteringsoverføring*	*ring*·e paw no·*te*·rings·aw·ver·*feu*·ring

How much does … cost?	*Hvor mye koster …?*	vor *mew*·e *kaws*·ter …
a (three)-minute call	*en (tre) minutters samtale*	en (trey) mee·*nu*·ters *sam*·ta·le
each extra minute	*hvert ekstra minutt*	veyrt *eks*·tra mee·*nut*

It's (15) kroner per (minute).
(Femten) kroner pr. (minutt). — (*fem*·ten) *kraw*·ner peyr (mee·*nut*)

post office

I want to send a …	*Jeg vil sende …*	yey vil *se*·ne …
fax	*en faks*	en faks
letter	*et brev*	et brev
parcel	*en pakke*	en *pa*·ke
postcard	*et postkort*	et *pawst*·kawrt

NORSK – communications & banking

I want to buy ...	*Kan jeg få ...*	kan yai faw ...
an envelope	*en konvolutt*	en kawn·vaw·*lut*
stamps	*frimerker*	*free*·mer·ker
Please send it (to Australia) by ...	*Vennligst send (til Australia) med ...*	*ven*·list sen (til ow·*stra*·lee·a) mey ...
airmail	*luftpost*	*luft*·pawst
express mail	*ekspresspost*	eks·*pres*·pawst
registered mail	*rekommandert post*	re·ko·man·*deyrt* pawst
surface mail	*overflatepost*	aw·ver·*fla*·te·pawst
Is there any mail for me?	*Er det post til meg?*	eyr de pawst til mai

bank

Where's a/an ...?	*Er det ...?*	eyr de ...
ATM	*en minibank*	en *mi*·nee·bank
foreign exchange office	*valutaveksling*	va·*lu*·ta·vek·sling
I'd like to ...	*Jeg vil gjerne ...*	yai vil *yer*·ne ...
Where can I ...?	*Hvor kan jeg ...?*	vor kan yai ...
arrange a transfer	*overføre*	aw·ver·*feu*·re
cash a cheque	*heve en sjekk*	*hey*·ve en sheyk
change a travellers cheque	*heve en reisesjekk*	*hey*·ve en *rai*·se·sheyk
change money	*veksle penger*	*vek*·sle *peyng*·er
get a cash advance	*få kontantforskudd*	faw kon·*tant*·fawr·skud
withdraw money	*ta ut penger*	ta oot *peyng*·er
What's the ...?	*Hva ...?*	va ...
charge for that	*koster det*	*kaws*·ter de
commission	*er gebyret*	eyr ge·*boo*·re
exchange rate	*er valutakursen*	eyr va·*lu*·ta·kur·sen
It's ...	*Det ...*	de ...
(12) kroner	*koster (tolv) kroner*	*kaws*·ter (tawl) *kraw*·ner
free	*er gratis*	eyr *gra*·tis

What time does the bank open?
Når åpner banken? — nawr *awp*·ner *ban*·ken

Has my money arrived yet?
Har pengene mine kommet ennå? — har *peng*·e·ne *mee*·ne *kaw*·met e·naw

communications & banking – NORWEGIAN

sightseeing

getting in

What time does it open/close?
Når åpner/stenger det? — nawr *awp*·ner/*steng*·er de

What's the admission charge?
Hvor mye koster det å komme inn? — vor *mew*·e *kos*·ter de aw *kaw*·me in

Is there a discount for children/students?
Er det barnerabatt/studentrabatt? — eyr de *bar*·ney·ra·bat/stu·*dent*·ra·bat

I'd like a ...	*Jeg vil gjerne ha ...*	yai vil *yer*·ne haa ...
catalogue	*en katalog*	en ka·ta·*lawg*
guide	*en guide*	en gaid
local map	*et lokalkart*	et lo·*kal*·kart

I'd like to see ...
Jeg vil gjerne se ... — yai vil *yer*·ne se ...

What's that?
Hva er det? — va eyr de

Can I take a photo?
Kan jeg ta bilde? — kan yai ta *bil*·dey

tours

When's the next ...?	*Når går neste ...?*	nawr gawr *nes*·te ...
day trip	*dagstur*	*dags*·toor
tour	*tur*	toor

Is ... included?	*Er ... inkludert?*	eyr ... ing·kloo·*deyrt*
accommodation	*losji*	lo·*shee*
the admission charge	*inngangsbillett*	*in*·gangs·bee·*let*
food	*mat*	maat
transport	*transport*	trans·*pawrt*

How long is the tour?
Hvor lang tid tar turen? — vor lang tee tar *too*·ren

What time should we be back?
Når vil vi være tilbake? — nawr vil vee *vey*·re til·*baa*·ke

sightseeing

castle	*slott*	slawt
cathedral	*katedral*	ka·te·*dral*
church	*kirke*	*shir*·ke
main square	*stortorget*	stor·*tawr*·ge
monastery	*kloster*	*klaws*·ter
monument	*monument*	maw·noo·*ment*
museum	*museum*	moo·*se*·um
old city	*gamlebyen*	gam·le·*boo*·en
palace	*slott*	slawt
ruins	*ruiner*	roo·*ee*·ner
stadium	*stadion*	*sta*·dee·on
statues	*statuer*	sta·*too*·er

shopping

enquiries

Where's a . . .?	*Hvor er det . . .?*	vor eyr de . . .
bank	*bank*	bank
bookshop	*bokhandel*	*bok*·han·del
camera shop	*fotobutikk*	*fo*·to·boo·tik
department store	*varemagasin*	va·re·ma·ga·*sin*
grocery store	*matbutikk*	*maat*·boo·tik
market	*marked*	*mar*·ked
newsagency	*kiosk*	shosk
supermarket	*matbutikk*	*maat*·boo·tik

Where can I buy (a padlock)?
Hvor kan jeg kjøpe (en hengelås)? — vor kan yai *sheu*·pe (en *heng*·e·laws)

I'm looking for . . .
Jeg leter etter . . . — yai *ley*·ter e·*ter* . . .

Can I look at it?
Kan jeg få se på det? kan yai faw se paw de

Do you have any others?
Har du andre? har doo *an*·dre

Does it have a guarantee?
Er det med garanti? eyr de mey ga·ran·*tee*

Can I have it sent overseas?
Kan jeg få det sendt til utlandet? kan yai faw de sent til *oot*·lan·de

Can I have my ... repaired?
Kan jeg få min ... reparert? kan yai faw meen ... re·paa·*rert*

It's faulty.
Den er ødelagt. den eyr *eud*·lagt

I'd like ..., please.	*Jeg vil gjerne ..., takk.*	yai vil *yer*·ne ... tak
a bag	*ha en veske*	haa en *veys*·ke
a refund	*ha refusjon*	haa re·foo·*shawn*
to return this	*returnere dette*	re·toor·*ne*·re *dey*·te

paying

How much is it?
Hvor mye koster det? vor *mew*·e *kaws*·ter de

Can you write down the price?
Kan du skrive ned prisen? kan doo *skree*·ve ned *pree*·sen

That's too expensive.
Det er for dyrt. de eyr fawr dewrt

What's your lowest price?
Hva er din absolutt laveste pris? va eyr deen ab·saw·*lut la*·ves·te prees

I'll give you (15) kroner.
Jeg gir deg (femten) kroner. yai geer dey (*fem*·ten) *kraw*·ner

There's a mistake in the bill.
Det er en feil på regningen. de eyr en fail paw *rai*·ning·en

Do you accept ...?	*Tar du imot ...?*	taar doo ee·*mot* ...
credit cards	*kredittkort*	kre·*dit*·kawrt
debit cards	*debetkort*	*dey*·bet·kawrt
travellers cheques	*reisesjekker*	*rai*·se·*shey*·ker

I'd like ..., please.	*Jeg vil gjerne ha igjen ..., takk.*	yai vil *yer*·ne haa ee·*yen* ... tak
a receipt	*kvittering*	kvee·*te*·ring
my change	*vekslepenger*	*vek*·sle·*peyng*·er

clothes & shoes

Can I try it on?
Kan jeg prove denne? kan yai *praw*·ve *dey*·ne

My size is (42).
Jeg bruker størrelse (førtito). yai *broo*·ker *steu*·rel·se (fawr·tee·*taw*)

It doesn't fit.
Den passer ikke. den *paa*·ser *i*·key

small	*liten*	*lee*·ten
medium	*medium*	*mey*·di·um
large	*stor*	stor

books & music

I'd like a ...	*Kan jeg få en ...?*	kan yai faw en ...
newspaper (in English)	*(engelsk) avis*	(*eyng*·elsk) a·*vees*
pen	*penn*	pen

Is there an English-language bookshop?
Finnes det en bokhandel med engelske bøker? *fi*·nes de en *bok*·han·del mey *eyng*·els·ke *beu*·ker

I'm looking for something by (Edvard Grieg/Henrik Ibsen).
Jeg ser etter noe av (Edvard Grieg/Henrik Ibsen). yai seyr *e*·ter *naw*·e av (*ed*·var grig/*hen*·rik *ip*·sen)

Can I listen to this?
Kan jeg høre på denne? kan yai *heu*·re paw *dey*·ne

photography

Could you ...?	*Kan du ...?*	kan doo ...
burn a CD from my memory card	*brenne en CD fra minnekortet*	*brey*·ne en *se*·de fra *mi*·ne·kawr·te
develop this film	*fremkalle*	*frem*·ka·le
load my film	*sette i film for meg*	*sey*·te ee film fawr mai
I need a/an ... film for this camera.	*Jeg vil gjerne ha ... film til dette kameraet.*	yai vil *yer*·ne haa ... film til *dey*·te *ka*·me·raa
APS	*APS*	aa·pe·*es*
B&W	*svart-hvitt*	*svart*·vit
colour	*farge*	*far*·ge
slide	*lysbilde*	*lews*·bil·de
(200) speed	*(tohundre) lukkerhastighet*	(*taw*·hun·dre) *lo*·ker·has·tee·*het*
When will it be ready?	*Når er den ferdig?*	nawr eyr den *fer*·dee

meeting people

greetings, goodbyes & introductions

Hello.	*God dag.*	go·*daag*
Hi.	*Hei.*	hai
Good night.	*God natt.*	go·*nat*
Goodbye.	*Ha det.*	*haa*·de
See you later.	*Vi sees senere.*	vee sees *se*·ne·re
Mr	*herr*	heyr
Mrs	*fru*	froo
Miss	*frøken*	*freu*·ken

How are you?
Hvordan har du det? — *vor*·dan haar doo de

Fine, thanks. And you?
Bra, takk. Og du? — braa tak aw doo

What's your name? | Hva heter du? | vaa *hey*·ter doo

What's your name?		
Hva heter du?		vaa *hey*·ter doo
My name is ...		
Jeg heter ...		yai *hey*·ter ...
I'm pleased to meet you.		
Hyggelig å treffe deg.		*hew*·ge·lee aw *tre*·fe dai
This is my ...	*Dette er min ...*	*dey*·te eyr meen ...
boyfriend	*kjæreste*	*shey*·re·ste
brother	*bror*	bror
daughter	*datter*	*da*·ter
father	*far*	faar
friend	*venn/venninne* m/f	ven/ve·*ni*·ne
girlfriend	*kjæreste*	*shey*·re·ste
husband	*mann*	man
mother	*mor*	mawr
partner (intimate)	*samboer*	*sam*·bo·er
sister	*søster*	*seus*·ter
son	*sønn*	seun
wife	*kone*	*kaw*·ne
Here's my ...	*Her er min ...*	heyr eyr meen ...
What's your ...?	*Hva er din ...?*	vaa eyr deen ...
address	*adresse*	a·*dre*·se
email address	*e-postadresse*	*ey*·post·a·dre·se
fax number	*faksnummer*	*faks*·no·mer
phone number	*telefonnummer*	te·le·*fon*·*no*·mer

occupations

What's your occupation?	*Hva driver du med?*	vaa *dree*·ver doo mey
I'm a/an ...	*Jeg er ...*	yai eyr ...
artist	*kunstner*	*koonst*·ner
businessperson	*forretningsdrivende*	faw·*ret*·nings·dri·ven·de
farmer	*bonde*	*baw*·ne
manual worker	*kropsarbeider*	*krawps*·ar·bai·der
office worker	*kontoransatt*	kon·*tor*·an·sat
scientist	*forsker*	*fawr*·sker
student	*student*	stu·*dent*
tradesperson	*håndtverker*	*hawnt*·ver·ker

background

Where are you from?	*Hvor er du fra?*	vor eyr doo fra
I'm from ...	*Jeg er fra ...*	yai eyr fraa ...
Australia	*Australia*	ow·*stra*·li·aa
Canada	*Canada*	*ka*·na·da
England	*England*	*eyng*·lan
Ireland	*Irland*	*ir*·lan
New Zealand	*Ny Zealand*	new *se*·lan
the USA	*USA*	oo·es·*aa*
Are you married?	*Er du gift?*	eyr doo yft
I'm married.	*Jeg er gift.*	yai eyr yft
I'm single.	*Jeg er enslig.*	yai eyr *en*·slee

age

How old ...?	*Hvor gammel ...?*	vor *ga*·mel er ...
are you	*du*	doo
is your daughter	*din datter*	din *da*·ter
is your son	*din sønn*	din seun

I'm ... years old.
Jeg er ... år gammel. yai eyr ... awr *ga*·mel

He/She is ... years old.
Han/Hun er ... år gammel. han/hun eyr ... awr *ga*·mel

feelings

I'm (not) ...	*Jeg ... (ikke).*	yai ... (*ee*·key)
Are you ...?	*Er du ...?*	eyr du ...
happy	*lykkelig*	*lu*·ke·lee
hot	*varm*	varm
hungry	*sulten*	*sool*·ten
sad	*nedfor*	*ney*·fawr
thirsty	*tørst*	teurst
tired	*trøtt*	treut
Are you cold?	*Fryser du?*	*fru*·ser doo
I'm (not) cold.	*Jeg fryser (ikke).*	yai *fru*·ser (*i*·key)

entertainment

going out

Where can I find ...?	*Hvor er det ...?*	vor eyr de ...
clubs	*klubber*	*kloo*·ber
gay venues	*homseklubber*	*hom*·se·*kloo*·ber
pubs	*barer*	*ba*·rer

I feel like going to a/the ...	*Jeg vil gjerne gå på ...*	yai vil *yer*·ne gaw paw ...
concert	*konsert*	kawn·*sert*
movies	*kino*	*shee*·naw
party	*fest*	fest
restaurant	*restaurant*	res·tu·*rang*
theatre	*teater*	te·*aa*·ter

interests

Do you like ...?	*Liker du ...?*	*lee*·ker doo ...
I (don't) like ...	*Jeg liker (ikke) ...*	yai *lee*·ker (*i*·key) ...
art	*kunst*	koonst
cooking	*matlaging*	*maat*·la·ging
movies	*å gå på kino*	aw gaw paw *shee*·naw
nightclubs	*nattklubber*	nat·*kloo*·ber
reading	*å lese*	aw *ley*·se
shopping	*å handle*	aw *hand*·le
sport	*sport*	spawrt
travelling	*å reise*	aw *rai*·se

Do you like to ...?	*Liker du å ...?*	*lee*·ker doo aw ...
dance	*danse*	*dan*·se
go to concerts	*gå på konserter*	gaw paw kawn·*ser*·ter
listen to music	*høre på musikk*	*heu*·re paw *moo*·sik

food & drink

finding a place to eat

Can you recommend a ...?	*Kan du anbefale en ...?*	kan doo *an*·be·fa·le en ...
bar	*bar*	baar
café	*kafé*	ka·*fe*
restaurant	*restaurant*	res·tu·*rang*
I'd like ..., please.	*Jeg vil gjerne ha ..., takk.*	yai vil *yer*·ne ha ... tak
a table for (four)	*et bord til (fire)*	et bawr til (*fee*·re)
the nonsmoking section	*på ikke-røyke*	paw *i*·key·*roy*·ke
the smoking section	*der man kan røyke*	deyr man kan *roy*·ke

ordering food

breakfast	*frokost*	*fro*·kost
lunch	*lunsj*	loonsh
dinner	*middag*	*mi*·da
snack	*noe godt*	*naw*·e gawt
today's menu	*dagens meny*	*da*·gens me·*ni*
today's special	*dagens rett*	*da*·gens ret
eat	*spise*	*spi*·se
drink	*drikke*	*dri*·ke

What would you recommend?
Hva vil du anbefale? — va vil doo *an*·be·fa·le

I'd like (the) ...	*Kan jeg få ..., takk.*	kan yai faw ... tak
bill	*regningen*	*rai*·ning·en
drink list	*vinlisten*	*veen*·lis·ten
menu	*menyen*	me·*new*·en
that dish	*den retten*	den *re*·ten

drinks

(cup of) coffee …	*(en kopp) kaffe …*	(en kawp) *kaa*·fe …
(cup of) tea …	*(en kopp) te …*	(en kawp) te …
with milk	*med melk*	mey melk
without sugar	*med sukker*	mey *soo*·ker
(orange) juice	*(appelsin)jus*	(a·pel·*seen*·)joos
soft drink	*brus*	broos
boiled water	*kokt vann*	kokt van
mineral water	*mineralvann*	mi·ne·*ral*·van
sparkling mineral water	*Farris*	*fa*·ris
water	*vann*	van

in the bar

I'll have …
Jeg vil ha … — yai vil haa …

I'll buy you a drink.
Jeg spanderer en dram på deg. — yai span·*de*·rer en dram paw dai

What would you like?
Hva vil du ha? — va vil doo ha

Cheers!
Skål! — skawl

brandy	*brandy*	*bran*·dee
cocktail	*cocktail*	*kawk*·tail
cognac	*konjakk*	kon·*yak*
a shot of (whisky)	*et glass (whisky)*	et glas (*vees*·ki)
a … of beer	*… øl*	… eul
bottle	*en flaske*	en *flas*·ke
glass	*et glass*	et glas
a bottle of …	*en flaske …*	en *flas*·ke …
a glass of …	*et glass …*	et glas …
red wine	*rødvin*	*reu*·veen
sparkling wine	*musserende vin*	mu·*sey*·ren·de veen
white wine	*hvitvin*	*veet*·veen

self-catering

What's the local speciality?
Hva er den lokale spesialiteten? — va eyr den lo·*ka*·le spe·see·a·lee·*te*·ten

What's that?
Hva er det? — va eyr de

How much is (a kilo of cheese)?
Hvor mye koster (et kilo ost)? — vor *mew*·e *kaws*·ter (et *shee*·lo ost)

I'd like …	*Jeg tar …*	yey taar …
(100) grams	*(hundre) gram*	(*hun*·dre) gram
(two) kilos	*(to) kilo*	(taw) *shee*·lo
(three) pieces	*(tre) stykker*	(trey) *stew*·ker
(six) slices	*(seks) skiver*	(seks) *shee*·ver

Less.	*Mindre.*	*min*·dre
Enough.	*Nok.*	nawk
More. (countable)	*Flere.*	*fley*·re
More. (uncountable)	*Mer.*	meyr

special diets & allergies

Is there a vegetarian restaurant near here?
Finnes det en vegetariansk restaurant i nærheten? — *fi*·nes dey en ve·ge·ta·ree·*ansk* res·tu·*rang* ee *neyr*·he·ten

Do you have vegetarian food?
Har du vegetariansk mat her? — har doo ve·ge·ta·ree·*ansk* maat heyr

Could you prepare a meal without …?	*Kan du lage maten uten …?*	kan doo *la*·ge *maa*·ten *oo*·ten …
butter	*smør*	smeur
eggs	*egg*	eg
meat stock	*kjøttbuljong*	sheut·bul·*yong*

I'm allergic to …	*Jeg er allergisk mot …*	yai eyr a·*ler*·gisk mot …
dairy produce	*melkeprodukt*	*mel*·ke·pro·*dukt*
gluten	*gluten*	*gloo*·ten
MSG	*MSG*	em·es·*ge*
nuts	*nøtter*	*neu*·ter
seafood	*sjømat*	*sheu*·maat

menu reader

arme riddere	ar·me·*ri*·de·re	*bread dipped in batter, fried & served with jam*
benløse fugler	ben·*leu*·se *foo*·ler	*rolled slices of veal stuffed with minced meat*
blodpudding	*blaw*·pu·ding	*black pudding*
bløtkake	*bleut*·ka·ke	*rich sponge layer cake with whipped cream*
brissel	*bri*·sel	*sweetbread*
dyrestek	*dew*·re·stek	*roast venison*
fårikål	*faw*·ree kawl	*lamb in cabbage stew*
fenalår n	*fey*·na·lawr	*cured leg of lamb*
fiskeboller	*fis*·ke·bo·ler	*fish dumpling*
fiskegrateng	*fis*·ke·gra·*teng*	*fish casserole*
fiskekake	*fis*·ke·ka·ke	*fried fish dumpling*
fiskepudding	*fis*·ke·poo·ding	*fish pâté fried in a pan*
flatbrød n	*flat* breu	*thin wafer of rye or barley*
fleskepannekake	*fles*·ke·pa·ne·*ka*·ke	*thick pancake with bacon, baked in the oven*
fleskepølse	*fles*·ke·*peul*·se	*pork sandwich spread*
fløtevaffel	*fleu*·te·*va*·fel	*cream-enriched waffle (served with jam)*
gaffelbiter	*ga*·fel·*bee*·ter	*salt- & sugar-cured sprat or herring fillets*
gammalost	*ga*·mel·ost	*hard cheese with strong flavour*
geitost	*geyt*·ost	*sweet brown goat cheese*
gravlaks	*grav*·laks	*salt- & sugar-cured salmon with dill (served with mustard sauce)*
gryte(rett)	*grew*·te(·ret)	*casserole*
julekake	*yu*·le·ka·ke	*rich fruit cake*
kalvetunge	*kal*·ve·tung·e	*calf's tongue*
kaviar	ka·vi·*ar*	*smoked cod-roe spread*

koldtbord n	*kolt*·bawr	*cold buffet (fish, meat, cheese & salad)*
kjøttkake	*sheut*·ka·ke	*small hamburger steak*
kjøttpålegg n	*sheut*·paw·leg	*cold meat cuts*
kjøttpudding	*sheut*·poo·ding	*meat loaf*
klippfisk	*klip*·fisk	*salted & dried cod*
kringle	*kring*·le	*ring-twisted bread with raisins*
kålruletter	*kawl*·ru·le·ter	*minced meat in cabbage leaves*
lapskaus	*laps*·kows	*thick stew of diced meat, potatoes, onions & other vegetables*
lefse	*lef*·se	*traditional thin griddle cake (without eggs)*
lutefisk	*lu*·te·fisk	*dried cod, boiled or steamed & served with potatoes, peas & white sauce*
medaljong	me·dal·*yong*	*small round fillet*
mysost	*mews*·ost	*brown whey cheese*
napoleonskake	na·*po*·le·ons·*ka*·ke	*custard slice*
pinnekjøtt	*pi*·ne·sheut	*smoked, salted & steamed mutton ribs*
plukkfisk	*plok*·fisk	*poached fish in white sauce*
postei	po·*stai*	*meat, liver or fish pâté*
pultost	*pult*·ost	*soft fermented cheese with caraway seeds*
pyttipanne	*pew*·tee·*pa*·ne	*leftover meat & potatoes fried with onions*
rakefisk	*ra*·ke·fisk	*cured & fermented fish (often trout)*
rislapper	*ris*·la·per	*small sweet rice cake*
rødgrøt	*reu*·grawt	*fruit pudding with custard*
sildesalat	*si*·le·sa·lat	*herring salad*
spekesild	*spe*·ke·sil	*salted, cured herring*
surkål	*soor*·kawl	*boiled cabbage flavoured with caraway seeds, sugar & vinegar*

emergencies

basics

Help!	*Hjelp!*	yelp
Stop!	*Stopp!*	stawp
Go away!	*Forsvinn!*	fawr·*svin*
Thief!	*Tyv!*	teev
Fire!	*Brann!*	bran
Watch out!	*Pass!*	pas

Call ...!	*Ring ...!*	ring ...
a doctor	*en lege*	en *le*·ge
an ambulance	*etter sykebil*	e·ter *sew*·ke·bil
the police	*politiet*	po·lee·*tee*·ay

It's an emergency!
Dette er en nødsituasjon! — de·tey eyr en *neud*·si·tu·a·*shawn*

Could you help me, please?
Kan du være så snill å hjelpe meg? — kan doo *vey*·re saw snil aw *yel*·pe mai

I have to use the telephone.
Jeg må låne telefonen. — yai maw *law*·ne te·le·*fo*·nen

I'm lost.
Jeg har gått meg vill. — yai har gawt mai vil

Where are the toilets?
Hvor er toalettene? — vor eyr to·aa·*le*·te·ne

police

Where's the police station?
Hvor er politistasjonen? — vor eyr po·lee·*tee*·sta·*shaw*·nen

I want to report an offence.
Jeg ønsker å rapportere noe ulovlig. — yai *eun*·sker aw ra·pawr·*te*·re *naw*·e oo·*lov*·lee

I have insurance.
Jeg har forsikring. — yai har fawr·*si*·kring

I've been ...	*Jeg er blitt ...*	yai eyr blit ...
assaulted	*overfalt*	*aw*·ver·falt
raped	*voldtatt*	*vol*·tat
robbed	*rana*	*ra*·na

I've lost my ...	*Jeg har mistet ...*	yai har *mis*·tet ...
backpack	*ryggsekken min*	*rewg*·se·ken meen
bags	*bagasjen min*	ba·*gaa*·shen meen
credit card	*kredittkortet mitt*	kre·*dit*·kawr·te mit
handbag	*vesken min*	*veys*·ken meen
jewellery	*smykkene mine*	*smew*·ke·ne *mee*·ne
money	*pengene mine*	*peng*·e·ne *mee*·ne
passport	*passet mitt*	*pa*·se mit
travellers cheques	*reisesjekkene mine*	*rai*·se·*shey*·ke·ne *mee*·ne
wallet	*lommeboken min*	*lo*·me·bo·ken meen

I want to contact my ...	*Vær så snill å la meg få kontakte ...*	veyr saw snil aw la mai faw kon·*tak*·te ...
consulate	*mitt konsulat*	mit kon·su·*lat*
embassy	*min ambassade*	meen am·ba·*sa*·de

health

medical needs

Where's the nearest ...?	*Hvor er nærmeste ...?*	vor eyr *neyr*·me·ste ...
dentist	*tannlege*	*tan*·le·ge
doctor	*lege*	*le*·ge
hospital	*sykehus*	*sew*·ke·hus
(night) pharmacist	*(nattåpent) apotek*	(*nat*·aw·pent) a·po·*tek*

I need a doctor (who speaks English).
Jeg trenger en lege (som snakker engelsk). — yai *tren*·ger en *le*·ge (som *sna*·ker *eyng*·elsk)

Could I see a female doctor?
Kan jeg få snakke med en kvinnelig lege? — kan yai faw *sna*·ke mey en *kvi*·ne·lee *le*·ge

I ran out of my medication.
Jeg har sluppet opp for medisiner. — yai har *slu*·pet awp fawr me·de·*see*·ner

symptoms, conditions & allergies

I'm sick.	*Jeg er syk.*	yai er sewk
It hurts here.	*Det gjør vondt her.*	de yeur vont heyr
I have nausea.	*Jeg er kvalm.*	yai er kvalm
I have (a) …	*Jeg har …*	yai har …
asthma	*astma*	*as*·ma
bronchitis	*bronkitt*	*bron*·kit
constipation	*torstoppelse*	fawr·*stuw*·pel·se
cough	*hoste*	*hos*·te
diarrhoea	*diaré*	dee·a·*re*
fever	*feber*	*fe*·ber
headache	*vondt i hodet*	vont ee *ho*·de
heart condition	*hjertefeil*	*yer*·te·fail
pain	*smerte*	*smer*·te
sore throat	*vondt i halsen*	vont ee *hal*·sen
toothache	*tannverk*	*tan*·verk
I'm allergic to …	*Jeg er allergisk mot …*	yai eyr a·*ler*·gisk mot …
antibiotics	*antibiotika*	an·ti·bi·*o*·ti·ka
anti-inflammatories	*betennelsesdempende middel*	be·*te*·nel·ses·*dem*·pen·de *mi*·del
aspirin	*Dispril*	dis·*pril*
bees	*bier*	*bi*·er
codeine	*kodein*	ko·de·*in*
penicillin	*penicillin*	pen·se·*lin*
antiseptic	*desinfeksjonsmiddel*	des·in·fek·*shawns*·mi·del
bandage	*bandasje*	ban·*da*·she
condoms	*kondom* n	kawn·*dom*
contraceptives	*prevensjonsmiddel*	pre·van·*shawns*·mi·del
diarrhoea medicine	*middel mot diaré*	*mi*·del mot dee·a·*re*
insect repellent	*myggspray*	*mewg*·sprai
laxatives	*avførende middel*	av·*feu*·ren·de *mi*·del
painkillers	*smertestillende*	*smer*·te·*sti*·len·de
rehydration salts	*salt-tabletter*	*salt*·*ta*·be·le·ter
sleeping tablets	*sovetabletter*	*saw*·ve·*ta*·be·le·ter

english–norwegian dictionary

In this dictionary, words are marked as n (noun), a (adjective), v (verb), sg (singular), pl (plural), inf (informal) and pol (polite) where necessary. Note that Norwegian nouns are either masculine, feminine or neuter. Masculine and feminine forms (known as 'common gender') take the indefinite article *en* (a) while the neuter forms take the article *et* (a). Every Norwegian noun needs to be learned with its indefinite article (*en* or *et*). Only in *Nynorsk* is the distinction between masculine and feminine still relevant, so we've only indicated the neuter nouns with ⓝ after the Norwegian word. Note also that the ending 't' is added to adjectives for the neuter form (ie when they accompany indefinite singular nouns). In some cases both forms of the adjective (ie ⓜ&ⓕ form and ⓝ form) are spelled out in full and separated with a slash.

A

accident *ulykke oo*·lew·ke
accommodation *losji* lo·*shee*
adaptor *adapter* a·*dap*·ter
address n *adresse* a·*dre*·se
after *etter e*·ter
air-conditioned *luftkjøling luft*·sheu·ling
airplane *fly* ⓝ flew
airport *flyplass flew*·plas
alcohol *alkohol* al·ko·*hol*
all *alt* alt
allergy *allergi* a·ler·*gee*
ambulance *sykebil sew*·ke·bil
and *og* aw
arm *arm* arm
ashtray *askebeger* as·ke·*be*·ger
ATM *minibank mee*·ni·bank

B

baby *baby bai*·bee
back (body) *rygg* rewg
backpack *ryggsekk rewg*·sek
bad *dårlig dawr*·lee
bag *bag* bag
baggage claim *bagasjeskranke* ba·*ga*·she·*skran*·ke
bank *bank* bank
bar *bar* bar
bathroom *bad* ⓝ baad
battery *batteri* ⓝ ba·te·*ree*
beautiful *vakker(t) va*·ker(t)
bed *seng* seng
beer *øl* eul
before *før* feur
behind *bak* bak
bicycle *sykkel sew*·kel
big *stor* stor
bill *regning rai*·ning
black *svart* svart
blanket *teppe* ⓝ *te*·pe
blood group *blodtype blo*·tew·pe
blue *blå(tt)* blaw(t)
boat *båt* bawt
book (make a reservation) v *bestille* be·*stee*·le
bottle *flaske flas*·ke
bottle opener *flaskeåpner flas*·ke·*awp*·ner
boy *gutt* goot
brakes (car) *bremser brem*·ser
breakfast *frokost fro*·kost
broken (faulty) *ødelagt eud*·lagt
bus *buss* bus
business *forretning* fo·*ret*·ning
buy *kjøpe sheu*·pee

C

café *kafé* ka·*fe*
camera *kamera* ⓝ *ka*·me·ra
camp site *campingplass keym*·ping·plas
cancel *avbestill av*·be·stil
can opener *boksåpner boks*·awp·ner
car *bil* beel
cash n *kontanter* kon·*tan*·ter
cash (a cheque) v *veksle (en sjekk) vek*·sle (en sheyk)
cell phone *mobiltelefon* mo·*beel*·te·le·*fon*
centre *sentrum* ⓝ *sen*·trum
change (money) v *veksle (penger) vek*·sle (*peyng*·er)
cheap *billig(t) bi*·lee
check (bill) *sjekk* sheyk
check-in n *sjekke inn shey*·ke in
chest *bryst* ⓝ brewst

child *barn* ⓝ barn
cigarette *sigarett* si·ga·*ret*
city *by* bew
clean a *ren(t)* ren(t)
closed *stengt* stengt
coffee *kaffe* *ka*·fe
coins *mynter* *mewn*·ter
cold a *kald(t)* kal(t)
collect call *noteringsoverføring* no·*te*·rings·aw·ver·*feu*·ring
come *komme* *kaw*·me
computer *datamaskin* *da*·ta·ma·*sheen*
condom *kondom* ⓝ kon·*dom*
contact lenses *kontaktlinse* kon·*takt*·lin·se
cook v *lage mat* *la*·ge maat
cost n *pris* pris
credit card *kredittkort* ⓝ kre·*dit*·kawrt
cup *kopp* en kawp
currency exchange *valutaveksling* va·*lu*·ta·*vek*·sling
customs (immigration) *toll* tawl

D

dangerous *farlig(t)* *far*·lee
date (time) *dato* *daa*·taw
day *dag* daag
delay n *forsinkelse* for·*sin*·kel·se
dentist *tannlege* *tan*·le·ge
depart *avreise* *av*·rai·se
diaper *bleie* *blai*·ey
dictionary *ordbok* *or*·bok
dinner *middag* *mi*·daa
direct *direkte* *di*·rek·te
dirty *skitten(t)* *shi*·ten(t)
disabled *funksjonshemmet* funk·*shons*·he·met
discount n *rabatt* ra·*bat*
doctor *lege* *le*·ge
double bed *dobbelseng* *daw*·bel·seng
double room *dobbeltrom* ⓝ *daw*·belt·rom
drink n *drikke* *dri*·ke
drive v *kjøre* *sheu*·re
drivers licence *førerkort* ⓝ *feu*·rer·kawrt
drug (illicit) *narkotika* nar·*ko*·ti·ka
dummy (pacifier) *smokk* smok

E

ear *øre* ⓝ *eu*·re
east *øst* eust
eat *spise* *spi*·se
economy class *økonomiklasse* eu·ko·no·*mi*·kla·se
electricity *elektrisitet* e·lek·tri·si·*tet*
elevator *heis* hais
email *e-post* *e*·post
embassy *ambassade* am·ba·*sa*·de
emergency *akuttmottak* ⓝ a·*kut*·mo·tak
English (language) *engelsk* *eyng*·elsk
entrance *inngang* *in*·gang
evening *kveld* kvel
exchange rate *vekslingskurs* *vek*·slings·kurs
exit n *utgang* *oot*·gang
expensive *dyr(t)* dewr(t)
express mail *ekspresspost* eks·*pres*·pawst
eye *øye* ⓝ *oy*·e

F

far *langt* langt
fast *rask(t)* rask(t)
father *far* far
film (camera) *film* film
finger *finger* *fin*·ger
first-aid kit *førstehjelpsskrin* ⓝ *feur*·ste·yelp·skrin
first class *førsteklasse* *feur*·ste·kla·se
fish n *fisk* fisk
food *mat* maat
foot *fot* fot
fork *gaffel* *ga*·fel
free (of charge) *gratis* *gra*·tis
friend *venn/venninne* ⓜ/ⓕ ven/ve·*ni*·ne
fruit *frukt* frookt
full *full(t)* ful(t)
funny *morsom(t)* *mawr*·som(t)

G

gift *gave* *ga*·ve
girl *jente* *yen*·te
glass (drinking) *glass* ⓝ glas
glasses *briller* *bri*·ler
go *gå* gaw
good *god(t)* go(t)
green *grønn(t)* greun(t)
guide n *guide* gaid

H

half n *halv(t)* hal(t)
hand *hånd* hawn
handbag *veske* *veys*·ke

happy *glad* glaa
have *ha* haa
he *han* han
head *hode* ⓝ *ho*·de
heart *hjerte* ⓝ *yer*·te
heat n *varme var*·me
heavy *tung(t)* tung(t)
help v *hjelp* yelp
here *her* heyr
high *høy(t)* hoy(t)
highway *motorvei maw*·tor·vey
hike v *tur* toor
holiday *ferie fe*·ree·e
homosexual n *homoseksuell ho*·mo·sek·su·el
hospital *sykehus* ⓝ *sew*·ke·hoos
hot *het(t)* heyt/het
hotel *hotell* ⓝ hoo·*tel*
hungry *sulten sul*·ten
husband *mann* man

I

I *jeg* yai
identification (card) *legitimasjon* le·gi·ti·ma·*shawn*
ill *syk* sewk
important *viktig vik*·tee
included *inkludert* in·kloo·*deyrt*
injury *skade ska*·de
insurance *forsikring* fawr·*si*·kring
Internet *Internett in*·ter·net
interpreter *translatør* tran·sla·*teur*

J

jewellery *smykke* ⓝ *smew*·ke
job *jobb* yob

K

key *nøkkel neu*·kel
kilogram *kilo* ⓝ *shee*·lo
kitchen *kjøkken* ⓝ *sheu*·ken
knife *kniv* kniv

L

laundry (place) *vaskeri* ⓝ vas·ke·*ree*
lawyer *advokat* ad·voo·*kat*
left (direction) *venstre ven*·strey
left-luggage office *gjenglemt bagasjeskranke* *yen*·glemt ba·*gaa*·she·skran·ke
leg *bein* bain
lesbian n *lesbisk les*·bisk
less *mindre min*·dre
letter (mail) *brev* ⓝ brev
lift (elevator) *heis* hais
light *lys* ⓝ lews
like v *like li*·ke
lock n *lås* laws
long *lang* lang
lost *mistet mis*·tet
lost-property office *bortkommet bagasjeskranke* *bawrt*·kaw·met ba·*gaa*·she·skran·ke
love v *elsker eyls*·ker
luggage *bagasje* ba·*gaa*·she
lunch *lunsj* leunsh

M

mail n *post* pawst
man *mann* man
map *kart* ⓝ kart
market *marked* ⓝ *mar*·ked
matches *fyrstikker fewr*·sti·ker
meat *kjøtt* sheut
medicine *medisin* me·de·*seen*
menu *meny* me·*new*
message *beskjed* be·*shey*
milk *melk* melk
minute *minutt* ⓝ mi·*nut*
mobile phone *mobiltelefon* mo·*beel*·te·le·*fon*
money *penger peyng*·er
month *måned maw*·ne
morning *morgen maw*·ren
mother *mor* mawr
motorcycle *motorsykkel maw*·tor·sew·kel
motorway *motorvei maw*·tor·vey
mouth *munn* mun
music *musikk* mu·*sik*

N

name *navn* ⓝ navn
napkin *tallerken* ta·*ler*·ken
nappy *bleie blai*·ey
near *nær* neyr
new *ny(tt)* new(t)

news *nyheter* *new*·he·ter
newspaper *avis* a·*vis*
night *natt* nat
no *nei* nai
noisy *bråkete* *braw*·ke·te
nonsmoking *ikke-røyke* *i*·key·*roy*·ke
north *nord* nor
Norway *Norge* *nawr*·gai
Norwegian (language) *norsk* nawrsk
Norwegian a *norsk* nawrsk
nose *nese* *ney*·se
now *nå* naw
number *nummer* ⓝ *no*·mer

O

oil (engine) *olje* *ol*·ye
old *gammel(t)* *ga*·mel(t)
one-way ticket *enveisbillett* *en*·veys·bee·*let*
open a *åpen(t)* *aw*·pen(t)
outside *utenfor* *u*·ten·fawr

P

package *pakke* *pa*·ke
paper *papir* ⓝ pa·*peer*
park (car) v *parkere* par·*key*·re
passport *pass* ⓝ pas
pay *betale* be·*ta*·le
pen *penn* pen
petrol *bensin* ben·*seen*
pharmacy *apotek* ⓝ a·po·*tek*
phonecard *telefonkort* ⓝ te·le·*fon*·kawrt
photo *foto* ⓝ *fo*·to
plate *tallerken* ta·*ler*·ken
police *politi* ⓝ po·lee·*tee*
postcard *postkort* ⓝ *pawst*·kawrt
post office *postkontor* ⓝ *pawst*·kawn·tawr
pregnant *gravid* gra·*veed*
price *pris* pris

Q

quiet *stille* *sti*·le

R

rain n *regn* rain
razor *barberhøvel* bar·*ber*·heu·vel
receipt n *kvittering* kvi·*te*·ring
red *rød(t)* reu(t)
refund n *refusjon* re·foo·*shawn*
registered mail *rekommandert post* re·ko·man·*deyrt* pawst
rent v *leie* *lai*·e
repair v *reparasjon* re·pa·ra·*shawn*
reservation *reservasjon* re·ser·va·*shawn*
restaurant *restaurant* res·tu·*rang*
return v *retur* re·*toor*
return ticket *returbillett* re·*toor*·bi·*let*
right (direction) *høyre* *heu*·rey
road *vei* vai
room *rom* ⓝ rom

S

safe a *trygg* trewg
sanitary napkin *bind* ⓝ bin
seat *sete* ⓝ *se*·te
send *sende* *sen*·de
service station *bensinstasjon* ben·*seen*·staa·*shawn*
sex *sex* seks
shampoo *sjampo* *sham*·po
share (a dorm) *dele* *de*·le
shaving cream *barberskum* bar·*ber*·skom
she *hun* hun
sheet (bed) *laken* ⓝ *la*·ken
shirt *skjorte* *shor*·te
shoes *sko* sko
shop n *butikk* boo·*tik*
short *kort* kawrt
shower n *dusj* dush
single room *enkeltrom* ⓝ *eyn*·kelt·rom
skin *hud* hood
skirt *skjørt* ⓝ sheurt
sleep v *sove* *saw*·ve
slowly *sakte* *sak*·te
small *liten/lite* *lee*·ten/*lee*·te
smoke (cigarettes) v *røyke* *roy*·ke
soap *såpe* *saw*·pe
some *noen* *naw*·en
soon *snart* snart
south *sør* seur
souvenir shop *suvenirbutikk* su·ve·*neer*·boo·tik
speak *snakke* *sney*·ke
spoon *skje* shai
stamp *frimerke* ⓝ *free*·mer·key

stand-by ticket *reservebillett* re·ser·vey·bee·let
station (train) *stasjon* staa·shawn
stomach *mage* ma·ge
stop v *stopp* stawp
stop (bus) n *busstopp* bus·stawp
street *gate* ga·te
student *student* stu·dent
sun *sol* sol
sunscreen *solfaktor* sol·fak·tor
swim v *svømme* sveu·me

T

tampons *tamponger* tam·pong·er
taxi *drosje* draw·shey
teaspoon *teskje* te·shey
teeth *tenner* te·ner
telephone n *telefon* te·le·fon
television *TV* te·ve
temperature (weather) *temperatur* tem·pe·ra·toor
tent *telt* ⓝ telt
that (one) *den* den
they *de* dey
thirsty *tørst* teurst
this (one) *denne/dette* dey·ne/dey·te
ticket *billett* bee·let
time *tid* teed
tired *trøtt* treut
tissues *papirserviett* pa·peer·ser·vee·et
today *i dag* ee dag
toilet *toalett* ⓝ to·aa·let
tomorrow *i morgen* ee maw·ren
tonight *i kveld* ee kvel
toothbrush *tannbørste* tan·beur·ste
toothpaste *tannkrem* tan·krem
torch (flashlight) *lommelykt* lo·mey·lewkt
tour n *tur* toor
tourist office *turistinformasjon* tu·reest·in·fawr·ma·shawn
towel *håndkle* ⓝ hawn·kle
train *tåg* ⓝ tawg
translate *oversette* aw·ver·se·te
travel agency *reisebyrå* ⓝ rai·se·bew·raw
travellers cheque *reisesjekker* rai·se·shey·ker
trousers *bukser* buk·ser
twin beds *to enkeltsenger* taw eyn·kelt·seng·er
tyre *dekk* ⓝ dek

U

underwear *undertøy* un·der·toy
urgent *haster* has·ter

V

vacant *ledig* le·dee
vacation *ferie* fe·ree·e
vegetable n *grønnsak* greun·sak
vegetarian a *vegetariansk* ve·ge·ta·ree·ansk
visa *visum* ⓝ vee·sum

W

waiter *kelner* kel·ner
walk v *gå* gaw
wallet *lommebok* lo·mey·bok
warm a *varm(t)* varm(t)
wash (something) *vaske* vas·ke
watch n *se* se
water *vann* van
we *vi* vee
weekend *helg* helg
west *vest* vest
wheelchair *rullestol* ru·le·stol
when *når* nawr
where *hvor* vor
white *hvit* veet
who *hvem* vem
why *hvorfor* vor·fawr
wife *kone* ko·ne
window *vindu* ⓝ vin·du
wine *vin* veen
with *med* mey
without *uten* u·ten
woman *kvinne* kvi·ne
write *skrive* skree·ve

Y

yellow *gul(t)* gool(t)
yes *ja* yaa
yesterday *i går* ee gawr
you sg inf *du* doo
you sg pol *De* dee
you pl *dere* dey·re

T
DICTIONARY

Portuguese

portuguese alphabet				
Aa aa	*Bb* be	*Cc* se	*Dd* de	*Ee* e
Ff *e*·fe	*Gg* je	*Hh* a·*gaah*	*Ii* ee	*Jj* *jo*·ta
Kk *ka*·pa	*Ll* *e*·le	*Mm* *e*·me	*Nn* *e*·ne	*Oo* o
Pp pe	*Qq* ke	*Rr* *e*·rre	*Ss* *e*·se	*Tt* te
Uu oo	*Vv* ve	*Ww* *da*·blyoo	*Xx* sheesh	*Yy* *eeps*·lon
Zz ze				

portuguese

introduction

Portuguese (*português* poor·too·*gesh*), the language which produced words such as *albino*, *brocade* and *molasses*, comes from the Romance language family and is closely related to Spanish, French and Italian. Descended from the colloquial Latin spoken by Roman soldiers, it's now used by over 200 million people worldwide.

Linguists believe that before the Roman invasion of the Iberian Peninsula in 218 BC, the locals of modern-day Portugal spoke a Celtic language. That local language was supplanted by the vernacular form of Latin (sometimes called 'Romance') spoken by the occupying forces under the Romans' 500-year rule of the province of Lusitania (present-day Portugal and Spanish Galicia). During this period, Portuguese also absorbed elements of the languages of invading Germanic tribes. The greatest influence on today's Portuguese, however, was a result of the Moorish invasion of the peninsula in AD 711. Arabic was imposed as the official language of the region until the expulsion of the Moors in 1249, and although Romance was still spoken by the masses, the Moorish language left its mark on the vocabulary. From the 16th century on, there were only minor changes to the language, mostly influences from France and Spain. The earliest written documents were composed in the 12th century, and the Portuguese used in 1572 by Luís de Camões (author of the first great Portuguese classic, *Os Lusíadas*) was already identifiable as the language of José Saramago's Nobel Prize-winning works in the 20th century.

The global distribution of the Portuguese language began during the period know as *Os Descobrimentos* (the Discoveries), the golden era of Portugal's colonial expansion into Africa, Asia and South America. In the 15th and 16th centuries, the peninsular nation was a world power and had enormous economic, cultural and political influence. The empire's reach can be seen today in the number of countries besides Portugal where Portuguese still has the status of an official language – Brazil, Madeira and the Azores in the Atlantic Ocean off Europe, Cape Verde, São Tomé and Príncipe, Guinea-Bissau, Angola and Mozambique (all in Africa), and Macau and East Timor in Asia.

While there are differences between European Portuguese and that spoken elsewhere, you shouldn't have many problems being understood throughout the Portuguese-speaking world. As the Portuguese say, *Quem não arrisca, não petisca* keng nowng a·*rreesh*·ka, nowng pe·*teesh*·ka (If you don't take a risk, you won't eat delicacies).

pronunciation

vowel sounds

The vowel sounds in Portuguese are quite similar to those found in English. Most vowel sounds in Portuguese also have a nasal version with an effect similar to the silent '-ng' ending in English, as in *amanhã* aa·ma·*nyang* (tomorrow), for example. The letter 'n' or 'm' at the end of a syllable or a tilde (~) in written Portuguese indicate that the vowel is nasal.

symbol	english equivalent	portuguese example	transliteration
a	run	*maçã*	ma·*sang*
aa	father	*tomate*	too·*maa*·te
ai	aisle	*pai*	pai
ay	say	*lei*	lay
e	bet	*cedo*	*se*·doo
ee	see	*fino*	*fee*·noo
o	pot	*sobre*	*so*·bre
oh	oh	*couve*	*koh*·ve
oo	book	*gato*	*ga*·too
ow	how	*Austrália*	ow·*shtraa*·lya
oy	toy	*noite*	*noy*·te

word stress

In Portuguese, stress generally falls on the second-to-last syllable of a word, though there are exceptions. If a written vowel has a circumflex (ˆ) or an acute (´) or grave (`) accent marked on it, this cancels the general rule and the stress falls on that syllable. When a word ends in a written *i*, *im*, *l*, *r*, *u*, *um* or *z*, or is pronounced with a nasalised vowel, the stress falls on the last syllable. Don't worry too much about it when using phrases from this book though – the stressed syllable is always italicised in our coloured pronunciation guides.

consonant sounds

Most of the consonant sounds in Portuguese are also found in English, and even *r* (rr) will be familiar to many people (it's similar to the French 'r'). Note that the letter *ç* ('c' with a cedilla) is pronounced as s rather than k.

symbol	english equivalent	portuguese example	transliteration
b	bed	*beber*	be·*ber*
d	dog	*dedo*	*de*·doo
f	fat	*faca*	*faa*·ka
g	go	*gasolina*	ga·zoo·*lee*·na
k	kit	*cama*	*ka*·ma
l	lot	*lixo*	*lee*·shoo
ly	million	*muralhas*	moo·*raa*·lyash
m	man	*macaco*	ma·*kaa*·koo
n	not	*nada*	*naa*·da
ng	ring (indicates the nasalisation of the preceding vowel)	*ambos,* *uns,* *amanhã*	*ang*·boosh, oongsh, aa·ma·*nyang*
ny	canyon	*linha*	*lee*·nya
p	pet	*padre*	*paa*·dre
r	like 'tt' in 'butter' said fast	*hora*	*o*·ra
rr	run (throaty)	*relva*	*rrel*·va
s	sun	*criança*	kree·*ang*·sa
sh	shot	*chave*	*shaa*·ve
t	top	*tacho*	*taa*·shoo
v	very	*vago*	*vaa*·goo
w	win	*água*	*aa*·gwa
y	yes	*edifício*	ee·dee·*fee*·syoo
z	zero	*camisa*	ka·*mee*·za
zh	pleasure	*cerveja*	serr·*ve*·zha

tools

language difficulties

Do you speak English?		
Fala inglês?		*faa*·la eeng·*glesh*
Do you understand?		
Entende?		eng·*teng*·de
I (don't) understand.		
(Não) Entendo.		(nowng) eng·*teng*·doo
What does (*bem-vindo*) mean?		
O que quer dizer (bem-vindo)?		oo ke ker dee·*zer* (beng·*veeng*·doo)

How do you ...?	*Como é que se ...?*	*ko*·moo e ke se ...
pronounce this	*pronuncia isto*	proo·noong·*see*·a *esh*·too
write (*ajuda*)	*escreve (ajuda)*	*shkre*·ve (a·*zhoo*·da)
Could you please ...?	*Podia ..., por favor?*	poo·*dee*·a ... poor fa·*vor*
repeat that	*repetir isto*	rre·pe·*teer eesh*·too
speak more slowly	*falar mais devagar*	fa·*laar* maish de·va·*gaar*
write it down	*escrever isso*	shkre·*ver ee*·soo

essentials

Yes.	*Sim.*	seeng
No.	*Não.*	nowng
Please.	*Por favor.*	poor fa·*vor*
Thank you (very much).	*(Muito) Obrigado/a.* m/f	(*mweeng*·too) o·bree·*gaa*·doo/a
You're welcome.	*De nada.*	de *naa*·da
Excuse me.	*Faz favor!*	faash fa·*vor*
Sorry.	*Desculpe.*	desh·*kool*·pe

numbers

0	*zero*	*ze*·roo	16	*dezasseis*	de·za·*saysh*
1	*um*	oong	17	*dezassete*	de·za·*se*·te
2	*dois*	doysh	18	*dezoito*	de·*zoy*·too
3	*três*	tresh	19	*dezanove*	de·za·*no*·ve
4	*quatro*	*kwaa*·troo	20	*vinte*	*veeng*·te
5	*cinco*	*seeng*·koo	21	*vinte e um*	*veeng*·te e oong
6	*seis*	saysh	22	*vinte e dois*	*veeng*·te e doysh
7	*sete*	*se*·te	30	*trinta*	*treeng*·ta
8	*oito*	*oy*·too	40	*quarenta*	kwa·*reng*·ta
9	*nove*	*no*·ve	50	*cinquenta*	seeng·*kweng*·ta
10	*dez*	desh	60	*sessenta*	se·*seng*·ta
11	*onze*	*ong*·ze	70	*setenta*	se·*teng*·ta
12	*doze*	*do*·ze	80	*oitenta*	oy·*teng*·ta
13	*treze*	*tre*·ze	90	*noventa*	no·*veng*·ta
14	*catorze*	ka·*tor*·ze	100	*cem*	seng
15	*quinze*	*keeng*·ze	1000	*mil*	meel

time & dates

What time is it?	*Que horas são?*	kee *o*·rash sowng
It's one o'clock.	*É uma hora.*	e *oo*·ma *o*·ra
It's (10) o'clock.	*São (dez) horas.*	sowng (desh) *o*·rash
Quarter past (10).	*(Dez) e quinze.*	(desh) e *keeng*·ze
Half past (10).	*(Dez) e meia.*	(desh) e *may*·a
Quarter to (10).	*Quinze para as (dez).*	*keeng*·ze *pa*·ra ash (desh)
At what time ...?	*A que horas ...?*	a ke *o*·rash ...
At ...	*Às ...*	ash ...
in the morning	*da manhã*	da ma·*nyang*
in the afternoon	*da tarde*	da *taar*·de
in the evening	*da noite*	da *noy*·te
Monday	*segunda-feira*	se·*goong*·da·*fay*·ra
Tuesday	*terça-feira*	*ter*·sa·*fay*·ra
Wednesday	*quarta-feira*	*kwaar*·ta·*fay*·ra
Thursday	*quinta-feira*	*keeng*·ta·*fay*·ra
Friday	*sexta-feira*	*saysh*·ta·*fay*·ra
Saturday	*sábado*	*saa*·ba·doo
Sunday	*domingo*	doo *meeng* goo

January	*Janeiro*	zha·*nay*·roo
February	*Fevereiro*	fe·*vray*·roo
March	*Março*	*maar*·soo
April	*Abril*	a·*breel*
May	*Maio*	*maa*·yoo
June	*Junho*	*zhoo*·nyoo
July	*Julho*	*zhoo*·lyoo
August	*Agosto*	a·*gosh*·too
September	*Setembro*	se·*teng*·broo
October	*Outubro*	oh·*too*·broo
November	*Novembro*	no·*veng*·broo
December	*Dezembro*	de·*zeng*·broo

What date is it today?
Qual é a data de hoje? — kwaal e a *daa*·ta de *o*·zhe

It's (18 October).
Hoje é dia (dezoito de Outubro). — *o*·zhe e *dee*·a (de·*zoy*·too de oh·*too*·broo)

since (May)	*desde (Maio)*	*desh*·de (*maa*·yoo)
until (June)	*até (Junho)*	a·*te* (*zhoo*·nyoo)
last ...		
night	*a noite passada*	a *noy*·te pa·*saa*·da
week	*a semana passada*	a se·*ma*·na pa·*saa*·da
month	*o mês passado*	oo mesh pa·*saa*·doo
year	*o ano passado*	oo *a*·noo pa·*saa*·doo
next ...		
week	*na próxima semana*	na *pro*·see·ma se·*ma*·na
month	*no próximo mês*	noo *pro*·see·moo mesh
year	*no próximo ano*	noo *pro*·see·moo *a*·noo
yesterday/tomorrow ...	*ontem/amanhã ...*	*ong*·teng/aa·ma·*nyang* ...
morning	*de manhã*	de ma·*nyang*
afternoon	*à tarde*	aa *taar*·de
evening	*à noite*	aa *noy*·te

PORTUGUÊS – tools

weather

What's the weather like?	*Como está o tempo?*	*ko*·moo shtaa oo *teng*·poo
It's …	*Está …*	shtaa …
cloudy	*enublado*	e·noo·*blaa*·doo
cold	*frio*	*free*·oo
hot	*muito quente*	*mweeng*·too *keng*·te
raining	*a chover*	a shoo·*ver*
snowing	*a nevar*	a ne·*vaar*
sunny	*sol*	sol
warm	*quente*	*keng*·te
windy	*ventoso*	veng·*to*·zoo
spring	*primavera* f	pree·ma·*ve*·ra
summer	*verão* m	ve·*rowng*
autumn	*outono* m	oh·*to*·noo
winter	*inverno* m	eenq·*ver*·noo

border crossing

I'm here …	*Estou …*	shtoh …
in transit	*em trânsito*	eng *trang*·zee·too
on business	*em negócios*	eng ne·*go*·syoosh
on holiday	*de férias*	de *fe*·ree·ash
I'm here for …	*Vou ficar por …*	voh fee·*kaar* poor …
(10) days	*(dez) dias*	(desh) *dee*·ash
(three) weeks	*(três) semanas*	(tresh) se·*ma*·nash
(two) months	*(dois) meses*	(doysh) *me*·zesh

I'm going to (Elvas).
Vou para (Elvas). voh *pa*·ra (*el*·vash)

I'm staying at the (Hotel Lisbon).
Estou no (Hotel Lisboa). shtoh noo (o·*tel* leezh·*bo*·a)

I have nothing to declare.
Não tenho nada a declarar. nowng *ta*·nyoo *naa*·da a de·kla·*raar*

I have something to declare.
Tenho algo a declarar. *ta*·nyoo *al*·goo a de·kla·*raar*

That's (not) mine.
Isto (não) é meu. *eesh*·too (nowng) e *me*·oo

transport

tickets & luggage

Where can I buy a ticket?
Onde é que eu compro o bilhete? — *ong*·de e ke *e*·oo *kong*·proo oo bee·*lye*·te

Do I need to book a seat?
Preciso de fazer reserva? — pre·*see*·zoo de fa·*zer* rre·*zer*·va

One ... ticket (to Braga), please.	*Um bilhete de ... (para Braga), por favor.*	oong bee·*lye*·te de ... (pra *braa*·ga) poor fa·*vor*
one-way	*ida*	*ee*·da
return	*ida e volta*	*ee*·da ee *vol*·ta

I'd like to ... my ticket, please.	*Queria ... o bilhete, por favor.*	ke·*ree*·a ... oo bee·*lye*·te poor fa·*vor*
cancel	*cancelar*	kang·se·*laar*
change	*trocar*	troo·*kaar*
collect	*cobrar*	koo·*braar*
confirm	*confirmar*	kong·feer·*maar*

I'd like a ... seat, please.	*Queria um lugar ... por favor.*	ke·*ree*·a oong loo·*gaar* ... poor fa·*vor*
nonsmoking	*de não fumadores*	de nowng foo·ma·*do*·resh
smoking	*para fumadores*	pra foo·ma·*do*·resh

How much is it?
Quanto é? — *kwang*·too e

Is there air conditioning?
Tem ar condicionado? — teng aar kong·dee·syoo·*naa*·doo

Is there a toilet?
Tem casa de banho? — teng *kaa*·za de *ba*·nyoo

How long does the trip take?
Quanto tempo é que leva a viagem? — *kwang*·too *teng*·poo e ke *le*·va a vee·*aa*·zheng

Is it a direct route?
É uma rota directa? — e *oo*·ma *rro*·ta dee·*re*·ta

I'd like a luggage locker.
Queria o depósito de bagagens. — ke·*ree*·a oo de·*po*·zee·too de ba·*gaa*·zhengsh

My luggage has been …	*A minha bagagem …*	a *mee*·nya ba·*gaa*·zheng …
damaged	*foi danificada*	foy da·nee·fee·*kaa*·da
lost	*perdeu-se*	per·*de*·oo·se
stolen	*foi roubada*	foy rroh·*baa*·da

getting around

Where does flight (TP 615) arrive/depart?
De onde pára/parte o voo (TP 615)? — de *ong*·de *paa*·ra/*paar*·te oo *vo*·oo (te pe saysh·*seng*·toosh e *keeng*·ze)

Where's (the) …?	*Onde é …?*	*ong*·de e …
arrivals hall	*a porta de chegada*	a *por*·ta de she·*gaa*·da
departures hall	*a porta de partida*	a *por*·ta de par·*tee*·da
duty-free shop	*a loja duty-free*	a *lo*·zha *doo*·tee·free
gate (12)	*a porta (doze)*	a *por*·ta (*do*·ze)

Is this the … to (Lisbon)?	*Este é o … para (Lisboa)?*	*esh*·te e oo … pra (leezh·*bo*·a)
boat	*barco*	*baar* koo
bus	*autocarro*	ow·to·*kaa*·rroo
plane	*avião*	a·vee·*owng*
train	*comboio*	kong·*boy*·oo

What time's the … bus?	*Quando é que sai o … autocarro?*	*kwang*·doo e ke sai oo … ow·to·*kaa*·rroo
first	*primeiro*	pree·*may*·roo
last	*último*	*ool*·tee·moo
next	*próximo*	*pro*·see·moo

At what time does it arrive/leave?
A que horas chega/sai? — a ke *o*·rash *she*·ga/sai

How long will it be delayed?
Quanto tempo é que vai chegar atrasado? — *kwang*·too *teng*·poo e ke vai she·*gaar* a·tra·*zaa*·doo

What station/stop is this?
Qual estação/paragem é este? — kwaal shta·*sowng*/pa·*raa*·zheng e *esh*·te

What's the next station/stop?
Qual é a próxima estação/paragem? — kwaal e a *pro*·see·ma shta·*sowng*/pa·*raa*·zheng

Does it stop at (Amarante)?
Pára em (Amarante)? — *paa*·ra eng (a·ma·*rang*·te)

Please tell me when we get to (Évora).
Por favor avise-me quando chegarmos a (Évora). — poor fa·*vor* a·*vee*·ze·me *kwang*·doo she·*gaar*·moosh a (*e*·voo·ra)

How long do we stop here?
Quanto tempo vamos ficar parados aqui? — *kwang*·too *teng*·poo *va*·moosh fee·*kaar* pa·*raa*·doosh a·*kee*

Is this seat available?
Este lugar está vago? — *esh*·te loo·*gaar* shtaa *va*·goo

That's my seat.
Este é o meu lugar. — *esh*·te e oo *me*·oo loo·*gaar*

I'd like a taxi . . .	*Queria chamar um táxi . . .*	ke·*ree*·a sha·*maar* oong *taak*·see . . .
at (9am)	*para as (nove da manhã)*	pra ash (*no*·ve da ma·*nyang*)
now	*agora*	a·*go*·ra
tomorrow	*amanhã*	aa·ma·*nyang*

Is this taxi available?
Este táxi está livre? — *esh*·te *taak*·see shtaa *lee*·vre

How much is it to . . .?
Quanto custa até ao . . . ? — *kwang*·too *koosh*·ta a·*te* ow . . .

Please put the meter on.
Por favor, ligue o taxímetro. — poor fa·*vor* *lee*·ge oo taak·*see*·me·troo

Please take me to (this address).
Leve-me para (este endereço), por favor. — *le*·ve·me *pa*·ra (*esh*·te eng·de·*re*·soo) poor fa·*vor*

Please . . .	*Por favor . . .*	poor fa·*vor* . . .
slow down	*vá mais devagar*	vaa maish de·va·*gaar*
stop here	*pare aqui*	*paa*·re a·*kee*
wait here	*espere aqui*	*shpe*·re a·*kee*

car, motorbike & bicycle hire

I'd like to hire a ...	*Queria alugar ...*	ke·*ree*·a a·loo·*gaar* ...
bicycle	*uma bicicleta*	*oo*·ma bee·see·*kle*·ta
car	*um carro*	oong *kaa*·rroo
motorbike	*uma mota*	*oo*·ma *mo*·ta
with ...	*com ...*	kong ...
a driver	*motorista*	moo·too·*reesh*·ta
air conditioning	*ar condicionado*	aar kong·dee·syoo·*naa*·doo
How much for ... hire?	*Quanto custa para alugar por...?*	*kwang*·too *koosh*·ta *pa*·ra a·loo·*gaar* poor ...
hourly	*hora*	*o*·ra
daily	*dia*	*dee*·a
weekly	*semana*	se·*ma*·na
air	*ar* m	aar
oil	*óleo* m	*o*·le·oo
petrol	*gasolina* f	ga·zoo·*lee*·na
tyres	*pneus* m pl	pe·*ne*·oosh

I need a mechanic.
Preciso de um mecânico. pre·*see*·zoo de oong me·*kaa*·nee·koo

I've run out of petrol.
Estou sem gasolina. shtoh seng ga·zoo·*lee*·na

I have a flat tyre.
Tenho um furo no pneu. *ta*·nyoo oong *foo*·roo noo pe·*ne*·oo

directions

Where's the ...?	*Onde é ...?*	*ong*·de e ...
bank	*o banco*	oo *bang*·koo
city centre	*o centro da cidade*	oo *seng*·troo da see·*daa*·de
hotel	*o hotel*	oo o·*tel*
market	*o mercado*	oo mer·*kaa*·doo
police station	*a esquadra da polícia*	a *shkwaa*·dra da poo·*lee*·sya
post office	*o correio*	oo koo·*rray*·oo
public toilet	*a casa de banho pública*	a *kaa*·za de *ba*·nyoo *poo*·blee·ka
tourist office	*o escritório de turismo*	oo shkree·*to*·ryoo de too·*reezh*·moo

Is this the road to (Sintra)?
Esta é a estrada para (Sintra)? — *esh*·ta e a *shtraa*·da *pa*·ra (*seeng*·tra)

Can you show me (on the map)?
Pode-me mostrar (no mapa)? — *po*·de·me moosh·*traar* (noo *maa*·pa)

How far is it?
A que distância fica? — a ke deesh·*tang*·sya *fee*·ka

How do I get there?
Como é que eu chego lá? — *ko*·moo e ke *e*·oo *she*·goo laa

Turn …	*Vire …*	*vee*·re …
at the corner	*na esquina*	na *shkee*·na
at the traffic lights	*nos semáforos*	noosh se·*maa*·foo·roosh
left	*à esquerda*	aa *shker*·da
right	*à direita*	aa dee·*ray*·ta

It's …	*É …*	e …
behind …	*atrás de …*	a·*traash* de …
far away	*longe*	*long*·zhe
here	*aqui*	a·*kee*
in front of …	*em frente de …*	eng *freng*·te de …
left	*à esquerda*	aa *shker*·da
near (to …)	*perto (de …)*	*per*·too (de …)
next to …	*ao lado de …*	ow *laa*·doo de …
on the corner	*na esquina*	na *shkee*·na
opposite …	*do lado oposto …*	doo *laa*·doo oo·*posh*·too …
right	*à direita*	aa dee·*ray*·ta
straight ahead	*em frente*	eng *freng*·te
there	*lá*	laa

by bus	*de autocarro*	de ow·to·*kaa*·rroo
by taxi	*de táxi*	de *taak*·see
by train	*de comboio*	de kong·*boy*·oo
on foot	*a pé*	a pe

north	*norte*	*nor*·te
south	*sul*	sool
east	*leste*	*lesh*·te
west	*oeste*	o·*esh*·te

signs

Entrada/Saída	eng·*traa*·da/sa·*ee*·da	**Entrance/Exit**
Aberto/Fechado	a·*ber*·too/fe·*shaa*·doo	**Open/Closed**
Há Vaga	aa *vaa*·ga	**Rooms Available**
Não Há Vaga	nowng aa *vaa*·ga	**No Vacancies**
Informação	eeng·for·ma·*sowng*	**Information**
Esquadra da Polícia	*shkwaa*·dra da poo·*lee*·sya	**Police Station**
Proibido	pro·ee·*bee*·doo	**Prohibited**
Casa de Banho	*kaa*·za de *ba*·nyoo	**Toilets**
Homens	*o*·mengsh	**Men**
Mulheres	moo·*lye*·resh	**Women**
Quente/Frio	*keng*·te/*free*·oo	**Hot/Cold**

accommodation

finding accommodation

Where's a ...?	*Onde é que há ...?*	*ong*·de e ke aa ...
camping ground	*um parque de campismo*	oong *paar*·ke de kang·*peezh*·moo
guesthouse	*uma casa de hóspedes*	*oo*·ma *kaa*·za de *osh*·pe·desh
hotel	*um hotel*	oong o·*tel*
youth hostel	*uma pousada de juventude*	*oo*·ma poh·*zaa*·da de zhoo·veng·*too*·de

Can you recommend somewhere ...?	*Pode recomendar algum lugar ...?*	*po*·de rre·koo·meng·*daar* aal·*goong* loo·*gaar* ...
cheap	*barato*	ba·*raa*·too
good	*bom*	bong
nearby	*perto daqui*	*per*·too da·*kee*

I'd like to book a room, please.
Eu queria fazer uma reserva, por favor. — e·oo ke·*ree*·a fa·*zer* *oo*·ma rre·*zer*·va poor fa·*vor*

I have a reservation.
Eu tenho uma reserva. — e·oo *ta*·nyoo *oo*·ma rre·*zer*·va

My name's ...
O meu nome é ... — oo *me*·oo *no*·me e ...

Do you have a ... room?	*Tem um quarto ...?*	teng oong *kwaar*·too ...
single	*de solteiro*	de sol·*tay*·roo
double	*de casal*	de ka·*zaal*
twin	*duplo*	*doo*·ploo
How much is it per ...?	*Quanto custa por ...?*	*kwang*·too *koosh*·ta poor ...
night	*noite*	*noy*·te
person	*pessoa*	pe·*so*·a
Can I pay by ...?	*Posso pagar com ...?*	*po*·soo pa·*gaar* kong ...
credit card	*cartão de crédito*	kar·*towng* de *kre*·dee·too
travellers cheque	*traveller cheque*	*tra*·ve·ler shek

I'd like to stay for (three) nights.
Para (três) noites. — *pa*·ra (tresh) *noy*·tesh

From (2 July) to (6 July).
De (dois de julho) até (seis de julho). — de (doysh de *zhoo*·lyoo) a·*te* (saysh de *zhoo*·lyoo)

Can I see it?
Posso ver? — *po*·soo ver

Am I allowed to camp here?
Posso acampar aqui? — *po*·soo a·kang·*paar* a·*kee*

Where can I find a camping ground?
Onde é o parque de campismo? — *ong*·de e oo *par*·ke de kang·*peesh*·moo

requests & queries

When/Where is breakfast served?
Quando/Onde é que servem o pequeno almoço? — *kwang*·doo/*ong*·de e ke *ser*·veng oo pe·*ke*·noo aal·*mo*·soo

Please wake me at (seven).
Por favor acorde-me às (sete). — poor fa·*vor* aa·*kor*·de·me aash (*se*·te)

Could I have my key, please?
Pode-me dar a minha chave, por favor? — *po*·de·me daar a *mee*·nya *shaa*·ve poor fa·*vor*

Can I get another (blanket)?
Pode-me dar mais um (cobertor)? — *po*·de·me daar maish oong (koo·ber·*tor*)

Is there a/an ...?	*Tem ...?*	teng ...
elevator	*elevador*	e·le·va·*dor*
safe	*cofre*	*ko*·fre
The room is too ...	*É demasiado ...*	e de·ma·zee·*aa*·doo ...
expensive	*caro*	*kaa*·roo
noisy	*barulhento*	ba·roo·*lyeng*·too
small	*pequeno*	pe·*ke*·noo
The ... doesn't work.	*... não funciona.*	... nowng foong·see·*o*·na
air conditioner	*O ar condicionado*	oo aar kong·dee·syoo·*naa*·doo
fan	*A ventoínha*	a veng·too·*ee*·na
toilet	*A sanita*	a sa·*nee*·ta
This ... isn't clean.	*Esta ... está suja.*	*esh*·ta ... shtaa *soo*·zha
pillow	*almofada*	aal·moo·*faa*·da
towel	*toalha*	*twaa*·lya
This sheet isn't clean.	*Este lençol está sujo.*	*esh*·te leng·*sol* shtaa *soo*·zho

checking out

What time is checkout?
A que horas é a partida? — a ke *o*·rash e a par·*tee*·da

Can I leave my luggage here?
Posso deixar as minhas malas aqui? — *po*·soo day·*shaar* ash *mee*·nyash *maa*·lash a·*kee*

Could I have my ..., please?	*Pode-me devolver ..., por favor?*	*po*·de·me de·vol·*ver* ... poor fa·*vor*
deposit	*o depósito*	oo de·*po*·zee·too
passport	*o passaporte*	oo paa·sa·*por*·te
valuables	*os objectos de valor*	oosh o·be·*zhe*·toosh de va·*lor*

communications & banking

the internet

Where's the local Internet café?
Onde fica um café da internet nas redondezas? — *ong*·de *fee*·ka oong ka·*fe* da eeng·ter·*net* nash rre·dong·*de*·zash

How much is it per hour?
Quanto custa por hora? — *kwang*·too *koosh*·ta pooro·ra

I'd like to ...	*Queria ...*	ke·*ree*·a ...
check my email	*ler o meu email*	ler oo *me*·oo ee·*mayl*
get Internet access	*ter acesso à internet*	ter a·*se*·soo aa eeng·ter·*net*
use a printer	*usar uma impressora*	oo·*zaar oo*·ma eeng·pre·*so*·ra
use a scanner	*usar um digitalizador*	oo·*zaar* oong dee·zhee·ta·lee·za·*dor*

mobile/cell phone

I'd like a ...	*Queria ...*	ke·*ree*·a ...
mobile/cell phone for hire	*alugar um telemóvel*	a·loo·*gaar* oong te·le·*mo*·vel
SIM card for your network	*cartão SIM para a sua rede*	kar·*towng* seeng *pa*·ra a *soo*·a *rre*·de

What are the rates?	*Qual é o valor cobrado?*	kwaal e oo va·*lor* koo·*braa*·doo

telephone

What's your phone number?
Qual é o seu número de telefone? — kwaal e oo *se*·oo *noo*·me·roo de te·le·*fo*·ne

The number is ...
O número é ... — oo *noo*·me·roo e ...

Where's the nearest public phone?
Onde fica o telefone público mais perto? — *ong*·de *fee*·ka o te·le·*fo*·ne *poo*·blee·koo maish *per*·too

I'd like to buy a phonecard.
Quero comprar um cartão telefónico. — *ke*·roo kong·*praar* oong kar·*towng* te·le·*fo*·nee·koo

I want to ...	*Quero ...*	*ke*·roo ...
call (Singapore)	*telefonar (para Singapura)*	te·le·foo·*naar* (*pa*·ra seeng·ga·*poo*·ra)
make a local call	*fazer uma chamada local*	fa·*zer oo*·ma sha·*maa*·da loo·*kaal*
reverse the charges	*fazer uma chamada a cobrar*	fa·*zer oo*·ma sha·*maa*·da a koo·*braar*

How much does ... cost?	*Quanto custa ...?*	*kwang*·too *koosh*·ta ...
a (three)-minute call	*uma ligação de (três) minutos*	*oo*·ma lee·ga·*sowng* de (tresh) mee·*noo*·toosh
each extra minute	*cada minuto extra*	*kaa*·da mee·*noo*·too *aysh*·tra

It's (30c) per (30) seconds.
(Trinta cêntimos) por (trinta) segundos.
(*treeng*·ta *seng*·tee·moosh) poor (*treeng*·ta) se·*goong*·doosh

post office

I want to send a ...	*Quero enviar ...*	ke·roo eng·vee·*aar* ...
fax	*um fax*	oong faks
letter	*uma carta*	*oo*·ma *kaar*·ta
parcel	*uma encomenda*	*oo*·ma eng·koo·*meng*·da
postcard	*um postal*	oong poosh·*taal*

I want to buy a/an ...	*Quero comprar um ...*	ke·*roo* kong·*praar* oong ...
envelope	*envelope*	eng·ve·*lo*·pe
stamp	*selo*	*se*·loo

Please send it (to Australia) by ...	*Por favor envie isto (para Australia) por ...*	poor fa·*vor* eng·*vee*·e *eesh*·too (*pa*·ra owsh·*traa*·lya) poor ...
airmail	*via aérea*	*vee*·a a·*e*·ree·a
express mail	*correio azul*	koo·*rray*·oo a·*zool*
registered mail	*registado/a* m/f	rre·zheesh·*taa*·doo/a
surface mail	*via terrestre*	*vee*·a te·*rresh*·tre

Is there any mail for me?
Há alguma correspondência para mim?
aa aal·*goo*·ma koo·rresh·pong·*deng*·sya *pa*·ra meeng

bank

Where's a/an ...?	*Onde é que há ...?*	*ong*·de e ke aa ...
ATM	*um caixa automático*	oong *kai*·sha ow·too·*maa*·tee·koo
foreign exchange office	*um câmbio*	oong *kang*·byoo

I'd like to ...	*Queria ...*	ke·*ree*·a ...
Where can I ...?	*Onde é que posso ...?*	*ong*·de e ke *po*·soo ...
arrange a transfer	*fazer uma transferencia*	faa·*zer oo*·ma trans·fe·*reng*·sya
cash a cheque	*trocar um cheque*	troo·*kaar* oong *she*·ke
change a travellers cheque	*trocar traveller cheque*	troo·*kaar tra*·ve·ler shek
change money	*trocar dinheiro*	troo·*kaar* dee·*nyay*·roo
get a cash advance	*fazer um levantamento adiantado*	fa·*zer* oong le·vang·ta·*meng*·too a·dee·ang·*taa*·doo
withdraw money	*levantar dinheiro*	le·vang·*taar* dee·*nyay*·roo

What's the ...?	*Qual é ...?*	kwaal e ...
commission	*a comissão*	a koo·mee·*sowng*
charge for that	*o imposto*	oo eeng·*posh*·too
exchange rate	*o câmbio do dia*	oo *kang*·byoo doo *dee*·a

It's ...	*É ...*	e ...
(12) euros	*(doze) euros*	(*do*·ze) e·*oo*·roosh
free	*gratuito*	gra·*twee*·too

What time does the bank open?
A que horas é que abre o banco? — a ke *o*·rash e ke *aa*·bre oo *bang*·koo

Has my money arrived yet?
O meu dinheiro já chegou? — oo *me*·oo dee·*nyay*·roo zhaa she·*goh*

sightseeing

getting in

What time does it open/close?
A que horas abre/fecha? — a ke *o*·rash *aa*·bre/*fe*·sha

What's the admission charge?
Qual é o preço de entrada? — kwaal e oo *pre*·soo de eng·*traa*·da

Is there a discount for children/students?
Tem desconto para crianças/ estudantes? — teng desh·*kong*·too *pa*·ra kree·*ang*·sash/ shtoo·*dang*·tesh

I'd like a …	*Queria um …*	ke·*ree*·a oong …
catalogue	*catálogo*	ka·*taa*·loo·goo
guide	*guia*	*gee*·a
local map	*mapa local*	*maa*·pa loo·*kaal*

I'd like to see …	*Eu gostava de ver …*	*e*·oo goosh·*taa*·va de ver …
What's that?	*O que é aquilo?*	oo ke e a·*kee*·loo
Can I take a photo?	*Posso tirar uma fotografia?*	*po*·soo tee·*raar oo*·ma foo·too·gra·*fee*·a

tours

When's the next …?	*Quando é …?*	*kwang*·doo e …
day trip	*o próximo passeio*	oo *pro*·see·moo pa·*say*·oo
tour	*a próxima excursão*	a *pro*·see·ma shkoor·*sowng*

Is … included?	*Inclui …?*	eeng·*kloo*·ee …
accommodation	*hospedagem*	osh·pe·*daa*·zheng
the admission charge	*preço de entrada*	*pre*·soo de eng·*traa*·da
food	*comida*	koo·*mee*·da
transport	*transporte*	trangsh·*por*·te

How long is the tour?
Quanto tempo dura a excursão? — *kwang*·too *teng*·poo *doo*·ra a shkoor·*sowng*

What time should we be back?
A que hora é que devemos estar de volta? — a ke *o*·ra e ke de·*ve*·moosh shtaar de *vol*·ta

sightseeing		
castle	*castelo* m	kash·*te*·loo
cathedral	*catedral* f	ka·te·*draal*
church	*igreja* f	ee·*gre*·zha
main square	*praça principal* f	*praa*·sa preeng·see·*paal*
monastery	*mosteiro* m	moosh·*tay*·roo
monument	*monumento* m	moo·noo·*meng*·too
museum	*museu* m	moo·*ze*·oo
old city	*cidade antiga* f	see·*daa*·de ang·*tee*·ga
palace	*palácio* m	pa·*laa*·syoo
ruins	*ruínas* f pl	rroo·*ee*·nash
stadium	*estádio* m	*shtaa*·dyoo
statues	*estátuas* f pl	shtaa·too·ash

shopping

enquiries

Where's a ...?	*Onde é ...?*	*ong*·de e ...
bank	*o banco*	oo *bang*·koo
bookshop	*a livraria*	a lee·vra·*ree*·a
department store	*loja de departamentos*	*lo*·zha de de·par·ta·*meng*·toosh
grocery store	*a mercearia*	a mer·see·a·*ree*·a
market	*o mercado*	oo mer·*kaa*·doo
newsagency	*o quiosque*	oo kee·*osh*·ke
supermarket	*o supermercado*	oo soo·per·mer·*kaa*·doo

Where can I buy (a padlock)?
Onde é que posso comprar (um cadeado)? — *ong*·de e ke *po*·soo kong·*praar* (oong ka·de·*aa*·doo)

I'm looking for ...
Estou à procura de ... — shtoh aa proo·*koo*·ra de ...

Can I look at it?
Posso ver? — *po*·soo ver

Do you have any others?
Tem outros? — teng *oh*·troosh

Does it have a guarantee?
Tem garantia? teng ga·rang·*tee*·a

Can I have it sent overseas?
Podem enviar para o estrangeiro? *po*·deng eng·vee·*aar pa*·ra oo shtrang·*zhay*·roo

Can I have my ... repaired?
Vocês consertam ... ? vo·*sesh* kong·*ser*·tang ...

It's faulty.
Tem defeito. teng de·*fay*·too

I'd like ..., please.	*Queria ..., por favor.*	ke·*ree*·a ... poor fa·*vor*
a bag	*um saco*	oong *saa*·koo
a refund	*ser reembolsado/a* m/f	ser rre·eng·bol·*saa*·doo/a
to return this	*devolver isto*	de·vol·*ver eesh*·too

paying

How much is it?
Quanto custa? *kwang*·too *koosh*·ta

Can you write down the price?
Pode escrever o preço? *po*·de shkre·*ver* oo *pre*·soo

That's too expensive.
Está muito caro. shtaa *mweeng*·too *kaa*·roo

What's your lowest price?
Qual é o seu último preço? kwaal e oo *se*·oo *ool*·tee·moo *pre*·soo

I'll give you (five) euros.
Dou-lhe (cinco) euros. *doh*·lye (*seeng*·koo) e·*oo*·roosh

There's a mistake in the bill.
Há um erro na conta. aa oong *e*·rroo na *kong*·ta

Do you accept ...?	*Aceitam ...?*	a·*say*·tang ...
credit cards	*cartão de crédito*	kar·*towng* de *kre*·dee·too
debit cards	*multibanco*	mool·tee·*bang*·koo
travellers cheques	*travellers cheques*	*tra*·ve·ler *she*·kesh

I'd like ..., please.	*Queria ..., por favor.*	ke·*ree*·a ... poor fa·*vor*
a receipt	*um recibo*	oong rre·*see*·boo
my change	*o troco*	oo *tro*·koo

clothes & shoes

Can I try it on?	*Posso experimentar?*	*po*·soo shpree·meng·*taar*
My size is (40).	*O meu número é (quarenta).*	oo *me*·oo *noo*·me·roo e (kwa·*reng*·ta)
It doesn't fit.	*Não serve.*	nowng *ser*·ve
small	*pequeno/pequena* m/f	pe·*ke*·noo/pe·*ke*·na
medium	*meio/meia* m/f	*may*·oo/*may*·a
large	*grande* m&f	*grang*·de

books & music

I'd like a ...	*Queria comprar ...*	ke·*ree*·a kong·*praar* ...
newspaper (in English)	*um jornal (em inglês)*	oong zhor·*naal* (eng eeng·*glesh*)
pen	*uma caneta*	*oo*·ma ka·*ne*·ta

Is there an English-language bookshop?
Há uma livraria de língua inglesa? — aa *oo*·ma lee·vra·*ree*·a de *leeng*·gwa eeng·*gle*·za

I'm looking for something by (Fernando Pessoa).
Estou à procura de qualquer coisa do (Fernando Pessoa). — shtoh aa proo·*koo*·ra de kwaal·*ker* *koy*·za doo (fer·*nang*·doo pe·*so*·a)

Can I listen to this?
Posso ouvir? — *po*·soo oh·*veer*

photography

I need a/an ... film for this camera.	*Preciso de filme ... para esta máquina.*	pre·*see*·zoo de *feel*·me ... *pa*·ra *esh*·ta *maa*·kee·na
APS	*sistema APS*	seesh·*te*·ma aa pe *e*·se
B&W	*a preto e branco*	a *pre*·too e *brang*·koo
colour	*a cores*	a *ko*·resh
slide	*de diapositivos*	de dee·a·po·zee·*tee*·voosh
(200) ASA	*de (duzentos) ASA*	de (doo·*zeng*·toosh) *aa*·za
When will it be ready?	*Quando fica pronto?*	*kwang*·doo *fee*·ka *prong*·too

Can you …?	*Pode …?*	*po*·de …
develop this film	*revelar este filme*	rre·ve·*laar esh*·te *feel*·me
load my film	*carregar o filme*	kaa·rre·*gaar* oo *feel*·me
transfer photos from my camera to CD	*transferir as fotografias da minha máquina para um CD*	trangsh·fe·*reer* ash foo·too·gra·*fee*·ash da *mee*·nya *maa*·kee·na *pa*·ra oong se·*de*

meeting people

greetings, goodbyes & introductions

Hello/Hi.	*Olá.*	o·*laa*
Good night.	*Boa noite.*	*bo*·a *noy*·te
Goodbye/Bye.	*Adeus.*	a·*de*·oosh
See you later.	*Até logo.*	a·*te lo*·goo
Mr	*Senhor*	se·*nyor*
Mrs	*Senhora*	se·*nyo*·ra
Ms	*Senhorita*	se·nyo·*ree*·ta
How are you?	*Como está?*	*ko*·moo shtaa
Fine. And you?	*Bem. E você?*	beng e vo·*se*
What's your name?	*Qual é o seu nome?*	kwaal e oo *se*·oo *no*·me
My name is …	*O meu nome é …*	oo *me*·oo *no*·me e …
I'm pleased to meet you.	*Prazer em conhecê-lo/conhecê-la.* m/f	pra·*zer* eng koo·nye·*se*·lo/koo·nye·*se*·la
This is my …	*Este é o meu …* m *Esta é a minha …* f	*esh*·te e oo *me*·oo … *esh*·ta e a *mee*·nya …
brother	*irmão*	eer·*mowng*
daughter	*filha*	*fee*·lya
father	*pai*	pai
friend	*amigo/a* m/f	a·*mee*·goo/a
husband	*marido*	ma·*ree*·doo
mother	*mãe*	maing
partner (intimate)	*companheiro/a* m/f	kong·pa·*nyay*·roo/a
sister	*irmã*	eer·*mang*
son	*filho*	*fee*·lyoo
wife	*espasa*	*shpo*·za

Here's my ...	*Aqui está o meu ...*	a·*kee* shtaa oo *me*·oo ...
What's your ...?	*Qual é o seu ...?*	kwaal e oo *se*·oo ...
address	*endereço*	eng·de·*re*·soo
email address	*email*	ee·*mayl*
fax number	*número de fax*	*noo*·me·roo de faaks
phone number	*número de telefone*	*noo*·me·roo de te·le·*fo*·ne

occupations

What's your occupation?
Qual é a sua profissão? kwaal e a *soo*·a proo·fee·*sowng*

I'm a/an ...	*Sou ...*	soh ...
artist	*artista* **m&f**	ar·*teesh*·ta
business person	*homem/mulher de negócios* **m/f**	*o*·meng/moo·*lyer* de ne·*go*·syoosh
farmer	*agricultor* **m&f**	a·gree·kool·*tor*
manual worker	*trabalhador* **m**	tra·ba·lya·*dor*
	trabalhadora **f**	tra·ba·lya·*do*·ra
office worker	*empregado/a de escritório* **m/f**	eng·pre·*gaa*·doo/a de shkree·*to*·ryoo
scientist	*cientista* **m&f**	see·eng·*teesh*·ta
student	*estudante* **m&f**	shtoo·*dang*·te
tradesperson	*comerciante* **m&f**	koo·mer·see·*aang*·te

background

Where are you from?	*De onde é?*	*dong*·de e
I'm from ...	*Eu sou ...*	*e*·oo soh ...
Australia	*da Austrália*	da owsh·*traa*·lya
Canada	*do Canadá*	doo ka·na·*daa*
England	*da Inglaterra*	da eeng·gla·*te*·rra
New Zealand	*da Nova Zelândia*	da *no*·va ze·*lang*·dya
the USA	*dos Estados Unidos*	doosh *shtaa*·doosh oo·*nee*·doosh

Are you married?	*É casado/a?* **m/f**	e ka·*zaa*·doo/a
I'm ...	*Eu sou ...*	*e*·oo soh ...
married	*casado/a* **m/f**	ka·*zaa*·doo/a
single	*solteiro/a* **m/f**	sol·*tay*·roo/a

age

How old . . .?	*Quantos anos . . .?*	*kwang*·toosh *a*·noosh . . .
are you	*tem*	teng
is your daughter	*tem a sua filha*	teng a *soo*·a *fee*·lya
is your son	*tem o seu filho*	teng oo *se*·oo *fee*·lyoo
I'm . . . years old.	*Tenho . . . anos.*	*ta*·nyoo . . . *a*·noosh
He/She is . . . years old.	*Ele/Ela tem . . . anos.*	e·le/e·la teng . . . *a*·noosh

feelings

I'm (not) . . .	*(Não) Estou . . .*	(nowng) shtoh . . .
Are you . . .?	*Está . . .*	shtaa . . .
cold	*com frio*	kong *free*·oo
happy	*feliz*	fe·*leesh*
hot	*com calor*	kong ka·*lor*
hungry	*com fome*	kong *fo*·me
OK	*bem*	beng
sad	*triste*	*treesh*·te
thirsty	*com sede*	kong *se*·de
tired	*cansado/a* m/f	kang·*saa*·doo/a

entertainment

going out

Where can I find . . .?	*Onde é que há . . .?*	*ong*·de e ke aa . . .
clubs	*discotecas*	deesh·koo·*te*·kash
gay/lesbian venues	*lugares de gays/lésbicas*	loo·*gaa*·resh de gaysh/*lezh*·bee·kash
pubs	*bares*	*ba*·resh
I feel like going to a . . .	*Está-me a apetecer ir a . . .*	*shtaa*·me a a·pe·te·*ser* eer a . . .
concert	*um concerto*	oong kong·*ser*·too
movies	*um filme*	oong *feel*·me
party	*uma festa*	*oo*·ma *fesh*·ta
restaurant	*um restaurante*	oong rresh·tow·*rang*·te
theatre	*uma peça de teatro*	*oo*·ma *pe*·sa de tee·*aa*·troo

interests

Do you like ...?	*Gosta de ...?*	*gosh*·ta de ...
I (don't) like ...	*Eu (não) gosto de ...*	e·oo (nowng) *gosh*·too de ...
art	*arte*	*aar*·te
cooking	*cozinhar*	koo·zee·*nyaar*
movies	*ver filmes*	ver *feel*·mesh
reading	*ler*	ler
sport	*fazer desporto*	fa·*zer* desh·*por*·too
travelling	*viajar*	vee·a·*zhaar*

Do you like to ...?	*Costuma ...?*	koosh·*too*·ma ...
dance	*ir dançar*	eer dang·*saar*
go to concerts	*ir a concertos*	eer a kong·*ser*·toosh
listen to music	*ouvir música*	oh·*veer* *moo*·zee·ka

food & drink

finding a place to eat

Can you recommend a ...?	*Pode-me recomendar um ...?*	*po*·de·me rre·koo·meng·*daar* oong ...
bar	*bar*	bar
café	*café*	ka·*fe*
restaurant	*restaurante*	rresh·tow·*rang*·te

I'd like ..., please.	*Queria uma ..., por favor.*	ke·*ree*·a *oo*·ma ... poor fa·*vor*
a table for (five)	*mesa para (cinco)*	*me*·za *pa*·ra (*seeng*·koo)
the (non)smoking section	*mesa de (não) fumador*	*me*·za de (nowng) foo·ma·*dor*

ordering food

breakfast	*pequeno almoço* m	pe·*ke*·noo aal·*mo*·soo
lunch	*almoço* m	aal·*mo*·soo
dinner	*jantar* m	zhang·*taar*
snack	*lanche* m	*lang*·she

What would you recommend?
O que é que recomenda? — oo ke e ke rre·koo·*meng*·da

I'd like (the) . . ., please.	*Queria . . ., por favor.*	ke·*ree*·a . . . poor fa·*vor*
bill	*a conta*	a *kong*·ta
drink list	*a lista das bebidas*	a *leesh*·ta dash be·*bee*·dash
menu	*um menu*	oong me·*noo*
that dish	*aquele prato*	a·*ke*·le *praa*·too

drinks

(cup of) coffee . . .	*(chávena de) café . . .*	(*shaa*·ve·na de) ka·*fe* . . .
(cup of) tea . . .	*(chávena de) chá . . .*	(*shaa*·ve·na de) shaa . . .
with milk	*com leite*	kong *lay*·te
without sugar	*sem açúcar*	seng a·*soo*·kar
(orange) juice	*sumo (de laranja)* m	*soo*·moo (de la·*rang*·zha)
soft drink	*refrigerante* m	rre·free·zhe·*rang*·te
. . . water	*água . . .*	*aa*·gwa . . .
hot	*quente*	*keng*·te
(sparkling) mineral	*mineral (com gás)*	mee·ne·*raal* (kong gaash)

in the bar

I'll have . . .	*Eu queria . . .*	*e*·oo ke·*ree*·a . . .
I'll buy you a drink.	*Eu pago-lhe uma bebida.*	*e*·oo *paa*·goo·lye *oo*·ma be·*bee*·da
What would you like?	*O que é que quer?*	oo ke e ke ker
Cheers!	*À nossa!*	aa *no*·sa
brandy	*brandy* f	*brang*·dee
cocktail	*cocktail* m	kok·*tayl*
a shot of (whisky)	*um copinho de (uísque)*	oong koo·*pee*·nyoo de (oo·*eesh*·kee)
a . . . of beer	*. . . de cerveja*	. . . de ser·*ve*·zha
bottle	*uma garrafa*	*oo*·ma ga·*rraa*·fa
glass	*um copo*	oong *ko*·poo
a bottle of . . . wine	*uma garrafa de vinho . . .*	*oo*·ma ga·*rraa*·fa de *vee*·nyoo . . .
a glass of . . . wine	*um copo de vinho . . .*	oong *ko*·poo de *vee*·nyoo . . .
red	*tinto*	*teeng*·too
sparkling	*espumante*	shpoo·*mang*·te
white	*branco*	*brang*·koo

self-catering

What's the local speciality?		
Qual é a especialidade local?		kwaal e a shpe·see·a·lee·*daa*·de loo·*kaal*
What's that?		
O que é aquilo?		oo ke e a·*kee*·loo
How much is (a kilo of cheese)?		
Quanto é (um quilo de queijo)?		*kwang*·too e (oong *kee*·loo de *kay*·zhoo)
I'd like ...	*Eu queria ...*	e·oo ke·*ree*·a ...
(200) grams	*(duzentos) gramas*	(doo·*zeng*·toosh) *graa*·mash
(two) kilos	*(dois) quilos*	(doysh) *kee*·loosh
(three) pieces	*(três) peças*	(tresh) *pe*·sash
(six) slices	*(seis) fatias*	(saysh) fa·*tee*·ash
Less.	*Menos.*	*me*·noosh
Enough.	*Chega.*	*she*·ga
More.	*Mais.*	maish

special diets & allergies

Is there a vegetarian restaurant near here?		
Há algum restaurante vegetariano perto daqui?		aa aal·*goong* rresh·tow·*rang*·te ve·zhe·ta·ree·*aa*·noo *per*·too da·*kee*
Do you have vegetarian food?		
Tem comida vegetariana?		teng koo·*mee*·da ve·zhe·ta·ree·*aa*·na
Could you prepare a meal without ...?	*Pode preparar sem ...?*	*po*·de pre·pa·*raar* seng ...
butter	*manteiga*	mang·*tay*·ga
eggs	*ovos*	*o*·voosh
meat stock	*caldo de carne*	*kaal*·doo de *kaar*·ne
I'm allergic to ...	*Eu sou alérgico/a a ...* m/f	*e*·oo soh a·*ler*·zhee·koo/a a ...
dairy produce	*produtos lácteos*	pro·*doo*·toosh *laak*·tee·oosh
gluten	*glúten*	*gloo*·teng
MSG	*MSG*	e·me·e·se·*zhe*
nuts	*oleaginosas*	o·lee·a·zhee·*no*·zash
seafood	*marisco*	ma·*reesh*·koo

menu reader

açorda f	a·*sor*·da	*bread-based thick soup, flavoured with garlic, coriander & olive oil*
alheiras f pl	a·*lyay*·rash	*bread, garlic, chilli & meat sausage*
arroz árabe m	a·*rrosh aa*·ra·be	*rice with raisins, nuts & dried fruit*
arroz de bacalhau m	a·*rrosh* de ba·ka·*lyow*	*rice with shredded salt cod*
assado de peixe m	a·*saa*·doo de *pay*·she	*mix of roasted or baked fish*
bacalhau no borralho m	ba·ka·*lyow* noo boo·*rraa*·lyoo	*salt cod steak wrapped in cabbage leaves & bacon*
bacalhau roupa-velha m	ba·ka·*lyow* rroh·pa·*ve*·lya	*mixture of cabbage, salt cod & potatoes, sautéed in olive oil & garlic*
bifana no pão f	bee·*fa*·na noo powng	*thin pork steak sandwich*
bitoque m	bee·*to*·ke	*steak or fillet with a fried egg on top*
bolo de mel m	*bo*·loo de mel	*rich molasses & spice cake with candied fruit & almonds*
borrachoes m pl	boo·rra·*shoyngsh*	*fried ring-shaped biscuits flavoured with brandy or white wine & cinnamon*
caldeirada f	kaal·day·*raa*·da	*soup-like stew, usually with fish*
chanfana f	shang·*fa*·na	*hearty stew with goat or mutton in heavy red wine sauce*
chouriço m	shoh·*ree*·soo	*garlicky pork sausage flavoured with red pepper paste*
coelho à cacador m	koo·e·lyoo aa ka·sa·*dor*	*rabbit stewed with wine & tomato*
cozido à Portuguesa m	koo·*zee*·doo aa poor·too·*ge*·za	*hearty meal with chunks of meats & sausages, vegetables, beans & rice*
dobrada f	doo·*braa*·da	*tripe with white beans & rice*
duchesse f	doo·*shes*	*puff pastry filled with whipped cream & topped with fruit*

escabeche m	shka·*be*·she	*raw meat or fish pickled in olive oil, vinegar, garlic & bay leaf*
favada à Portuguesa f	fa·*vaa*·da aa poor·too·*ge*·za	*stew of fava beans, sausage & sometimes poached eggs*
feijoada f	fay·*zhwaa*·da	*bean stew with sausages or other meat*
francesinha f	frang·se·*zee*·nya	*ham, sausage & cheese in a tomato-cream sauce, on slices of bread*
gaspacho m	gash·*paa*·shoo	*chilled tomato & garlic bread soup with olive oil, vinegar & oregano*
jesuítas m pl	zhe·zoo·*ee*·tash	*puff pastry with baked meringue icing*
manjar branco m	mang·*zhaar brang*·koo	*coconut-milk & prunes pudding with syrup poured over the top*
migas f pl	*mee*·gash	*a side dish, usually bread flavoured with olive oil, garlic & spices & fried*
morgados m pl	mor·*gaa*·doosh	*sweetmeats made with almonds & figs*
pastéis de feijão m pl	pash·*taysh* de fay·*zhowng*	*rich lima bean & almond mixture in flaky pastry shells*
pataniscas de bacalhau f pl	pa·ta·*neesh*·kash de ba·ka·*lyow*	*seasoned salt cod fritters*
prato de grão m	*praa*·too de growng	*chickpea stew flavoured with tomato, garlic, bay leaf & cumin*
salada de atum f	sa·*laa*·da de a·*toong*	*salad of tuna, potato, peas, carrots & eggs in an olive oil & vinegar dressing*
salame de chocolate m	sa·*la*·me de shoo·koo·*laa*·te	*dense chocolate fudge roll studded with bits of biscuits, served sliced*
sopa de pedra f	*so*·pa de *pe*·dra	*vegetable soup with red beans, onions, potatoes, pig's ear, bacon & sausages*
tecolameco m	te·koo·la·*me*·koo	*rich orange & almond cake*
tripas à moda do Porto f pl	*tree*·pash aa *mo*·da doo *por*·too	*slow-cooked dried beans, trotters, tripe, chicken, vegetables & sausages*

emergencies

basics

Help!	*Socorro!*	soo·*ko*·rroo
Stop!	*Stop!*	stop
Go away!	*Vá-se embora!*	*vaa*·se eng·*bo*·ra
Thief!	*Ladrão!*	la·*drowng*
Fire!	*Fogo!*	*fo*·goo
Watch out!	*Cuidado!*	kwee·*daa*·doo
Call . . .!	*Chame . . .!*	*shaa*·me . . .
a doctor	*um médico*	oong *me*·dee·koo
an ambulance	*uma ambulância*	*oo*·ma ang·boo·*lang*·sya
the police	*a polícia*	a poo·*lee*·sya

It's an emergency.
É uma emergência. — e *oo*·ma ee·mer·*zheng*·sya

Could you help me, please?
Pode ajudar, por favor? — *po*·de a·zhoo·*daar* poor fa·*vor*

Can I use the telephone?
Posso usar o seu telefone? — *po*·soo oo·*zaar* oo *se*·oo te·le·*fo*·ne

I'm lost.
Estou perdido/a. m/f — shtoh per·*dee*·doo/a

Where are the toilets?
Onde é a casa de banho? — *ong*·de e a *kaa*·za de *ba*·nyoo

police

Where's the police station?
Onde é a esquadra da polícia? — *ong*·de e a *shkwaa*·dra da poo·*lee*·sya

I want to report an offence.
Eu quero denunciar um crime. — e·oo *ke*·roo de·noong·see·*aar* oong *kree*·me

I have insurance.
Eu estou coberto/a pelo seguro. m/f — e·oo shtoh koo·*ber*·too/a *pe*·loo se·*goo*·roo

I've been assaulted.	*Eu fui agredido/a.* m/f	e·oo fwee a·gre·*dee*·doo/a
I've been raped.	*Eu fui violado/a.* m/f	e·oo fwee vee·oo·*laa*·doo/a
I've been robbed.	*Eu fui roubado/a.* m/f	e·oo fwee rroh·*baa*·doo/a

I've lost my ...	*Eu perdi ...*	e·oo per·*dee*
My ... was/were stolen.	*Roubaram ...*	rroh·*baa*·rang ...
backpack	*a minha mochila*	a *meeng*·nya moo·*shee*·la
bags	*os meus sacos*	oosh *me*·oosh *saa*·koosh
credit card	*o meu cartão de crédito*	oo *me*·oo kar·*towng* de *kre*·dee·too
handbag	*a minha bolsa*	a *mee*·nya *bol*·sa
jewellery	*as minhas jóias*	ash *mee*·nyash *zhoy*·ash
money	*o meu dinheiro*	oo *me*·oo dee·*nyay*·roo
passport	*o meu passaporte*	oo *me*·oo paa·sa·*por*·te
travellers cheques	*os meus travellers cheques*	oosh *me*·oosh *tra*·ve·ler *she*·kesh
wallet	*a minha carteira*	a *mee*·nya kar·*tay*·ra

I want to contact my ...	*Eu quero contactar com ...*	e·oo *ke*·roo kong·tak·*taar* kong ...
consulate	*o meu consulado*	oo *me*·oo kong·soo·*laa*·doo
embassy	*a minha embaixada*	a *mee*·nya eng·bai·*shaa*·da

health

medical needs

Where's the nearest ...?	*Qual é ... mais perto?*	kwaal e ... maish *per*·too
dentist	*o dentista*	oo deng·*teesh*·ta
doctor	*o médico* m *a médica* f	oo *me*·dee·koo a *me*·dee·ka
hospital	*o hospital*	oo osh·pee·*taal*
(night) pharmacist	*a farmácia (de serviço)*	a far·*maa*·sya (de ser·*vee*·soo)

I need a doctor (who speaks English).
Eu preciso de um médico (que fale inglês). — e·oo pre·*see*·zoo de oong *me*·dee·koo (que *faa*·le eeng·*glesh*)

Could I see a female doctor?
Posso ser vista por uma médica? — *po*·soo ser *veesh*·ta poor *oo*·ma *me*·dee·ka

I've run out of my medication.
Os meus medicamentos acabaram. — oosh *me*·oosh me·dee·ka·*meng*·toosh a·ka·*baa*·rowng

symptoms, conditions & allergies

I'm sick.	*Estou doente.*	shtoh doo·*eng*·te
It hurts here.	*Dói-me aqui.*	*doy*·me a·*kee*
I have (a) ...	*Eu tenho ...*	e·oo *ta*·nyoo ...
asthma	*asma*	*ash*·ma
bronchitis	*bronquite*	brong·*kee*·te
constipation	*prisão de ventre*	pree·*zowng* de *veng*·tre
cough	*tosse*	*to*·se
diarrhoea	*diarreia*	dee·a·*rray*·a
fever	*febre*	*fe*·bre
headache	*dor de cabeça*	dor de ka·*be*·sa
heart condition	*problemas cardíacos*	proo·*ble*·mash kar·*dee*·a·koosh
nausea	*náusea*	*now*·zee·a
pain	*dor*	dor
sore throat	*dores de garganta*	*do*·resh de gar·*gang*·ta
toothache	*uma dor de dentes*	*oo*·ma dor de *deng*·tesh
I'm allergic to ...	*Eu sou alérgico/a a* m/f	e·oo soh a·*ler*·zhee·koo/a a ...
antibiotics	*antibióticos*	ang·tee·bee·*o*·tee·koosh
anti-inflammatories	*anti-inflamatórios*	ang·tee·eeng·fla·ma·*to*·ryoosh
aspirin	*aspirina*	ash·pee·*ree*·na
bees	*abelhas*	a·*be*·lyash
codeine	*codeína*	ko·de·*ee*·na
penicillin	*penicilina*	pe·nee·see·*lee*·na
antiseptic	*antiséptico* m	ang·tee·*se*·tee·koo
bandage	*ligadura* f	lee·ga·*doo*·ra
condoms	*preservativos* m pl	pre·zer·va·*tee*·voosh
contraceptives	*contraceptivos* m pl	kong·tra·se·*tee*·voosh
diarrhoea medicine	*remédio para diarreia* m	re·*me*·dyo *pa*·ra dee·a·*rray*·a
insect repellent	*repelente* m	rre·pe·*leng*·te
laxatives	*laxantes* m pl	la·*shang*·tesh
painkillers	*comprimidos para as dores* m pl	kong·pree·*mee*·doosh *pa*·ra ash *do*·resh
rehydration salts	*sais rehidratantes* m pl	saish rre·ee·dra·*tang*·tesh
sleeping tablets	*pílulas para dormir* f pl	*pee*·loo·laash *pa*·ra door·*meer*

english–portuguese dictionary

Portuguese nouns and adjectives in this dictionary have their gender indicated with ⓜ (masculine) and ⓕ (feminine). If it's a plural noun, you'll also see pl. Words are also marked as v (verb), n (noun), a (adjective), pl (plural), sg (singular), inf (informal) and pol (polite) where necessary.

A

accident *acidente* ⓜ a·see·*deng*·te
accommodation *hospedagem* ⓕ osh·pe·*daa*·zheng
adaptor *adaptador* ⓜ a·da·pe·ta·*dor*
address *endereço* ⓜ eng·de·*re*·soo
after *depois* de·*poysh*
air conditioned *com ar condicionado* kong aar kong·dee·syoo·*naa*·doo
airplane *avião* ⓜ a·vee·*owng*
airport *aeroporto* ⓜ a·e·ro·*por*·too
alcohol *alcoól* ⓜ al·ko·*ol*
all a *todo/a* ⓜ/ⓕ *to*·doo/a
allergy *alergia* ⓕ a·ler·*zhee*·a
ambulance *ambulância* ⓕ ang·boo·*lang*·sya
and *e* e
ankle *tornozelo* ⓜ toor·noo·*ze*·loo
arm *braço* ⓜ *braa*·soo
ashtray *cinzeiro* ⓜ seeng·*zay*·roo
ATM *caixa automático* ⓜ *kai*·sha ow·too·*maa*·tee·koo

B

baby *bebé* ⓜ&ⓕ be·*be*
back (body) *costas* ⓕ pl *kosh*·tash
backpack *mochila* ⓕ moo·*shee*·la
bad *mau/má* ⓜ/ⓕ *ma*·oo/maa
bag *saco* ⓜ *saa*·koo
baggage claim *balcão de bagagens* ⓜ bal·*kowng* de ba·*gaa*·zhengsh
bank *banco* ⓜ *bang*·koo
bar *bar* ⓜ baar
bathroom *casa de banho* ⓕ *kaa*·za de *ba*·nyoo
battery *pilha* ⓕ *pee*·lya
beautiful *bonito/a* ⓜ/ⓕ boo·*nee*·too/a
bed *cama* ⓕ *ka*·ma
beer *cerveja* ⓕ ser·*ve*·zha
before *antes* *ang*·tesh
behind *atrás* a·*traash*
bicycle *bicicleta* ⓕ bee·see·*kle*·ta
big *grande* ⓜ&ⓕ *grang*·de
bill *conta* ⓕ *kong*·ta
black *preto/a* ⓜ/ⓕ *pre*·too/a
blanket *cobertor* ⓜ koo·ber·*tor*
blood groop *grupo sanguíneo* ⓜ *groo*·poo sang·*gwee*·nee·oo
blue *azul* a·*zool*
boat *barco* ⓜ *baar*·koo
book (make a reservation) v *reservar* rre·zer·*vaar*
bottle *garrafa* ⓕ ga·*rraa*·fa
bottle opener *saca-rolhas* ⓜ *saa*·ka·*rro*·lyash
boy *menino* ⓜ me·*nee*·noo
brake (car) *travão* ⓜ tra·*vowng*
breakfast *pequeno almoço* ⓜ pe·*ke*·noo aal·*mo*·soo
broken (faulty) *defeituoso/a* ⓜ/ⓕ de·fay·too·*o*·zoo/a
bus *autocarro* ⓜ ow·to·*kaa*·roo
business *negócios* ⓜ pl ne·*go*·syoosh
buy *comprar* kong·*praar*

C

café *café* ⓜ ka·*fe*
camera *máquina fotográfica* ⓕ *maa*·kee·na foo·too·*graa*·fee·ka
camp site *parque de campismo* ⓜ *paar*·ke de kang·*peezh*·moo
cancel *cancelar* kang·se·*laar*
can opener *abre latas* ⓜ *aa*·bre *laa*·tash
car *carro* ⓜ *kaa*·rroo
cash *dinheiro* ⓜ dee·*nyay*·roo
cash (a cheque) v *levantar (um cheque)* le·vang·*taar* (oong *she*·ke)
cell phone *telemóvel* ⓜ te·le·*mo*·vel
centre *centro* ⓜ *seng*·troo
change (money) v *trocar* troo·*kaar*
cheap *barato/a* ba·*raa*·too/a
check (bill) *conta* ⓕ *kong*·ta
check-in *check-in* ⓜ shek·*eeng*
chest *peito* ⓜ *pay*·too
child *criança* ⓜ&ⓕ kree·*ang*·sa
cigarette *cigarro* ⓜ see·*gaa*·rroo
city *cidade* ⓕ see·*daa*·de
clean a *limpo/a* ⓜ/ⓕ *leeng*·poo/a

closed *fechado/a* ⓜ/ⓕ fe·*shaa*·doo/a
coffee *café* ⓜ ka·*fe*
coins *moedas* ⓕ pl moo·*e*·dash
cold a *frio/a* ⓜ/ⓕ *free*·oo/a
collect call *ligação a cobrar* ⓕ lee·ga·*sowng* a koo·*braar*
come *vir* veer
computer *computador* ⓜ kong·poo·ta·*dor*
condom *preservativo* ⓜ pre·zer·va·*tee*·voo
contact lenses *lentes de contacto* ⓜ pl
leng·tesh de kong·*taak*·too
cook v *cozinhar* koo·zee·*nyaar*
cost *preço* ⓜ *pre*·soo
credit card *cartão de crédito* ⓜ kar·*towng* de *kre*·dee·too
cup *chávena* ⓕ *shaa*·ve·na
currency exchange *câmbio* ⓜ *kang*·byoo
customs (immigration) *alfândega* ⓕ aal·*fang*·de·ga

D

dangerous *perigoso/a* ⓜ/ⓕ pe·ree·*go*·zoo/a
date (time) *data* ⓕ *daa*·ta
day *dia* ⓜ *dee*·a
delay n *atraso* ⓜ a·*traa*·zoo
dentist *dentista* ⓜ&ⓕ deng·*teesh*·ta
depart *partir* par·*teer*
diaper *fralda* ⓕ *fraal*·da
dictionary *dicionário* ⓜ dee·syoo·*naa*·ryoo
dinner *jantar* ⓜ zhang·*taar*
direct *directo/a* ⓜ/ⓕ dee·*re*·too/a
dirty *sujo/a* ⓜ/ⓕ *soo*·zhoo/a
disabled *deficiente* de·fee·see·*eng*·te
discount *desconto* ⓜ desh·*kong*·too
doctor *médico/a* ⓜ/ⓕ *me*·dee·koo/a
double bed *cama de casal* ⓕ *ka*·ma de ka·*zaal*
double room *quarto de casal* ⓜ *kwaar*·too de ka·*zaal*
drink *bebida* ⓕ be·*bee*·da
drive v *conduzir* kong·doo·*zeer*
drivers licence *carta de condução* ⓕ
kaar·ta de kong·doo·*sowng*
drugs (illicit) *droga* ⓕ *dro*·ga
dummy (pacifier) *chupeta* ⓕ shoo·*pe*·ta

E

ear *orelha* ⓕ o·*re*·lya
east *leste* *lesh*·te
eat *comer* koo·*mer*
economy class *classe económica* ⓕ
klaa·se ee·koo·*no*·mee·ka
electricity *electricidade* ⓕ ee·le·tree·see·*daa*·de
elevator *elevador* ⓜ ee·le·va·*dor*
email *email* ⓜ ee·*mayl*
embassy *embaixada* ⓕ eng·bai·*shaa*·da
emergency *emergência* ⓕ ee·mer·*zheng*·sya
English (language) *inglês* ⓜ eeng·*glesh*
entrance *entrada* ⓕ eng·*traa*·da
evening *noite* ⓕ *noy*·te
exchange rate *taxa de câmbio* ⓕ *taa*·sha de *kang*·byoo
exit *saída* ⓕ saa·*ee*·da
expensive *caro/a* ⓜ/ⓕ *kaa*·roo/a
express mail *correio azul* ⓜ koo·*rray*·oo a·*zool*
eye *olho* ⓜ *o*·lyoo

F

far *longe* *long*·zhe
fast *rápido/a* ⓜ/ⓕ *rraa*·pee·doo/a
father *pai* ⓜ pai
film (camera) *filme* ⓜ *feel*·me
finger *dedo* ⓜ *de*·doo
first-aid kit *estojo de primeiros socorros* ⓜ
shto·zhoo de pree·*may*·roosh soo·*ko*·rroosh
first class *primeira classe* ⓕ pree·*may*·ra *klaa*·se
fish *peixe* ⓜ *pay*·she
food *comida* ⓕ koo·*mee*·da
foot *pé* ⓜ pe
fork *garfo* ⓜ *gaar*·foo
free (of charge) ⓐ *grátis* *graa*·teesh
friend *amigo/a* ⓜ/ⓕ a·*mee*·goo/a
fruit *fruta* ⓕ *froo*·ta
full *cheio/a* ⓜ/ⓕ *shay*·oo/a
funny *engraçado/a* ⓜ/ⓕ eng·gra·*saa*·doo/a

G

gift *presente* ⓜ pre·*zeng*·te
girl *menina* ⓕ me·*nee*·na
glass (drinking) *copo* ⓜ *ko*·poo
glasses *óculos* ⓜ pl *o*·koo·loosh
go *ir* eer
good *bom/boa* ⓜ/ⓕ bong/*bo*·a
green *verde* *ver*·de
guide n *guia* ⓜ *gee*·a

H

half *metade* ⓕ me·*taa*·de
hand *mão* ⓕ mowng
handbag *mala de mão* ⓕ *maa*·la de mowng
happy *feliz* ⓜ&ⓕ fe·*leesh*

have *ter* ter
he *ele* e·le
head *cabeça* ⓕ ka·be·sa
heart *coração* ⓜ koo·ra·*sowng*
heat *calor* ⓜ ka·*lor*
heavy *pesado/a* ⓜ/ⓕ pe·*zaa*·doo/a
help v *ajudar* a·zhoo·*daar*
here *aqui* a·*kee*
high *alto/a* ⓜ/ⓕ *aal*·too/aa
highway *autoestrada* ⓕ ow·to·*shtraa*·da
hike v *caminhar* ka·mee·*nyaar*
holiday *feriado* ⓜ fe·ree·*aa*·doo
homosexual n&a *homosexual* ⓜ&ⓕ o·mo·sek·soo·*aal*
hospital *hospital* ⓜ osh·pee·*taal*
hot *quente* *keng*·te
hotel *hotel* ⓜ o·*tel*
hungry *faminto/a* ⓜ/ⓕ fa·*meeng*·too/a
husband *marido* ⓜ ma·*ree*·doo

I

I *eu* e·oo
identification (card) *bilhete de identidade* ⓜ bee·*lye*·te de ee·deng·tee·*daa*·de
ill *doente* ⓜ&ⓕ doo·*eng*·te
important *importante* ⓜ&ⓕ eeng·por·*tang*·te
included *incluído/a* ⓜ/ⓕ eeng·kloo·*ee*·doo/a
injury *ferimento* ⓜ fe·ree·*meng*·too
insurance *seguro* ⓜ se·*goo*·roo
Internet *internet* ⓕ eeng·ter·*net*
interpreter *intérprete* ⓜ&ⓕ eeng·*ter*·pre·te

J

jewellery *ourivesaria* ⓕ oh·ree·ve·za·*ree*·a
job *emprego* ⓜ eng·*pre*·goo

K

key *chave* ⓕ *shaa*·ve
kilogram *quilograma* ⓜ kee·loo·*graa*·ma
kitchen *cozinha* ⓕ koo·*zee*·nya
knife *faca* ⓕ *faa*·ka

L

laundry (place) *lavandaria* ⓕ la·vang·da·*ree*·a
lawyer *advogado/a* ⓜ/ⓕ a·de·voo·*gaa*·doo/a
left (direction) *esquerda* ⓕ *shker*·da
left-luggage office *perdidos e achados* ⓜ pl per·*dee*·doosh ee aa·*shaa*·doosh
leg *perna* ⓕ *per*·na
lesbian n&a *lésbica* ⓕ *lezh*·bee·ka
less *menos* *me*·noosh
letter (mail) *carta* ⓕ *kaar*·ta
lift (elevator) *elevador* ⓜ ee·le·va·*dor*
light *luz* ⓕ loosh
like v *gostar* goosh·*taar*
lock *tranca* ⓕ *trang*·ka
long *longo/a* ⓜ/ⓕ *long*·goo/a
lost *perdido/a* ⓜ/ⓕ per·*dee*·doo/a
lost-property office *gabinete de perdidos e achados* ⓜ gaa·bee·*ne*·te de per·*dee*·doosh ee a·*shaa*·doosh
love v *amar* a·*maar*
luggage *bagagem* ⓕ ba·*gaa*·zheng
lunch *almoço* ⓜ aal·*mo*·soo

M

mail *correio* ⓜ koo·*rray*·oo
man *homem* ⓜ *o*·meng
map *mapa* ⓜ *maa*·pa
market *mercado* ⓜ mer·*kaa*·doo
matches *fósforos* ⓜ pl *fosh*·foo·roosh
meat *carne* ⓕ *kaar*·ne
medicine *medicamentos* ⓜ pl me·dee·ka·*meng*·toosh
menu *ementa* ⓕ ee·*meng*·ta
message *mensagem* ⓕ meng·*saa*·zheng
milk *leite* ⓜ *lay*·te
minute *minuto* ⓜ mee·*noo*·too
mobile phone *telemóvel* ⓜ te·le·*mo*·vel
money *dinheiro* ⓜ dee·*nyay*·roo
month *mês* ⓜ mesh
morning *manhã* ⓕ ma·*nyang*
mother *mãe* ⓕ maing
motorcycle *mota* ⓕ *mo*·ta
motorway *autoestrada* ⓕ ow·to·*shtraa*·da
mouth *boca* ⓕ *bo*·ka
music *música* ⓕ *moo*·zee·ka

N

name *nome* ⓜ *no*·me
napkin *guardanapo* ⓜ gwar·da·*naa*·poo
nappy *fralda* ⓕ *fraal*·da
near *perto* *per*·too
neck *pescoço* ⓜ pesh·*ko*·soo
new *novo/a* ⓜ/ⓕ *no*·voo/a
news *notícias* ⓕ pl noo·*tee*·syash

newspaper *jornal* ⓜ zhor·*naal*
night *noite* ⓕ *noy*·te
no *não* nowng
noisy *barulhento/a* ⓜ/ⓕ ba·roo·*lyeng*·too/a
nonsmoking *não-fumador* nowng·foo·ma·*dor*
north *norte* *nor*·te
nose *nariz* ⓜ na·*reesh*
now *agora* a·*go*·ra
number *número* ⓜ *noo*·me·roo

O

oil (engine) *petróleo* ⓜ pe·*tro*·lyoo
old *velho/a* ⓜ/ⓕ *ve*·lyoo/a
one-way ticket *bilhete de ida* ⓜ bee·*lye*·te de *ee*·da
open a *aberto/a* ⓜ/ⓕ a·*ber*·too/a
outside *fora* *fo*·ra

P

package *embrulho* ⓜ eng·*broo*·lyoo
paper *papel* ⓜ pa·*pel*
park (car) v *estacionar* shta·syoo·*naar*
passport *passaporte* ⓜ paa·sa·*por*·te
pay *pagar* pa·*gaar*
pen *caneta* ⓕ ka·*ne*·ta
petrol *gasolina* ⓕ ga·zoo·*lee*·na
pharmacy *farmácia* ⓕ far·*maa*·sya
phonecard *cartão telefónico* ⓜ
kar·*towng* te·le·*fo*·nee·koo
photo *fotografia* ⓕ foo·too·gra·*fee*·a
plate *prato* ⓜ *praa*·too
police *polícia* ⓕ poo·*lee*·sya
Portugal *Portugal* ⓜ poor·too·*gaal*
Portuguese (language) *português* ⓜ poor·too·*gesh*
postcard *postal* ⓜ poosh·*taal*
post office *correio* ⓜ koo·*rray*·oo
pregnant *grávida* ⓕ *graa*·vee·da
price *preço* ⓜ *pre*·soo

Q

quiet *calado/a* ⓜ/ⓕ ka·*laa*·doo/a

R

rain *chuva* ⓕ *shoo*·va
razor *gilete* ⓕ zhee·*le*·te
receipt *recibo* ⓜ rre·*see*·boo
red *vermelho/a* ⓜ/ⓕ ver·*me*·lyoo/a
refund *reembolso* ⓜ rre·eng·*bol*·soo
registered mail *correio registado* ⓜ
koo·*rray*·oo re·zhee·*shtaa*·doo
rent v *alugar* a·loo·*gaar*
repair v *consertar* kong·ser·*taar*
reservation *reserva* ⓕ rre·*zer*·va
restaurant *restaurante* ⓜ rresh·tow·*rang*·te
return v *voltar* vol·*taar*
return ticket *bilhete de ida e volta* ⓜ
bee·*lye*·te de *ee*·da ee *vol*·ta
right (direction) *direita* ⓕ dee·*ray*·ta
road *estrada* ⓕ *shtraa*·da
room *quarto* ⓜ *kwaar*·too

S

safe a *seguro/a* ⓜ/ⓕ se·*goo*·roo/a
sanitary napkin *penso higiénico* ⓜ
peng·soo ee·zhee·*e*·nee·koo
seat *assento* ⓜ a·*seng*·too
send *enviar* eng·vee·*aar*
service station *posto de gasolina* ⓜ
posh·too de ga·zoo·*lee*·na
sex *sexo* ⓜ *sek*·soo
shampoo *champô* ⓜ shang·*poo*
share (a dorm) *partilhar* par·tee·*lyaar*
shaving cream *creme de barbear* ⓜ
kre·me de bar·bee·*aar*
she *ela* *e*·la
sheet (bed) *lençol* ⓜ leng·*sol*
shirt *camisa* ⓕ ka·*mee*·za
shoes *sapatos* ⓜ pl sa·*paa*·toosh
shop n *loja* ⓕ *lo*·zha
short *curto/a* ⓜ/ⓕ *koor*·too/a
shower n *chuveiro* ⓜ shoo·*vay*·roo
single room *quarto de solteiro* ⓜ
kwaar·too de sol·*tay*·roo
skin *pele* ⓕ *pe*·le
skirt *saia* ⓕ *sai*·a
sleep v *dormir* door·*meer*
slowly *vagarosamente* va·ga·ro·za·*meng*·te
small *pequeno/a* ⓜ/ⓕ pe·*ke*·noo/a
smoke (cigarettes) v *fumar* foo·*maar*
soap *sabonete* ⓜ sa·boo·*ne*·te
some *uns/umas* ⓜ/ⓕ pl oongsh/*oo*·mash
soon *em breve* eng *bre*·ve
south *sul* sool
souvenir shop *loja de lembranças* ⓕ
lo·zha de leng·*brang*·sash
speak *falar* fa·*laar*

spoon *colher* ⓕ koo·*lyer*
stamp *selo* ⓜ *se*·loo
stand-by ticket *bilhete sem garantia* ⓜ
bee·*lye*·te seng ga·rang·*tee*·a
station (train) *estação* ⓕ shta·*sowng*
stomach *estômago* ⓜ *shto*·ma·goo
stop v *parar* pa·*raar*
stop (bus) *paragem* ⓕ pa·*raa*·zheng
street *rua* ⓕ *rroo*·a
student *estudante* ⓜ&ⓕ shtoo·*dang*·te
sun *sol* ⓜ sol
sunscreen *protecção anti-solar* ⓕ
proo·te·*sowng* ang·tee·soo·*laar*
swim v *nadar* na·*daar*

T

tampons *tampões* ⓜ pl tang·*powngsh*
taxi *táxi* ⓜ *taak*·see
teaspoon *colher de chá* ⓕ koo·*lyer* de shaa
teeth *dentes* ⓜ pl *deng*·tesh
telephone *telefone* ⓜ te·le·*fo*·ne
television *televisão* ⓕ te·le·vee·*zowng*
temperature (weather) *temperatura* ⓕ
teng·pe·ra·*too*·ra
tent *tenda* ⓕ *teng*·da
that (one) *aquele/a* ⓜ/ⓕ a·*ke*·le/a
they *eles/elas* ⓜ/ⓕ *e*·lesh/*e*·lash
thirsty *sedento/a* ⓜ/ⓕ se·*deng*·too/a
this (one) *este/a* ⓜ/ⓕ *esh*·te/a
throat *garganta* ⓕ gar·*gang*·ta
ticket *bilhete* ⓜ bee·*lye*·te
time *tempo* ⓜ *teng*·poo
tired *cansado/a* ⓜ/ⓕ kang·*saa*·doo/a
tissues *lenços de papel* ⓜ pl *leng*·soosh de pa·*pel*
today *hoje* *o*·zhe
toilet *casa de banho* ⓕ *kaa*·za de *ba*·nyoo
tomorrow *amanhã* aa·ma·*nyang*
tonight *hoje à noite* *o*·zhe aa *noy*·te
toothbrush *escova de dentes* ⓕ *shko*·va de *deng*·tesh
toothpaste *pasta de dentes* ⓕ *paash*·ta de *deng*·tesh
torch (flashlight) *lanterna eléctrica* ⓕ
lang·*ter*·na ee·*le*·tree·ka
tour n *excursão* ⓕ shkoor·*sowng*
tourist office *escritório de turismo* ⓜ
shkree·*to*·ryoo de too·*reezh*·moo
towel *toalha* ⓕ *twaa*·lya
train *comboio* ⓜ kong·*boy*·oo
translate *traduzir* tra·doo·*zeer*
travel agency *agência de viagens* ⓕ
a·*zheng*·sya de vee·*aa*·zhengsh
travellers cheque *travellers cheque* ⓜ *tra*·ve·ler shek
trousers *calças* ⓕ pl *kaal*·sash
twin beds *camas gémeas* ⓕ pl *ka*·mash *zhe*·me·ash
tyre *pneu* ⓜ pe·*ne*·oo

U

underwear *roupa interior* ⓕ *rroh*·pa eeng·te·ree·*or*
urgent *urgente* ⓜ&ⓕ oor·*zheng*·te

V

vacant *vago/a* ⓜ/ⓕ *vaa*·goo/a
vacation *férias* ⓕ pl *fe*·ree·ash
vegetable *legume* ⓜ le·*goo*·me
vegetarian a *vegetariano/a* ⓜ/ⓕ ve·zhe·ta·ree·*a*·noo/a
visa *visto* ⓜ *veesh*·too

W

waiter *criado/a de mesa* ⓜ/ⓕ kree·*aa*·doo/a de *me*·za
walk v *caminhar* ka·mee·*nyaar*
wallet *carteira* ⓕ kar·*tay*·ra
warm a *morno/a* ⓜ/ⓕ *mor*·noo/a
wash (something) *lavar* la·*vaar*
watch *relógio* ⓜ rre·*lo*·zhyoo
water *água* ⓕ *aa*·gwa
we *nós* nosh
weekend *fim-de-semana* ⓜ feeng·de·se·*ma*·na
west *oeste* o·*esh*·te
wheelchair *cadeira de rodas* ⓕ ka·*day*·ra de *rro*·dash
when *quando* *kwang*·doo
where *onde* *ong*·de
white *branco/a* ⓜ/ⓕ *brang*·koo/a
who *quem* keng
why *porquê* poor·*ke*
wife *esposa* ⓕ *shpo*·za
window *janela* ⓕ zha·*ne*·la
wine *vinho* ⓜ *vee*·nyoo
with *com* kong
without *sem* seng
woman *mulher* ⓕ moo·*lyer*
write *escrever* shkre·*ver*

Y

yellow *amarelo/a* ⓜ/ⓕ a·ma·*re*·loo/a
yes *sim* seeng
yesterday *ontem* *ong*·teng
you inf sg/pl *tu/vocês* too/vo·*sesh*
you pol sg/pl *você/vós* vo·*se*/vosh

Spanish

spanish alphabet

Aa a	*Bb* be	*Cc* the	*Chch* che	*Dd* de
Ee e	*Ff* e·fe	*Gg* khe	*Hh* *a*·che	*Ii* ee
Jj *kho*·ta	*Kk* ka	*Ll* *e*·le	*LLll* *e*·lye	*Mm* *e*·me
Nn *e*·ne	*Ññ* *e*·nye	*Oo* o	*Pp* pe	*Qq* koo
Rr *e*·re	*Ss* *e*·se	*Tt* te	*Uu* oo	*Vv* *oo*·ve
Ww *oo*·ve *do*·vle	*Xx* *e*·kees	*Yy* ee·*grye*·ga	*Zz* *the*·ta	

spanish

introduction

The lively and picturesque language of Cervantes' *Don Quijote* and Almodóvar's movies, Spanish (*espanol* es·pa·*nyol*), or Castilian (*castellano* kas·te·*lya*·no), as it's also called in Spain, has over 390 million speakers worldwide. Outside Spain, it's the language of most of Latin America and the West Indies and is also spoken in the Philippines and Guam, in some areas of the African coast and in the US.

Spanish belongs to the Romance group of languages – the descendents of Latin – together with French, Italian, Portuguese and Romanian. It's derived from Vulgar Latin, which Roman soldiers and merchants brought to the Iberian Peninsula during the period of Roman conquest (3rd to 1st century BC). By 19 BC Spain had become totally Romanised and Latin became the language of the peninsula in the four centuries that followed. Thanks to the Arabic invasion in AD 711 and the Arabs' continuing presence in Spain during the next eight centuries, Spanish has also been strongly influenced by Arabic, although mostly in the vocabulary. Today's Castilian is spoken in the north, centre and south of Spain. Completing the colourful linguistic profile of the country, Basque (*euskera* e·*oos*·ke·ra), Catalan (*catalán* ka·ta·*lan*) and Galician (*gallego* ga·*lye*·go) are also official languages in Spain, though Castilian covers by far the largest territory.

Besides the shared vocabulary of Latin origin that English and Spanish have in common, there's also a large corpus of words from the indigenous American languages that have entered English via Spanish. After Columbus' discovery of the New World in 1492, America's indigenous languages had a considerable impact on Spanish, especially in words to do with flora, fauna and topography (such as *tobacco, chocolate, coyote, canyon,* to name only a few).

Even if you're not familiar with the sound of Spanish through, say, the voices of José Carreras or Julio Iglesias, you'll be easily seduced by this melodic language and have fun trying to roll your *rr*'s like the locals. You may have heard the popular legend about one of the Spanish kings having a slight speech impediment which prompted all of Spain to mimick his lisp. Unfortunately, this charming explanation of the lisping 's' is only a myth – it's actually due to the way Spanish evolved from Latin and has nothing to do with lisping monarchs at all. So, when you hear someone say *gracias* *gra*·thyas, they're no more lisping than when you say 'thank you' in English.

pronunciation

vowel sounds

Vowels are pronounced short and fairly closed. The sound remains level, and each vowel is pronounced as an individual unit. There are, however, a number of cases where two vowel sounds become very closely combined (so-called diphthongs).

symbol	english equivalent	spanish example	transliteration
a	run	*agua*	*a*·gwa
ai	aisle	*bailar*	bai·*lar*
ay	say	*seis*	says
e	bet	*número*	*noo*·me·ro
ee	see	*día*	*dee*·a
o	pot	*ojo*	*o*·kho
oo	zoo	*gusto*	*goo*·sto
ow	how	*autobús*	ow·to·*boos*
oy	toy	*hoy*	oy

word stress

Spanish words have stress, which means you emphasise one syllable of a word over another. Here's a rule of thumb: when a written word ends in *n*, *s* or a vowel, the stress falls on the second-last syllable. Otherwise, the final syllable is stressed. If you see an accent mark over a syllable, it cancels out this rule and you just stress that syllable instead. You needn't worry about this though, as the stressed syllables are always italicised in our pronunciation guides.

consonant sounds

Remember that in Spanish the letter *h* is never pronounced. The Spanish *v* sounds more like a b, said with the lips pressed together. When ending a word, *d* is pronounced soft, like a th, or it's so slight it doesn't get pronounced at all. Finally, try to roll your *r*'s, especially at the start of a word and in words with *rr*.

symbol	english equivalent	spanish example	transliteration
b	bed	*barco*	*bar*·ko
ch	cheat	*chica*	*chee*·ka
d	dog	*dinero*	dee·*ne*·ro
f	fat	*fiesta*	*fye*·sta
g	go	*gato*	*ga*·to
k	kit	*cabeza, queso*	ka·*be*·tha, *ke*·so
kh	loch (harsh and guttural)	*jardín, gente*	khar·*deen*, *khen*·te
l	lot	*lago*	*la*·go
ly	million	*llamada*	lya·*ma*·da
m	man	*mañana*	ma·*nya*·na
n	not	*nuevo*	*nwe*·vo
ny	canyon	*señora*	se·*nyo*·ra
p	pet	*padre*	*pa*·dre
r	like 'tt' in 'butter' said fast	*hora*	*o*·ra
rr	run (but stronger and rolled)	*ritmo, burro*	*rreet*·mo, *boo*·rro
s	sun	*semana*	se·*ma*·na
t	top	*tienda*	*tyen*·da
th	thin	*Barcelona, manzana*	bar·the·*lo*·na man·*tha*·na
v	soft 'b', between 'v' and 'b'	*abrir*	a·*vreer*
w	win	*guardia*	*gwar*·dya
y	yes	*viaje*	*vya*·khe

language difficulties

Do you speak English?		
¿Habla inglés?		*ab*·la een·*gles*
Do you understand?		
¿Me entiende?		me en·*tyen*·de
I (don't) understand.		
(No) Entiendo.		(no) een·*tyen*·do
What does (*cuenta*) mean?		
¿Qué significa (cuenta)?		ke seeg·nee·*fee*·ka (*kwen*·ta)

How do you ...?	*¿Cómo se ...?*	*ko*·mo se ...
pronounce this word	*pronuncia esta palabra*	pro·*noon*·thya *es*·ta pa·*lab*·ra
write (*ciudad*)	*escribe (ciudad)*	es·*kree*·be (thee·oo·*da*)

Could you please ...?	*¿Puede ..., por favor?*	*pwe*·de ... por fa·*vor*
repeat that	*repetir*	rre·pe·*teer*
speak more slowly	*hablar más despacio*	ab·*lar* mas des·*pa*·thyo
write it down	*escribirlo*	es·kree·*beer*·lo

essentials

Yes.	*Sí.*	see
No.	*No.*	no
Please.	*Por favor.*	por fa·*vor*
Thank you (very much).	*(Muchas) Gracias.*	(*moo*·chas) *gra*·thyas
You're welcome.	*De nada.*	de *na*·da
Excuse me.	*Perdón/Discúlpeme.*	per·*don*/dees·*kool*·pe·me
Sorry.	*Lo siento.*	lo *syen*·to

numbers

0	*cero*	*the*·ro	16	*dieciséis*	dye·thee·*seys*
1	*uno*	*oo*·no	17	*diecisiete*	dye·thee·*sye*·te
2	*dos*	dos	18	*dieciocho*	dye·thee·*o*·cho
3	*tres*	tres	19	*diecinueve*	dye·thee·*nwe*·ve
4	*cuatro*	*kwa*·tro	20	*veinte*	*veyn*·te
5	*cinco*	*theen*·ko	21	*veintiuno*	veyn·tee·*oo*·no
6	*seis*	seys	22	*veintidós*	veyn·tee·*dos*
7	*siete*	*sye*·te	30	*treinta*	*treyn*·ta
8	*ocho*	*o*·cho	40	*cuarenta*	kwa·*ren*·ta
9	*nueve*	*nwe*·ve	50	*cincuenta*	theen·*kwen*·ta
10	*diez*	dyeth	60	*sesenta*	se·*sen*·ta
11	*once*	*on*·the	70	*setenta*	se·*ten*·ta
12	*doce*	*do*·the	80	*ochenta*	o·*chen*·ta
13	*trece*	*tre*·the	90	*noventa*	no·*ven*·ta
14	*catorce*	ka·*tor*·the	100	*cien*	thyen
15	*quince*	*keen*·the	1000	*mil*	mil

time & dates

What time is it?	*¿Qué hora es?*	ke *o*·ra es
It's one o'clock.	*Es la una.*	es la *oo*·na
It's (10) o'clock.	*Son (las diez).*	son (las dyeth)
Quarter past (one).	*Es (la una) y cuarto.*	es (la *oo*·na) ee *kwar*·to
Half past (one).	*Es (la una) y media.*	es (la *oo*·na) ee *me*·dya
Quarter to (one).	*Es (la una) menos cuarto.*	es (la *oo*·na) *me*·nos *kwar*·to
At what time ...?	*¿A qué hora ...?*	a ke *o*·ra ...
At ...	*A las ...*	a las ...
am	*de la mañana*	de la ma·*nya*·na
pm	*de la tarde*	de la *tar*·de
Monday	*lunes*	*loo*·nes
Tuesday	*martes*	*mar*·tes
Wednesday	*miércoles*	*myer*·ko·les
Thursday	*jueves*	*khwe*·ves
Friday	*viernes*	*vyer*·nes
Saturday	*sábado*	*sa*·ba·do
Sunday	*domingo*	do·*meen*·go

January	*enero*	e·ne·ro
February	*febrero*	fe·*bre*·ro
March	*marzo*	*mar*·tho
April	*abril*	a·*breel*
May	*mayo*	*ma*·yo
June	*junio*	*khoo*·nyo
July	*julio*	*khoo*·lyo
August	*agosto*	a·*gos*·to
September	*septiembre*	sep·*tyem*·bre
October	*octubre*	ok·*too*·bre
November	*noviembre*	no·*vyem*·bre
December	*diciembre*	dee·*thyem*·bre

What date is it today?
¿Qué día es hoy? ke *dee*·a es oy

It's (18 October).
Es (el dieciocho de octubre). es (el dye·thee·*o*·cho de ok·*too*·bre)

since (May)	*desde (mayo)*	*des*·de (*ma*·yo)
until (June)	*hasta (junio)*	*as*·ta (*khoo*·nyo)
last …		
night	*anoche*	a·*no*·che
week	*la semana pasada*	la se·*ma*·na pa·*sa*·da
month	*el mes pasado*	el mes pa·*sa*·do
year	*el año pasado*	el *a*·nyo pa·*sa*·do
next …	*… que viene*	… ke *vye*·ne
week	*la semana*	la se·*ma*·na
month	*el mes*	el mes
year	*el año*	el *a*·nyo
yesterday/tomorrow …	*ayer/mañana por la …*	a·*yer*/ma·*nya*·na por la …
morning	*mañana*	ma·*nya*·na
afternoon	*tarde*	*tar*·de
evening	*noche*	*no*·che

weather

What's the weather like?	*¿Qué tiempo hace?*	ke *tyem*·po *a*·the
It's …		
cloudy	*Está nublado.*	es·*ta* noo·*bla*·do
cold	*Hace frío.*	*a*·the *free*·o
hot	*Hace calor.*	*a*·the ka·*lor*
raining	*Está lloviendo.*	es·*ta* lyo·*vyen*·do
snowing	*Está nevando.*	es·*ta* ne·*van*·do
sunny	*Hace sol.*	*a*·the sol
warm	*Hace calor.*	*a*·the ka·*lor*
windy	*Hace viento.*	*a*·the *vyen*·to
spring	*primavera* f	pree·ma·*ve*·ra
summer	*verano* m	ve·*ra*·no
autumn	*otoño* m	o·*to*·nyo
winter	*invierno* m	een·*vyer*·no

border crossing

I'm here …	*Estoy aquí …*	es·*toy* a·*kee* …
in transit	*en tránsito*	en *tran*·see·to
on business	*de negocios*	de ne·*go*·thyos
on holiday	*de vacaciones*	de va·ka·*thyo*·nes
I'm here for …	*Estoy aquí por …*	es·*toy* a·*kee* por …
(10) days	*(diez) días*	(dyeth) *dee*·as
(three) weeks	*(tres) semanas*	(tres) se·*ma*·nas
(two) months	*(dos) meses*	(dos) *me*·ses

I'm going to (Salamanca).
Voy a (Salamanca). voy a (sa·la·*man*·ka)

I'm staying at the (Flores Hotel).
Me estoy alojando en (hotel Flores). me es·*toy* a·lo·*khan*·do en (o·*tel flo*·res)

I have nothing to declare.
No tengo nada que declarar. no *ten*·go *na*·da ke dek·la·*rar*

I have something to declare.
Quisiera declarar algo. kee·*sye*·ra dek·la·*rar al*·go

That's (not) mine.
Eso (no) es mío. eso (no) es *mee*·o

tools – SPANISH

transport

tickets & luggage

Where can I buy a ticket?
¿Dónde puedo comprar un billete? — *don*·de *pwe*·do kom·*prar* oon bee·*lye*·te

Do I need to book a seat?
¿Tengo que reservar? — *ten*·go ke rre·ser·*var*

One ... ticket to (Barcelona), please.	*Un billete ... a (Barcelona), por favor.*	oon bee·*lye*·te ... a (bar·the·*lo*·na) por fa·*vor*
one-way	*sencillo*	sen·*thee*·lyo a
return	*de ida y vuelta*	de *ee*·da ee *vwel*·ta

I'd like to ... my ticket.	*Me gustaría ... mi billete.*	me goos·ta·*ree*·a ... mee bee·*lye*·te
cancel	*cancelar*	kan·the·*lar*
change	*cambiar*	kam·*byar*
confirm	*confirmar*	kon·feer·*mar*

I'd like a ... seat.	*Quisiera un asiento ...*	kee·*sye*·ra oon a·*syen*·to ...
nonsmoking	*de no fumadores*	de no foo·ma·*do*·res
smoking	*de fumadores*	de foo·ma·*do*·res

How much is it?
¿Cuánto cuesta? — *kwan*·to *kwes*·ta

Is there air conditioning?
¿Hay aire acondicionado? — ai *ai*·re a·kon·dee·thyo·*na*·do

Is there a toilet?
¿Hay servicios? — ai ser·*vee*·thyos

How long does the trip take?
¿Cuánto se tarda? — *kwan*·to se *tar*·da

Is it a direct route?
¿Es un viaje directo? — es oon *vya*·khe dee·*rek*·to

I'd like a luggage locker.
Quisiera un casillero de consigna. — kee·*sye*·ra oon ka·see·*lye*·ro de kon·*seeg*·na

My luggage has been ...	*Mis maletas han sido ...*	mees ma·*le*·tas an *see*·do ...
damaged	*dañadas*	da·*nya*·das
lost	*perdidas*	per·*dee*·das
stolen	*robadas*	rro·*ba*·das

getting around

Where does flight (G10) arrive/depart?
¿Dónde llega/sale el vuelo (G10)? — *don*·de *lye*·ga/*sa*·le el *vwe*·lo (khe dyeth)

Where's the ...?	*¿Dónde está...?*	*don*·de es·*ta* ...
arrivals hall	*el hall de partidas*	el hol de par·*tee*·das
departures hall	*el hall de llegadas*	el hol de lye·*ga*·das
duty-free shop	*la tienda libre de impuestos*	la *tyen*·da *lee*·bre de eem·*pwe*·stos
gate (12)	*la puerta (doce)*	la *pwer*·ta (*do*·the)

Is this the ... to (Valencia)?	*¿Es el ... para (Valencia)?*	es el ... *pa*·ra (va·*len*·thya)
boat	*barco*	*bar*·ko
bus	*autobús*	ow·to·*boos*
plane	*avión*	a·*vyon*
train	*tren*	tren

What time's the ... bus?	*¿A qué hora es el ... autobús?*	a ke *o*·ra es el ... ow·to·*boos*
first	*primer*	pree·*mer*
last	*último*	*ool*·tee·mo
next	*próximo*	*prok*·see·mo

At what time does it arrive/leave?
¿A qué hora llega/sale? — a ke *o*·ra *lye*·ga/*sa*·le

How long will it be delayed?
¿Cuánto tiempo se retrasará? — *kwan*·to *tyem*·po se rre·tra·sa·*ra*

What station/stop is this?
¿Cuál es esta estación/parada? — kwal es *es*·ta es·ta·*thyon*/pa·*ra*·da

What's the next station/stop?
¿Cuál es la próxima estación/parada? — kwal es la *prok*·see·ma es·ta·*thyon*/pa·*ra*·da

Does it stop at (Aranjuez)?
¿Para en (Aranjuez)? — *pa*·ra en (a·*ran*·khweth)

Please tell me when we get to (Seville).
¿Puede avisarme cuando lleguemos a (Sevilla)? — *pwe*·de a·vee·*sar*·me *kwan*·do lye·*ge*·mos a (se·*vee*·lya)

How long do we stop here?
¿Cuánto tiempo vamos a parar aquí? — *kwan*·to *tyem*·po *va*·mos a pa·*rar* a·*kee*

Is this seat available?
¿Está libre este asiento? — es·*ta lee*·bre *es*·te a·*syen*·to

That's my seat.
Ése es mi asiento. — *e*·se es mee a·*syen*·to

I'd like a taxi …	*Quisiera un taxi …*	kee·*sye*·ra oon *tak*·see …
at (9am)	*a (las nueve de la mañana)*	a (las *nwe*·ve de la ma·*nya*·na)
now	*ahora*	a·*o*·ra
tomorrow	*mañana*	ma·*nya*·na

Is this taxi available?
¿Está libre este taxi? — es·*ta lee*·bre *es*·te *tak*·see

How much is it to …?
¿Cuánto cuesta ir a …? — *kwan*·to *kwes*·ta eer a …

Please put the meter on.
Por favor, ponga el taxímetro. — por fa·*vor pon*·ga el tak·*see*·me·tro

Please take me to (this address).
Por favor, lléveme a (esta dirección). — por fa·*vor lye*·ve·me a (*es*·ta dee·rek·*thyon*)

Please …	*Por favor …*	por fa·*vor* …
slow down	*vaya más despacio*	*va*·ya mas des·*pa*·thyo
stop here	*pare aquí*	*pa*·re a·*kee*
wait here	*espere aquí*	es·*pe*·re a·*kee*

car, motorbike & bicycle hire

I'd like to hire a …	*Quisiera alquilar …*	kee·*sye*·ra al·*kee*·lar …
bicycle	*una bicicleta*	*oo*·na bee·thee·*kle*·ta
car	*un coche*	oon *ko*·che
motorbike	*una moto*	*oo*·na *mo*·to

with …	*con …*	kon …
a driver	*chófer*	*cho*·fer
air conditioning	*aire acondicionado*	*ai*·re a·kon·dee·thyo·*na*·do
antifreeze	*anticongelante*	an·tee·kon·khe·*lan*·te
snow chains	*cadenas de nieve*	ka·*de*·nas de *nye*·ve

How much for … hire?	*¿Cuánto cuesta el alquiler por …?*	*kwan*·to *kwes*·ta el al·*kee*·ler por …
hourly	*hora*	*o*·ra
daily	*día*	*dee*·a
weekly	*semana*	se·*ma*·na

air	*aire* **m**	*ai*·re
oil	*aceite* **m**	a·*they*·te
petrol	*gasolina* **f**	ga·so·*lee*·na
tyres	*neumáticos* **f pl**	ne·oo·*ma*·tee·kos

I need a mechanic.
Necesito un mecánico. ne·the·*see*·to oon me·*ka*·nee·ko

I've run out of petrol.
Me he quedado sin gasolina. me e ke·*da*·do seen ga·so·*lee*·na

I have a flat tyre.
Tengo un pinchazo. *ten*·go oon peen·*cha*·tho

directions

Where's the …?	*¿Dónde está/ están …?* **sg/pl**	*don*·de es·*ta*/ es·*tan* …
bank	*el banco* **sg**	el *ban*·ko
city centre	*el centro de la ciudad* **sg**	el *then*·tro de la thee·oo·*dad*
hotel	*el hotel* **sg**	el o·*tel*
market	*el mercado* **sg**	el mer·*ka*·do
police station	*la comisaría* **sg**	la ko·mee·sa·*ree*·a
post office	*el correos* **sg**	el ko·*rre*·os
public toilet	*los servicios* **pl**	los ser·*vee*·thyos
tourist office	*la oficina de turismo* **sg**	la o·fee·*thee*·na de too·*rees*·mo

Is this the road to (Valladolid)?

¿Se va a (Valladolid) por esta carretera? — se va a (va·lya·do·*lee*) por *es*·ta ka·rre·*te*·ra

Can you show me (on the map)?

¿Me lo puede indicar (en el mapa)? — me lo *pwe*·de een·dee·*kar* (en el *ma*·pa)

What's the address?

¿Cuál es la dirección? — *kwal* es la dee·rek·*thyon*

How far is it?

¿A cuánta distancia está? — a *kwan*·ta dees·*tan*·thya es·*ta*

How do I get there?

¿Cómo se llega ahí? — *ko*·mo se *lye*·ga a·*ee*

Turn ...	*Doble ...*	*do*·ble ...
at the corner	*en la esquina*	en la es·*kee*·na
at the traffic lights	*en el semáforo*	en el se·*ma*·fo·ro
left	*a la izquierda*	a la eeth·*kyer*·da
right	*a la iderecha*	a la de·*re*·cha

It's ...	*Está ...*	es·*ta* ...
behind ...	*detrás de ...*	de·*tras* de ...
far away	*lejos*	*le*·khos
here	*aquí*	a·*kee*
in front of ...	*enfrente de ...*	en·*fren*·te de ...
left	*por la izquierda*	por la eeth·*kyer*·da
near (to ...)	*cerca (de ...)*	*ther*·ka (de ...)
next to ...	*al lado de ...*	al *la*·do de ...
opposite ...	*frente a ...*	*fren*·te a ...
right	*por la derecha*	por la de·*re*·cha
straight ahead	*todo recto*	*to*·do *rrek*·to
there	*ahí*	a·*ee*

by bus	*por autobús*	por *ow*·to·boos
by taxi	*por taxi*	por *tak*·see
by train	*por tren*	por tren
on foot	*a pie*	a pye

north	*norte* m	*nor*·te
south	*sur* m	soor
east	*este* m	*es*·te
west	*oeste* m	o·*es*·te

signs		
Acceso/Salida	ak·*the*·so/sa·*lee*·da	**Entrance/Exit**
Abierto/Cerrado	a·*byer*·to/the·*rra*·do	**Open/Closed**
Hay Lugar	ai loo·*gar*	**Rooms Available**
No Hay Lugar	no ai loo·*gar*	**No Vacancies**
Información	een·for·ma·*thyon*	**Information**
Comisaría de Policía	ko·mee·sa·*ree*·a de po·lee·*thee*·a	**Police Station**
Prohibido	pro·ee·*bee*·do	**Prohibited**
Servicios	ser·*vee*·thyos	**Toilets**
Caballeros	ka·ba·*lye*·ros	**Men**
Señoras	se·*nyo*·ras	**Women**
Caliente/Frío	ka·*lyen*·te/*free*·o	**Hot/Cold**

accommodation

finding accommodation

Where's a ...?	*¿Dónde hay ...?*	*don*·de ai
camping ground	*un terreno de cámping*	oon te·*rre*·no de *kam*·peeng
guesthouse	*una pensión*	*oo*·na pen·*syon*
hotel	*un hotel*	oon o·*tel*
youth hostel	*un albergue juvenil*	oon al·*ber*·ge khoo·ve·*neel*
Can you recommend somewhere ...?	*¿Puede recomendar algún sitio ...?*	*pwe*·de rre·ko·men·*dar* al·*goon see*·tio ...
cheap	*barato*	ba·*ra*·to
good	*bueno*	*bwe*·no
nearby	*cercano*	ther·*ka*·no

I'd like to book a room, please.
Quisiera reservar una habitación. kee·*sye*·ra rre·ser·*var oo*·na a·bee·ta·*thyon*

I have a reservation.
He hecho una reserva. e e·cho *oo*·na rre·*ser*·va

My name's ...
Me llamo ... me *lya*·mo ...

accommodation – SPANISH

Do you have a ... room?	*¿Tiene una habitación ...?*	*tye*·ne *oo*·na a·bee·ta·*thyon* ...
single	*individual*	een·dee·vee·*dwal*
double	*doble*	*do*·ble
twin	*con dos camas*	kon dos *ka*·mas
How much is it per ...?	*¿Cuánto cuesta por ...?*	*kwan*·to *kwes*·ta por ...
night	*noche*	*no*·che
person	*persona*	per·*so*·na
Can I pay by ...?	*¿Puedo pagar con ...?*	*pwe*·do pa·*gar* con ...
credit card	*tarjeta de crédito*	tar·*khe*·ta de *kre*·dee·to
travellers cheque	*cheque de viajero*	*che*·ke de vya·*khe*·ro

I'd like to stay for (three) nights/weeks.
Quisiera quedarme por (tres) noches/semanas. — kee·*sye*·ra ke·*dar*·me por (tres) *no*·ches/se·*ma*·nas

From (July 2) to (July 6).
Desde (el dos de julio) hasta (el seis de julio). — *des*·de (el dos de *khoo*·lyo) *as*·ta (el seys de *khoo*·lyo)

Can I see it?
¿Puedo verla? — *pwe*·do *ver*·la

Am I allowed to camp here?
¿Se puede acampar aquí? — se *pwe*·de a·kam·*par* a·*kee*

Is there a camp site nearby?
¿Hay un terreno de cámping cercano? — ai oon te·*rre*·no de *kam*·peeng ther·*ka*·no

requests & queries

When/Where's breakfast served?
¿Cuándo/Dónde se sirve el desayuno? — *kwan*·do/*don*·de se *seer*·ve el de·sa·*yoo*·no

Please wake me at (seven).
Por favor, despiérteme a (las siete). — por fa·*vor* des·*pyer*·te·me a (las *sye*·te)

Could I have my key, please?
¿Me puede dar la llave, por favor? — me *pwe*·de dar la *lya*·ve por fa·*vor*

Can I get another (blanket)?
¿Puede darme otra (manta)? — *pwe*·de *dar*·me *ot*·ra (*man*·ta)

Is there a/an ...?	*¿Hay ...?*	ai ...
elevator	*ascensor*	as·then·*sor*
safe	*una caja fuerte*	*oo*·na *ka*·kha *fwer*·te
The room is too ...	*Es demasiado ...*	es de·ma·*sya*·do ...
expensive	*cara*	*ka*·ra
noisy	*ruidosa*	rrwee·*do*·sa
small	*pequeña*	pe·*ke*·nya
The ... doesn't work.	*No funciona ...*	no foon·*thyo*·na ...
air conditioning	*el aire acondicionado*	el *ai*·re a·kon·dee·thyo·*na*·do
fan	*el ventilador*	el ven·tee·la·*dor*
toilet	*el retrete*	el rre·*tre*·te
This ... isn't clean.	*Esta ... no está limpia.*	es·ta ... no es·*ta leem*·pya
pillow	*almohada*	al·*mwa*·da
sheet	*sábana*	*sa*·ba·na
towel	*toalla*	to·*a*·lya

checking out

What time is checkout?
¿A qué hora hay que dejar libre la habitación? — a ke *o*·ra ai ke de·*khar* *lee*·bre la a·bee·ta·*thyon*

Can I leave my luggage here?
¿Puedo dejar las maletas aquí? — *pwe*·do de·*khar* las ma·*le*·tas a·*kee*

Could I have ..., please?	*¿Me puede dar ..., por favor?*	me *pwe*·de dar ... por fa·*vor*
my deposit	*mi depósito*	mee de·*po*·see·to
my passport	*mi pasaporte*	mee pa·sa·*por*·te
my valuables	*mis objetos de valor*	mees ob·*khe*·tos de va·*lor*

communications & banking

the internet

Where's the local Internet café?
¿Dónde hay un cibercafé cercano? — *don*·de ai oon thee·ber·ka·*fe* ther·*ka*·no

How much is it per hour?
¿Cuánto cuesta por hora? — *kwan*·to *kwes*·ta por *o*·ra

I'd like to ...	*Quisiera ...*	kee·*sye*·ra ...
check my email	*revisar mi correo electrónico*	rre·vee·*sar* mee ko·*re*·o e·lek·*tro*·nee·ko
get Internet access	*usar el Internet*	oo·*sar* el *een*·ter·net
use a printer	*usar una impresora*	oo·*sar* *oo*·na eem·pre·*so*·ra
use a scanner	*usar un escáner*	oo·*sar* oon es·*ka*·ner

mobile/cell phone

I'd like a ...	*Quisiera ...*	kee·*sye*·ra ...
mobile/cell phone for hire	*un móvil para alquilar*	oon *mo*·veel *pa*·ra al·kee·*lar*
SIM card for your network	*una tarjeta SIM para su red*	*oo*·na tar·*khe*·ta seem *pa*·ra soo rred
What are the rates?	*¿Cuál es la tarifa?*	kwal es la ta·*ree*·fa

telephone

What's your phone number?
¿Cuál es su/tu número de teléfono? pol/inf — kwal es soo/too *noo*·me·ro de te·*le*·fo·no

The number is ...
El número es ... — el *noo*·me·ro es ...

Where's the nearest public phone?
¿Dónde hay una cabina telefónica? — *don*·de ai *oo*·na ka·*bee*·na te·le·*fo*·nee·ka

I'd like to buy a phonecard.
Quiero comprar una tarjeta telefónica. — *kye*·ro kom·*prar* *oo*·na tar·*khe*·ta te·le·*fo*·nee·ka

I want to ...	*Quiero ...*	*kye*·ro ...
call (Singapore)	*hacer una llamada (a Singapur)*	a·*ther oo*·na lya·*ma*·da (a seen·ga·*poor*)
make a local call	*hacer una llamada local*	a·*ther oo*·na lya·*ma*·da lo·*kal*
reverse the charges	*hacer una llamada a cobro revertido*	a·*ther oo*·na lya·*ma*·da a *ko*·bro rre·ver·*tee*·do

How much does ... cost?	*¿Cuánto cuesta ...?*	*kwan*·to *kwes*·ta ...
a (three)-minute call	*una llamada de (tres) minutos*	*oo*·na lya·*ma*·da de (tres) mee·*noo*·tos
each extra minute	*cada minuto extra*	*ka*·da mee·*noo*·to *ek*·stra

It's (one euro) per (minute).
(Un euro) por (un minuto). (oon *e*·oo·ro) por (oon mee·*noo*·to)

post office

I want to send a ...	*Quisiera enviar ...*	kee·*sye*·ra en·vee·*ar* ...
fax	*un fax*	oon faks
letter	*una carta*	*oo*·na *kar*·ta
parcel	*un paquete*	oon pa·*ke*·te
postcard	*una postal*	*oo*·na pos·*tal*

I want to buy ...	*Quisiera comprar ...*	kee·*sye*·ra kom·*prar* ...
an envelope	*un sobre*	oon *so*·bre
stamps	*sellos*	*se*·lyos

Please send it (to Australia) by ...	*Por favor, mándelo (a Australia) por ...*	por fa·*vor man*·de·lo (a ows·*tra*·lya) por ...
airmail	*vía aérea*	*vee*·a a·*e*·re·a
express mail	*correo urgente*	ko·*rre*·o oor·*khen*·te
registered mail	*correo certificado*	ko·*rre*·o ther·tee·fee·*ka*·do
surface mail	*vía terrestre*	*vee*·a te·*rres*·tre

Is there any mail for me?
¿Hay alguna carta para mí? ai al·*goo*·na *kar*·ta *pa*·ra mee

bank

Where's a/an …?	*¿Dónde hay …?*	*don*·de ai …
ATM	*un cajero automático*	oon ka·*khe*·ro ow·to·*ma*·tee·ko o
foreign exchange office	*una oficina de cambio*	*oo*·na o·fee·*thee*·na de *kam*·byo

I'd like to …	*Me gustaría …*	me *goos*·ta·*ree*·a …
cash a cheque	*cambiar un cheque*	kam·*byar* oon *che*·ke
change a travellers cheque	*cobrar un cheque de viajero*	ko·*brar* oon *che*·ke de vee·a·*khe*·ro
change money	*cambiar dinero*	kam·*byar* dee·*ne*·ro
get a cash advance	*obtener un adelanto*	ob·te·*ner* oon a·de·*lan*·to
withdraw money	*sacar dinero*	sa·*kar* dee·*ne*·ro

What's the …?	*¿Cuál es …?*	kwal es …
commission	*la comisión*	la ko·mee·*syon*
exchange rate	*el tipo de cambio*	el *tee*·po de *kam*·byo

It's (12) euros.	*Es (doce) euros.*	es (*do*·the) *e*·oo·ros
It's free.	*Es gratis.*	es *gra*·tees

What's the charge for that?
¿Cuánto hay que pagar por eso? — *kwan*·to ai ke pa·*gar* por *e*·so

What time does the bank open?
¿A qué hora abre el banco? — a ke *o*·ra *a*·bre el *ban*·ko

Has my money arrived yet?
¿Ya ha llegado mi dinero? — ya a lye·*ga*·do mee dee·*ne*·ro

sightseeing

getting in

What time does it open/close?
¿A qué hora abren/cierran? — a ke *o*·ra *ab*·ren/*thye*·rran

What's the admission charge?
¿Cuánto cuesta la entrada? — *kwan*·to *kwes*·ta la en·*tra*·da

Is there a discount for children/students?
¿Hay descuentos para niños/estudiantes? — ai des·*kwen*·tos *pa*·ra *nee*·nyos/es·too·*dyan*·tes

I'd like a ...	*Quisiera ...*	kee·*sye*·ra ...
catalogue	*un catálogo*	oon ka·*ta*·lo·go
guide	*una guía*	*oo*·na *gee*·a
(local) map	*un mapa (de la zona)*	oon *ma*·pa (de la *tho*·na)

I'd like to see ...	*Me gustaría ver ...*	me goos·ta·*ree*·a ver ...
What's that?	*¿Qué es eso?*	ke es *e*·so
Can I take a photo?	*¿Puedo tomar un foto?*	*pwe*·do to·*mar* un *fo*·to

tours

When's the next day trip?
¿Cuándo es la próxima excursión de un día? — *kwan*·do es la *prok*·see·ma eks·koor·*syon* de oon *dee*·a

When's the next tour?
¿Cuándo es el próximo recorrido? — *kwan*·do es ela *prok*·see·mo rre·ko·*rree*·do

Is ... included?	*¿Incluye ...?*	een·*kloo*·ye ...
accommodation	*alojamiento*	a·lo·kha·*myen*·to
the admission charge	*entrada*	en·*tra*·da
food	*comida*	ko·*mee*·da
transport	*transporte*	trans·*por*·te

How long is the tour?
¿Cuánto dura el recorrido? — *kwan*·to *doo*·ra el rre·ko·*rree*·do

What time should we be back?
¿A qué hora tenemos que volver? — a ke *o*·ra te·*ne*·mos ke vol·*ver*

sightseeing

castle	*castillo* m	kas·*tee*·lyo
cathedral	*catedral* f	ka·te·*dral*
church	*iglesia* f	ee·*gle*·sya
main square	*plaza mayor* f	*pla*·tha ma·*yor*
monastery	*monasterio* m	mo·na·*ste*·ryo
monument	*monumento* m	mo·noo·*men*·to
museum	*museo* m	moo·*se*·o
old city	*casco antiguo* m	*kas*·ko an·*tee*·gwo
palace	*palacio* m	pa·*la*·thyo
ruins	*ruinas* f pl	*rrwee*·nas
stadium	*estadio* m	es·*ta*·dyo
statues	*estatuas* f pl	es·*ta*·twas

shopping

enquiries

Where's a ...?	*¿Dónde está ...?*	don·de es·*ta* ...
bank	*el banco*	el *ban*·ko
bookshop	*la librería*	la lee·bre·*ree*·a
camera shop	*la tienda de fotografía*	la *tyen*·da de fo·to·gra·*fee*·a
department store	*el centro comercial*	el *then*·tro ko·mer·*thyal*
grocery store	*la tienda de comestibles*	la *tyen*·da de ko·mes·*tee*·bles
market	*el mercado*	el mer·*ka*·do
newsagency	*el quiosco*	el *kyos*·ko
supermarket	*el supermercado*	el soo·per·mer·*ka*·do

Where can I buy (a padlock)?
¿Dónde puedo comprar (un candado)? — don·de *pwe*·do kom·*prar* (oon kan·*da*·do)

I'm looking for ...
Estoy buscando ... — es·*toy* boos·*kan*·do ...

Can I look at it?
¿Puedo verlo? — *pwe*·do *ver*·lo

Do you have any others?
¿Tiene otros? — *tye*·ne *o*·tros

Does it have a guarantee?
¿Tiene garantía? — *tye*·ne ga·ran·*tee*·a

Can I have it sent overseas?
¿Pueden enviarlo por correo a otro país? — *pwe*·den en·vee·*ar*·lo por ko·*rre*·o a *o*·tro pa·*ees*

Can I have my ... repaired?
¿Puede reparar mi ... aquí? — *pwe*·de rre·pa·*rar* mee ... a·*kee*

It's faulty.
Es defectuoso. — es de·fek·too·*o*·so

I'd like ..., please.	*Quisiera ..., por favor.*	kee·*sye*·ra ... por fa·*vor*
a bag	*una bolsa*	*oo*·na *bol*·sa
a refund	*que me devuelva el dinero*	ke me de·*vwel*·va el dee·*ne*·ro
to return this	*devolver esto*	de·vol·*ver es*·to

paying

How much is it?
¿Cuánto cuesta esto? — *kwan*·to *kwes*·ta *es*·to

Can you write down the price?
¿Puede escribir el precio? — *pwe*·de es·kree·*beer* el *pre*·thyo

That's too expensive.
Es muy caro. — es mooy *ka*·ro

What's your lowest price?
¿Cuál es su precio más bajo? — kwal es soo *pre*·thyo mas *ba*·kho

I'll give you (five) euros.
Te daré (cinco) euros. — te da·*re* (*theen*·ko) *e*·oo·ros

There's a mistake in the bill.
Hay un error en la cuenta. — ai oon e·*rror* en la *kwen*·ta

Do you accept ...?	*¿Aceptan ...?*	a·*thep*·tan ...
credit cards	*tarjetas de crédito*	tar·*khe*·tas de *kre*·dee·to
debit cards	*tarjetas de débito*	tar·*khe*·tas de *de*·bee·to
travellers cheques	*cheques de viajero*	*che*·kes de vya·*khe*·ro

I'd like ..., please.	*Quisiera ..., por favor.*	kee·*sye*·ra ... por fa·*vor*
a receipt	*un recibo*	oon rre·*thee*·bo
my change	*mi cambio*	mee *kam*·byo

clothes & shoes

Can I try it on?	*¿Me lo puedo probar?*	me lo *pwe*·do *pro*·bar
My size is (40).	*Uso la talla (cuarenta).*	*oo*·so la *ta*·lya (kwa·*ren*·ta)
It doesn't fit.	*No me queda bien.*	no me *ke*·da byen

small	*pequeño/a* **m/f**	pe·*ke*·nyo/a
medium	*mediano/a* **m/f**	me·*dya*·no/a
large	*grande* **m&f**	*gran*·de

books & music

I'd like a ...	*Quisiera un ...*	kee·*sye*·ra oon ...
newspaper (in English)	*periódico (en inglés)*	pe·*ryo*·dee·ko (en een·*gles*)
pen	*bolígrafo*	bo·*lee*·gra·fo

Is there an English-language bookshop?
¿Hay alguna librería en inglés? — ai al·*goo*·na lee·bre·*ree*·a en een·*gles*

I'm looking for something by (Enrique Iglesias).
Estoy buscando algo de (Enrique Iglesias). — es·*toy* boos·*kan*·do *al*·go de (en·*ree*·ke ee·*gle*·syas)

Can I listen to this?
¿Puedo escuchar esto aquí? — *pwe*·do es·koo·*char* es·to a·*kee*

photography

Can you ...?	*¿Puede usted ...?*	*pwe*·de oos·*ted* ...
burn a CD from my memory card	*copiar un disco compacto de esta tarjeta de memoria*	ko·*pyar* oon *dees*·ko kom·*pak*·to de *es*·ta tar·*khe*·ta de me·*mo*·rya
develop this film	*revelar este carrete*	rre·ve·*lar es*·te ka·*rre*·te
load my film	*cargar el carrete*	kar·*gar* el ka·*rre*·te

I need a ... film for this camera.	*Necesito película ... para esta cámara.*	ne·the·*see*·to pe·*lee*·koo·la ... *pa*·ra *es*·ta *ka*·ma·ra
APS	*APS*	a pe *e*·se
B&W	*en blanco y negro*	en *blan*·ko y *ne*·gro
colour	*en color*	en ko·*lor*
slide	*para diapositivas*	*pa*·ra dya·po·see·*tee*·vas
(200) speed	*de sensibilidad (doscientos)*	de sen·see·bee·lee·*da* (dos·*thyen*·tos)

When will it be ready?	*¿Cuándo estará listo?*	*kwan*·do es·ta·*ra lees*·to

meeting people

greetings, goodbyes & introductions

Hello/Hi.	*Hola.*	*o*·la
Good night.	*Buenas noches.*	*bwe*·nas *no*·ches
Goodbye/Bye.	*Adiós.*	a·*dyos*
See you later.	*Hasta luego.*	*as*·ta *lwe*·go
Mr	*Señor*	se·*nyor*
Mrs	*Señora*	se·*nyo*·ra
Miss	*Señorita*	se·nyo·*ree*·ta
How are you?	*¿Qué tal?*	ke tal
Fine, thanks.	*Bien, gracias.*	byen *gra*·thyas
And you?	*¿Y Usted/tú?* **pol/inf**	ee oos·*te*/too
What's your name?	*¿Cómo se llama Usted?* **pol**	*ko*·mo se *lya*·ma oos·*te*
	¿Cómo te llamas? **inf**	*ko*·mo te *lya*·mas
My name is …	*Me llamo …*	me *lya*·mo …
I'm pleased to meet you.	*Mucho gusto.*	*moo*·cho *goos*·to
This is my …	*Éste/Ésta es mi …* **m/f**	*es*·te/a es mee …
boyfriend	*novio*	*no*·vyo
brother	*hermano*	er·*ma*·no
daughter	*hija*	*ee*·kho
father	*padre*	*pa*·dre
friend	*amigo/a* **m/f**	a·*mee*·go/a
girlfriend	*novia*	*no*·vya
husband	*marido*	ma·*ree*·do
mother	*madre*	*ma*·dre
partner (intimate)	*pareja*	pa·*re*·kha
sister	*hermana*	er·*ma*·na
son	*hijo*	*ee*·kho
wife	*esposa*	es·*po*·sa
Here's my …	*Éste/Ésta es mi …* **m/f**	*es*·te/a es mee …
What's your …?	*¿Cuál es su/tu …?* **pol/inf**	kwal es soo/too …
address	*dirección* **f**	dee·rek·*thyon*
email address	*dirección de email* **f**	dee·rek·*thyon* de *ee*·mayl
fax number	*número de fax* **m**	*noo*·me·ro de faks
phone number	*número de teléfono* **m**	*noo*·me·ro de te·*le*·fo·no

occupations

What's your occupation?	*¿A qué se dedica Usted?* pol	a ke se de·*dee*·ka oos·*te*
	¿A qué te dedicas? inf	a ke te de·*dee*·kas
I'm a/an ...	*Soy un/una ...* m/f	soy oon/*oo*·na ...
artist	*artista* m&f	ar·*tees*·ta
business person	*comerciante* m&f	ko·mer·*thyan*·te
farmer	*agricultor* m	a·gree·kool·*tor*
	agricultora f	a·gree·kool·*to*·ra
manual worker	*obrero/a* m/f	o·*bre*·ro/a
office worker	*oficinista* m&f	o·fee·thee·*nees*·ta
scientist	*científico/a* m/f	thyen·*tee*·fee·ko/a
student	*estudiante* m&f	es·too·*dyan*·te
tradesperson	*artesano/a* m/f	ar·te·*sa*·no/a

background

Where are you from?	*¿De dónde es Usted?* pol	de *don*·de es oos·*te*
	¿De dónde eres? inf	de *don*·de e·res
I'm from ...	*Soy de ...*	soy de ...
Australia	*Australia*	ow·*stra*·lya
Canada	*Canadá*	ka·na·*da*
England	*Inglaterra*	een·gla·*te*·rra
New Zealand	*Nueva Zelanda*	*nwe*·va the·*lan*·da
the USA	*los Estados Unidos*	los es·*ta*·dos oo·*nee*·dos
Are you married?	*¿Estás casado/a?* m/f	es·*tas* ka·*sa*·do/a
I'm married.	*Estoy casado/a.* m/f	es·*toy* ka·*sa*·do/a
I'm single.	*Soy soltero/a.* m/f	soy sol·*te*·ro/a

age

How old ...?	*¿Cuántos años ...?*	*kwan*·tos *a*·nyos ...
are you	*tienes* inf	*tye*·nes
is your daughter	*tiene su hija* pol	*tye*·ne soo *ee*·kha
is your son	*tiene su hijo* pol	*tye*·ne soo *ee*·kho
I'm ... years old.	*Tengo ... años.*	*ten*·go ... *a*·nyos
He/She is ... years old.	*Tiene ... años.*	*tye*·ne ... *a*·nyos

feelings

I'm (not) …	*(No) Tengo …*	(no) *ten*·go …
Are you …?	*¿Tiene Usted …?* pol	*tye*·ne oos·*te* …
	¿Tienes …? inf	*tye*·nes …
cold	*frío*	*free*·o
hot	*calor*	ka·*lor*
hungry	*hambre*	*am*·bre
thirsty	*sed*	se

I'm (not) …	*(No) Estoy …*	(no) es·*toy* …
Are you …?	*¿Está Usted …?* pol	es·*ta* oos·*te* …
	¿Estás …? inf	es·*tas* …
happy	*feliz* m&f	fe·*leeth*
OK	*bien* m&f	byen
sad	*triste* m&f	*trees*·te
tired	*cansado/a* m/f	kan·*sa*·do/a

entertainment

going out

Where can I find …?	*¿Dónde hay …?*	*don*·de ai …
clubs	*clubs nocturnos*	kloobs nok·*toor*·nos
gay venues	*lugares gay*	loo·*ga*·res gai
pubs	*bares*	*ba*·res

I feel like going to a/the …	*Tengo ganas de ir …*	*ten*·go *ga*·nas de eer …
concert	*a un concierto*	a oon kon·*thyer*·to
movies	*al cine*	al *thee*·ne
party	*a una fiesta*	a *oo*·na *fyes*·ta
restaurant	*a un restaurante*	a oon rres·tow·*ran*·te
theatre	*al teatro*	al te·*a*·tro

interests

Do you like ...	*¿Le/Te gusta ...?* **pol/inf**	le/te *goos*·ta ...
I (don't) like ...	*(No) Me gusta ...*	(no) me *goos*·ta ...
art	*el arte*	el *ar*·te
movies	*el cine*	el *thee*·ne
reading	*leer*	le·*er*
sport	*el deporte*	el de·*por*·te
travelling	*viajar*	vya·*khar*
Do you like to ...?	*¿Le/Te gusta ...?* **pol/inf**	le/te *goos*·ta ...
dance	*ir a bailar*	eer a bai·*lar*
go to concerts	*ir a conciertos*	eer a kon·*thyer*·tos
listen to music	*escuchar música*	es·koo·*char moo*·see·ka

food & drink

finding a place to eat

Can you recommend a ...?	*¿Puede recomendar un ...?*	*pwe*·de rre·ko·men·*dar* oon ...
bar	*bar*	bar
café	*café*	ka·*fe*
restaurant	*restaurante*	rres·tow·*ran*·te
I'd like ..., please.	*Quisiera ..., por favor.*	kee·*sye*·ra ... por fa·*vor*
a table for (two)	*una mesa para (dos)*	*oo*·na *me*·sa *pa*·ra (dos)
the (non)smoking section	*(no) fumadores*	(no) foo·ma·*do*·res

ordering food

breakfast	*desayuno* **m**	de·sa·*yoo*·no
lunch	*comida* **f**	ko·*mee*·da
dinner	*almuerzo* **m**	al·*mwer*·tho
snack	*tentempié* **m**	ten·tem·*pye*

What would you recommend?
¿Qué recomienda? ke rre·ko·*myen*·da

I'd like (the) ...	*Quisiera ..., por favor.*	kee·*sye*·ra ... por fa·*vor*
bill	*la cuenta*	la *kwen*·ta
drink list	*la lista de bebidas*	la *lees*·ta de be·*bee*·das
menu	*el menú*	el me·*noo*
that dish	*ese plato*	*e*·se *pla*·to

drinks

(cup of) coffee ...	*(taza de) café ...*	(*ta*·tha de) ka·*fe* ...
(cup of) tea ...	*(taza de) té ...*	(*ta*·tha de) te ...
with milk	*con leche*	kon *le*·che
without sugar	*sin azúcar*	seen a·*thoo*·kar
(orange) juice	*zumo de (naranja)* **m**	*zoo*·mo de (na·*ran*·kha)
soft drink	*refresco* **m**	rre·*fres*·ko
... water	*agua ...*	*a*·gwa ...
boiled	*hervida*	er·*vee*·da
(sparkling) mineral	*mineral (con gas)*	mee·ne·*ral* (kon gas)

in the bar

I'll have ...	*Para mí ...*	*pa*·ra mee ...
I'll buy you a drink.	*Te invito a una copa.* **inf**	le/te een·*vee*·to a *oo*·na *ko*·pa
What would you like?	*¿Qué quieres tomar?* **inf**	ke *kye*·res to·*mar*
Cheers!	*¡Salud!*	sa·*loo*
brandy	*coñac* **m**	ko·*nyak*
cocktail	*combinado* **m**	kom·bee·*na*·do
red-wine punch	*sangría* **f**	san·*gree*·a
a shot of (whisky)	*chupito de (güisqui)*	choo·*pee*·to de (*gwees*·kee)
a ... of beer	*una ... de cerveza*	*oo*·na ... de *ther*·ve·tha
bottle	*botella*	bo·*te*·lya
glass	*caña*	*ka*·nya
a bottle/glass of ... wine	*una botella/copa de vino ...*	*oo*·na bo·*te*·lya/*ko*·pa de *vee*·no ...
red	*tinto*	*teen*·to
sparkling	*espumoso*	es·poo·*mo*·so
white	*blanco*	*blan*·ko

self-catering

What's the local speciality?
¿Cuál es la especialidad de la zona? — kwal es la es·pe·thya·lee·*da* de la *tho*·na

What's that?
¿Qué es eso? — ke es *e*·so

How much is (a kilo of cheese)?
¿Cuánto vale (un kilo de queso)? — *kwan*·to *va*·le (oon *kee*·lo de *ke*·so)

I'd like ...	*Póngame ...*	*pon*·ga·me ...
(200) grams	*(doscientos) gramos*	(dos·*thyen*·tos) *gra*·mos
(two) kilos	*(dos) kilos*	(dos) *kee*·los
(three) pieces	*(tres) piezas*	(tres) *pye*·thas
(six) slices	*(seis) lonchas*	(seys) *lon*·chas

Less.	*Menos.*	*me*·nos
Enough.	*Basta.*	*ba*·sta
More.	*Más.*	mas

special diets & allergies

Is there a vegetarian restaurant near here?
¿Hay un restaurante vegetariano por aquí? — ai oon rres·tow·*ran*·te ve·khe·ta·*rya*·no por a·*kee*

Do you have vegetarian food?
¿Tienen comida vegetariana? — *tye*·nen ko·*mee*·da ve·khe·ta·*rya*·na

Could you prepare a meal without ...?	*¿Me puede preparar una comida sin ...?*	me *pwe*·de pre·pa·*rar* *oo*·na ko·*mee*·da seen ...
butter	*mantequilla*	man·te·*kee*·lya
eggs	*huevos*	*we*·vos
meat stock	*caldo de carne*	*kal*·do de *kar*·ne

I'm allergic to ...	*Soy alérgico/a ...* **m/f**	soy a·*ler*·khee·ko/a ...
dairy produce	*a los productos lácteos*	a los pro·*dook*·tos *lak*·te·os
gluten	*al gluten*	al *gloo*·ten
MSG	*al glutamato monosódico*	al gloo·ta·*ma*·to mo·no·*so*·dee·ko
nuts	*a las nueces*	a las *nwe*·thes
seafood	*a los mariscos*	a los ma·*rees*·kos

menu reader

aceitunas rellenas f pl	a·they·*too*·nas rre·*lye*·nas	*stuffed olives*
albóndigas f pl	al·*bon*·dee·gas	*meatballs*
almejas f pl	al·*me*·khas	*clams*
arroz con leche m	a·*rroth* kon *le*·che	*rice pudding*
atún m	a·*toon*	*tuna*
bacalao m	ba·ka·*low*	*salted cod*
beicon con queso m	*bey*·kon kon *ke*·so	*cold bacon with cheese*
berberechos m pl	ber·be·*re*·chos	*cockles*
boquerones fritos m pl	bo·ke·*ro*·nes *free*·tos	*fried anchovies*
butifarra f	boo·tee·*fa*·rra	*thick sausage*
calamares m pl	ka·la·*ma*·res	*squid*
camarón m	ka·ma·*ron*	*shrimp • small prawn*
cangrejo m	kan·*gre*·kho	*crab*
caracol m	ka·ra·*kol*	*snail*
cazuela f	ka·*thwe*·la	*casserole*
champiñones m pl	cham·pee·*nyo*·nes	*mushrooms*
charcutería f	char·koo·te·*ree*·a	*cured pork meats*
chorizo m	cho·*ree*·tho	*spicy red or white sausage*
churrasco m	choo·*rras*·ko	*grilled meat in a tangy sauce*
churro m	*choo*·rro	*long, deep-fried doughnut*
cocido m	ko·*thee*·do	*stew of chickpeas, pork & chorizo*
cuajada f	kwa·*kha*·da	*milk junket with honey*
ensaladilla f	en·sa·la·*dee*·lya	*vegetable salad*
escabeche m	es·ka·*be*·che	*pickled or marinated fish*
estofado m	es·to·*fa*·do	*stew*

fideos m pl	fee·*de*·os	*thin pasta noodles with sauce*
flan m	flan	*crème caramel*
gachos m pl	*ga*·chos	*type of porridge*
gazpacho m	gath·*pa*·cho	*cold soup with garlic, tomato & vegetables*
helado m	e·*la*·do	*ice cream*
jamón m	kha·*mon*	*ham*
langosta f	lan·*gos*·ta	*spiny lobster*
langostino m	lan·gos·*tee*·no	*large prawn*
lomo m	*lo*·mo	*pork loin • sausage*
longaniza f	lon·ga·*nee*·tha	*dark pork sausage*
magdalena f	mag·da·*le*·na	*fairy cake (often dunked in coffee)*
mejillones m pl	me·khee·*lyo*·nes	*mussels*
natillas f pl	na·*tee*·lyas	*creamy milk dessert*
ostras f pl	*os*·tras	*oysters*
paella f	pa·*e*·lya	*rice & seafood dish (sometimes with meat)*
peregrina f	pe·re·*gree*·na	*scallop*
pescaíto frito m	pes·*kai*·to *free*·to	*tiny fried fish*
picadillo m	pee·ka·*dee*·lyo	*minced meat*
pinchitos m pl	peen·*chee*·tos	*Moroccan-style kebabs*
pulpo m	*pool*·po	*octopus*
salchicha f	sal·*chee*·cha	*fresh pork sausage*
sobrasada f	so·bra·*sa*·da	*soft pork sausage*
tortilla española f	tor·*tee*·lya es·pa·*nyo*·la	*potato omelette*
trucha f	*troo*·cha	*trout*
zarzuela f	thar·*thwe*·la	*fish stew*

emergencies

basics

Help!	*¡Socorro!*	so·*ko*·ro
Stop!	*¡Pare!*	*pa*·re
Go away!	*¡Váyase!*	*va*·ya·se
Thief!	*¡Ladrón!*	lad·*ron*
Fire!	*¡Fuego!*	*fwe*·go
Watch out!	*¡Cuidado!*	kwee·*da*·do

Call ...!	*¡Llame a ...!*	*lya*·me a ...
a doctor	*un médico*	oon *me*·dee·ko
an ambulance	*una ambulancia*	*oo*·na am·boo·*lan*·thya
the police	*la policía*	la po·lee·*thee*·a

It's an emergency.
Es una emergencia. es *oo*·na e·mer·*khen*·thya

Could you help me, please?
¿Me puede ayudar, por favor? me *pwe*·de a·yoo·*dar* por fa·*vor*

I have to use the telephone.
Necesito usar el teléfono. ne·the·*see*·to oo·*sar* el te·*le*·fo·no

I'm lost.
Estoy perdido/a. m/f es·*toy* per·*dee*·do/a

Where are the toilets?
¿Dónde están los servicios? *don*·de es·*tan* los ser·*vee*·thyos

police

Where's the police station?
¿Dónde está la comisaría? *don*·de es·*ta* la ko·mee·sa·*ree*·a

I want to report an offence.
Quiero denunciar un delito. *kye*·ro de·noon·*thyar* oon de·*lee*·to

I have insurance.
Tengo seguro. *ten*·go se·*goo*·ro

I've been assaulted.	*He sido asaltado/a.* m/f	e *see*·do a·sal·*ta*·do/a
I've been raped.	*He sido violado/a.* m/f	e *see*·do vee·o·*la*·do/a
I've been robbed.	*Me han robado.*	me an rro·*ba*·do

I've lost my ...	*He perdido ...*	e per·*dee*·do ...
backpack	*mi mochila*	mee mo·*chee*·la
bags	*mis maletas*	mees ma·*le*·tas
credit card	*mi tarjeta de crédito*	mee tar·*khe*·ta de *kre*·dee·to
handbag	*mi bolso*	mee *bol*·so
jewellery	*mis joyas*	mees *kho*·yas
money	*mi dinero*	mee dee·*ne*·ro
passport	*mi pasaporte*	mee pa·sa·*por*·te
travellers cheques	*mis cheques de viajero*	mees *che*·kes de vya·*khe*·ro
wallet	*mi cartera*	mee kar·*te*·ra

I want to contact my ...	*Quiero ponerme en contacto con mi ...*	*kye*·ro po·*ner*·me en kon·*tak*·to kon mee ...
consulate	*consulado*	kon·soo·*la*·do
embassy	*embajada*	em·ba·*kha*·da

health

medical needs

Where's the nearest ...?	*¿Dónde está el ... más cercano?*	*don*·de es·*ta* el ... mas ther·*ka*·no
dentist	*dentista*	den·*tees*·ta
doctor	*médico*	*me*·dee·ko
hospital	*hospital*	os·pee·*tal*

Where's the nearest (night) pharmacist?
¿Dónde está la farmacia (de guardia) más cercana? — *don*·de es·*ta* la far·*ma*·thya (de *gwar*·dya) mas ther·*ka*·na

I need a doctor (who speaks English).
Necesito un médico (que hable inglés). — ne·the·*see*·to oon *me*·dee·ko (ke *a*·ble een·*gles*)

Could I see a female doctor?
¿Puede examinarme una médica? — *pwe*·de ek·sa·mee·*nar*·me *oo*·na *me*·dee·ka

I've run out of my medication.
Se me terminaron los medicamentos. — se me ter·mee·*na*·ron los me·dee·ka·*men*·tos

symptoms, conditions & allergies

I'm sick.	*Estoy enfermo/a.* m/f	es·*toy* en·*fer*·mo/a
It hurts here.	*Me duele aquí.*	me *dwe*·le a·*kee*
I have (a) ...	*Tengo ...*	*ten*·go ...
asthma	*asma*	*as*·ma
bronchitis	*bronquitis*	bron·*kee*·tees
constipation	*estreñimiento*	es·tre·nyee·*myen*·to
cough	*tos*	tos
diarrhoea	*diarrea*	dya·*rre*·a
fever	*fiebre*	*fye*·bre
headache	*dolor de cabeza*	do·*lor* de ka·*be*·tha
heart condition	*una condición cardíaca*	*oo*·na kon·dee·*thyon* kar·*dee*·a·ka
nausea	*náusea*	*now*·se·a
pain	*dolor*	do·*lor*
sore throat	*dolor de garganta*	do·*lor* de gar·*gan*·ta
toothache	*dolor de muelas*	do·*lor* de *mwe*·las

I'm allergic to ...	*Soy alérgico/a a ...* m/f	soy a·*ler*·khee·ko/a a ...
antibiotics	*los antibióticos*	los an·tee·*byo*·tee·kos
anti-inflammatories	*los anti-inflamatorios*	los *an*·tee·een·fla·ma·*to*·ryos
aspirin	*la aspirina*	la as·pee·*ree*·na
bees	*las abejas*	las a·*be*·khas
codeine	*la codeina*	la ko·de·*ee*·na
penicillin	*la penicilina*	la pe·nee·thee·*lee*·na

antiseptic	*antiséptico* m	an·tee·*sep*·tee·ko
bandage	*vendaje* m	ven·*da*·khe
condoms	*condones* m pl	kon·*do*·nes
contraceptives	*anticonceptivos* m pl	an·tee·kon·thep·*tee*·vos
diarrhoea medicine	*medicina para diarrea* f	me·dee·*thee*·na *pa*·ra dya·*rre*·a
insect repellent	*repelente de insectos* m	re·pe·*len*·te de een·*sek*·tos
laxatives	*laxantes* m pl	lak·*san*·tes
painkillers	*analgésicos* m pl	a·nal·*khe*·see·kos
rehydration salts	*sales rehidratantes* f pl	*sa*·les re·eed·ra·*tan*·tes
sleeping tablets	*pastillas para dormir* f pl	pas·*tee*·lyas *pa*·ra dor·*meer*

english–spanish dictionary

Spanish nouns in this dictionary, and adjectives affected by gender, have their gender indicated by ⓜ (masculine) or ⓕ (feminine). If it's a plural noun, you'll also see pl. Words are also marked as v (verb), n (noun), a (adjective), pl (plural), sg (singular), inf (informal) and pol (polite) where necessary.

A

accident *accidente* ⓜ ak·thee·*den*·te
accommodation *alojamiento* ⓜ a·lo·kha·*myen*·to
adaptor *adaptador* ⓜ a·dap·ta·*dor*
address *dirección* ⓕ dee·rek·*thyon*
after *después de* des·*pwes* de
air-conditioned *con aire acondicionado* kon *ai*·re a·kon·dee·thyo·*na*·do
airplane *avión* ⓜ a·*vyon*
airport *aeropuerto* ⓜ ay·ro·*pwer*·to
alcohol *alcohol* ⓜ al·*col*
all a *todo/a* *to*·do/a
allergy *alergia* ⓕ a·*ler*·khya
ambulance *ambulancia* ⓕ am·boo·*lan*·thya
ankle *tobillo* ⓜ to·*bee*·lyo
and *y* ee
arm *brazo* ⓜ *bra*·tho
ashtray *cenicero* ⓜ the·nee·*the*·ro
ATM *cajero automático* ka·*khe*·ro ow·to·*ma*·tee·ko

B

baby *bebé* ⓜ be·*be*
back (body) *espalda* ⓕ es·*pal*·da
backpack *mochila* ⓕ mo·*chee*·la
bad *malo/a* ⓜ/ⓕ *ma*·lo/a
bag *bolso* ⓜ *bol*·so
baggage claim *recogida de equipajes* ⓕ rre·ko·*khee*·da de e·kee·*pa*·khes
bank *banco* ⓜ *ban*·ko
bar *bar* ⓜ bar
bathroom *baño* ⓜ *ba*·nyo
battery (general) *pila* ⓕ *pee*·la
battery (car) *batería* ⓕ ba·te·*ree*·a
beautiful *hermoso/a* ⓜ/ⓕ er·*mo*·so/a
bed *cama* ⓕ *ka*·ma
beer *cerveza* ⓕ ther·*ve*·tha
before *antes* *an*·tes
behind *detrás de* de·*tras* de
bicycle *bicicleta* ⓕ bee·thee·*kle*·ta
big *grande* *gran*·de
bill *cuenta* ⓕ *kwen*·ta
black *negro/a* ⓜ/ⓕ *ne*·gro/a
blanket *manta* ⓕ *man*·ta
blood group *grupo sanguíneo* ⓜ *groo*·po san·*gee*·neo
blue *azul* a·*thool*
boat *barco* ⓜ *bar*·ko
book (make a reservation) v *reservar* rre·ser·*var*
bottle *botella* ⓕ bo·*te*·lya
bottle opener *abrebotellas* ⓜ a·bre·bo·*te*·lyas
boy *chico* ⓜ *chee*·ko
brakes (car) *frenos* ⓜ pl *fre*·nos
breakfast *desayuno* ⓜ des·a·*yoo*·no
broken (faulty) *roto/a* ⓜ/ⓕ *ro*·to/a
bus *autobús* ⓜ ow·to·*boos*
business *negocios* ⓜ pl ne·*go*·thyos
buy *comprar* kom·*prar*

café *café* ⓜ ka·*fe*
camera *cámara (fotográfica)* ⓕ *ka*·ma·ra (fo·to·*gra*·fee·ka)
camp site *cámping* ⓜ *kam*·peen
cancel *cancelar* kan·the·*lar*
can opener *abrelatas* ⓜ a·bre·*la*·tas
car *coche* ⓜ *ko*·che
cash *dinero en efectivo* ⓜ dee·*ne*·ro en e·fek·*tee*·vo
cash (a cheque) v *cambiar (un cheque)* kam·*byar* (oon *che*·ke)
cell phone *teléfono móvil* ⓜ te·*le*·fo·no *mo*·veel
centre *centro* ⓜ *then*·tro
change (money) v *cambiar* kam·*byar*
cheap *barato/a* ⓜ/ⓕ ba·*ra*·to/a
check (bill) *cuenta* ⓕ *kwen*·ta
check-in *facturación de equipajes* ⓕ fak·too·ra·*thyon* de e·kee·*pa*·khes
chest *pecho* ⓜ *pe*·cho
child *niño/a* ⓜ/ⓕ *nee*·nyo/a
cigarette *cigarillo* ⓜ thee·ga·*ree*·lyo
city *ciudad* ⓕ theew·*da*
clean a *limpio/a* ⓜ/ⓕ *leem*·pyo/a

closed *cerrado/a* ⓜ/ⓕ the·*rra*·do/a
coffee *café* ⓜ ka·*fe*
coins *monedas* ⓕ pl mo·*ne*·das
cold a *frío/a* ⓜ/ⓕ *free*·o/a
collect call *llamada a cobro revertido* ⓕ
lya·*ma*·da a *ko*·bro re·ver·*tee*·do
come *venir* ve·*neer*
computer *ordenador* ⓜ or·de·na·*dor*
condom *condones* ⓜ pl kon·*do*·nes
contact lenses *lentes de contacto* ⓜ pl
len·tes de kon·*tak*·to
cook v *cocinar* ko·thee·*nar*
cost *precio* ⓜ *pre*·thyo
credit card *tarjeta de crédito* ⓕ
tar·*khe*·ta de *kre*·dee·to
cup *taza* ⓕ *ta*·tha
currency exchange *cambio de dinero* ⓜ
kam·byo de dee·*ne*·ro
customs (immigration) *aduana* ⓕ a·*dwa*·na

D

dangerous *peligroso/a* ⓜ/ⓕ pe·lee·*gro*·so/a
date (time) *fecha* ⓕ *fe*·cha
day *día* ⓜ *dee*·a
delay *demora* ⓕ de·*mo*·ra
dentist *dentista* ⓜ/ⓕ den·*tees*·ta
depart *salir de* sa·*leer* de
diaper *pañal* ⓜ pa·*nyal*
dictionary *diccionario* ⓜ deek·thyo·*na*·ryo
dinner *cena* ⓕ *the*·na
direct *directo/a* ⓜ/ⓕ dee·*rek*·to/a
dirty *sucio/a* ⓜ/ⓕ *soo*·thyo/a
disabled *minusválido/a* ⓜ/ⓕ mee·noos·*va*·lee·do/a
discount *descuento* ⓜ des·*kwen*·to
doctor *doctor/doctora* ⓜ/ⓕ dok·*tor*/dok·*to*·ra
double bed *cama de matrimonio* ⓕ
ka·ma de ma·tree·*mo*·nyo
double room *habitación doble* ⓕ a·bee·ta·*thyon* *do*·ble
drink *bebida* ⓕ be·*bee*·da
drive v *conducir* kon·doo·*theer*
drivers licence *carnet de conducir* ⓜ
kar·*ne* de kon·doo·*theer*
drugs (illicit) *droga* ⓕ *dro*·ga
dummy (pacifier) *chupete* ⓜ choo·*pe*·te

E

ear *oreja* ⓕ o·*re*·kha
east *este* *es*·te
eat *comer* ko·*mer*
economy class *clase turística* ⓕ *kla*·se too·*rees*·tee·ka
electricity *electricidad* ⓕ e·lek·tree·thee·*da*
elevator *ascensor* ⓜ as·then·*sor*
email *correo electrónico* ⓜ ko·*rre*·o e·lek·*tro*·nee·ko
embassy *embajada* ⓕ em·ba·*kha*·da
emergency *emergencia* ⓕ e·mer·*khen*·thya
English (language) *inglés* ⓜ een·*gles*
entrance *entrada* ⓕ en·*tra*·da
evening *noche* ⓕ *no*·che
exchange rate *tipo de cambio* ⓜ *tee*·po de *kam*·byo
exit *salida* ⓕ sa·*lee*·da
expensive *caro/a* ⓜ/ⓕ *ka*·ro/a
express mail *correo urgente* ⓜ ko·*rre*·o oor·*khen*·te
eye *ojo* ⓜ *o*·kho

F

far *lejos* *le*·khos
fast *rápido/a* ⓜ/ⓕ *rra*·pee·do/a
father *padre* ⓜ *pa*·dre
film (camera) *carrete* ⓜ ka·*rre*·te
finger *dedo* ⓜ *de*·do
first-aid kit *maletín de primeros auxilios* ⓜ
ma·le·*teen* de pree·*me*·ros ow·*ksee*·lyos
first class *de primera clase* de pree·*me*·ra *kla*·se
fish *pez* ⓜ peth
food *comida* ⓕ ko·*mee*·da
foot *pie* ⓜ pye
fork *tenedor* ⓜ te·ne·*dor*
free (of charge) *gratis* *gra*·tees
friend *amigo/a* ⓜ/ⓕ a·*mee*·go/a
fruit *fruta* ⓕ *froo*·ta
full *lleno/a* ⓜ/ⓕ *lye*·no/a
funny *gracioso/a* ⓜ/ⓕ gra·*thyo*·so/a

G

gift *regalo* ⓜ rre·*ga*·lo
girl *chica* ⓕ *chee*·ka
glass (drinking) *vaso* ⓜ *va*·so
glasses *gafas* ⓕ pl *ga*·fas
go *ir* eer
good *bueno/a* ⓜ/ⓕ *bwe*·no/a
green *verde* *ver*·de
guide n *guía* ⓜ/ⓕ *gee*·a

H

half *mitad* ⓕ mee·*tad*
hand *mano* ⓕ *ma*·no
handbag *bolso* ⓜ *bol*·so

happy *feliz* fe·*leeth*
have *tener* te·*ner*
he *él* el
head *cabeza* ⓕ ka·*be*·tha
heart *corazón* ⓜ ko·ra·*thon*
heat *calor* ⓜ ka·*lor*
heavy *pesado/a* ⓜ/ⓕ pe·*sa*·do/a
help v *ayudar* a·yoo·*dar*
here *aquí* a·*kee*
high *alto/a* ⓜ/ⓕ *al*·to/a
highway *autovía* ⓕ ow·to·*vee*·a
hike v *ir de excursión* eer de eks·koor·*syon*
holiday *vacaciones* ⓕ pl va·ka·*thyo*·nes
homosexual *homosexual* ⓜ/ⓕ o·mo·se·*kswal*
hospital *hospital* ⓜ os·pee·*tal*
hot *caliente* ka·*lyen*·te
hotel *hotel* ⓜ o·*tel*
hungry *hambriento/a* ⓜ/ⓕ am·bree·*en*·to/a
husband *marido* ⓜ ma·*ree*·do

I

I *yo* yo
identification (card) *carnet de identidad* ⓜ kar·*net* de ee·den·tee·*da*
ill *enfermo/a* ⓜ/ⓕ en·*fer*·mo/a
important *importante* eem·por·*tan*·te
included *incluido* een·kloo·*ee*·do
injury *herida* ⓕ e·*ree*·da
insurance *seguro* ⓜ se·*goo*·ro
Internet *Internet* ⓜ *een*·ter·net
interpreter *intérprete* ⓜ/ⓕ een·*ter*·pre·te

J

jewellery *joyas* ⓕ pl *kho*·yas
job *trabajo* ⓜ tra·*ba*·kho

K

key *llave* ⓕ *lya*·ve
kilogram *kilogramo* ⓜ *kee*·lo·gra·mo
kitchen *cocina* ⓕ ko·*thee*·na
knife *cuchillo* ⓜ koo·*chee*·lyo

L

laundry (place) *lavadero* ⓜ la·va·*de*·ro
lawyer *abogado/a* ⓜ/ⓕ a·bo·*ga*·do/a
left (direction) *izquierda* ⓕ eeth·*kyer*·da
left-luggage office *consigna* ⓕ kon·*seeg*·na
leg *pierna* ⓕ *pyer*·na
lesbian *lesbiana* ⓕ les·bee·*a*·na
less *menos* *me*·nos
letter (mail) *carta* ⓕ *kar*·ta
lift (elevator) *ascensor* ⓜ as·then·*sor*
light *luz* ⓕ looth
like v *gustar* goos·*tar*
lock *cerradura* ⓕ the·rra·*doo*·ra
long *largo/a* ⓜ/ⓕ *lar*·go/a
lost *perdido/a* ⓜ/ⓕ per·*dee*·do/a
lost-property office *oficina de objetos perdidos* ⓕ o·fee·*thee*·na de ob·*khe*·tos per·*dee*·dos
love v *querer* ke·*rer*
luggage *equipaje* ⓜ e·kee·*pa*·khe
lunch *almuerzo* ⓜ al·*mwer*·tho

M

mail *correo* ⓜ ko·*rre*·o
man *hombre* ⓜ *om*·bre
map *mapa* ⓜ *ma*·pa
market *mercado* ⓜ mer·*ka*·do
matches *cerillas* ⓕ pl the·*ree*·lyas
meat *carne* ⓕ *kar*·ne
medicine *medicina* ⓕ me·dee·*thee*·na
menu *menú* ⓜ me·*noo*
message *mensaje* ⓜ men·*sa*·khe
milk *leche* ⓕ *le*·che
minute *minuto* ⓜ mee·*noo*·to
mobile phone *teléfono móvil* ⓜ te·*le*·fo·no *mo*·veel
money *dinero* ⓜ dee·*ne*·ro
month *mes* ⓜ mes
morning *mañana* ⓕ ma·*nya*·na
mother *madre* ⓕ *ma*·dre
motorcycle *motocicleta* ⓕ mo·to·thee·*kle*·ta
motorway *autovía* ⓕ ow·to·*vee*·a
mouth *boca* ⓕ *bo*·ka
music *música* ⓕ *moo*·see·ka

N

name *nombre* ⓜ *nom*·bre
napkin *servilleta* ⓕ ser·vee·*lye*·ta
nappy *pañal* ⓜ pa·*nyal*
near *cerca* *ther*·ka
neck *cuello* ⓜ *kwe*·lyo
new *nuevo/a* ⓜ/ⓕ *nwe*·vo/a
news *noticias* ⓕ pl no·*tee*·thyas
newspaper *periódico* ⓜ pe·*ryo*·dee·ko

night *noche* ⓕ *no*·che
no *no* no
noisy *ruidoso/a* ⓜ/ⓕ rrwee·*do*·so/a
nonsmoking *no fumadores* no foo·ma·*do*·res
north *norte* ⓜ *nor*·te
nose *nariz* ⓕ na·*reeth*
now *ahora* a·*o*·ra
number *número* ⓜ *noo*·me·ro

O

oil (engine) *aceite* ⓜ a·*they*·te
old *viejo/a* ⓜ/ⓕ *vye*·kho/a
one-way ticket *billete sencillo* ⓜ bee·*lye*·te sen·*thee*·lyo
open a *abierto/a* ⓜ/ⓕ a·*byer*·to/a
outside *exterior* ⓜ eks·te·*ryor*

P

package *paquete* ⓜ pa·*ke*·te
paper *papel* ⓜ pa·*pel*
park (car) v *estacionar* es·ta·thyo·*nar*
passport *pasaporte* ⓜ pa·sa·*por*·te
pay *pagar* pa·*gar*
pen *bolígrafo* ⓜ bo·*lee*·gra·fo
petrol *gasolina* ⓕ ga·so·*lee*·na
pharmacy *farmacia* ⓕ far·*ma*·thya
phonecard *tarjeta de teléfono* ⓕ
tar·*khe*·ta de te·*le*·fo·no
photo *foto* ⓕ *fo*·to
plate *plato* ⓜ *pla*·to
police *policía* ⓕ po·lee·*thee*·a
postcard *postal* ⓕ pos·*tal*
post office *correos* ⓜ ko·*rre*·os
pregnant *embarazada* ⓕ em·ba·ra·*tha*·da
price *precio* ⓜ *pre*·thyo

Q

quiet *tranquilo/a* ⓜ/ⓕ tran·*kee*·lo/a

R

rain *lluvia* ⓕ *lyoo*·vya
razor *afeitadora* ⓕ a·fey·ta·*do*·ra
receipt *recibo* ⓜ rre·*thee*·bo
red *rojo/a* ⓜ/ⓕ *rro*·kho/a
refund *reembolso* ⓜ rre·em·*bol*·so
registered mail *correo certificado* ⓜ
ko·*rre*·o ther·tee·fee·*ka*·do
rent v *alquilar* al·kee·*lar*
repair v *reparar* rre·pa·*rar*
reservation *reserva* ⓕ rre·*ser*·va
restaurant *restaurante* ⓜ rres·tow·*ran*·te
return v *volver* vol·*ver*
return ticket *billete de ida y vuelta* ⓜ
bee·*lye*·te de *ee*·da ee *vwel*·ta
right (direction) *derecha* de·*re*·cha
road *carretera* ⓕ ka·rre·*te*·ra
room *habitación* ⓕ a·bee·ta·*thyon*

S

safe a *seguro/a* ⓜ/ⓕ se·*goo*·ro/a
sanitary napkin *compresas* ⓕ pl kom·*pre*·sas
seat *asiento* ⓜ a·*syen*·to
send *enviar* en·vee·*ar*
service station *gasolinera* ⓕ ga·so·lee·*ne*·ra
sex *sexo* ⓜ *se*·kso
shampoo *champú* ⓜ cham·*poo*
share (a dorm) *compartir* kom·par·*teer*
shaving cream *espuma de afeitar* ⓕ
es·*poo*·ma de a·fey·*tar*
she *ella* ⓕ *e*·lya
sheet (bed) *sábana* ⓕ *sa*·ba·na
shirt *camisa* ⓕ ka·*mee*·sa
shoes *zapatos* ⓜ pl tha·*pa*·tos
shop *tienda* ⓕ *tyen*·da
short *corto/a* ⓜ/ⓕ *kor*·to/a
shower *ducha* ⓕ *doo*·cha
single room *habitación individual* ⓕ
a·bee·ta·*thyon* een·dee·vee·*dwal*
skin *piel* ⓕ pyel
skirt *falda* ⓕ *fal*·da
sleep v *dormir* dor·*meer*
slowly *despacio* des·*pa*·thyo
small *pequeño/a* ⓜ/ⓕ pe·*ke*·nyo/a
smoke (cigarettes) v *fumar* foo·*mar*
soap *jabón* ⓜ kha·*bon*
some *alguno/a* ⓜ/ⓕ al·*goo*·no/a
soon *pronto* *pron*·to
south *sur* ⓜ soor
souvenir shop *tienda de recuerdos* ⓕ
tyen·da de re·*kwer*·dos
Spain *España* ⓕ es·*pa*·nya
Spanish (language) *español/castellano* ⓜ
es·pa·*nyol*/kas·te·*lya*·no
speak *hablar* a·*blar*
spoon *cuchara* ⓕ koo·*cha*·ra
stamp *sello* ⓜ *se*·lyo

stand-by ticket *billete de lista de espera* ⓜ bee·*lye*·te de *lees*·ta de es·*pe*·ra
station (train) *estación* ⓕ es·ta·*thyon*
stomach *estómago* ⓜ es·*to*·ma·go
stop v *parar* pa·*rar*
stop (bus) *parada* ⓕ pa·*ra*·da
street *calle* ⓕ *ka*·lye
student *estudiante* ⓜ/ⓕ es·too·*dyan*·te
sun *sol* ⓜ sol
sunscreen *crema solar* ⓕ *kre*·ma so·*lar*
swim v *nadar* na·*dar*

T

tampons *tampones* ⓜ pl tam·*po*·nes
taxi *taxi* ⓜ *tak*·see
teaspoon *cucharita* ⓕ koo·cha·*ree*·ta
teeth *dientes* ⓜ pl *dyen*·tes
telephone *teléfono* ⓜ te·*le*·fo·no
television *televisión* ⓕ te·le·vee·*syon*
temperature (weather) *temperatura* ⓕ tem·pe·ra·*too*·ra
tent *tienda (de campaña)* ⓕ *tyen*·da (de kam·*pa*·nya)
that (one) *ése/a* ⓜ/ⓕ *e*·se/a
they *ellos/ellas* ⓜ/ⓕ *e*·lyos/*e*·lyas
thirsty *sediento/a* ⓜ/ⓕ se·dee·*en*·to/a
this (one) *éste/a* ⓜ/ⓕ *es*·te/a
throat *garganta* ⓕ gar·*gan*·ta
ticket *billete* ⓜ bee·*lye*·te
time *tiempo* ⓜ *tyem*·po
tired *cansado/a* ⓜ/ⓕ kan·*sa*·do/a
tissues *pañuelos de papel* ⓜ pl pa·*nywe*·los de pa·*pel*
today *hoy* oy
toilet *servicio* ⓜ ser·*vee*·thyo
tomorrow *mañana* ma·*nya*·na
tonight *esta noche* *es*·ta *no*·che
toothbrush *cepillo de dientes* ⓜ the·*pee*·lyo de *dyen*·tes
toothpaste *pasta dentífrica* ⓕ *pas*·ta den·*tee*·free·ka
torch (flashlight) *linterna* ⓕ leen·*ter*·na
tour *excursión* ⓕ eks·koor·*syon*
tourist office *oficina de turismo* ⓕ o·fee·*thee*·na de too·*rees*·mo
towel *toalla* ⓕ to·*a*·lya
train *tren* ⓜ tren
translate *traducir* tra·doo·*theer*
travel agency *agencia de viajes* ⓕ a·*khen*·thya de *vya*·khes
travellers cheque *cheque de viajero* ⓜ *che*·ke de vya·*khe*·ro
trousers *pantalones* ⓜ pl pan·ta·*lo*·nes
twin beds *dos camas* ⓕ pl dos *ka*·mas
tyre *neumático* ⓜ ne·oo·*ma*·tee·ko

U

underwear *ropa interior* ⓕ *rro*·pa een·te·*ryor*
urgent *urgente* oor·*khen*·te

V

vacant *vacante* va·*kan*·te
vacation *vacaciones* ⓕ pl va·ka·*thyo*·nes
vegetable *verdura* ⓕ ver·*doo*·ra
vegetarian a *vegetariano/a* ⓜ/ⓕ ve·khe·ta·*rya*·no/a
visa *visado* ⓜ vee·*sa*·do

W

waiter *camarero/a* ⓜ/ⓕ ka·ma·*re*·ro/a
walk v *caminar* ka·mee·*nar*
wallet *cartera* ⓕ kar·*te*·ra
warm a *templado/a* ⓜ/ⓕ tem·*pla*·do/a
wash (something) *lavar* la·*var*
watch *reloj de pulsera* ⓜ rre·*lokh* de pool·*se*·ra
water *agua* ⓕ *a*·gwa
we *nosotros/nosotras* ⓜ/ⓕ no·*so*·tros/ no·*so*·tras
weekend *fin de semana* ⓜ feen de se·*ma*·na
west *oeste* ⓜ o·*es*·te
wheelchair *silla de ruedas* ⓕ *see*·lya de *rrwe*·das
when *cuando* *kwan*·do
where *donde* *don*·de
white *blanco/a* ⓜ/ⓕ *blan*·ko/a
who *quien* kyen
why *por qué* por *ke*
wife *esposa* ⓕ es·*po*·sa
window *ventana* ⓕ ven·*ta*·na
wine *vino* ⓜ *vee*·no
with *con* kon
without *sin* seen
woman *mujer* ⓕ moo·*kher*
write *escribir* es·kree·*beer*

Y

yellow *amarillo/a* a·ma·*ree*·lyo/a
yes *sí* see
yesterday *ayer* a·*yer*
you sg inf/pol *tú/Usted* too/oos·*te*
you pl *vosotros/vosotras* ⓜ/ⓕ vo·*so*·tros/vo·*so*·tras

Swedish

swedish alphabet				
Aa aa	*Bb* bey	*Cc* sey	*Dd* dey	*Ee* ey
Ff ef	*Gg* gey	*Hh* hoh	*Ii* ee	*Jj* yoy
Kk koh	*Ll* el	*Mm* em	*Nn* en	*Oo* oh
Pp pey	*Qq* ku	*Rr* er	*Ss* es	*Tt* tey
Uu u	*Vv* vey	*Ww* *do*·belt vey	*Xx* eks	*Yy* ew
Zz set	*Åå* aw	*Ää* e	*Öö* eu	

introduction

The Swedish language (*svenska sven*·ska) gave us *ombudsman* and *smorgasbord*, which just confirms the image of the Swedes as a nation that's good at making the most of life in more ways than one. As a member of the Germanic language family, Swedish shares common roots with English and German. German, in particular, has influenced Swedish in the form of numerous loanwords. However, the closest relatives of Swedish are, of course, the other Scandinavian languages, Danish and Norwegian – all of them descendants of Old Norse, which started branching out from the 9th century and the Viking age.

The oldest inscriptions in Old Norse, dating from the same period, used the runic alphabet and were written on stone or wood. The missionaries who introduced Christianity in the 12th century brought the Roman alphabet (and the custom of writing on parchment) to the emerging Scandinavian languages, but some modification was necessary to represent the specific vowel sounds, so additional letters were eventually developed. The turning point in the evolution of Swedish coincided with the achievement of independence from Danish rule in 1526, when the first translation of the New Testament appeared. The modern literary language was shaped after the first Swedish translation of the whole Bible, known as *Gustav Vasas Bibel* as it was published under the patronage of King Gustav Vasa in 1541.

The standard language or *Rikssvenska* reek·*sven*·ska (lit: kingdom-Swedish) is based on the central dialects from the area around Stockholm. Some of the rural dialects that are spoken across the country are quite diverse – for example, *Skånska skawn*·ska, spoken in the southern province of Skåne, has flatter vowel sounds (and sounds a lot more like Danish), whereas *Dalmål daal*·mawl, spoken in the central region of Dalarna, has a very up-and-down sound.

Interestingly, Swedish doesn't have official status in Sweden itself, but it does in neighbouring Finland. This is easily explained though – Swedish is the national language of Sweden, spoken by the majority of residents (around 8.5 million), and it simply wasn't felt necessary to enforce its use by law. Finland, on the other hand, was part of Sweden from the mid-14th century until 1809, and Swedish was the language of administration. Today, it shares official status with Finnish and is a mandatory subject in schools, but it's the first language for only about 300,000 people or 6% of Finland's population. PS: any traveller to Sweden should know that the Swedish Chef from the Muppets doesn't really speak Swedish at all.

pronunciation

vowel sounds

Swedish vowel sounds can be either short or long – generally the stressed vowels are long, except when they are followed by double consonants, in which case they are short. The vowels in unstressed syllables are also short.

symbol	english equivalent	swedish example	transliteration
a	run	*glass*	glas
aa	father	*glas*	glaas
ai	aisle	*kaj*	kai
aw	saw	*gå*	gaw
e	bet	*vän*	ven
air	hair	*gärna*	*yair*·na
ee	see	*hit*	heet
eu	nurse	*söt*	seut
ew	ee pronounced with rounded lips	*nytt*	newt
ey	as in 'bet', but longer	*heta*	*hey*·ta
i	hit	*hitta*	*hi*·ta
o	pot	*kopp*	kop
oh	oh	*bott*	boht
oo	zoo	*kul*	kool
u	put	*buss*	bus

consonant sounds

Most Swedish consonants sounds are similar to their English counterparts. One exception is the fh sound (a breathy sound pronounced with rounded lips, like saying 'f' and 'w' at the same time), but with a little practice, you'll soon get it right.

symbol	english equivalent	swedish example	transliteration
b	bed	*bil*	beel
ch	cheat	*tjur*	choor
d	dog	*dyr*	dewr
f	fat	*filt*	filt
fh	f pronounced with rounded lips	*sjuk*	fhook
g	go	*gård*	gawrd
h	hat	*hård*	hawrd
k	kit	*kung*	kung
l	lot	*land*	land
m	man	*man*	man
n	not	*nej*	ney
ng	ring	*sång*	sawng
p	pet	*penna*	*pe*·na
r	red	*rosa*	*roh*·sa
s	sun	*sol*	sohl
sh	shot	*första*	*feush*·ta
t	top	*tröja*	*tror*·ya
v	very	*vit*	veet
y	yes	*jag*	yaag

word stress

In Swedish, stress usually falls on the first syllable in a word, but sometimes it falls on two syllables. It's important to get the stress right, as it can change the meaning of words (eg *anden* *an*·den 'duck' versus *anden* *an·den* 'spirit'). Words borrowed from other languages are often stressed on the last syllable (eg *bibliotek* bib·li·o·*tek* 'library'). In this chapter, the stressed syllables are always in italics.

language difficulties

Do you speak English?		
Talar du engelska?		*taa*·lar doo *eng*·el·ska
Do you understand?		
Förstår du?		feur·*shtawr* doo
I (don't) understand.		
Jag förstår (inte).		yaa feur·*shtawr* (*in*·te)
What does (*snus*) mean?		
Vad betyder (snus)?		vaad be·*tew*·der (snoos)

How do you ...?	*Hur ...?*	hoor ...
pronounce this	*uttalar man detta*	*ut*·taa·lar man *de*·ta
write (*spårvagn*)	*skrivar man (spårvagn)*	*skree*·var man (*spawr*·vangn)

Could you please ...?	*Kan du vara snäll och ...?*	*kan* doo vaa·ra snel o ...
repeat that	*upprepa det*	*up*·rey·pa det
speak more slowly	*tala lite långsammare*	*taa*·la *lee*·te *lawng*·sa·ma·re
write it down	*skriva ner det*	*skree*·va *neyr* de

essentials

Yes.	*Ja.*	yaa
No.	*Nej.*	ney
Please.	*Tack.*	tak
Thank you (very much).	*Tack (så mycket).*	tak (saw *mew*·ke)
You're welcome.	*Varsågod.*	var·sha·*gohd*
Excuse me.	*Ursäkta mig.*	oor·*shek*·ta mey
Sorry.	*Förlåt.*	feur·*lawt*

numbers

0	*noll*	nol	16	*sexton*	*seks*·ton
1	*ett*	et	17	*sjutton*	*fhu*·ton
2	*två*	tvaw	18	*arton*	*ar*·ton
3	*tre*	trey	19	*nitton*	*ni*·ton
4	*fyra*	*few*·ra	20	*tjugo*	*shoo*·go
5	*fem*	fem	21	*tjugoett*	shoo·go·*et*
6	*sex*	seks	22	*tjugotvå*	shoo·go·*tvaw*
7	*sju*	fhoo	30	*trettio*	*tre*·tee
8	*åtta*	*o*·ta	40	*fyrtio*	*fewr*·tee
9	*nio*	*nee*·oh	50	*femtio*	*fem*·tee
10	*tio*	*tee*·oh	60	*sextio*	*seks*·tee
11	*elva*	*el*·va	70	*sjuttio*	*fhu*·tee
12	*tolv*	tolv	80	*åttio*	*o*·tee
13	*tretton*	*tre*·ton	90	*nittio*	*ni*·tee
14	*fjorton*	*fyor*·ton	100	*ett hundra*	et *hun*·dra
15	*femton*	*fem*·ton	1000	*ett tusen*	et *too*·sen

time & dates

What time is it?	*Hur mycket är klockan?*	hur *mew*·ke air *klo*·kan
It's one o'clock.	*Klockan är en.*	*klo*·kan air *eyn*
It's (two) o'clock.	*Klockan är (två).*	*klo*·kan air (*tvaw*)
Quarter past (one).	*Kvart över (en).*	*kvart eu*·ver (eyn)
Half past (one).	*Halv (två).* (lit: half two)	halv (tvaw)
Quarter to (nine).	*Kvart i (nio).*	kvart ee (*nee*·oh)
At what time ...?	*Hur dags ...?*	hur daks ...
At (10) o'clock.	*Klockan (tio).*	*klo*·kan (*tee*·oh)
am	*förmiddagen (f m)*	*feur*·mi·daa·gen
pm	*eftermiddagen (e m)*	*ef*·ter·mi·daa·gen
Monday	*måndag*	*mawn*·daa
Tuesday	*tisdag*	*tees*·taa
Wednesday	*onsdag*	*ohns*·daa
Thursday	*torsdag*	*torsh*·daa
Friday	*fredag*	*frey*·daa
Saturday	*lördag*	*leur*·daa
Sunday	*söndag*	*seun*·daa

January	*januari*	ya·nu·*aa*·ree
February	*februari*	fe·bru·*aa*·ree
March	*mars*	mars
April	*april*	a·*preel*
May	*maj*	mai
June	*juni*	*yoo*·nee
July	*juli*	*yoo*·lee
August	*augusti*	aw·*gus*·tee
September	*september*	sep·*tem*·ber
October	*oktober*	ok·*toh*·ber
November	*november*	noh·*vem*·ber
December	*december*	dey·*sem*·ber

What date is it today?
Vilket datum är det idag? — *vil*·ket *daa*·tum air de ee·*daag*

It's (15 December).
Det är (femtonde December). — de air (*fem*·ton·de dey·*sem*·ber)

since (May)	*sedan (maj)*	seyn (mai)
until (June)	*till (juni)*	til (*yoo*·nee)
last ...		
night	*igår kväll*	ee·*gawr kvel*
week	*förra veckan*	*feu*·ra *ve*·kan
month	*förra månaden*	*feu*·ra *maw*·na·den
year	*förra året*	*feu*·ra *aw*·ret
next ...	*nästa ...*	*nes*·ta ...
week	*vecka*	*ve*·ka
month	*månad*	*maw*·nad
year	*år*	awr
yesterday ...	*igår ...*	ee·*gawr* ...
morning	*morse*	*mor*·she
afternoon	*eftermiddag*	*ef*·ter·mi·daag
evening	*kväll*	kvel
tomorrow ...	*imorgon ...*	ee·*mor*·ron ...
morning	*bitti*	*bi*·ti
afternoon	*eftermiddag*	*ef*·ter·mi·daag
evening	*kväll*	kvel

weather

What's the weather like?	*Hur är vädret?*	hur air *vey*·dret
It's …		
cold	*Det är kallt.*	de air kalt
cloudy	*Det är molnigt.*	de air *mol*·nit
hot	*Det är het.*	de air heyt
raining	*Det regnar.*	de *reng*·nar
snowing	*Det snöar.*	de *sneu*·ar
sunny	*Solen skiner.*	*soh*·len *fhee*·ner
warm	*Det är varmt.*	de air varmt
windy	*Det blåser.*	de *blaw*·ser
spring	*vår*	vawr
summer	*sommar*	*so*·mar
autumn	*höst*	heust
winter	*vinter*	*vin*·ter

border crossing

I'm here …	*Jag är …*	yaa air …
in transit	*i transit*	i *tran*·sit
on business	*på affärsresa*	paw a*fairsh*·rey·sa
on holiday	*på semester*	paw se·*mes*·ter
I'm here for …	*Jag stannar här …*	yaa *sta*·nar hair …
(10) days	*(tio) dagar*	(*tee*·oh) *daa*·gar
(three) weeks	*(tre) veckor*	(*trey*) *ve*·kor
(two) months	*(två) månader*	(*tvaw*) *maw*·na·der

I'm going to (Trelleborg).
Jag resar till (Trelleborg). — yaa *rey*·sa til (tre·le·*bory*)

I'm staying at the (Grand Hotel).
Jag bor på (Grand Hotell). — yaa bor paw (grand hoh·*tel*)

I have nothing to declare.
Jag har ingenting att förtulla. — yaa har *ing*·en·ting at feur·*tu*·la

I have something to declare.
Jag har något att förtulla. — yaa har *naw*·got at feur·*tu*·la

That's (not) mine.
Det är (inte) min. — de air (*in*·te) min

transport

tickets & luggage

Where can I buy a ticket?		
Var kan jag köpa en biljett?		*var* kan yaa *sheu*·pa eyn bil·*yet*
Do I need to book a seat?		
Måste man boka?		*maw*·ste man *boh*·ka
One … ticket (to Stockholm), please.	*Jag skulle vilja ha en … (till Stockholm).*	yaa *sku*·le *vil*·ya haa eyn … (til *stok*·holm)
one-way	*enkelbiljett*	*en*·kel·bil·*yet*
return	*returbiljett*	re·*toor*·bil·*yet*
I'd like to … my ticket, please.	*Jag vill gärna … min biljett.*	yaa vil *yair*·na … min bil·*yet*
cancel	*upphäva*	*up*·hey·va
change	*ändra*	*en*·dra
collect	*hämta*	*hem*·ta
confirm	*bekräfta*	be·*kref*·ta
I'd like a … seat, please.	*Jag vill gärna ha en … plads.*	yaa vil *yair*·na haa eyn … plads
nonsmoking	*icke-rökande*	*i*·ke·reu·kan·de
smoking	*rökande*	*reu*·kan·de
How much is it?		
Hur mycket kostar det?		hoor *mew*·ke *kos*·tar de
Is there air conditioning?		
Finns det luft-konditionering?		fins de *luft*·kon·di·fho·*ney*·ring
Is there a toilet?		
Finns det en toalett?		fins de eyn toh·aa·*let*
How long does the trip take?		
Hur länge undgår resan?		hoor *leng*·e *und*·gawr *rey*·san
Is it a direct route?		
Är det en direktförbindelse?		air de eyn dee·*rekt*·feur·bin·del·se
I'd like a luggage locker.		
Jag vill gärna få ett låsbara skåp till mit bagage.		yaa vil *yair*·na faw et *laws*·ba·ra *skawp* til mit ba·*gaash*

My luggage has been ...	*Mit bagage är blivit ...*	mit ba·*gaash* air *blee*·vit ...
damaged	*skadat*	*skaa*·dat
lost	*förlorat*	feur·*loh*·rat
stolen	*stulit*	*stoo*·lit

getting around

Where does flight (SK403) arrive/depart?
Var ankommar/avgår flyg (SK403)? — var *an*·ko·mar/*aav*·gawr flewg (es koh *few*·ra nol trey)

Where's (the) ...?	*Var finns ...?*	var fins ...
arrivals hall	*ankomsthallen*	*an*·komst·ha·len
departures hall	*avgångshallen*	*aav*·gawngs·ha·len
duty free shop	*en duty-free affär*	eyn *dyoo*·tee·*free* a·*fair*
gate (12)	*gate (tolv)*	gayt (tolv)

Is this the ... to (Stockholm)?	*Är den här ... till (Stockholm)?*	air den hair ... til (*stok*·holm)
boat	*båten*	*baw*·ten
bus	*bussen*	*bu*·sen

Is this the ... to (Stockholm)?	*Är det här ... till (Stockholm)?*	air de hair ... til (*stok*·holm)
plane	*planet*	*plaa*·net
train	*tåget*	*taw*·get

What time's the ... bus?	*När går ...?*	nair gawr ...
first	*första bussen*	*feursh*·ta *bu*·sen
last	*sista bussen*	*sis*·ta *bu*·sen
next	*nästa buss*	*nes*·ta bus

At what time does it arrive/leave?
Hur dags anländer/avgår den? — hoor daks *an*·len·der/*aav*·gawr deyn

How long will it be delayed?
Hur mycket är det försenat? — hoor *mew*·ket air dey feur·*shey*·nat

What station/stop is this?
Vilken station/hållplats är denna? — *vil*·ken sta·*fhohn*/*hawl*·plats air *dey*·na

What's the next station/stop?
Vilken är nästa station/hållplats? — *vil*·ken air *nes*·ta sta·*fhohn*/*hawl*·plats

Does it stop at (Lund)?
Stannar den på (Lund)? — *sta*·nar deyn paw (lund)

Please tell me when we get to (Linköping).
Kan du säga till när vi kommer till (Linköping)? — kan doo *say*·ya *til* nair vee *ko*·mer til (*lin*·sheu·ping)

How long do we stop here?
Hur länge stannar vi här? — hoor *leng*·e *sta*·nar vee hair

Is this seat available?
Är denna plads ledig? — air *dey*·na plats *ley*·dig

That's my seat.
Det är min plads. — de air *min* plats

I'd like a taxi ...	*Jag vill gärna få en taxi ...*	yaa vil *yair*·na faw eyn *tak*·see ...
at (9am)	*klockan (nio på morgonen)*	*klo*·kan (*nee*·oh paw *mo*·ro·nen)
now	*nu*	noo
tomorrow	*imorgon*	ee·*mo*·ron

Is this taxi available?
Är denna taxi ledig? — air *dey*·na *tak*·see *ley*·di

How much is it to ...?
Vad kostar det till ...? — vaad *kos*·tar de til ...

Please put the meter on.
Kan du kör på taxametern? — kan doo sheur paw tak·sa·*mey*·tern

Please take me to (this address).
Kan du köra mig till (denna address)? — kan doo *sheu*·ra mey til (*dey*·na a·*dres*)

Please ...	*Kan du ...?*	kan doo ...
slow down	*sakta ner*	*sak*·ta neyr
stop here	*stanna här*	*sta*·na hair
wait here	*vänta här*	*ven*·ta hair

car, motorbike & bicycle hire

I'd like to hire a ...	*Jag vill hyra en ...*	yaa vil *hew*·ra eyn ...
bicycle	*cykel*	*sew*·kel
car	*bil*	beel
motorbike	*motorcykel*	*moh*·tor·sew·kel

with ...	*med ...*	meyd ...
a driver	*chaufför*	fho·*feur*
air conditioning	*luft-konditionering*	*luft*·kon·di·fho·*ney*·ring
antifreeze	*kylarvätska*	*shew*·lar·vet·ska
snow chains	*snökedja*	*sneu*·she·dya

How much for ... hire?	*Hur mycket kostar det ...?*	hoor *mew*·ke *kos*·tar de ...
hourly	*per timma*	peyr *ti*·ma
daily	*per dag*	peyr *daag*
weekly	*per vecka*	peyr *ve*·ka

air	*luft*	luft
oil	*olja*	*ol*·ya
petrol	*bensin*	ben·*seen*
tyres	*däck* n	dek

I need a mechanic.
Jag behöver en mekaniker. — yaa be·*heu*·ver eyn me·*kaa*·ni·ker

I've run out of petrol.
Jag har ingen bensin kvar. — yaa har *ing*·en ben·*seen* kvar

I have a flat tyre.
Jag har fått punktering. — yaa har fawt punk·*tey*·ring

directions

Where's the ...?	*Var ligger ...?*	var *li*·ger ...
bank	*banken*	*ban*·ken
city centre	*centrum*	*sen*·trum
hotel	*hotellet*	hoh·*te*·let
market	*salutorget*	*saa*·loo *tor*·yet
police station	*polisen*	poh·*lee*·sen
post office	*posten*	*pos*·ten
public toilet	*en offentlig toalett*	eyn o·*feynt*·lig toh·aa·*let*
tourist office	*turistinformationen*	too·*rist*·in·for·ma·*fhoh*·nen

Is this the road to (Göteborg)?
Går den här vägen till (Göteborg)? — gawr den hair *vey*·gen til (yeu·te·*bory*)

Can you show me (on the map)?
Kan du visa mig (på kartan)? — kan doo *vee*·sa mey (paw *kar*·tan)

What's the address?
Vilken adress är det? — *vil*·ken a·*dres* air de

How far is it?
Hur långt är det? — hoor *lawngt* air de

How do I get there?
Hur kommer man dit? — hoor *ko*·mar man *deet*

Turn ...	*Sväng ...*	sveng ...
at the corner	*vid hörnet*	veed *heur*·net
at the traffic lights	*vid trafikljuset*	veed tra·*feek*·yoo·set
left/right	*till vänster/höger*	til *ven*·ster/*heu*·ger

It's ...	*Det är ...*	de air ...
behind ...	*bakom ...*	*baa*·kom ...
far away	*långt*	lawngt
here	*här*	hair
in front of ...	*framför ...*	*fram*·feur ...
left	*till vänster*	til *ven*·ster
near (to ...)	*nära (på ...)*	*nair*·ra (paw ...)
next to ...	*bredvid ...*	breyd·*veed* ...
on the corner	*vid hörnet*	veed *heur*·net
opposite ...	*mitt emot ...*	mit ey·*moht* ...
right	*till höger*	til *heu*·ger
straight ahead	*rakt fram*	raakt fram
there	*där*	dair

by boat	*med båt*	me *bawt*
by bus	*med buss*	me *bus*
by taxi	*med taxi*	me *tak*·see
by train	*med tåg*	me *tawg*
on foot	*till fods*	til fohts

north	*nord*	nord
south	*syd*	sewd
east	*öst*	eust
west	*väst*	vest

signs		
Ingång/Utgång	*in*·gawng/*oot*·gawng	Entrance/Exit
Öppet/Stängt	*eu*·pet/stengt	Open/Closed
Lediga Rum	*ley*·di·ga *rum*	Rooms Available
Fullt/Inga Lediga Rum	fult/*ing*·a *ley*·di·ga *rum*	No Vacancies
Information	in·for·ma·*fhohn*	Information
Polisstation	poh·*lees*·sta·*fhohn*	Police Station
Förbjudet	feur·*byoo*·det	Prohibited
Toaletter	toh·aa·*le*·ter	Toilets
Herrar	*her*·ar	Men
Damer	*daa*·mer	Women
Varm/Kall	varm/kal	Hot/Cold

accommodation

finding accommodation

Where's a ...?	*Var finns det ...?*	var fins de ...
camping ground	*en campingplats*	cyn *kam*·ping·*plats*
guesthouse	*ett gästhus*	et *yest*·hoos
hotel	*ett hotell*	et hoh·*tel*
youth hostel	*ett vandrarhem*	et *van*·drar·hem

Can you recommend somewhere ...?	*Kan ni rekommendera något ...?*	kan nee re·ko·men·*dey*·ra *naw*·got ...
cheap	*billigt*	*bi*·lit
good	*bra*	braa
nearby	*i närheten*	ee *nair*·hey·ten

I'd like to book a room, please.
Jag skulle vilja boka ett rum. — yaa *sku*·le *vil*·ya *boh*·ka et rum

I have a reservation.
Jag har bokat. — yaa har *boh*·kat

My name's ...
Jag heter ... — yaa *hey*·ter ...

Do you have a . . . room?	*Har ni . . . ?*	har nee . . .
single	*ett enkeltrum*	et *en*·kelt·rum
double	*ett dubbeltrum*	et *du*·belt·rum
twin	*ett rum med två sängar*	et rum me tvaw *seng*·ar

How much is it per . . . ?	*Hur mycket kostar det per . . . ?*	hoor *mew*·ket *kos*·tar de peyr . . .
night	*natt*	nat
person	*person*	*peyr*·shohn

Can I pay by . . . ?	*Tar ni . . . ?*	taar nee . . .
credit card	*kreditkort*	kre·*deet*·kort
travellers cheque	*resecheckar*	*rey*·se·*she*·kar

I'd like to stay for (two) nights.
Jag tänker stanna (två) dagar. — yaa *ten*·kar *sta*·na (tvaw) *daa*·gar

From (July 2) to (July 6).
Från (annan Juli) till (sjätte Juli). — frawn (*a*·nen *yoo*·lee) til (*fhe*·te *yoo*·lee)

Can I see it?
Kan jag få se rummet? — kan yaa *faw* se *ru*·met

Am I allowed to camp here?
Får jag campa här? — fawr yaa *kam*·pa hair

Is there a campsite nearby?
Finns det någon campingplats i närheten? — fins de nawn *kam*·ping·*plats* ee *nair*·hey·ten

requests & queries

When/Where is breakfast served?
När/Var serveras frukost? — nair/var ser·*vey*·ras *froo*·kost

Please wake me at (seven).
Kan ni väcka mig klockan (sju). — kan nee *ve*·ka mey *klo*·kan (fhoo)

Could I have my key, please?
Jag vill gärna ha min nyckel. — yaa vil *yair*·na haa min *new*·kel

Can I get another (blanket)?
Kan jag få en (filt) till? — kan yaa fawr eyn (filt) *till*

Is there an elevator/a safe?
Finns det en hiss/förvaringsbox? — fins de eyn his/feur·*vaa*·rings·boks

The room is too …	*Rummet är för …*	*ru*·met air feur …
expensive	*dyrt*	dewrt
noisy	*bullrigt*	*bul*·rit
small	*litet*	*lee*·tet

The … doesn't work.	*… funkar inte.*	… *fun*·kar *in*·te
air conditioning	*Luftkonditioneringen*	*luft*·kon·di·fho·*ney*·ring·en
fan	*Fläkten*	*flek*·ten
toilet	*Toaletten*	toh·aa·*le*·ten

This … isn't clean.	*Denna … är inte ren.*	*dey*·na … air *in*·te reyn
pillow	*kudde*	*ku*·de
sheet	*lakan*	*laa*·kan
towel	*handduk*	*han*·duk

checking out

What time is checkout?
Hur dags måste man checka ut? — hoor daks *maw*·ste man *she*·ka ut

Can I leave my luggage here?
Kan jag lämna min bagage här? — kan yaa *lem*·na min ba·*gaash* hair

Could I have my …, please?	*Kan jag få …?*	kan yaa fawr …
deposit	*min depositionsavgift*	min de·poh·si·*fhohns*·aav·yift
passport	*mitt pass*	mit pas
valuables	*mina värdesaker*	*mee*·na *vair*·de·saa·ker

communications & banking

the internet

Where's the local Internet café?
Var finns det lokala Internet kaféet? — var fins de loh·*kaa*·la *in*·ter·net ka·*fey*·et

How much is it per hour?
Hur mycket kostar det per timma? — hoor *mew*·ke *kos*·tar de par *ti*·ma

I'd like to ...	*Jag skulle vilja ...*	yaa *sku*·le *vil*·ya ...
check my email	*kolla min e-post*	*ko*·la min *ey*·post
get Internet access	*koppla upp mig till Internetet*	*kop*·la *up* mey til *in*·ter·ne·tet
use a printer	*använda en printer*	*an*·ven·da eyn *prin*·ter
use a scanner	*använda en scanner*	*an*·ven·da eyn *ska*·ner

mobile/cell phone

I'd like a ...	*Jag skulle vilja ha ...*	yaa *sku*·le *vil*·ya *haa* ...
mobile/cell phone for hire	*en mobil telefon till hyra*	eyn moh·*beel* te·le·*fohn* til *hew*·ra
SIM card for your network	*ett sim-kort till detta nätverk*	et *sim*·kort til *de*·ta *neyt*·verk
What are the rates?	*Vad är prisarna?*	vaad air *pree*·sar·na

telephone

What's your phone number?
Vad är ditt telefonnummer? — vaad air dit te·le·*fohn*·nu·mer

The number is ...
Numret är ... — *num*·ret air ...

Where's the nearest public phone?
Var ligger närmaste publiktelefon? — var *li*·ger *nair*·ma·ste pub·*leek*·te·le·*fohn*

I'd like to buy a phonecard.
Jag skulle vilja ha ett telefonkort. — yaa *sku*·le *vil*·ya *haa* et te·le·*fohn*·kort

I want to ...	*Jag skulle vilja ...*	yaa *sku*·le *vil*·ya ...
call (Singapore)	*ringa till (Singapore)*	*ring*·a til (*sing*·a·poor)
make a local call	*ringa lokalt*	*ring*·a loh·*kaalt*
reverse the charges	*göra ett ba-samtal*	*yeu*·ra et *be*·*aa*·sam·taal
How much does ... cost?	*Hur mycket kostar ...?*	hoor *mew*·ke *kos*·tar ...
a (three)-minute call	*ett (tre)minuter-samtal*	et (*trey*·)mi·noo·te·*sham*·taal
each extra minute	*varje extra minut*	*var*·ye *eks*·tra mi·*noot*

It's (three) kronor per minute.
(Tre) kronor per minut. — (tre) *kroh*·nor par mi·*noot*

post office

I want to send a …	*Jag skulle vilja skicka ett …*	yaa *sku*·le *vil*·ya *fhi*·ka et …
fax	*fax*	faks
letter	*brev*	breyv
parcel	*paket*	pa·*keyt*
postcard	*vykort*	*vew*·kort
I want to buy …	*Jag skulle vilja ha …*	yaa *sku*·le *vil*·ya *haa* …
an envelope	*kuvert*	koo·*ver*
stamps	*frimärken*	*free*·mair·ken
Please send it (to Australia) by …	*Var snäll och skicka den (till Australien) …*	var snel o *fhi*·ka deyn (til o·*straa*·lyen) …
airmail	*med flygpost*	me *flewg*·post
express mail	*express*	eks·*pres*
registered mail	*som rekommenderat brev*	som re·ko·men·*dey*·rat breyv
surface mail	*som ytpost*	som *ewt*·post
Is there any mail for me?	*Finns det post til mig?*	fins de post til mey

bank

Where's a/an …?	*Var finns det en …?*	var fins de eyn …
ATM	*bankomat*	ban·koh·*maat*
foreign exchange office	*utländsk valuta*	*oot*·lensk va·*loo*·ta
I'd like to …	*Jag skulle vilja …*	yaa *sku*·le *vil*·ya …
arrange a transfer	*överföra pengar*	eu·ver·fer·ra *peng*·ar
cash a cheque	*lösa in en check*	*leu*·sa in eyn shek
change a travellers cheque	*växla resecheckar*	*veks*·la *rey*·se·she·kar
change money	*växla pengar*	*veks*·la *peng*·ar
get a cash advance	*ta ut kontant på mitt bankkort*	taa oot kon·*tant* paw mit *bank*·kort
withdraw money	*dra ut pengar*	draa oot *peng*·ar
What's the …?	*Vad är …?*	vaad air …
charge for that	*belastningen för det*	be·*last*·ning·en feur de
exchange rate	*växelkursen*	*vek*·sel·koor·shen

It's ...	*Det är ...*	de air ...
(25) kronor	*(tjugofem) kronor*	(shoo·go·*fem*) *kroh*·nor
free	*gratis*	*graa*·tis

What time does the bank open?
Hur dags öppnar banken? — hoor daks *eup*·nar *ban*·ken

Has my money arrived yet?
Är mina pengar kommit än? — air *mee*·na *peng*·ar *ko*·mit en

sightseeing

getting in

What time does it open/close?
Hur dags öppnar/stänger de? — hoor daks *eup*·nar/*steng*·ar dom

What's the admission charge?
Hur mycket kostar det i inträde? — hoor *mew*·ke *kos*·tar de i *in*·trey·de

Is there a discount for children/students?
Finns det barnrabatt/studentrabatt? — fins de *barn*·ra·bat/stoo·*dent*·ra·bat

I'd like a ...	*Jag skulle vilja ha en ...*	yaa *sku*·le *vil*·ya *haa* eyn ...
catalogue	*katalog*	ka·ta·*lohg*
guide	*resehandbok*	*rey*·se·hand·bohk
local map	*lokal karta*	loh·*kaal kar*·ta
I'd like to see ...	*Jag skulle vilja se ...*	yaa *sku*·le *vil*·ya *se* ...
What's that?	*Vad är det?*	vaad air *de*
Can I take a photo?	*Får jag fotografera?*	fawr yaa foh·toh·gra·*fey*·ra

tours

When's the next ...?	*När avgår nästa ...?*	nair *aav*·gawr *nes*·ta ...
day trip	*dagsturen*	*daks*·too·ren
tour	*turen*	*too*·ren
Is ... included?	*Inkluderas ...*	in·kloo·*dey*·ras ...
accommodation	*logi*	lo·*shee*
the admission charge	*inträden*	*in*·trey·den
food	*mat*	maat
transport	*transport*	tran·*sport*

How long is the tour?
Hur länge undgår turen? — hoor *leng*·e *oon*·gawr *too*·ren

What time should we be back?
Hur dags kommer vi tillbaka? — hoor *daks ko*·mar vee til·*baa*·ka

sightseeing		
castle	*slott* n	slot
cathedral	*domkyrka*	*dom*·shewr·ka
church	*kyrka*	*shewr*·ka
main square	*stortorget* n	*stor*·tor·yet
monastery	*kloster* n	*klos*·ter
monument	*monument* n	mo·noo·*ment*
museum	*museum/museet* n	moo·*sey*·oom/moo·*sey*·et
old city	*gamla stan*	*gam*·la *staan*
palace	*palats*	pa·*lats*
ruins	*ruiner*	roo·*ee*·ner
stadium	*idrottsplats*	*i*·drots·plats
statues	*statyer*	sta·*tew*·er

shopping

enquiries

Where's a ...?	*Var finns det ...?*	var finns de ...
bank	*en bank*	eyn bank
bookshop	*en bokhandel*	eyn *bohk*·han·del
camera shop	*en fotoaffär*	eyn *fo*·toh·a·fair
department store	*ett varuhus*	et *va*·roo·hus
grocery store	*en livsmedelsaffär*	eyn *leevs*·mey·dels·a·fair
market	*en torghandel*	eyn *tory*·han·del
newsagency	*en pressbyrå*	eyn *pres*·bew·raw
supermarket	*ett snabbköp*	et *snab*·sheup

Where can I buy a (padlock)?	
Var kan jag köpa ett (hänglås)?	var kan yaa *sheu*·pa et (*heng*·laws)
I'm looking for …	
Jag letar efter …	yaa *ley*·tar *ef*·ter …
Can I look at it?	
Får jag se den?	fawr yaa *se* deyn
Do you have any others?	
Har ni några andra?	har nee *naw*·ra *an*·dra
Does it have a guarantee?	
Har den garanti?	har deyn ga·ran·*tee*
Can I have it sent overseas?	
Kan jag få den skickat utomlands?	kan yaa fawr deyn *fhi*·kat *oo*·tom·lants
Can I have (my backpack) repaired?	
Kan jag får (min ryggsäck) reparerad?	kan yaa fawr (min *rewg*·sek) re·pa·*rey*·rad
It's faulty.	
Den är felaktig.	deyn air *fey*·lak·ti

I'd like …, please.	*Jag vill gärna …*	yaa vil *yair*·na …
a bag	*ha en kasse*	ha eyn *ka*·se
a refund	*få en återbäring*	faw eyn *aw*·ter·bai·ring
to return this	*återlämna denna*	*aw*·ter·lem·na *dey*·na

paying

How much is it?	
Hur mycket kostar det?	hoor *mew*·ke *kos*·tar de
Can you write down the price?	
Kan du skriva ner priset?	kan du *skree*·va neyr *pree*·set
That's too expensive.	
Det är för dyrt.	de air feur *dewrt*
What's your lowest price?	
Vad är dit lägste pris?	vaad air dit *leyg*·ste prees
I'll give you (50) kronor.	
Jag ger dig (femtio) kronor.	yaa yer dey (*fem*·ti) *kroh*·nor
There's a mistake in the bill.	
Det är ett fel på räkningen.	de air et *fel* paw *reyk*·ning·en

Do you accept ...?	*Tar ni ...?*	tar nee ...
credit cards	*kreditkort*	kre·*deet*·kort
debit cards	*betalkort*	be·*taal*·kort
travellers cheques	*resecheckar*	*rey*·se·she·kar
I'd like ..., please.	*Jag vill gärna ha ...*	yaa vil *yair*·na ha ...
a receipt	*ett kvitto*	et *kvi*·to
my change	*min växel*	min *vek*·sel

clothes & shoes

Can I try it on?	*Får jag pröva den?*	fawr yaa *preu*·va deyn
My size is (40).	*Min storlek är (fyrtio).*	min *stor*·leyk air (*fewr*·tee)
It doesn't fit.	*Den passar inte.*	deyn *pa*·sar *in*·te
small	*liten*	*lee*·ten
medium	*medelstor*	*mey*·del·stor
large	*stor*	stor

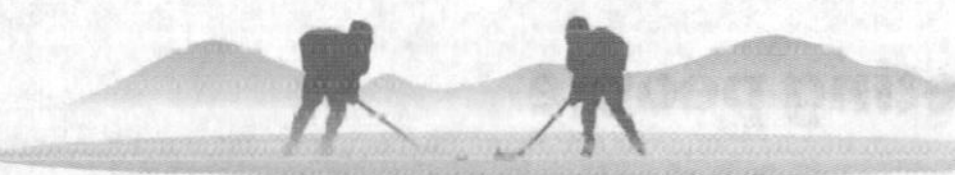

books & music

I'd like a ...	*Jag skulle vilja ha en ...*	yaa *sku*·le *vil*·ya *haa* eyn ...
newspaper (in English)	*(engelsk) tidning*	(*eng*·elsk) *teed*·ning
pen	*penna*	*pe*·na

Is there an English-language bookshop?
Finns det an bokhandel med böcker på engelska? — fins de eyn *bohk*·han·del me *beu*·ker paw *eng*·el·ska

I'm looking for something by (Henning Mankell).
Jag letar efter något av (Henning Mankell). — yaa *ley*·tar *ef*·ter nawt aav (*he*·ning *man*·kel)

Can I listen to this?
Kan jag få höra denna? — kan yaa faw *heu*·ra *dey*·na

photography

Could you ...?	*Kan du ...?*	kan doo ...
burn a CD from my memory card	*bränna en CD från min memory kort*	*bre*·na eyn *se*·*de* frawn min *me*·mo·ree kort
develop this film	*framkalla denna filmen*	*fram*·ka·la *dey*·na *fil*·men
load my film	*ladda film i min kamera*	*la*·da *film* i min *kaa*·me·ra

I need a ... film for this camera.	*Jag skulle vilja ha en ... till den här kameran.*	yaa *sku*·le *vil*·ya *haa* eyn ... til deyn hair *kaa*·me·ra
APS	*APS-film*	*aa*·pe·*es*·film
B&W	*svart-vit film*	*svart*·vit film
colour	*färg film*	fairg film
slide	*dia-film*	*dee*·a·film
(200) speed	*(tvåhundra)-film*	(tvaw·*hund*·ra)·film

When will it be ready?	*När är den klar?*	nair air deyn klaar

meeting people

greetings, goodbyes & introductions

Hello.	*Hej.*	hey
Hi.	*Hejså.*	*hey*·saw
Good night.	*Godnatt.*	goh·*nat*
Goodbye.	*Adjö./Hej då.*	aa·*yeu*/*hey* daw
See you later.	*Vi ses senare.*	vee seys *sey*·na·re

Mr	*herr*	her
Mrs	*fru*	froo
Miss	*fröken*	*freu*·ken

How are you?	*Hur står det till?*	hoor stawr de til
Fine, thanks. And you?	*Bra, tack. Och dig?*	braa tak o dey
What's your name?	*Vad heter du?*	vaad *hey*·ter doo
My name is ...	*Jag heter ...*	yaa *hey*·ter ...
I'm pleased to meet you.	*Trevligt att träffas.*	*treyv*·lit at *tre*·fas

This is my …	*Detta är min …*	de·ta air min …
boyfriend	*pojkvän*	*poyk*·ven
brother	*bror*	bror
daughter	*dotter*	*do*·ter
father	*far*	far
friend	*vän/väninna* m/f	ven/ve·*ni*·na
girlfriend	*flickvän*	*flik*·ven
husband	*man*	man
mother	*mor*	mor
partner (intimate)	*partner*	*part*·ner
sister	*syster*	*sews*·ter
son	*son*	sohn
wife	*fru*	froo

Here's my …	*Här är min …*	hair air min …
What's your …?	*Vad är din …?*	vaad air din …
address	*adress*	a·*dres*
email address	*e-post adress*	*ey*·post a·*dres*
Here's my …	*Här är mitt …*	hair air mit …
What's your …?	*Vad är ditt …?*	vaad air dit …
fax number	*fax-nummer*	*faks*·nu·mer
phone number	*telefonnummer*	te·le·*fohn*·nu·mer

occupations

What's your occupation?	*Vad har du för yrke?*	vaad har doo feur *ewr*·ke
I'm a/an …	*Jag är …*	yaa air …
artist	*konstnär*	*konst*·nair
business person	*affärsman*	a·*fairsh*·man
office worker	*kontorist*	kon·to·*rist*
scientist	*naturvetare*	na·*toor*·vey·ta·re
tradesperson	*detaljhandlare*	de·*taly*·hand·la·re

meeting people – SWEDISH

background

Where are you from?	*Varifrån kommer du?*	*var*·ee·frawn *ko*·mer doo
I'm from ...	*Jag kommer från ...*	yaa *ko*·mer frawn ...
Australia	*Australien*	o·*straa*·lyen
Canada	*Kanada*	*ka*·na·da
England	*England*	*eng*·land
New Zealand	*Nya Zealand*	*new*·a *sey*·land
the USA	*USA*	oo·es·*aa*
Are you married?	*Är du gift?*	air doo yift
I'm married.	*Jag är gift.*	yaa air yift
I'm single.	*Jag är ogift.*	yaa air *oh*·yift

age

How old ...?	*Hur gammal ...?*	hoor *ga*·mal ...
are you	*är du*	air doo
is your daughter	*är din dotter*	air din *do*·ter
is your son	*är din son*	air din sohn

I'm ... years old.
Jag är ... år gammal. yaa air ... awr *ga*·mal

He/She is ... years old.
Han/Hon är ... år gammal. han/hon air ... awr *ga*·mal

feelings

I'm (not) ...	*Jag är (inte) ...*	yaa air (*in*·te) ...
Are you ...?	*Är du ...?*	air doo ...
happy	*glad*	glaad
hot	*varm*	varm
hungry	*hungrig*	*hung*·greeg
sad	*ledsen*	*le*·sen
thirsty	*törstig*	*teur*·shteeg
tired	*trött*	treut
Are you cold?	*Fryser du?*	*frew*·ser doo
I'm (not) cold.	*Jag fryser (inte).*	yaa *frew*·ser (*in*·te)
Are you OK?	*Mår du bra?*	mawr doo *braa*
I'm (not) OK.	*Jag mår (inte) bra.*	yaa mawr (*in*·te) braa

entertainment

going out

Where can I find ...?	*Var finns ...?*	var fins ...
clubs	*klubbarna*	*klu*·bar·na
gay venues	*gayklubbarna*	*gay*·klu·bar·na
pubs	*pubbarna*	*pu*·bar·na
I feel like going to a/the ...	*Jag vil gärna gå på ...*	yaa vil *yair*·na gaw paw ...
concert	*konsert*	kon·*seyr*
movies	*bio*	*bee*·oh
party	*fest*	fest
restaurant	*restaurang*	res·taw·*rang*
theatre	*teater*	tee·*ay*·ter

interests

Do you like ...?	*Tycker du om ...?*	*tew*·ker doo om ...
I (don't) like ...	*Jag tycker (inte) om ...*	yaa *tew*·ker (*in*·te) om ...
art	*konst*	konst
cooking	*att laga mat*	at *laa*·ga *maat*
movies	*film*	film
nightclubs	*natklubbar*	*nat*·klu·bar
reading	*att läsa*	at *ley*·sa
shopping	*att shoppa*	at *sho*·pa
sport	*sport*	sport
travelling	*att resa*	at *rey*·sa
Do you like to ...?	*Tycker du om att ...?*	*tew*·ker doo om at ...
dance	*dansa*	*dan*·sa
go to concerts	*gå på konsert*	gaw paw kon·*seyr*
listen to music	*lyssna på musik*	*lews*·na paw moo·*seek*

food & drink

finding a place to eat

Can you recommend a ...?	*Kan du anbefalla en ...?*	kan doo *an*·be·fa·la eyn ...
bar	*bar*	bar
café	*kafé*	ka·*fey*
restaurant	*restaurang*	res·taw·*rang*
I'd like ..., please.	*..., tack.*	... tak
a table for (four)	*Ett bord för (fyra)*	et bord feur (*few*·ra)
the nonsmoking section	*Rökfria avdelningen*	*reuk*·free·a *aav*·del·ning·en
the smoking section	*Rökavdelningen*	*reuk*·aav·del·ning·en

ordering food

breakfast	*frukost*	*froo*·kost
lunch	*lunch*	lunsh
dinner	*middag*	*mi*·daa
snack	*mellanmål* n	*me*·lan·mawl
today's special	*dagens rätt*	*daa*·gens ret

What would you recommend?
Vad skulle ni anbefalla? vaad *sku*·le nee *an*·be·fa·la

I'd like (the) ...	*Jag skulle vilja ha ...*	yaa *sku*·le *vil*·ya *haa* ...
bill	*räkningen*	*reyk*·ning·en
drink list	*dryckslistan*	*driks*·lis·tan
menu	*menyn*	me·*newn*
that dish	*den maträtt*	deyn *maat*·ret

drinks

(cup of) coffee …	*(en kopp) kaffe …*	(eyn kop) *ka*·fe …
(cup of) tea …	*(en kopp) te …*	(eyn kop) *tey* …
with milk	*med mjölk*	me myeulk
without sugar	*utan socker*	*oo*·taan *so*·ker
(orange) juice	*(apelsin)juice*	(a·pel·*seen*·)djoos
soft drink	*läsk*	lesk
boiled water	*kokt vatten* n	kohkt *va*·ten
mineral water	*mineralvatten* n	mi·ne·*raal*·va·ten
water	*vatten* n	*va*·ten

in the bar

I'll have …
Jag vill ha … — yaa vil haa …

I'll buy you a drink.
Jag köper dig en drink. — yaa *sheu*·per dey eyn *drink*

What would you like?
Vad vill du ha? — vaad vil doo *haa*

Cheers!
Skål! — skawl

brandy	*brandy*	*bran*·dee
cocktail	*cocktail*	*kok*·tayl
cognac	*cognac*	*kon*·yak
a shot of (whisky)	*2 cl (whiskey)*	tvaw *sen*·ti·ley·ter (*vis*·kee)
a … of beer	*… öl*	… eul
bottle	*en flaska*	eyn *flas*·ka
glass	*ett glass*	et glaas
a bottle of …	*en flaska …*	eyn *flas*·ka …
a glass of …	*ett glas …*	et glaas …
red wine	*rödvin*	*reud*·veen
sparkling wine	*mousserande vin*	moo·*sey*·ran·de veen
white wine	*vitt vin*	vit veen

self-catering

What's the local speciality?
Vad är den lokala specialiteten? — vaad air deyn loh·*kaa*·la spe·si·a·li·*tey*·ten

What's that?
Vad är det? — vaad air de

How much is (a kilo of cheese)?
Hur mycket kostar (en kilo ost)? — hoor *mew*·ke *kos*·tar (eyn *shee*·loh ohst)

I'd like ...	*Jag vil ha ...*	yaa vil ha ...
(100) grams	*(hundra) gram*	(*hun*·dra) gram
(two) kilos	*(två) kilo*	(*tvaw*) *shee*·loh
(three) pieces	*(tre) styck*	(*trey*) stewk
(six) slices	*(sex) skivor*	(*seks*) *fhee*·vor

Less.	*Mindre.*	*min*·dre
Enough.	*Det räcker.*	de *re*·ker
More.	*Mera.*	*mey*·ra

special diets & allergies

Is there a vegetarian restaurant near here?
Finns det en vegetarisk restaurang i närheten? — fins de eyn ve·ge·*taa*·risk res·taw·*rang* ee *nair*·hey·ten

Do you have vegetarian food?
Har ni vegetarisk mat? — har nee ve·ge·*taa*·risk maat

Could you prepare a meal without ...?	*Kan ni laga en maträtt utan ...?*	kan nee *laa*·ga eyn *maat*·ret *oo*·tan ...
butter	*smör*	smeur
eggs	*ägg*	eg
meat stock	*köttspad*	*sheut*·spaad

I'm allergic to ...	*Jag är allergisk mot ...*	yaa air al·*leyr*·gisk moht ...
dairy produce	*mejeriprodukter*	me·ye·*ree*·pro·*dook*·ter
gluten	*gluten*	*gloo*·ten
MSG	*MSG*	em·es·*gee*
nuts	*nötter*	*neu*·ter
seafood	*fisk och skaldjur*	fisk o *skaal*·yoor

ärtsoppa	*airt*·so·pa	*yellow pea soup with pork*
biff á la Lindström	*bif* a la *lind*·streum	*patties of minced meat & beetroot, served with a fried egg*
blodpudding med lingon	*blohd*·*pu*·ding me *ling*·on	*black pudding with lingonberry jam*
böckling	*beuk*·ling	*smoked herring*
falukorv	*faa*·lu·*korv*	*lean sausage cut in thick slices & fried*
glass	glas	*ice cream*
gravad lax	*graa*·vad *laks*	*cured salmon*
grönsakssoppa	*greun*·saaks·*so*·pa	*vegetable soup*
gryta	*grew*·ta	*casserole*
havskräftor	*haavs*·*kref*·tor	*prawns*
hönssoppa	*heuns*·*so*·pa	*chicken soup*
inlagd sill	*in*·lagt *sil*	*pickled herring*
isterband n	*is*·ter·band	*sausage of pork, beef & barley grains*
Janssons frestelse	*yan*·sons *fres*·tel·se	*potato, onion & anchovy, oven-baked with lots of cream*
kåldolmar	*kawl*·dol·mar	*stuffed cabbage leaves*
kalops	ka·*lops*	*meat casserole with onions & allspice*
kålsoppa med frikadeller	*kawl*·*so*·pa me fri·ka·*de*·ler	*cabbage soup with boiled meatballs (usually pork)*
kanelbulle	ka·*neyl*·*bu*·le	*sweet roll with cinnamon & cardamom*
kavring	*kaav*·ring	*dark sweetened rye bread*
knäckebröd n	*kne*·ke·*breud*	*crispbread, usually rye*
köttbullar	*sheut*·bu·lar	*meatballs*
köttsoppa	*sheut*·so·pa	*beef broth with meat & vegetables*

lövbiff	*leuv*·bif	*very thinly sliced beef*
mazarin	ma·za·*reen*	*pastry with almond paste filling*
nässelsoppa	*ne*·sel·*so*·pa	*nettle soup with a hard-boiled egg*
nyponsoppa	*new*·pon·*so*·pa	*rosehip soup, eaten with cream*
ostkaka	*ost*·kaa·ka	*cheese cake*
pannbiff med lök	*pan*·bif me *leuk*	*minced beef patties with fried onion*
prinsesstårta	prin·*ses*·tawr·ta	*layered sponge cake with jam, cream & custard filling, covered with marzipan*
pyttipanna	*pew*·ti·*pa*·na	*diced meat, boiled potatoes & onion, fried & served with beetroot & a fried egg*
rågbröd n	*rawg*·breud	*rye bread*
raggmunkar	*rag*·mun·kar	*pancakes made from grated potatoes*
räkor	*rey*·kor	*shrimps*
råstekt potatis	*raw*·*stekt* poh·*taa*·tis	*potato slices fried in oil*
renskav n	*reyn*·skaav	*thinly sliced reindeer meat*
ris á la malta n	*rees* a la *mal*·ta	*rice with whipped cream & orange*
schwartzwaldstårta	*shvarts*·valds·*tawr*·ta	*meringue, cream & chocolate cake*
skalpotatis	*skaal*·poh·*taa*·tis	*potatoes boiled in their jackets*
småländsk ostkaka	*smaw*·lands *awst*·kaa·ka	*baked curd cake with almonds*
sockerkaka	*so*·ker·kaa·ka	*sponge cake flavoured with lemon*
sotare	*soh*·ta·re	*lightly salted & grilled herring*
sötlimpa	*seut*·lim·pa	*sweetened brown loaf*
stuvad potatis	*stoo*·vad poh·*taa*·tis	*potatoes in white sauce*
svampsoppa	*svamp*·*so*·pa	*mushroom soup*
tunnbröd n	*tun*·breud	*very thin crisp or soft barley bread*
viltgryta	vilt·*grew*·ta	*game casserole*
vörtbröd n	*vert*·breud	*rye bread flavoured with wort (a herb)*

emergencies

basics

Help!	*Hjälp!*	yelp
Stop!	*Stanna!*	*sta*·na
Go away!	*Försvinn!*	feur·*shvin*
Thief!	*Ta fast tjuven!*	ta fast *shoo*·ven
Fire!	*Elden är lös!*	*el*·den air *leus*
Watch out!	*Se upp!*	se up
Call . . . !	*Ring . . . !*	ring . . .
a doctor	*efter en doktor*	*ef*·ter en *dok*·tor
an ambulance	*efter en ambulans*	*ef*·ter en am·boo·*lans*
the police	*polisen*	poh·*lee*·sen

It's an emergency!
Det är ett nödsituation! — de air et *neud*·si·too·a·fhohn

Could you help me, please?
Kan du hjälpa mig? — kan doo *yel*·pa mai

I have to use the telephone.
Jag måste använda telefonen. — yaa *maws*·te *an*·ven·da te·le·*foh*·nen

I'm lost.
Jag har gått vilse. — yaa har got *vil*·se

Where are the toilets?
Var är toaletten? — var air toh·aa·*le*·ten

police

Where's the police station?
Var är polisstationen? — var air poh·*lees*·sta·*fhoh*·nen

I want to report an offence.
Jag vill anmäla ett brott. — yaa vil *an*·mey·la et brot

I have insurance.
Jag har försäkring. — yaa har feur·*shey*·kring

I've been assaulted.
Jag är blivit utsatt för övervåld. — yaa air *blee*·vit *ut*·sat feur *eu*·ver·vawld

I've been …	*Jag har blivit …*	yaa har *blee*·vit …
raped	*våldtagen*	*vol*·taa·gen
robbed	*rånad*	*raw*·nad

I've lost my …	*Jag har förlorat …*	yaa har feur·*loh*·rat …
backpack	*min ryggsäck*	min *rewk*·sek
bags	*mina väskor*	*mee*·na *ves*·kor
credit card	*min kreditkort*	min kre·*deet*·kort
handbag	*min handväska*	min *hand*·ves·ka
jewellery	*mina smycken*	*mee*·na *smew*·ken
money	*mina pengar*	*mee*·na *peng*·ar
passport	*mitt pass*	mit pas
travellers cheques	*mina resecheckar*	*mee*·na *rey*·se·she·kar
wallet	*min plånbok*	min *plawn*·bohk

I want to contact my …	*Jag vill kontakta …*	yaa vil kon·*tak*·ta …
consulate	*mitt konsulat*	mit kon·soo·*laat*
embassy	*min ambassad*	min am·ba·*saad*

health

medical needs

Where's the nearest …?	*Var är närmaste …?*	var air *nair*·ma·ste …
dentist	*tandläkaren*	*tand*·ley·ka·ren
doctor	*doktorn*	*dok*·torn
hospital	*sjukhuset*	*fhook*·hu·set
(night) pharmacist	*(natt)apoteket*	(*nat*·)a·poh·*te*·ket

I need a doctor (who speaks English).
Jag behöver en läkare (som talar engelska). — yaa be·*heu*·ver eyn *ley*·ka·re (som *taa*·lar *eng*·el·ska)

Could I see a female doctor?
Kan jag få träffa en kvinnlig läkare? — kan yaa faw *tre*·fa eyn *kvin*·li *ley*·ka·re

I've run out of my medication.
Jag har ingen medikament kvar. — yaa har *ing*·en me·di·ka·*ment* kvar

symptoms, conditions & allergies

I'm sick.	*Jag är sjuk.*	yaa air fhook
It hurts here.	*Det gör ont här.*	de yeur ont hair
I have nausea.	*Jag mår illa.*	yaa mawr *i*·la
I have (a) …	*Jag har …*	yaa haa …
asthma	*astma*	*ast*·maa
bronchitis	*bronkit*	bron·*keet*
constipation	*förstoppning*	feur·*shtop*·ning
cough	*en hosta*	eyn *hoh*·sta
diarrhoea	*diarré*	dee·a·*rey*
fever	*feber*	*fey*·ber
headache	*huvudvärk*	*hoo*·vud·vairk
heart condition	*en hjärttillstånd*	eyn *yairt*·til·stawnd
pain	*ont*	ont
sore throat	*ont i halsen*	ont ee *hal*·sen
toothache	*tandvärk*	*tand*·verk
I'm allergic to …	*Jag är allergisk mot …*	yaa air a·*leyr*·gisk moht …
antibiotics	*antibiotika*	an·tee·bee·*oh*·ti·ka
anti-inflammatories	*anti-inflammatoriska medel*	*an*·tee·in·fla·ma·*toh*·ri·ska *mey*·del
aspirin	*magnecyl*	mag·ne·*sewl*
bees	*bin*	been
codeine	*kodein*	*koh*·deen
penicillin	*penicillin*	pe·ne·si·*leen*
antiseptic	*antiseptiskt medel* **n**	an·tee·*sep*·tiskt *mey*·del
bandage	*förband* **n**	feur·*band*
condoms	*kondomer*	kon·*doh*·mer
diarrhoea medicine	*medel mot diarré* **n**	*mey*·del moht dee·a·*rey*
insect repellent	*insektsmedel* **n**	*in*·sekts·mey·del
laxatives	*laxermedel* **n**	*lak*·ser·mey·del
painkillers	*smärtstillande medel* **n**	*smairt*·sti·lan·de *mey*·del
rehydration salts	*vätskeersätt-ningsmedel* **n**	*vet*·ske·*er*·set·nings·*mey*·del
sleeping tablets	*sovmedel* **n**	*sohv*·mey·del

english–swedish dictionary

In this dictionary, words are marked as n (noun), a (adjective), v (verb), sg (singular), pl (plural), inf (informal) and pol (polite) where necessary. Note that Swedish nouns are either masculine, feminine or neuter. Masculine and feminine forms (known as 'common gender') take the indefinite article *en* (a) while the neuter forms take the article *ett* (a). Every Swedish noun needs to be learned with its indefinite article (*en* or *ett*). We've only indicated the neuter nouns with ⓝ after the Swedish word. Note also that the ending 't' is added to adjectives for the neuter form (ie when they accompany indefinite singular nouns). In some cases both forms of the adjective (ie ⓜ&ⓕ form and ⓝ form) are spelled out in full and separated with a slash.

A

accident *olycka* *oh*·lew·ka
accommodation *husrum* ⓝ *hus*·rum
adaptor *adapter* a·*dap*·ter
address n *adress* a·*dres*
after *efter* *ef*·ter
air-conditioned *luftkonditionerad/luftkonditionerat* *luft*·kon·di·fho·*ney*·rad/*luft*·kon·di·fho·*ney*·rat
airplane *flygplan* ⓝ *flewg*·plaan
airport *flygplats* *flewg*·plats
alcohol *alkohol* al·ko·*hohl*
all *alla* *a*·la
all (everything) n *allt* alt
allergy *allergi* a·ler·*gee*
ambulance *ambulans* am·bu·*lans*
and *och* ok
ankle *vrist* vrist
arm *arm* arm
ashtray *askfat* ⓝ ask·*faat*
ATM *bankomat* bang·koh·*maat*

B

baby *baby* *bey*·bee
back (body) *rygg* rewg
backpack *ryggsäck* *rewg*·sek
bad *dålig(t)* *dawr*·lig/*dawr*·lit
bag *väska* *ves*·ka
baggage claim *bagageavhämtning* ba·*gaash*·aav·hemt·ning
bank *bank* bank
bar *bar* baar
bathroom *badrum* ⓝ *baad*·rum
battery *batteri* ⓝ ba·te·*ree*
beautiful *vacker(t)* *va*·ker(t)
bed *säng* seng
beer *öl* ⓝ eul
before *framför* *fram*·feur
behind *bakom* *baa*·kom
bicycle *cykel* *sew*·kel
big *stor(t)* stawr(t)
bill *räkning* *reyk*·ning
black *svart* svart
blanket *filt* filt
blood group *blodgrupp* *blohd*·grup
blue *blå(tt)* blaw/blot
boat *båt* bawt
book (make a reservation) v *boka* *boh*·ka
bottle *flaska* *flas*·ka
bottle opener *flasköppnare* *flask*·eup·na·re
boy *pojke* *poy*·ke
brakes (car) *bromsar* *brom*·sar
breakfast *frukost* *froo*·kost
broken (faulty) *sönder* *seun*·der
bus *buss* bus
(do) business *handla* *hand*·la
buy *köpa* *sheu*·pa

C

café *kafé* ⓝ ka·*fey*
camera *kamera* *kaa*·me·ra
camp site *campingplats* *kam*·ping·plats
cancel *upphäva* *up*·hey·va
can opener *burköppnare* *burk*·eup·na·re
car *bil* beel
cash n *kontant* kon·*tant*
cash (a cheque) v *lösa in (en check)* *leu*·sa in (eyn *shek)*
cell phone *mobiltelefon* moh·*beel*·te·le·fohn
centre *center* ⓝ *sen*·ter
change (money) v *växla (pengar)* *veyk*·sla (*peng*·ar)
cheap *billig(t)* *bi*·lig/*bi*·lit
check (bill) *räkning* *reyk*·ning

check-in *incheckning in*·chek·ning
chest *bröst* ⓝ breust
child *barn* ⓝ barn
cigarette *cigarett* si·ga·*ret*
city *storstad stawr*·staad
clean a *ren(t)* reyn(t)
closed *stängd/stängt* stengd/stengt
coffee *kaffe* ⓝ *ka*·fe
coins *mynt* ⓝ mewnt
cold a *kylig(t) shew*·lig/*shew*·lit
collect call *ba-samtal* ⓝ *be*·*aa*·sam·taal
come *komma ko*·ma
computer *dator daa*·tor
condom *kondom* kon·*dohm*
contact lenses *kontaktlinser kon*·takt·lin·ser
cook v *laga mat laa*·ga *maat*
cost n *kostnad kost*·nad
credit card *kreditkort* ⓝ kre·*deet*·kort
cup *kopp* kop
currency exchange *växel veyk*·sel
customs (immigration) *tullen tu*·len

D

dangerous *farlig(t) far*·lig/*far*·lit
date (time) *datum* ⓝ *daa*·tum
day *dag* daag
delay *dröjsmål* ⓝ *dreuys*·mawl
dentist *tandläkare tand*·ley·ka·re
depart *avresa aav*·rey·sa
diaper *blöja bleu*·ya
dictionary *ordbok ord*·bohk
dinner *middag mi*·daag
direct *direkt* dee·*rekt*
dirty *smutsig(t) smut*·sig/*smut*·sit
disabled *handikappad han*·dee·ka·pad
discount n *rabatt* ra·*bat*
doctor *läkare ley*·ka·re
double bed *dubbelsäng du*·bel·seng
double room *dubbelt rum* ⓝ *du*·belt rum
drink n *dricka dri*·ka
drive v *köra sheu*·ra
drivers licence *körkort* ⓝ *sheur*·kort
drug (illicit) *narkotika* nar·*koh*·ti·ka
dummy (pacifier) *napp* nap

E

ear *öra eu*·ra
east *öst* eust
eat *äta ey*·ta
economy class *ekonomiklass* e·ko·noh·*mee*·klas
electricity *elektricitet* ey·lek·tri·si·*teyt*
elevator *hiss* his
email *e-post ey*·post
embassy *ambassad* am·ba·*saad*
emergency *nödsituation* ⓝ *neud*·si·too·a·fhohn
English (language) *engelska eng*·el·ska
entrance *ingång in*·gawng
evening *kväll* kvel
exchange rate *växelkurs veyk*·sel·kursh
exit n *utgång oot*·gawng
expensive *dyr(t)* dewr(t)
express mail *expresspost* eks·*pres*·post
eye *öga* ⓝ *eu*·ga

F

far *långt* lawngt
fast *snabb(t)* snab(t)
father *far* faar
film (camera) *film* film
finger *finger* ⓝ *fing*·er
first-aid kit *förbandslåda* feur·*bants*·law·da
first class *första klass feu*·shta klas
fish n *fisk* fisk
food *mat* maat
foot *fot* foht
fork *gaffel ga*·fel
free (of charge) *gratis graa*·tis
friend *vän/vännina* ⓜ/ⓕ ven/ve·*ni*·na
fruit *frukt* frukt
full *fylld/fyllt* fewld/fewlt
funny *rolig(t) roh*·lig/*roh*·lit

G

gift *gåva gaw*·va
girl *flicka fli*·ka
glass (drinking) *glas* ⓝ glaas
glasses *glasögon* ⓝ *glaa*·seu·gon
go *åka aw*·ka
good *bra* braa
green *grön(t)* greun(t)
guide n *guide* gaid

H

half n *halv* halv
hand *hand* hand

handbag *handväska hand·vey·ska*
happy *glad* glaad
have *ha* haa
he *han* han
head *huvud* ⓝ *hoo·vud*
heart *hjärta yair·ta*
heat n *hetta he·ta*
heavy *tung(t)* tung(t)
help v *hjälp* yelp
here *här* hair
high *hög(t)* heug(t)
highway *huvudväg hoo·vud·veyg*
hike v *fotvandra foht·van·dra*
holiday *semester se·mes·ter*
homosexual n&a *homosexuell* hoh·moh·sek·soo·*el*
hospital *sjukhus* ⓝ *fhook·hoos*
hot *varm(t)* varm(t)
hotel *hotell* ⓝ hoh·*tel*
hungry *hungrig(t) hung·grig/hung·grit*
husband *man* man

I

I *jag* yaag
identification (card) *identitetskort* ⓝ ee·den·ti·*teyts*·kort
ill *sjuk(t)* fhook(t)
important *viktig(t) vik·tig/vik·tit*
included *inklusiv* in·kloo·*seev*
injury *skada skaa·da*
insurance *försäkring* feu·*shey*·kring
Internet *Internet* ⓝ *in*·ter·net
interpreter *tolk* tolk

J

jewellery *smycke* ⓝ *smew·ke*
job *arbete* ⓝ *aar*·bey·te

K

key *nyckel new·kel*
kilogram *kilo(gram)* ⓝ *shee*·loh(·gram)
kitchen *kök* ⓝ sheuk
knife *kniv* kneev

L

laundry (place) *tvättstuga tvet·*stoo·ga
lawyer *advokat* ad·voh·*kaat*
left (direction) *vänster ven·ster*
left-luggage office *resgodsinlämning reys·*gohds·in·lem·ning
leg *ben* ⓝ beyn
lesbian a *lesbisk lez·*bisk
less *mindre min·*dre
letter (mail) *brev* ⓝ breyv
lift (elevator) *hiss* his
light *ljus* ⓝ yoos
like v *tycka om tew·*ka om
lock n *lås* laws
long *lång(t)* lawng(t)
(be) lost (of a person) *vilse vil·*se
(be) lost (of property) *borta bor·*ta
lost-property office *hittegodsexpedition hi·*te·gohds·eks·pe·di·*fhohn*
love v *älska el·ska*
luggage *bagage* ⓝ ba·*gaash*
lunch *lunch* lunsh

M

mail n *post* post
man *man* man
map *karta kar·*ta
market *marknad/torg* ⓝ *mark·*naad/tory
matches *tändstickor ten·*sti·kor
meat *kött* ⓝ sheut
medicine *medicin* me·di·*seen*
menu *meny/matsedel* me·*new*/*maat*·sey·del
message *bud* ⓝ bood
milk *mjölk* myeulk
minute *minut* mi·*noot*
mobile phone *mobiltelefon* moh·*beel*·te·le·fohn
money *pengar peng·*ar
month *månad maw·*nad
morning *morgon mor·*gon
mother *mor* mawr
motorcycle *motorcykel moh·*tor·sew·kel
motorway *motorväg moh·*tor·veyg
mouth *mun* mun
music *musik* moo·*seek*

N

name *namn* ⓝ namn
napkin *servett* seyr·*vet*
nappy *blöja bleu·*ya
near *nära nair·*a

neck *hals* hals
new *ny(tt)* new(t)
news *nyheter* *new*·hey·ter
newspaper *tidning* *teed*·ning
night *natt* nat
no *nej* ney
noisy *bullrig(t)* *bul*·rig/*bul*·rit
nonsmoking *icke-rökande* *i*·ke·reu·kan·de
north *nord* nord
nose *näsa* ney·sa
now *nu* noo
number *nummer* ⓝ *nu*·mer

O

oil (engine) *olja* *ol*·ya
old *gammal(t)* *ga*·mal(t)
one-way ticket *enkelbiljett* *en*·kel·bil·*yet*
open a *öppen/öppet* *eu*·pen/*eu*·pet
outside *utanför* *oo*·tan·feur

P

package *paket* ⓝ pa·*keyt*
paper *papper* ⓝ *pa*·per
park (car) v *parkera* par·*key*·ra
passport *pass* ⓝ pas
pay *betala* be·*taa*·la
pen *penna* *pe*·na
petrol *bensin* ben·*seen*
pharmacy *apotek* ⓝ a·poh·*teyk*
phonecard *telefonkort* ⓝ te·le·*fohn*·kort
photo *foto* ⓝ *foh* toh
plate *tallrik* *tal*·reek
police *polis* poh·*lees*
postcard *postkort* ⓝ *post*·*kort*
post office *posten* *pos*·ten
pregnant *gravid* gra·*veed*
price *pris* prees

Q

quiet *stilla* *stil*·la

R

rain n *regn* rengn
razor *rakhyvel* *raak*·hew·vel
receipt *kvitto* ⓝ *kvi*·toh
red *röd/rött* reud/reut
refund n *återbäring* *aw*·ter·bair·ing
registered mail *värdeförsändelse* *vair*·de·feu·*shen*·del·se
rent v *hyra* *hew*·ra
repair v *reparera* re·pa·*rey*·ra
reservation *beställning* be·*stel*·ning
restaurant *restaurang* res·taw·*rang*
return v *återvända* *aw*·ter·ven·da
return ticket *returbiljett* rey·*toor*·bil·*yet*
right (direction) *höger* *heu*·ger
road *väg* veyg
room *rum* ⓝ rum

S

safe a *trygg(t)* trewg(t)
sanitary napkin *dambinda* *daam*·bin·da
seat *sittplats* *sit*·plats
send *skicka* *fhi*·ka
service station *bensinstation* ben·*seen*·sta·fhohn
sex *samlag* ⓝ *sam*·laag
shampoo *schampo* ⓝ *fham*·poo
share (a dorm) *dela* *dey*·la
shaving cream *rakkräm* *raak*·kreym
she *hon* hoon
sheet (bed) *lakan* ⓝ *luu*·kan
shirt *skjorta* *fhor*·ta
shoes *skor* skor
shop n *affär* a·*fair*
short *kort* kort
shower n *dusch* doosh
single room *enkelt rum* ⓝ *en*·kelt rum
skin *hud* hood
skirt *kjol* shohl
sleep v *sova* *soh*·va
slowly *sakta* *sak*·ta
small *liten/litet* *lee*·ten/*lee*·tet
smoke (cigarettes) v *röka* *reu*·ka
soap *tvål* tvawl
some *någon/något* *naw*·gon/*naw*·got
soon *snart* snart
south *syd* sewd
souvenir shop *souvenir affär* su·ve·*neer* a·*fair*
speak *tala* *taa*·la
spoon *sked* fheyd
stamp *frimärke* ⓝ *free*·mair·ke
stand-by ticket *standbybiljett* *stand*·bai·bil·*yet*
station (train) *(järnvägs)station* (*yairn*·veyks·)sta·*fhohn*

stomach *mage* *maa*·ge
stop v *stanna/hålla* *sta*·na/*haw*·la
stop (bus) n *(buss)hållplats* (*bus*·)*hawl*·plats
street *gata* *gaa*·ta
student *studerande* stoo·*dey*·ran·de
sun *sol* sohl
sunscreen *solkräm* *sohl*·kreym
Sweden *Sverige* *sve*·rya
Swedish (language) *svenska* *sven*·ska
Swedish a *svensk(t)* svensk(t)
swim v *simma* *si*·ma

T

tampons *tampong* tam·*pong*
taxi *taxi* *tak*·see
teaspoon *tesked* *tey*·fheyd
teeth *tänder* *te*·ner
telephone n *telefon* te·le·*fohn*
television *TV* *tey*·*vey*
temperature (weather) *temperatur* tem·pe·ra·*toor*
tent *tält* ⓝ telt
that (one) *den* ⓜ&ⓕ/*det* ⓝ deyn/dey
they *dem* dom
thirsty *törstig(t)* *teush*·tig/*teush*·tit
this (one) *den här* ⓜ&ⓕ/*det här* ⓝ den *hair*/dey *hair*
throat *strupe* *stroo*·pe
ticket *biljett* bil·*yet*
time *tid* teed
tired *trött* treut
tissues *näsdukar* *neys*·doo·kar
today *i dag* i *daag*
toilet *toalett* toh·aa·*let*
tomorrow *imorgon* ee·*mor*·ron
tonight *i kväll* ee *kvel*
toothbrush *tandborste* *tand*·beu·shte
toothpaste *tandkräm* *tand*·kreym
torch (flashlight) *ficklampa* *fik*·lam·pa
tour n *tur* toor
tourist office *turistbyrå* too·*rist*·bew·raw
towel *badduk* *baad*·dook
train *tåg* ⓝ tawg
translate *översätta* *eu*·ve·se·ta
travel agency *resebyrå* *rey*·se·bew·raw
travellers cheque *resecheck* *rey*·se·shek
trousers *byxor* *bewk*·sor
twin beds *två sängar* tvaw *seng*·ar
tyre *däck* ⓝ dek

U

underwear *underkläder* *un*·der·kley·der
urgent *angelägen/angeläget* *an*·ye·ley·gen/*an*·ye·ley·get

V

vacant *ledig(t)* *ley*·dig/*ley*·dit
vacation *semester* se·*mes*·ter
vegetable n *grönsak* *greun*·saak
vegetarian a *vegetarian* ve·ge·taa·ree·*aan*
visa *visum* ⓝ *vee*·sum

W

waiter *servitör* ser·vi·*teur*
Waiter! *Vaktmästern!* *vakt*·mes·tern
walk v *gå* gaw
wallet *plånbok* *plawn*·bohk
warm a *varm(t)* varm(t)
wash (something) *tvätta* *tve*·ta
watch n *klocka* *klo*·ka
water *vatten* ⓝ *va*·ten
we *vi* vee
weekend *helg* hely
west *väst* vest
wheelchair *rullstol* *rul*·stohl
when *när* nair
where *var* var
white *vit(t)* veet/vit
who *vem* vem
why *varför* *var*·feur
wife *fru* froo
window *fönster* *feun*·ster
wine *vin* ⓝ veen
with *med* meyd
without *utan* *oo*·taan
woman *kvinna* *kvi*·na
write *skriva* *skree*·va

Y

yellow *gul(t)* gul(t)
yes *ja* yaa
yesterday *igår* i·*gawr*
you sg inf *du* doo
you sg pol & pl *ni* nee

Turkish

turkish alphabet				
Aa a	*Bb* be	*Cc* je	*Çç* che	*Dd* de
Ee e	*Ff* fe	*Gg* ge	*Ğğ* yu·*moo*·shak ge	*Hh* he
Iı uh	*İi* ee	*Jj* zhe	*Kk* ke	*Ll* le
Mm me	*Nn* ne	*Oo* o	*Öö* er	*Pp* pe
Rr re	*Ss* se	*Şş* she	*Tt* te	*Uu* oo
Üü ew	*Vv* ve	*Yy* ye	*Zz* ze	

turkish

TÜRKÇE

introduction

Turkish (*Türkçe tewrk*·che) – the language which traces its roots as far back as 3500 BC, has travelled through Central Asia, Persia, North Africa and Europe and been written in both Arabic and Latin script – has left us words like *yogurt*, *horde*, *sequin* and *bridge* (the game) along the way. But how did it transform itself from a nomad's tongue spoken in Mongolia into the language of modern Turkey, with a prestigious interlude as the diplomatic language of the Ottoman Empire?

The first evidence of the Turkish language, which is a member of the Ural-Altaic language family, was found on stone monuments from the 8th century BC, in what's now Outer Mongolia. In the 11th century, the Seljuq clan invaded Asia Minor (Anatolia) and imposed their language on the peoples they ruled. Over time, Arabic and Persian vocabulary was adopted to express artistic and philosophical concepts and Arabic script began to be used. By the 14th century, another clan – the Ottomans – was busy establishing the empire that was to control Eurasia for centuries. In their wake, they left the Turkish language. There were then two levels of Turkish – ornate Ottoman Turkish, with flowery Persian phrases and Arabic honorifics (words showing respect), used for diplomacy, business and art, and the language of the common Turks, which still used 'native' Turkish vocabulary and structures.

When the Ottoman Empire fell in 1922, the military hero, amateur linguist and historian Kemal Atatürk came to power and led the new Republic of Turkey. With the backing of a strong language reform movement, he devised a phonetic Latin script that reflected Turkish sounds more accurately than Arabic script. On 1 November 1928, the new writing system was unveiled: within two months, it was illegal to write Turkish in the old script. In 1932 Atatürk created the *Türk Dil Kurumu* (Turkish Language Society) and gave it the brief of simplifying the Turkish language to its 'pure' form of centuries before. The vocabulary and structure was completely overhauled. As a consequence, Turkish has changed so drastically that even Atatürk's own speeches are barely comprehensible to today's speakers of *öztürkçe* ('pure Turkish').

With 70 million speakers worldwide, Turkish is the official language of Turkey and the Turkish Republic of Northern Cyprus (recognised as a nation only by the Turkish government). Elsewhere, the language is also called *Osmanlı* os·*man*·luh, and is spoken by large populations in Germany, Bulgaria, Macedonia, Greece and the '-stans' of Central Asia. So start practising and you might soon be complimented with *Ağzına sağlık!* a·zuh·*na* sa·*luhk* (lit: health to your mouth) – 'Well said!'

pronunciation

vowel sounds

Most Turkish vowel sounds can be found in English, although in Turkish they're generally shorter and slightly harsher. When you see a double vowel, such as *saat* sa·*at* (hour), you need to pronounce both vowels.

symbol	english equivalent	turkish example	transliteration
a	run	*abide*	a·bee·*de*
ai	aisle	*hayvan*	hai·*van*
ay	say	*ney*	nay
e	bet	*ekmek*	ek·*mek*
ee	see	*ile*	ee·le
eu	nurse	*özel*	eu·*zel*
ew	ee pronounced with rounded lips	*üye*	ew·*ye*
o	pot	*oda*	o·*da*
oo	zoo	*uçak*	oo·*chak*
uh	ago	*ıslak*	uhs·*lak*

word stress

In Turkish, the stress generally falls on the last syllable of the word. Most two-syllable placenames, however, are stressed on the first syllable (eg *Kıbrıs kuhb*·ruhs), and in three-syllable placenames the stress is usually on the second syllable (eg *İstanbul* ees·*tan*·bool). Another common exception occurs when a verb has a form of the negative marker *me* (*me* me, *ma* ma, *mı* muh, *mi* mee, *mu* moo, or *mü* mew) added to it. In those cases, the stress goes onto the syllable before the marker – eg *gelmiyorlar gel*·mee·yor·lar (they're not coming). You don't need to worry too much about this, as the stressed syllable is always in italics in our coloured pronunciation guides.

TÜRKÇE – pronunciation

consonant sounds

Most Turkish consonants sound the same as in English, so they're straightforward to pronounce. The exception is the Turkish r, which is always rolled. Note also that *ğ* is a silent letter which extends the vowel before it – it acts like the 'gh' combination in 'weigh', and is never pronounced.

symbol	english equivalent	turkish example	transliteration
b	bed	*bira*	*bee*·ra
ch	cheat	*çanta*	chan·*ta*
d	dog	*deniz*	de·*neez*
f	fat	*fabrika*	fab·ree·*ka*
g	go	*gar*	gar
h	hat	*hala*	ha·*la*
j	joke	*cadde*	jad·*de*
k	kit	*kadın*	ka·*duhn*
l	lot	*lider*	lee·*der*
m	man	*maç*	mach
n	not	*nefis*	ne·*fees*
p	pet	*paket*	pa·*ket*
r	red (rolled)	*rehber*	reh·*ber*
s	sun	*saat*	sa·*at*
sh	shot	*şarkı*	shar·*kuh*
t	top	*tas*	tas
v	van (but softer, between 'v' and 'w')	*vadi*	va·*dee*
y	yes	*yarım*	ya·*ruhm*
z	zero	*zarf*	zarf
zh	pleasure	*jambon*	zham·*bon*

pronunciation – TURKISH

language difficulties

Do you speak English?
İngilizce konuşuyor musunuz? — een·gee·*leez*·je ko·noo·*shoo*·yor moo·soo·*nooz*

Do you understand?
Anlıyor musun? — an·*luh*·yor moo·*soon*

I understand.
Anlıyorum. — an·*luh*·yo·room

I don't understand.
Anlamıyorum. — an·*la*·muh·yo·room

What does (*kitap*) mean?
(Kitap) ne demektir? — (kee·*tap*) ne de·*mek*·teer

How do you pronounce this?
Bunu nasıl telaffuz edersiniz? — boo·*noo na*·suhl te·laf·*fooz* e·*der*·see·neez

How do you write (*yabancı*)?
(Yabancı) kelimesini nasıl yazarsınız? — (ya·ban·*juh*) ke·lee·me·see·*nee* *na*·suhl ya·*zar*·suh·nuhz

Could you please ...?	*Lütfen ...?*	*lewt*·fen ...
repeat that	*tekrarlar mısınız*	tek·*rar*·lar muh·suh·*nuhz*
speak more slowly	*daha yavaş konuşur musunuz*	da·*ha* ya·*vash* ko·noo·*shoor* moo·soo·*nooz*
write it down	*yazar mısınız*	ya·*zar* muh·suh·*nuhz*

essentials

Yes.	*Evet.*	e·*vet*
No.	*Hayır.*	*ha*·yuhr
Please.	*Lütfen.*	*lewt*·fen
Thank you (very much). pol	*(Çok) Teşekkür ederim.*	(chok) te·shek·*kewr* e·*de*·reem
Thanks. inf	*Teşekkürler.*	te·shek·kewr·*ler*
You're welcome.	*Birşey değil.*	beer·*shay* de·*eel*
Excuse me.	*Bakar mısınız?*	ba·*kar* muh·suh·*nuhz*
Sorry.	*Özür dilerim.*	eu·*zewr* dee·*le*·reem

numbers

0	*sıfır*	suh·*fuhr*	16	*onaltı*	*on*·al·*tuh*
1	*bir*	beer	17	*onyedi*	*on*·ye·*dee*
2	*iki*	ee·*kee*	18	*onsekiz*	*on*·se·*keez*
3	*üç*	ewch	19	*ondokuz*	*on*·do·*kooz*
4	*dört*	deurt	20	*yirmi*	yeer·*mee*
5	*beş*	besh	21	*yirmibir*	yeer·*mee*·beer
6	*altı*	al·*tuh*	22	*yirmiiki*	yeer·*mee*·ee·*kee*
7	*yedi*	ye·*dee*	30	*otuz*	o·*tooz*
8	*sekiz*	se·*keez*	40	*kırk*	kuhrk
9	*dokuz*	do·*kooz*	50	*elli*	el·*lee*
10	*on*	on	60	*altmış*	alt·*muhsh*
11	*onbir*	*on*·beer	70	*yetmiş*	yet·*meesh*
12	*oniki*	*on*·ee·*kee*	80	*seksen*	sek·*sen*
13	*onüç*	*on*·ewch	90	*doksan*	dok·*san*
14	*ondört*	*on*·deurt	100	*yüz*	yewz
15	*onbeş*	*on*·besh	1000	*bin*	been

time & dates

What time is it?	*Saat kaç?*	sa·*at* kach
It's one o'clock.	*Saat bir.*	sa·*at* beer
It's (10) o'clock.	*Saat (on).*	sa·*at* (on)
Quarter past (10).	*(Onu) çeyrek geçiyor.*	(o·*noo*) chay·*rek* ge·*chee*·yor
Half past (10).	*(On) buçuk.*	(on) boo·*chook*
Quarter to (11).	*(Onbire) çeyrek var.*	(*on*·bee·*re*) chay·*rek* var
At what time ...?	*Saat kaçta ...?*	sa·*at* kach·*ta* ...
At ...	*Saat ...*	sa·*at* ...
am (morning)	*sabah*	sa·*bah*
pm (afternoon)	*öğleden sonra*	er·le·*den son*·ra
pm (evening)	*gece*	ge·*je*
Monday	*Pazartesi*	pa·*zar*·te·see
Tuesday	*Salı*	sa·*luh*
Wednesday	*Çarşamba*	char·sham·*ba*
Thursday	*Perşembe*	per·shem·*be*
Friday	*Cuma*	joo·*ma*
Saturday	*Cumartesi*	joo·*mar*·te·see
Sunday	*Pazar*	pa·*zar*

January	*Ocak*	o·*jak*
February	*Şubat*	shoo·*bat*
March	*Mart*	mart
April	*Nisan*	nee·*san*
May	*Mayıs*	ma·*yuhs*
June	*Haziran*	ha·zee·*ran*
July	*Temmuz*	tem·*mooz*
August	*Ağustos*	a·oos·*tos*
September	*Eylül*	ay·*lewl*
October	*Ekim*	e·*keem*
November	*Kasım*	ka·*suhm*
December	*Aralık*	a·ra·*luhk*

What date is it today?
Bugün ayın kaçı? — *boo*·gewn a·*yuhn ka*·chuh

It's (18 October).
(Onsekiz Ekim). — (*on*·se·*keez* e·*keem*)

since (May)	*(Mayıs'tan) beri*	(ma·yuhs·*tan*) be·*ree*
until (June)	*(Haziran'a) kadar*	(ha·zee·ra·*na*) ka·*dar*
yesterday	*dün*	dewn
today	*bugün*	*boo*·gewn
tonight	*bu gece*	boo ge·*je*
tomorrow	*yarın*	*ya*·ruhn
last/next ...	*geçen/gelecek ...*	ge·*chen*/ge·le·*jek* ...
night	*gece*	ge·*je*
week	*hafta*	haf·*ta*
month	*ay*	ai
year	*yıl*	yuhl
yesterday/tomorrow ...	*dün/yarın ...*	dewn/*ya*·ruhn ...
morning	*sabah*	sa·*bah*
afternoon	*öğleden sonra*	eu·le·*den son*·ra
evening	*akşam*	ak·*sham*

weather

What's the weather like?	*Hava nasıl?*	ha·*va na*·suhl
It's ...	*Hava ...*	ha·*va* ...
cloudy	*bulutlu*	boo·loot·*loo*
cold	*soğuk*	so·*ook*
hot	*sıcak*	suh·*jak*
raining	*yağmurlu*	ya·moor·*loo*
snowing	*kar yağışlı*	kar ya·uhsh·*luh*
sunny	*güneşli*	gew·nesh·*lee*
warm	*ılık*	uh·*luhk*
windy	*rüzgarlı*	rewz·gar·*luh*
spring	*ilkbahar*	*eelk*·ba·har
summer	*yaz*	yaz
autumn	*sonbahar*	*son*·ba·har
winter	*kış*	kuhsh

border crossing

I'm here ...	*Ben ...*	ben ...
in transit	*transit yolcuyum*	tran·*seet* yol·*joo*·yoom
on business	*iş gezisindeyim*	eesh ge·zee·seen·*de*·yeem
on holiday	*tatildeyim*	ta·teel·*de*·yeem
I'm here for ...	*Ben ... buradayım*	ben ... boo·ra·*da*·yuhm
(10) days	*(on) günlüğüne*	(on) gewn·lew·ew·*ne*
(three) weeks	*(üç) haftalığına*	(ewch) haf·ta·luh·uh·*na*
(two) months	*(iki) aylığına*	(ee·*kee*) ai·luh·uh·*na*

I'm going to (Sarıyer).
(Sarıyer'e) gidiyorum. — (sa·*ruh*·ye·re) gee·dee·*yo*·room

I'm staying at the (Divan).
(Divan'da) kalıyorum. — (dee·van·da) ka·luh·*yo*·room

I have nothing to declare.
Beyan edecek hiçbir şeyim yok. — be·*yan* e·de·*jek* heech beer she·*yeem* yok

I have something to declare.
Beyan edecek bir şeyim var. — be·*yan* e·de·*jek* beer she·*yeem* var

That's (not) mine.
Bu benim (değil). — boo be·*neem* (de·*eel*)

transport

tickets & luggage

Where can I buy a ticket?		
Nereden bilet alabilirim?		ne·re·den bee·*let* a·*la*·bee·lee·reem
Do I need to book a seat?		
Yer ayırtmam gerekli mi?		yer a·yuhrt·*mam* ge·rek·*lee* mee
One ... ticket to (Bostancı), please.	*(Bostancı'ya) ... lütfen.*	(bos·*tan*·juh·ya) ... *lewt*·fen
one-way	*bir gidiş bileti*	beer gee·*deesh* bee·le·*tee*
return	*gidiş-dönüş bir bilet*	gee·deesh·deu·*newsh* beer bee·*let*
I'd like to ... my ticket, please.	*Biletimi ... istiyorum.*	bee·le·tee·*mee* ... ees·*tee*·yo·room
cancel	*iptal ettirmek*	eep·*tal* et·teer·*mek*
change	*değiştirmek*	de·eesh·teer·*mek*
collect	*almak*	al·*mak*
confirm	*onaylatmak*	o·nai·lat·*mak*
I'd like a ... seat, please.	*... bir yer istiyorum.*	... beer yer ees·*tee*·yo·room
nonsmoking	*Sigara içilmeyen kısımda*	see·*ga*·ra ee·*cheel*·me·yen kuh·suhm·*da*
smoking	*Sigara içilen kısımda*	see·*ga*·ra ee·*chee*·len kuh·suhm·*da*
How much is it?		
Şu ne kadar?		shoo ne ka·*dar*
Is there air conditioning?		
Klima var mı?		*klee*·ma var muh
Is there a toilet?		
Tuvalet var mı?		too·va·*let* var muh
How long does the trip take?		
Yolculuk ne kadar sürer?		yol·joo·*look* ne ka·*dar* sew·*rer*
Is it a direct route?		
Direk güzergah mı?		dee·*rek* gew·zer·*gah* muh
Where's the luggage locker?		
Emanet dolabı nerede?		e·ma·*net* do·la·*buh* ne·re·de

My luggage has been …	*Bagajım …*	ba·ga·*zhuhm* …
damaged	*zarar gördü*	za·*rar* geu·*dew*
lost	*kayboldu*	kai·bol·*doo*
stolen	*çalındı*	cha·luhn·*duh*

getting around

Where does flight (TK0060) arrive?
(TK0060) sefer sayılı uçak nereye iniyor? — (*te*·ka suh·*fuhr* suh·*fuhr* alt·*muhsh*) se·*fer* sa·yuh·*luh* oo·*chak* *ne*·re·ye ee·*nee*·yor

Where does flight (TK0060) depart?
(TK0060) sefer sayılı uçak nereden kalkıyor? — (*te*·ka suh·*fuhr* suh·*fuhr* alt·*muhsh*) se·*fer* sa·yuh·*luh* oo·*chak* *ne*·re·den kal·*kuh*·yor

Where's (the) …?	*… nerede?*	… *ne*·re·de
arrivals hall	*Gelen yolcu bölümü*	ge·*len* yol·*joo* beu·lew·*mew*
departures hall	*Giden yolcu bölümü*	gee·*den* yol·*joo* beu·lew·*mew*
duty-free shop	*Gümrüksüz satış mağazası*	gewm·rewk·*sewz* sa·*tuhsh* ma·a·za·*suh*
gate (12)	*(Oniki) numaralı kapı*	(*on*·ee·*kee*) noo·ma·ra·*luh* ka·*puh*

Is this the … to (Sirkeci)?	*(Sirkeci'ye) giden … bu mu?*	(*seer*·ke·jee·ye) gee·*den* … boo moo
boat	*vapur*	va·*poor*
bus	*otobüs*	o·to·*bews*
plane	*uçak*	oo·*chak*
train	*tren*	tren

What time's the … bus?	*… otobüs ne zaman?*	… o·to·*bews* ne za·*man*
first	*İlk*	eelk
last	*Son*	son
next	*Sonraki*	son·ra·*kee*

At what time does it arrive/leave?
Ne zaman varır/kalkacak? — ne za·*man* va·*ruhr*/kal·ka·*jak*

How long will it be delayed?
Ne kadar gecikecek? — ne ka·*dar* ge·jee·ke·*jek*

What station/stop is this?
Bu hangi istasyon/durak? — boo *han*·gee ees·tas·*yon*/doo·*rak*

What's the next station/stop?
Sonraki istasyon/durak hangisi? — son·ra·*kee* ees·tas·*yon*/doo·*rak han*·gee·see

Does it stop at (Kadıköy)?
(Kadıköy'de) durur mu? — (ka·*duh*·kay·de) doo·*roor* moo

Please tell me when we get to (Beşiktaş).
(Beşiktaş'a) vardığımızda lütfen bana söyleyin. — (be·*sheek*·ta·sha) var·duh·uh·muhz·*da lewt*·fen ba·*na* say·*le*·yeen

How long do we stop here?
Burada ne kadar duracağız? — boo·ra·*da* ne ka·*dar* doo·ra·*ja*·uhz

Is this seat available?
Bu koltuk boş mu? — boo kol·*took* bosh moo

That's my seat.
Burası benim yerim. — boo·ra·*suh* be·*neem* ye·*reem*

I'd like a taxi ...	*... bir taksi istiyorum.*	... beer tak·*see* ees·*tee*·yo·room
at (9am)	*(Sabah dokuzda)*	(sa·*bah* do·kooz·*da*)
now	*Hemen*	*he*·men
tomorrow	*Yarın*	*ya*·ruhn

Is this taxi available?
Bu taksi boş mu? — boo tak·*see* bosh moo

How much is it to ...?
... ne kadar? — ... ne ka·*dar*

Please put the meter on.
Lütfen taksimetreyi çalıştırın. — *lewt*·fen tak·*see*·met·re·yee cha·luhsh·*tuh*·ruhn

Please take me to (this address).
Lütfen beni (bu adrese) götürün. — *lewt*·fen be·*nee* (boo ad·re·*se*) geu·*tew*·rewn

Please ...	*Lütfen ...*	*lewt*·fen ...
slow down	*yavaşlayın*	ya·vash·*la*·yuhn
stop here	*burada durun*	boo·ra·*da doo*·roon
wait here	*burada bekleyin*	boo·ra·*da* bek·*le*·yeen

car, motorbike & bicycle hire

I'd like to hire a ...	*Bir ... kiralamak istiyorum.*	beer ... kee·ra·la·*mak* ees·*tee*·yo·room
bicycle	*bisiklet*	bee·seek·*let*
car	*araba*	a·ra·*ba*
motorbike	*motosiklet*	mo·to·seek·*let*
with ...		
a driver	*şoförlü*	sho·feur·*lew*
air conditioning	*klimalı*	klee·ma·*luh*
How much for ... hire?	*... kirası ne kadar?*	... kee·ra·*suh* ne ka·*dar*
hourly	*Saatlık*	sa·at·*luhk*
daily	*Günlük*	gewn·*lewk*
weekly	*Haftalık*	haf·ta·*luhk*
air	*hava*	ha·*va*
oil	*yağ*	ya
petrol	*benzin*	ben·*zeen*
tyres	*lastikler*	las·teek·*ler*

I need a mechanic.
Tamirciye ihtiyacım var. — ta·meer·jee·*ye* eeh·tee·ya·*juhm* var

I've run out of petrol.
Benzinim bitti. — ben·*zee*·neem beet·*tee*

I have a flat tyre.
Lastiğim patladı. — las·tee·eem pat·la·*duh*

directions

Where's the ...?	*... nerede?*	... *ne*·re·de
bank	*Banka*	ban·*ka*
city centre	*Şehir merkezi*	she·*heer* mer·ke·*zee*
hotel	*Otel*	o·*tel*
market	*Pazar yeri*	pa·*zar* ye·*ree*
police station	*Polis karakolu*	po·*lees* ka·ra·ko·*loo*
post office	*Postane*	pos·*ta*·ne
public toilet	*Umumi tuvalet*	oo·moo·*mee* too·va·*let*
tourist office	*Turizm bürosu*	too·*reezm* bew·ro·*soo*

Is this the road to (Taksim)?
(Taksim'e) giden yol bu mu? — (*tak*·see·me) gee·*den* yol boo moo

Can you show me (on the map)?
Bana (haritada) gösterebilir misiniz? — ba·*na* (ha·ree·ta·*da*) geus·te·*re*·bee·leer mee·seen·*neez*

What's the address?
Adresi nedir? — ad·re·*see ne*·deer

How far is it?
Ne kadar uzakta? — ne ka·*dar* oo·zak·*ta*

How do I get there?
Oraya nasıl gidebilirim? — o·ra·*ya na*·suhl gee·*de*·bee·lee·reem

Turn …	*… dön.*	… deun
at the corner	*Köşeden*	keu·she·*den*
at the traffic lights	*Trafik ışıklarından*	tra·*feek* uh·shuhk·la·ruhn·*dan*
left/right	*Sola/Sağa*	so·*la*/sa·*a*

It's …		
behind …	*… arkasında.*	… ar·ka·suhn·*da*
far away	*Uzak.*	oo·*zak*
here	*Burada.*	boo·ra·*da*
in front of …	*… önünde.*	… eu·newn·*de*
left	*Solda.*	sol·*da*
near …	*… yakınında.*	… ya·kuh·nuhn·*da*
next to …	*… yanında.*	… ya·nuhn·*da*
on the corner	*Köşede.*	keu·she·*de*
opposite …	*… karşısında.*	… kar·shuh·suhn·*da*
right	*Sağda.*	sa·*da*
straight ahead	*Tam karşıda.*	tam kar·shuh·*da*
there	*Şurada.*	shoo·ra·*da*

by bus	*otobüslü*	o·to·bews·*lew*
by taxi	*taksili*	tak·see·*lee*
by train	*trenli*	tren·*lee*
on foot	*yürüyerek*	yew·rew·ye·*rek*

north	*kuzey*	koo·*zay*
south	*güney*	gew·*nay*
east	*doğu*	do·*oo*
west	*batı*	ba·*tuh*

signs

Giriş/Çıkış	gee·*reesh*/chuh·*kuhsh*	**Entrance/Exit**
Açık/Kapalı	a·*chuhk*/ka·pa·*luh*	**Open/Closed**
Boş Oda	bosh o·*da*	**Rooms Available**
Boş Yer Yok	bosh yer yok	**No Vacancies**
Danışma	da·nuhsh·*ma*	**Information**
Polis Karakolu	po·*lees* ka·ra·ko·*loo*	**Police Station**
Yasak	ya·*sak*	**Prohibited**
Tuvaletler	too·va·let·*ler*	**Toilets**
Erkek	er·*kek*	**Men**
Kadın	ka·*duhn*	**Women**
Sıcak/Soğuk	suh·*jak*/so·*ook*	**Hot/Cold**

accommodation

finding accommodation

Where's a ...?	*Buralarda nerede ... var?*	boo·ra·lar·*da* *ne*·re·de ... var
camping ground	*kamp yeri*	kamp ye·*ree*
guesthouse	*misafirhane*	mee·*sa*·feer·ha·ne
hotel	*otel*	o·*tel*
youth hostel	*gençlik hosteli*	gench *leek* hos·te·*lee*
Can you recommend somewhere ...?	*... bir yer tavsiye edebilir misiniz?*	... beer yer tav·see·*ye* e·*de*·bee·leer mee·see·*neez*
cheap	*Ucuz*	oo·*jooz*
good	*İyi*	ee·*yee*
nearby	*Yakın*	ya·*kuhn*

I'd like to book a room, please.
Bir oda ayırtmak istiyorum lütfen. — beer o·*da* a·yuhrt·*mak* ees·*tee*·yo·room *lewt*·fen

I have a reservation.
Rezervasyonum var. — re·zer·vas·yo·*noom* var

My name's ...
Benim ismim ... — be·*neem* ees·*meem* ...

Do you have a … room?	*… odanız var mı?*	… o·da·*nuhz* var muh
single	*Tek kişilik*	tek kee·shee·*leek*
double	*İki kişilik*	ee·*kee* kee·shee·*leek*
twin	*Çift yataklı*	cheeft ya·tak·*luh*
How much is it per …?	*… ne kadar?*	… ne ka·*dar*
night	*Geceliği*	ge·je·lee·*ee*
person	*Kişi başına*	kee·*shee* ba·shuh·*na*
Can I pay by …?	*… ile ödeyebilir miyim?*	… ee·*le* eu·de·*ye*·bee·leer mee·*yeem*
credit card	*Kredi kartı*	*kre*·dee kar·*tuh*
travellers cheque	*Seyahat çeki*	se·ya·*hat* che·*kee*

I'd like to stay for (three) nights.
Kalmak istiyorum (üç) geceliğine. kal·*mak* ees·*tee*·yo·room (ewch) ge·je·lee·ee·*ne*

From (2 July) to (6 July).
(İki Temmuz'dan) (ee·*kee* tem·mooz·*dan*)
(altı Temmuz'a) kadar. (al·*tuh* tem·moo·*za*) ka·*dar*

Can I see it?
Görebilir miyim. geu·*re*·bee·leer mee·*yeem*

Am I allowed to camp here?
Burada kamp yapabilir miyim? boo·ra·*da* kamp ya·*pa*·bee·leer mee·*yeem*

Where can I find a camping ground?
Kamp alanı nerede? kamp a·la·*nuh ne*·re·de

requests & queries

When/Where is breakfast served?
Kahvaltı ne zaman/ nerede veriliyor? kah·val·*tuh* ne za·*man*/ *ne*·re·de ve·ree·*lee*·yor

Please wake me at (seven).
Lütfen beni (yedide) kaldırın. *lewt*·fen be·*nee* (ye·dee·*de*) kal·*duh*·ruhn

Could I have my key, please?
Anahtarımı alabilir miyim? a·nah·ta·ruh·*muh* a·*la*·bee·leer mee·*yeem*

Can I get another (blanket)?
Başka bir (battaniye) alabilir miyim? bash·*ka* beer (bat·*ta*·nee·ye) a·*la*·bee·leer mee·*yeem*

Is there an elevator/a safe?
Asansör/Kasanız var mı? a·san·*seur*/ka·sa·*nuhz* var muh

The room is too …	*Çok …*	chok …
expensive	*pahalı*	pa·ha·*luh*
noisy	*gürültülü*	gew·rewl·tew·*lew*
small	*küçük*	kew·*chewk*

The … doesn't work.	*… çalışmıyor.*	… cha·*luhsh*·muh·yor
air conditioning	*Klima*	*klee*·ma
fan	*Fan*	fan
toilet	*Tuvalet*	too·va·*let*

This … isn't clean.	*Bu … temiz değil.*	boo … te·*meez* de·*eel*
pillow	*yastık*	yas·*tuhk*
sheet	*çarşaf*	char·*shaf*
towel	*havlu*	hav·*loo*

checking out

What time is checkout?
Çıkış ne zaman? — chuh·*kuhsh* ne za·*man*

Can I leave my luggage here?
Eşyalarımı burada bırakabilir miyim? — esh·ya·la·ruh·*muh* boo·ra·*da* buh·ra·*ka*·bee·leer mee·*yeem*

Could I have my …, please?	*… alabilir miyim lütfen?*	… a·*la*·bee·leer mee·*yeem lewt*·fen
deposit	*Depozitomu*	de·po·zee·to·*moo*
passport	*Pasaportumu*	pa·sa·por·too·*moo*
valuables	*Değerli eşyalarımı*	de·er·*lee* esh·ya·la·ruh·*muh*

communications & banking

the internet

Where's the local Internet café?
En yakın internet kafe nerede? — en ya·*kuhn* een·ter·*net* ka·*fe* ne·re·de

How much is it per hour?
Saati ne kadar? — sa·a·*tee* ne ka·*dar*

I'd like to …	… istiyorum.	… ees·tee·yo·room
check my email	E-postama bakmak	e·pos·ta·ma bak·mak
get Internet access	İnternete girmek	een·ter·ne·te geer·mek
use a printer	Printeri kullanmak	preen·te·ree kool·lan·mak
use a scanner	Tarayıcıyı	ta·ra·yuh·juh·yuh

mobile/cell phone

I'd like a …	… istiyorum.	… ees·tee·yo·room
mobile/cell phone for hire	Cep telefonu kiralamak	jep te·le·fo·noo kee·ra·la·mak
SIM card for your network	Buradaki şebeke için SİM kart	boo·ra·da·kee she·be·ke ee·cheen seem kart

What are the rates?	Ücret tarifesi nedir?	ewj·ret ta·ree·fe·see ne·deer

telephone

What's your phone number?
Telefon numaranız nedir? te·le·fon noo·ma·ra·nuhz ne·deer

The number is …
Telefon numarası … te·le·fon noo·ma·ra·suh …

Where's the nearest public phone?
En yakın telefon kulübesi nerede? en ya·kuhn te·le·fon koo·lew·be·see ne·re·de

I'd like to buy a phonecard.
Telefon kartı almak istiyorum. te·le·fon kar·tuh al·mak ees·tee·yo·room

I want to …	… istiyorum.	… ees·tee·yo·room
call (Singapore)	(Singapur'u) aramak	(seen·ga·poo·roo) a·ra·mak
make a local call	Yerel bir görüşme yapmak	ye·rel beer geu·rewsh·me yap·mak
reverse the charges	Ödemeli görüşme yapmak	eu·de·me·lee ger·rewsh·me yap·mak

How much does … cost?	… ne kadar eder?	… ne ka·*dar* e·*der*
a (three)-minute call	*(Üç) dakikalık konuşma*	(ewch) da·kee·ka·*luhk* ko·noosh·*ma*
each extra minute	*Her ekstra dakika*	her eks·*tra* da·kee·*ka*

It's (10) *yeni kuruş* per minute.
Bir dakikası (on) yeni kuruş. beer da·kee·ka·*suh* (on) ye·*nee* koo·*roosh*

post office

I want to send a …	*Bir … göndermek istiyorum.*	beer … geun·der·*mek* ees·*tee*·yo·room
fax	*faks*	faks
letter	*mektup*	mek·*toop*
parcel	*paket*	pa·*ket*
postcard	*kartpostal*	kart·pos·*tal*
I want to buy a/an …	*… satın almak istiyorum.*	… sa·*tuhn* al·*mak* ees·*tee*·yo·room
envelope	*Zarf*	zarf
stamp	*Pul*	pool
Please send it (to Australia) by …	*Lütfen … (Avustralya'ya) gönderin.*	*lewt*·fen … (a·voos·*tral*·ya·ya) geun·*de*·reen
airmail	*hava yoluyla*	ha·*va* yo·*looy*·la
express mail	*ekspres posta*	eks·*pres* pos·*ta*
registered mail	*taahhütlü posta*	ta·ah·hewt·*lew* pos·*ta*
surface mail	*deniz yoluyla*	de·*neez* yo·*looy*·la
Is there any mail for me?	*Bana posta var mı?*	ba·*na* *pos*·ta var muh

bank

Where's a/an …?	*… nerede var?*	… *ne*·re·de var
ATM	*Bankamatik*	ban·ka·ma·*teek*
foreign exchange office	*Döviz bürosu*	deu·*veez* bew·ro·*soo*

I'd like to …	*… istiyorum.*	… ees·*tee*·yo·room
cash a cheque	*Çek bozdurmak*	chek boz·door·*mak*
change a travellers cheque	*Seyahat çeki bozdurmak*	se·ya·*hat* che·*kee* boz·door·*mak*
change money	*Para bozdurmak*	pa·*ra* boz·door·*mak*
get a cash advance	*Avans çekmek*	a·*vans* chek·*mek*
withdraw money	*Para çekmek*	pa·*ra* chek·*mek*

What's the …?	*… nedir?*	… *ne*·deer
charge for that	*Ücreti*	ewj·re·*tee*
commission	*Komisyon*	ko·mees·*yon*
exchange rate	*Döviz kuru*	deu·*veez* koo·*roo*

It's …		
(12) euros	*(Oniki) euro.*	(*on*·ee·*kee*) yoo·*ro*
(25) lira	*(Yirmibeş) lira.*	(yeer·*mee*·besh) lee·*ra*
free	*Ücretsiz.*	ewj·ret·*seez*

What time does the bank open?
Banka ne zaman açılıyor? — *ban*·ka ne za·*man* a·chuh·*luh*·yor

Has my money arrived yet?
Param geldi mi? — pa·*ram* gel·*dee* mee

sightseeing

getting in

What time does it open/close?
Saat kaçta açılır/kapanır? — sa·*at* kach·*ta* a·chuh·*luhr*/ka·pa·*nuhr*

What's the admission charge?
Giriş ücreti nedir? — gee·*reesh* ewj·re·*tee* *ne*·deer

Is there a discount for children/students?
Çocuk/Öğrenci indirimi var mı? — cho·*jook*/eu·ren·*jee* een·dee·ree·*mee* var muh

I'd like a …	*… istiyorum.*	… ees·*tee*·yo·room
catalogue	*Katalog*	ka·ta·*log*
guide	*Rehber*	reh·*ber*
local map	*Yerel Harita*	ye·*rel* ha·ree·*ta*

I'd like to see ...	*... görmek istiyorum.*	... geur·*mek* ees·*tee*·yo·room
What's that?	*Bu nedir?*	boo *ne*·deer
Can I take a photo?	*Bir fotoğrafınızı çekebilir miyim?*	beer fo·to·ra·fuh·nuh·*zuh* che·*ke*·bee·leer mee·*yeem*

tours

When's the next ...?	*Sonraki ... ne zaman?*	son·ra·*kee* ... ne za·*man*
day trip	*gündüz turu*	gewn·*dewz* too·*roo*
tour	*tur*	toor
Is ... included?	*... dahil mi?*	... da·*heel* mee
accommodation	*Kalacak yer*	ka·la·*jak* yer
the admission charge	*Giriş*	gee·*reesh*
food	*Yemek*	ye·*mek*
transport	*Ulaşım*	oo·la·*shuhm*

How long is the tour?
Tur ne kadar sürer? — toor ne ka·*dar* sew·*rer*

What time should we be back?
Saat kaçta dönmeliyiz? — sa·*at* kach·*ta* deun·me·*lee*·yeez

sightseeing

castle	*kale*	ka·*le*
church	*kilise*	kee·lee·*se*
main square	*meydan*	may·*dan*
monument	*anıt*	a·*nuht*
mosque	*cami*	ja·*mee*
museum	*muze*	mew·*ze*
old city	*eski şehir*	es·*kee* she·*heer*
palace	*saray*	sa·*rai*
ruins	*harabeler*	ha·ra·be·*ler*
stadium	*stadyum*	*stad*·yoom
statue	*heykel*	hay·*kel*
Turkish bath	*hamam*	ha·*mam*

shopping

enquiries

Where's a ...?	*... nerede?*	... *ne*·re·de
bank	*Banka*	*ban*·ka
bookshop	*Kitapçı*	kee·tap·*chuh*
camera shop	*Fotoğrafçı*	fo·to·raf·*chuh*
department store	*Büyük mağaza*	bew·*yewk* ma·a·*za*
grocery store	*Bakkal*	bak·*kal*
market	*Pazar yeri*	pa·*zar* ye·*ree*
newsagency	*Gazete bayii*	ga·*ze*·te ba·yee·*ee*
supermarket	*Süpermarket*	sew·*per*·mar·ket

Where can I buy (a padlock)?
Nereden (asma kilit) alabilirim? — *ne*·re·den (as·*ma* kee·*leet*) a·*la*·bee·lee·reem

I'm looking for ...
... istiyorum. — ... ees·*tee*·yo·room

Can I look at it?
Bakabilir miyim? — ba·*ka*·bee·leer mee·*yeem*

Do you have any others?
Başka var mı? — bash·*ka* var muh

Does it have a guarantee?
Garantisi var mı? — ga·ran·tee·*see* var muh

Can I have it sent overseas?
Yurt dışına gönderebilir misiniz? — yoort duh·shuh·*na* geun·de·*re*·bee·leer mee·see·*neez*

Can I have my ... repaired?
... burada tamir ettirebilir miyim? — ... boo·ra·*da* ta·*meer* et·tee·*re*·bee·leer mee·*yeem*

It's faulty.
Arızalı. — a·ruh·za·*luh*

I'd like ..., please.	*... istiyorum lütfen.*	... ees·*tee*·yo·room *lewt*·fen
a bag	*Çanta*	chan·*ta*
a refund	*Para iadesi*	pa·*ra* ee·a·de·*see*
to return this	*Bunu iade etmek*	boo·*noo* ee·a·*de* et·*mek*

paying

How much is it? *Ne kadar?*	ne ka·*dar*
Can you write down the price? *Fiyatı yazabilir misiniz?*	fee·ya·*tuh* ya·*za*·bee·leer mee·see·*neez*
That's too expensive. *Bu çok pahalı.*	boo chok pa·ha·*luh*
Is that your lowest price? *Son fiyatınız bu mu?*	son fee·ya·tuh·*nuhz* boo moo
I'll give you (30) lira. *(Otuz) lira veririm.*	(o·*tooz*) lee·*ra* ve·*ree*·reem
There's a mistake in the bill. *Hesapta bir yanlışlık var.*	he·sap·*ta* beer yan·luhsh·*luhk* var

Do you accept ...?	*... kabul ediyor musunuz?*	... ka·*bool* e·*dee*·yor moo·soo·*nooz*
credit cards	*Kredi kartı*	*kre*·dee kar·*tuh*
debit cards	*Banka kartı*	*ban*·ka kar·*tuh*
travellers cheques	*Seyahat çeki*	se·ya·*hat* che·*kee*

I'd like ..., please.	*... istiyorum lütfen.*	... ees·*tee*·yo·room *lewt*·fen
a receipt	*Makbuz*	mak·*booz*
my change	*Paramın üstünü*	pa·ra·*muhn* ews·tew·*new*

clothes & shoes

Can I try it on?	*Deneyebilir miyim?*	de·ne·*ye*·bee·leer mee·*yeem*
My size is (42).	*(Kırkiki) beden giyiyorum.*	(kuhrk·ee·*kee*) be·*den* gee·*yee*·yo·room
It doesn't fit.	*Olmuyor.*	*ol*·moo·yor

small	*küçük*	kew·*chewk*
medium	*orta*	or·*ta*
large	*büyük*	bew·*yewk*

books & music

I'd like a ...	*... istiyorum.*	... ees·*tee*·yo·room
newspaper (in English)	*(İngilizce) bir gazete*	(een·gee·*leez*·je) beer ga·*ze*·te
pen	*Tükenmez kalem*	tew·ken·*mez* ka·*lem*

Is there an English-language bookshop?
İngilizce yayın satan bir dükkan var mı?
een·gee·*leez*·je ya·*yuhn* sa·*tan* beer dewk·*kan* var muh

I'm looking for something by (Yaşar Kemal).
(Yaşar Kemal'in) albümlerine bakmak istiyorum.
(ya·*shar* ke·mal·*een*) al·bewm·le·ree·*ne* bak·*mak* ees·*tee*·yo·room

Can I listen to this?
Bunu dinleyebilir miyim?
boo·*noo* deen·le·*ye*·bee·leer mee·*yeem*

photography

Can you ...?	*... misiniz?*	... mee·see·*neez*
develop this film	*Bu filmi basabilir*	boo feel·*mee* ba·*sa*·bee·leer
load my film	*Filmi makineye takabilir*	feel·*mee* ma·kee·ne·*ye* ta·*ka*·bee·leer
transfer photos from my camera to CD	*Kameramdaki fotoğrafları CD'ye aktarabilir*	ka·me·ram·da·*kee* fo·to·raf·la·*ruh* *see*·dee·ye ak·ta·*ra*·bee·leer

I need a/an ... film for this camera.	*Bu kamera için ... film istiyorum.*	boo ka·me·*ra* ee·*cheen* ... feelm ees·*tee*·yo·room
APS	*APS*	a·pe·*se*
B&W	*siyah-beyaz*	see·*yah*·be·yaz
colour	*renkli*	renk·*lee*
slide	*slayt*	slayt
(200) speed	*(ikiyüz) hızlı*	(ee·*kee*·yewz) huhz·*luh*

When will it be ready? *Ne zaman hazır olur?* ne za·*man* ha·*zuhr* o·*loor*

meeting people

greetings, goodbyes & introductions

Hello.	*Merhaba.*	mer·ha·ba
Hi.	*Selam.*	se·*lam*
Good night.	*İyi geceler.*	ee·*yee* ge·je·*ler*
Goodbye. (by person leaving)	*Hoşçakal.* **inf**	hosh·*cha*·kal
	Hoşçakalın. **pol**	hosh·*cha*·ka·luhn
Goodbye. (by person staying)	*Güle güle.*	gew·*le* gew·*le*
See you later.	*Sonra görüşürüz.*	*son*·ra ger·rew·*shew*·rewz
Mr	*Bay*	bai
Mrs/Miss	*Bayan*	ba·*yan*
How are you?	*Nasılsın?* **inf**	*na*·suhl·suhn
	Nasılsınız? **pol**	*na*·suhl·suh·nuhz
Fine. And you?	*İyiyim. Ya sen/siz?* **inf/pol**	ee·*yee*·yeem ya sen/seez
What's your name?	*Adınız ne?* **inf**	a·duh·*nuhz* ne
	Adınız nedir? **pol**	a·duh·*nuhz ne*·deer
My name is ...	*Benim adım ...*	be·*neem* a·*duhm* ...
I'm pleased to meet you.	*Tanıştığımıza sevindim.*	ta·nuhsh·tuh·uh·muh·*za* se·veen·*deem*
This is my ...	*Bu benim ...*	boo be·*neem* ...
brother	*kardeşim*	kar·de·*sheem*
daughter	*kızım*	kuh·*zuhm*
father	*babayım*	ba·ba·*yuhm*
friend	*arkadaşım*	ar·ka·da·*shuhm*
husband	*kocam*	ko·*jam*
mother	*anneyim*	an·ne·*yeem*
partner (intimate)	*partnerim*	part·ne·*reem*
sister	*kız kardeşim*	kuhz kar·de·*sheem*
son	*oğlum*	o·*loom*
wife	*karım*	ka·*ruhm*
Here's my ...	*İşte benim ...*	eesh·*te* be·*neem* ...
(email) address	*(e-posta) adresim*	(*e*·pos·ta) ad·re·*seem*
fax number	*faks numaram*	faks noo·ma·*ram*
phone number	*telefon numaram*	te·le·*fon* noo·ma·*ram*

What's your ...?	*Sizin ... nedir?*	see·*zeen* ... *ne*·deer
(email) address	*(e-posta) adresiniz*	(e·pos·ta) ad·re·see·*neez*
fax number	*faks numaranız*	faks noo·ma·ra·*nuhz*
phone number	*telefon numaranız*	te·le·*fon* noo·ma·ra·*nuhz*

occupations

What's your occupation?	*Mesleğiniz nedir?* pol	mes·le·ee·*neez ne*·deer
	Mesleğin nedir? inf	mes·le·*een ne*·deer
I'm a/an ...	*Ben ...*	ben ...
artist	*sanatçıyım* m&f	sa·nat·*chuh*·yuhm
business person	*iş adamıyım* m	ish a·da·*muh*·yuhm
	kadınıyım f	ka·duh·*nuh*·yuhm
farmer	*çiftçiyim* m&f	cheeft·*chee*·yeem
manual worker	*işçiyim* m&f	eesh·*chee*·yeem
office worker	*memurum* m&f	me·*moo*·room
scientist	*bilim adamıyım* m&f	bee·*leem* a·da·*muh*·yuhm

background

Where are you from?	*Nerelisiniz?* pol	*ne*·re·lee·see·neez
	Nerelisin? inf	*ne*·re·lee·seen
I'm from ...	*Ben ...*	ben ...
Australia	*Avustralya'lıyım*	a·voos·*tral*·ya·luh·yuhm
Canada	*Kanada'lıyım*	ka·*na*·da·luh·yuhm
England	*İngiltere'liyim*	een·geel·*te*·re·lee·yeem
the USA	*Amerika'lıyım*	a·*me*·ree·ka·luh·yuhm
Are you married?	*Evli misiniz?*	ev·*lee* mee·see·*neez*
I'm married/single.	*Ben evliyim/bekarım.*	ben ev·*lee*·yeem/be·*ka*·ruhm

age

How old ...?	*Kaç ...?*	kach ...
are you	*yaşındasın* inf	ya·shuhn·*da*·suhn
is your son	*yaşında oğlunuz*	ya·shuhn·*da* o·loo·*nooz*
is your daughter	*yaşında kızınız*	ya·shuhn·*da* kuh·zuh·*nuhz*
I'm ... years old.	*Ben ... yaşındayım.*	ben ... ya·shuhn·*da*·yuhm
He/She is ... years old.	*O ... yaşında.*	o ... ya·shuhn·*da*

feelings

I'm/I'm not …		
cold	*Üşüdüm./ Üşümedim.*	ew·shew·*dewm*/ ew·*shew*·me·deem
happy	*Mutluyum./ Mutlu değilim.*	moot·*loo*·yoom/ moot·*loo* de·ee·leem
hot	*Sıcakladım./ Sıcaklamadım.*	suh·jak·la·*duhm*/ suh·jak·*la*·ma·duhm
hungry	*Açım./Aç değilim.*	*a*·chuhm/ach de·*ee*·leem
sad	*Üzgünüm./ Üzgün değilim.*	ewz·gew·*newm*/ ewz·*gewn* de·ee·leem
thirsty	*Susadım./Susamadım.*	soo·sa·*duhm*/soo·*sa*·ma·duhm
tired	*Yorgunum./ Yorgun değilim.*	yor·*goo*·noom/ yor·*goon* de·ee·leem
Are you …?		
cold	*Üşüdün mü?*	ew·shew·*dewn* mew
happy	*Mutlu musun?*	moot·*loo* moo·*soon*
hot	*Sıcakladın mı?*	suh·jak·la·*duhn* muh
hungry	*Aç mısın?*	ach muh·*suhn*
sad	*Üzgün musun?*	ewz·*gewn* moo·*soon*
thirsty	*Susadın mı?*	soo·sa·*duhn* muh
tired	*Yorgun musun?*	yor·*goon* moo·*soon*

entertainment

going out

Where can I find …?	*Buranın … nerede?*	boo·ra·*nuhn* … *ne*·re·de
clubs	*kulüpleri*	koo·lewp·le·*ree*
gay venues	*gey kulüpleri*	gay koo·lewp·le·*ree*
pubs	*birahaneleri*	bee·ra·ha·ne·le·*ree*
I feel like going to a/the …	*… gitmek istiyor.*	… geet·*mek* ees·*tee*·yor
concert	*Konsere*	kon·se·*re*
movies	*Sinemaya*	see·ne·ma·*ya*
party	*Partiye*	par·tee·*ye*
restaurant	*Restorana*	res·to·ra·*na*
theatre	*Oyuna*	o·yoo·*na*

interests

Do you like ...?	*... sever misin?*	... se·*ver* mee·*seen*
I like ...	*... seviyorum.*	... se·*vee*·yo·room
I don't like ...	*... sevmiyorum.*	... *sev*·mee·yo·room
art	*Sanat*	sa·*nat*
movies	*Sinemaya gitmeyi*	see·ne·ma·*ya* geet·me·*yee*
reading	*Okumayı*	o·koo·ma·*yuh*
sport	*Sporu*	spo·*roo*
travelling	*Seyahat etmeyi*	se·ya·*hat* et·me·*yee*

Do you ...?	*... misin/misiniz?* inf/pol	... mee·*seen*/mee·see·*neez*
dance	*Dans eder*	dans e·*der*
go to concerts	*Konserlere gider*	kon·ser·le·*re* gee·*der*
listen to music	*Müzik dinler*	mew·*zeek* deen·*ler*

food & drink

finding a place to eat

Can you recommend a ...?	*İyi bir ... tavsiye edebilir misiniz?*	ee·*yee* beer ... tav·see·*ye* e·*de*·bee·leer mee·see·*neez*
bar	*bar*	bar
café	*kafe*	ka·*fe*
restaurant	*restoran*	res·to·*ran*

I'd like ..., please.	*... istiyorum.*	... ees·*tee*·yo·room
a table for (five)	*(Beş) kişilik bir masa*	(besh) kee·shee·*leek* beer ma·*sa*
the nonsmoking section	*Sigara içilmeyen bir yer*	see·*ga*·ra ee·*cheel*·me·yen beer yer
the smoking section	*Sigara içilen bir yer*	see·*ga*·ra ee·chee·*len* beer yer

ordering food

breakfast	*kahvaltı*	kah·val·*tuh*
lunch	*öğle yemeği*	eu·*le* ye·me·*ee*
dinner	*akşam yemeği*	ak·*sham* ye·me·*ee*
snack	*hafif yemek*	ha·*feef* ye·*mek*

What would you recommend?		
Ne tavsiye edersiniz?		ne tav·see·*ye* e·*der*·see·neez
I'd like (a/the) ...	*... istiyorum.*	... ees·*tee*·yo·room
bill	*Hesabı*	he·sa·*buh*
drink list	*İçecek listesini*	ee·che·*jek* lees·te·see·*nee*
menu	*Menüyü*	me·new·*yew*
that dish	*Şu yemeği*	shoo ye·me·*ee*

drinks

(cup of) coffee ...	*(fincan) kahve ...*	(feen·*jan*) kah·*ve* ...
(cup of) tea ...	*(fincan) çay ...*	(feen·*jan*) chai ...
with milk	*sütlü*	sewt·*lew*
without sugar	*şekersiz*	she·ker·*seez*
(orange) juice	*(portakal) suyu*	(por·ta·*kal*) soo·*yoo*
soft drink	*alkolsüz içecek*	al·kol·*sewz* ee·che·*jek*
sparkling mineral water	*maden sodası*	ma·*den* so·da·*suh*
still mineral water	*maden suyu*	ma·*den* soo·*yoo*
(hot) water	*(sıcak) su*	(suh·*jak*) soo

in the bar

I'll have ...	*... alayım.*	... a·la·*yuhm*
I'll buy you a drink.	*Sana içecek alayım.*	sa·*na* ee·che·*jek* a·la·*yuhm*
What would you like?	*Ne alırsınız?*	ne a·*luhr*·suh·nuhz
Cheers!	*Şerefe!*	she·re·*fe*
brandy	*brendi*	*bren*·dee
cocktail	*kokteyl*	kok·*tayl*
cognac	*konyak*	kon·*yak*
a shot of (whisky)	*bir tek (viski)*	beer tek (*vees*·kee)
a bottle/glass of beer	*bir şişe/bardak bira*	beer shee·*she*/bar·*dak* bee·ra
a bottle/glass of ... wine	*bir şişe/bardak ... şarap*	beer shee·*she*/bar·*dak* ... sha·*rap*
red	*kırmızı*	kuhr·muh·*zuh*
sparkling	*köpüklü*	keu·pewk·*lew*
white	*beyaz*	be·*yaz*

self-catering

What's the local speciality?
Bu yöreye has yiyecekler neler? — boo yeu·re·*ye* has yee·ye·jek·*ler* ne·ler

What's that?
Bu nedir? — boo *ne*·deer

How much (is a kilo of cheese)?
(Bir kilo peynir) Ne kadar? — (beer kee·*lo* pay·*neer*) ne ka·*dar*

I'd like ...	*... istiyorum.*	... ees·*tee*·yo·room
(200) grams	*(İkiyüz) gram*	(ee·*kee*·yewz) gram
(two) kilos	*(İki) kilo*	(ee·*kee*) kee·*lo*
(three) pieces	*(Üç) parça*	(ewch) par·*cha*
(six) slices	*(Altı) dilim*	(al·*tuh*) dee·*leem*

Less.	*Daha az.*	da·*ha* az
Enough.	*Yeterli.*	ye·ter·*lee*
More.	*Daha fazla.*	da·*ha* faz·*la*

special diets & allergies

Where's a vegetarian restaurant?
Buralarda vejeteryan restoran var mı? — boo·ra·lar·*da* ve·zhe·ter·*yan* res·to·*ran* var muh

Do you have vegetarian food?
Vejeteryan yiyecekleriniz var mı? — ve·zhe·ter·*yan* yee·ye·jek·le·ree·*neez* var muh

Is it cooked with ...?	*İçinde ... var mı?*	ee·cheen·*de* ... var muh
butter	*tereyağ*	te·*re*·ya
eggs	*yumurta*	yoo·moor·*ta*
meat stock	*et suyu*	et soo·*yoo*

I'm allergic to ...	*... alerjim var.*	... a·ler·*zheem* var
dairy produce	*Süt ürünlerine*	sewt ew·rewn·le·ree·*ne*
gluten	*Glutene*	gloo·te·*ne*
MSG	*Mono sodyum glutamata*	mo·*no* sod·*yoom* gloo·ta·ma·*ta*
nuts	*Çerezlere*	che·rez·le·*re*
seafood	*Deniz ürünlerine*	de·*neez* ew·rewn·le·ree·*ne*

menu reader

asma yaprağında sardalya	as·*ma* yap·ra·uhn·*da* sar·*dal*·ya	*sardines in vine leaves*
baklava	bak·la·*va*	*pastry stuffed with pistachio & walnuts*
biber dolması	bee·*ber* dol·ma·*suh*	*stuffed capsicum*
börek	beu·*rek*	*sweet or savoury dishes with a thin crispy pastry*
bumbar	boom·*bar*	*sausage made of rice & meat stuffed in a large sheep or lamb gut*
cacık	ja·*juhk*	*yogurt, mint & cucumber mix*
cevizli bat	je·veez·*lee* bat	*salad of bulgur, lentils, tomato paste & walnuts*
çevirme	che·veer·*me*	*eggplant, chicken, rice & pistachio dish*
çoban salatası	cho·*ban* sa·la·ta·*suh*	*tomato, cucumber & capsicum salad*
çökertme	cheu·kert·*me*	*steak on potatoes with yogurt*
dolma	dol·*ma*	*vine or cabbage leaves stuffed with rice*
erik aşı	e·*reek* a·*shuh*	*plum dish with prunes, rice & sugar*
gökkuşağı salatası	*gcuk*·koo·sha·uh sa·la·ta·*suh*	*salad of macaroni, capsicum, mushrooms, pickles & salami*
gül tatlısı	gewl tat·luh·*suh*	*fried pastry in lemon sherbet*
halim aşı	ha·*leem* a·*shuh*	*soup of chickpeas, meaty bones, wheat & tomato*
hamsi tava	ham·*see* ta·*va*	*fried, corn-breaded anchovies with onion & lemon*
höşmerim	heush·me·*reem*	*walnut & pistachio pudding*
humus	hoo·*moos*	*mashed chickpeas with sesame oil, lemon & spices*
imam bayıldı	ee·*mam* ba·yuhl·duh	*eggplant, tomato & onion dish*

kadayıf	ka·da·*yuhf*	*dessert of dough soaked in syrup with a layer of sour cream*
kapuska	ka·poos·*ka*	*cold dish of onion, tomato paste & cabbage*
karaş	ka·*rash*	*berry, grape & nut pudding*
kebab/kebap	ke·*bab*/ke·*bap*	*skewered meat & vegetables cooked on an open fire*
keşkül	kesh·*kewl*	*almond, coconut & milk pudding*
köfte	keuf·*te*	*mincemeat or bulgur balls*
kulak çorbası	koo·*lak* chor·ba·*suh*	*meat dumplings boiled in stock*
lokum	lo·*koom*	*Turkish delight*
musakka	moo·sak·*ka*	*vegetable & meat pie*
pastırma	pas·tuhr·*ma*	*pressed beef preserved in spices*
paşa pilavı	pa·*sha* pee·la·*vuh*	*potato, egg & capsicum salad*
patlıcan karnıyarık	pat·luh·*jan* kar·*nuh*·ya·ruhk	*eggplant stuffed with minced meat*
pirpirim çorbası	*peer*·pee·reem chor·ba·*suh*	*chickpea, bean & lentil soup*
pişmaniye	peesh·*ma*·nee·ye	*dessert of sugar, flour & soapwort*
revani	re·*va*·nee	*semolina, vanilla & cream cake*
soğuk çorba	so·*ook* chor·*ba*	*cold soup of yogurt, rice & capsicum*
sucuk	soo·*jook*	*spicy sausage*
susamlı şeker	soo·sam·*luh* she·*ker*	*sugar-coated peanuts & almonds*
sütlaç	sewt·*lach*	*rice pudding*
şiş kebab	sheesh ke·*bab*	*meat skewered on an open fire*
tarhana	tar·ha·*na*	*yogurt, onion, flour & chilli mix*
topik	to·*peek*	*chickpeas, pistachios, flour & currants topped with sesame sauce*
tulumba tatlısı	too·*loom*·ba tat·luh·*suh*	*fluted fritters served in sweet syrup*
yuvarlama	yoo·var·la·*ma*	*chickpea & mince dumpling soup*

emergencies

basics

Help!	*İmdat!*	eem·dat
Stop!	*Dur!*	door
Go away!	*Git burdan!*	geet boor·*dan*
Thief!	*Hırsız var!*	huhr·*suhz* var
Fire!	*Yangın var!*	*yan*·guhn var
Watch out!	*Dikkat et!*	*deek*·kat et
Call ...!	*... çağırın!*	... cha·*uh*·ruhn
a doctor	*Doktor*	dok·*tor*
an ambulance	*Ambulans*	am·boo·*lans*
the police	*Polis*	po·*lees*

It's an emergency!
Bu acil bir durum. — boo a·*jeel* beer *doo*·room

Could you help me, please?
Yardım edebilir misiniz lütfen? — yar·*duhm* e·*de*·bee·leer mee·see·*neez lewt*·fen

Can I use your phone?
Telefonunuzu kullanabilir miyim? — te·le·fe·noo·noo·*zoo* kool·la·*na*·bee·leer mee·*yeem*

I'm lost.
Kayboldum. — kai·bol·*doom*

Where are the toilets?
Tuvaletler nerede? — too·va·let·*ler ne*·re·de

police

Where's the police station?
Polis karakolu nerede? — po·*lees* ka·ra·ko·*loo ne*·re·de

I want to report an offence.
Şikayette bulunmak istiyorum. — shee·ka·yet·*te* boo·loon·*mak* ees·*tee*·yo·room

I have insurance.
Sigortam var. — see·gor·*tam* var

I've been ...	*Ben ...*	ben ...
assaulted	*saldırıya uğradım*	sal·duh·ruh·*ya* oo·ra·*duhm*
raped	*tecavüze uğradım*	te·ja·vew·*ze* oo·ra·*duhm*
robbed	*soyuldum*	so·yool·*doom*

I've lost my ...	*... kayıp.*	... ka·*yuhp*
My ... was/were stolen.	*... çalındı.*	... cha·luhn·*duh*
backpack	*Sırt çantası*	suhrt chan·ta·*suh*
bags	*Çantalar*	chan·ta·*lar*
credit card	*Kredi kartı*	*kre*·dee kar·*tuh*
handbag	*El çantası*	el chan·ta·*suh*
jewellery	*Mücevherler*	mew·jev·her·*ler*
money	*Para*	pa·*ra*
passport	*Pasaport*	pa·sa·*port*
travellers cheques	*Seyahat çekleri*	se·ya·*hat* chek·le·*ree*
wallet	*Cüzdan*	jewz·*dan*

I want to contact my ...	*... görüşmek istiyorum.*	... geu·rewsh·*mek* ees·*tee*·yo·room
consulate	*Konsoloslukla*	kon·so·los·*look*·la
embassy	*Elçilikle*	el·chee·*leek*·le

health

medical needs

Where's the nearest ...?	*En yakın ... nerede?*	en ya·*kuhn* ... *ne*·re·de
dentist	*dişçi*	deesh·*chee*
doctor	*doktor*	dok·*tor*
hospital	*hastane*	has·*ta*·ne
(night) pharmacist	*(nöbetçi) eczane*	(neu·bet·*chee*) ej·*za*·ne

I need a doctor (who speaks English).
(İngilizce konuşan) — (een·gee·*leez*·je ko·noo·*shan*)
Bir doktora ihtiyacım var. — beer dok·to·*ra* eeh·tee·ya·*juhm* var

Could I see a female doctor?
Bayan doktora görünebilir miyim? — ba·*yan* dok·to·*ra* geu·rew·*ne*·bee·leer mee·*yeem*

I've run out of my medication.
İlacım bitti. — ee·la·*juhm* beet·*tee*

symptoms, conditions & allergies

I'm sick.	*Hastayım.*	has·*ta*·yuhm
It hurts here.	*Burası ağrıyor.*	boo·ra·*suh* a·*ruh*·yor
I have a toothache.	*Dişim ağrıyor.*	dee·*sheem* a·*ruh*·yor
I have (a) ...	*Bende ... var.*	ben·*de* ... var
asthma	*astım*	as·*tuhm*
bronchitis	*bronşit*	bron·*sheet*
constipation	*kabızlık*	ka·buhz·*luhk*
cough	*öksürük*	euk·sew·*rewk*
diarrhoea	*ishal*	ees·*hal*
fever	*ateş*	a·*tesh*
headache	*baş ağrısı*	bash a·ruh·*suh*
heart condition	*kalp rahatsızlığı*	kalp ra·hat·suhz·luh·*uh*
nausea	*bulantı*	boo·lan·*tuh*
pain	*ağrı*	a·*ruh*
sore throat	*boğaz ağrısı*	bo·*az* a·ruh·*suh*
I'm allergic to ...	*... alerjim var.*	... a·ler·*zheem* var
antibiotics	*Antibiyotiklere*	an·tee·bee·yo·teek·le·*re*
anti-inflammatories	*Anti-emflamatuarlara*	an·*tee*·em·fla·ma·too·ar·la·ra
aspirin	*Aspirine*	as·pee·ree·*ne*
bees	*Arılara*	a·ruh·la·*ra*
codeine	*Kodeine*	ko·de·ee·*ne*
penicillin	*Penisiline*	pe·nee·see·lee·*ne*
antiseptic	*antiseptik*	an·tee·sep·*teek*
bandage	*bandaj*	ban·*dazh*
condoms	*prezervatifler*	pre·zer·va·teef·*ler*
contraceptives	*doğum kontrol hapı*	do·*oom* kon·*trol* ha·*puh*
diarrhoea medicine	*ishal ilacı*	ees·*hal* ee·la·*juh*
insect repellent	*sinek kovucu*	see·*nek* ko·voo·*joo*
laxatives	*müsil ilacı*	mew·*seel* ee·la·*juh*
painkillers	*ağrı kesici*	a·*ruh* ke·see·*jee*
rehydration salts	*rehidrasyon tuzları*	re·heed·ras·*yon* tooz·la·*ruh*
sleeping tablets	*uyku hapı*	ooy·*koo* ha·*puh*

english–turkish dictionary

Words in this dictionary are marked as a (adjective), n (noun), v (verb), sg (singular), pl (plural), inf (informal) and pol (polite) where necessary.

A

accident *kaza* ka·*za*
accommodation *kalacak yer* ka·la·*jak* yer
adaptor *adaptör* a·dap·*teur*
address n *adres* ad·*res*
after *sonra* *son*·ra
air conditioning *klima* *klee*·ma
airplane *uçak* oo·*chak*
airport *havaalanı* ha·*va*·a·la·nuh
alcohol *alkol* al·*kol*
all *hepsi* *hep*·see
allergy *alerji* a·ler·*zhee*
ambulance *ambulans* am·boo·*lans*
and *ve* ve
ankle *ayak bileği* a·*yak* bee·le·ee
arm *kol* kol
ashtray *kül tablası* kewl tab·la·*suh*
ATM *bankamatik* ban·ka·ma·*teek*

B

baby *bebek* be·*bek*
back (body) *sırt* suhrt
backpack *sırt çantası* suhrt chan·ta·*suh*
bad *kötü* keu·*tew*
bag *çanta* *chan*·ta
baggage claim *bagaj konveyörü* ba·*gazh* kon·ve·yeu·*rew*
bank *banka* *ban*·ka
bar *bar* bar
bathroom *banyo* *ban*·yo
battery *pil* peel
beautiful *güzel* gew·*zel*
bed *yatak* ya·*tak*
beer *bira* *bee*·ra
before *önce* *eun*·je
behind *arkasında* ar·ka·suhn·*da*
bicycle *bisiklet* bee·seek·*let*
big *büyük* bew·*yewk*
bill *hesap* he·*sap*
black *siyah* see·*yah*
blanket *battaniye* bat·*ta*·nee·ye
blood group *kan gurubu* kan goo·roo·*boo*
blue *mavi* *ma*·vee
boat *vapur* va·*poor*
book (make a reservation) v *yer ayırtmak* yer a·yuhrt·*mak*
bottle *şişe* shee·*she*
bottle opener *şişe açacağı* shee·*she* a·cha·ja·*uh*
boy *oğlan* o·*lan*
brakes (car) *fren* fren
breakfast *kahvaltı* kah·val·*tuh*
broken (faulty) *bozuk* bo·*zook*
bus *otobüs* o·to·*bews*
business *iş* eesh
buy *satın almak* sa·*tuhn* al·*mak*

C

café *kafe* ka·*fe*
camera *kamera* ka·*me*·ra
camp site *kamp yeri* kamp ye·*ree*
cancel *iptal etmek* eep·*tal* et·*mek*
can opener *konserve açacağı* kon·ser·*ve* a·cha·ja·*uh*
car *araba* a·ra·*ba*
cash n *nakit* na·*keet*
cash (a cheque) v *(çek) bozdurmak* (chek) boz·door·*mak*
cell phone *cep telefonu* jep te·le·fo·*noo*
centre n *merkez* mer·*kez*
change (money) v *bozdurmak* boz·door·*mak*
cheap *ucuz* oo·*jooz*
check (bill) *fatura* fa·*too*·ra
check-in n *giriş* gee·*reesh*
chest *göğüs* geu·*ews*
child *çocuk* cho·*jook*
cigarette *sigara* see·*ga*·ra
city *şehir* she·*heer*
clean a *temiz* te·*meez*
closed *kapalı* ka·pa·*luh*
coffee *kahve* kah·*ve*
coins *madeni para* ma·de·*nee* pa·*ra*
cold a *soğuk* so·*ook*
collect call *ödemeli telefon* eu·de·me·*lee* te·le·*fon*
come *gelmek* gel·*mek*

computer *bilgisayar* beel·gee·sa·*yar*
condom *prezervatif* pre·zer·va·*teef*
contact lenses *kontak lens* kon·*tak* lens
cook v *pişirmek* pee·sheer·*mek*
cost n *fiyat* fee·*yat*
credit card *kredi kartı* *kre*·dee kar·*tuh*
cup *fincan* feen·*jan*
currency exchange *döviz kuru* deu·*veez* koo·*roo*
customs (immigration) *gümrük* gewm·*rewk*

D

dangerous *tehlikeli* teh·lee·ke·*lee*
date (time) *tarih* ta·*reeh*
day *gün* gewn
delay n *gecikme* ge·jeek·*me*
dentist *dişçi* deesh·*chee*
depart *ayrılmak* ai·ruhl·*mak*
diaper *bebek bezi* be·*bek* be·*zee*
dictionary *sözlük* seuz·*lewk*
dinner *akşam yemeği* ak·*sham* ye·me·*ee*
direct *direk* dee·*rek*
dirty *kirli* keer·*lee*
disabled *özürlü* eu·zewr·*lew*
discount n *indirim* een·dee·*reem*
doctor *doktor* dok·*tor*
double bed *iki kişilik yatak* ee·*kee* kee·shee·*leek* ya·*tak*
double room *iki kişilik oda* ee·*kee* kee·shee·*leek* o·*da*
drink n *içecek* ee·che·*jek*
drive v *sürmek* sewr·*mek*
drivers licence *ehliyet* eh·lee·*yet*
drugs (illicit) *uyuşturucu* oo·yoosh·too·roo·*joo*
dummy (pacifier) *emzik* em·*zeek*

E

ear *kulak* koo·*lak*
east *doğu* do·*oo*
eat *yemek* ye·*mek*
economy class *ekonomi sınıfı* e·ko·no·*mee* suh·nuh·*fuh*
electricity *elektrik* e·lek·*treek*
elevator *asansör* a·san·*seur*
email *e-posta* e·pos·ta
embassy *elçilik* el·chee·*leek*
emergency *acil durum* a·*jeel* doo·*room*
English (language) *İngilizce* een·gee·*leez*·je
entrance *giriş* gee·*reesh*
evening *akşam* ak·*sham*
exchange rate *döviz kuru* deu·*veez* koo·*roo*
exit n *çıkış* chuh·*kuhsh*
expensive *pahalı* pa·ha·*luh*
express mail *ekspres posta* eks·*pres* pos·*ta*
eye *göz* geuz

F

far *uzak* oo·*zak*
fast *hızlı* huhz·*luh*
father *baba* ba·*ba*
film (camera) *film* feelm
finger *parmak* par·*mak*
first-aid kit *ilk yardım çantası*
eelk yar·*duhm* chan·ta·*suh*
first class *birinci sınıf* bee·reen·*jee* suh·*nuhf*
fish n *balık* ba·*luhk*
food *yiyecek* yee·ye·*jek*
foot *ayak* a·*yak*
fork *çatal* cha·*tal*
free (of charge) *ücretsiz* ewj·ret·*seez*
friend *arkadaş* ar·ka·*dash*
fruit *meyve* may·*ve*
full *dolu* do·*loo*
funny *komik* ko·*meek*

G

gift *hediye* he·dee·*ye*
girl *kız* kuhz
glass (drinking) *bardak* bar·*dak*
glasses *gözlük* geuz·*lewk*
go *gitmek* geet·*mek*
good *iyi* ee·*yee*
green *yeşil* ye·*sheel*
guide n *rehber* reh·*ber*

H

half n *yarım* ya·*ruhm*
hand *el* el
handbag *el çantası* el chan·ta·*suh*
happy *mutlu* moot·*loo*
have *sahip olmak* sa·*heep* ol·*mak*
he *o* o
head *baş* bash
heart *kalp* kalp
heat n *ısı* uh·*suh*
heavy *ağır* a·*uhr*
help v *yardım etmek* yar·*duhm* et·*mek*
here *burada* boo·ra·*da*
high *yüksek* yewk·*sek*

highway *otoyol* o·to·yol
hike v *uzun yürüyüşe çıkmak* oo·*zoon* yew·rew·yew·*she* chuhk·*mak*
holiday *tatil* *ta*·teel
homosexual *homoseksüel* ho·*mo*·sek·sew·el
hospital *hastane* has·*ta*·ne
hot *sıcak* suh·*jak*
hotel *otel* o·*tel*
hungry *aç* ach
husband *koca* ko·*ja*

I

I *ben* ben
identification (card) *kimlik kartı* keem·*leek* kar·*tuh*
ill *hasta* has·*ta*
important *önemli* eu·nem·*lee*
included *dahil* da·*heel*
injury *yara* ya·*ra*
insurance *sigorta* see·*gor*·ta
Internet *internet* een·ter·*net*
interpreter *tercüman* ter·jew·*man*

J

jewellery *mücevherler* mew·jev·her·*ler*
job *meslek* mes·*lek*

K

key *anahtar* a·nah·*tar*
kilogram *kilogram* kee·log·*ram*
kitchen *mutfak* moot·*fak*
knife *bıçak* buh·*chak*

L

laundry (place) *çamaşırlık* cha·ma·shuhr·*luhk*
lawyer *avukat* a·voo·*kat*
left (direction) *sol* sol
left-luggage office *emanet bürosu* e·ma·*net* bew·ro·soo
leg *bacak* ba·*jak*
lesbian *lezbiyen* lez·bee·*yen*
less *daha az* da·*ha* az
letter (mail) *mektup* mek·*toop*
lift (elevator) *asansör* a·san·*seur*
light n *ışık* uh·*shuhk*
like v *sevmek* sev·*mek*
lock n *kilit* kee·*leet*
long *uzun* oo·*zoon*
lost *kayıp* ka·*yuhp*
lost-property office *kayıp eşya bürosu* ka·*yuhp* esh·*ya* bew·ro·soo
love v *aşık olmak* a·*shuhk* ol·*mak*
luggage *bagaj* ba·*gazh*
lunch *öğle yemeği* eu·*le* ye·me·*ee*

M

mail n *mektup* mek·*toop*
man *adam* a·*dam*
map *harita* ha·ree·*ta*
market *pazar* pa·*zar*
matches *kibrit* keeb·*reet*
meat *et* et
medicine *ilaç* ee·*lach*
menu *yemek listesi* ye·*mek* lees·te·*see*
message *mesaj* me·*sazh*
milk *süt* sewt
minute *dakika* da·kee·*ka*
mobile phone *cep telefonu* jep te·le·fo·*noo*
money *para* pa·*ra*
month *ay* ai
morning *sabah* sa·*bah*
mother *anne* *an*·ne
motorcycle *motosiklet* mo·to·seek·*let*
motorway *paralı yol* pa·ra·*luh* yol
mouth *ağız* a·*uhz*
music *müzik* mew·*zeek*

N

name *ad* ad
napkin *peçete* pe·*che*·te
nappy *bebek bezi* be·*bek* be·*zee*
near *yakında* ya·kuhn·*da*
neck *boyun* bo·*yoon*
new *yeni* ye·*nee*
news *haberler* ha·ber·*ler*
newspaper *gazete* ga·*ze*·te
night *gece* ge·*je*
no *hayır* *ha*·yuhr
noisy *gürültülü* gew·rewl·tew·*lew*
nonsmoking *sigara içilmeyen* see·*ga*·ra ee·*cheel*·me·yen
north *kuzey* koo·*zay*
nose *burun* boo·*roon*
now *şimdi* *sheem*·dee
number *sayı* sa·*yuh*

O

oil (engine) *yağ* ya
old (object/person) *eski/yaşlı* es·*kee*/yash·*luh*
one-way ticket *gidiş bilet* gee·*deesh* bee·*let*
open a *açık* a·*chuhk*
outside *dışarıda* duh·sha·ruh·*da*

P

package *ambalaj* am·ba·*lazh*
paper *kağıt* ka·*uht*
park (car) v *park etmek* park et·*mek*
passport *pasaport* pa·sa·*port*
pay *ödemek* eu·de·*mek*
pen *tükenmez kalem* tew·ken·*mez* ka·*lem*
petrol *benzin* ben·*zeen*
pharmacy *eczane* ej·*za*·ne
phonecard *telefon kartı* te·le·*fon* kar·*tuh*
photo *fotoğraf* fo·to·*raf*
plate *tabak* ta·*bak*
police *polis* po·*lees*
postcard *kartpostal* kart·pos·*tal*
post office *postane* pos·*ta*·ne
pregnant *hamile* ha·mee·*le*
price *fiyat* fee·*yat*

Q

quiet *sakin* sa·*keen*

R

rain n *yağmur* ya·*moor*
razor *traş makinesi* trash ma·kee·ne·*see*
receipt n *makbuz* mak·*booz*
red *kırmızı* kuhr·muh·*zuh*
refund n *para iadesi* pa·*ra* ee·a·de·*see*
registered mail *taahhütlü posta* ta·ah·hewt·*lew* *pos*·ta
rent v *kiralamak* kee·ra·la·*mak*
repair v *tamir etmek* ta·*meer* et·*mek*
reservation *rezervasyon* re·zer·vas·*yon*
restaurant *restoran* res·to·*ran*
return v *geri dönmek* ge·*ree* deun·*mek*
return ticket *gidiş-dönüş bilet*
gee·deesh·deu·*newsh* bee·*let*
right (direction) *doğru yön* do·*roo* yeun

road *yol* yol
room *oda* o·*da*

S

safe a *emniyetli* em·nee·yet·*lee*
sanitary napkin *hijyenik kadın bağı*
heezh·ye·*neek* ka·*duhn* ba·*uh*
seat *yer* yer
send *göndermek* geun·der·*mek*
service station *benzin istasyonu*
ben·*zeen* ees·tas·yo·*noo*
sex *seks* seks
shampoo *şampuan* sham·poo·*an*
share (a dorm) *paylaşmak* pai·lash·*mak*
shaving cream *tıraş kremi* tuh·*rash* kre·*mee*
she *o* o
sheet (bed) *çarşaf* char·*shaf*
shirt *gömlek* geum·*lek*
shoes *ayakkabılar* a·yak·ka·buh·*lar*
shop n *dükkan* dewk·*kan*
short *kısa* kuh·*sa*
shower n *duş* doosh
single room *tek kişilik oda* tek kee·shee·*leek* o·*da*
skin *cilt* jeelt
skirt *etek* e·*tek*
sleep v *uyumak* oo·yoo·*mak*
slowly *yavaşça* ya·vash·*cha*
small *küçük* kew·*chewk*
smoke (cigarettes) v *sigara içmek*
see·*ga*·ra eech·*mek*
soap *sabun* sa·*boon*
some *biraz* bee·raz
soon *yakında* ya·kuhn·*da*
south *güney* gew·*nay*
souvenir shop *hediyelik eşya dükkanı*
he·dee·ye·*leek* esh·*ya* dewk·ka·*nuh*
speak *konuşmak* ko·noosh·*mak*
spoon *kaşık* ka·*shuhk*
stamp *pul* pool
stand-by ticket *açık bilet* a·*chuhk* bee·*let*
station (train) *istasyon* ees·tas·*yon*
stomach *mide* mee·*de*
stop v *durmak* door·*mak*
stop (bus) n *durağı* doo·ra·*uh*
street *sokak* so·*kak*
student *öğrenci* eu·ren·*jee*
sun *güneş* gew·*nesh*

sunscreen *güneşten koruma kremi* gew·nesh·ten ko·roo·ma kre·mee
swim v *yüzmek* yewz·mek

T

tampons *tamponlar* tam·pon·lar
taxi *taksi* tak·see
teaspoon *çay kaşığı* chai ka·shuh·uh
teeth *dişler* deesh·ler
telephone n *telefon* te·le·fon
television *televizyon* te·le·veez·yon
temperature (weather) *derece* de·re·je
tent *çadır* cha·duhr
that (one) *şunu/onu* shoo·noo/o·noo
they *onlar* on·lar
thirsty *susamış* soo·sa·muhsh
this (one) *bunu* boo·noo
throat *boğaz* bo·az
ticket *bilet* bee·let
time *zaman* za·man
tired *yorgun* yor·goon
tissues *kağıt mendil* ka·uht men·deel
today *bugün* boo·gewn
toilet *tuvalet* too·va·let
tomorrow *yarın* ya·ruhn
tonight *bu gece* boo ge·je
toothbrush *diş fırçası* deesh fuhr·cha·suh
toothpaste *diş macunu* deesh ma·joo·noo
torch (flashlight) *el feneri* el fe·ne·ree
tour n *tur* toor
tourist office *turizm bürosu* too·reezm bew·ro·soo
towel *havlu* hav·loo
train *tren* tren
translate *çevirmek* che·veer·mek
travel agency *seyahat acentesi* seya·hat a·jen·te·see
travellers cheque *seyahat çeki* se·ya·hat che·kee
trousers *pantolon* pan·to·lon
Turkey *Türkiye* tewr·kee·ye
Turkish (language) *Türkçe* tewrk·che
Turkish Republic of Northern Cyprus (TRNC) *Kuzey Kıbrıs Türk Cumhuriyeti (KKTC)* koo·zay kuhb·ruhs tewrk joom·hoo·ree·ye·tee (ka·ka·te·je)
twin beds *çift yatak* cheeft ya·tak
tyre *lastik* las·teek

U

underwear *iç çamaşırı* eech cha·ma·shuh·ruh
urgent *acil* a·jeel

V

vacant *boş* bosh
vacation *tatil* ta·teel
vegetable n *sebze* seb·ze
vegetarian a *vejeteryan* ve·zhe·ter·yan
visa *vize* vee·ze

W

waiter *garson* gar·son
walk v *yürümek* yew·rew·mek
wallet *cüzdan* jewz·dan
warm a *ılık* uh·luhk
wash (something) *yıkamak* yuh·ka·mak
watch n *saat* sa·at
water *su* soo
we *biz* beez
weekend *hafta sonu* haf·ta so·noo
west *batı* ba·tuh
wheelchair *tekerlekli sandalye* te·ker·lek·lee san·dal·ye
when *ne zaman* ne za·man
where *nerede* ne·re·de
white *beyaz* be·yaz
who *kim* keem
why *neden* ne·den
wife *karı* ka·ruh
window *pencere* pen·je·re
wine *şarap* sha·rap
with *ile* ee·le
without *-sız/-siz/-suz/-süz* ·suhz/·seez/·sooz/·sewz
woman *kadın* ka·duhn
write *yazı yazmak* ya·zuh yaz·mak

yellow *sarı* sa·ruh
yes *evet* e·vet
yesterday *dün* dewn
you sg inf *sen* sen
you sg pol & pl *siz* seez

INDEX

festivals in western europe

On the last weekend of June, **Denmark** hosts one of Europe's biggest rock music festivals – the Roskilde Festival. The Copenhagen Jazz Festival, with 10 days of music in early July, presents a wide range of Danish and international jazz, blues and fusion music.

The Amsterdam Fantastic Film Festival, held in April, is a feast of fantasy, horror and science fiction movies. On the *Nationale Molendag* (National Mill Day) in May, nearly every working windmill in the **Netherlands** opens its doors to visitors.

The Cannes Film Festival in May is the world's most glitzy cinema event and a feast for the paparazzi. Another spectacle is the *Tour de France*, the famous bicycle race through **France** and the neighbouring countries, which ends in Paris in July.

The Berlin Love Parade in June is the largest techno party in the world. Hordes of tourists come to **Germany** for the famous beer festival in Munich, the *Oktoberfest* – one of Europe's biggest and most drunken parties, from late September to early October.

The Hellenic Festival in Athens, the major summer arts festival in **Greece**, features international music, dance and theatre. Το φεστιβάλ κρασιού (the wine festival) is held in early September in Dafni, west of Athens, to celebrate the grape harvest.

The San Remo Music Festival in March has been running in **Italy** since 1951 and was the inspiration for the Eurovision Song Contest. The Italian Gran Prix, organised in September at Monza, is one of the oldest circuits in Formula One.

Påske (Easter) is the occasion for the Sami people (Lapps) of **Norway** to organise colourful celebrations with reindeer races and chanting concerts in April. *Jonsok* (Midsummer's Eve) is celebrated with bonfires and dancing on the beach around 23 June.

Festas das Cruzes (Festival of the Crosses), held in May in Barcelos, **Portugal**, is known for processions, folk music and regional handicrafts. In June, Santarém hosts the *Feira Nacional da Agricultura* (National Agricultural Fair) with bullfighting and folk music.

In June, Pamplona combines the *San Fermíne* festivities with macho posturing and running bulls, drawing TV crews from all over the world to **Spain**. *Semana Santa* (Holy Week) in April brings parades of holy images and huge crowds, notably in Seville.

On 30 April or *Valborgsmässoafton* (Walpurgis Night), **Sweden** celebrates the coming of spring with choral songs and huge bonfires. The Stockholm Water Festival in August is a major event with all sorts of activities including sport, music and fireworks.

Şeker Bayramı (Sweets Festival) is a three-day festival in **Turkey** at the end of the Muslim lunar month of Ramadan. *Kurban Bayramı* (Sacrifice Festival), two months after Ramadan, lasts for four days during which people make animal sacrifices.